5th June 2009,

Thank-you for being our usher

Love

Niki

&

Sabina

x

HALIFAX TOWN

FROM BALL TO LILLIS

– A Complete Record –

DESERT ISLAND FOOTBALL HISTORIES

Halifax Town: From Ball to Lillis – A Complete Record	1-874287-26-0
Portsmouth: From Tindall to Ball – A Complete Record	1-874287-25-2
Colchester Utd: Graham to Whitton – A Complete Record	1-874287-27-9
Bristol City: The Modern Era – A Complete Record	1-874287-28-7
Coventry City: The Elite Era – A Complete Record	1-874287-03-1
Luton Town: The Modern Era – A Complete Record	1-874287-05-8
Hereford United: The League Era – A Complete Record	1-874287-18-X
West Ham: From Greenwood to Redknapp – Match by Match	1-874287-19-8
Wimbledon: From Southern League to Premiership	1-874287-09-0
Wimbledon: From Wembley to Selhurst	1-874287-20-1
Aberdeen: The European Era – A Complete Record	1-874287-11-2
The Story of the Rangers 1873-1923	1-874287-16-3
The Story of the Celtic 1888-1938	1-874287-15-5
History of the Everton Football Club 1878-1928	1-874287-14-7
The Romance of the Wednesday 1867-1926	1-874287-17-1
Red Dragons in Europe – A Complete Record	1-874287-01-5
The Book of Football: A History to 1905-06	1-874287-13-9
England: The Quest for the World Cup – A Complete Record	1-897850-40-9
Scotland: The Quest for the World Cup – A Complete Record	1-897850-50-6
Ireland: The Quest for the World Cup – A Complete Record	1-897850-80-8

HALIFAX TOWN

FROM BALL TO LILLIS
— A Complete Record —

Series Editor: Clive Leatherdale
Series Consultant: Leigh Edwards

Johnny Meynell

DESERT ISLAND BOOKS LIMITED

First Published in 1999

DESERT ISLAND BOOKS LIMITED
89 Park Street, Westcliff-on-Sea, Essex SS0 7PD
United Kingdom
www.desertislandbooks.com

British Library Cataloguing-in-Publication Data
A catalogue record for this book is available from the British Library

ISBN 1-874287-26-0

Printed in Great Britain
by
Biddles Ltd, Guildford

Photographs in this book are reproduced courtesy of
Halifax *Evening Courier*: pages 65, 67 (top), 68 (top), 70 (top), 360.
Keith Middleton: pages 71 (bottom), 72, 73, 74, 75, 76, 77,
147, 148, 149, 150, 151, 152, 153, 154, 155, 156, 157, 158, 159, 160.

CONTENTS

4. FINANCIAL WOES – 1981-1987

5. LIVING ON BORROWED TIME – 1987-1993

5. THE CONFERENCE AND BACK – 1993-1999

PREFACE

When I first arrived at Halifax Town I never thought that twenty years later I would have the privilege to be asked to write a preface for such an interesting book on the club's history.

I have many happy memories but the outstanding time for me and the club was when Halifax Town were drawn at home in the third round of the FA Cup against Malcolm Allison's £1.5 million side, Manchester City.

I remember arriving at the ground on 5 January 1980 to see the supporters with forks and even towels trying to dry up the pitch! It was like a mud bath but this typified the spirit of the supporters that Halifax Town has always had.

There was a massive crowd of over 12,000 to see David take on Goliath in front of a televised audience and I shall never forget for the rest of my life scoring the winning goal in a 1-0 victory.

Halifax Town have always held a special place in my heart as it was one of the best clubs I had ever been at. It is one of the first results I look for every Saturday. It was a painful experience to see them relegated to the Conference League but what a great pleasure to see them get back into Football League status, where they always belong.

This book is a compilation of Halifax Town's disasters and triumphs and I am sure that in the future there will be many more successes to come.

PAUL HENDRIE

AUTHOR'S NOTE

Saturday, 24 February 1979 was the day that changed my life. That was the day that BBC's 'Grandstand' announced that ailing Halifax Town had won at Port Vale to record only their second win of the season. I was acutely aware of Halifax Town's sorry plight, and promised myself that I would attend their next home match. There was no turning back. The following Saturday I took my place in the small Patron's Stand and watched the Shaymen defeat Portsmouth. Thus began my love affair with Halifax Town which, though often strained, has always been undying.

I choose to relay this story simply because all of us who regularly attend the Shay have our stories as to how we came to be following the fortunes of Halifax Town. Doubtless for hundreds of you, your first match is covered between the ends of this book.

When I was commissioned by Clive Leatherdale in November 1998 to write this book on Halifax Town – the latest in the series of footballing histories published by Desert Island Books – it was an opportunity too good to turn down. The work, though, was immense. This book covers in detail thirty-one seasons (and almost as many managers), and encompasses many highs and, sadly, many more lows. It begins with the historic 1968-69 season when Halifax Town, under Alan Ball, won their first promotion, and ends with their first season back in the Football League following their Conference championship of 1998. In between, it is often a tale of woe, but nevertheless it makes for compulsive reading.

For the most part, I have gone alone while writing this book, though I am grateful to several individuals who have assisted me. Firstly, I must thank Keith Middleton for supplying many of the photographs, and Ian Rushworth and the *Halifax Evening Courier* for allowing the use of others. Leigh Edwards, the doyen of football historians, helped me with missing statistics, as did Andy Pinfield of the Halifax Town commercial department. I am also grateful to chairman Jim Brown and Halifax Town for backing me on this project, and for the publicity which they gave to it.

Then, of course, there is my long-suffering wife Denise, who has been supportive of my efforts while at the same time admitting to being glad when it was all over. She is, however, looking forward to the two dozen red roses she made me promise to buy her upon completion. And last but not least, there are the Halifax Town players and managers, good or bad, that have enabled this story to be told.

JOHNNY MEYNELL, September 1999

INTRODUCTION

If the pioneers of Halifax Town could have seen the troubles that lay ahead for the club over the years, they might not have bothered. Beset for the most part by lack of support, lack of money and, not least, lack of success, the club has stumbled from one crisis to another. When Halifax Town were facing relegation to the Unibond League in 1977, it seemed to many to be the natural progression for the club.

In 1911, when Halifax Town had been formed, certain townsfolk here cast an envious eye over neighbouring sides Leeds United, Bradford's City and Park Avenue and the recently formed Huddersfield Town. In those days the local folk were concerned that football followers were travelling out of Halifax to watch these sides. Over the years, envy continued to exist as all these local rivals at one time or another flirted with the top flight, with Leeds United and Bradford City currently Premiership members.

A letter written by a Mr AE Jones, published in the Halifax *Courier* on 20 April, 1911 has always been recognised as the real catalyst behind the creation of Halifax Town FC. Together with Joe McClelland, the club's first secretary, and Dr Howie Muir, the first president, they saw no reason why the club could not emulate the feats of their near neighbours. But whereas the other West Yorkshire sides shook off the competition of their rugby counterparts, in Halifax it was a different story. The rugby club had stood alone since 1873 and, with success coming at regular intervals, Halifax Town were, for the most part, living in their shadow. Rivalry always existed – there was opposition from rugby followers to the creation of the football club in 1911 – but has intensified following Halifax RFLC's success in the 1980s.

Perhaps just as frustrating for Halifax Town supporters is the fact that fellow perennial strugglers in the Football League's basement – where Town have spent most of their life – have had their moments. The likes of Crewe, Stockport and Tranmere – against whom Town were consistent victors – have all risen up the League whilst Halifax have continued to struggle. Worse, while those clubs were in the ascendancy, Town actually dropped out of the League and were on the verge of becoming the forgotten men.

Despite the ambitions of Messrs Jones, McClelland and Muir back in 1911, success for Halifax Town has often been about survival. And though silverware has come their way, it has only been in the form of the West Riding Senior Cup, won in the competition's heyday in 1959, 1962 and 1967, and more recently the

Yorkshire and Humberside Cup in 1990 and 1993. Many managers have tried and failed – too many to mention here – but Alex Raisbeck took the club close to Division Two in 1935. That was the season after his side had been humbled 0-13 at Stockport, a result that saw Town enter the record books for all the wrong reasons, the heaviest defeat any club has suffered in Football League history.

Notable famous players to have worn Town's colours include former England international wingers Fred Pentland (in the Midland League days) and Freddie Tunstall in the 1930s. Other players such as Ernest Dixon, Tim Coleman, Albert Valentine, Alex South and George Whitelaw have been crowd favourites, but collectively, as a team, Halifax Town had always flattered to deceive.

In 1966, after a spell as coach, Vic Metcalfe became the latest manager to chance his fortunes with Halifax Town. In November 1967 his side was going quite well, but following a disagreement with the directors on team policy he resigned. Alan Ball was thereupon installed as the twelfth incumbent of the hot seat, with chairman Alan Maden saying: 'I believe he will be the greatest capture Halifax Town has ever made.'

Alan Ball inherited a useful side that included the likes of John Pickering, Ivan Hampton, Jeff Lee, David Shawcross, Bob Wallace, Les Massie, Phil McCarthy and Tony Flower. He improved it by signing goalkeeper Alex Smith before that season was out, and the platform for success was at last in place. Upon his arrival at the Shay, Ball had promised Second Division football within five years. It was a noble prediction, but having seen so many managers fail before him, the Halifax supporters had every right to be sceptical.

1

GLORY DAYS 1968-1972

LEAGUE DIVISION 4	**1968-69**
Division 4	2nd (promoted)
League Cup	1st Round
FA Cup	4th Round

There are some Halifax Town supporters who believe, with some justification, that the finest side ever to represent the club was that put together by Alan Ball Snr during the 1968-69 season. Yet there are others who, whilst acknowledging its achievements, believe that the club went on to produce more talented sides.

Alan Ball might have been the first to agree that his promotion-winning side had its limitations, but what he produced was a set of players that knew how to work hard for each other, and for a full ninety minutes. If the team lacked flair, it certainly wasn't found wanting for fitness, for that was the key to his success. During the season, it would be hard to find as fit a side in the Fourth Division, or even the whole Football League for that matter.

Ball had claimed when he first took over as manager in November 1967 that promotion was his number one priority. To achieve it, however, he needed to strengthen his squad. Ray Holt had been sold to Scunthorpe, so Ball brought in Burnley full-back Mick Buxton and a couple of internationals in half-back Mick Meagan (Republic of Ireland) and forward Ian Lawther (Northern Ireland). Meagan had had a lengthy career in the First Division with Everton, but arrived at the Shay from Huddersfield, whilst Lawther was signed from Brentford, having started his career with Sunderland.

Yet Halifax made a poor start to the new season, not only losing their opening two league fixtures, but also crashing out of the League Cup to Second Division Hull City 0-3 at the Shay. There was also something of a shock when one of the club's most loyal servants, full-back Malcolm Russell – he was the only player still at the club who was part of the team relegated in 1963 – expressed a desire to move on. After playing in only two games, he went to

Southport in exchange for a useful £7,000, but for the player himself, it was probably the biggest mistake of his career.

£1,250 of that transfer money was used to bring a young centre-half to the Shay. Chris Nicholl, rejected by Burnley, was then turning out for non-league Witton Albion, but the vintage Ball knew a talented player when he saw one, and Nicholl quickly adapted to league football, becoming part of a mean defence that included a new full-back partnership of Ivan Hampton and Mick Buxton. The team began to settle down and results improved, save for a 0-4 reversal at the Shay by Darlington. When Doncaster were beaten in a thriller on 26 October, Town moved up to sixth. Ball's insistence that his side was 'going places' began to be taken seriously.

That defeat of Doncaster brought a few smiles around the Shay, for the club revealed a record loss for the year ending 31 March 1968 of £15,886. Chairman Alan Maden, emphasised that there was 'no crisis at the Shay'. He felt that the situation the club found itself in was simply a challenge.

Alan Ball loved challenges, and he was presented with one of sorts when Town were given a tricky First Round tie at West Midlands League side Bilston in the FA Cup. With a good run in the competition a necessity, if only to bring some money into the coffers, Town were locked at 1-1 with twelve minutes to go, until two late goals saw them through to Round Two. In view of the financial situation, the directors probably welcomed a replay at Crewe, following a 1-1 draw at the Shay, and rubbed their hands with glee when they beat the Railwaymen in extra-time.

That replay at Gresty Road would be the last match Buxton completed that season. The following week at Peterborough, on a freezing pitch, the referee elected to start the game, only to abandon it at half-time. But Town had already paid a heavy price. Buxton had broken his leg, and would not return to the first team until the following season. Ball had to act, and did so by taking Rotherham United full-back Andy Burgin on loan, before securing him permanently the following March for £2,000.

Whilst Town's run in the FA Cup was a distraction from their league efforts, it was, at least, an exciting one. But when they were drawn away at Fourth Division Swansea Town in Round Three, it could hardly have been called a glamour tie. A tricky game, certainly, but Les Massie's late strike proved enough, and Town moved into the fourth round where they were, thankfully, paired with a First Division side in the form of Stoke City. Whether the players had this game on their minds or not, they failed to win any of the four league games that preceded it, and that included another 0-4 home defeat, this time by York City. Some supporters pointed to Town's small squad of players, and wondered whether it was actually geared up for a promotion push.

Ivan Hampton was unfortunate to be injured in the game against Bradford City, and was therefore forced to sit out the cup-tie at the Victoria Ground, where Town came so close to winning. The bumper crowd that turned up for the replay at the Shay, whilst disappointed at the scoreline – Town lost 0-3 – at least did much to top up the coffers. Once out of the Cup, the Shaymen were left to concentrate on the league, but with so many games to fit in extra pressure was put on the players to achieve results. But they were up to the task. A goalless draw in the Shay mud against Chester at least showed that they were suffering no hangovers from the defeat by Stoke.

In February, Ball added to his small squad by signing, initially on loan but later permanently in a £3,000 deal, Bury's Lammie Robertson. The newcomer did not have to wait long for his first start in Town's colours, but at the same time, another Town player was ending a fifty-week wait for his. Mark Pearson, one of Manchester United's Busby Babes, made his first start against Colchester and scored a memorable glancing header as the Shaymen won their first game in the league for six matches.

A goalless draw at Lincoln looked worthy enough, until it was pointed out that Town had only scored four goals in their last eight matches. But that was what Town were about. Nick a goal if they could, then defend resolutely to protect it, as single-goal victories over Darlington and Grimsby indicated. In April, Town managed to record 3-0 wins over both Workington and Newport. The points accumulated strengthened their position, but even at this late stage fourteen clubs were still in with a realistic chance of gaining one of the four promotion places. A 0-0 draw at second-placed Colchester may have been unspectacular, but Town did at least prevent their opponents from scoring at home for the first time since August. Not surprisingly, other teams began to take serious notice of Town's exploits.

Attendances began to increase as the folk of Halifax latched on to the possibility of Town gaining promotion. Victory over Brentford moved them into fifth position and set them up nicely for a crunch derby at Rochdale, another team with one eye on Division Three. They were lying second, with the same number of points as Town, but it was Dale who strengthened their own position with a 1-0 win in front of Spotland's biggest crowd of the season, 13,266. Defeat by Dennis Butler's solitary strike, in off the post, meant that with just four games left, Town really could not afford any more slip-ups.

Did You Know?

Bob Suter is the oldest player ever to appear for Halifax. He was 48 years and 288 days when he turned out at Darlington on 24 April 1929.

By the time Rochdale visited the Shay for the return fixture, Town's chances had improved with a win over Aldershot and a draw at York. With Doncaster already assured of the title, the Shaymen knew that victory would guarantee that they would join Rovers in Division Three the following season. An incredible 17,186 packed into the Shay, and in a tension-charged atmosphere, a headed goal by Massie – who else? – fourteen minutes from time was enough to secure promotion, the first in the club's history.

Town moved into second place, but Rochdale's victory over Southend two days later enabled them to leap-frog over the Shaymen. However, a sterile 0-0 draw at relegated Bradford Park Avenue on 12 May in the final game was enough for Town to reclaim that runners-up spot.

But Halifax Town's season was not quite over. Two days later they were beaten 0-5 by Don Revie's Leeds United – they were League Champions, making it a good year for West Yorkshire – in a West Riding Senior Cup-tie. Afterwards the players left for a treat – a European tour, as Ball had promised if promotion was achieved. The three games in Belgium, France and Luxembourg saw Town draw (1-1) with Namur, then beat Hayange (3-0), and Jeannesse (2-1). The tour was not without incident. The morning after the first game, Mark Pearson walked out of the team's Luxembourg headquarters before breakfast and headed home along with Ivan Hampton, who was ordered to leave because he claimed he was 'bored'. The following day, Pearson, always a controversial character, was sacked, and this soured somewhat an historic season, one that up to that point had seen Halifax Town claim their finest hour.

Match of the Season 1968-69

Stoke City 1 Halifax Town 1

FA Cup, 4th Round, 25 January 1969

The *Halifax Evening Courier* described this as 'Town's greatest display in years', and the 4,000 fans who travelled to the Victoria Ground may not wish to argue. Although still a Fourth Division side – albeit a good one – Halifax Town belied their lowly status by putting on a performance that many First Division sides would have been proud of. The Shaymen actually came close to winning.

Stoke City were hardly the biggest name in English football, but they were a useful Division One side, having been promoted in 1963. They were in the throws of their golden period – mirroring in a way Town's own success over a similar period – reaching the FA Cup semi-finals in 1971 and then winning the League Cup the following year, their first honour.

Their side had been assembled by Tony Waddington, who had been in charge since 1960 after eight years as a coach, then assistant manager, and included a couple of star players. In goal was England World Cup winner Gordon Banks, soon to be hailed as the best in the world, and in the forward line was George Eastham, formerly of Newcastle and Arsenal, but famed for daring to take on the Football League over 'freedom of contract' in 1961. Stoke had moved into the Fourth Round after negotiating a tricky tie at York, coming through as 2-0 winners, whilst Town's path had, of course, been a little longer and taken in more games. Now, the two teams met for the first time since 1953 when Town won 1-0 at the Shay in the same competition.

This was a game that Town manager Alan Ball was particularly looking forward to. He had been a coach at the Victoria Ground for two years before arriving at the Shay, but his team selection was hampered by injuries to key players. Ivan Hampton, Jeff Lee and Mick Buxton were all ruled out, so into the side came Mick Meagan, playing his first game since victory over Crewe in Round Three. Former Manchester United player Mark Pearson had to settle for a place on the bench.

It hardly mattered. Town more than matched their First Division opponents, with young Chris Nicholl the game's outstanding player. But when Stoke skipper Peter Dobing headed in from close range following a corner with ten minutes left, Town's efforts looked to have been in vain. That is until Nicholl back-headed one of Phil McCarthy's long throws for Les Massie to score the equaliser with Banks isolated. His goal somehow inspired Town to go for the kill and they could have nicked it. Ian Lawther headed over the bar, then with less than two minutes remaining, Massie went through on the left only to see Banks prove equal to his cross-shot.

Small clubs usually only get one chance at beating the top sides. It was true in this case, as a Terry Conroy hat-trick saw off Town's challenge at the Shay three days later. But at least Halifax had done well financially out of the competition, creating some interest among the Halifax people along the way. The replay at the Shay was watched by 24,891, and they paid new record receipts of £5,849, beating the £4,898 for the Town v Spurs Cup-tie in 1953.

LEAGUE DIVISION 3	**1969-70**
Division 3	18th
League Cup	2nd Round
FA Cup	1st Round

Mark Pearson and Ivan Hampton were not the only players to leave the Shay during the close season. Mick Meagan, after only one season here, took up the opportunity of becoming player-manager of League of Ireland side Drogheda, where amazingly he would win the last of his seventeen Irish caps. Halifax Town still awaited its first full international. And there was a change on the management side when Clive Baker, assistant coach for five years, moved to Rotherham United. Town offered his post to the former Leeds and Scotland ace Bobby Collins, but he declined it, and in the end, George Kirby, a player who had taken in Everton, Southampton, Coventry and Plymouth along his travels, took it on.

Alan Ball stated that his main priority for the forthcoming season was survival in the Third Division, and he added quality to his squad to help ensure it. Dave Lennard, having been released by Bolton, had travelled with Town on a pre-season tour of Ireland – Meagan's Drogheda side had provided the opposition in one of the games – and after impressing, became one of two close-season signings. The second was another Bolton player, former England international Freddie Hill. On 15 July, Town paid a new club record £6,000 for his services, and while he was in action here, it seemed money well spent.

Both Hill and Lennard took their place in Town's side that kicked off the new season in the home game against Shrewsbury at the Shay. Town won 1-0, but the club was concerned at the low attendance. Alas, apart from the local derbies that always attracted higher gates, this was as good as it was going to get. Town had won without Les Massie – he was top scorer in both his previous seasons here – who was named only as substitute. Two weeks into the season, still not having signed a new contract, Massie was sold to Bradford Park Avenue for £1,750, a move that came as a shock to many supporters. The 'Massie Affair' would raise its head intermittently whenever Town found goals hard to come by, the first such period, as it happened, being immediately after he was sold. Five games into the league programme, that opening day win was their only one, with just three goals scored.

Massie was not the only player to leave in controversial circumstances. After Town had gained a creditable point from a 1-1 draw at leaders Luton, Hatters' manager Harry Haslam, having been impressed by the performance of Chris Nicholl, immediately made an offer for the young centre-half. Half an hour after the final whistle a deal was struck, and Nicholl became a Luton player, netting Town a record £30,000. Like the sale of Massie, Nicholl's transfer met with a great deal of criticism from the fans, but chairman Alan Maden defended the club's actions, saying that Luton had made an offer which Town were not in a position to turn down.

The Shaymen had progressed to the second round of the League Cup, where they were drawn away at First Division West Ham, a side that included England World Cup winners Bobby Moore, Martin Peters and hat-trick hero Geoff Hurst. Town performed well at Upton Park despite going down 2-4, and their performance hinted at nothing to suggest how they would capitulate against Fulham two weeks later. Fulham had been in the First Division themselves only two seasons earlier, so remained quite an attraction, especially with the mercurial former England skipper Johnny Haynes in their side. In an amazing game, they trounced the Shaymen 8-0 at the Shay, with Steve Earle writing himself into the record books by scoring five goals.

Alex Smith, his confidence shattered, took time to get over this hammering, and Alan Ball saw fit to omit him – the first time Smith had been dropped in his career. John Connaughton was drafted in on loan from Wilf McGuiness's Manchester United and made his debut in a 1-0 win at high-flying Torquay. But overall, Town's form was giving cause for concern. At the end of October, no sooner had Ball scotched rumours that he was about to take over at Notts County, than he re-signed old Shay favourite Bill Atkins from Portsmouth in a new record deal worth £9,000. This resulted in Hugh Ryden, a disappointment this season, moving to Southport the following week.

Atkins made his second Halifax Town debut in a 3-1 win over a Rochdale side seeking its ninth consecutive win. Town hit something of a purple patch. They suffered only one defeat out of eleven games and by February had moved away from the relegation zone and into the top half of the table. Interest in the FA Cup had ended disappointingly, meantime, with defeat at Fourth Division Chester in a replay after a 3-3 draw at the Shay. But that was not the only disappointment that Halifax Town would suffer around this time. Their best player, Freddie Hill, broke three toes in a friendly with Sunderland on 19 January (Halifax won 4-0) and as things transpired, he would never play for the club again.

Hill's lay-off was offset somewhat by the arrival on 22 January of crafty outside-right Dave Chadwick from Bournemouth, another big-money buy at £7,000. His performances were appreciated by the Shay faithful, who, despite the improved results, continued to drift away. Chadwick made his debut in a 3-0 win over relegation-bound Barrow, one of the season's high points, but Town's good run could not last. Despite taking two forwards on loan, firstly Stoke City's former Northern Ireland international Roy Vernon, then Peter Graham from Barnsley, only three wins were recorded from the last nineteen games. Relegation had only been talked about lightly at the Shay, but in the end it was avoided by just four points. In early March they had been clear of the drop zone by ten points. Their last victory, indeed, was on 28 March, but it was a memorable one. A diving header by Chadwick right on half-time was enough to see off then division leaders Brighton at the Shay.

Town wound up the season with four consecutive defeats. By this time the people of Halifax had already lost interest, with less than 2,000 turning up for the visit of Walsall on the last day. Vice-chairman David Waithman, who had resigned from the board at the end of October, two months after Alan Walton had quit, had expressed his concerns then over the lack of support Halifax Town were enjoying. Things had not improved.

It had been in some ways a strange season – where else would a player who missed almost half the fixtures through injury be voted by the supporters as their Player of the Season, as Freddie Hill was? – but to be fair, it can be argued that a team should be judged over a full league programme. Alan Ball had wanted Town to remain a Division Three side come the end of the season, and so to that end at least he had to be satisfied with Town's eighteenth place finish.

Match of the Season 1969-70

Halifax Town 0 Fulham 8

Division 3, 16 September 1969

When Halifax Town were promoted to the Third Division, one of the most eagerly awaited fixtures was the visit to the Shay of Fulham. The Cottagers, under Bill Dodgin Jnr, found themselves in the same division but had entered it from the opposite direction, having finished bottom of Division Two the previous season.

One of the reasons why Fulham were such a big attraction was that only two seasons earlier they had been in the First Division, which they had occupied since 1959. Their fall from grace had been dramatic, and the meeting of these clubs was like the coming together of two worlds. Another reason was that they still had in their side the legendary Johnny Haynes, a former England skipper – he won 56 caps – and noted as one of the best passers of the ball the English game had seen.

Did You Know?

Halifax keeper Alex Smith played in Accrington Stanley's final League game in 1962 before the Lancashire club folded.

Town's manager recognised Fulham's threat and said so before the game. 'When this Fulham side really gets going, someone is going to get such a hiding,' he predicted, but surely he could never have imagined that they would run up such a score. Yet Town fans today still talk about the game and claim that it wasn't as one-sided as the scoreline suggests. True enough, for if Town had taken even half the chances that were presented to them, then the result would have been totally different.

Though Haynes was the star attraction, it was Steve Earle who left an indelible mark on the game, as he helped himself to five goals and put himself into the record books with the highest individual tally away from home. He scored his first after thirteen minutes, converting Stan Horne's pass – Town's David Shawcross had been unlucky to see his pass rebound off the referee in the build-up – and netted his fifth and Fulham's eighth in the 67th minute. Other goals came from Barry Lloyd and two from Republic of Ireland international Jimmy Conway, his first a penalty after Andy Burgin had brought him down. Haynes strutted his stuff before being replaced after eighty minutes by Dave Roberts.

Halifax Town were already in the record books after a 0-13 defeat at Stockport in 1934, and this defeat ensured them another entry, the heaviest-ever home defeat in Football League history. Fulham, for their part, confirmed themselves as one of the division's top sides, but would miss out on instant promotion, finishing fourth. They would, however, go up the following season, with the Shaymen not far behind.

LEAGUE DIVISION 3	**1970-71**
Division 3	3rd
League Cup	2nd Round
FA Cup	1st Round

No sooner had the 1969-70 season finished, then Town were to lose the services of their star player. Despite being missed for almost half of the season, the supporters were looking forward to seeing the best of Freddie Hill. But on 8 May, he took up the chance of returning to the First Division with Manchester City, then under the wings of Joe Mercer and the flamboyant Malcolm Allison, and moved to Maine Road in a record Shay deal worth £12,000.

Alan Ball retained the rest of the squad, but within weeks of the 1969-70 season finishing he too had left the club. Speculation had been rife ever since Preston had sacked manager Bobby Seith that Ball would be one of the favourites to take over. This was realised when, on 22 May, Ball moved to Deepdale, to a club that, on the face of it, had better prospects than Halifax Town. Ball took trainer Harry Hubbick – he had been at the Shay for seven years - with him.

Chairman Alan Maden described the loss of Ball as a 'body blow', but there was no shortage of applicants for the now vacant post of manager. Halifax Town received over fifty, but in the end the board decided to promote from within, and George Kirby, after a year as coach, moved into his first managerial hot-seat. He immediately installed Arthur Cox as coach, moving from a similar position at Aston Villa, and made Andy Burgin captain.

Kirby felt no need to delve into the transfer market immediately, despite the money available from the sale of Freddie Hill. But he did promise the Town supporters that, with the same players at his disposal – except for David Shawcross, who was advised to quit the game on medical advice – he would put the accent on attack. His one big surprise was the inclusion of young Keith Brierley in the forward line, but having nurtured him for a year in the reserves, Kirby had no doubts as to his ability.

As fate would have it, Kirby and his mentor Alan Ball met on the season's opening day at Preston, where the sides fought out a 1-1 draw. Town built on this, and when they defeated Doncaster on 11 September they moved into second place. A thrilling victory over local rivals Bradford City also carried them into the second round of the League Cup, and a meeting with Brian Clough's Derby County – former Town favourite Willie Carlin was in their side – at the Baseball Ground. Town lost 1-3, but fought all the way and were a credit to the Third Division. In November, Kirby returned to Derby to sign centre-half Tony Rhodes, a reserve, but who had played against Town in that match.

It was not just the new strip of tangerine shirts and blue shorts that was getting Town noticed in the league. A comprehensive 4-1 victory over Plymouth was one result among many that had other teams taking note. True, Chesterfield let Town off lightly with a 5-0 hammering, but the following week, Town's defeat of Preston, making steady progress towards the summit under Ball, was no fluke. Even after an indifferent spell, Town geared themselves up and came through with flying colours against an Aston Villa side playing in the Third Division for the first time. The Shaymen's 2-1 home win suggested that they could more than compete with the biggest clubs.

Tony Rhodes' arrival in a £7,000 deal coincided with the departure of coach Arthur Cox, who defected to Preston. His replacement at the Shay was Brian Green, who moved from Barrow, and though he lasted at Halifax longer than Cox, it was not by much. By the end of March, Green had headed for Kuwait, where a coaching post awaited him, so into his shoes stepped Mick Buxton, who had been advised to quit the game following two broken legs.

An unbeaten run in the New Year saw Town move among the promotion chasers, with Fulham, Preston and Villa – all clubs on sound financial footings – also in contention. Two draws and two wins in February earned Kirby his – and Town's – first Manager of the Month award, as the Shaymen moved into third spot. Then, during March, Town were put to the test, but proved equal to all that was thrown at them. They beat second-placed Fulham at the Shay, then seven days later held Aston Villa to a 1-1 draw at Villa Park in front of an attendance of 33,522.

Ultimately, Town would miss out on promotion by finishing third – three clubs were not promoted from Division Three until 1974 – and they probably looked back at the home defeat by Mansfield on 20 March as the game that cost them most. Dudley Roberts' headed goal did the damage, and after that Town were always chasing Preston and Fulham, while Villa, surprisingly, slipped out of the race. Halifax kept up the pressure on the leading two, however, and promotion was still a possibility with three games to go. But luck deserted Town at Torquay on 28 April, where they went down 0-2. The players returned to the dressing room knowing that the dream was over.

Still, Town's finishing position was creditable for a club that had on its books just sixteen professionals. They had scored more goals – 74 – than any other team in the division, and their right to compete in the following season's Watney Cup competition was some

Did You Know?

The Shay has hosted rugby, speedway, baseball, boxing, wrestling, target golf, athletics, and in 1963 – when the pitch froze over – public ice-skating!

compensation. But promotion was not the only thing that Town missed out on during the 1970-71 season. Car manufacturers Ford were giving away huge prizes in a Sporting League, based on fair play and goal-scoring. As the season entered its closing stages, Town were in contention for the £30,000 prize money for second place. But only the first 42 league games counted, and with three of Town's last four matches away from home (away goals counted double and Town's three more would have been enough) they were unable to overtake Crewe, and they ended up with nothing.

It was that sort of season. Even in the final of the West Riding Cup, played on 10 May, Town succumbed to Huddersfield Town at Leeds Road, who won thanks to an early Frank Worthington goal. The Shaymen had defeated an accomplished-looking Leeds United side in the semi-final, but like in everything else, were denied at the final hurdle. In retrospect, the 1970-71 campaign was something of a watershed. Subsequent events prior to the coming season perhaps suggested that Halifax Town would never get another chance of going so close.

Match of the Season 1970-71

Aston Villa 1 Halifax Town 1

Division 3, 13 March 1971

March was a massive month for Halifax Town. An unbeaten run of eleven league games had seen them move into the promotion frame, and they needed to keep the momentum going. On 6 March they had beaten fellow title contenders Fulham 2-1 at the Shay (revenge for the previous season's 0-8 thrashing), and now, seven days later, they travelled to meet Aston Villa.

Following relegation the previous season, Villa found themselves in Division Three for the first time, but manager Vic Crowe had already given their supporters a season to remember by taking his side to the League Cup final, beating First Division Manchester United and Burnley on the way. Villa had lost 0-2 to Tottenham at Wembley, but now, back in the league, they were still in with a chance of promotion at the first attempt. They went into this game, their first at home since that final, looking to end a run of three games without a win.

A good result here for the Shaymen would not only keep them in touch with the top, but would also illustrate just how far they had come since promotion two seasons earlier. But it was a daunting prospect. This was their first ever visit to Villa Park, and the huge crowd that was expected was realised when 33,522, the highest figure in the division so far that season (it would be broken the following week when derby rivals Walsall provided Villa's opposition) packed into the ground.

But how Town responded. Although the home side controlled the early stages and went in front, Town fought back, grabbed an equaliser, then hung on for a memorable draw. It was Fred Turnbull, on loan at Halifax the previous season, who put Villa ahead in the 31st minute. It was his second goal of the season – ironically his first had been in their 1-2 defeat at the Shay – and came after Alex Smith had failed to cut out Chico Hamilton's low right-wing corner. Town were relieved to see McMahon's header five minutes before the break ruled out because old warhorse Andy Lochhead was offside, but in the 62nd minute, they were level when Dave Chadwick planted the ball low into the right-hand corner of the net.

Villa piled on the pressure late on but Town held firm and the game ended a draw. At the same time, however, leaders Preston won at Rochdale, and second placed Fulham beat Rotherham, to increase their lead over Town, lying third. As the season went into April, Town remained the main challengers, as Villa faltered, but they were always playing catch-up.

LEAGUE DIVISION 3	**1971-72**
Division 3	17th
League Cup	2nd Round
FA Cup	1st Round

George Kirby, unsurprisingly, retained all the players that had performed so well the previous season, and there was talk – naturally – of the club going one better this time around. The side began its preparations for the forthcoming season with a short tour, once again, of Ireland, before playing hosts to one of the biggest clubs in the world, Manchester United, in the Watney Cup.

This was a tournament for each division's top scorers not involved in Europe or promotion, and the game at the Shay kicked off a new season covered by the BBC's 'Match of the Day'. The bumper 19,765 crowd – and later that evening millions on TV – witnessed one of the shocks of the season as a star-studded Manchester United side that included George Best, Bobby Charlton and Denis Law were beaten 2-1 by an enthusiastic Town side.

Four days later, the Shaymen were beaten in the semi-finals 0-2 at home by a ruthless West Bromwich Albion, now under the guidance of future England coach Don Howe. Colin Suggett scored both West Brom's goals. George Kirby, however, was preparing to say his farewells to his players and the fans. When Second Division Watford lost manager Ken Furphy to Blackburn Rovers, it was to Halifax Town and Kirby that they turned for a replacement. Watford were hardly a glamour club, but they were without doubt bigger than Halifax, and so on 5 August, the day after Town's exit from the Watney Cup, Kirby announced that he was leaving, and he took up the post at Vicarage Road the following week.

In June, chairman Alan Maden had resigned, which meant that his successor Arthur Smith, a Nottingham-based businessman, found that his first job was to appoint Kirby's successor. The board interviewed among others Jack Crompton, the Manchester United trainer, but on 10 August, just four days before the new league season was due to start, plumped for Barrow coach Ray Henderson, appointing him as the new Halifax Town manager.

Henderson pledged attacking football – he reckoned in the Kirby mould – but made no promises as to how the team would fare. He privately believed that Town were not yet geared to Second Division soccer, should they get there this time, but alas, neither he nor his team even got close.

The 1971-72 season was disappointing to say the least, yet it promised much to start with. Only one game was lost from the first five, and after disposing of local rivals Rochdale at the third attempt in the League Cup, Town performed admirably at St James' Park despite losing 1-2 at First Division Newcastle United. The Magpies' latest hotshot No 9, Malcolm Macdonald, was one of the scorers.

With hindsight, the rot seemed to set in after a game that Town dominated but in which they ended up with nothing. Aston Villa would go on to clinch the title, but at the Shay on 18 September they were decidedly second best, only to steal the points with a late Ray Graydon goal. Town barely recovered. Despite taking winger John Farley on loan from George Kirby's Watford – he proved a success with three goals from six games – the club was not helped by the shock transfer of the popular Dave Lennard – albeit for a welcome club record £30,500 – to Blackpool on 7 October. Shortly afterwards, Henderson lost the services of coach Mick Buxton, who left to join forces with Kirby at Watford. At least the appointment of his successor, George Mulhall, the former Aberdeen, Sunderland and Scotland international, would prove to be a significant one for Halifax Town.

Mulhall took up his coaching duties on 18 October, by which time Town had cascaded down the table. In an effort to stem the tide, Henderson took midfielder Johnny Johnston on loan from Blackpool, then delved into the transfer market, buying firstly outside-right Frank Brogan, then forward Terry Shanahan, both from Ipswich Town, for £4,000 and £8,000 respectively. Cruelly, Town were denied the services of Brogan after he broke his leg in a challenge with Plymouth's Steve Davey at the Shay in only his third game. He would not play again that season.

Town were lying sixteenth and looking forward to a morale-boosting run in the FA Cup when they travelled to Northern Premier League outfit Wigan Athletic for their first-round match. But their season went from bad to worse as the home side ran up a two-goal half-time lead, which Town, despite a late rally, found too much to pull back.

Out of the Cup, Henderson's response on 2 December was to break the club transfer record by signing Blackpool's Fred Kemp for £13,500. Slowly, he was trying to mould his own team, but results were hardly improving. After defeat at Rochdale in late January, Town lay nineteenth, just two places above the relegation zone, and pressure from the fans reached such a pitch that the board and management held a public talk-in, where they outlined their hopes for the club. The players responded with their highest victory of the season, but Dave Chadwick's goal in their 4-1 win over Wrexham was also his last for the Shaymen. He had earlier expressed a desire to leave, and on 24 February he did so, moving to Bournemouth for £12,000, a somewhat meagre sum for a player of such high talent.

Did You Know?

Ian Lawther signed for Halifax Town from Brentford in 1968 in the House of Commons. The Brentford chairman was a Member of Parliament.

The lowest point of Town's league season was undoubtedly their 0-5 defeat, and the manner in which they succumbed to it, at the hands of Brighton at the Shay. On this showing, Town were looking relegation certainties, but three consecutive wins at the end of March and the beginning of April did much to ease such fears. However, they were still not safe from the drop when they went into their last home game of the season against Shrewsbury. The ensuing goalless draw ensured their survival, but Town's return of only one win from their last nine games gave cause for concern. The side finished 17th, just two points clear of relegation. Attendance figures, too, were worrying, for they had begun to dip regularly below the 3,000 mark, and the directors felt the need to take drastic action. On 16 May, just four days after picking his last Halifax Town team that season – it was for a West Riding Senior Cup Final, in which Town lost 3-4 to First Division Leeds United – Henderson was sacked.

Ray Henderson was unlucky. The side was always going to find it hard to match the achievements of the previous term, and the sale of some of the top players was not necessarily his responsibility. He sought replacements, and in Frank Brogan found a good one. It must have been heartbreaking for Henderson to see him break his leg so early on.

Arthur Smith had begun the season appointing a new manager. He would spend part of the summer starting the process all over again.

Match of the Season 1971-72

Halifax Town 2 Manchester United 1

Watney Cup, 1st Round, 31 July 1971

Sponsorship came to British soccer with the advent of mini-competitions such as the Watney Invitation Cup and Texaco Cup for a short spell in the early 1970s. The Watney Cup, as it was more simply known, had been inaugurated in 1970 and was open to the two highest scoring clubs from each division which neither qualified for Europe or gained promotion.

In 1971, Halifax Town qualified for the competition by finishing third in Division Three, having scored 74 goals, with Wrexham, ninth, joining them, having netted 72. The reward for their free-scoring exploits was a plum home tie with First Division Manchester United, a game that kicked off a new series of BBC's 'Match of the Day'.

United had finished a disappointing eighth but were still one of the biggest names in world football. However, despite winning the European Cup only three years earlier, their side was generally regarded as being past its peak. In an attempt to bring back the glory days, they had recruited Frank O'Farrell from Leicester City as manager, and this was his first match in charge.

This Manchester United side still contained many star names, not least the 'holy trinity' of Denis Law, George Best and Bobby Charlton, and they all played in this game. The folk of Halifax were not used to being in such illustrious company, so they turned up in numbers and with thousands of United followers, a minority of which terrorised the town centre, the game produced a crowd of 19,765. This figure has never been bettered since at the Shay.

It was a day the Town fans will never forget. Bill Atkins' glancing header gave the Shaymen the lead after only three minutes, but in the 25th minute Willie Morgan missed the chance to equalise when Alex Smith saved his penalty-kick. A minute later, Bob Wallace succeeded where Morgan had failed by converting his penalty (David Sadler had felled Lammie Robertson in the box) to make it 2-0.

United reduced the arrears with the game's third penalty, George Best this time taking responsibility after Tony Rhodes had brought him down, but the Shaymen held out for a memorable win. Defeat for United, however, did not seem to worry them unduly. They stormed the First Division and looked likely championship contenders before 'burning up' dramatically after the turn of the year.

For Town, this was as good as it got this season. Though no one knew it at the time, manager George Kirby was entering his last week here as manager before heading for Watford. His last game in charge was a 0-2 defeat in the semi-final against a no-nonsense West Bromwich Albion side.

HALIFAX TOWN: Smith, Burgin, Lee, Wallace, Pickering, Rhodes, Chadwick, Atkins, Robertson, Lennard, Holmes.
MANCHESTER UNITED: Stepney, Fitzpatrick, Dunne, Crerand (Burns), James, Sadler, Morgan, Gowling (Kidd), Charlton, Law, Best.

2

AGAINST THE ODDS 1972-1976

LEAGUE DIVISION 3	**1972-73**
Division 3	20th
League Cup	1st Round
FA Cup	2nd Round

Without a manager to draw up the club's summer list of retained players, but with the knowledgeable George Mulhall around to assist them, the directors retained all but one of the professionals who had featured in the disappointing 1971-72 season. Missing was Bob Wallace, who, having asked for a transfer, moved to Chester for £4,000.

Mulhall seemed an obvious choice as the next manager, and on 28 June the board put their faith in him. This was Mulhall's first managerial post. He immediately went to Hartlepool to bring former Newcastle half-back Ken Hale to the Shay. Hale originally came as coach, but such was the side's plight later in the season that he re-registered as a player to help Town out of their crisis. Mulhall's only other significant signing in the close season was that of Johnny Quinn from Rotherham United.

Halifax Town travelled to Scotland for a short tour before the new season kicked off. The supporters were heartened not only by the victories over Arbroath and Cowdenbeath, but also because Frank Brogan was now fit and raring to go. Town's league programme opened with a single-goal victory at Brentford – Terry Shanahan netted a late winner – and after the first four games, two wins and two draws saw Town on top of the Division Three table. Defeat by Fourth Division Bury in the League Cup was disappointing, though it was hardly the end of the world, and after two successive defeats by Bournemouth and Chesterfield, Town returned to the top, briefly, after a 3-0 win at Scunthorpe.

Then things started to go wrong. By the end of September, the side had slipped into mid-table, and by the end of the following month, had dropped as low as eighteenth. Confidence was being drained away, and November saw things slip from bad to worse, both on and off the field. A friendly at Blyth, no doubt intended to help boost morale, had the adverse effect – Town lost 2-4. Then on 16 November, both chairman Arthur Smith and director Arthur Mitchell failed to be re-elected to the board. Smith had been criticised over financial matters, and offered no satisfactory explanation as to why the accounts for 1970-71 had been prepared so late, nor when last season's would be ready. Vice-chairman Percy Albon took over the running of the club, and Harry Taylor returned to the board to fill Albon's former position.

A recurrence of a knee injury would keep Alex Smith out of the side until February, so reserve keeper Barry White – having been at the club since November 1970 – was called up for his first prolonged spell. His first game was at Barnsley in the first round of the FA Cup, and he did his utmost to earn Town their replay, which they won. But as the team prepared for the their second-round game at Scunthorpe three weeks later, the club rocked supporters by selling Bill Atkins to Rochdale. The timing of his transfer – the deal was actually completed on the morning of the Scunthorpe match – was questionable, and did nothing to help the team as they slipped to a 2-3 defeat at the Old Show Ground. Mulhall had claimed that Atkins did not fit into his plans, but the fans felt they had a right to know just what those plans were.

A week after the cup defeat, Mulhall exchanged Lammie Robertson for Brighton's former Northern Ireland international Willie Irvine, plus £23,000. Doubtless Irvine would have made his debut at York on 16 December, had the Town boss not successfully called the match off on account of five of his players going down with flu. But when Irvine did appear in the side, his contribution was minimal, as Town's miserable run of games without a win extended to fourteen. By the turn of the year, Halifax were in the relegation zone.

Looking for fresh impetus, Mulhall signed Ken Hale on as a player, and he made his debut in Town's first home win in the league since August – 1-0 over bottom club Scunthorpe, their cup conquerors. But it was a flash in the pan. Despite adding to the squad John Wilkie, a £1,000 signing from Highland League side Ross County, Town's fortunes hardly improved. Mulhall actually saw fit to transfer-list Dave Verity, Terry Shanahan, Frank Brogan and Keith Brierley – the last-named actually went on loan to Yeovil Town – and in February Mulhall suspended young Alan Waddle for a 'breach of club discipline'. But a further run of six games without a win meant the situation was becoming desperate, with Town now lying next to bottom.

Did You Know?

In 1971 v Bury, Town were refused permission to play a tape of a Cup final crowd. It was feared Town would turn up the volume when they had the ball.

A promising run in March – four unbeaten games including three wins – hinted at a revival. But at the beginning of April, Mulhall admitted that avoiding relegation looked a forlorn hope. Not that Town waved the white flag. Shanahan put himself back in favour with a hat-trick as Town defeated Brentford 3-2, though he might have wished there had been a bigger crowd to see him do it. The attendance of 970 was at that time the lowest-ever first-team attendance in the Shay's history.

With four games left, however, Halifax were five points adrift from safety. There were only two points for a win in those days, remember, and Town looked out for the count. They could not afford any more slip-ups, so were fortunate that the first three of their remaining fixtures were at home. Still, it was remarkable that they should first beat Charlton, then Southend, then, in their last home game of the season, Bournemouth. Those six points set Halifax up for the final showdown at Fellows Park, home of Walsall.

It was all or nothing: only victory would enable Town to avoid the drop and send Rotherham down instead. Town had to make do without Trevor Womble – he had played in ten games on loan from Rotherham, but under the circumstances, was recalled by the Millmoor club. In one of the most dramatic evenings in Halifax's history, Alan Waddle's headed goal proved enough. Town moved out of the bottom four and relegated Rotherham on the slimmest of margins – goal-average. It had been the mother and father of all the great escapes.

Immediately, Mulhall looked to the new season by promoting Quinn to assistant coach, and then announced a retained list of twelve other players. Released were Brogan and Brierley, together with reserves Barry Holmes – he had actually been at the Shay since 1966 – Jim McKernan and Michael Swaine.

Match of the Season 1972-73

Walsall 0 Halifax Town 1

Division 3, 1 May 1973

Just two years after going so close to Division Two, Halifax Town's Third Division survival – for the time being at least – rested on their last game of the season away at Walsall. The incredible thing was that going into the game they were still in with a chance, for only three weeks earlier, they had looked certainties for the drop when they lay next to bottom of the table, five points adrift of safety.

Amazingly, after three consecutive home wins, the situation had dramatically altered, and Town travelled to Fellows Park knowing that victory – and nothing else – would ensure their survival, whilst condemning Rotherham to relegation along with Brentford, Swansea and Scunthorpe.

Manager George Mulhall seemingly never had his doubts. On the day of the match, he said, 'I am confident, and so are the players, that we can get a result. And by that I mean a win. We have to treat it as a home game, since only two points will do.' The only thing in Town's favour was that Bill Moore's Walsall side had nothing to play for, having crossed the safety threshold with a couple of games left to play. Professional pride, however, would prevent Walsall from simply handing Town the points.

The thousand or so Halifax supporters who made the journey to the Midlands were in wonderland when Alan Waddle rose to head in Johnny Quinn's hanging cross in the 35th minute. But nerves were tested to the limit when, in the second half, Chris Jones fired wide from a dangerous position. Five minutes from time Alex Smith had to make a fingertip save from Saddlers' sub Brian Caswell.

The Shaymen hung on, their Houdini-act complete, but for Rotherham it was a cruel way to be relegated. Goal-average had decided the issue, with Town's more favourable, 0.83 to Rotherham's 0.78, meaning Halifax stopped up by 0.05 of a goal. In the dressing room, apparently, Mulhall had his players observing two minutes' silence for Jim McAnearney's side, but relegation would mean the Millers' boss would lose his job.

Alan Waddle's goal, despite being only his third of the season, was probably the most important one he would ever score. But it turned out to be his last significant contribution in Town's colours. During the summer, Liverpool manager Bill Shankly took him to Anfield, where relegation was a word never used.

LEAGUE DIVISION 3	**1973-74**
Division 3	9th
League Cup	2nd Round
FA Cup	2nd Round

It was no secret that Alan Waddle, after a number of promising displays, was a wanted man. At the beginning of June, Halifax Town put a £46,000 price tag on the head of the player whom George Mulhall had reckoned had saved the club from relegation, and three weeks later, that is what reigning League Champions Liverpool paid for him. Bill Shankly was looking for an understudy for John Toshack, and Waddle's 6ft 3in frame more than fitted the bill.

Also leaving the Shay was Jeff Lee, a loyal servant, who had signed for Halifax Town originally as an amateur way back in 1964. The previous season, Lee had been awarded a benefit match – Preston provided the opposition in November and won 4-3 – but although he had been retained by Mulhall, Lee fancied a change, and Peterborough United paid £6,000 for his services.

New players included a straight replacement for Waddle in Welsh Under-23 international Dave Gwyther, a regular tormentor of the Shaymen. He cost £10,000 from Swansea City, and was probably more the finished article than Waddle was. David Ford, a former England Under-23 international and FA Cup finalist and scorer with Sheffield Wednesday, actually joined from Sheffield United, David Pugh was a £6,000 buy from Chesterfield, whilst Gerry McDonald arrived on a free having been released by Blackburn Rovers. Then, just two days before the new season was due to start, Mulhall rushed back from a scouting mission in Scotland to secure Huddersfield Town winger Alan Jones in a £4,500 deal.

Halifax Town's start to the league programme was unspectacular, three straight draws setting the tone for the rest of the season. The first win arrived at Oakwell, where Town disposed of Fourth Division Barnsley in the first round of the League Cup, but only after a replay. The first league win, against Charlton, came at the sixth attempt, and coincided with Pugh taking over the captaincy after Mulhall had claimed that John Pickering was 'too quiet'.

Charlton would gain ample revenge two weeks later when they won 5-2 at the Valley, one of two early season hammerings suffered by Town – Grimsby had won 4-1 at Blundell Park on 11 September. Town were hardly setting the division alight, and their second round League Cup-tie with Wolverhampton Wanderers at the Shay was probably a welcome distraction. Wolves were a useful First Division outfit, and had been UEFA Cup finalists the previous season (they lost over two legs to Tottenham Hotspur). Their current side included internationals Derek Dougan (Northern Ireland) – he was chairman of the PFA – John Richards (England) and future Town manager Jim McCalliog (Scotland). On the night, Town matched their opponents for long periods, only to go down 0-3, with Fred Kemp missing a crucial penalty at 0-1. Wolves would not look back in the competition, going on to beat Manchester City 2-1 in the final at Wembley.

Just how many of the 8,222 who watched that match at the Shay got in without paying is not clear, but doubtless quite a few did. At their AGM on 18 October, Halifax Town announced they were losing around £600 per week, but Mulhall was quick to accuse the board about their attitude towards ground security. There were many 'hidden' parts of the ground where gate-crashers, especially young boys, could sneak in for free, but alas, this problem would not be addressed properly for several years. Until it was, Halifax Town would keep on losing money.

Dave Worthington, who began his career at the Shay in 1962, returned to the fold on loan from Grimsby. He played his part in a six-match unbeaten run that culminated in a 6-1 defeat of Northern Premier League Frickley Colliery in the first round of the FA Cup. Frickley, cheered on by around 1,000 supporters, included in their side former Town winger Archie Taylor, but they were clearly second best on the day. Dave Gwyther scored a headed hat-trick as Halifax Town ran up their highest score since defeating Bishop Auckland 7-0 in an FA Cup replay in 1967.

Towards the end of 1973, Ted Heath's Conservative Government had been hit by an energy crisis that had resulted in the three-day week. The Football League tried to help out by allowing games to kick-off an hour earlier, thereby avoiding the necessity of using floodlights. One game that remained a 3pm kick-off was Town's first-ever league meeting with Huddersfield Town at Leeds Road on Boxing Day. The Shaymen lost 0-4, but they put it out of their system with a useful run over the holiday period. They even managed to hold leaders Bristol Rovers to a goalless draw, and for a short time there was optimistic talk on the terraces of promotion.

Because of the energy crisis, the board – it now included John Crowther – had discussed the possibility of Sunday soccer. Once the Football League sanctioned this experiment, Town played three games at the Shay on the Sabbath, the first being a 1-1 draw with Southport, then managed by Alan Ball, following his sacking from Preston the previous season. There were obvious comparisons in attendances at the Shay with those at Thrum Hall, where Halifax RLFC played hosts to New Hunslet. 4,178 turned up for the soccer, whilst only 1,302 attended the rugby, thereby pouring scorn on those who believed that Halifax has always been a rugby town.

Town's two other Sunday games saw them defeat Walsall 3-1, then lose 0-1 to Cambridge, for whom ex-Shayman Dave Lennard scored the only goal. Brighton, now managed by Brian Clough following a dramatic exit from Derby County, turned down Town's request to play on the Sunday, citing a lack of rail services as their reason.

The last three months of the season were especially difficult. When Alan Jones underwent a cartilage operation, Town's professional staff was cut to just fourteen players. Mulhall was fortunate to sign Huddersfield's David Smith on deadline day on a month's loan, but in view of Town's plight Smith would stay at the Shay until the end of the season. Still, content with his efforts at keeping Town's head above the water, the board at long last offered Mulhall a two-year contract – until then he was not under contract – which on 18 March he accepted. One of his next tasks was to oblige the League to postpone Town's game at Bournemouth on 29 March because he was down to just ten fit players, including both keepers.

Unexpectedly, given the circumstances, Town ended the season with an eight-match unbeaten run, saving the best game till last. Then, having fallen behind, they defeated an already promoted York side in a thrilling contest. Following the drama of the previous term, George Mulhall had worked wonders to steer Town to a praiseworthy ninth position, and most importantly in the eyes of many Shay supporters, one place higher than Huddersfield Town.

Upon the season's close, Mulhall released Wilkie – he would return to Ross County – McDonald, and John Pickering, whom he described as 'a tremendous professional'. Open to offers were Terry Shanahan and Fred Kemp, the latter eventually moving to Hereford for a four-figure fee in June, having never really settled in Halifax in two and a half years here.

Match of the Season 1973-74

Halifax Town 1 Southport 1

Division 3, 27 January 1974

On the face of it, this was just another run-of-the-mill fixture between two Third Division sides, neither of whom were making waves. Town were placed comfortably in mid-table, whilst Southport were fighting a losing relegation battle. But what made this game unique, as far as Halifax Town was concerned, was that it was the first ever played at the Shay on a Sunday.

Did You Know?

In the 1971 Watney Cup, Halifax Town experimented with wearing numbers on the front of their shirts. It was quickly abandoned.

Because of the energy crisis, the Football Association had ordered all games to kick off early so as to avoid power cuts. Then, in late December, they sanctioned Sunday football for the first time. On Sunday, 4 January, four FA Cup-ties had been played, with Cambridge's meeting with Oldham the first to kick off.

The Halifax Town board had toyed with the idea of Sunday soccer, and at a meeting on 14 January decided to give it a try. Their next scheduled weekend home game, against Southport, would be put back a day with a 2.30pm start, but their decision upset Halifax RLFC, who were playing New Hunslet up at Thrum Hall that same afternoon 'If there was any honour between the clubs, Town should keep to Saturday. After all, we were in first,' muttered their secretary, Bill Hughes.

Undeterred, Town went ahead with their plan, and the game was watched by a welcome 4,178 – this compared to their Saturday average of 2,921 – whilst the rugby club, rightly aggrieved, attracted barely 1,000. One person missing from the match was Southport caretaker-manager Alan Ball, the former Town boss, who had failed to meet up with the team bus on the way. Yet without him, his side collected only its sixth and last away point of the season. Jim Fryatt, put clear by Alex Russell, coolly scored five minutes after Dave Gwyther had converted Johnny Quinn's 74th-minute cross.

Attendance-wise, Town's two further Sunday games, against Walsall and Cambridge, were also above average. The same could not be said of the results. But though the people of Halifax had taken to Sunday soccer, it would be another twenty seasons before Town would play another Sunday game at the Shay.

LEAGUE DIVISION 3	**1974-75**
Division 3	17th
League Cup	2nd Round
FA Cup	2nd Round

If George Mulhall was to carry Halifax Town on to better things, he would have to do it without his assistant Ken Hale, who returned to his former club Hartlepool at the beginning of June to take over as manager. Mulhall thought he had solved that particular problem when he promoted Johnny Quinn to player-coach, but deep inside, he knew things were not quite as he would have wanted them to be.

New players at the club were striker Steve Downes and left-back John Collins from Chesterfield and Portsmouth respectively – each costing £6,000 – and midfielder Ricky Moir from Shrewsbury. Town's professional staff was increased to fifteen with the additions of trialist Paul Luckett and groundstaff boy Mark Harold, but there was disappointment when former skipper Andy Burgin asked for a transfer. Though he would appear in Town's opening five games, he would finally get his wish, moving to Blackburn Rovers for a £14,500 fee.

Whether or not he believed his own words, Mulhall stated publicly that Halifax would be a force to be reckoned with this season. Early results suggested they might. As well as moving into the second round of the League Cup, following a 2-1 win at Barnsley, Town were unbeaten in their first three league games and had looked particularly accomplished when beating Crystal Palace – a First Division side only two seasons previously – 3-1 at home. Smarting from defeat, Palace boss Malcolm Allison retorted that the Shay facilities were a disgrace, and Town shouldn't even be in the Football League. Even so, it was the Shaymen who had the chance to go top in their next game, although as they would do so often, they proceeded to blow it big style, crashing 0-4 at Southend.

Oxford defender Nick Lowe had been signed on loan. He played in the Shaymen's 0-3 defeat at Stoke City in the second round of the League Cup, where Terry Conroy, a tormentor of the Shayman for a number of years, scored a hat-trick. The result suggested an easy ride for the First Division side, but it was never that. Town actually acquitted themselves quite well, but the successive defeats in the league that followed gave cause for concern. Mulhall was exasperated in his efforts to improve things, but with only a small squad to work with, this was nigh on impossible. On 18 September, fed up and disillusioned, he tendered his resignation, claiming that Halifax Town wasn't for him. Second Division Bolton, however, evidently were, for within a month he teamed up with Ian Greaves at Burnden Park.

Into Mulhall's shoes stepped Johnny Quinn – he was appointed caretaker manager for the 0-1 defeat at Blackburn – but having being given the job on a permanent basis on 23 September he immediately attempted to have Town's game at Peterborough postponed as he had only twelve players at his disposal. The Football League refused permission, so, undeterred, Quinn pressed Barry White into action as an emergency sweeper. This would be the first of four outfield appearances made by Town's reserve keeper, as injuries cut the squad down to the bare minimum.

While Town slithered down the table – defeat at Aldershot left them twentieth – Quinn added new faces to his squad. The Chesterfield pair of midfielder Ray McHale and centre-back Albert Phelan signed up, with want-away Terry Shanahan moving in the opposite direction. Then Kenny Blair arrived, originally on loan from Dave Mackay's Derby County – he would sign permanently in November – to compensate for the loss of Nick Lowe, who had been recalled by Oxford. Another extra player was acquired when Syd Farrimond arrived from Tranmere Rovers to take up his duties as coach. Farrimond registered as a player in case of emergencies, but Town had to fork out £500 for his extra services.

Whilst results were generally disappointing, the one shining light in the side was the form of striker Dave Gwyther. He was playing so well that Quinn suggested the Welsh FA take a look at him with a view to Wales' European Championship qualifying game with Hungary at the end of October.

A five-match unbeaten run took Town up to eighteenth, but their revival ended with a bang at Gillingham. There were hopes that a run in the FA Cup might spark some interest among supporters, but though the team won at Barnsley in the first round, a shallow performance at non-league Stafford Rangers led to an embarrassing 1-2 defeat, the winning goal coming in injury-time. Town therefore missed out on the chance of pulling a big club that would have brought in extra revenue. And how the club needed it. The directors claimed they only had enough money to keep the club going until the end of February, and might have to sell their best players to survive beyond that.

At the turn of the year, Town still hovered just above the relegation zone. A 0-4 defeat at Wrexham told no lies. Though Quinn signed a full-back from Colchester confusingly named Alex Smith – the same as Halifax's goalkeeper – and took on loan Bobby Scaife (Middlesbrough) and Bobby Campbell (Aston Villa), defeat at Preston on 8 February dropped Town to 22nd in the table.

Did You Know?

Between 1965 and 1971, the four corners of the pitch had to be taken up whenever speedway meetings were held on the perimeter cinder track.

Then suddenly, Town found the form that would ultimately save them. A five-game unbeaten run included a 2-1 victory over neighbours Huddersfield – they were bottom and having harder times than Halifax. This run lifted Halifax out of the relegation zone and was a prelude to an even better run to the season's close, in which they only lost two of their last nine games. The drop was avoided. Safety was actually guaranteed at Brighton on 16 April – four games from the season's end – where Town slugged out a goalless draw.

The retained list was announced before the last game of the season. Only Ricky Moir was released, but omitted from the list was the name of Johnny Quinn. He had not actually played since February, but he knew by now the extent of the demands of being manager of Halifax Town. Quinn retired as a player in order to give himself the best chance of turning the club around. However, as he was to find to his cost, this would be beyond him.

Match of the Season 1974-75

Halifax Town 3 Preston North End 0

Division 3, 2 November 1974

If George Mulhall had resigned back in September because he was fed up, supporters might have forgiven his successor Johnny Quinn had he done likewise. Town failed to find any sort of consistency and flirted with relegation for too long. Though this was ultimately avoided, supporters must have wondered why relegation was ever an issue, for they knew that on their day Halifax Town were more than a match for anybody. This game with Preston was a case in point.

At the end of August, under Mulhall, Town had blown away Crystal Palace 3-1 at the Shay. Then, following eleven games without a win, Quinn saw his side tear Southend apart. Three games on, the players prepared for the visit of Preston, a team expected to give them a rough ride.

Having retired from playing in 1973, Manchester United legend Bobby Charlton had gone into management at Deepdale, but his first season had ended in relegation to the Third Division. In an attempt to win promotion at the first time of asking, Charlton had decided to put his boots on again, and for a while it looked as if his magic might turn the tables. After only one defeat in the first eight games, Preston had hit the top spot in late September, and just prior to this Shay meeting had gone back to the top on the back of three consecutive wins.

Charlton included in his side two of his former United team-mates, David Sadler and Nobby Stiles – Stiles was substitute – both of whom had played in the 1968 European Cup triumph over Benfica. But Town were unconcerned. They tore into Preston and by half-time had the game as good as won. Ricky Moir opened the scoring midway through the half, then Ray McHale made it 2-0, blasting the ball past the wall when Dave Gwyther touched a twice-taken free-kick to him. Right on half-time, Gwyther rolled the ball across for on-loan Kenny Blair – he would sign for Town the following week from Derby – to score his first goal in Town's colours.

Though no goals followed after the break – as if they were needed – Town had done enough to secure the points. But they could not follow up this fine victory with more of the same. As was their wont, they crashed 0-4 at Gillingham in their next match and continued their battle against relegation. For Bobby Charlton, whose previous appearance at the Shay, incidentally, was in Manchester United's Watney Cup defeat, his Preston side would struggle to come to terms with this setback. They would lose their next three matches, and at the season's close finished a disappointing sixth.

LEAGUE DIVISION 3	**1975-76**
Division 3	24th (relegated)
League Cup	2nd Round
FA Cup	3rd Round

Johnny Quinn prepared for his first full season in charge – at least that's what he hoped it would be – by strengthening his squad with a number of new faces. First to arrive was 22-year-old goalkeeper Terry Gennoe from Bury. Gennoe only had three league games behind him, but looked promising enough for Town to shell out £3,000 for him. He was joined by young forward Derek Bell from Derby County, and trialist Dave Harris (Oldham Athletic), who was later offered a contract. Following a trans-Atlantic phone call, Town also received an assurance that former Tranmere midfielder Tommy Veitch would be joining the club. Veitch was currently playing for Denver in the NASL, and he duly arrived in September.

Fashion-wise, the club did away with the blue and tangerine strip they had worn for the past two seasons and returned to the more traditional blue shirts and white shorts, and for a while the change looked to have rubbed off on the players' performances. Despite an opening day home defeat by relegated Millwall – they would return to the Second Division at the first attempt – Town shrugged off the loss to win their next three matches. This carried them to third in the table. These wins sparked an eight-game unbeaten run, which kept the team tucked in behind the leaders.

In the League Cup, Town had disposed of Fourth Division Hartlepool United 5-3 on aggregate before entertaining First Division strugglers Sheffield United. The Blades' 4-2 victory in a game held up for a while by spectacular flashes of lightning, was actually their first win of the season. Town emerged with credit from the defeat, which was no less than what supporters expected, considering the team's positive start in the league.

Sadly, the rot seemed to set in following defeat at Swindon, Town's first reverse on their travels. This was followed by a home defeat at the hands of Hereford United, and after losing 1-3 to Crystal Palace in early November the Shaymen had slipped to sixteenth. The poor run was halted with victory over Preston, but Town were hardly convincing, and grey clouds loomed over the Shay.

In these circumstances Town were glad of a good run in the FA Cup. Top non-league side Altrincham were seen off at the Shay. Town then made sure there was no repeat of the previous season's embarrassment, gaining revenge over Stafford Rangers, 3-1 in their own back yard. Having reached the third round for the first time since 1969, Town bowed out at Bobby Robson's First Division Ipswich Town, losing 1-3, but in the light of what Ipswich were to achieve over the next few years, this was no disgrace.

Meanwhile, form in the league saw no improvement. Town dropped to eighteenth at Christmas, before a 1-0 victory at Rotherham temporarily lifted the gloom. That goal was scored by Dave Gwyther, a significant one as it turned out, for it was his last for the club. He had already asked for a move, and would eventually get one, though it would not be Johnny Quinn who finally sold him.

Goalkeeper Terry Gennoe, without being outstanding, had kept his place in the side, but when he pulled a hip muscle in training this prompted a recall for Alex Smith. But with Smith in the side, Town failed to win a game, and by the time Gennoe returned in February, Halifax were next to bottom and had a new manager.

With results giving continued cause for concern, Quinn's position had come under scrutiny. On 19 January he told the board that if the team did not improve in their next three games he would have to buy new players. Following a home defeat by Shrewsbury, Quinn fielded ten of that side in a reserve fixture at Doncaster, a game that was lost 1-2. Present that night was Alan Ball, and it was here that he was approached with a view to making a return to the Shay as manager.

Quinn was shocked to read about this in a Sunday newspaper, and the story was backed up by the Halifax *Evening Courier* the following day. That evening, 2 February, the board sacked him. Quinn, who had no contract, felt he had been stabbed in the back, and the manner of his dismissal provoked outrage from the fans. Chairman Percy Albon defended the board's decision: 'We were losing spectators, and the position was becoming critical.'

Alan Ball thereby began his second stint as Halifax manager, but defeat in his first game, ironically at Preston, the club for which he had left the Shay in 1970, dumped Town into the relegation zone for the first time. The enormity of Ball's task was put into perspective when Town lost at home to bottom club Mansfield, who would eventually pull clear. After selling Gwyther for £17,000 (actually on the morning of that match) he brought in new players, possibly too many too soon. Midfield hardman Jimmy McGill arrived from Hull City, and forward Mickey Bullock from Orient, both for £5,000, whilst another experienced forward, George Jones, cost £2,000 from Oldham Athletic. Shortly afterwards, right-back Bobby Flavell arrived from Burnley for £6,000, with John Overton coming on loan from Aston Villa.

Ball kidded the supporters that Town could and would avoid relegation. Results suggested otherwise, apart from a magnificent performance at leaders Hereford, where Town pulled off one of the shocks of the season, winning 2-1. But it was as if the players had put all their efforts into this one game. Town only managed to win two more games from their last eleven, but such was the tightness of the situation at the bottom that relegation was not confirmed until the penultimate match – a home defeat by Aldershot.

The last game was a rearranged fixture with Colchester, the original on 10 April having been postponed because Town had seven players down with flu. The delay only prolonged the agony. The fans stayed away in numbers, with a pathetic 856 watching the match. Failure to win it – Town managed a draw – meant they finished bottom. For several seasons relegation had looked on the cards, but in the end, after a seven-year gap, the man who had taken Halifax Town out of the Fourth Division was deemed responsible by taking them back into it.

If relegation wasn't bad enough, the season ended on an even sourer note when long-serving keeper Alex Smith asked to be released following a row over his benefit match. The board originally offered assistance in arranging it, then seemed to change their minds, and told Smith to sort everything out himself. Feeling aggrieved, Smith joined Preston North End, while namesake full-back Alex Smith, Ken Blair, Mark Harrold, David Pugh, Tommy Veitch, Steve Downes and David Ford were also invited by Ball to find new clubs.

Match of the Season 1975-76

Hereford United 1 Halifax Town 2

Division 3, 17 March 1976

As the season moved into March, Halifax Town's position in the league had become critical. They were staring relegation to the Fourth Division in the face. A home draw with Gillingham and defeat by Swindon hardly helped their cause, for they were left 23rd in the table. Colchester's 2-0 win over Aldershot then dumped Town on the bottom, and the team needed a visit to Edgar Street, home of Hereford, like a hole in the head.

This was Hereford's fourth season in the league following their election to Division 4 in 1972, and manager John Sillett had them making great strides to the Second Division. Top of the table, three points clear of nearest rivals Crystal Palace and with two games in hand, the destiny of the title was in their own hands. Perhaps when the Shaymen came to town, Hereford felt a little over-confident.

Did You Know?

John Pickering holds the club's record of 367 League appearances, established between 1967 and 1974. He then signed for Barnsley.

To say that Town's victory was a shock would be to undermine the performance of the players on view. Unexpected, maybe. But the only real surprise on the night was that Town did not win by more.

That Hereford were a good side, no one was in any doubt, but the best of the clear-cut chances fell to the Shaymen. George Jones twice, and Mickey Bullock both missed good first-half opportunities, but it was Jones who was on hand to give the Shaymen a deserved lead. In the 63rd minute he volleyed in after the overlapping Bobby Flavell, recently signed from Burnley, sent over the cross. Two minutes later, Jones went close again when his header thumped against the bar.

When John Galley equalised with eight minutes remaining he must have thought he had got his side out of jail. He was lucky that Jimmy Lindsay's mis-hit shot fell nicely for him, but unlucky when Alex Smith pulled off a super save near the end. Deep into injury-time, of which referee John Hough somehow found seven minutes, on loan John Overton netted a dramatic winner. Playing only his second game for Town, he was on hand to steer in Jones's angled shot past Kevin Charlton and send the Shaymen into ecstasy.

Victory, of course, whilst moving them off the bottom, kept Town's season alive. There was still a lot to do. Too much in fact, to avoid the drop. Hereford, on the other hand, did not dwell on their setback. They won 3-2 at Bury in their next match, and, suffering just one more defeat – they went down at Cardiff in front of 35,549 spectators – won the championship at a canter, six points clear.

FAMILIAR FACES 1976-1981

LEAGUE DIVISION 4	**1976-77**
Division 4	21st (sought re-election)
League Cup	1st Round
FA Cup	3rd Round

Back in the Fourth Division for the first time since 1969, Alan Ball did not intend Halifax Town staying there for long. At the club's Annual General Meeting on 29 July, he spoke of bouncing back at the first attempt. 'I think we have a chance,' he told the members.

As well as those players released, Ball had also lost skipper Tony Rhodes, sold to Southport for £2,000, and John Collins to Sheffield Wednesday for £4,000, but he still felt his new signings would make his side a force to be reckoned with. First to arrive was the experienced Huddersfield midfielder Jimmy Lawson. Shortly afterwards, Lawson's colleague, Bobby Hoy, followed him to the Shay, though he would be hampered all season by a knee injury. Johnny Johnston, a midfielder, arrived from Southport. Plucked from non-league London football was goalkeeper Mick Leonard. Full-back Paul Kent, released by Norwich, was taken on trial. Central defenders Dave Rylands (Hereford United) and Jack Trainer (Cork Hibernian) also joined the club in time for a pre-season tour of Scotland, as did Bradford-based Roland Gregoire, a young midfielder.

The tour was not a success and did not bode well for the coming season. Of four matches played, three were lost – Elgin City (1-4), Dunfermline (1-2) and Hamilton (1-4). Back home, the supporters must have been concerned, and their worst fears were about to be realised. Town never posed a challenge for promotion. Indeed, they were in trouble virtually from Day One.

The Shaymen kicked off their season with home and away legs against Darlington in the League Cup, but with the aggregate scores level, a third meeting was necessary. When the Quakers won 2-1 after extra-time at the Shay on 30 August, it was hardly a shock, considering Town's awful start to their league programme.

Halifax had begun with a 2-3 home defeat by Bournemouth. The game attracted only 1,711, the first time in the club's history that the attendance had dropped below 2,000 on the opening day for a league game. Town were still looking for their first win after their sixth match. They had also been hit by injury to Rylands and the sale of Ray McHale to Swindon Town and Alan Jones to Blackburn Rovers for £8,000 and £7,000 respectively. Ball acted by signing Oldham front-runner Joe Carroll, initially on loan, before he joined permanently in November.

With the fans staying away, the club tried to entice them back by experimenting with Friday-night football for the visit of Hartlepool on 24 September. The result? A 1-0 win, Town's first success of the season, but the attendance was the lowest at the Shay so far – only 1,393. This, however, was not to be the lowest of the season.

October saw a host of more new faces arrive and these coincided with an upturn in Town's fortunes. Defender Lee Bradley arrived from Stockport and midfielder Jim McCann was taken on loan from Nottingham Forest, now managed by Brian Clough. Ball then signed the Chester pair of full-back Tony Loska and centre-half Chris Dunleavy in a deal totalling £10,000. Dunleavy made his debut against Doncaster, opening the scoring in a 6-0 victory, which equalled Halifax's highest-ever League score.

Town enjoyed a seven-match unbeaten run that carried them out of the re-election zone and into the third round of the FA Cup. They had seen off Stafford – these clubs had drawn each other for the third successive season – albeit after a replay, then defeated Third Division Preston 1-0 at home. Although Town hoped for a big name in Round Three, the nearest they came to one was England manager Don Revie, who attended the Shay for the visit of Second Division Luton. He was spying on defender Paul Futcher, but though Luton were hardly glamorous opposition – they had been in the First Division only two seasons earlier – they proved too good for Town and won courtesy of John Aston's first-half goal.

When Town returned to league action, it was back to their bad old ways, and with crowds continuing to dwindle, the club invited fans to travel to away games in company with the players – for the privilege of which the fans had to pay! The directors then took drastic action to curb the wage bill. On 26 January, all 21 players were put up for sale, with Kent being the first player to leave after having his contract cancelled.

Town ended a run of seven games without a win by hammering lowly Workington 6-1 on 5 February, after which Town appeared to be keeping their heads above water. Ball started looking ahead to the following season, threatening to quit if he failed to lift Town out of the Fourth Division, but he really needed to address the present situation, which actually was getting worse. April was a disastrous month, with four successive defeats heaping the pressure back on the side. A 0-3 defeat at Doncaster highlighted the club's problems. With Gennoe already ruled out with a broken nose, Leonard failed a fitness test just before the game, so trainer Brain Hendy had to rush to the home of 16-year-old trialist Roman Chmilowsky, and somehow get him to Belle Vue forty minutes before kick-off. In case the youngster failed to show up in time, Johnny Johnston was placed on stand-by.

A sequence of poor results meant the re-election issue loomed ever larger. Town went into the last game with their fate still in their own hands, knowing that victory over Southport – who were already condemned along with Hartlepool and Workington – would ensure their safety. But Town could only manage a 1-1 draw, and three days later Bobby Flavell was left to rue a penalty miss that could have rendered Newport's one outstanding game meaningless. Newport defeated bottom side Workington three days later to leap-frog over Town, thus condemning them to re-election, just one year after dropping out of Division Three.

Chairman Percy Albon had expected Town's fortunes to improve after their poor start, but in February had come close to resigning. Now he knew that a trip to the Cafe Royal in London was necessary for the League's Annual Meeting. He was confident Town would be re-elected, but non-league clubs had made a pact of sorts to increase the chances of toppling one of existing League clubs. Wimbledon would carry the Southern League banner, free from the added competition of perennially strong rivals Yeovil and Kettering. Late in the day Altrincham of the Northern Premier League threw their hat into the ring

Match of the Season 1976-77

Halifax Town 6 Doncaster Rovers 0

Division 4, 2 November 1976

After being relegated from Division Three, Town boss Alan Ball reckoned his players had a good chance of making a swift return. Three months into the season, he might have felt differently. With only two wins from their first thirteen games, not to mention elimination from the League Cup at the hands of Darlington, Town's priority was not so much gaining promotion as avoiding the re-election zone, which, as it happened, is where they found themselves when this game was played.

Did You Know?

In June 1974, Town supporter Brenda England finished 3rd in Yorkshire TV's 'Yorkshire Women's Shouting Championships'

In an effort to buck up his team, Ball recruited full-back Tony Loska and central defender Chris Dunleavy from Chester in a combined deal worth £10,000. Loska had played his part in Town's 2-1 victory over Stockport in his first game, and three days later Dunleavy was set for his debut in this meeting with Doncaster.

Like the Shaymen, Doncaster had made an inauspicious start. Lying eighteenth, they had mustered just four wins, but one of these had been a 4-0 hammering of Darlington. Rovers also had a player to watch in striker Peter Kitchen, who had netted eight league goals so far, one more than the whole Halifax side.

The chances, therefore, of the Shaymen equalling their own club record win, set in 1955 when Bradford Park Avenue were humbled 6-0, seemed improbable. Nevertheless, this Yorkshire derby attracted a heartening 2,350 spectators – admittedly there were a few from Doncaster – but they were treated to a scintillating Town performance, and some good goals, too. The Shaymen's only real scares came, inevitably, from Kitchen, who hit the post at 0-2, then later, with the game lost, a point-blank header saved by Gennoe. Otherwise, it was all Town.

Dunleavy quickly made his mark in Town's colours, scoring with a powerful header off Loska's free-kick after only six minutes, and seven minutes later Hoy scored a simple goal when Reed skied a clearance into his path. Hoy's second goal, which made it 3-0, was made by Bullock. He then turned provider, crossing for a spread-eagled Joe Carroll to head in right on half-time.

Two goals in three minutes completed the scoring. First came Bullock's 58th-minute header off Johnny Johnston's centre. Then a fortuitous cross by Jimmy Lawson, intended for Bullock, was knocked in by keeper Dennis Peacock. One more goal would equal the senior club record, set in 1967, when Town defeated Bishop Auckland 7-0 in the FA Cup, but it was not forthcoming. Still, Ball was a happy man. 'It's a great feeling,' he beamed afterwards, as his side climbed out of the bottom four. Later, his team would put six past Workington, but these were isolated highs in what was a very disappointing season.

This thrashing evidently did not affect Doncaster unduly. Their pride might have been hurt, but they responded by winning their next three matches, and, but for their poor start, may have figured in the promotion frame instead of finishing a moderate eighth.

LEAGUE DIVISION 4	**1977-78**
Division 4	20th
League Cup	1st Round
FA Cup	1st Round

Halifax Town – and Alan Ball – breathed a huge sigh of relief when they were re-elected at the Football League's Annual Meeting on 17 June, polling the most votes, 44. Happy, too, were Hartlepool (43) and Southport (37), for they also held onto their Football League status, but not so Workington. This was their fourth successive re-application, and the League clearly felt a change was overdue. With Wimbledon's reputation growing in non-league circles, especially after a marvellous FA Cup run in 1974-75, they were elected with 27 votes, six more than Workington.

Alan Ball made just two pre-season signings. The fans had expected something a little more radical, and who could blame them? There was concern, too, that the newcomers were both central defenders, with Tommy Horsfall arriving from Cambridge United and Terry Alcock from Port Vale. When the side got down to business, they looked to be starting as they had left off, with an inglorious defeat in the League Cup at the hands of Rochdale. Once Halifax lost the second leg at the Shay to bow out 2-3 on aggregate, Ball went to Huddersfield to strengthen his midfield by signing the experienced Steve Smith.

Though far from fully fit, Smith took his place in the Town line-up for their opening league game at, as fate decreed, newly elected Wimbledon. The Shaymen played their part in a thrilling contest, equalising near the end for a 3-3 draw. Three days later, a 3-0 win over Hartlepool had some fans believing that maybe Town were on to something special this season, after all. How wrong could they be?

Northampton brought them back to earth by winning 1-0 at the Shay, and Town slipped down the table at an alarming rate. As results went from bad to worse, Ball admitted he did not know what to do for the best, and from October was left to fend for himself for a while after coach Syd Farrimond left to join Second Division Sunderland. Farrimond would be influential in Sunderland's purchase of Town's young Roland Gregoire in November for £5,000, but meantime, following eleven games without a win, Town lay next to bottom.

Bristol Rovers' striker Wayne Powell arrived on loan – Town might have bought him had they been able to afford the £10,000 asking price – and he made his debut, and scored the winner, in a 2-1 win over fellow strugglers Southport. But Town could not build on this, and three consecutive defeats left the situation as desperate as it could be. Drastic action was called for.

Behind the scenes, the club had appointed lifelong supporter Tony Thwaites as commercial manager, but a month or so later he would be working under a new chairman. At the board meeting on 31 October, Percy Albon resigned, claiming that he had been neglecting his plumbing business. Demolition contractor Andrew Delaney, on the board since May, took over as Halifax Town's latest chairman.

Ball knew his own position was hanging in the balance following a 0-2 home defeat by Newport. Two days later, on 14 November, the board decided enough was enough. Having won just two of the first seventeen league games, Ball was dismissed. 'Due to a lack of satisfactory results, Mr Ball's contract has been brought to an end,' read the club statement. Ball responded by saying the sack did not surprise him, only the timing of it. Two weeks earlier, he had been told he had a month to improve the results. Delaney obviously decided he could not wait that long.

Jimmy Lawson was handed the caretaker role of player-manager, and his first game in charge was a West Riding Senior Cup-tie at Huddersfield. The performance was encouraging – Halifax drew the game 1-1 but lost 4-5 on penalties – and in the next game the Shaymen came from behind to beat Aldershot 2-1 at the Shay, with Lawson prompting every move. Defeat seven days later at Chesterfield in the FA Cup did not deter the board. Having already seen a marked improvement in performances they appointed Lawson full-time manager on 29 November.

The players responded to Lawson and strung together a run of eight unbeaten matches. This enabled them to climb out of the bottom four. It was ironic, rather than coincidental, that when Mickey Bullock was officially appointed coach in January, the team slipped into their old ways and Town found themselves back in the re-election zone.

Problems on the field, then, and more off it. At the club's Annual General Meeting on 19 December, Andrew Delaney had revealed that Town had made a loss on the year ending 31 March 1977 of £36,000. With the club continuing to lose money he reckoned Town needed minimum gates of 4,000 to survive. One solution, as was often the case over the years, was to sell their best players. On 21 February, goalkeeper Terry Gennoe, who had been the centre of much transfer talk since the summer, moved to Lawrie McMenemy's Southampton for a much-needed £35,000, the Second Division side obviously not deterred after Gennoe had conceded five goals at Southend four days previously.

Did You Know?

In the 1974-75 season, Halifax had identical attendances – 2,063 – for consecutive home games versus Plymouth and Grimsby.

Some of that money was made available for new players. Lawson had already secured Huddersfield winger Francis Firth on a free transfer, but went back to his former club to pay £10,000 for striker Bob Mountford, as well as obtaining Barnsley defender Peter Burke in a £4,000 deal. By the end of March, results once again had picked up, and Town climbed as high as fifteenth, re-election worries seemingly banished.

That was not quite the case, but Town did avoid the indignity of having to go cap-in-hand again to the League. This was due to gaining a point in their penultimate game, a physical 1-1 draw with champions Watford, managed by Graham Taylor – he would take them all the way to the First Division – and financed by pop star Elton John. Town lost their last game at Swansea, who thus clinched promotion, and ended the season in twentieth place, four points clear of the re-election zone.

It had been a close shave, but Lawson had somehow steered his ship to safety. His retained list reflected the confidence he had in his players – only Terry Alcock was released, Tommy Horsfall having moved to Dover in March for a small fee. With former Huddersfield defender Geoff Hutt having signed from York City before the season's close for £4,000, Lawson felt he had every right to be confident for the new season.

But no sooner had the curtain fallen than the directors were making waves. In a cost-cutting exercise, they decided to withdraw youth sides from the Lancashire League and the Halifax and District League, and then stated they were prepared to listen to offers for star player Bobby Flavell. Finances as ever were dictating matters, and in light of the traumas that the 1978-79 campaign would bring, the club viewed the launch of the Shaymaker Lottery on 18 April as a godsend.

Match of the Season 1977-78

Halifax Town 2 Aldershot 1

Division 4, 19 November 1977

With Halifax Town lying next to bottom of Division Four, and the board having dispensed with the services of Alan Ball, it was Jimmy Lawson who was handed the unenviable task of trying to revive the club's fortunes. Lawson was one of the most popular players at the Shay, and had been voted Player of the Year in his first season. His appointment, on a temporary basis initially, was hardly headline news. The nation was more interested in England's build-up for a vital World Cup qualifying match with Italy at Wembley.

Lawson wanted the job on a permanent basis, and evidently the players wanted him to have it, too. They had given their all for him in a West Riding Senior Cup-tie at Leeds Road – the Shaymen lost 4-5 on penalties to Huddersfield – but it was in the League where results mattered most. With only two wins so far, Town were desperate for points.

Tom McAnearney's Aldershot, on the other hand, were going well. Second in the table, they had suffered only three defeats and with hotshot John Dungworth in their side – he was a close-season signing from Huddersfield – were certainly not expected to lose here. But facing a side with a new manager is always a dangerous prospect, and the Shaymen were clearly geared up for this game.

Having chosen his team, Lawson now wanted to run the show, and he was at the heart of all the best moves as a rejuvenated Halifax put on a performance not seen for a long time. So it was against the run of play that Aldershot took the lead after 23 minutes with a goal scored by Malcolm Crosby from outside the box. Town protested that Murray Brodie had been offside, but referee George Tyson ignored their appeals. Brodie had been lying injured for fully two minutes and was hardly interfering with play.

That goal proved only a minor setback for the Shaymen. Within three minutes, Jack Trainer had headed in Derek Bell's corner. Halifax were unlucky not be leading at the break after Johnny Johnston's shot came back off a post.

Town reserved their winner for the 70th minute. The goal stemmed from a free-kick. Steve Smith tapped the ball to Bobby Flavell, and his goal-bound shot caught Shots' Wynne Hooper before flying in. With Town continuing to dominate, there was no way back for the visitors. Victory was confirmed, the start of an eight-match unbeaten league run that not only helped secure Lawson the job he wanted, but also went a long way to helping Town steer clear of re-election at the season's close.

LEAGUE DIVISION 4	**1978-79**
Division 4	23rd (sought re-election)
League Cup	1st Round
FA Cup	1st Round

There were rumours during the summer of 1978 that Halifax Town were on the verge of folding. The council had refused to sell the Shay to the club in case – should Town ever fail to be re-elected to the Football League – they attempted to sell it for redevelopment. This refusal had startled some supporters, who may have viewed the club's ownership of the Shay as their only means of survival. Secretary David Holland, however, was quick to reassure them that there was 'no question of the club folding.'

Another rumour doing the rounds centred on the future of defender-cum-midfielder Bobby Flavell. Jimmy Lawson did not want to lose him, but when Chesterfield offered £25,000 for him at the beginning of August, Flavell was on his way. Lawson, though, was quick to spend all that money on Huddersfield Town's midfield dynamo Kevin Johnson – who thus became Town's most expensive player – but after only 46 minutes of his debut in a League Cup-tie at Walsall he damaged ankle ligaments and was sidelined for three weeks. Town lost the second leg at the Shay to go out of the competition 1-4 on aggregate, but Lawson wasn't unduly worried. After all, Walsall were a Division Three side.

The Town boss had instilled a strict dress code – this included club blazers – and discipline at the Shay, and for the new season introduced a new all-white playing strip. 'A touch of the Real Madrid's' the *Evening Courier* proclaimed it, but that, unfortunately was as far as the similarities went with the Spanish giants. True, Town were unlucky to lose their opening league game 2-4 at Barnsley – new signing Jon Nixon made a quick return to Oakwell – but they looked sluggish in beating Stockport three days later, and seven successive defeats ensued as Town crashed towards the foot of the table. A combination of poor form and bad weather that played havoc with the football programme meant Town would not win again until February.

During Town's descent, Lawson decided to leave himself out of the side so he could better identify the source of the problems, but he still failed to come up with any solutions. He saw fit to give promising youngster Mick Kennedy his league debut, but after Town touched bottom on 25 September – Rochdale's draw with Wimbledon gave them that unenviable distinction – only 985 spectators turned up for the visit of Crewe. Town at least ended their losing sequence in that game, albeit in a goalless draw.

Did You Know?

6 players earned full caps after leaving Town – Meagan, Kennedy (Ireland), Galloway (Scotland), Knill (Wales), Nicholl and Campbell (Northern Ireland).

October saw two Huddersfield players joining the club. Centre-back Arnold Sidebottom, formerly of Manchester United, arrived first, then striker Bobby Campbell – he had been here on loan from Aston Villa four seasons earlier – joined him, along with his reputation for hard living and mischief. These latest arrivals brought the number of ex-Huddersfield players at the Shay to eight, but the day after Campbell's arrival, Derek Bell left the club for Barnsley for £30,000. It was money Halifax could not turn down. Part of that deal saw Mick Prendergast arrive on loan, but during his short time at the Shay, he would play under two managers.

October also saw Halifax enter into the music business. Tommy Degnan, a clubland singer from Glasgow, released a record entitled 'Shaymen of Halifax'. He sang about Town being 'the best team in Yorkshire' but just days after it hit the shops, Town lost 0-3 at home to Port Vale and slumped to bottom again.

Following three further defeats, the directors felt action needed to be taken. At the board meeting of 30 October, although chairman Andrew Delaney said he was not thinking of a change, that is exactly what the board went for. Lawson was sacked as manager. He was retained as a player, but though he remained at the club for the rest of the season, he never featured in the first team again. A short-list of five was drawn up, and on 3 November George Kirby returned to the fold following a successful spell in Iceland to start his second stint as manager. But, as Alan Ball found out before him, he would find the going a lot harder the second time around.

Kirby watched the side in action the following day at Hereford, where Mickey Bullock picked the team. The game ended 2-2. But Kirby could not work miracles overnight, and by the turn of the year, Town were still anchored at the foot of the table, and had been knocked out of the FA Cup by Carlisle.

Town were denied any immediate chance of closing the gap on the clubs above them as the winter weather caused postponements nationwide for weeks on end. The situation got so bad that the Football League eventually extended the season by two weeks. At the Shay, snow lay several feet deep and the club employed a bulldozer at one point in their vain efforts to get the pitch ready. No soccer meant no money coming in, so Halifax Town, whose finances were hit harder than any other club in the League, were grateful to their Shaymaker Lottery for keeping things ticking over.

When the side did return to action, on 10 February, they went down at Crewe – lying 22nd – a result that left the Shaymen twelve points behind the Railwaymen, with Rochdale in 23rd place, six points better off than Town. Halifax started to make up ground two weeks later with a 1-0 victory at Port Vale, albeit through a Bill Bentley own-goal, but victory did not come without a heavy price. Keeper Mick Leonard had his jaw broken, but fortunately Town were able to take Preston's John Kilner on loan until the end of the season.

On 3 March the Shaymen prepared for their first home game since 16 December – almost three months earlier. The visitors were promotion-chasing Portsmouth, who were clear favourites to win. The match attracted a welcome 1,741 spectators, who saw Town pull off a shock 2-0 victory. Repeat performances, however, were rare. Town managed to win a second away game, at Stockport, then later beat another of the promotion sides, Wimbledon, at the Shay. These were isolated highlights as Town crammed in their fixtures thick and fast. But the chances of Town escaping the clutches of re-election were fast fading, and the inevitable became reality when, with five games still to play, they went down 0-1 at Reading, who themselves clinched promotion. Immediately, Town prepared a blueprint for their case at the Football League's Annual Meeting.

If re-election could not be avoided, then George Kirby's next aim was to avoid finishing bottom. Town set their eyes on Crewe, who had gone into free-fall. On 9 May, with Halifax playing their third game in six days, a Kevin Johnson goal was enough to beat Hereford and lift Town off the bottom. Town still had two home games left and they could have put daylight between themselves and Crewe, but in the end the challenge for the wooden spoon went to the wire. Lee Bradley, one of seven players not retained by the club – Trainer, Loska, Johnston, Nixon, Carroll and Jimmy Lawson were the others – signed off with two goals in the final match, a 2-3 defeat by Scunthorpe. With Crewe losing to Rochdale on the same evening, Town finished above them on goal-difference.

Arnold Sidebottom had already been released to play cricket for Yorkshire, but Bobby Campbell left the club in more controversial circumstances. Warned about his drinking habits, he pushed Kirby to the limits, and was sacked by the club before the final game. For Campbell, being shown the door at the Shay would not destroy his career – he would go on to break Bradford City's goalscoring records and go with Northern Ireland to the 1982 World Cup finals – but he had proved to be a headache Halifax Town could have done without. The club's own future now rested with the chairmen of the other 91 Football League clubs.

Match of the Season 1978-79

Halifax Town 2 Portsmouth 0

Division 4, 3 March 1979

It was not just the result that made this match memorable. The mere fact that Halifax Town were playing at the Shay at all was significant. It was actually their first home fixture since being defeated by Wigan Athletic on 16 December, almost three months previously. The Arctic weather that plagued the football programme had put paid to seven scheduled Shay matches.

This game, too, was in doubt the day before, but once referee Burden had passed the pitch fit to play, Town boss George Kirby was hopeful for a bumper crowd. He had several reasons: the Halifax supporters had been starved of their football; Portsmouth were attractive opposition; and Town had won their second game of the season seven days earlier at Port Vale.

This Portsmouth side was a shadow of that which had won the League Championship in 1949 and 1950 but were still regarded a big name. And in manager Jimmy Dickinson, they retained connections with those halcyon days. He had played a record 764 league games for them between 1946 and 1965, winning 48 England caps in the bargain, but having gone into management he had been responsible for taking the club into the Fourth Division for the first time.

When Portsmouth arrived at the Shay, they were handily placed for a swift return, though they had slipped to fourth after being top in January. Seven days earlier they had lost at home to Grimsby and were keen to make amends. Odds favoured them, with Town stranded at the foot of the table, and it was Pompey who had the best of the early exchanges. Future England defender Steve Foster headed against the bar, but it was the Shaymen who got the breaks. When they were awarded a free-kick, Kevin Johnson's shot was heading for the left-hand corner until the ball caught Peter Ellis and flew into the other side of the net with keeper Mellor – an FA Cup finalist with Fulham four seasons earlier – stranded. Six minutes later, Johnson met Francis Firth's cross and guided the ball inside the far post.

Town had further chances to make the game safe, but had to contend with the rough-arm tactics of a Portsmouth side that got more and more frustrated. At one point, George Kirby remonstrated with the referee, but in the end cuts and bruises were but a small price to pay for two valuable well-earned points. It was Town's first home win since the second Saturday of the season, and saw them close the gap slightly to four points over next-to-bottom Rochdale.

LEAGUE DIVISION 4	**1979-80**
Division 4	18th
League Cup	1st Round
FA Cup	4th Round

Halifax Town survived the Football League's Annual Meeting, but were concerned that they only picked up 37 votes, the fewest of the four clubs up for re-election. Doncaster (50), Crewe (49) and Darlington (43) were comfortably voted back in, but non-league Altrincham and Kettering must have been devastated at polling only thirteen and twelve votes respectively.

Town's directors viewed re-election as a 'fresh start' and made £45,000 available to George Kirby for team strengthening. The Town boss spent wisely, capturing young Aston Villa defender David Evans for £22,500 – he was appointed skipper – and Paul Hendrie from Bristol Rovers for £5,000. Hendrie was a midfielder who had played in the top division with Birmingham City. Kirby also secured the experienced midfielder Tony Geidmintis (Northampton) and Port Vale centre-half Dave Harris on free transfers. There was, in addition, talk of Icelandic international Arni Sveinsson joining the club. Hopes were raised, but the player, whom Kirby knew from his time spent out in Iceland, never boarded the plane.

Despite encouraging performances in the League Cup against Division Three side Shrewsbury Town – the home leg was drawn 2-2 before the Shaymen lost 0-1 at Gay Meadow – supporters may have been forgiven for thinking it was a case of 'as you were'. Town failed to win any of their first three league games. But results during September brightened the outlook, as the side went through the month unbeaten in six games, earning Kirby the division's Manager of the Month award. This was his second such honour whilst at Halifax Town (his first had been nine seasons earlier).

September was not without its hitches. Kirby lost his secretary David Holland, who left for a job outside football (he was replaced by Mike Walker, who was in turn succeeded by Martin Firth in January). Two weeks later goalkeeper Mick Leonard moved to Notts County for £35,000. Town went back to Preston to buy John Kilner in a deal worth £12,500. Kilner's registration was not cleared in time for Town's home game with Hereford – Mickey Bullock's car broke down on the way to the Football League headquarters at Lytham St Anne's – so into the side came Johnny Hough, a non-contract player. Hough played for top amateur Halifax side Irish Democratic Club, but he performed soundly as Town won 1-0. Later in the month Johnson broke his leg in a crude challenge by Hartlepool's Bob Newton, and would not play again for almost a year. It was around this time that Kirby turned down a £25,000 bid from Hereford for Kevin Johnson: the manager rated the player in the £100,000-price bracket!

On the day George Kirby was named as Manager of the Month, Town beat Newport 2-1 to rise to fifth. Two weeks later, with the crowds flocking back to the Shay, Town became the first side to beat Walsall. But although the squad had been bolstered by signing centre-back Malcolm Goodman from Bromsgrove Rovers and local lad Andy Whiteley, Town could not sustain their challenge. Kirby made further signings, including John Thomas, on loan from Everton, former Preston striker John Smith via Los Angeles Hawks, and Vernon Allatt from Hednesford Town (Allatt cost £6,500), but the injection of fresh blood could not halt Town's slide.

With league form deteriorating, Town at least allayed fears of a shock in the FA Cup when they defeated non-league Scarborough 2-0 at the Shay. No sooner had Halifax secured a draw at Walsall in the next round than the winners were paired with First Division Manchester City. Town needed two replays to get past Walsall, after extra-time.

Two days later, on Boxing Day, the Shaymen produced another memorable performance, beating high-flying neighbours Huddersfield 2-1 in front of 10,061. That turned out to be the last ever five-figure gate for a league match at the Shay. That figure was exceeded in the FA Cup just ten days later, when an all-ticket 12,599 packed the stadium for the visit of Malcolm Allison and his multi-million pound Manchester City outfit.

Leaving no stone unturned, George Kirby enlisted the aid of hypnotist Romark. But chances of a giant-killing lay more in the state of the mudbath pitch than anything else. Halifax duly provided that upset, courtesy of Paul Hendrie's solitary strike, but that game was a prelude to off-the-field problems. Chairman Andrew Delaney missed the match in protest over directors Jack Turner and Robert Hanson, whom he claimed were not pulling their weight. At an emergency board meeting, these two resigned from the board, leaving it just three strong, although the addition of John Goldthorpe in March brought it back up to four.

The spotlight was on Town for three weeks leading up to the fourth round tie at Bolton, so much so that even defeat at bottom-placed Crewe, seven days after the Manchester City win, merited a mention. Around 6,000 supporters made the trip to Burnden Park, but there was to be no repeat shock. Bolton, struggling in Division One, won 2-0, though Town were far from disgraced. Just where all those supporters disappeared to when Town next played at home was a mystery: on 9 February just 1,939 turned up for the visit of

Bournemouth. That disappointing figure was mirrored only by Town's miserable run-in to the end of the season.

With his reputation enhanced by the cup run, manager George Kirby was offered a three-year contract. His reward was to watch his side taken apart by Huddersfield, who hit five goals on their way to the Fourth Division title. How Kirby must have envied his counterpart that day, former Town full-back Mick Buxton, for the Shaymen won only one of their last thirteen matches, slipping from eleventh to eighteenth.

After the nightmarish events of the previous season, Kirby had intended this campaign to be one of consolidation, prior to making a promotion surge in 1980-81. With this in mind, there was some surprise at the players Kirby released. Tony Geidmintis had been forced to quit after being diagnosed with an irregular heartbeat. But who knows, John Smith, Peter Burke and Geoff Hutt may all have offered something to the cause. Bob Mountford left for Australia, and Chris Dunleavy, having also been originally released, was re-signed before jetting out to join him at Christmas. By which time Kirby expected his promotion push to be in full swing.

Match of the Season 1979-80

Halifax Town 1 Manchester City 0

FA Cup, 3rd Round, 5 January 1980

Halifax Town's most famous victory? Those who witnessed it would probably not disagree.

Having finally seen off Walsall in the second round, the Shaymen now earned the right to play hosts to First Division Manchester City. The match was all-ticket, with the crowd limit set at 16,500. Yorkshire TV were there to film it, which meant that the game kicked off at 2pm on the account of the Shay's modest floodlights. Inevitably, the TV people were keeping their fingers crossed for an upset. They were not to be disappointed.

Whether the game should or should not have gone ahead is a matter of debate. If the Cup itself was not already a leveller, then the boggy Shay pitch, following the thawing of a week's frost, made it even more so, and doubtless favoured the Shaymen. But after an early morning inspection referee Michael Lowe was happy to give the game the nod, whereupon City's general manager Tony Book rushed back to report to the rest of the party staying at the Ainley Hilton Hotel, Elland, just what to expect.

Manchester City were already beginning to lose their way. Championship runners-up to Liverpool in 1977, they had since re-appointed Malcolm Allison as team manager – he had been coach to Joe Mercer when the club enjoyed its golden period in the late 1960s and early 70s – and he had started to dismantle the team. Allison replaced stars Asa Hartford, Dave Watson and Mick Channon with youngsters Tommy Caton, Dave Bennett and Nicky Reid, and also spent lavishly. Teenager Mick Robinson had cost £750,000 from Preston, whilst Steve Daley, who cost a staggering £1,150,000 – Allison would later claim that it was chairman Peter Swales who did the deal while he was away – became Britain's then costliest player when signed from Wolves. Altogether, the City side that Allison put out that day cost over £3 million: George Kirby's side a mere £61,000.

The part that TV hypnotist Romark played in Town's win has, somewhat unjustly, been overstated. True, George Kirby twice had him 'talk' to all the Town players except one – the Town boss reckoned John Kilner was so good he did not need any help – but it was Halifax's keeper who turned out to be the game's shining light. He made two superb first-half saves, from Bobby Shinton's snap-shot and from a vicious volley by Mick Robinson. Then, in the 65th minute, he somehow blocked Shinton's scooped effort from five yards out.

Not that City had it all their own way. England international keeper Joe Corrigan had to be alert to palm Andy Stafford's corner onto the bar; then right on half-time the City keeper did well to keep out a stinging drive from Town skipper David Evans. Paul Hendrie, too, had Corrigan worried twice early on, and the Town midfielder must have thought he had blown his chance. In the end, though, he would not be denied.

With fifteen minutes remaining, a throw-in out on the left ended with Stafford sending over a low cross to John Smith. He played the ball first time for Hendrie, who manoeuvred himself goal-side of the defence and swept a low shot past Corrigan into the right-hand corner. It was a gem of a goal – Kirby would later put it in the Kevin Keegan mould – and for Hendrie himself, it propelled him into the national spotlight, as well as into Halifax folklore.

The closing minutes were nerve-wracking for the Shay fans but Town hung on for the shock of that season's FA Cup. By kicking-off early, Halifax booked their place in the Fourth Round while other teams were still playing. They bowed out of the Cup at Bolton, but their moment of glory could never be denied them. For Malcolm Allison, however, further misery awaited. Though he saw out the season, he would be sacked the following October, branded a failure. His successor, John Bond, would have fleeting success, however, taking the side to Wembley for the 1981 final.

LEAGUE DIVISION 4	**1980-81**
Division 4	23rd (sought re-election)
League Cup	1st Round
FA Cup	1st Round

This was Halifax Town's promotion year. Or at least that's what George Kirby intended. What actually unfolded was another depressing season during which there was as much action – probably more, in fact – off the field as there was on it as the club stumbled from one crisis to another.

Kirby signed the players he felt might serve him well, but all came on free transfers. Defenders Clive Nattrass (Darlington) and Ken Burton (Chesterfield) – Burton had played in the First Division with Sheffield Wednesday – were joined by utility player Steve Ward from Northampton. Then, at the end of June, Kirby's own job description changed when he set a trend by becoming the first paid chief executive and member of the board, with responsibilities for much else besides running the team.

One of his immediate tasks was to persuade Mick Kennedy to remain at the Shay. The midfielder, obviously desiring a higher grade of football, declined a new contract, and refused to train with the club. Bristol Rovers and Chelsea showed initial interest, but on 6 August Kennedy moved to Huddersfield Town for a record £50,000. His departure left Kirby with a void he was unable to fill.

Seeking a fresh image, Town reverted to the more traditional blue shirts and white shorts. But as was becoming customary, they bowed out of the League Cup at the first hurdle, with relegated Bury winning 1-0 at the Shay for a 3-2 aggregate win. The arrival of Tranmere midfielder Tommy O'Neil, once with Manchester United, helped lift the mood at the Shay, but not for long. Mansfield's 2-0 win on the league's opening day was as bad a start as Kirby, or the fans, could have wished for.

The Town boss was becoming increasingly frustrated in his efforts to sign new players, particularly strikers. The previous term he had failed to land the likes of Fred Binney (Exeter) and Simon Garner (Blackburn). Now, just before Town's second league game, at Peterborough, Everton's Imre Varadi – who had actually been listed in the match programme – suddenly decided against signing after all. Before long, Portsmouth's Derek Showers would also turn the club down. No doubt Kirby found the signings of Mickey Bullock's nephew, Simon, and his own son Simon a little smoother.

Early season results continued to be generally poor. A 4-2 victory over Bury was spectacular, a single-goal win over Scunthorpe less so, but before Town knew where they were, they were bottom of the table. Even the long-awaited return after injury of Kevin Johnson failed to inspire the team, and he would struggle to find the form that made him such an outstanding player before breaking his leg.

Behind the scenes, an almighty upheaval was brewing. At the board meeting of 26 August, chairman Andrew Delaney resigned (director Arthur Mitchell followed suit days later) and was succeeded by John Crowther. Andrew Hodgson joined the board shortly afterwards. But Crowther's term at the helm was to be short-lived. In November, he was in talks with his counterpart at Halifax Rugby League Club, Bill Hughes, with a view to ground-sharing up at Thrum Hall. However, at a further meeting of the Town board, on 17 November, it was decided to curtail any further discussions on the subject. Three days later, Crowther resigned, citing his own poor health, though many speculated upon the real reasons. The upshot was that John Goldthorpe found himself appointed Town's third chairman of the season.

Meantime, in an attempt to strengthen his team, Kirby missed the defeat at Torquay in order to sign Barnsley striker Tommy Graham for £20,000, and midfielder Jimmy McIlwraith, just released by Bury. These two starred in Town's next game, a 3-1 win over York, but four days later the same side crumbled embarrassingly 1-5 against high-flyers Southend at the Shay. There were calls for Kirby's head – a petition was even drawn up for one game – but the Town manager carried on regardless.

He considered Town unfortunate not to earn a replay at Third Division Hull City in the first round of the FA Cup. True, his side had performed well, but still lost 1-2 at Boothferry Park. But with results in the league of primary concern, the pressure was well and truly on as Town continued to struggle. Worrying, too, was the fact that the crowds were staying away. For the home game with Bournemouth on 29 November, only 987 had bothered to turn up.

Watching Halifax Town's sorry plight with interest was Don Robinson, chairman of non-league Scarborough. On 17 December he made an audacious £80,000 offer – the total cost of Halifax Town's shares – to take over the club. His intention seemed to be to move Halifax Town to Seamer Road and use his own club as a reserve side in the Alliance Premier League. New Town chairman John Goldthorpe reacted by saying: 'I am treating this thing with disdain and will not lose any sleep over it.' Still, with the threat hanging over the club, Town strengthened their own position when millionaire Sam Rorke, owner of a deer-park at Holywell Green, joined the board on Christmas Eve, along with builders' merchant David Sharp. The pair of them actually sat down with Robinson, but the outcome was that Halifax Town would retain its own identity and carry on fighting. On 19 January, Sam Rorke took over as chairman – Goldthorpe would eventually leave the board in March – and John Crowther returned as vice-chairman, with responsibility for public relations. He would have to work overtime.

Back in December, Bobby Flavell had rejoined the club – he would make just one appearance before being sacked for 'disciplinary matters'. On New Year's Day, centre-half Billy Ayre signed from Hartlepool with Kevin Johnson going in the opposite direction. Walsall goalkeeper Ian Turner – an FA Cup winner with Southampton in 1976 – came on loan, and days after Rorke took over as chairman, Town breezed to a 2-0 win over Stockport as an air of optimism crept over the Shay.

It never amounted to much. Despite taking Bournemouth midfielder Brian Chambers till the end of the season and earning successive victories over Crewe and fellow strugglers Hereford in March, consecutive defeats by Northampton (at the Shay), Hartlepool and Darlington meant that re-election was unavoidable. Town tried to remain upbeat, and after avoiding defeat in their final three matches, set about the task of impressing other Football League chairmen. To this end, they issued a brochure outlining their plans for the Shay.

Sam Rorke upset the Halifax Dukes Speedway Club in March by demanding a hike in their rent – a similar dispute in 1986 would see the Dukes switch to Odsal. He also sought to buy the Shay from the council for £75,000 – Town were currently paying £500 per year rent, plus rates – and proposed new floodlights, a badminton court, and a restaurant among his ideas for redeveloping the ground. John Crowther was then set the onerous task of lobbying the other chairmen, but, having done so, felt confident that Halifax Town would be re-elected at the Football League's Annual Meeting.

Match of the Season 1980-81

Halifax Town 2 Stockport County 0

Division 4, 24 January 1981

The installation of millionaire deer-park owner Sam Rorke as chairman might have heralded the dawning of a new era for Halifax Town. That is what he himself hoped for. Though he admitted he knew little about football, he saw the club as a business and wanted it to operate on business principles. To his credit, he authorised expensive improvements to the ground, but, more than anything, he wanted to improve the club's image on the field.

Did You Know?

In 1975-76, Dave Gwyther scored Town's goal in a 1-0 win at Rotherham, then later in the season scored Rotherham's only goal in a 1-0 win at the Shay.

By now, Town were looking re-election certainties, lying next to bottom of the division. But the visit of Stockport was the first home game since Rorke took over. He was out to make a big impression. He sent the players into local schools to hand out free tickets, and was so successful that around 1,000 children contributed to the biggest gate of the season. There was a lively pre-match atmosphere, and the players kicked plastic footballs into the crowd as a goodwill gesture. Then it was down to the action, and Halifax Town could not – and would not – let the fans down.

Jim McGuigan's Stockport, like Town, were struggling, and arrived at the Shay lying 21st, having lost six out of their last seven games. Even had they been top of the table, they would probably have struggled to live with the Shaymen in this sort of form. Actually, Town performed as if they were top, and gave no indication that they were heading for yet another re-election.

Town included in their side goalkeeper Ian Turner, on loan from Walsall, but he was hardly needed as they dominated from the off. As early as the sixth minute, Tommy Graham had a goal disallowed for offside, but ten minutes later Vernon Allatt scored his second goal for the club, an accurate shot from eighteen yards that gave keeper David Lawson no chance. Allatt later had a goal disallowed himself, but he was the architect of Town's second goal in the 58th minute. He slipped his marker, drew Lawson, then pulled the ball across for Graham to score his third goal in four matches.

The crowd were loving it. The margin of victory could have been wider as the Shaymen created chance after chance. No further goals followed, though at the end, the players returned to the dressing room happy in the knowledge that they had shown the form of which they knew they were capable. A climb out of the bottom four looked a formality, but alas, Town had flattered only to deceive. The three successive draws that followed hinted at some sort of revival, but it was wins that the Shaymen needed. They managed only five more before the season's close. Stockport's form was hardly better than Town's but they won more games and avoided re-election by three points.

4

FINANCIAL WOES 1981-1987

LEAGUE DIVISION 4	**1981-82**
Division 4	19th
League Cup	1st Round
FA Cup	1st Round

Halifax Town were re-elected to the Football League at the Annual Meeting with 41 votes. With Tranmere polling 48, and Hereford and York 46 each, Town had once again received the fewest of the four League clubs, but though Alliance Premier champions Altrincham were expected to put in a strong challenge, they came nowhere, receiving only fifteen nominations.

Doubtless manager George Kirby was relieved, but he would not be for long. With the directors ever fearful of a repeat season, they decided he should go. On 30 June, chairman Sam Rorke met Kirby and sought his resignation. When he refused – Kirby had another two years of his contract still to run – Rorke sacked him on the spot. Few were surprised. Despite the glories the previous season in the FA Cup, it was the league that was the bread and butter, and, in that, Kirby had failed miserably.

More than forty applications were received for the vacancy, but from a shortlist of six, the board made the surprising decision of promoting from within. Coach Mickey Bullock was installed as the new manager, but would have a hard time in this, his first season.

With Kirby already having released Dave Harris, Carl Dryhurst, Andy Stafford, Brian Chambers and his own son Simon, Bullock cancelled the contracts of Kenny Burton and Clive Nattress, then sought replacements. Left-back Everton Carr arrived from Leicester City and midfielder Glyn Chamberlain from Chesterfield, but the biggest signing Bullock made was that of young striker Bobby Davison from neighbours Huddersfield at a cost of £20,000. Billy Ayre was also promoted to player-coach, whilst in the boardroom, the familiar face of Jack Turner returned, eighteen months after Andrew Delaney had forced him out.

The 1934-35 side that came close to achieving promotion

A practice game at the Shay, August 1938

Halifax Town line-up in January 1953

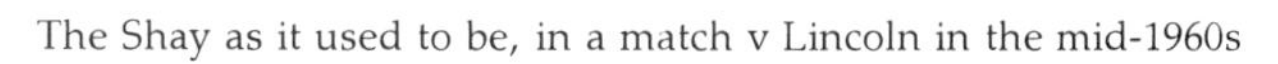

The Shay as it used to be, in a match v Lincoln in the mid-1960s

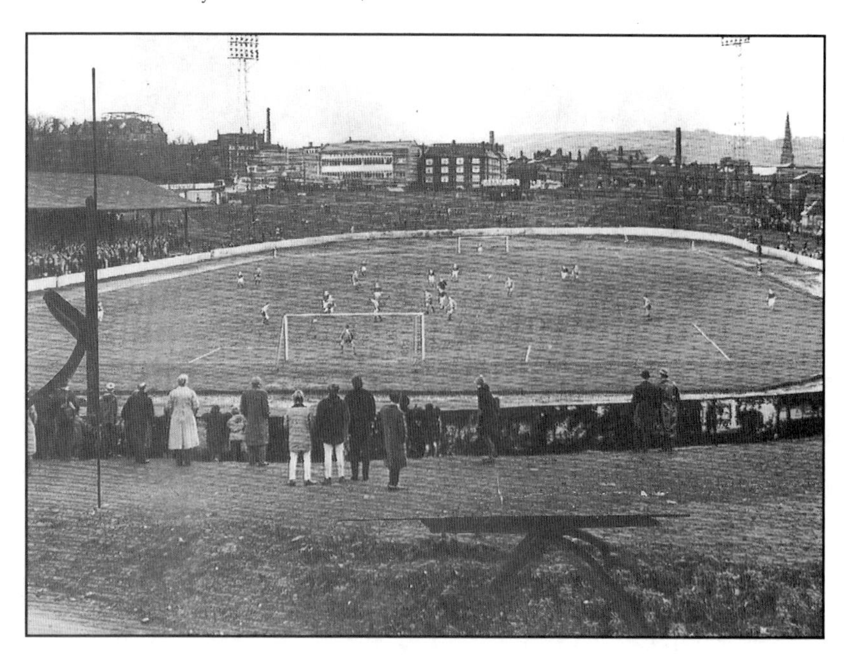

Halifax's successful 1968-69 side won promotion and glory in the FA Cup

Souvenir supplement to the match programme v Stoke in FA Cup (January 1969)

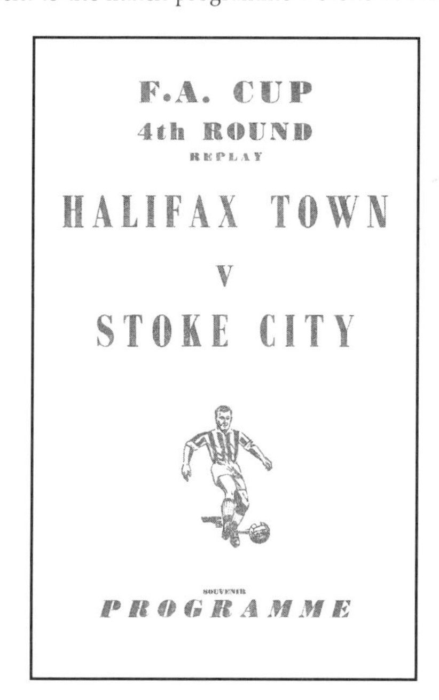

George Kirby's entertaining team of 1970-71 that almost reached Division Two

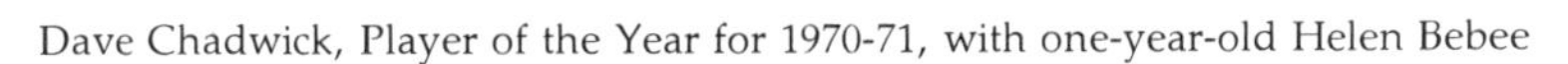

Dave Chadwick, Player of the Year for 1970-71, with one-year-old Helen Bebee

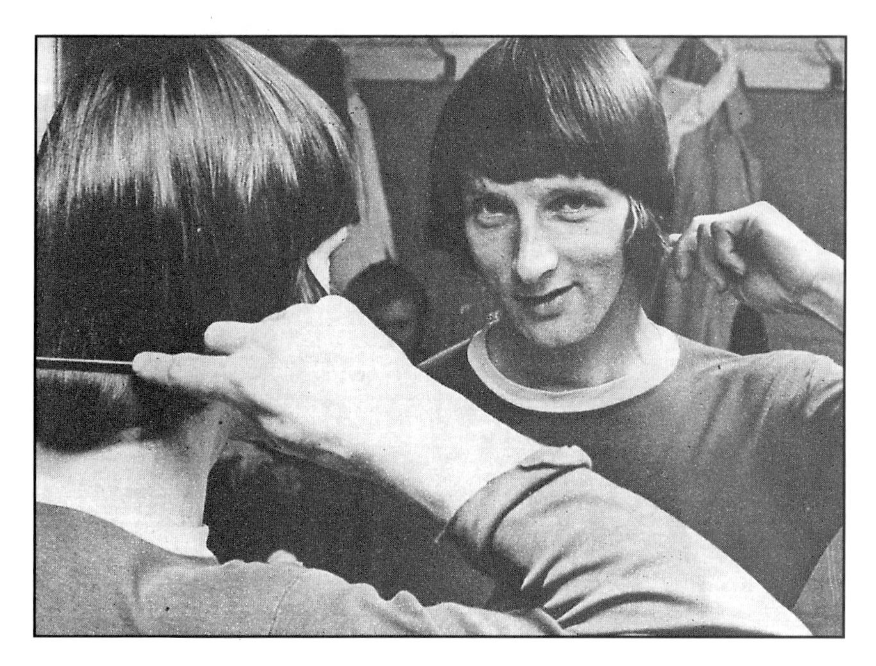

Bill Atkins' hair grows, as does Town's good run during the 1970-71 season

Match programme for Halifax v Manchester United in the Watney Cup (July 1971)

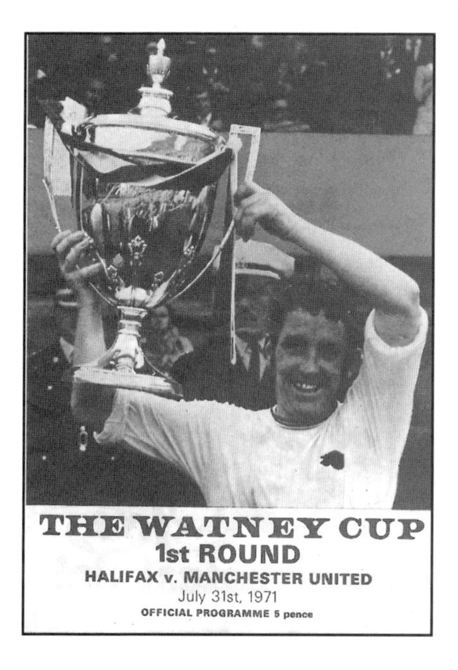

George Best in action for Manchester United in the Watney Cup (July 1971)

Match programme for the Wolves League Cup-tie at the Shay (October 1973)

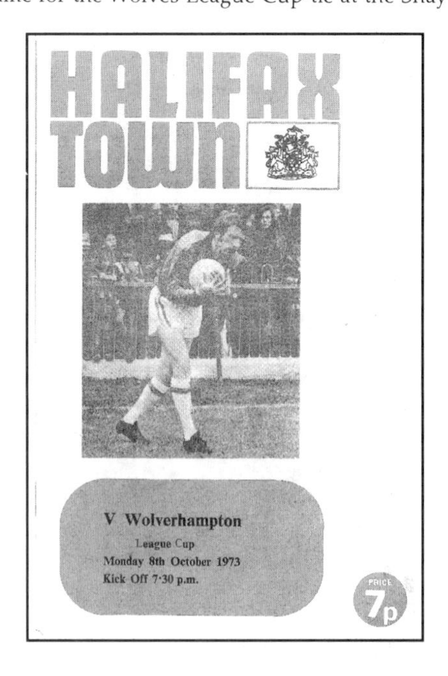

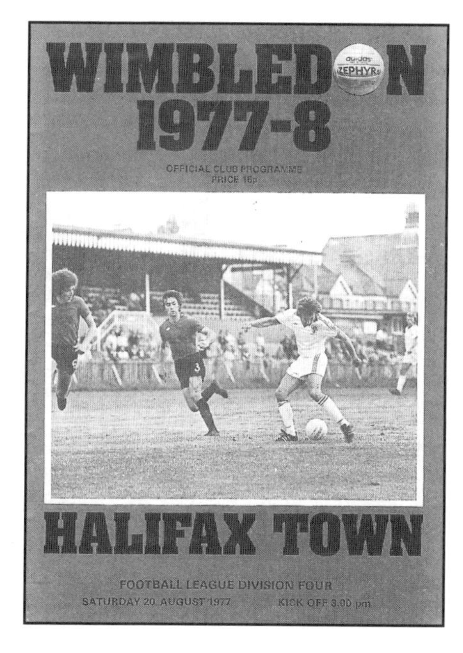

Halifax are the opponents for Wimbledon's first ever league match (August 1977)

Bob Mountford scores a rare Halifax goal, against Aldershot (November 1978)

John Kilner and Peter Burke repel a Portsmouth attack at the Shay (March 1979)

Paul Hendrie nets against Manchester City in the FA Cup (January 1980)

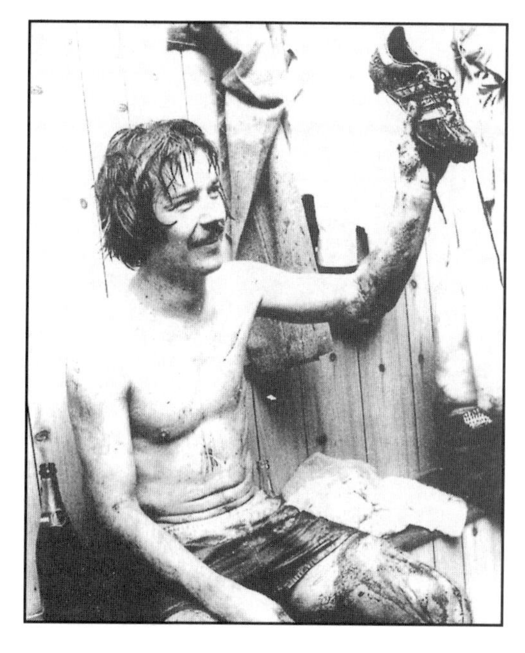

Paul Hendrie and the boot that kicked Man City out of the FA Cup (January 1980)

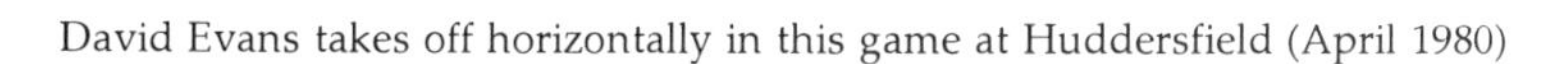

David Evans takes off horizontally in this game at Huddersfield (April 1980)

Franny Firth scores the only goal against Scunthorpe (September 1980)

Paul Hendrie and Gary Peters toss. Wimbledon's last visit to the Shay (May 1983)

Barry Gallagher terrifies the Doncaster defence (February 1984)

Steve Thornber hoofs clear at Northampton (September 1984)

Mickey Hazard scores Spurs' first goal v Town in the Milk Cup (October 1984)

Barry Gallagher (No 10) equalises against Burnley in the FA Cup (December 1984)

Town defend against Bury in the snow (January 1985)

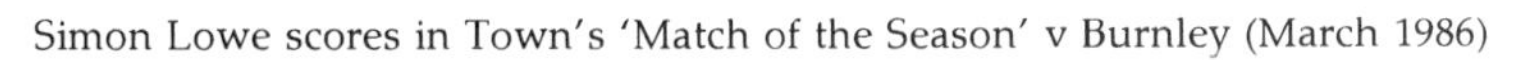

Simon Lowe scores in Town's 'Match of the Season' v Burnley (March 1986)

Sam Rorke had helped fund the new £50,000 floodlights, which were switched on for the first time on 10 August in a friendly with League of Ireland side Cliftonville. But in the next Shay friendly, Huddersfield fans ran amok, some gaining free access by breaching the porous perimeter of the ground. Rorke vowed to improve security at the Shay, and included a nine-feet-high perimeter fence among the list of improvements. The Shay was to undergo a face-lift, with the entrance to the ground put under tarmac, and the old Shay Club replaced by a restaurant, Chimes.

With the Football League introducing three points for a win, it was imperative that teams went for maximum points, but though Town played some attractive football, results failed to materialise, and they soon found themselves in their customary lowly position. In the League Cup, too, despite encouraging performances over Tommy Docherty's Third Division Preston, Town failed to make Round Two. It was a frustrating start for Bullock. Following a 2-3 defeat at Hartlepool he saw fit to transfer-list John Kilner, Jimmy McIlwraith, Vernon Allatt and Francis Firth.

Kilner kept his place for Town's next game, but his confidence was shattered as Blackpool scored seven. Bullock responded by taking Lee Smelt from Nottingham Forest, initially on loan before securing him in a £10,000 deal. Immediately fortunes improved.

As one keeper arrived, so another left, but the surprise was that it was not the hapless Kilner, but young reserve Bobby Mimms. Having served his apprenticeship, Mimms had signed professional forms in August. After starring against Rotherham United reserves on 2 September, Millers' boss Emlyn Hughes came back for him, paying £15,000 in November, not bad for a player who had yet to feature in Halifax's first team.

November also saw Tommy O'Neil break his leg in a 2-1 victory over Mansfield, and Town bow out of the FA Cup, losing 0-3 at home to Peterborough. The following month Bullock stiffened his midfield by securing Steve Spooner from Derby. Spooner made his debut in the defeat at Wigan, but this turned out to be Town's last game for a month. Heavy snow put paid to three matches up to the turn of the year. It was the last thing the club needed. Dark clouds were looming over the Shay as attention suddenly focussed on Town's off-field financial plight.

The balance sheet for the year ending 31 March showed that Town had made a loss of £34,062, and were now £112,000 in the red. With attendances averaging only around the 1,800 mark, Sam Rorke was concerned enough to call a public meeting at the Civic Theatre on 11 January, where he put this question to those present: 'Do the people of Calderdale want a Football League club?'

Did You Know?

Jimmy Lawson was relegated with Huddersfield in 1972, 1973 and 1975, and was with Halifax when they had to apply for re-election in 1977.

Around 2,000 turned up – among them TV presenters John Helm and Derek Dougan, Leeds boss Allan Clarke, and the Mayor, Councillor Eric Whitehead. Rorke urged those present to pledge money, setting a survival target of £100,000, with a deadline of six weeks. But by the end of February, the money raised totalled only £13,845, and Rorke was adamant that the die was cast. On 1 March, he summoned a press conference, and with tears in his eyes told reporters that the club was up for sale.

What a difference a day makes. Less than 24 hours later, Rorke joined forces with Mickey Bullock with the battle-cry: 'We carry on.' Rorke insisted that, provided the club could see out the season – they would seek to cut the wage bill – they could kick off the following season with a clean sheet. But his rallying call was undermined by Jimmy McIlwraith's revelations in the *Sun* that he was earning £350 a week, whilst most players were on just £120. Bullock suspended McIlwraith without pay for two weeks, a fine which was doubled when the player twice failed to report to the club.

Meantime, Halifax Town had found some form. A nine-match unbeaten run had enabled the team to creep out of the re-election zone. Seven of those games, however, were draws, and Town would have made better progress had they not gifted opponents late goals to deprive themselves of victory, as at Bournemouth and Tranmere, then later against Darlington at the Shay.

There was a recall for Kilner when Lee Smelt fractured a knuckle in training, but after playing in Town's best win of the season – 4-1 over Stockport – Kilner conceded ten in two games against Bradford City and Sheffield United. Town slid back to 23rd. Smelt, fit again, was restored, and a six-match unbeaten run saw Town once again climb out of the danger zone. Though the team lost heavily at York on 7 May, Rochdale's defeat at Hull the following day meant that, with two games still to play, Town were safe.

Mickey Bullock would look back on the season with satisfaction. Not only had re-election been avoided, but the average attendance had gone up. Town had experimented three times with Friday night football, which had proved successful, as the supporters rallied to Sam Rorke's call. And Bobby Davison had ended up top scorer with 21 goals – the first Town player to pass the twenty mark since Les Massie in 1967-68. In a season that almost saw the club fold, Davison would prove to be the jewel that would keep Town alive.

Match of the Season 1981-82

Sheffield United 2 Halifax Town 2

Division 4, 2 January 1982

In a season that saw Halifax Town draw a record 22 matches, it could be argued that they made life hard for themselves by conceding too many late goals when victory was within their grasp. Early season games at the Shay had seen both Peterborough and Bournemouth score late equalisers, whilst Town also had victories denied in the return at Bournemouth and at Tranmere, and in home games with Aldershot and Darlington.

One game in which Town were happy to gain a point, however, was this one at Bramall Lane, home of high-flying Sheffield United. The Blades' fall from grace – only six seasons earlier they had been in Division One – had been dramatic, and they now found themselves in the Fourth Division for the first time. Managed by former FA Cup winner Ian Porterfield – he had scored the only goal in Sunderland's win over Leeds in 1973 – United were not expected to remain long in the soccer basement. Indeed, when Town travelled to meet them, United were second, their promotion charge well on course. The Blades included in their side the experienced Stewart Houston (ex-Manchester United and Scotland), whilst up front they called upon the deadly duo of Keith Edwards and Bob Hatton. Hatton had starred in the First Division for Birmingham City and had over 200 goals to his name.

On a pitch resembling a bog, the game had everything. Hatton headed the Blades into the lead, then Paul Richardson was sent off for kicking out at Steve Ward. The decision prompted a disgruntled fan to hit referee Vic Callow in the face with a snowball minutes after the interval. But in the 65th minute, United doubled their lead through Tony Kenworthy's penalty after Steve Spooner had handled Hatton's header.

Town had always looked threatening, however, and against United's ten men, they reduced the arrears when substitute Francis Firth – on the field a matter of seconds – whipped over a cross for Ward to head home. With six minutes remaining, Ward equalised when the ball fell to him following David Evans' free-kick.

Sheffield United deemed the draw, naturally, as two points dropped. But by losing just one game between then and the end of the season they nicked the title from Wigan Athletic. Town, on the other hand, were fighting battles on and off the field, both of which they would eventually overcome. The result here was perhaps the inspiration they needed.

LEAGUE DIVISION 4	**1982-83**
Division 4	11th
Milk Cup	1st Round
FA Cup	1st Round

At the end of 1981-82 Mickey Bullock released John Kilner, Jimmy McIlwraith, the unfortunate Tommy O'Neil, and – to most people's surprise – Tommy Graham, who had weighed in with a useful eight goals. Glyn Chamberlain rejected new terms and left the club, as did striker Vernon Allatt. He joined Bolton, but would return to the Shay in November after scoring prolifically in Bolton's reserves. But there was a major shock in July when centre-half and coach Billy Ayre joined Mansfield Town in a deal worth £17,500.

Bullock worked hard to seek replacements. Tony Smith arrived from Peterborough to take Ayre's place. Striker Dave Staniforth came from Bradford City and took over the coaching duties. Other new players were full-backs Keith Nobbs from Middlesbrough and the experienced Mick Wood, like Staniforth, from Bradford City. Midfielder Jimmy Hallybone (Orient) and young forward Martin Nuttall (Oldham) also joined.

There were changes at the top, too. On 2 June, chairman Sam Rorke stood down after a turbulent 500 days in office. He said nothing, but John Crowther pointed out the strains Rorke had been under as Town's plight worsened. Town were still £140,000 in the red but Crowther explained that no one was pushing the club for money. Even so, Town welcomed a sponsorship deal with kitchen manufacturers Macdee: for the first time the players would have a sponsor emblazoned across the front of their shirts.

Town's build-up to the new campaign included a 2-3 defeat by Leeds United in the West Riding Senior Cup final, after extra-time, and two games in the Football League's new Group Cup. Bobby Davison scored the only goal against Hull and grabbed a hat-trick against Hartlepool. But when it mattered, Town looked all over the place as they lost 0-1 at Colchester on the opening day. They raised their game against Second Division Derby County in the Milk Cup, the new guise of the League Cup following a sponsorship deal with the Milk Marketing Board. Staniforth netted a late winner as Town won the first leg at the Shay, and at the Baseball Ground in the return, almost made it into Round Two. Trailing 0-2 at half-time, Town hit back to go ahead on aggregate, until a Glen Skivington goal took the game into extra-time. Though Town eventually lost on the night 2-5, Mickey Bullock was rightly proud of his players, and for one of them, Bobby Davison – scorer of both Town's goals – his performance was one that probably changed his career.

In the league, a draw with Mansfield and wins over Darlington and Swindon meant Town could go top when they entertained Aldershot. This was one of Halifax's few Saturday games this season, the club having opted for Friday night football. But their efforts at Derby appeared to have drained the players. They crashed 1-3 against the Shots, and thereafter slid down the table. Matters were not helped when keeper Lee Smelt broke a finger in that game with Aldershot – Oxford United's John Butcher came on loan – but Smelt was back in the side when Town were humiliated 0-3 at home to Crewe. That result dumped them in the re-election zone.

The Shaymen made it eleven games without a win when they drew at home to Hereford, one of the few teams below them. That result rendered all the more remarkable the events of the following week, when Town turned the tables at Plough Lane, home of high-flying Wimbledon. Having returned from Bolton, Vernon Allatt starred up front with Davison, who netted a hat-trick as Town won 4-2, inflicting on the Dons their first home defeat.

Perhaps only Halifax Town could cap that magnificent victory by losing at home the following week to non-league North Shields in the FA Cup. The goal that beat them was a pot-shot out of the blue from Bede McCaffrey, worthy of winning any game. Town just wished it hadn't been here, for a run in the Cup was badly needed to ease their mounting financial plight. Attendances had dropped to the 1,000 mark.

The timing, therefore, of Derby boss Peter Taylor's decision to spy on Davison in Town's next game at Hartlepool could not have been better. Town won 2-1, but though Davison failed to score Taylor had been impressed. 'I saw enough to convince me that he can do a good job,' he explained. Derby's original offer for the player of just £50,000 was rejected by Halifax – Bullock himself rated the striker at £200,000 – but following an improved offer, Davison travelled with John Crowther to Derby on 1 December to put pen to paper. The fee? A reputed Town club record £98,000.

Later, Bullock confided that had Davison not gone when he did, the club would have folded, with the Inland Revenue clamouring for around £70,000 in tax arrears.

Without a fixture when the second round of the FA Cup came around, Halifax arranged a Friday night friendly with Manchester United – Bullock was a former team-mate at Oxford United with Reds' boss Ron Atkinson. A meagre crowd of 1,070 turned up to see United win 3-2. It was disappointing for the sparse crowd that the only noted United player on view was international full-back John Gidman. But for those with an eye for the future, Mark Hughes and Peter Beardsley both played.

There were even fewer spectators for Town's next home game, a sorry defeat by Tranmere being watched by just 912. But then something clicked. The departure of Bobby Davison had an unexpected effect. A draw at high-flying Hull was followed by a 3-1 victory over Scunthorpe. During January and February, Town put together a six-match winning run, their best since 1964. This not only hoisted them out of relegation danger – Town climbed as high as eighth – it also had supporters chanting for promotion.

The run ended at Chester, and thereafter Town struggled. The Shaymen were not helped by injuries to Evans, Hendrie, Staniforth and Nuttall. In the short term, Bullock took on loan midfielders David Wilkes (Barnsley) and Glen Skivington (Derby). In the long term, he signed Bradford City's free-kick expert Barry Gallagher, while off-loading Everton Carr to Rochdale. Town still failed to find any consistency. They enjoyed a 3-1 victory at Torquay – a beaming Bullock described the performance as the best since he took over – but were hammered 1-6 at Aldershot three days later.

Town rounded off the season by holding champions Wimbledon to a draw – the Dons extending their unbeaten run to 21 games – then beat Stockport in their final match. Town finished the season eleventh, their highest Division Four placing since 1968-69, and by recent standards a top-half position was most welcome. Bullock reckoned Town would do even better the following term.

Match of the Season 1982-83

Wimbledon 2 Halifax Town 4

Division 4, 13 November 1982

Wimbledon's elevation to the top flight in 1986, and the fact that (to date) they have stayed there, surprised most people within the game. In many ways, the feats of this unfashionable club have surpassed the achievements of giants Liverpool and Manchester United. Their 'Crazy Gang' spirit has kept them competing ever since in the First Division, now the Premiership.

Wimbledon's climb up the Football League ladder began in 1982-83, when, under former player Dave 'Harry' Bassett, they not only clinched promotion from the Fourth Division, but won the title eight points clear of second placed Hull. But while they beat most sides in the division, one they could not get the better of was Halifax Town. The Shaymen had been Wimbledon's opponents for their first ever league match, back in August 1977, and claimed a draw to spoil the newcomers' party. Now, in this, their last visit to Plough Lane, they were about to party-poop again.

Did You Know?

Kevin Johnson kept Kevin Keegan out of the Doncaster Schoolboys team, when Johnson was a year younger than Keegan!

To say that this victory for Town was unexpected would be an understatement. Most people – probably a few of the players themselves – thought they were travelling to Plough Lane to make up the numbers. Town had not won for eleven games, home or away, and confidence was as low as expected for a side that lay 22nd in the table. The Dons, on the other hand, had already staked their promotion claims, though they went into this game having lost their last two matches, at Colchester and Hartlepool.

This fixture, on the face of it, presented Wimbledon with the perfect opportunity to get back on track, but with Town employing a sweeper system, Wimbledon found them hard to break down. Their efforts were hampered by the loss of leading scorer John Leslie after half an hour, whilst at the other end, Town's own leading scorer made his presence felt.

In Bobby Davison's short time at Halifax, this game undoubtedly provided his finest hour. His hat-trick was his first in the league, and Wimbledon had no answer to him. He opened the scoring in the 42nd minute with a first-time strike after Vernon Allatt and Paul Hendrie had combined to set him up, and made it 2-0 seven minutes after half-time, when Hendrie sent him clear. Allatt made it 3-0 following some slack defending, whilst Wayne Entwistle's goal only served to give the home side false hopes of a fightback. Davison completed his hat-trick in the 68th minute, finishing off a Steve Spooner-inspired move with a first-time shot. Wimbledon did make the score slightly more respectable when Dean Thomas scored a late penalty after Malcolm Goodman had handled, but some of the home supporters were already heading for home by then.

This was a monumental victory. The last time the Shaymen had scored four goals away from home was when they defeated Workington by the same score in February 1958. Davison's hat-trick was Halifax Town's first in the league since Terry Shanahan's against Brentford in April 1973, and the first away from home since John Parks scored all Town's goals in a 3-1 win at Hartlepool in April 1967.

But, as was typical of Halifax at this time, they followed up this notable scalp by losing theirs to non-league North Shields seven days later.

LEAGUE DIVISION 4	**1983-84**
Canon Division 4	21st (sought re-election)
Milk Cup	1st Round
FA Cup	1st Round

Mickey Bullock's expectations for an improved season might have been enhanced had he been able to strengthen his squad with the players he wanted. Having released Malcolm Goodman and Jimmy Hallybone, Bullock acquired forwards Jeff Cook from Plymouth (a target for George Kirby four years earlier), Stewart Mell from Doncaster, and midfielder Neil Hanson from Preston. Though Vernon Allatt moved to Rochdale for £2,000, the Town boss struggled in vain to keep want-away Steve Spooner at the Shay. Spooner eventually moved to Chesterfield in exchange for £11,500, and further headaches lay in store for Bullock. Alderhot striker Mark Sandford signed for the club before breaking down in training with a recurrence of a knee problem – his contract had to be cancelled in September. Sheffield Wednesday's Gordon Owen, having had a pair of boots bought for him, turned his back on Halifax and signed for Cardiff instead.

Despite a morale-boosting 2-0 win over Leeds United in the West Riding Senior Cup – Illingworth teenager Mark Greenway kept former England winger Peter Barnes under wraps – the Shaymen made a disappointing start to the season. Two victories in the first nine league games left them languishing in nineteenth place. And they fell yet again at the first hurdle in the Milk Cup, this time to Darlington. Town lost the first leg 0-1 at the Shay, but looked to have turned things around at Feethams, taking a two-goal lead, before Darlington hit back with three goals in twenty minutes to take the tie 4-2 on aggregate.

On 31 August, Halifax Town had announced a record profit of £40,008 – as opposed to a record loss of £97,627 the previous term – though profits had included the money from the sale of Bobby Davison. Town were still £177,882 in the red, and deep in trouble. With his side struggling, Bullock's £12,000 bid for Alan Little was accepted by Torquay, only for Town to pull out when a long-standing debt meant they could not afford him. Luckily for Bullock, he would be able to acquire the midfield general in November on a free transfer.

October's wins over Peterborough and Crewe lifted the Shaymen up to eighth, but that was as good as it got. Despite taking Burnley's former England 'B' international Joe Gallagher on loan, Town went into free-fall. Alan Little actually arrived in the middle of a run of six consecutive defeats, as Town dropped into the re-election zone for the first time. But that was not all. As North Shields had done twelve months earlier, Northern League Whitby Town came to the Shay and knocked Halifax out of the FA Cup. This had looked unlikely when Dave Evans gave Town a 2-0 lead in the 58th minute, but there was no excuse for the way the Shaymen caved in and handed the non-leaguers victory.

With confidence obviously low, the side ended their poor run with a draw at fellow strugglers Rochdale, and followed that up by defeating promotion hopefuls Blackpool at the Shay. With striker Steve Cooper arriving on loan from Birmingham City, Town extended their unbeaten run to seven games in the New Year, though it took a last-gasp goal from Tony Smith to earn them a home point against Wrexham in a wretched display.

It was teenager Steve Thornber, with his first touch in league football, who saved the day when he scored Town's second equaliser in the next match at the Shay, against Chester, but this was only the prelude to their worst spell of the season. February and March brought four consecutive league defeats, among them hammerings of 2-5 at Aldershot and 1-6 at Crewe, and there was also a 0-2 defeat at Tranmere in the first round of the new Associate Members Cup. But the worst result was still to come. With keeper Lee Smelt ruled out through injury, Manchester student Kieron Vesey was drafted in goal for only his second game at Mansfield, but he was left shell-shocked as the Stags found it all too easy and romped to a 7-1 win.

Mickey Bullock was dismayed at losing Paul Hendrie and Dave Staniforth, both long-term injury casualties. The pressure increased on the manager, particularly after a 1-4 defeat at runaway league leaders York City. But three days later, on Easter Monday, his players responded magnificently, beating Rochdale 5-0 at the Shay, with Barry Gallagher helping himself to four goals as Town moved temporarily out of the re-election zone. Further home wins over Chesterfield and, in their final game, 4-1 over Colchester, saw Halifax move out of the bottom four once again. But the season had yet to run its course. Wrexham, who had three games left, could still overhaul the Shaymen if they mustered seven points from them.

Even before the club's immediate future was decided, supporters knew they would have to do without several key players. On 17 May, the retained list showed seven major omissions. Incredibly, Lee Smelt, David Evans, Tony Smith, Mick Wood, Martin Nuttall, Stewart Mell and player-coach David Staniforth were all given free transfers, with John Crowther admitting that the severe financial situation had forced the club's hand.

Did You Know?

Halifax Town's mascot is Freddy Fox, after a fox was spotted running about at the Shay.

Three days later, Wrexham, who had started to make up the points on Town with victory over Chesterfield and a draw at Crewe, thrashed mid-table Tranmere 5-1 to leap above the Shaymen on goal-difference. It meant Halifax now needed to make their fourth re-election application in the last eight years, and although the Mayor, councillor John Bradley, canvassed all the other 91 Football League clubs asking for support, there was yet again the feeling that Halifax's time might be up. Along with their own recent poor history, and all-too-familiar financial plight, Alliance Premier League champions Maidstone United were preparing a strong case. Should they be elected, they were pledging to make £300,000 available to launch an immediate challenge for Division Four honours.

Match of the Season 1983-84

Halifax Town 5 Rochdale 0

Division 4, 23 April 1984

As another season entered its final weeks, the Shaymen were staring re-election straight in the face. A crushing 1-7 defeat at Mansfield had indicated just how poor a side they had become. Table-toppers York had had no trouble in putting four past them just days before the Rochdale fixture. Halifax were desperate for the points, but the visit of fellow strugglers Rochdale did not guarantee any. Their manager Jimmy Greenhoff had resigned in March. Now under player-manager Les Chapman, who had been put in temporary charge, Rochdale were equally desperate for the points, and this Easter Monday game promised, if anything, a tense battle, with no quarter asked or given.

The Shaymen, and Barry Gallagher in particular, were delighted, then, to find Rochdale in such charitable mood. Town ran up their biggest score since beating Workington 6-1 in February 1977, and Gallagher scored four goals himself, the first Town player to do so since Des Frost scored all the goals in a 4-1 win at Lincoln in February 1951.

Despite including former Manchester City and England defender Mike Doyle in their side, Rochdale were all over the place, and Town could easily have won by more. Yet despite scoring four, Gallagher was modest about his achievement. He claimed afterwards that he was simply in the right place at the right time for three of his goals – isn't that the trait of a good goalscorer? – whilst his first was something of a fluke, a corner-kick that sailed straight in. But Gallagher was not complaining. His second goal was a spectacular finish at the far post following a cross from Jeff Cook, his third was made by Paul Hendrie, who had robbed Paul Heaton, and Gallagher's last was a comic-cut goal, Doyle's back-pass to keeper Steve Conroy leaving him with an open goal.

As Gallagher grabbed the headlines, his strike partner Stewart Mell seemed almost forgotten. Yet it was he who actually opened the scoring in the fifteenth minute, outpacing the defence before guiding the ball past the advancing Conroy – the game's best goal. It was also the significant breakthrough.

Though poles apart in this game, both Halifax and Rochdale would not be so at the end of the season. Rochdale's fate would be sealed first, but Wrexham's late surge meant that Town, too, would join them at the Football League's Annual Meeting in June, when they would seek yet again re-election.

LEAGUE DIVISION 4	**1984-85**
Canon Division 4	21st (sought re-election)
Milk Cup	2nd Round
FA Cup	2nd Round

Halifax Town need not have worried. At the Football League's Annual Meeting on 8 June, though there was no real glory in it, Town and Chester each polled a maximum 52 votes. Rochdale (50) and Hartlepool (32) were also re-elected, whilst the challenge of Maidstone was overlooked, as they received just 22 votes.

A relieved Mickey Bullock said, 'Now I can get on with the business of getting players,' but having had to release so many of his best, he now found himself locked in a battle to keep the fans' favourite, Paul Hendrie. Bullock had been told to trim the wage bill: he now asked Hendrie to take a £1,000 per annum pay cut. Hendrie couldn't afford it, refused to re-sign, and eventually moved to Stockport for £1,500, the amount settled by tribunal after Bullock had valued him at £5,000. Also to reject new terms was Keith Nobbs, who moved back to the north-east with Hartlepool.

Bullock's new signings were a contrasting, but affordable, mix of kids and veterans. Defender Alan Knill (Southampton), midfielder Chris Moyses (Lincoln City), and forwards Simon Lowe (Barnsley) and Paul Sanderson (Chester) all brought limited Football League experience. Defenders Cyril Podd and Garry Watson, both from Bradford City – Podd had made a record 502 league appearances for the Bantams – were in the twilight years of their careers. So too, it has to be said, were Billy Ayre, who rejoined the club in his old capacity as player-coach, having been released by Mansfield, and former Manchester United and Republic of Ireland international keeper Paddy Roche. He was signed from Brentford, yet despite being 33, Roche would probably display the best form of his career with the Shaymen.

Halifax announced the new club sponsors as Madeley's, the DIY company, but on the field they made a dreadful start, losing their opening three league games. The side kept supporters' interest alive by making it to the second round of the Milk Cup for the first time since 1975. They did it the hard way, being held by Chesterfield at home in the first leg before playing above themselves at Saltergate and winning 2-1. Their reward in Round Two was a money-spinner over two legs with Division One glamour side Tottenham Hotspur, managed by Peter Shreeve.

When Spurs arrived at the Shay for the first leg, they did so as First Division leaders after winning at Aston Villa. Included in Spurs' side were household names such as former England keeper

Ray Clemence, current international Gary Mabbutt, and Garth Crooks. Town, with only two wins under their belts, lay sixteenth in Division Four, but the game was considered attractive enough for the BBC 'Sporstnight' cameras to capture the action. Disappointingly for the BBC, there was no shock result. Though the Shaymen created a number of early openings, they were overwhelmed 1-5 with Crooks netting a hat-trick. The second leg was a formality for Spurs – they won 4-0 at White Hart Lane – but Town's bankers were happy with over £30,000 the club made from the two games.

In the league, Town were in a familiar position near the division's basement. After losing 0-1 to Darlington at the Shay on 19 October – Town's fourth consecutive league defeat – they hit rock bottom, three points adrift of the team above them. The directors knew they had to take action: at a board meeting three days later they decided Mickey Bullock should go. It was not a decision they made lightly – the meeting itself lasted over three hours – but Bullock, after almost nine years at the club, was disgusted at his treatment. He felt, with some justification, that he had been made a scapegoat for the club's poor position, and left the club a bitter man.

Billy Ayre was given temporary charge of the team, but he made it known he wanted the job on a permanent basis. A 3-1 victory at Colchester and a draw at Torquay did his chances no harm, but immediately after beating Mansfield to move off the bottom of the table the directors unveiled the new manager as the former Bradford City and Derby County coach Mick Jones. In a personal telephone call to John Crowther, Nottingham Forest boss Brain Clough had recommended Jones, saying he was the second best manager in the Football League – after himself, of course!

Mick Jones appointed Ayre as his right-hand man and made a good start. His first game was a 2-0 victory over non-league Goole Town in the FA Cup – the win was marred by a broken leg for Paul Kendall – and this was followed up by successive wins over Crewe and Port Vale which lifted Town up to seventeenth. But then the good run ended. Despite taking Adrian Shaw on loan from Forest – he eventually signed for a four-figure fee in March – Town lost at Burnley in the FA Cup and suffered four defeats in the league to slip once more into the re-election zone.

Town's poor sequence was halted by a morale-boosting draw at Blackpool. The following week the side pulled off one of the biggest shocks of the season by beating leaders Bury 4-1 at the Shay. But though bad weather saw Town lose their momentum, they put on a refreshing display in the Freight Rover Trophy, where Jones blooded youngsters Robert Hunt, Paul Fleming, John Francis and

Did You Know?

Only one player in Halifax Town's history had a surname beginning with the letter 'I' – Willie Irvine

Dean Martin. Town beat Darlington 4-1 in the first leg, but then inexplicably, a more experienced line-up in the return was humiliated 0-7 at Feethams.

Mick Jones was finding the going tough. He sought to bolster the defence by signing centre-half Steve Brookes from non-league Barrow, and added firepower to the forward line with former Leeds United and Bradford City striker David McNiven, who had returned from a spell with Pittsburgh Spirit in Canada. But results hardly improved. The situation was not helped by attendances which barely topped the one-thousand mark. Some games failed even to reach four figures. Tranmere's visit was watched by just 914, and only 890 saw Torquay win 1-0.

On 20 April, with Town lying next to bottom, chairman Jack Turner decided to stand down – he would remain a director. John Crowther began his second spell at the helm, with Roger Newby his vice-chairman. The board by now consisted of eleven. Its other members were Tom Dawson, Derick Wilkinson, John Robinson, Tom McLean, Colin Wood, Eddie Walton, Dr David Lord and Frank Hinchliffe. Some supporters quipped that the Board XI looked stronger than the team itself.

For Crowther, it must have been like a recurring nightmare to see Town fighting against re-election yet again. The players raised hopes of avoiding this by wining their final three matches, which included a terrific 3-0 win at Stockport. Upon the final whistle in the last game, having defeated Swindon at the Shay on a Friday night, the Town supporters invaded the pitch and saluted their heroes. They wrongly believed their team was safe after moving out of the re-election zone. The following day Southend beat bottom club Torquay 1-0 to leapfrog above the Shaymen. Shades of Wrexham twelve months previously. Town were condemned to another re-election bid on goal-difference.

Match of the Season 1984-85

Halifax Town 4 Bury 1

Division 4, 12 January 1985

In another season of disappointments, Halifax Town still found it within themselves to pull off one of the shocks of the season. For whichever way it was looked at, this hammering of Bury was a shock, with the Shaymen proving that when they put their minds to it, they could match anyone in the division.

Not that Bury were just anyone. Under player-manager Martin Dobson – he had taken over from Jim Iley the previous March – Bury had finished a moderate fifteenth in 1984, but now, having recruited a couple of old heads, they were setting the pace. Like Dobson, Leighton James (ex-Burnley, Derby and Wales) and Trevor Ross (Arsenal and Everton) may have been past their best. But they could still play a bit, and together with the prolific goalscoring talents of Craig Madden, it was not hard to see why Bury arrived at the Shay two points clear at the top of the table.

The Shakers had won their previous four matches, whilst Town had lost four of their last five, including a 0-3 home defeat by Hartlepool. So when Madden slid in to score his fifteenth goal of the season after 23 minutes the result looked a formality, especially as Bury had dominated the game up to that point. But in tricky conditions – a blanket of snow covered the pitch – Town drew level in the 39th minute and after taking the lead early in the second half, they grew in confidence.

Hero for the Shaymen was Simon Lowe. He only had three league goals to his name so far this season, but he was about to double his tally in this game. He nipped in at the near post to turn in Barry Gallagher's cross for the equaliser, then, in the 52nd minute, headed into an empty net after Garry Watson had kept his cool and centred perfectly when Bury keeper David Brown had fumbled the ball.

The visitors, as one might expect, came back strongly, and Roche had to make magnificent saves off two Entwistle headers, but Town were not finished. Badly in need of points to escape the re-election clutches, they went 3-1 up in the 84th minute when Gallagher rose above Brown, John Bramhall and Andy Hill, to head home, then finished the job off in injury-time. Gallagher created the last goal and might have scored it himself after rounding Brown, but instead, unselfishly, he set up Lowe, who duly scored one of the easiest goals of his career to complete his hat-trick.

Martin Dobson's side would struggle to cope with the shock of this defeat. They succumbed at Colchester the following week, and eventually lost their grip on the leadership. At the season's close, however, they would gain promotion by finishing fourth.

LEAGUE DIVISION 4	**1985-86**
Canon Division 4	20th
Milk Cup	1st Round
FA Cup	1st Round

Halifax Town's fifth re-election application could, and perhaps should, have been their last. But they were fortunate to have so many sympathisers within the Football League. They were voted back in with 48 votes, while non-league Enfield, the Gola League champions – the new name of the Alliance Premier League - received just eight. Northampton (52 votes), Stockport and Torquay, with 50 votes each, were also re-elected, but not for much longer could clubs like these count on the 'old pals act' to retain their league status. The following year, the League decided to introduce automatic exchange between the bottom club in Division Four and the winners of the Gola League.

There was one surprising omission from Mick Jones' first retained list, that of skipper Alan Little. Also shown the door were David McNiven, Steve Brookes, Jeff Cook, Chris Moyses, Garry Watson and Mark Greenway. But there was no shortage of quality with the players Jones brought in. The experienced Billy Kellock arrived from Peterborough, winger Gary Nicholson (Mansfield Town), defender Phil Brown (Hartlepool United) – Brown would be appointed skipper – and exciting young forward David Longhurst from Nottingham Forest.

All these players, however, were joining a club in a mess. As well as their poor recent league record, Halifax Town had revealed debts of £193,000, and had been hit harder than most when, following the Bradford City fire disaster the previous May, new regulations necessitated expensive ground improvements at the Shay. A Ground Improvement Fund, headed by Northampton businessman Chris Stephenson, was launched on 14 July, but for the first three matches at the Shay, all standing areas were closed off.

Doubtless such restrictions had a bearing on attendances. Only 890 turned up for the first leg of Town's Milk Cup-tie with Second Division Hull City. The Shaymen actually performed creditably in that game, drawing 1-1, but were humbled in the return at Boothferry Park. In the league, they made a pleasing start, with three wins from the opening six matches putting Halifax among the leaders. But then they lost their way completely. They went on a run of thirteen games without a win, and a 0-4 defeat at Northampton left them in 23rd place. At one point, Jones told his players, 'Work together or leave,' but if he was expecting an immediate positive response, he was to be disappointed.

Did You Know?

Town broke their own transfer record when they sold Rick Holden (£125,000), Lee Richardson (£175,000) and Wayne Allison (£250,000) – all to Watford.

November saw Town bow out of the FA Cup at home to Scunthorpe, despite taking an early lead, but in early December their run of terrible results was ended when Simon Lowe scored the only goal to sink Hereford. Victories should also have been achieved in Town's next two games, but they squandered a two-goal lead at Swindon and lost 2-3; then worse, at Scunthorpe, they allowed the home side to claw back three goals to earn a point. As the season went into January, Town once again looked doomed to re-election.

Mick Jones knew he needed new players, but with hardly any money in the kitty, he had to rectify the situation himself. Splitting the proceeds 50-50 with Martin House, a home in Boston Spa for the terminally ill, he undertook a sponsored walk to Preston, where the Shaymen were playing on 11 January, to buy a player. Perhaps viewing this as an incentive, the Shaymen won at Deepdale courtesy of a Billy Kellock header.

That victory did not immediately win back the fans, who had been conspicuous by their absence. The home game with Colchester at the end of January attracted just 989, but that was not the lowest at the Shay that season. A meaningless Freight Rover Trophy game with Lincoln (Scunthorpe had already won the group) had been postponed several times because of bad weather. It was hurriedly arranged for the afternoon of 11 February, and was watched by a mere 150 – the official figure – though a head-count by the *Courier* reporter put the figure at a more precise 122.

With the arrival of striker Barry Diamond from Rochdale and central defender Mick Galloway on loan from Mansfield – Galloway would eventually be signed for £1,500 with money raised from Mick Jones' sponsored walk – Town's league fortunes during February and March changed dramatically. The side won six games out of seven and climbed out of the bottom four to a lofty sixteenth, the best performances of this sequence being a 5-2 home win over Wrexham and a David Longhurst-inspired 3-1 victory at Burnley. But the good run could not last. It came to an end at Rochdale and Town struggled thereafter, slipping back into their old losing ways.

All the while, the Town directors had been examining ways of taking the club forward, with another ground-sharing scheme with the rugby club top of the agenda. The two parties sat down for talks in January with the main option being for Halifax Town to move up to Thrum Hall. Inevitably, as in 1981, the talks broke down, but at least relations between the two football codes had improved greatly. At the beginning of the season, Halifax RLFC chairman David Brook had launched a scathing attack on Halifax Town in the *Evening Courier*. But when the Thrum Hall floodlights were blown down by gale-force winds, the Town board were quick to allow the rugby club to play one of its games at the Shay. On 22 January, Widnes beat Halifax 15-8 on an historic night when Rugby League was staged at the Shay for the first time.

The season was turning into a nightmare for the soccer lovers. Whilst Halifax Town struggled to the end, the rugby club was making great strides for the League Championship. They clinched it on 20 April by drawing with Featherstone Rovers, but days later the Shaymen responded by slipping again into the bottom four, following defeat at Hereford. The consequences of another re-election bid were unthinkable, but the players tried to allay any fears by beating Port Vale 2-0 to move up to eighteenth. With two games left to play, Town were still far from safe, but after losing at home to Swindon, they were relieved to see Exeter go down at home to Crewe the following day. That meant that Town could lose their final home game – which, unsurprisingly, they did – and know that re-election would not be necessary. Both Halifax and Exeter had 54 points, but when Rochdale drew their outstanding fixture at Peterborough it left the Grecians to drop into the re-election zone.

Halifax Town saw out those final anxious weeks of the season without a chairman. At the end of April John Crowther had resigned, thus ending an association with the club that stretched back to 1974, following a personal attack on him by a fellow director: 'I have resigned because the backing of the board should have been unquestioned,' he said. He added that boardroom difficulties 'had made my position untenable'. But perhaps, on reflection, Crowther might like to think he got out at the right time. Halifax Town's *annus horribilis* was just about to begin.

Match of the Season 1985-86

Burnley 1 Halifax Town 3

Division 4, 22 March 1986

Back in 1976, Burnley were a First Division club with facilities to match. But having already sold a whole host of top players – Dave Thomas, Leighton James and Martin Dobson, to name but three – they were falling on hard times. Following relegation that year, they had yo-yoed between Divisions Two and Three, before falling through the trap-door into the Fourth in 1985. Some Halifax Town supporters followed their demise with sadistic glee, and with Burnley now in the same division as the Shaymen, quickly took to them as Public Enemy Number One.

Over the ensuing years, however, it was the Clarets who generally held the upper hand. But in this 1985-86 season, it was Halifax who enjoyed the better of the exchanges. Back in October, they had been denied victory when Neil Grewcock fired in a late long-range equaliser, but in this return at Turf Moor, Town made sure there was no chance of a repeat.

Star of the show was undoubtedly David Longhurst, as he put on a virtuoso display – it was probably his finest in a Town shirt – and capped it with a brilliant solo goal late on. By which time he had already run ragged a Burnley defence that included former Leeds United star's Peter Hampton and Kevin Hird, had a hand in Town's first two goals, and showed why manager Mick Jones rated him so highly.

Despite his performance, it was Burnley who took the lead in the thirteenth minute when Hampton fired in from 24 yards, but within five minutes, Town were level, and never looked back. Longhurst nipped between two defenders on the left and cut into the box to set up Gary Nicholson. Then, in the 26th minute, Longhurst played a major part in Town's second goal. He controlled Paul Sanderson's corner at the near post, turned, then fired in a shot that keeper Joe Neenan could not hold. Simon Lowe was only too happy to turn the loose ball over the line.

For the most part, Burnley looked a demoralised lot. The club was £800,000 in debt, and the players seemed to be affected by it all. Or was it just Longhurst whom they were more concerned with? Either way, there was nothing they could do to prevent his goal that gave Town a 3-1 lead. Beating two players in the air, he controlled the ball just inside the centre-circle then set off on his run. Defenders were alerted to the danger, but it was too late. Longhurst homed in on goal, drew the keeper, waltzed round him, then planted the ball into the roof of the net. It was one of the finest goals ever scored by a Halifax Town player.

Ten minutes later, the final whistle blew. The Town supporters claimed revenge for defeat here by the same score in the FA Cup the previous term, although this probably was not on the players' minds. They were more concerned that they had kept an impressive run going – it now stood at six wins from seven games – and moved them out of the bottom four, and ultimately to safety.

Of Longhurst's goal, the supporters who saw it would treasure it for ever, and would use it as their perfect epitaph to a player who would die on the pitch while playing for York in September 1990.

LEAGUE DIVISION 4	**1986-87**
Today Division 4	15th
Littlewoods Cup	1st Round
FA Cup	1st Round

With Halifax RLFC celebrating their first championship since 1965, under the presidency of David Brook, Halifax Town fans were hoping the appointment of their new chairman might have a similar effect at the Shay. On 12 June, John Madeley, a partner with club sponsors Madeley DIY Ltd, was installed as John Crowther's successor, and immediately stated his ambitions: 'I assure the people of Calderdale I will bring them the success they deserve. We are going to put Halifax Town on the football map.'

Top scorer Billy Kellock was not offered a new contract by Mick Jones, and he, Barry Gallagher, Steve Ward, Paul Kendall and Cec Podd, were released. Jones was also resigned to losing the jewel in his crown, David Longhurst, who was stalling over a new contract. It required Madeley's intervention to persuade the Town striker to stay. Next, Madeley announced a new sponsorship deal, this time with paint manufacturers Valspar. Jones also brought two new players to the club, leggy defender Dave Robinson from Hartlepool, and striker Russell Black from Sheffield United.

It was Black who scored the game's only goal at the Shay, after only 90 seconds, against Aldershot, as Town ended a 14-year wait for opening-day success. In the League Cup, now sponsored by Littlewoods, the Shaymen pushed neighbours Huddersfield all the way. Though Halifax lost the first leg at Leeds Road 1-3, they went two goals up at the Shay to take the tie into extra-time. The Terriers then scored twice to go through to Round Two.

Alas, no. Despite opening-day success, the side lost their next seven matches. Four weeks into the season, following a 0-2 home defeat by Stockport, Town found themselves bottom of the table. In some games they had thrown points away, such as at Preston where, with 22 minutes to go, they led 2-0; and in others, injuries had played their part. When Jones' squad had been pared to the bone, he had had to play teenage goalkeeper Phil Whitehead and student winger Rick Holden at Burnley, and his side slumped 0-3. It was a frustrating time, but at least in Holden, Jones had a player who would prove to be the find of the season.

Jones recruited Hull midfielder Mick Matthews and keeper Paul Gregory on loan from Scunthorpe. They made their debuts in a 3-6 home defeat by Northampton. Town recovered to beat Swansea in their next game to move off the bottom, but looming on the horizon was the biggest financial crisis to hit the club since it was formed.

While Town put a decent run of results together in October, by the end of the month the club was on the verge of extinction. A month earlier, they had been given six months to pay off a £76,000 tax debt, but now, with total debts exceeding £300,000, Madeley called in the accounting firm Peat, Marwick and Mitchell to examine the books. Madeley claimed there was no money in which to bale the club out, and the odds were against Halifax Town surviving. On 12 November, accountant Tony Richmond told shareholders that irregularities appeared to have been found in the club's financial operations.

Following an appeal on BBC's 'Grandstand', Town had been inundated with offers of help. When Exeter visited the Shay on 4 November, however, it was billed as Halifax Town's last ever game. Town won 2-0 and carried on regardless. The only thing that threatened the visit of Bolton in the first round of the FA Cup was an unpaid electricity bill. The Yorkshire Electricity Board had pulled the plug on the floodlights, but reconnected them when Town's commercial department stumped up the money. Halifax failed to make Round Two, but it took Bolton three pulsating games before they earned the right to play Tranmere in the next round.

All the while, though, Town's financial predicament was becoming ever more critical. The key to Town's survival seemingly lay with the lease to the Shay, but with Calderdale Council unwilling to part with it, there seemed to be no way forward. In November, an Edinburgh property company, headed by Michael Knighton, offered to build a £3 million sports complex in exchange for the ground, whilst in January, construction group Marshall's of Elland put forward a package to save the club.

On 3 December a letter appeared in the *Evening Courier* from Mick Jones, in which he claimed the council were letting the club die. On 12 December, John Madeley called a public meeting at the Civic Theatre to air ideas designed to save the club. Councillors present were given a rough ride, but the main outcome of the evening was the launch of the Save Halifax Association Lifeline (SHAL), fronted by supporters Colin Richardson and Jack Haymer. They put forward a five-year plan to construct a sports centre at the Shay, paid for by fans who would pay monthly amounts into the fund, but the long and short of it was that the money simply went to meet Halifax Town's running costs.

Mick Jones contributed to that meeting, but on 18 December he quit the club for the apparent security of the assistant manager's post at Peterborough United, where Noel Cantwell was in charge. The following day Billy Ayre was at last handed the job he had always wanted. Despite the crisis, he got off to great start, with the

Shaymen going unbeaten for six games and moving up to eleventh, at which point Ayre actually went on record as saying that he believed the side was good enough to go up.

On 19 January, the High Court put Halifax Town into the hands of accountant Tony Richmond. The following day Town lost 0-4 in the Freight Rover Trophy at home to Middlesbrough, the club for whom Richmond had acted as liquidator the previous season. In early March, Marshall's of Elland came back with an offer to pay off Town's £400,000 debts and build a new stadium near the North Bridge Leisure Centre. Marshall's had insisted all along, however, that they intended to build a superstore on the Shay for Gateway Foodstores. When the council rejected their plans, Marshall's, who had been injecting cash into Halifax Town in the hope of landing a contract, pulled out of any rescue deal.

The club stumbled along, on and off the field. Town were one of several clubs in the frame for automatic demotion to the Vauxhall Conference, whilst SHAL helped meet the club's weekly running costs. But money was running out, and with the council insisting that it was not going to help – money was still owed from a loan in March 1984 – Halifax Town looked doomed yet again. Fortunately, Calderdale Council were about to do a massive U-turn.

At a meeting on 8 April, the council came up with a deal, agreed by a large majority, to save Halifax Town. The brainchild of Labour councillor David Helliwell, it involved donating the club £210,000, buying back the lease of the Shay – it was valued at £150,000 – taking control of the club until the new season, and, except for John Madeley, removing the present board. Creditors later agreed to wipe out almost £200,000 in debts, and Halifax Town suddenly found itself on its soundest footing since formation in 1911.

An advisory committee was set up to run the club until 31 August, and a relieved Billy Ayre felt the club could only go one way – upwards. And how it needed to. At this point, Halifax Town were living completely in the shadow of Halifax RLFC, who, at the end of April, followed up their 1986 championship win with victory over St Helens in the Challenge Cup Final at Wembley. While they were winning trophies, Ayre could only content himself with the fact his side had comfortably staved off demotion – that sad distinction fell to Lincoln, who hit rock bottom for the first time on the last day – as the Shaymen finished a commendable fifteenth.

But Halifax Town did win its first ever championship, when their Under-19s clinched the Northern Intermediate League, in the process seeing off Leeds, Newcastle and Sunderland. Players such as Phil Whitehead, Wayne Allison, Lee Richardson, Dean Martin, Bobby Barr and Phil Sharpe had all appeared in the first team this season. With Billy Barr, Toby Paterson and Paul and Jimmy Willis waiting in the wings, the future of Halifax Town looked bright.

Match of the Season 1986-87

Tranmere Rovers 3 Halifax Town 4

Division 4, 13 March 1987

In what was a difficult season for a variety of reasons, Halifax Town were involved in several high-scoring games during 1986-87, only to come off second best in most. There was the 3-6 home defeat by Northampton and a 3-5 defeat at Rochdale. Immediately after this exciting win at Tranmere, Town would lose 3-4 at home to Wolves.

Victory over Tranmere, it must be said, was unexpected. Although Rovers were hardly the best team in the division – they were little better than Town at the time – the Shaymen went into the game on the back of seven games without a win. They had lost five of these and failed to score in their last three matches. Tranmere had had problems, too, but after sacking Halifax-born player-manager Frank Worthington in February, had picked up slightly under player-boss Ronnie Moore.

It was Moore who fired Tranmere into the lead after only four minutes, at which point the writing looked on the wall. But amazingly, after 27 minutes Billy Ayre's side had blitzed their hosts with three goals to turn the game on its head. Dave Longhurst set up Dean Martin for a 16th-minute equaliser, Mick Matthews scored with a vicious 25-yard drive that went in off the underside of the bar, then skipper Phil Brown scored at the second attempt to put Town 3-1 up.

At the interval, Halifax's lead had been reduced to one goal after Ian Muir netted his 21st of the season, but Town dug deep to protect it in the second half. Hero on the night was young keeper Phil Whitehead, who made a series of fine saves, despite having cracked his head against the post following a sickening challenge by Moore just after the restart.

The game was held up for four minutes while Whitehead received treatment, but after keeping out all that Tranmere threw at them, Town then stunned the home side with a fourth goal, this time scored by on-loan Tommy Sword with a header off Brown's free-kick in the 82nd minute. And that more or less sealed a famous victory, Town's first four-goal haul away from home since beating Wimbledon in November 1982. Steve Mungall had the last word though, with a driven cross in the final minute, which Graham Bell claimed he touched in.

5

LIVING ON BORROWED TIME 1987-1993

LEAGUE DIVISION 4	**1987-88**
Barclays Division 4	18th
Littlewoods Cup	1st Round
FA Cup	3rd Round

With Calderdale Council holding 76 per cent of the club's shares, and creditors accepting eighteen pence in the pound, Halifax Town went into the new season with a clean slate. But their problems were not quite over. The council also bought back the lease on the Shay (paying former chairman Sam Rorke £13,000, as he had money tied up in the lease) – then, so to speak, kicked Halifax Town out, giving them use of it only on match days. While all administrative affairs were conducted at new headquarters at Old Crossleyans Rugby Union Club, this meant the players could no longer train on the Shay pitch, nor did they have exclusive rights to the stadium's treatment facilities. Groundsman Northern Southernwood was also dismissed, but this backfired when the pitch, for so long immaculate, deteriorated so badly that for most of the season it had to be covered in sand.

The council had saved the club, but were not helping the team. Nor were they co-operative when the club put forward names for the composition of a new board of directors. Along with John Madeley, former player Dave Worthington, Chris Calvert, Martin Chippendale and George Watson met councillors on 18 August. Talks came to nothing. Madeley, with his associates resigned from Halifax Town, leaving the caretaker board that had been running the club with just two members, Rod Thomas and Jack Haymer.

Billy Ayre felt that the recent upheavals were deterring players from coming to the club. Having released Gary Nicholson, Paul Sanderson, Craig Farnaby and Barry Diamond, he succeeded in signing midfielder Stewart Ferebee from York, and Neil Matthews – he had been on loan at the Shay in 1986 – from Grimsby. But Ayre was dealt a body-blow when fans' favourite David Longhurst moved to Northampton for £40,000. Alan Knill went to Swansea for £15,000 after saying that Halifax Town lacked ambition.

For the first time, the Football League allowed the use of two substitutes, and in their opening league game Town put theirs to good use. Town played out a 2-2 draw with relegated Darlington at the Shay. Matthews' appearance in that game, however, would cost the club dearly. Though signed a month before the season began, his forms were not sent to the Football League headquarters in time, and for fielding an ineligible player Town were fined £500 in November and deducted one point. And although Halifax bowed out over two legs to York in the Littlewoods Cup, victories at Wolves – who were also in the Fourth Division at that time – and at home to Newport and Swansea kept them up with the front runners. When Phil Brown's header gave them a 2-1 win over Tranmere, Town moved into fourth, just one point behind the leaders.

While home form continued to be impressive, away form was less so, and the Shaymen's challenge faltered. Through September and October, Town lost five out of six matches on their travels, and there was the fear that they might carry this form into the FA Cup when they were drawn away at non-league Billingham Sythonia.

In the week preceding that match. Town lost their unbeaten home record to Colchester and left-back Frankie Harrison with a broken leg. Centre-back Mick Galloway moved to Scottish Premier League outfit Hearts for £60,000. The money was welcome, but did not make Halifax Town flush – half of the fee went to Mansfield as part of their sell-on clause.

Without two of their best players, the Shaymen travelled to meet Billingham, the tie having been switched to Hartlepool's Victoria Ground. When Billingham led 2-1, Town looked to be on the receiving end of yet another cup shock, but they rallied late on to turn the game round and win 4-2.

In the second round, Town were given a tricky tie at Third Division Grimsby Town – where they had already lost in the Freight Rover Trophy – but held out for a goalless draw. In the replay Town won 2-0 and move into the third round for the first time since 1979-80. They would face First Division giants Nottingham Forest.

By then, having taken Sunderland defender Mick Heathcote on loan, Town were enjoying an unbeaten run of four games, so there was the potential for another giant-killing act in the mould of Manchester City. But Forest were no mugs. Brian Clough brought his players up to look at the pitch, commented that he wished he had brought his bucket and spade, then watched his team stroll – if that is the right term on such a sandy surface – to a 4-0 win. The Shaymen never got a look in.

Did You Know?

Workington's first Football League game was against Town in 1951. In 1977, Workington were replaced by Wimbledon, whose first opponents were Town!

Following that defeat, Town blew hot and cold. One week they lost to bottom side Newport, then the next they beat table-toppers Wolves. But though they were not making any noises in the league, interest was growing in the Freight Rover Trophy, which had changed its name to the Sherpa Van in mid-season.

The *Evening Courier* dubbed it 'The Wembley Dream'. Having finished top of a qualifying group that contained Grimsby and Scunthorpe, Town beat Chesterfield 2-1 at the Shay, then Darlington by the same score at Feethams, to move into the Northern Area semi-finals. There they were paired with Burnley. In a never-to-be-forgotten encounter, Town drew 0-0 after extra-time, before losing 3-5 on penalties.

Making his Town debut in that game was striker Peter Duffield, on loan from Sheffield United. He would remain at the club until the end of the season, and score some valuable goals, but one player on his way out was winger Rick Holden. There had never been any doubt that he would better himself, and when First Division Watford came in with a £150,000 offer, Town could not refuse it. Holden completed his transfer on 23 March.

With yet another of Town's star players gone, and league form on the wane – Town won only three of their last fifteen matches – crowds began to dwindle. Only 866 were present for the visit of Hartlepool, the lowest in the league that season. The previous summer, the council had reckoned that Halifax Town would lose around £85,000 over the course of the season. But for the sales of Longhurst, Galloway, Knill and Holden, they surely would have.

Match of the Season 1987-88

Burnley 0 Halifax Town 0

Sherpa Van Trophy, 8 March 1988

The competition that began life as the Football League Group Cup, then the Associate Members' Cup, was now under the guise of the Sherpa Van Trophy. For all teams, the early stages were poorly supported, with interest only mounting once there was the glimmer of Wembley's Twin Towers.

Over the years, Halifax Town's record in the competition was actually quite good. They regularly progressed beyond the qualifying stage, and this season showed signs that they might even go all the way. They had topped their group, thanks mainly to a 3-0 home win over Scunthorpe, before a crowd of just 686. In the knockout stage, they had seen off Chesterfield and Darlington to reach the Northern Area semi-final for the first time. Standing between them and a place in the Northern final were the local enemy, Burnley.

Brian Miller's Clarets had got this far by overcoming Tranmere and Rochdale in their group, then beating both Chester and Bury. For the meeting with Halifax, they enjoyed home advantage, but for the Shaymen, this mattered little. They were being cheered on by an army of around 1,000 mad-keen supporters who were not too bothered at having to make the twenty-mile journey across the Pennines.

The 10,222 that watched the game were treated to a classic, with the action fast and furious, and no quarter asked or given. It was the Shaymen, though, who looked the better side. They eventually outfought the home side, created the better openings, and in the last half-hour of the ninety minutes, almost dominated the proceedings. Town included debutant Peter Duffield, on loan from Sheffield United, and it was from his cross in the 85th minute that Town came closest to scoring. Skipper Phil Brown met it, but his header came back off the bar.

The game went to extra-time, but there were still no goals, and in the end, a pulsating game came down to penalties. It was there that Town's dreams ended. With Burnley's Ray Deakin, Shaun McGory, Ian Britton and George Oghani all scoring with their kicks, and Brown, Dean Martin and Mick Matthews netting for Town, the Clarets led 4-3. There were gasps on the terraces when boss Billy Ayre instructed keeper Paddy Roche to take Town's next kick, especially as strikers Duffield, Neil Matthews, Wayne Allison, Terry McPhillips and Rick Holden were all eligible to take one. Roche crashed his kick against the crossbar. All it needed was for Paul Comstive to net Burnley's last kick – which he did – to ensure his side went through.

Roche and Halifax Town were left cursing that penalty miss. The *Evening Courier* described it as 'folly', but Burnley were not complaining. They overcame Preston in the two-legged Northern final to meet Wolves in the final at Wembley. There, luck deserted Burnley. Steve Bull and Andy Mutch scored Wolves' goals.

BURNLEY: Pearce, Daniel, Deakin, Britton, Davis, Gardner, (McGory), Farrell, Oghani, Taylor, Comstive, Grewcock (Hoskin).
HALIFAX: Roche, Brown, Barr, Matthews M, Fleming (Matthews N), Richardson, Martin, Thornber (McPhillips), Duffield, Allison, Holden.

LEAGUE DIVISION 4	**1988-89**
Barclays Division 4	21st
Littlewoods Cup	1st Round
FA Cup	3rd Round

Billy Ayre contemplated his retained list while on holiday in Majorca, then decided to release Paul Kendall, Adrian Shaw and Russell Black. Stewart Ferebee, who had had a wretched year with injuries, was given a monthly contract in an effort to prove himself, but he never played again and eventually had to retire.

The Town boss was not slow to bring new players to the club. There were experienced central defenders John Bramhall (Rochdale) and Alan Whitehead (York), full-back David Logan (Nothampton), and midfielder Phil Horner (Leicester City). All these arrived on free transfers, but Ayre did dip into the club's funds to bring Barnsley's Chris Hedworth to the Shay for £10,000. Hedworth was an obviously talented player, but unfortunate with injuries. And that was not the end of Ayre's recruitment drive. Following a pre-season friendly with Harrogate Town, so impressed was he with their young striker Andy Watson, that he signed him as well.

The new intake helped compliment a squad that now included several youngsters making the transition from youth to first team. Paul Fleming and Dean Martin had already featured in the side over the last three seasons, but the likes of Wayne Allison, Lee Richardson, Phil Whitehead and Billy Barr would come to the fore during this campaign, and in the long run would help to keep the club afloat.

During the summer, Douglas Moody had joined the board as vice-chairman to Rod Thomas, with Jack Haymer being made director of football. A working committee had been set up by Jim Brown of the club's new sponsors J&J Fee, whose primary aim had been to make money for Halifax Town and keep the club viable. The administrative heart of the football club now moved out of the Old Crossleyans and into new premises near the town centre.

The Shaymen, despite a number of players out through injury or suspension, made a flying start to the season with a 2-0 win at Torquay, then drew 1-1 at Scarborough in the Littlewoods Cup. On the eve of their first home game, Liburd Henry was taken on loan from Watford. He played, but could not prevent Town going down 1-2 to 'the enemy' Burnley.

Town bowed out of the Littlewoods Cup without losing a game, though Scarborough could consider themselves fortunate at the Shay to hold out, after extra-time, for a 2-2 draw to go through on the away-goals rule. The Shaymen put in plenty of effort, but not so much in their next game. They went down 1-4 at Exeter, but Ayre was angered to find that three players had broken club rules, and had been drinking less than 48 hours before that match. Neil Matthews, Mick Matthews and David Logan were all suspended without pay and banned from any contact with the club for two weeks. Mick Matthews and Logan would leave shortly afterwards. Town played out a 3-3 draw with Carlisle, a game that with a full-strength team they would surely have won. Ayre was unrepentant, however. Under the same circumstances, he claimed, 'I would have done the same again.' On the bright side, young striker Terry McPhillips netted his first senior hat-trick in that match.

Though Town were not winning regularly, they were scoring goals, and in October they hit a purple patch. The *Evening Courier* tagged it 'The Great Halifax Town Goal Rush' as, first, Wrexham were beaten 4-1 at the Shay. Then, following defeat at Cambridge, Town scored thirteen goals in three games to head the Football League's scoring charts. After twelve games, they had scored 31 goals, with the prolific McPhillips level with Arsenal's Alan Smith at the top of the individual charts.

In November, chairman Rod Thomas stood down. Douglas Moody took over the club with Jack Haymer becoming chairman – this was not unexpected as they were now the sole members of the board. But on the pitch, Halifax Town kept scoring goals. In the FA Cup, a typical poached goal by McPhillips was enough to put them into the second round at the expense of York City. Town were drawn away at non-league Altrincham. They went into that game having failed to score for the first time all season, suffering a 0-1 home defeat to Exeter seven days earlier. But in front of the BBC 'Match of the Day' cameras, they did a professional job at Altrincham and won 3-0 – and that without McPhillips, who was injured.

In the third round for a second successive season, the Shaymen obviously hoped for another big-name club. Alas, they were paired with Altrincham's Conference rivals Kettering Town. This was not an easy game by any means, and certainly did not guarantee a passage to Round Four. But when Town drew at Rockingham Road, they must have thought the hard work had been done. Not so. With First Division Charlton awaiting the winners, Town tossed away all their advantages in the replay, surrendering a 2-1 lead to go down 2-3, with Robbie Cooke, not for the first time, proving a thorn in their side.

The rot began to set in. Although the Shaymen put five past Scunthorpe at the beginning of January, that was the last of the good times. Only four more matches were won between then and at the end of the season, and there was even talk, however hushed, of relegation to the Conference. Town's last hope of salvaging their season was in the Sherpa Van Trophy. They had finished above Huddersfield and Scunthorpe to move into the knockout stage. Darlington were beaten 3-0 in the first round, but the Shaymen blew it in front of an unusually high – and optimistic – crowd at the Shay against an efficient Blackpool side on 21 February, losing 0-2.

Interest in the side began to wane as the team struggled. Matters were not helped when one of their young riches, Lee Richardson, left for Watford in February for a new club record fee of £175,000 plus. Halifax also lost the on-loan services of Chris Pullan, but took on his younger brother Nick, who had been turning out for Emley. Town also offered non-contract forms to forward Graham Broadbent, a local league player.

Town saw the season out with ten games without a win, but thankfully for them and their suffering supporters, relegation was avoided after Darlington claimed bottom place. Town's draw at Crewe in their penultimate match meant that mathematically they could not be caught.

There had been more board-room changes in February, when Douglas Moody resigned, thus leaving Jack Haymer as its sole member. Jim Brown was elected chairman, with Billy Ayre made managing director, and Barry Dawson and Pam Burton co-opted onto the board. Pam Burton, a schoolteacher, thus became Halifax Town's first female director.

A new board with new ideas would perhaps engender better fortunes. Some chance. With money still tight, Town would always be restricted, and it looked as if the club's future was already mapped out. The worst days were still ahead of them and Town would find survival their sole objective. Still, they could always sell a player or two to keep things ticking over ...

Match of the Season 1988-89

Doncaster Rovers 1 Halifax Town 4

Division 4, 21 October 1988

The early months of the season had seen Halifax Town hit the headlines with their goalscoring exploits. But though they were at one stage scoring and picking up points for fun at the Shay, their away form was unproductive. True, they were still scoring, but usually they found their opponents scoring more. They had won at Torquay on the opening day, but somehow that elusive second away win proved elusive. Until, that is, one barmy Friday night at Doncaster.

Did You Know?

Derek Bell, who was transferred to Barnsley in October 1978, was still Town's leading scorer by March. He had scored three goals.

October was the month Halifax Town hit the top of the goal-scoring charts. They travelled to Belle Vue for this fixture on the back of a 4-1 home win over Rochdale. Victory was hoped for, but in light of their recent away form, not necessarily expected. Dave Mackay's Doncaster Rovers had won three games on the trot. What unfolded, however, was something akin to a bombing raid.

The game kicked off at 7.30. By 7.44 it was as good as over, as the Shaymen blitzed their hosts with four quick-fire goals. The player grabbing the headlines at this time was young striker Terry McPhillips, and typically it was he who started the ball rolling. In the ninth minute, he turned in the loose ball after Rovers' keeper Paul Malcolm parried Wayne Allison's shot. Within a minute, Town were two up, when Malcolm this time failed to hold McPhillips shot, leaving Andy Watson to fire in his first goal of the season.

A minute later it was 3-0. Town forced a corner from the restart, and when Mick Matthews floated the ball over, there was his namesake Neil to head home. Neither the Town fans nor the home supporters could believe it, but the Shaymen were not finished. Three minutes later, Paul Raven slipped up, and McPhillips punished him to net his second goal. With fourteen minutes played, Town led 4-0.

The goal spree was over, but it should not have been. Allison, Dean Martin and Watson all missed inviting chances within the first thirty minutes – perhaps they were getting complacent. It was ironic that the next to score were Rovers, courtesy of an indirect free-kick on the six-yard line, awarded for high kicking by Neil Matthews. Ronnie Robinson crashed the ball home, but already it was a case of too little too late.

Half-time came, the players lost the momentum, and the second half proved to be a drab affair. Town had already done enough, and were content to sit on their lead, though Doncaster had little idea of how to keep the contest alive. McPhillips shot straight at the keeper, thereby wasting the opportunity to register his second hat-trick of the season.

Halifax's next opponents were Peterborough United at the Shay. Their manager Mick Jones admitted to being frightened of Halifax, and his worst fears were realised when, after a goalless first half, Town rattled in five goals after the break. The goal train was still rolling.

LEAGUE DIVISION 4	**1989-90**
Barclays Division 4	23rd
Littlewoods Cup	2nd Round
FA Cup	2nd Round

Despite such a poor finish to 1988-89, many supporters held the opinion that with the addition of three or four new players there was no insurmountable reason why Halifax Town could not challenge, if not for promotion, then certainly the play-offs. Billy Ayre released four players: keeper Paddy Roche – his departure was the only real surprise – Colin Blain, Bobby Barr, and Frankie Harrison. Harrison actually stayed at the club as a player after being appointed Gerry Brook's assistant with the youth team. But what the fans did not expect was to lose two more of the club's better players. First to leave was defender Dave Robinson to Peterborough United for £100,000. Then, on 17 July, striker Wayne Allison joined former colleagues Rick Holden and Lee Richardson at Watford. He cost the Vicarage Road outfit, managed by Steve Harrison, £250,000. Allison's sale yet again broke Halifax Town's transfer record.

Town chairman Jim Brown, acknowledging the criticism received for selling these two players, defended the decision, adding: 'I want to stress that we didn't need to sell, and that the money will be used for team strengthening in any way the manager sees fit.' So Ayre in turn spent a club record £40,000 to bring Leyton Orient striker Ian Juryeff to the Shay. Juryeff joined new team-mates Mitch Cook, a defender from Scarborough who had himself cost £22,500, and several free-transfers – goalkeeper David Brown (Preston), and midfielders Derek Hall (Southend) and Brian Butler (Stockport).

Juryeff made his league debut as a 76th-minute substitute. Those fourteen minutes were enough for him to head the fourth goal against a Hartlepool side that looked relegation certainties. After three games unbeaten, Town moved into second place, and the fans could have been forgiven for getting carried away. The team's performances indicated that this could actually be Town's year.

Carlisle United had also been beaten 3-1 in the Littlewoods Cup. Following Town's backs-to-the-wall performance in the return leg, the Shaymen moved into the second round 3-2 on aggregate. But by the time they met Second Division Middlesbrough in Round Two, the early season sparkle had begun to desert them. For the first leg at Ayresome Park, Billy Ayre asked his players to keep it tight, but Middlesbrough, buoyed by an early Bernie Slaven goal, ran up four goals to leave the second leg academic.

As had happened so many times before, Town plummeted down the table. Having beaten Torquay in their third game, they won only one of their next eight league fixtures. At Chesterfield, they contrived to throw away a 3-1 lead and lose 3-4. Despite playing well enough, they were not getting the points. But in an underpar performance, Town beat Rochdale in their next game and embarked on a run of four matches unbeaten to climb the table to sixteenth. They also defeated Lincoln City in the Leyland DAF Cup, the new name for the Sherpa Van. Town travelled to Marston Road for an FA Cup-tie with Stafford Rangers in understandably good spirits, despite having just lost at home to Southend.

Conference side Stafford were always going to give the Shaymen a run for their money, as they had in three cup-ties in the 1970s, and even the most ardent Town fan agreed that their own side were lucky on this occasion. Leading 2-1, Stafford had the chance to wrap the game up, before being sunk by two Phil Horner headed goals. Halifax's luck, though, ran out in the second round. Town were drawn to meet Darlington, a League side in all but name, but now plying their trade in the Conference. Darlington's 3-0 win over the Shaymen illustrated why they would make a return to Division Four at the first attempt.

Troubled times now lay ahead for Halifax Town and Billy Ayre. Chairman Jim Brown claimed it was costing £750,000 a year to run the club. A row between Ayre and Ian Juryeff, which became public knowledge, ended with the striker sold to Hereford the following week for £50,000. Town at least had made a £10,000 profit on him, as Bulls' boss Ian Bowyer paid out a club record to secure him. And in the league, the Shaymen lost the art of winning – the defeat at Darlington hung round their necks like a millstone – and slipped to 21st just after the turn of the year.

Juryeff was not the only player to leave the Shay. In January, centre-half John Bramhall joined Scunthorpe, but new players were not long in coming. Dominic Naylor arrived from Watford, initially on loan. He was joined later by Tony Fyfe, a forward from Carlisle, and an old – 'old' being the operative word – favourite in Tommy Graham. These two made their debuts in a 4-2 win over Wrexham. A run of five games unbeaten, including three victories, eased the pressure on Billy Ayre.

The manager was offered more salvation in the Leyland DAF Cup. Despite losing a group game at Chesterfield, Town had finished top of it. In the knockout stage, Town drew 1-1 with York City at the Shay, but went through 7-6 on penalties, with 18-year old Craig Fleming netting the decisive kick after he had come on as a 111th minute substitute. In the second round, they always looked to have the beating of Stockport, and did so eventually after extra-time 3-1 to progress once again into the Northern semi-final. The

Did You Know?

In 1979-80, Halifax Town were the only Yorkshire club to make it through to the Fourth Round of the FA Cup.

competition at last began to grab the attention of the supporters, with the *Evening Courier* labelling it 'The Wembley Dream' yet again, but at Doncaster on 20 February Town came a cropper, losing 0-3. The dream was over.

Town, with on loan Jim Gannon from Sheffield United in the side, recovered to beat Maidstone in their next game, but time was catching up with Billy Ayre. No sooner had he sold keeper Phil Whitehead to Barnsley for £60,000, than his side endured five consecutive defeats to leave them just two points clear of bottom place. Following defeat at home to Lincoln City on 20 March, supporters milled onto the pitch calling for his head. Jim Brown decided to terminate his contract 'by mutual consent'. Ayre's association with Halifax Town had come to an abrupt end, but whilst his record this term was disappointing, he could always claim to have kept the club afloat by giving youngsters such as Lee Richardson and Wayne Allison their chance. The supporters had much to thank him for.

The board now turned to former Manchester United, Southampton and Scotland international Jim McCalliog to rescue the club. In June 1989 McCalliog had been chosen to run Halifax Town's Football in the Community scheme, but now took over as caretaker boss for the visit of Chesterfield. The game ended 1-1. Forty minutes before Town's game at Rochdale, McCalliog was appointed full-time manager, with Tommy Graham acting as player-coach.

Jim Brown never had any doubts. 'He'll pull us clear,' he predicted, and was proved right as McCalliog steered the side to safety with three crucial away wins. Rochdale was the first, Doncaster the third, when McCalliog's half-time team talk transformed a 0-3 deficit into a 4-3 victory. In the end, relegation to the Conference was avoided by six points, leaving Colchester United as the unfortunate side to make the dreaded drop.

Match of the Season 1989-90

Doncaster Rovers 3 Halifax Town 4

Division 4, 21 April 1990

Older Halifax fans might recall a game played against Swindon Town at the Shay in September 1962, when Town rallied to win 4-3 after trailing by three goals with less than twenty minutes to go. It was one of the most sensational games Halifax Town have ever been involved in.

In April 1990, the Shaymen were once again fighting to stave off relegation, this time to the Vauxhall Conference. They badly needed a win, no matter how, if they were to pull themselves clear.

Doncaster were managed by Billy Bremner, who was having his second spell at the club. Rovers were also desperate for points. At kick-off, they lay just one place above the Shaymen, who were 21st.

Bremner must have been happy with his side's first-half performance. They had taken the lead after five minutes. Town's offside trap had been sprung and Lee Turnbull scored from 25 yards. The lead was doubled in the 21st when Turnbull rounded David Brown and crossed to give John Muir a simple header. Five minutes later it was 3-0 when David Harle unselfishly set up Neil Grayson. Town had been outplayed, and by the end of the half, had mustered only one effort on goal, a shot from Andy Watson that hit the post.

During the interval, Town boss Jim McCalliog, in the job for just a few weeks, was reported to have 'raised his voice', but his final instruction before they went back out was to 'keep playing football'. Within two minutes of the restart the fightback was underway.

Mitch Cook began it with a curling free-kick that Rovers keeper Mark Samways dropped over the goal-line. Town did not look back. In the 66th minute, Billy Barr cut in from the right, beat a couple of defenders, and fired home from inside the box. A minute later, McCalliog switched Barr for striker Nick Richardson, and it was the substitute who levelled the scores with nine minutes to go. His goal came after Neil Matthews had flicked on Brian Butler's corner. The home side looked stunned. They were already having to cope with the loss of injured defender Rufus Brevett, and, while they were still trying to regroup, the Shaymen scored a sensational winner.

Just four minutes remained when Mitch Cook flighted the ball over. Butler latched onto it on the right-hand side of the penalty area and struck a mighty shot that gave Samways no chance. The fightback was complete, and the small band of travelling supporters went delirious.

The two clubs traded places in the league, but neither were yet safe. The Shaymen secured their own survival with a goalless draw against Burnley in their next match. Shell-shocked Doncaster promptly lost a crucial six-pointer with bottom side Colchester, but eventually gained the points they needed. Colchester lost their last two matches and went out of the League.

LEAGUE DIVISION 4	**1990-91**
Barclays Division 4	22nd
Rumbelows Cup	2nd Round
FA Cup	2nd Round

No sooner had the season ended than Jim McCalliog appointed former Doncaster and Rochdale stopper Brian Taylor as his right-hand man. Taylor had been working as a coach with the PFA, and between them they set about rejuvenating Halifax Town. Their abilities were called into question when strikers Andy Watson and Neil Matthews were sold to Swansea and Stockport respectively, and though the money was welcome – Watson fetched £60,000, Matthews £70,000 – supporters wondered just how these players were going to be replaced.

McCalliog began rebuilding by recruiting Barnsley centre-back Paul Futcher for £30,000. Futcher was a former England Under-21 international and had played in the First Division with Luton and Manchester City. Midfielder Tony Gregory came from Sheffield Wednesday, and McCalliog also brought back David Evans, who had spent six successful seasons with Bradford City. Also arriving during the close season was a trialist goalkeeper, Jonathan Gould, son of the much-travelled Bobby.

A pre-season tour of Scotland went reasonably well. Town also won at Grimsby and Bradford City, as well as drawing at Hull to move into the final of the Diamik Yorkshire and Humberside Cup. But the bookies were unimpressed. On the eve of the new league season they offered odds of 66-1 on the Shaymen winning promotion. The next worst odds were for Doncaster, Scarborough and Wrexham, who were quoted at 33-1.

The bookies obviously knew something. Halifax Town made the worst start in their history, and were soon bottom of the pile. There was no concern about drawing their opening fixture 0-0 at home to a strong Stockport side which had missed out on the play-offs, but after eight games Town were still looking for their first league goal. McCalliog was already under fire.

Despite being punchless in the league, the Shaymen had progressed to the second round of the Rumbelows Cup – the new sponsors of the League Cup – at the expense of Lincoln City, Town's 2-0 win at the Shay proved just enough over the two legs. They managed two more goals over two legs against arguably the biggest – though at this stage not the best – club in English football, Manchester United, who boasted in their side international stars Neil Webb, Mark Hughes, Gary Pallister, Paul Ince and Brian McClair. David Evans scored a direct free-kick as Town lost the first leg 1-3 at the Shay in front of a near-capacity 6,841 crowd, and Tony Gregory scored as Town went down 1-2 at Old Trafford.

Town even lifted their first trophy since winning the West Riding Senior Cup in 1967, when they won the Yorkshire and Humberside Cup on 11 September. Graham Broadbent came off the bench to net the winner in injury-time as Town sealed a 3-2 extra time win at Rotherham United. But the goals would not flow in the league.

During September, McCalliog sold Chris Hedworth and Phil Horner for a combined £27,500 to Blackpool, where Billy Ayre was now assistant manager. He then spent £50,000 to bring Ian Juryeff back from Hereford, thus breaking Town's club record outlay, previously held by the same player. On 4 October, McCalliog traded Tony Fyfe and £20,000 for Carlisle's Steve Norris. Norris scored in his second game, ironically against Carlisle, but it was Halifax lad Billy Barr who netted Town's first goal of the season as they ran out surprising winners 3-0.

Though results in the main barely improved, there were some extraordinary games. Not the least of these was a 5-3 victory over Blackpool, which came hard on a 0-4 defeat at Hereford. The form of Norris, who could not stop scoring, gave everyone hope that Town could haul themselves off the foot of the table. McCalliog's ever-changing team now included ex-Bradford City winger Mark Ellis and they finally moved off the bottom following a 2-0 win over Rochdale on 21 December – only their fourth win of the season.

Hopes were raised in the FA Cup, when Town beat fellow strugglers Wrexham 3-2 at the Shay before drawing at Third Division Rotherham in the second round. The hard work seemed to have been done, but Town proceeded to blow their chances in the replay, losing 1-2. Disappointment there, and more was to follow in the New Year. The commanding Paul Futcher was loaned and eventually sold to Grimsby for £10,000 – rumours centred on a fall-out with McCalliog – and without him the Shaymen returned to the bottom. They went eleven games without a win, culminating in a 1-5 thrashing at Maidstone on 27 February.

Brief respite had been found in the Leyland DAF Cup, when Town topped Rotherham and Scarborough in their group, but in the first round of the knockout stage they were beaten 0-1 by Blackpool. Town now concentrated their efforts on the league, but good news awaited. The Football League, having reduced the First Division to twenty clubs, decided to revert back to 22. The knock-on effect meant that nobody would be relegated from Division Four, despite the fact that the Conference champions would be promoted. Even so, finishing bottom was not what Halifax Town wanted.

Did You Know?

In June 1980, George Kirby went to present prizes at a Sport For All The Family Day. He was turned away – the organisers did not recognise him.

A week after the mauling at Maidstone, unpredictable Town beat Walsall 5-2 in an extraordinary game – they were two goals down after three minutes, and played Tommy Graham in goal after Jonanthan Gould suffered facial injuries. The upturn continued throughout March. After drawing another improbable match, 4-4 at Scunthorpe, Town beat Wrexham to move off the bottom. After signing Bradford City winger Kevin Megson, Town did just enough to steer clear of bottom place. Wrexham finished wooden spoonists, though they would now live to fight another day.

Other than the form of teenager Craig Fleming, who came of age and was ever-present, the main feature of Halifax Town's season was the goalscoring of Steve Norris. In the closing weeks Norris was in the running for at least two records. Albert Valentine's 56-year old Halifax Town record of 34 league goals in one season was under threat, but Norris needed a hat-trick in the final game to equal it, and missed it by two. There was also the distinction of being the Football League's top scorer, but in the end, by scoring 32 – Norris had scored two for Carlisle before coming to the Shay – he fell short of Millwall's Teddy Sheringham by one goal. Norris did, however, finish as the Fourth Division's leading marksman, beating off the challenge of Hartlepool's Joe Allon.

Norris's achievements helped disguise what a terrible season it had been for Halifax Town. It was clear that the team was not good enough. But if that invited concern, even more worrying was the future of the club itself. At the end of May, it was revealed that Halifax Town had run up debts of £40,000. Though one councillor, Tom McElroy, described it as 'peanuts', it was enough to prompt Calderdale Council to announce it was selling its 76 per cent share-holding. With the season barely over, only the appointment of an administrator looked like saving Halifax Town.

Match of the Season 1990-91

Carlisle United 0 Halifax Town 3

Division 4, 13 October 1990

In terms of goalscoring, it was the worst start to a season in Football League history. Halifax Town, after eight games, had yet to register their first goal. Manager Jim McCalliog was adamant it was only a matter of time before things started to get better, but he moved into the transfer market to speed things up. Striker Steve Norris was signed in exchange for an out-of-sorts Tony Fyfe, and the outcome was, at least for Norris, spectacular.

In only his second game for the Shaymen, Norris lined up against his old club at Brunton Park – Fyfe, back at Carlisle for a second spell would reappear as a substitute. Norris helped his new team break their duck, and in turn, earn their first win of the season. Yet it was not he who scored the first goal. That distinction was reserved for Halifax born, Halifax supporter, and now Halifax player Billy Barr, when, in the tenth minute, he crashed the ball home from twenty yards after Ian Juryeff had laid it back to him.

This goal suddenly gave the handful of travelling supporters something to cheer about – thirteen hours and eighteen minutes of league action had passed since Neil Matthews netted against Stockport in the final game of the previous season. More joy awaited. Eight minutes later, Norris profited from a cross by Juryeff, beating Colin Methven to the ball to tuck it under keeper Priestley. By half-time, Town were in dreamland. Tommy Graham had arrived at the back post to crash the ball home after Norris had flicked on Barr's cross.

After the break, Carlisle, after a tongue-lashing from manager Clive Middlemass, took the game to the Shaymen, created chances, but failed to take them. Town survived, then hit back, and might have increased their lead.

After his goal that ended the drought, Billy Barr came under the national spotlight, but in an interview on BBC's Radio Five, he got a bit carried away. He believed that Town would now start climbing the table, and saw no reason why they could not make a serious assault on promotion. Anybody knows that one swallow does not make a summer, and that was particularly true in this case.

LEAGUE DIVISION 4	**1991-92**
Barclays Division 4	20th
Rumbelows Cup	1st Round
FA Cup	1st Round

On 3 June, Calderdale Council, no longer wanting to be burdened by shares in a club that was running at a loss, applied to the High Court to appoint an administrator to run the club. Talks had been held with potential buyers, but as none were considered suitable, the council felt that this action was their only option. Before they knew it, five more bids came for their 76 per cent shares. On 15 June the council announced that they were to sell out to Jim Brown and the owners of a local bathroom makers Aquarius – David Greenwood and Bob Asprey – at a knockdown price of £1,000. The deal was confirmed at a council meeting four days later, the only stipulation being that Jim Brown would pay off all outstanding debts by February. Councillor David Helliwell looked back on the council's involvement with Halifax Town and said, 'Our link with the club as a major shareholder has succeeded in that it helped Halifax Town to continue over a difficult period.'

With Halifax Town's future secure – until the next time, that is – and a new sponsorship deal confirmed with Paraglas, Jim McCalliog was given the go-ahead to buy new players with money made available. But the Town boss was not having it easy. Having already released Mark Ellis, and Dean Martin, he found Brian Butler wanting away and rising star Craig Fleming rejecting new terms. Fleming eventually moved to First Division Oldham Athletic, and better things, for £80,000, whilst his older brother Paul, who had been at the Shay since leaving school, also took the chance to move on. He signed for Mansfield Town in exchange for £10,000.

McCalliog brought in four new players in the close season. The first was Bradford City utility man Greg Abbott for £25,000. Abbott was joined by two players from Scarborough, full-back Alan Kamara, and Steve Richards. McCalliog described Richards as 'the best centre-half in the Fourth Division' – at £25,000 he probably needed to be. Last but not least, McCalliog brought in young Rochdale defender Chris Lucketti.

Steve Norris scored for fun during a pre-season tour of Scotland, but when the gloves came off it became a familiar story. Despite winning their second league game, at Maidstone, Town soon found themselves near the foot of the table. This was all the more surprising, considering their performances over two legs in the Rumbelows Cup against Second Division Tranmere. Town led 3-1 at the Shay before losing 3-4, but in the return at Prenton Park, they recovered to take the tie into extra-time, before losing 3-4 again on the night. The 6-8 overall score suggested goals galore this season.

This was half right. The Shaymen lost 0-3 at Walsall and 0-4 to Rotherham, although they did win 3-1 at Aldershot, a club about to receive their last rites. But with Town still looking for their first home win, they lost 1-3 to Mansfield. Never mind that the result sent the Stags to the top: it was the final straw for the Town board.

On 2 October, McCalliog and his assistant Brian Taylor were sacked, with chairman Jim Brown citing failure to win at home – they had played six league and cup games – as the reason. McCalliog had struggled the previous season, albeit with a team he could not really call his own, but things had not improved even with a host of new players of his choosing.

The following day, the former Newcastle United and Southampton stopper John McGrath – 'a great motivator' the board reckoned – was installed as the new Town boss. McGrath recruited Oshor Williams, the ex-Stockport, Port Vale and Preston winger, as his assistant. McGrath had previously turned round the fortunes of ailing clubs Port Vale and Preston, both of which he guided to promotion from the Fourth Division on shoestring budgets. It was hoped that he could display similar magic at the Shay.

There was, however, no immediate change in fortunes. A creditable draw was gained at Lincoln, but the size of McGrath's task was evident when Town lost 0-3 at home to Chesterfield. McGrath sought to bolster his defence, starting with a goalkeeper, and forked out £47,500 for Swansea City's Lee Bracey. The new boss then acquired Dudley Lewis on loan from neighbours Huddersfield.

When bubbly midfielder Ronnie Hildersley, who had played under McGrath at Preston, returned from a stint in Canada, he too was snapped up. Hildersley made a big impact in his second game, scoring a sensational late equaliser at non-league Witton in the FA Cup. It helped to keep the club's season alive – very briefly – for there was no joy in the replay at the Shay. Witton won 2-1, all the goals coming in extra-time, and the fans already were fast losing interest. They voted with their feet for Town's next home game, with only 881 turning up for the visit of Wrexham, although those that stayed away missed an absolute cracker as Town won 4-3.

By Christmas, though Halifax had signed left-back Paul Wilson from Northampton Town for £30,000, they still languished in sixteenth place. Then, despite getting the New Year off to a good start by winning at Doncaster, they failed to win again until March. The fans had their own explanation for Town's plight, most pinpointing the sale of Steve Norris as the major reason. Though Norris was not as prolific this time around, he was still the side's leading scorer, and without him goals were always going to be hard to come by. But McGrath needed money for teambuilding, and in Norris he had the player who could help fund it. In January, McGrath loaned him to Chesterfield. A fee of £33,000 was then agreed, leaving Town supporters not only shocked, but angry that he had been let go so cheaply.

In February, midfielders Jason Hardy (Burnley) and Kevin Donovan (Huddersfield Town) arrived on loan, but results did not improve. The following month, McGrath came up with another surprise, selling Steve Richards to Doncaster. McGrath evidently did not rate Richards as highly as McCalliog had done. The upshot was that Town pulled off probably their best win of the season, a 3-1 home win against promotion-chasing Barnet on 21 March. However, only two more victories were recorded before the end of the season, and the Shaymen could not even rely on the Autoglass Trophy to restore their pride. For the first time in six seasons, they failed to reach the knockout stage, after losing to Scunthorpe on 7 January. But although no one was being relegated – the Football League intended to increase membership to 94 clubs – there was no room for complacency. With crowds at the Shay still the lowest in the Football League and the club continuing to lose money, the fate that befell Aldershot came as a clear warning. Aldershot were wound up in the High Court on 25 March, just days after playing what was to be their last league match, a 0-2 defeat at Cardiff.

All fixtures against Aldershot were expunged from the records, including Town's 3-1 win at the Recreation Ground in September. That left Town with only ten victories to their name, and worse, only 34 goals – the lowest total Halifax had ever recorded since their formation. The future was ominous. John McGrath may have pulled rabbits from hats at Port Vale and Preston, but he needed a different kind of magic to sort out Halifax Town.

Match of the Season 1991-92

Tranmere Rovers 4 Halifax Town 3

Rumbelows Cup, 1st Round, 2nd Leg, 27 August 1991

Town's two Rumbelows Cup-ties with First Division Tranmere Rovers in August were the worst possible tonic, for they suggested a thrill-a-minute season in prospect. True, in both games, Town came off second best, but their performances home and away suggested league points would be easy to come by.

Tranmere were a useful outfit, having clinched the Division Three title only months previously. Manager John King had further

Did You Know?

Halifax Town were drawn at home in the First Round of the FA Cup for six consecutive seasons between 1981 and 1986.

strengthened the side by tempting Republic of Ireland and former Liverpool striker John Aldridge back to England following a stint in Spain with Real Sociedad. Aldridge had 191 league goals to his name – he had scored prolifically for Newport and Oxford before moving to Anfield – but would be remembered as the first player to miss a penalty in an FA Cup final, as he did against Wimbledon in 1988. Whilst abroad, he had changed his style somewhat. His penalty run-up now included a little shuffle, and Town fans had been the first ones to witness it on English soil when he scored two penalties in the first leg at the Shay as Tranmere won 4-3.

In that game, the Shaymen had led 2-0 and 3-1. In the second leg they also found themselves 3-1 up to lead on aggregate. Town announced their intentions when Billy Barr turned the ball in at the far post after five minutes. But although Aldridge equalised six minutes later, Barr restored Town's lead on the night when he hammered in a loose ball.

There were no further goals in the first half, but after the break there was no end of drama. In the 51st minute, Rovers' skipper Mark Hughes was sent off for a professional foul on Ian Juryeff, and from the resultant free-kick, Graham Cooper curled the ball home off the far post. Town now led 3-1, and with a man advantage seemingly had the tie in the bag. Not so. Tranmere regrouped, played a 3-3-3 formation and within five minutes pulled a goal back when Jim Steel powered home a header. No more goals followed in normal time, though had Aldridge – shuffle and all – not fired a 73rd-minute penalty wide after he had been brought down, the extra half-hour may not have been needed.

With the score 6-6 on aggregate, the game went to extra-time. Town had their chances and considered themselves unlucky not to go through. Steve Norris hit the post and Nick Richardson had a shot cleared off the line by Dave Higgins. But at the end of the first period, the tie swung back in Tranmere's favour when Steel scored his second, a tap-in. A minute from the end, Aldridge arrived in the box to score his second.

The Shaymen bowed out, gallant losers. Manager Jim McCalliog was rightly proud of the effort his players had shown, even if they had lost to a team with ten men. Once again, Halifax Town had merely flattered to deceive.

LEAGUE DIVISION 3	**1992-93**
Barclays Division 3 (New Style)	22nd (relegated)
Coca-Cola Cup	1st Round
FA Cup	1st Round

John McGrath gave the supporters an inkling that it was going to be another tough season when he went on record as saying, 'We know we need to bring in players with more quality, but we have no money, so one or two will have to leave.' He had already released Graham Cooper, Ian Hutchinson and the injury-prone Tony Gregory. David Evans left after declining the offer of running the youth team (which was then controversially scrapped) and McGrath endeavoured to offload a few more. The first was Nick Richardson, who moved to Cardiff City for £35,000.

In his attempt to improve the squad, McGrath brought in players he had worked with previously – strikers John Thomas and Nigel Greenwood, free transfers from Hartlepool and Preston respectively. Ian Thompstone, a defender-cum-striker, arrived from Exeter City, whilst Mick Matthews, who had been at the Shay earlier, was signed on the eve of the season from Hull City. McGrath's biggest coup, however, was that of the former Liverpool, Brighton and Southampton midfield hardman Jimmy Case, winner of four League Championships and two European Cups. Case was one of the biggest names ever to play for the club, having been released by Bournemouth, and took up his position as player-coach.

Owing to the creation of the breakaway Premier League, the Football League had been restructured. There were now only three divisions in the League. Town made a sensational start with a 3-2 win at Rochdale – soccer nomad Howard Gayle was surprise substitute for the Shaymen – but though the clientele was changing, the story began to look pretty much the same. After five games, Town were bottom of the pack, and had been ousted from the Coca-Cola Cup, the latest sponsors of the League Cup, by Hartlepool United.

Ian Juryeff, having played just two games this term, moved to Darlington – he had cost Town £50,000, but left on a free. McGrath secured the services of a ball-playing midfielder in Jason Peake from Leicester City, and brought back Jason Hardy in a permanent deal. Town hoisted themselves up to mid-table and gave hope for better things on 26 September with a 5-2 success at Northampton. Three of the goals were scored by Thompstone: this was the first time Halifax had scored five away from home since beating Workington 5-0 in April 1960. Things appeared to be going well, but worrying times lay in store. Once again, Town were hit by yet another financial crisis.

With low crowds, the club was losing money. On 6 October, Jim Brown announced that Halifax Town were £100,000 in the red, and were a month away from possible closure. The fans were asked to rally round for the next three home games, with the board stating that it would review the situation the following month.

What they needed was increased gates and further progress in the league. What they got was exactly the opposite. Victory over Gillingham on 24 October, which actually took Town up to tenth, was watched by the lowest crowd of the season, and that win turned out to be the Shaymen's last until January. Worse, just when the club desperately needed a good Cup run to generate income, they were eliminated in the first round. Town's 1-4 defeat at non-league Marine was one of the most humiliating experiences ever felt by club and supporters, and the anger was vented at John McGrath. Two days later, the board, which by now comprised Jim Brown, David Greenwood, John Stockwell and Brian Boulton, met in crisis session. All they did was decide to carry on until the New Year.

By then, McGrath had gone. Following a home defeat by Barnet on 5 December – Town's seventh game without a win – he jumped ship. 'I have stopped enjoying he job,' he said. 'My leaving might just help the club. A fresh person at the helm might just solve some of their problems.' Ever a joker – he was a familiar face on the after-dinner circuit – McGrath had stopped smiling, but the seeds of Town's downfall had been well and truly planted.

Oshor Williams went with him. Most fans expected Jimmy Case to be handed the job of manager – he did, after all, seem the obvious choice – but they were in for a surprise. The board promoted the popular Mick Rathbone to the job, his first such appointment. Rathbone had had a lengthy career as a player with Birmingham, Blackburn and Preston, and had slipped quietly into the Shay as physio the previous May. To say he would find the going hard would be an understatement.

Rathbone's first game in charge saw Town lose 0-5 at Huddersfield in the Autoglass Trophy. He responded by signing forward Linton Brown from Guiseley and midfielder Mike Williams on loan from Sheffield Wednesday. But still Town could not find a winning formula.

Dave Ridings and Dave Christie were added to the squad. Both made their debuts in a 3-0 win at Darlington – Town's first win in thirteen league and cup games – with Ridings scoring twice. Ridings would also score a brace the following week against Northampton. His goals that day saved a point, but he would not score again that season.

On 15 December, the board announced that the club would see the season out, regardless of the financial plight, but that did not stop players being offloaded. In January, the impressive Linton Brown moved to Hull City, and at the end of the month Paul Wilson signed for Burnley for £30,000. He was worth more, but it was a case of needs must. As Town embarked on another awful losing run, Jimmy Case moved to Wrexham at the end of February. Eight defeats from nine games had left Halifax three off the bottom and in real trouble: to end up last meant being relegated to the Conference. It was now imperative that Town's fortunes changed immediately.

At this point the *Evening Courier*, sensing the gravity of the situation, launched a 'Staying Alive League Lifeline' campaign, and drummed up support for the home game against Shrewsbury on 20 March. They gave away discount entry vouchers, and a carnival atmosphere was ensured with the Friendly Brass Band performing, balloons handed out, and a fireworks display before the match (though in the sunshine the effects were far from spectacular!). A bumper gate of 3,872 turned out: they witnessed a thunderbolt goal from Billy Barr, but not a Town win, as Shrewsbury spoilt the party by gaining a draw.

Town lost their next game, at which joint leading scorer Ian Thompstone was surprisingly sold to Scunthorpe for £10,000. Rathbone brought in unknown quantities – Peter Craven (Guiseley) and Nigerian international Godfrey Obebo, on trial from Bury. The situation, however, remained critical, and though victories at Doncaster and Wrexham lifted the side off the bottom, Town were stuck in a real dogfight along with Gillingham, Torquay and Northampton. A terrible 0-4 defeat in their penultimate home game by Walsall meant the writing on was on the wall, and after losing 0-2 at Gillingham the following week – those three points secured the Gills' own safety – the game was almost up. Town's own future rested on the last match, but matters were not entirely in their own hands.

Rathbone all along had tried to inspire his players by saying they were lucky to be playing in so many cup finals. The home game with Hereford proved to be the biggest of them all. But like most of the others, it was one they lost. Northampton's win at Shrewsbury meant Derek Hall's goal for the Bulls was ultimately inconsequential, and the 7,451 that turned up saw the Shaymen's 72-year association with the Football League come to end. Halifax Town finished bottom and were demoted to the Vauxhall Conference. Had so many turned up on a regular basis, it may never have come to this.

Did You Know?

Up to 1998-99, Phil Whitehead was Town's youngest ever player when he kept goal at Burnley on 27 September 1986, aged 16 years and 284 days.

Match of the Season 1992-93

Halifax Town 0 Hereford United 1

Division 4, 8 May 1993

To many supporters, Halifax Town's date with destiny had been on the cards for a number of years. The dismal times they had endured over the last four seasons had culminated in this. Many felt that the Shaymen had been living on borrowed time, but now that time was almost up. Former chairman John Crowther argued that the introduction of automatic promotion and relegation with the Vauxhall Conference had actually prolonged Town's existence. Re-election would, after all, have been necessary in each of the four previous seasons. Now, going into their final game of 1992-93, relegation was staring them in the face.

It did not really help their cause that the game was played at home – Town had won only three at the Shay all season, compared with six on their travels. But the opponents were only Hereford, a team that in normal circumstances even this Halifax team should have been able to beat. Hereford, too, had briefly flirted with relegation, but had banished any fears several weeks earlier. They had nothing to play for as such, though player-manager Greg Downs insisted that they would treat the game as any other.

Even if Town won, it would not guarantee survival. They were hoping that Shrewsbury, who needed to win to make the play-offs, would beat Northampton, the only team that Town could overhaul. The situation was clear. Halifax had to win and Northampton had to lose if the two clubs were to swap places.

The bumper crowd of 7,451 – kick-off was delayed ten minutes to accommodate them – was composed of diehards, casuals, the interested and the ghoulish. Most were behind the Shaymen, and the players gave it their all. In the end, however, their all was not good enough.

Dave Ridings went close early on, but a last-ditch tackle by Gareth Davies forced him to shoot wide from close range. Billy Barr tried his luck from 25 yards, only to see the ball fly wide. But in truth, Hereford keeper Alan Judge was rarely troubled, and it was his counterpart Lee Bracey who made the save of the match when he tipped over a stinging drive from Owen Pickard.

Although Town had failed to break through by half-time, there was hope that just a single goal might be enough, especially when news filtered through that Shrewsbury had scored twice against Northampton. But dreams of a great escape vanished after 61 minutes when Derek Hall, ironically a former Town player, side-footed home Darren Rowbotham's pass for what turned out to be the only goal. It evoked memories of Denis Law's goal for Manchester City in 1974 that condemned his beloved Manchester United. But here there was no pitch invasion, and Hall himself, unlike Law, went on to complete the match.

Town had under half an hour in which to save the game, and they had their chances. A cross-cum-shot from Peter Craven hit the bar, Jason Hardy skewed wide, and substitute Nigel Greenwood might have had a hat-trick. Judge denied him his best chance, making a point-blank save with time almost up.

By then, the Shay fans knew that Northampton had turned the tables at Gay Meadow, and that the end was nigh. Silence enveloped the terraces, and upon the final whistle, fans streamed onto the pitch, many in tears. When they finally comprehended what had happened, they united in defiant mood. 'We'll be back,' they chanted. Chairman Jim Brown came out to say that, indeed, the club would make all-out efforts to get back.

Amidst all this misery and soul-searching, it was sad that Mick Rathbone, one of football's Mr Nice Guys, should be seen as the man who took Town into the Conference. A jack-of-all-trades, he could now add relegation to an already crammed CV, but no one really laid the blame at his feet. In the end, and in typical fashion, Rathbone paid tribute to his 'great bunch of guys' that had fought so gallantly in vain, saying, 'If they can come through an experience like this they have great futures ahead of them.' Except for a small handful – only Jamie Paterson and Chris Lucketti would forge any degree of success – most would fade into football obscurity. There was a time when it looked like Halifax Town might do the same.

As for Hereford United, their time would come.

6

THE CONFERENCE AND BACK 1993-1999

VAUXHALL CONFERENCE	**1993-94**
GM Vauxhall Conference	13th
FA Cup	2nd Round
FA Trophy	3rd Round

Nobody was under any illusions as to the size of the task faced by Halifax Town as they attempted to regain their Football League status at the first attempt. The standard in the Conference was high – Town had learned that to their cost in recent FA Cup defeats by Kettering Town and Witton Albion – and Halifax would quickly have to adapt to the physical approach adopted by most teams.

The club might have wished to remain full-time, and the players might have pledged themselves to Halifax Town's cause – though not Mick Matthews or John Thomas, both of whom had been released – but evidently not all meant what they said. Russell Bradley quickly moved to Scunthorpe United, while Jason Hardy, Jason Peake and Chris Lucketti expressed their intention to get back into the Football League as soon as possible.

For the board of directors, as for everyone, the Conference was uncharted waters. Peter Wragg had spent nine years with Macclesfield Town and had hoisted them up into the Conference in his first season at Moss Rose, and it was to him that Halifax turned in an effort to make an immediate challenge. While Mick Rathbone reverted to his old role as physio – he also took on the mantel of assistant-manager and registered as a player – Wragg took up his duties in June and sought out players that he knew he needed.

Wragg introduced defenders Elfyn Edwards (Macclesfield Town) and Martin Filson (Stalybridge Celtic) – they had played for Wrexham and Tranmere in the league – and forwards Jimmy Cameron (Winsford United) and Shaun Constable (Scunthorpe United). Macclesfield midfielder Colin Lambert was also signed, though his Town debut would be delayed through injury. Pre-season went well, with Town battling through to the final of the Yorkshire and

Humberside Cup – they were in effect defending it, as it had not been contested since Town won it three years earlier – but Wragg knew that this would count for nothing in the Conference. He had gone on record as saying that it would take Town at least ten games before they won their first match, but this had not gone down well with some supporters who accused Wragg of being too negative.

Negative or not, Wragg was not far out, as Town found the going tough. They opened with a frustrating 0-0 draw with Kettering, but after eight games they were still looking for their first win and had sunk to next to bottom in the table. They had also lost the services of keeper Lee Bracey, who moved to Bury for £25,000 after the first game, though Wragg responded by snapping up a popular replacement in Darren Heyes from Rochester.

But while Town struggled to adapt to life in the Conference, they retained the Yorkshire Cup by beating Frank Stapleton's Bradford City at Valley Parade. With a superlative display, they ran out 4-2 winners with goals coming, in order, from Constable, an own-goal by Noel Blake, Steve Saunders and Jamie Paterson. Saunders and Dave Hanson, newly signed from Altrincham and Bury, made their debuts in that match, and hopes carried over into the next fixture. But Town were in for a rude awakening, as Runcorn tore them apart at Canal Street, winning 5-0.

When the Shaymen eventually broke their Conference duck, they did so in style, winning 6-2 at Woking, the first time a Halifax side had scored as many away since beating Knaresborough by the same score in December 1911 in the old Yorkshire Combination. Then, as if to confirm it was no fluke, they scored six the following week too, this time against Telford, but they could not keep the goal-flood going. Town failed to win any of the next five matches and languished in eighteenth place.

With Chris Lucketti having joined Bracey at Bury at a cost of £50,000, Wragg signed Craig Boardman from Peterborough as a replacement. Boardman made his debut in a 3-0 win over Bromsgrove. He was fortunate that Town's next match was an eagerly awaited FA Cup-tie with First Division West Bromwich Albion at the Shay. The game was screened live by Sky television on a Sunday afternoon, and Town grabbed the headlines after their giant-killing 2-1 win.

The Shaymen lost 1-5 at Stockport in the next round – they found it hard to cope with the 6ft 7in frame of Kevin Francis – but Wembley still beckoned, more realistically, in the FA Trophy, which commenced in January. Town had by now lost the services – temporarily they thought, permanently as it turned out – of Steve Saunders, brought down by a mystery illness, but they had recruited a new keeper in Richard Wilmot (Scunthorpe United) and a replacement striker, Steve Burr (Stafford Rangers). In the first round, Town saw off local side Emley before making the trip to Spennymoor United in the next. When the Shaymen won again 2-1, their unbeaten run of league and cup matches had been extended to eight, but the board were seemingly unimpressed. Concerned that Town had not made any impact in the Conference, chairman Jim Brown summoned Wragg to tell him he was sacked. Wragg was astonished, though a part-time manager – for that is what he was – running a full-time club was deemed by the board to be unacceptable. The outcome had seemed on the cards for a while.

John Bird, former boss at both Hartlepool United and York City – in his playing days he had been a tough central defender with Preston and Newcastle United – was quickly installed as the new manager, but he got off to a terrible start. Bird saw his new side toss away the lead before going down 2-3 at Telford, then watched in disbelief as Town scrambled a draw at Runcorn in the FA Trophy before losing the replay miserably 0-2 at the Shay.

Bird set about recruiting his own players. Left-back Steve Prindiville arrived from Wycombe Wanderers and Lincoln City forward Tony Lormor came on loan. Centre-back Alex Jones arrived next from Rochdale, with Jason Peake making the journey in the opposite direction. But as all hopes of the Conference title, and with it promotion, long since disappeared, Bird looked ahead to the following season. Peter Craven had already gone to Preston, and Elfyn Edwards joined Southport in April, while Bird looked at trialists Nigel Smith (Farsley Celtic), Geoff Horsfield (Scarborough), and Pat O'Toole (Shamrock Rovers) – O'Toole had previously been with Leicester City – though none at this stage proved successful.

The closing weeks of the season were uninspired. Town eventually ended their first Conference season thirteenth, and this poor showing was reflected in the attendances. An unprecedented 643 turned up for the visit of Dagenham at the end of April. The club was again fast losing money, and having made the bold decision to remain full-time for a second season, barring success on the pitch these mounting debts would surely catch up with them.

Match of the Season 1993-94

Halifax Town 2 West Brom 1

FA Cup, 1st Round, 14 November 1993

Just when Halifax Town needed a boost, the FA Cup presented one, pairing them with West Bromwich Albion in what was argua-

Did You Know?

During 1988-89, Halifax had three pairs of brothers on their books – Billy and Bobby Barr, Lee and Nick Richardson, and Paul and Craig Fleming.

bly the plum draw of the first round. Certainly Sky TV thought so, for this was the game they elected to screen live on the Sunday. Halifax Town stood to make around £40,000 from the game and its spin-offs, and welcomed every penny.

West Brom were renowned as a cup team, having won the FA Cup on six occasions, the most recent being in 1968 when a Jeff Astle goal was enough to beat Everton. And though they now languished in the new First Division, manager Keith Burkinshaw boasted fine Cup credentials. He had been in charge at Tottenham in 1981 when they triumphed over Manchester City, and again the following year, when Spurs retained the Cup, beating Queen's Park Rangers. But in substitute Nicky Reid, they also had a player who, when on the books of Manchester City, had tasted defeat at the Shay in 1980. Reid hoped that lightning would not strike twice, at least for himself.

But Reid's worst fears were realised when, with the game barely six minutes old, Jason Peake danced through the Baggies' defence to slot home Town's opening goal. Then, after 36 minutes, a sweeping move involving Peake and Jamie Paterson led to Steve Saunders racing away. With Kieran O'Regan in pursuit, Saunders clipped the ball past the advancing keeper and shot into the far corner. The Town fans could not believe their eyes.

Halifax keeper Darren Hayes had had to make some fine saves to keep West Brom at bay in the first half. But Town were indebted to left-back Peter Craven for protecting that two-goal lead when he cleared off the goal-line on the stroke of half-time.

After the interval, the visitors came back strongly, but were almost down and out by the time they finally broke through. There were nine minutes remaining when O'Regan returned the ball into the box from the left, and Andy Hunt fended off Elfyn Edwards to head the ball past Heyes. Hunt received two broken teeth for his pains. The goal set up a nail-biting finish.

The Shaymen held out for a famous win, and the players and manager Peter Wragg rightly milked the attention heaped on them. West Bromwich Albion might not have had as high a profile as Manchester United or Manchester City – both of whom had been slayed at the Shay over the years – but that did not make victory any less sweeter.

VAUXHALL CONFERENCE	**1994-95**
GM Vauxhall Conference	8th
FA Cup	2nd Round
FA Trophy	1st Round

This was a make or break season for Halifax Town, and the directors knew it. They laid their cards on the table, made money available for new players, and hoped that the gamble would pay off. If it did not, and Town failed to win the Conference, then the consequences were set to be catastrophic.

The one big surprise during the summer was the departure of Billy Barr to Crewe. Most people reckoned he would stay at Halifax throughout his playing career, but when the opportunity arose, he could not resist moving back into the big time. Others on their way were Shaun Constable and Kevin Megson, but there would be no shortage of newcomers to the Shay for the new season.

The list was so long it could almost have filled a telephone directory. They included Andy Flounders, Dave Lancaster (who cost £10,000, £2,000 of which was met by the Supporters Club, who had organised a 'Sign A Striker Appeal'), Andy Kiwomya, Grant Leitch, Lee Fowler and much-travelled Gary Worthington, son of former Town player Dave.

After six games Town were unbeaten, thereby setting a welcome club record from the start of the season. Town had got off to a flyer with a 3-1 win at Woking, despite playing over half the match without the dismissed David German. Other fine performances had seen them beat Bromsgrove 4-2 and Southport 2-0, both at the Shay. Town went sixth, three points behind the leaders.

Home defeat by Conference newcomers Farnborough was a low – Town could have gone second in the table – but this was the start of an inconsistent spell. On the one hand, they beat Dagenham 4-1 away and Bath 4-2, whilst on the other they lost abysmally at Southport 0-4. At the end of October, Town had dropped to tenth.

The club had been banking on big support, but the fans were staying away, perhaps sensing that the title was already out of reach. Town's 6-0 win over Stafford Rangers was watched by just 750. What the club needed was a good run in the FA Cup. For the first time since 1923, Town had to survive a qualifying round. It was played on 22 October, the earliest Town had competed in the competition since their pre-Football League days. At least they had the satisfaction of seeing off the challenge of Lancaster City, winning 3-1 at the Shay. Runcorn presented stiffer opposition in the First Round proper, but after drawing at the Shay, Town – with Colin Lambert outstanding – won the replay 3-1 after extra-time.

That replay was staged at Witton Albion's Wincham Park, fire having gutted part of Runcorn's Canal Street ground.

Two old favourites had reappeared at the club – Dean Martin, on loan from Scunthorpe United, and full-back Paul Fleming, though neither played against Mansfield at the Shay in Round Two. Martin's clearance had not come through, whilst Fleming was cup-tied, having played as a substitute for Guiseley earlier in the competition. Without these players, Town were held to a 0-0 draw. Jamie Paterson was not around for the replay. On 11 December he made what was viewed at the time as a dream move, signing for Scottish Premier League outfit Falkirk for £40,000.

With Graham Taylor's Wolves awaiting the winners, the Shaymen lost the replay at Field Mill 1-2, falling to Paul Holland's injury-time goal, after Dave Lancaster had put Town ahead in the first half. At least the FA Cup had provided a welcome distraction from the rigours of Conference football. Not so welcome were other distractions, such as the future of the Shay itself.

In mid-November, plans were submitted to Calderdale Council by the Yorkshire Rider bus company for a supermarket at the Shay. On 18 November Jim Brown threatened to quit as chairman if the council failed to approve plans for ground improvements – new Football League regulations meant the winners of the Conference would only be promoted if their ground was deemed suitable. This precipitated an intense debate in Halifax as to the best site for a super stadium. Correspondence in the *Evening Courier* ran for weeks, with proposals for upgrading the Shay and Halifax RLFC's Thrum Hall presented. In January 1995, the council backed Thrum Hall as the site of a new super stadium. Halifax Town's board locked themselves in talks with their rugby counterparts to try to drive the plans to fruition.

With the Shay-Thrum Hall debate in full flow, Town tried to put their title hopes back on track. A 2-1 win at Gateshead was their fourth game unbeaten, and following defeat at Altrincham on New Years' Eve, they won their next four matches to go fifth. Despite signing centre-back Mick Trotter at the end of December, Town slipped embarrassingly out of the FA Trophy at Bamber Bridge, a club that was playing parks football only a few years earlier. Town were then found wanting in the league against lowly Dagenham and Merthyr, both of whom left the Shay with a point.

On the night that Town threw away two home points against Dagenham, councillors were voting down the proposed shopping development at the Shay by the Yorkshire Rider. As Jim Brown backed plans for a move to Thrum Hall, the sale of the Shay was the only way to finance the super stadium. With those plans now thrown out of the window, the chairman saw no alternative but to quit, and did so on 27 February, thus ending a period of more than six years at the helm. Having realistically lost out both on promotion and a new ground, and with the financial noose tightening, Town had now also lost their chairman.

On 6 March, Brighouse textile owner John Stockwell took over the chairmanship, with Brian Boulton stepping up to vice-chairman. The following day Town lost a crucial fixture with runaway Conference leaders Macclesfield. Town had hoped to catch them, but after the 0-1 defeat they gave up the ghost. Promotion took a back seat to survival. Dave Lancaster moved to Bury, Andy Kiwomya was shortly sold to Scunthorpe and Lee Fowler released to Telford. Assistant manager Mick Rathbone, too, was surplus to requirements. John Bird described Rathbone's sacking as 'the hardest decision I have ever had to make'.

On 15 March, Halifax Town revealed a tax bill of £100,000 and total debts of £175,000. Accountants advised the club to go into voluntary liquidation. The club vowed to see out the present season. After that, no one could quite be sure.

Despite losing 1-5 at Kettering, Town recovered to beat Welling 4-0, and actually climbed to third place following a goalless draw at Bath. New players included keeper Stuart Ford, on loan from Scarborough, and young striker Elliott Beddard, a trialist from Middlesbrough. Simon Johnson would later join from Armthorpe Welfare. But the off-field dramas affected the team. Town went six games without a win, and with the future of the club looking ever more unlikely, financial backers were called upon to help save the club. John Stockwell announced that unless something turned up, Town would fold at the end of the season. The final home game against Kidderminster Harriers on 29 April was actually billed as Town's last ever at the Shay, and following the 1-2 defeat hundreds of fans poured onto the pitch to plead for the club to be saved. A 'Fighting Fund' was set up, and Stockwell urged supporters to attend a critical meeting three days later.

On 2 May, around 250 supporters rolled up at Arden Road Social Club where they did their bit to secure the club's future. Stockwell announced that an initial target of £30,000 for the Inland Revenue had to be found immediately. Half of that money had already been raised, but amid astonishing scenes, a further £15,000 was raised by the supporters on that one night, and Stockwell knew he had bought the club a little more time.

Halifax travelled to Runcorn for the last match of the season. Following a 3-0 win – Dave Hanson netted his first senior hat-trick – the fans streamed onto the pitch chanting 'There'll always be the

Shaymen'. It was inconceivable to think that the club could wrap up, but though the wolves had been kept from the door, there was still much work to be done.

The club was then hit by a further crisis. The Vauxhall Conference demanded a £75,000 bond – money Halifax Town did not have – if they were to take their place the following season. Now, not only did the club have to find money to pay off existing debts, John Stockwell also had to do some smooth talking to ensure the club had a league to play in – should they still be around.

Match of the Season 1994-95

Runcorn 0 Halifax Town 3

Vauxhall Conference, 8 May 1995

With the club's future in doubt, Halifax Town went into their last game intent on making it one to remember. There was nothing at stake for either side, and under normal circumstances this game might have been a typically mundane end-of-season contest. But now it might bring the curtain down on Halifax Town FC, in which case players and supporters were determined to sign off in style.

Town fans were out in force at Canal Street. Around 400 had made the journey – many of them having dipped into their own funds days earlier to keep the Inland Revenue off Town's back – and they helped record Runcorn's highest crowd of the season, 985.

It was a scorching day, almost as hot as Town's performance. Every man gave it their all, including 17-year-old Noel Horner, who was drafted in for his debut, but it was Dave Hanson up front who made all the headlines. He signed off – literally as it turned out – with his first senior hat-trick.

The first half was a battle, in keeping with most games involving John Carroll's side. After the break, Town stepped into overdrive, and won the game in a 22-minute spell. Hanson scored his first goal when Linnets keeper Mark Morris failed to hold Steve Prindiville's shot. Hanson then galloped away when put through by Colin Lambert for his second goal. Hanson was fizzing, but reserved his best goal till last, shrugging off the challenge of Paul Robertson and Peter Ellis and firing into the top corner from 25 yards.

Upon the final whistle, the Town fans crammed behind that goal streamed across to the other side of the pitch where they gathered at the players' tunnel to salute their heroes. In scenes reminiscent of those at the Shay when Town were relegated, they chanted 'There'll always be the Shayman'. In football, supporters can be the most knowledgeable people, and in this case they were right.

VAUXHALL CONFERENCE	**1995-96**
GM Vauxhall Conference	15th
FA Cup	4th Qualifying Round
FA Trophy	2nd Round

Chairman John Stockwell emerged from his meeting with Conference chiefs on 12 May with a weight off his shoulders. Not only had he persuaded them to waive the £75,000 bond they had demanded; he also learned that all Conference clubs were now entitled to £250,000 for ground improvements, courtesy of the Football Trust.

Of course, Town were not completely out of the woods. At the end of May they agreed to a Compulsory Voluntary Arrangement that would run for 3½ years. This would provide security against any creditor trying to force the club from trading. Calderdale Council, which was owed £40,000 in rent, responded, insisting that Town paid in advance for the use of the Shay before each home game.

During the summer the club and its supporters worked hard to raise money. Former player Dave Worthington, who would be appointed commercial manager, drummed up the support of luminaries such as Eric Cantona, Matt Le Tissier, Gary Lineker, Alan Hansen and Tim Flowers. Each autographed Town shirts, and these eventually fetched £3,000 at auction.

Chris Holland, who had been on the board since 1993, was owner of Holland Decorators in Scunthorpe, who became the club's new sponsors. This was a bonus, for the club had decided it had no choice but to go part-time. The backlash came in the form of an exodus of players leaving the Shay. Alex Jones, Craig Boardman, Colin Lambert, Paul Fleming, and David German all fixed themselves up with new clubs, as did Dave Hanson, who after playing in a couple of pre-season friendlies for Town, joined Lambert at Conference newcomers Hednesford Town.

Hednesford happened to be Town's first opponents come the opening day of the season. They were a progressive club, who had celebrated winning the Beazer Homes League by moving to a new ground at Keys Park. Halifax Town became Hednesford's first visitors, and its first victims, as the newcomers won 3-0. Lambert scored one of the goals.

John Bird, having had to rebuild, included seven debutants in that game. His biggest capture had been that of the former Republic of Ireland midfielder Kieran O'Regan from West Bromwich Albion. The others were defenders Simon Thompson (Scarborough) and Paul Stoneman (Blackpool), the versatile Jon Brown (Exeter City), forwards Lee Ludlow (Notts County) and Michael Midwood

(Huddersfield Town). Another new face, goalkeeper Andy Woods – he was a former Oldham Athletic trainee – was forced into action for the second game against reigning champions Macclesfield Town, but Town put any selection problems behind them to pull off a 1-0 win. This victory, however, failed to inspire the side. Two defeats followed, and inconsistent form meant Town looked mid-table material, at best.

Bird added more new players during September. Shaun Constable returned, while local midfielder John Hendrick – he had impressed for Liversedge in a pre-season friendly – and forward Gary Brook (Boston United) made their first appearances for the club. Paul Smith – he was Lincoln City's longest serving player at the time – and Richard Annan (Guiseley), plus another local lad, Karl Cochrane, bolstered the squad as Bird sought consistency. For a time it worked, with the Shaymen putting together a seven-match unbeaten run which kept them in touch with the leaders. But key departures disrupted progress. Before the end of the year Steve Prindiville, Gary Worthington and Simon Thompson all left for struggling Dagenham. Bird later admitted that letting them go might have been an error.

An abject 1-3 home defeat by Runcorn on 16 December saw the side slip to tenth, and though the New Year started promisingly with a goalless draw at Southport and a 3-0 win over Dagenham – there was even victory over Southport in the FA Trophy – it was downhill all the way after that. The rot started with a 0-4 defeat at Gateshead in the Spalding Cup. By the end of January, Town had been knocked out of two other cup competitions. Bromsgrove won at the Shay in the second round of the FA Trophy – a game Town had been expected to win – and there was an embarrassing defeat at Farsley Celtic in the West Riding County Cup, a competition in which Town realistically should have progressed far. In the Conference, Halifax simply forgot the art of winning. Town slid down the table, and the gate for the visit of Stalybridge was a paltry 509 – the lowest attendance at the Shay in the Conference. A few days later Town lost 0-7 at Macclesfield.

John Bird hoped it was just a one-off result, but sadly it was not. Despite a morale-boosting win at Morecambe, and the inclusions of Lincoln City loanees Paul Mudd and Tony Daws, Town crashed 1-6 at Kidderminster. The Town boss had had enough. As Bird departed on 20 March, he explained: 'I have never been the type to walk away from things but I think that, given the problems the club has had over the season, it might help.' Bird had been a tireless worker, but the transition from full to part-time had presented him with obstacles he could not overcome.

Did You Know?

Ian Juryeff twice broke Town's transfer record, first signing in Aug 89 from Orient for £40,000, then in Dec 89 when signing from Hereford for £50,000.

As a stop-gap measure the board asked George Mulhall to take up the reins a second time (following his managerial stint between 1972 and 1974). Having provided his expertise in various capacities at Bolton, Bradford City and Huddersfield, he had returned to the Shay in May 1995 as youth coach. He now took up the role of caretaker boss, promoting Kieran O'Regan to be his assistant.

O'Regan fancied himself for the job, and indeed applied for it, but was content to wait. In the meantime, he and Mulhall tried to steady the ship. The team went unbeaten for five matches. Before the fifth of these, at Telford, the players were introduced to new boss John Carroll and his right-hand man, Billy Rodaway.

Having been sacked by Runcorn in November, Carroll was a surprising choice, but Stockwell was insistent that he was the right man. 'He was in great demand and had in fact been offered three jobs – that was why we couldn't wait. At 36, he is at the right age to take us forward,' he explained.

Carroll's first game in charge was Town's last at home, a 2-2 draw with high-flying Woking, and they ended the season in style with 1-0 win at Bromsgrove, thus extending to seven the team's unbeaten run. Then the new manager looked forward to the new season, and stated that no players would be shown the door. Every one would be given a chance.

Match of the Season 1995-96

Halifax Town 1 Macclesfield Town 0

Vauxhall Conference, 22 August 1995

After all the uncertainties of the summer, Halifax Town lived to fight another day. But having lost so many players, there were obvious concerns as to how John Bird's new look side would fare. Things did not look good when the side lost heavily at Hednesford on the opening day, and if that was not bad enough, their second game was against Macclesfield Town.

Sammy McIlroy's Macc had won the Conference by a mile the previous season, but like Kidderminster before them, had been denied entry into the Football League because improvements to their Moss Rose ground failed to meet the 1 January deadline. Macclesfield's players would find it tougher going this time around, but at this early stage of the season Macc were viewed as the top side in the Conference.

John Bird intended to field an unchanged side. But when goalkeeper Darren Heyes and left-back Steve Prindiville found themselves stuck in traffic on the M1, Bird was forced into hasty changes. In came young keeper Andy Woods for his first game – the eighth player to make his debut this season – and Bird gave a start up front to Michael Midwood.

It mattered not. With Woods looking assured, the Shaymen played their part in a thriller, which for the neutral, had just about everything. The game saw chances galore at both ends, a missed penalty in the first half by Macc's Karl Margison – he missed by so much that it would have come as no surprise had he not been asked to take another – and a sending off for Neil Howarth. There was even a disallowed goal for Town's Simon Thompson – and at this point, despite all the excitement, a goalless draw looked on the cards.

That is until the 85th minute. When Martin McDonald's pass went astray, Paul Stoneman gathered the loose ball and surged forward. Thirty yards form goal he chanced his luck and hit a low drive past Macc keeper Karl Williams. It may be a football cliché, but Stoneman's goal was good enough to win any game. Which, as it happened in this case, it did.

VAUXHALL CONFERENCE	**1996-97**
GM Vauxhall Conference	19th
FA Cup	2nd Qualifying Round
FA Trophy	2nd Round

With John Carroll offering all the players the chance to prove themselves, he must have been pleased that, with the exception of Paul Smith, who left to join the police force, everyone else elected to stay and fight for their places.

This did not stop Carroll bringing in his own players. These were plentiful in number, and it soon became clear that Carroll was out for building his own side as quickly as possible. He returned to Runcorn to sign defender Andy Lee and midfielder Ian McInerney. Two players returned to the Shay – Paul Mudd and Gary Worthington. The directors also brought back old favourite Bobby Davison from Rotherham United, and dipped into their pockets to raise £10,000 to sign Stafford Rangers striker Mick Norbury. Things looked promising, and even chairman John Stockwell was confident of a top four finish.

After the first game, though, he might have felt differently. Town suffered their worst-ever opening-day defeat when they went down 0-6 at reigning champions Stevenage, who, like Macclesfield and Kidderminster before them, had been denied entry into the Football League.

Confidence was restored with a home draw with Altrincham and a 4-1 victory over Slough, but then Town fell into free-fall. Pressure mounted on Carroll as his side lost four of their next five matches to find themselves next to bottom. To make matters worse, Carroll found the supporters ganging up against him as they incessantly chanted for Kieran O'Regan to take his place.

Carroll hoped for respite in the FA Cup, which because of their recent poor record in the competition, Town were forced to enter at the first qualifying stage. But their 3-2 win at Oldham Town was far from convincing, and having lost 0-3 at home to Telford in the Conference, temperatures on the terraces reached boiling point as Town were dumped out of the Cup by Bishop Auckland. The visitors strolled to a 4-1 win, and disgusted fans poured onto the pitch upon the final whistle to call for Carroll's head. Vice-chairman Chris Holland – he had taken over from Brian Boulton in May – tried to appease them. But when the fans refused to disperse, a delegation was allowed in to confront Carroll and the directors. A constructive discussion followed.

The result? Pretty much more of the same, as Town failed to win another game until the end of November. This was despite changes to the playing staff. Michael Midwood left for Hong Kong via Accrington, while Heyes and Trotter were loaned out to VS Rugby – both eventually stopped there – and Bobby Davison went on loan to Guiseley. John Hendrick, too, decided to quit, claiming he was disillusioned with football. Meantime, in came keeper Paul Gibson, on loan from Manchester United, Macclesfield hard-man Kevin Hulme, originally on loan but signed permanently in December, and striker Geoff Horsfield for a second spell after being signed for a four-figure fee from Witton Albion.

With the side next to bottom, Town slumped to probably their most embarrassing defeat when Harrogate Railway won 2-1 at the Shay in the West Riding County Cup. The Shaymen were undone by a bizarre extra-time winner from Harrogate keeper Mark Fenton, once on the books at Halifax Town, whose long punt downfield bounced over Andy Woods. On 10 December, Town had something to cheer about when they won the final of the West Riding Senior Cup. Having accepted the challenge of holders Bradford City, a goal from Gary Worthington in extra-time gave the Shaymen a 2-1 win and the Cup.

John Carroll added defenders Paul Cox (Gresley Rovers) and Derek Goulding (Southport), and winger Darren Lyons (Winsford United) to the squad, but results in the Conference did not improve. Assistant-manager Billy Rodaway pointed to the FA Trophy in which he felt Town could have a good run. But he was wrong. After winning at Stalybridge Celtic in the first round, they were humbled 0-3 at Gloucester City. Renewed calls for Carroll to be sacked were intensified seven days later after bottom-placed Bath won 5-4 at the Shay to claim their first away win of the season. Within a couple of hours of the final whistle Carroll and Rodaway had left the club by 'mutual consent'. Although never a popular choice as manager, Carroll could rightly claim that he was never really given a chance. He was quick to point out where he felt the trouble lay: 'I feel I have been let down by the players and I don't think that at this moment I can get any more out of them.'

The following day, George Mulhall and Kieran O'Regan stepped into the breach again, with John Stockwell saying, 'The crowd have been screaming for this for a long time and now I hope they get behind the team.' He later told the pair that should they keep Town in the Conference, then the job was theirs.

With leading scorer Mick Norbury pressed into action as an emergency centre-back, Town won their next three matches to ease their plight at the bottom. But the spectre of relegation to the Unibond League hovered menacingly. Town released Derek Goulding, but signed Doncaster's Jamie Murphy, and Murphy scored on his debut in a 2-0 win over Southport on Good Friday. But the losing run returned. After defeat in their final away game at Rushden – Town's seventh consecutive game without a win - Mulhall admitted: 'We have a mountain to climb.' Town responded by coming back from 1-3 down to draw 3-3 with champions-elect Macclesfield at the Shay. Struggling with Bath to avoid the drop, Town needed to win their last home game with Stevenage to guarantee safety.

Town beat Stevenage 4-2 to preserve their Conference status, after which Mulhall and O'Regan were rewarded with a one-year contract. They released Bobby Davison, Gary Worthington, Paul Mudd and Paul Cox, whose three sendings-off epitomised Town's awful disciplinary record. Mick Norbury's last-day hat-trick did not prevent his being sold to Hednesford.

Attention now turned to upgrading the Shay. Back in August, the *Evening Courier* had envisioned a super sports stadium at the Shay. This involved both Halifax Town and the rugby club, now trading under the name of Halifax Blue Sox, to suit the new Super League image, playing at the Shay. In September, Calderdale Council agreed to develop the ground. When Town played Southport in March, the club launched the 'Shaybuilder Premier Bond Club' for Phase One of the redevelopment programme. £70,000 needed to be raised to match the sum pledged by the directors. But if Halifax slipped out of the Conference, the scheme would be deemed a sheer waste.

Match of the Season 1996-97

Halifax Town 4 Stevenage Borough 2

Vauxhall Conference, 3 May 1997

Though relegation from the Conference seemed unthinkable, by the last day of the season it loomed large. Just four years after dropping out of the Football League, the nightmare scenario had arisen again, and the threat of life in the Unibond League and almost total oblivion hovered over Halifax Town.

Unlike 1993, the Shaymen had one thing in their favour. Though they were fighting with Bath City to avoid the last relegation place – Bromsgrove and Altrincham were already condemned – survival at least was in their own hands. But with only one point separating Town from Bath, only victory for the Shaymen would guarantee safety.

On the face of it, however, Town had a harder task than Bath, for while the Romans were playing at home to Northwich, Town's

Did You Know?

Town's Steve Norris scored over half his team's goals in 1990-91, the first time this had been done since Bournemouth's Ted McDougall in 1971-72.

opponents were third-placed Stevenage, who had beaten the Shaymen 6-0 on the opening day of the season.

This do-or-die contest was not for the faint-hearted, especially after Paul Stoneman turned Robbie Mutchell's cross into his own net. But urged on by an anxious Shay crowd, Town responded with Mick Norbury capitalising on Darren Lyons' corner.

At this point, news came through that Bath were losing 0-2, and things looked good for Town. But they fell behind again when Barry Hayles waltzed through the defence to shoot under Andy Woods. Within two minutes Town had drawn level for a second time when Norbury converted Paul Mudd's cross. Half-time came with the score 2-2.

But the drama had only just begun. Town went in front when they were fortuitously awarded an indirect free-kick inside the box (the ref deemed Dean Hooper's touch to former Town keeper Richard Wilmot a back-pass). Lyons touched the ball to Norbury, who crashed it home to complete his hat-trick. But then Town lost their way completely, living on their nerves as news filtered through that Bath had turned their game round and were now leading 3-2.

Town's fate could have been sealed had Stevenage's Mark Smith not blazed over from six yards after Woods fumbled a corner. But with the Town fans baying for the final whistle, sub Geoff Horsfield latched onto Mudd's through ball and fired home from eighteen yards. Town fans surged onto the pitch to celebrate, but the game was not yet over. They eventually returned to the terraces, but thirty seconds later they were back when the ref blew for full-time.

VAUXHALL CONFERENCE	**1997-98**
GM Vauxhall Conference	1st (promoted)
FA Cup	4th Qualifying Round
FA Trophy	2nd Round

While George Mulhall and Kieran O'Regan set about building the squad for the forthcoming season, serious negotiations were under way regarding building work at the Shay, which needed to be complete if Halifax Town hoped to return to the Football League by winning the Conference. But following the traumas of the previous campaign, the chances of this seemed remote to say the least. Even the bookies, who rarely get it wrong, initially quoted odds of 66-1.

The knowledgeable George Mulhall made a number of astute close-season signings, not least that of the former Bradford City and Huddersfield Town defender Peter Jackson on a free transfer from Chester City. Two new full-backs would transform into exciting wing-backs – Andy Thackeray (Rochdale) and Mark Bradshaw (Macclesfield Town). There were also welcome returns for the popular Craig Boardman (Stalybridge Celtic) and Jamie Paterson, who arrived from Scunthorpe after his Falkirk adventure had not worked out. Andy Woods, however, walked out on the club, claiming he needed a year off. Mulhall enticed him back, but by then Lee Martin, signed from Rochdale, had made the goalkeeping position his own.

After a promising series of friendlies, which included a 2-1 win over First Division Huddersfield, Halifax were given a tough start to the new season. Their first three games were all away from home, but they came through unscathed, capitalising on victory at Hayes with draws at Slough and Southport. The results may not have been spectacular, but they were the platform upon which the rest of the season was built.

Town's first win came over Welling, after which they hardly looked back. The 3-0 win at Telford had George Mulhall describing Town's display as awesome, and things just got better. Geoff Horsfield grabbed two goals in that match, but went one better in the next game against Yeovil, who were hammered 6-1 at the Shay in a game brought forward because of the funeral of Diana, Princess of Wales, the following day. Town were now top of the Conference.

Plans regarding the development of the Shay took a giant step forward during the half-time interval of that Yeovil game, when directors of Halifax Town and Halifax Blue Sox signed an agreement to share the Shay. Although no precise date had been given for work to start on Phase One – the Hunger Hill terracing – at least the signs were there that progress was being made.

The Shaymen carried on doing their bit on the field, not only beating all before them in the Conference, with Horsfield scoring for fun, but also crushing all-comers to the Shay in the FA Cup. Droylsden, Leigh RMI and Ossett Town were all easily accounted for, but while things appeared to be going well, obstacles still needed to be overcome, the first of which was the loss of influential Peter Jackson.

When neighbours Huddersfield sacked their manager, Brian Horton, it was to Jackson that they turned as a replacement. Though approached before Town's home game with Kettering, Jackson played in that match and helped the Shaymen to a 3-0 win, but two days later, he was installed as Huddersfield's new manager. Halifax were powerless to prevent it, as a clause had been written into Jackson's contract allowing him to leave should a managerial post come available, and the Huddersfield job was a dream for him. Even so, John Stockwell claimed Town had been 'mugged' in the way the Jackson deal was done.

Was it coincidence that Town should lose their first game without Jackson? It happened at Stalybridge in the Spalding Cup. Mulhall responded by signing the former Coventry and Newcastle defender Brian Kilcline – he had been released in the summer by Mansfield – as a replacement for Jackson. Kilcline slotted in well, but questions were suddenly being asked of the Shaymen. After gaining a point at third-placed Morecambe, a game which saw a thousand Town fans make the journey to Christie Park, Town were knocked off top-spot following a heavy defeat at Cheltenham, and bowed out of the FA Cup at Unibond League side Gainsborough. With hindsight, however, defeat in the Cup may have been a blessing in disguise.

The Shaymen soon got back on track, winning five of their next six matches to go seven points clear, only to hit their second sticky patch in December. Defeat at Leek was followed by three successive draws, one of which was at bottom-placed Gateshead, managed by John Carroll.

On 5 January, Blakedell Construction began work on Phase One of the ground development, the Hunger Hill end of the ground, but this soon turned into a race against time, as the 31 March deadline approached. Meanwhile, on the pitch, despite bowing out of the FA Trophy at the hands of Slough, in the Vauxhall Conference Halifax imply got on with the job of winning, and by the time they travelled to Rushden & Diamonds they held a massive ten-point lead. This was shortened after Town, with Woods making a rare start, were cut to shreds and lost 0-4. Mulhall would not call upon Woods again.

Did You Know?

In 1992-93 John McGrath invented Benny the Cat, saying there was no money to feed it. Torquay fans arrived with tins of cat food, so Town got a real cat!

Town responded with wins at Dover and Yeovil and victory over Farnborough at the Shay to edge them nearer to their ultimate prize. In March, Mulhall added ex-Shay favourite Andy Kiwomya to the squad, and he came on as a substitute as Town hammered Morecambe 5-1. This result set themselves up nicely for the visit of second-placed Rushden four days later. Town blew Brian Talbot's side away with one of the most devastating displays of the season, not reflected in the 2-0 scoreline. Surely nothing could stop the Shaymen now!

Making his only appearance for Town in that game was Stoke City's on-loan keeper Phil Morgan, who had come in for the injured Lee Martin. When Morgan was recalled by Stoke the following week, Mulhall went to Airdrie to capture the former Oldham keeper Andy Rhodes, and Rhodes played his part in the final assault. So too, would Dave Hanson, who returned to the Shay from Leyton Orient at the beginning of April.

On 2 April came the news that all connected with Halifax Town were waiting for. Upon inspection of the completed North Terrace, Football League officials deemed it suitable and announced that, should Town win the Conference, they would be accepted back. The capacity had been raised from just under 4,000 to 7,400. Chris Whalley of the Football League ground-grading committee said, 'This is clearly a forward looking club, and we will welcome them into the league.' (Phase Two – the Bus Garage End – would be completed, incidentally, in October).

The new terracing was used for the first time against Woking, Town's 1-0 win putting them thirteen points clear. The only conceivable threat now came from fifth-placed Cheltenham, who had a number of games in hand. But with Cheltenham enjoying a run in the FA Trophy – they would go on to win it – it was surely asking too much of them to make up the lost ground. And in any case, they had to rely on Town slipping up.

The Shaymen nearly did against Southport on Easter Monday, but down to ten men after O'Regan's sending-off and trailing 2-3, Dave Hanson popped up with two late goals to win the match. Victory at Kidderminster five days later would mean the Conference title, and with it promotion, was theirs.

The task was duly completed in style, with Andy Rhodes saving a penalty before goals from Horsfield – inevitably – and Jamie

Paterson sealed a 2-0 win in front of a travelling army of fans over 1,500 strong. As the referee blew the final whistle, they poured onto the pitch, knowing that Town's five-year exile was over.

Understandably, the last three games proved to be anti-climatic. Town lost at Northwich, but managed to keep their unbeaten home record intact, playing a 1-1 draw with Cheltenham prior to being presented with the Conference trophy. Disappointingly, Town's season ended with a 2-6 defeat at Welling, but Geoff Horsfield's goal ensured he finished as the Conference's top scorer with thirty goals, one ahead of Rushden's Darren Collins.

But at the moment of Town's finest hour, there were rumblings behind the scenes. Two days after the Cheltenham game, Halifax Town announced a £20,000 sponsorship deal with the Nationwide Building Society. The players paraded the Conference trophy on an open-top bus decked in Nationwide banners as they headed to the Town Hall for a civic reception. This understandably upset director Chris Holland, whose firm was still the club's official sponsors. Holland resigned from the board. Days later, reserve coach Dave Worthington also quit, claiming he had been snubbed at the civic reception. It almost went unnoticed that Gary Brook, Brian Kilcline, Darren Lyons, Andy Kiwomya, Andy Woods, and later Noel Horner, had all been released by the club, but at a time when they should have been basking in their glory, the worst of the troubles were just about to begin.

Match of the Season 1997-98

Kidderminster Harriers 0 Halifax Town 2

Vauxhall Conference, 18 April 1998

In a season full of highs, picking out one single match is not an easy thing to do. But for the sheer sense of occasion, the game at Aggborough against Kidderminster just nicks it, for it was here on an unforgettable day that Town clinched the Conference title.

At kick-off, only fifth-placed Cheltenham had any chance of catching Town, but despite their games in hand they were thirteen points adrift. Victory for the Shaymen over Kidderminster meant Town could not be overtaken.

Not that Town expected an easy ride. Although Kidderminster had had a disappointing season – they had been Conference champions in 1994 – manager Graham Allner had his players fired up, determined not to let the Shaymen clinch the title on their ground. But the words of their secretary Roger Barlow that 'Town won't win the title here' were like a red rag to a bull, and were just the spur

Did You Know?

In 1996 Halifax had a groundsman called Phil Garside. Back in the 1920s his grandfather – Bob Suter – was also groundsman at the Shay.

Town needed – particularly with around 1,500 supporters making the journey, many of whom rubbished Barlow's comments.

There was obvious tension, though, especially as Kidderminster dominated the early stages, and Andy Rhodes was forced into making fine saves. The best of these came when Brian Kilcline upended Mike Bignall in the box to concede a penalty. Rhodes, however, proved equal to Ian Arnold's kick and beat the ball away.

The goal that Town's fans were waiting for came three minutes before the break. Martin Weir's back-pass was too strong for keeper Darren Steadman, who failed to gather the ball cleanly, allowing Geoff Horsfield to nip in, round a defender, and crash the ball high into the net.

After half-time, Kidderminster saw plenty of the ball, but the best chances fell to the Shaymen. They were desperate for a second goal to ease the nerves, and ten minutes from time they got it. Fittingly, it came from Jamie Paterson, a member of the side relegated five years previously, and what a strike it was. Paterson cut inside, then hit a low shot with his right foot – his wrong foot – from 25 yards that beat the keeper at the left-hand post.

The goal reduced Paterson to tears, while on the terraces behind Andy Rhodes' goal, the Town fans went delirious. Ten minutes later, upon the final whistle, they gathered at the tunnel to salute the players and the manager. 'There's only one George Mulhall,' they cried, and the man who had masterminded Town's success reappeared to huge cheers.

The celebrations would go on long into the night back in Halifax. It was, after all, a novel experience for the fans, whose numbers, as the season progressed, had grown in number. But whilst they were enjoying themselves, doubtless somewhere in a darkened canteen, Kidderminster secretary Roger Barlow was eating his words.

LEAGUE DIVISION 3	**1998-99**
Nationwide Division 3	10th
Worthington Cup	2nd Round
FA Cup	1st Round

Chris Holland and Dave Worthington were not the only ones to resign during the close season. But whilst their departures were caused by personal disagreements, that of chairman John Stockwell on 7 June was put down to the fact that he needed a rest. 'It is extremely time-consuming and time for someone else to take the reins of responsibility. Quite truthfully I am tired,' said Stockwell.

Chris Holland may have resigned, but a change of heart saw him not only return to the board, but also take over the chairmanship, with Jim Brown, who had returned as a director in 1996, elected vice-chairman. The popular Holland promised a bright future for the club. He saw his first job as being to persuade George Mulhall to stay on as manager. Mulhall had hinted that he wanted another year in the job anyway, so this seemed a formality. Mulhall, indeed, agreed to a new one-year deal with a view to stepping up as director of football, allowing him to groom Kieran O'Regan as his successor. Matters, though, were about to take a different course.

Mulhall and O'Regan had already signed defender Mark Sertori from Scunthorpe and goalkeeper Tim Carter from Millwall. But seeds of discontent were sowed by the signing of Halifax-born Peter Butler from West Brom as player-coach. Butler had family ties with Jim Brown. For reasons unclear to this day, on 3 August Mulhall announced he was standing down.

With the new season only days away, the board hastily installed O'Regan as the new manager. O'Regan promoted Andy May, who had arrived as coach to the reserve and youth teams, as his assistant. But personality clashes continued. For some reason Butler was missing from the official team photo-call, and the installation of Jim Brown as chairman received mixed reactions. Rightly or wrongly, the club felt that it was necessary to have at the helm a local man – Chris Holland was based in Scunthorpe – but the undercurrent of unrest persisted for practically the whole season.

The players, however, forgot about the politics, and got off to a flier. Under a baking sun, a makeshift side including Richard Lucas (Hartlepool), Steve Murphy (Huddersfield), and Ian Duerden (Burnley) won 2-0 at Peterborough on the opening day, and followed up by defeating pre-season title favourites Brentford at the Shay seven days later. After four games, Town were unbeaten – they beat Shrewsbury on a Friday night to go top overnight – and had progressed into the second round of the Worthington Cup at the expense of Second Division Wrexham. Despite having a man sent off in both legs – Butler at the Shay on his debut – Town went through on penalties after the aggregate scores ended 2-2. Keeper Lee Martin proved to be the hero on the night by making the decisive save from Dave Brammer.

Town had started the season without the injured Jamie Paterson, but he returned in September as Town maintained their challenge. Paterson scored against First Division Bradford City in the Worthington Cup – Halifax bowed out after losing both legs – and scored two more as Town pulled off their best win of the season, winning 4-0 at leaders Scunthorpe in early October.

During the Conference-winning season, striker Horsfield had become the hottest property outside the Football League, and he now continued where he had left off. Kevin Keegan, now in charge at Fulham, moved to take Horsfield, a former brickie, to Craven Cottage. Though Horsfield initially rejected Fulham's terms, he soon completed his record £300,000 transfer.

Without Horsfield's fire-power, Town looked set to struggle. But Marc Williams (Bangor City) and Nottingham Forest's on loan Steve Guinan came into the side. Town rallied to go top following a stormy 3-2 win over Chester on 10 November. The game saw a mass brawl, for which Kevin Hulme was suspended by the club for his part. Hulme missed the next match at Manchester City in the FA Cup, a game screened live on a Friday night by Sky TV. The cup-tie evoked memories of the 1980 clash between the two sides, but alas for Town there was never a chance of a repeat shock win. They under-performed and lost 0-3.

The Shaymen remained top of Division Three going into December, but then began to lose their way. O'Regan gave youngsters Chris Newton and defender James Stansfield a run in the team, and signed Lee Power from Plymouth. After winning at Brighton, Town failed to win any of their next seven matches. Frustrated fans vented their anger at the chairman.

At the beginning of February, O'Regan signed a new contract. Results, however, continued to be patchy, and Town began to lose sight of the play-off placings that for so long seemed within their grasp. O'Regan took Craig Etherington (West Ham) and Gareth Grant (Bradford City) on loan, and forked out £35,000 to Notts County for striker Justin Jackson.

Shortly afterwards, Marc Williams moved to York for £30,000, but his was not the only departure from the club. Despite encouraging results at high-flying Cardiff and Brentford, Town had slipped to eleventh by the time Rochdale arrived on Easter Monday. Rochdale had earlier won at the Shay in the Auto Windscreen Shield,

Bolton defend desperately at the Shay in the FA Cup (November 1986)

Dave Robinson back-heads the ball v Billingham in the FA Cup (November 1987)

Harrison, Ferebee and Holden prepare to examine Forest in FA Cup (January 1988)

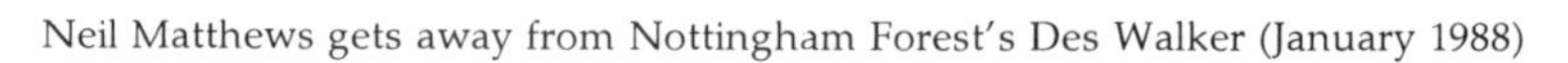

Neil Matthews gets away from Nottingham Forest's Des Walker (January 1988)

Terry McPhillips gets stuck in against Torquay (May 1988)

Andy Watson is about to head into Kettering's goal in the FA Cup (January 1989)

Bramhall, Robinson and Matthews lay siege to Hartlepool's goal (March 1989)

John Bramhall and Ian Juryeff attack the Maidstone goal (November 1989)

Craig Fleming climbs above Grimsby's Gary Birtles (April 1990)

Barr scores at Carlisle, Town's first league goal in their ninth match (October 1990)

Keeper Jonathan Gould, covered in blood, is led off v Walsall (March 1991)

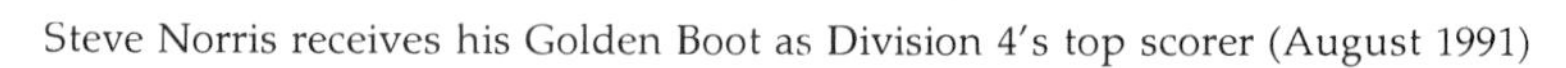

Steve Norris receives his Golden Boot as Division 4's top scorer (August 1991)

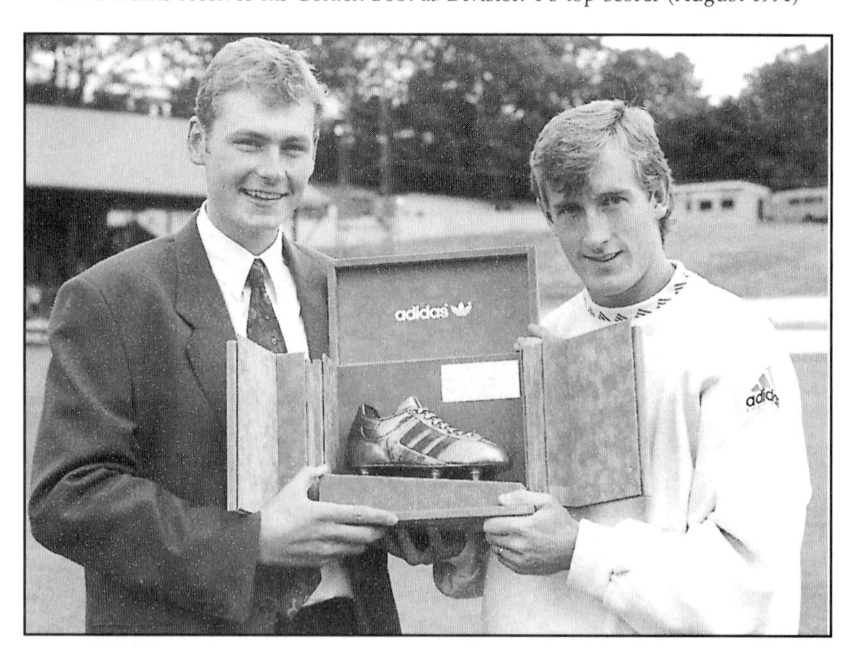

Neil Matthews helps out his defence v Gillingham (October 1991)

Jonathan Gould punches clear at Witton Albion in the FA Cup (November 1991)

Nick Richardson heads towards the Barnet goal (March 1992)

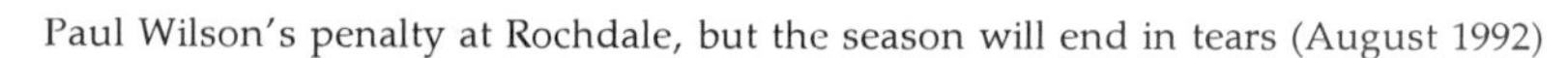
Paul Wilson's penalty at Rochdale, but the season will end in tears (August 1992)

The late Justin Fashanu of Torquay beats Russell Bradley (November 1992)

Dave Ridings goes close v Hereford. The Vauxhall Conference beckons (May 1993)

Martin Filson v Hull City in the Yorkshire Electricity Cup (August 1993)

Town's first ever away fixture in the Conference, v Southport (August 1993)

Where's the ball? Jimmy Cameron and a Southport player don't know (August 1993)

Peake, Filson and Cameron pressurise the Southport goal (August 1993)

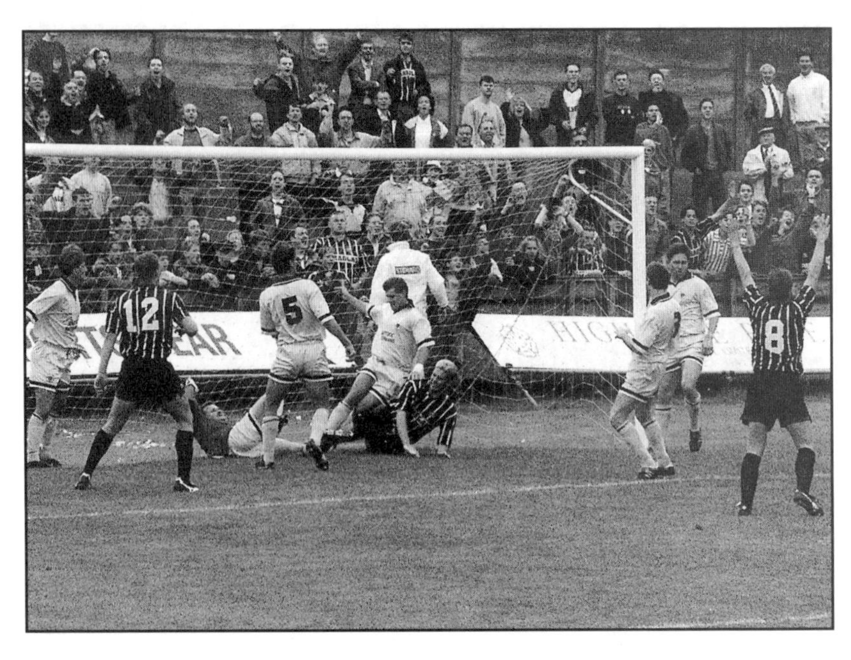

Yeovil survive this assault on their goal (September 1993)

Steve Saunders scores against West Brom in the FA Cup (November 1993)

Did You Know?

Halifax Town have twice been paid tribute on record – by Tommy Degnan in 1978, and by the Grumbleweeds when Town won the Conference in 1998.

but in a drab league fixture Town drew 0-0. Though they were still only three points off a play-off spot, performances suggested the side was heading in only one direction – downwards.

Still, the sacking of O'Regan and his assistant Andy May the following day came out of the blue. Always a popular player, whatever his credentials as a manager, O'Regan's dismissal divided the fans, and Jim Brown was compelled to defend the board's actions in the *Evening Courier*.

Halifax Town turned to Dave Worthington, who over the years had served the club as player, commercial manager and coach, to guide the side through until the end of the season. Worthington, a staunch Halifax supporter, felt the play-offs were still a possibility, and indeed, despite losing heavily in his first game at Cambridge, steered them into seventh place by winning three of the next four matches. But home defeat by bottom-of-the-table Scarborough, who would ultimately drop into the Conference, all but sealed Town's fate. The team travelled to Exeter for the final game knowing that only a victory would help them make the play-offs, and then only if Swansea failed to win their home game. Town's 1-2 defeat made it all academic – they slipped to tenth as things turned out.

Whether Dave Worthington fancied the manager's post full-time – and he never denied that he did not – the club began to look elsewhere. Former internationals Frank Stapleton and Alvin Martin were linked with the job, but it soon emerged that Mark Lillis, assistant to Brian Laws at Scunthorpe, was the man the directors wanted. Lillis, though, was still focusing on taking Scunthorpe into Division Two via the play-offs. On 2 June, four days after The Iron had completed their mission by beating Leyton Orient 1-0 at Wembley, Lillis was installed as the new Halifax Town manager.

Lillis arrived at a club that was at last showing some ambition. In May, Town smashed their own transfer record by signing striker Chris Tate for £150,000 and plans were afoot to build a new stand at the Shay by January 2000. As the 1999-2000 season approached, Town were the division's highest spenders, having shelled out a further £45,000 for Cardiff's Graham Mitchell. And with keeper Tony Parks, full-backs Matt Russell (Scarborough) and Marc Jules (Chesterfield), midfielder Steve Gaughan (Darlington) and forward Robbie Painter (Rochdale) replacing outgoing Lee Martin, Andy Thackeray, Jon Brown and Dave Hanson, expectations were high.

Match of the Season 1998-99

Halifax Town 3 Chester 2

Division 3, 10 November 1998

Even as Halifax Town celebrated promotion to the Third Division, there was talk in some quarters of 'doing a Macclesfield' – that is, promotion to Division Two at the first attempt. Three months and eighteen games into the season, that talk was given substance as Town won this fixture to go top of the table.

Halifax had hit top spot briefly back in September, and had sustained their promotion form into November. Though not playing eye-catching football – certainly not on a par with that shown in the Conference – what kept them among the leaders was their fighting spirit, most recently put to good effect when they played a 3-3 draw with Cambridge at the Shay. That spirit came to the fore again in this game with Chester, though at times that spirit was carried to excess.

Though Town came from behind to regain the leadership of the division, the game will best be remembered for a mass brawl in the 55th minute that involved players from both sides, as well as members of the Chester bench. The outcome was red cards for Chris Priest and Kevin Hulme. Hulme felt he was the innocent party, though he did retaliate, having had to jump out of the way of Priest's tackle. So incensed was he by his dismissal that he set about retribution in the tunnel. His actions led to Halifax Town suspending him for two matches and fining him two weeks' wages.

The game stood at 1-1 at this point. Jamie Paterson's spectacular 25-yarder had given Town the lead in an otherwise lacklustre first half, but the visitors had hit back after half-time through Luke Bennett after ex-Shayman Nick Richardson dispossessed Paul Stoneman just inside the Town half.

It was then that tempers flared. After peace had been restored, Chester took the lead when unmarked John Murphy headed in from six yards. Town regrouped, and it was the unlikely figure of right-wing-back Andy Thackeray who turned out to be their match-winner. First, he arrived in the box to curl the ball into the top corner, then, five minutes later, he was there again, this time sticking out a leg to divert home Jamie Murphy's free-kick.

It was hardly surprising that the Town fans got carried away, dreaming of another promotion. The legacy of a small squad, and no natural goalscorer following the departure of Geoff Horsfield, eventually caught up with them. But it was good while it lasted.

GUIDE TO SEASONAL SUMMARIES

Col 1: Match number (for league fixtures); Round (for cup-ties).
e.g. 2:1 means 'Second round; first leg.'
e.g. 4R means 'Fourth round replay.'

Col 2: Date of the fixture and whether Home (H), Away (A), or Neutral (N).

Col 3: Opposition.

Col 4: Attendances. Home gates appear in roman; Away gates in *italics*.
Figures in **bold** indicate the largest and smallest gates, at home and away.
Average home and away attendances appear after the final league match.

Col 5: Respective league positions of Halifax and their opponents after the match.
Halifax's position appears on the top line in roman.
Their opponents' position appears on the second line in *italics*.
For cup-ties, the division and position of opponents is provided.
e.g. *2:12* means the opposition are twelfth in Division 2.

Col 6: The top line shows the result: W(in), D(raw), or L(ose).
The second line shows Halifax's cumulative points total.

Col 7: The match score, Halifax's given first.
Scores in **bold** indicate Halifax's biggest league win and heaviest defeat.

Col 8: The half-time score, Halifax's given first.

Col 9: The top lines shows Halifax's scorers and times of goals in roman.
The second line shows opponents' scorers and times of goals in *italics*.
A 'p' after the time of a goal denotes a penalty; 'og' an own-goal.
The third line gives the name of the match referee.

Team line-ups: Halifax line-ups appear on the top line, irrespective of whether they are home or away. Opposition teams appear on the second line in *italics*.
Players of either side who are sent off are marked !
Halifax players making their league debuts are displayed in **bold**.

Substitutes: Names of substitutes appear only if they actually took the field.
A player substituted is marked *
A second player substituted is marked ^
A third player substituted is marked "
These marks do not indicate the sequence of substitutions.

N.B. For clarity, all information appearing in *italics* relates to opposing teams.

No	Date		Att	Pos	Pt	F-A	H-T	Scorers, Times, and Referees	1	2	3	4	5	6	7	8	9	10	11	12 sub used
1	A	SOUTHEND			L	1-2	1-0	Shawcross 30	Smith	Russell	Hampton	**Meagan**	Pickering	Shawcross	Ryden	Massie	Morris	Wallace	McCarthy	
	10/8		*10,406*		0			*McKinven 68, Smillie 76*	*Leslie*	*Bentley*	*Birks*	*McMillan*	*Stone*	*Kurila*	*Clayton*	*Best*	*Smillie*	*Chisnell*	*McKinven*	
								Ref: P Walters	It's a disappointing start, as Ernie Shepherd's side are better on the day and actually look fitter. Shawcross scores against the run of play, then the Shaymen play defensively. Unmarked John McKinven makes the breakthrough, then Andy Smillie seals it following a well-worked move.											
2	H	LINCOLN		23	L	0-1	0-0		Smith	Hampton	**Buxton**	Meagan	Pickering	Shawcross	Ryden	Massie	**Lawther**	Wallace	McCarthy	
	17/8		4,416	*1*	0			*Corner 62*	*Kennedy*	*Taylor*	*Pedon*	*Smith J*	*Harford*	*Hubbard*	*Hughes*	*Kearns*	*Corner*	*Lewis*	*Smith D*	
								Ref: J Quinn	Following the heavy defeat by Hull in the League Cup, the Shaymen play better but still come off second best. The Imps look dangerous, and their goal by Norman Corner, from a corner, comes as no real surprise. The ball is touched to him by Ray Harford – who comes from Halifax.											
3	A	ALDERSHOT		13	W	2-0	1-0	Ryden 30, 64	Smith	Hampton	Buxton	Meagan	Pickering	Shawcross	Ryden	Massie	Lawther	Wallace	Morris	
	24/8		*4,449*	*12*	2				*Dickie*	*Walden*	*Hawes*	*McAnearney*	*Rafferty*	*Walker*	*Walton*	*Wilson*	*Howarth*	*Gowans*	*Burton**	*Newman*
								Ref: R Paine	Town steal both points but Ball isn't complaining. His team is up and running. Keeper Alan Dickie fails to hold Shawcross's header and Ryden profits. Town survive when Buxton makes an amazing goal-line clearance off Jack Howarth, and then Massie sets Ryden up for his second.											
4	A	NOTTS CO		8	W	2-1	0-1	Massie 74, Lawther 89	Smith	Hampton	Buxton	Meagan	Pickering	Shawcross	Ryden	Massie	Lawther	Wallace	McCarthy	
	28/8		*4,980*	*22*	4			*Bradd 19*	*Rose*	*Ball*	*Smith K*	*Smith J*	*Needham*	*Gibson*	*Wilson*	*Bates*	*Bradd*	*Murphy Jim*	*Pring*	
								Ref: E Jennings	County boss Bill Gray is under pressure and will soon lose his job. Town never give up, even after they fall behind to rising star Les Bradd's effort. Ryden this time makes both goals, a free-kick touched in by Massie and a cross spectacularly headed in by Ian Lawther at the far post.											
5	H	BRADFORD PA		3	W	3-0	2-0	Shawcross 11, 30p, Wallace 57	Smith	Hampton	Buxton	Meagan	Pickering	Shawcross	Ryden	Massie	Lawther	Wallace	McCarthy	
	31/8		4,679	*22*	6				*Hardie*	*Andrews*	*Hudson*	*Drury*	*Harris*	*Singleton*	*Down*	*Hemstock**	*Draper*	*Darfield*	*Cockburn*	*Booker*
								Ref: T Pallister	Another manager soon to be on his way is Bradford's former England international Jack Rowley. Here it is all a bit too easy for the Shaymen. Shawcross gets his first off one of McCarthy's famous long throws. His second comes via the penalty spot after Tony Harris up-ends Meagan.											
6	H	DARLINGTON		14	L	**0-4**	0-2		Smith	Hampton	Buxton	Meagan	Pickering	Shawcross	Ryden	Morris*	Lawther	Wallace	McCarthy	**Pearson**
	7/9		5,058	*1*	6			*O'Neil 5, Hale 42p, 84, Felton 60*	*Moor*	*Peverell*	*Keeble*	*O'Neil*	*Albeson*	*Jacques*	*Sproates*	*Felton*	*Robson*	*Hale*	*Kirk*	
								Ref: A Morrissey	What a calamity! Town are already behind when Pickering brings down Harry Kirk for Ken Hale's penalty. A dreadful mix-up between Smith and Hampton lets in Ken Felton for 0-3. Hale's second is a cracking 30-yarder. Despite this trouncing Ball is adamant: 'We're going places.'											
7	A	NEWPORT			L	0-2	0-1		Smith	Hampton	Buxton	Pickering	**Nicholl**	Shawcross	Ryden	Massie	Lawther	Wallace*	McCarthy	Pearson
	14/9		***1,564***		6			*McClelland 36, Hill 50p*	*Weare*	*McLaughlin*	*King*	*Wood*	*Deacy*	*Rowland*	*Robinson*	*Hill*	*Buck*	*Wookey*	*McClelland*	
								Ref: C Nicholls	After heavy rain the ref gives the go-ahead just 30 minutes before kick-off. Debutant Nicholl makes a steady debut and he will go on to greater things. John McClelland converts McLaughlin's cross for Newport's first, then Pickering, again, concedes a penalty, fouling Henry Robinson.											
8	A	WORKINGTON			D	1-1	0-0	Massie	Smith	Hampton	Buxton	Pickering	Nicholl	Lee	Ryden	Massie	Lawther	Shawcross	McCarthy	
	18/9		*4,292*		7			*Tyrer 47*	*Rogan*	*Ogilvie*	*Butler*	*Geidmintis*	*Spencer*	*Middlemass*	*Banks*	*Griffin*	*Tyrer*	*Tinnion*	*Holliday*	
								Ref: G Singleton	Town only have eleven fit men so the team picks itself. Workington, under new manager Brian Doyle, are going well. Alan Tyrer, ex-Everton, gives them the lead, and only a magnificient save from Smith denies Brian Tinnion. At the other end Massie's shot into the corner gets a point.											
9	H	WREXHAM		12	W	2-0	1-0	Lawther 2, 55	Smith	Buxton	McCarthy	Pickering	Nicholl	Lee	Ryden	Massie	Lawther	Shawcross	**Parry**	
	21/9		**2,674**	*21*	9				*Livsey*	*Ingle*	*Bermingham*	*Davis*	*May*	*Bradbury*	*Beanland*	*Moir*	*Charnley*	*Smith R*	*Kinsey*	
								Ref: P Baldwin	Beleagured Wrexham are in for a long hard season. Manager Alvan Williams resigned five days ago but his protégé John Neal, now in charge, can't stop the rot here. Town, however, are unconvincing, but Lawther, heading in Ryden's cross and trialist Parry's corner, saves the day.											
10	A	SWANSEA		13	L	0-1	0-0		Smith	Buxton	McCarthy	Pickering	Nicholl	Wallace	Ryden	Massie	Lawther	Shawcross	Parry	
	28/9		*7,431*	*6*	9			*Williams 47*	*John*	*Laurence*	*Gomersall*	*Thomas*	*Nurse*	*Slee*	*Evans*	*Williams H*	*Gwyther*	*McMorran*	*Screen*	
								Ref: T Lockett	On this sort of form it's easy to see why Billy Lucas's Swansea side are among the early season pace-setters. Yet despite dominating they only manage one goal. It comes from long-serving Herbert Williams, who heads in Jim McMorran's free-kick, though Town feel Smith is impeded.											
11	A	SCUNTHORPE		11	W	1-0	0-0	Lawther	Smith	Hampton	Buxton	Pickering	Nicholl	Lee*	Ryden	Massie	Lawther	Shawcross	McCarthy	Wallace
	4/10		*3,828*	*20*	11				*Barnard*	*Foxton*	*Hemstead*	*Davison*	*Holt*	*Welbourne*	*Wilson*	*Harvey*	*Deere*	*Heath*	*Punton*	
								Ref: D Fieldsend	Town's sensible approach to this game starts talk of promotion. It may be a bit premature but their performance here is impressive. Lawther's flicked header off McCarthy's corner is enough to win it. The ref somehow finds eight minutes of injury-time. Iron sub Keegan fails to get on.											

No	Venue	Opponents	Att	Pos	Pts	F-A	H-T	Scorers, Times, and Referees	1	2	3	4	5	6	7	8	9	10	11	subs used
12	H	NOTTS CO			W	3-1	3-0	McCarthy 27, 39, Massie 40	Smith	Hampton	Buxton	Pickering	Nicholl	Lee	Ryden	Massie	Lawther	Shawcross	McCarthy	
8/10			3,630		13			*Bradd 88*	*Rose*	*Ball*	*Worthington*	*Farmer*	*Needham*	*Gibson*	*Pring*	*Murphy Jim**	*Bradd*	*Masson*	*Bates*	*Oakes*
								Ref: P Partridge	The Shaymen inflict an early season double over County. McCarthy's second goal, a spectacular shot from 18 yards that swerves and dips, puts them in control. Massie nips in before half-time. After the break Lawther hits the post before Don Masson sets up Bradd for a late consolation.											
13	H	PETERBOROUGH		8	W	2-1	0-1	Nicholl 48, Massie 80	Smith	Hampton	Buxton	Pickering	Nicholl	Lee	Ryden	Massie	Lawther	Shawcross	McCarthy	
12/10			4,075	*19*	15			*Pyatt 13*	*Millington*	*Noble*	*Crawford*	*Ricketts*	*Wile*	*Wright*	*Brace*	*Downes*	*Hall*	*Pyatt*	*Thompson*	
								Ref: A Green	Jim Iley's Posh give Town a fright. They score a real route-one goal through John Pyatt – his first and last career goal – and in the next minute Smith has to save with his legs from Stuart Brace. Town respond through Nicholl's header, and Massie, a gift supplied by Tony Millington.											
14	A	PORT VALE		9	D	1-1	1-0	Lawther 17	Smith	Hampton	Buxton	Pickering	Nicholl	Meagan	Ryden*	Massie	Lawther	Shawcross	McCarthy	Lee
19/10			*4,493*	*17*	16			*Morris 58*	*Hickson*	*Boulton*	*Wilson*	*Goodfellow*	*Sproson*	*King*	*Morris*	*Cullerton*	*Chapman*	*Gough*	*Williams*	
								Ref: P Walters	After recent trouble here the police keep guard on the players' bus. Town, therefore, do well not to win! Vale's Mick Cullerton hits the post early on before Town's Lawther hooks the ball in. The home side are allowed an equaliser when Roy Sproson heads down for Mick Morris.											
15	H	DONCASTER		6	W	**4-1**	1-1	Shawcr's 6, McCarthy 51, 72, Massie 53	Smith	Hampton	Buxton	Pickering	Nicholl	Meagan	Lee	Massie	Lawther	Shawcross	McCarthy	
26/10			6,734	*4*	18			*Jeffrey 40*	*Gavan*	*Haselden*	*Clish*	*Rabjohn*	*Robertson*	*Flowers*	*Usher*	*Jeffrey*	*Regan*	*Johnson*	*Gilfillan*	
								Ref: G Singleton	Two fancied teams draw the highest attendance at the Shay so far. They witness some classic goals, not least Shawcross's impudent back-heel. Rovers' prolific Alick Jeffrey heads in a corner, but the game is all but over just after half-time. McCarthy wraps it up with a fierce cross-shot.											
16	A	CHESTERFIELD		10	L	0-2	0-1		Smith	Hampton	Buxton	Pickering	Nicholl	Meagan	Lee*	Massie	Lawther	Shawcross	McCarthy	Wallace
4/11			*4,400*	*19*	18			*Randall 12, Bishop 90*	*Humphries*	*Holmes*	*Hickton*	*Pugh*	*Finnigan*	*Phelan*	*Moore*	*Randall*	*Moss*	*Bell*	*Bishop*	
								Ref: R Tinkler	Jimmy McGuigan has his Chesterfield side fired up for this one. When Kevin Randall fires in from twelve yards they have something to hang on to. Town in theory are still in the hunt until Peter Bishop's breakaway goal. But they can't play as badly again. 'We were terrible,' – Ball.											
17	H	BRADFORD C		10	D	1-1	0-0	Lawther 90	Smith	Hampton	Buxton	Pickering	Nicholl	Meagan	Lee	Massie	Lawther	Shawcross	McCarthy	
9/11			7,429	*6*	19			*Rackstraw 53*	*Liney*	*Lightowler*	*Cooper*	*Stowell*	*Hallett*	*Leighton*	*Hall*	*Ham*	*Rackstraw*	*Middleton*	*Walker*	
								Ref: D Fieldsend	A new season's best attendance at the Shay for this derby. It's an ill-tempered affair and the ref sees fit to book four players. City look to be heading for victory thanks to Charlie Rackstraw's sidefooted goal. But with the seconds ticking away Lawther crashes in McCarthy's corner.											
18	H	EXETER		8	W	2-1	1-1	Shawcross 2, Massie 54	Smith	Hampton	Buxton	Pickering	Nicholl	Meagan	**Flower**	Massie	Lawther	Shawcross	McCarthy	
23/11			3,186	*15*	21			*Whatling 1*	*Shearing*	*Smyth*	*Blain*	*Crawford*	*Harvey*	*Newman*	*Corr*	*Pleat*	*Kirkham*	*Curtis*	*Whatling*	
								Ref: V Batty	Alan Ball has just signed a new three-year contract, but probably hasn't reached the dug-out before Exeter's Keith Whatling strikes from close range. Shawcross's header is Town's swift reply. Massie pounces for 2-1. Pickering makes a desperate goal-line clearance to protect the lead.											
19	A	BRENTFORD		9	D	1-1	0-1	Hampton 81	Smith	Hampton	Buxton*	Pickering	Nicholl	Meagan	Flower	Massie	Lawther !	Shawcross	McCarthy	Wallace
30/11			*6,000*	*7*	22			*Mansley 35*	*Brodie*	*Nelmes*	*Jones*	*Hawley*	*Gelsop*	*Richardson*	*Neilson*	*Ross*	*Kirby*	*Fenton*	*Mansley*	
								Ref: C Thomas	Lawther becomes Town's 15th player to be sent off since the War, for remarks made to a linesman. Two minutes later Smith punches out but Alan Mansley heads the ball back. Nicholl has a goal ruled out but Town's ten men deservedly draw level when Flower crosses for Hampton.											
20	H	PORT VALE		7	W	2-1	2-0	Nicholl 35, Massie 38	Smith	Hampton	**Burgin**	Pickering	Nicholl	Wallace	Flower	Massie	Lawther	Shawcross	Lee	
21/12			3,806	*21*	24			*Chapman 56*	*Ball*	*Logan*	*Wilson*	*Goodfellow*	*Sproson*	*King*	*Gough*	*Chapman*	*Newton*	*Cullerton**	*Williams*	*James*
								Ref: A Bone/W Raine	The Shaymen move closer to the top but lowly Vale's luck is out. They feel Nicholl is offside when he crashes in the first, while Massie takes advantage of a deflection for the second. On the hard ground, referee Bone suffers cramp and is replaced by linesman Raine after 25 minutes.											
21	H	SCUNTHORPE		5	W	2-0	1-0	Lawther 71, Shawcross 87	Smith	Hampton	Burgin	Pickering	Nicholl	Wallace	Flower	Massie	Lawther	Shawcross	Lee	
26/12			7,268	*18*	26				*Barnard*	*Hemstead*	*Taylor*	*Davidson*	*Melbourne*	*Barker*	*Wilson*	*Kerr*	*Cassidy*	*Keegan*	*Punton*	
								Ref: D Pugh	The referee consults both managers before the game as the ground has frozen over. Ron Ashman doesn't want to play it and feels vindicated as both sets of players struggle. Town score twice, although Barnard is at fault for the second, allowing Shawcross' shot to slip through his hands.											
22	H	YORK		11	L	**0-4**	0-2	*[Boyer 80]*	Smith	Hampton	Burgin	Pickering	Nicholl	Wallace	Flower*	Massie	Lawther	Shawcross	McCarthy	Ryden
11/1			5,512	*19*	26			*Coleman 35, MacDougall 42, Carr 58,*	*Widdowson*	*Kelly*	*Richardson*	*Carr*	*Topping*	*Burrows*	*Taylor*	*Coleman*	*MacDougall*	*Hodgson*	*Boyer*	
								Ref: M Fussey	Alan Ball misses this defeat. He's spying on cup foes Stoke. York are getting into form and their victory is no fluke. Former Town star Archie Taylor takes the corner from which Ted MacDougall puts his side in firm control. Graham Carr's fierce volley could have gone anywhere.											
23	A	DONCASTER		9	D	0-0	0-0		Smith	Hampton	Burgin	Pickering	Nicholl	Wallace	Flower	Massie	Lawther	Shawcross*	McCarthy	Lee
14/1			*8,656*	*5*	27				*Ogston*	*Wilcockson*	*Clish*	*Flowers*	*Robertson*	*Haselden*	*Usher*	*Rabjohn*	*Webber*	*Jeffrey*	*Gilfillan*	
								Ref: D Laing	Lawrie McMenemy is building a Rovers side that is hard to beat. Town put the York nightmare behind them but they are hanging on. In the last ten minutes Stuart Robertson sees a header hit the top of the bar, then has a goal ruled out for pushing. Chris Nicholl gets his first booking.											

No	Date		Att	Pos	Pt	F-A	H-T	Scorers, Times, and Referees	1	2	3	4	5	6	7	8	9	10	11	12 sub used
24	A	BRADFORD C		9	D	1-1	1-0	Flower 18	Smith	Hampton*	Burgin	Pickering	Nicholl	Wallace	Flower	Massie	Lawther	Shawcross	McCarthy	Lee
	18/1		*7,917*	*11*	28			*Bannister 61*	*Liney*	*Atkins*	*Bayliss*	*Stowell*	*Hallett*	*Leighton*	*Hall*	*Ham*	*Rackstraw*	*Middleton*	*Bannister*	
								Ref: R Barker	The Shaymen's controlled performance isn't quite enough to earn victory in this thrilling derby. They take the lead when Flower prods the ball under Pat Liney. Bruce Bannister equalises following a corner. Shortly afterwards Liney has to react to keep out Lawther's long-range effort.											
25	H	CHESTER		10	D	0-0	0-0		Smith	Burgin	Meagan	Pickering	Nicholl	Wallace	Flower	Massie	Lawther	Shawcross	McCarthy	
	1/2		4,181	*7*	29				*Carling*	*Sear*	*Bennett*	*Ashworth*	*Turner*	*Sutton*	*Jones*	*Draper*	*Talbot*	*Brodie*	*Provan*	
								Ref: A Jones	It is questionable whether this game should be played at all. The pitch is a quagmire, and continuous rain, sleet and snow only makes it worse. Chances therefore are rare. The best opportunity falls to Flower late on but his deceptive cross is tipped over by much-travelled Terry Carling.											
26	A	PETERBOROUGH		8	D	0-0	0-0		Smith	Burgin	Meagan	Pickering	Nicholl	Wallace	Flower	Massie	Lawther	Shawcross	McCarthy	
	5/2		*5,618*	*18*	30				*Millington*	*Noble*	*Crawford*	*Wright*	*Wile*	*Iley*	*Hellawell*	*Comny*	*Hall*	*Thompson*	*Robson*	
								Ref: K Markham	The Posh were only relegated last season because of financial irregularities but they are finding the going tough. It's a rearranged game – the original fixture was abandoned after Mick Buxton broke a leg. Here, their player-manager Jim Iley has the best chance but Smith saves well.											
27	H	SOUTHEND		11	D	1-1	0-0	Nicholl 51	Smith	Burgin	Meagan	Pickering	Nicholl	Wallace	Flower	Massie	Lawther	Shawcross	**Robertson**	
	1/3		3,522	*10*	31			*Best 84*	*Roberts*	*Lindsey*	*Birks*	*Bentley*	*Beasley*	*Kurila*	*Clayton*	*Best*	*Moore*	*Hamilton*	*Chambers*	
								Ref: T Pallister	After a five-week lay-off Town return to action but play well below their best. Massie has a first-half effort ruled out. Lawther is offside. Chris Nicholl, however, heads in on-loan Robertson's free-kick. The points look safe until unmarked Billy Best makes the most of a lucky rebound.											
28	H	COLCHESTER		10	W	2-1	2-1	Pearson 30, Massie 33	Smith	Meagan	Burgin	Pickering	Nicholl	Wallace	Massie	Pearson	Lawther	Shawcross	McCarthy	
	4/3		3,400	*4*	33			*Shawcross 16 (og)*	*Macedo*	*Mochan*	*Hall*	*Brown**	*Bickles*	*Joslyn*	*Simpson*	*Oliver*	*Light*	*Gibbs*	*Dyson*	*Price*
								Ref: R Darlington	The Shay fans at last get to see former Busby Babe Mark Pearson start his first game – 50 weeks after he signed. His glancing header levels the scores. The tricky wind is responsible for Shawcross's headed own-goal. He makes amends, though by supplying the pass for Massie's winner.											
29	A	LINCOLN		11	D	0-0	0-0		Smith	Meagan	Burgin	Pickering	Nicholl	Robertson	Massie	Pearson*	Lawther	Shawcross	McCarthy	Wallace
	8/3		*6,974*	*4*	34				*McClelland*	*Taylor*	*Peden*	*Smith J*	*Harford*	*Grummett*	*Hughes**	*Hubbard*	*Jeffrey*	*Smith D*	*Lewis*	*Kearns*
								Ref: F Nicholson	Ron Gray's Imps side is going well but Alan Ball has his side well organised to cope. Alex Smith is the busier keeper but it's only routine stuff he has to deal with. Former Shayman Jim Smith is in the Lincoln side. In the last ten minutes Shawcross and Wallace nearly win it for Town.											
30	A	CHESTER		11	D	2-2	0-1	Lawther 82, Massie 88	Smith	Burgin	Meagan	Pickering	Nicholl	Robertson	Flower	Massie	Lawther	Shawcross	McCarthy	
	12/3		*4,277*	*5*	35			*Provan 3, Talbot 49*	*Carling*	*Jones R**	*Cheetham*	*Ashworth*	*Turner*	*Brodie*	*Dearden*	*Sutton*	*Talbot*	*Draper*	*Provan*	*Evans*
								Ref: S Kayley	Ken Roberts is disappointed to see his promotion hopefuls throw away a two-goal lead. Unmarked Drew Provan and Gary Talbot, intercepting McCarthy's backpass, put Chester in control. But Lawther slots home, and when Massie heads in at the far post Town's late show is complete.											
31	H	CHESTERFIELD		11	D	0-0	0-0		Smith	Hampton	Burgin	Pickering	Nicholl	Robertson	Flower	Massie	Lawther	Shawcross	McCarthy	
	25/3		4,377	*18*	36				*Humphreys*	*Hickton*	*Lumsden*	*Pugh*	*Moyes*	*Phelan*	*Moore*	*Randall*	*Moss*	*Wright*	*Bishop*	
								Ref: T Hill	There is concern that the Shaymen are not scoring enough goals. They've now scored only six in the last ten league games. Robertson skims the bar in the eighth minute, but that's as close as Town go. Hampton returns – and gets booked. Fortunately results elsewhere are favourable.											
32	A	DARLINGTON		10	W	1-0	0-0	Flower 71	Smith	Hampton	Burgin	Pickering	Nicholl	Robertson	Flower	Massie	Lawther	Shawcross	McCarthy	
	29/3		*5,081*	*8*	38				*Moor*	*Peverell*	*Chapman*	*Sproates*	*Albeson*	*Jacques*	*Lee*	*Melling*	*Robson*	*Solan*	*Gauden*	
								Ref: H Ellis	Tony Flower has a habit of scoring important goals. This one may prove priceless. Burgin makes it for him when he goes on a solo run. Massie is playing against his old club. He'd love to score and goes close when his 25-yarder hits the post with three minutes left. Robertson is booked.											
33	A	GRIMSBY			W	1-0	1-0	Massie 7	Smith	Hampton	Burgin	Pickering	Nicholl	Robertson	Flower	Massie	Lawther	Shawcross	McCarthy	
	4/4		*7,662*		40				*Macey*	*Worthington*	*Duncliffe*	*Kennedy*	*Jobling*	*Ross*	*Brace*	*Boylan*	*Walker*	*Hickman*	*Cockburn*	
								Ref: R Cussons	Grimsby's player-manager Bobby Kennedy tastes defeat for the first time in seven games since joining from Man City. Re-election for them is still a major concern. For Town, though, the promotion dream is still alive. But John Macey may feel he could have saved Massie's early drive.											
34	H	SWANSEA		7	W	2-1	0-1	Massie 81, Lawther 88	Smith	Hampton	Burgin	Pickering	Nicholl	Robertson	Flower	Massie	Lawther	Shawcross*	McCarthy	Wallace
	5/4		6,155	*11*	42			*Nurse 26*	*John*	*Lawrence*	*Gomersall*	*Williams A*	*Rosser*	*Nurse*	*Evans*	*Grey*	*Williams H*	*Screen*	*Slattery*	
								Ref: G Singleton	Welsh international Mel Nurse's extraordinary free-kick from the centre-circle, misjudged by Smith, gives Swansea something to protect. They defend resolutely, but victory is denied them in a frantic last nine minutes. Massie levels it and Lawther wins it, both goals made by McCarthy.											

No	Date	Opponent	Att	Pos	Res / Pts	F-A	H-T	Scorers, Times, and Referees	1	2	3	4	5	6	7	8	9	10	11	12 sub used
35	H	WORKINGTON		6	W	3-0	1-0	Shawcross 36, Flower 68, Lawther 70	Smith	Hampton	Burgin	Pickering	Nicholl	Robertson	Flower	Massie	Lawther	Shawcross*	McCarthy	Wallace
	7/4		6,965	*11*	44			D Laing	*Williams*	*Geidmintis*	*Wilson*	*Spratt*	*Ogilvie*	*Flynn*	*Traill*	*Tyrer*	*Barlow*	*Graham*	*Holliday*	
									Workington have drifted out of the promotion race. They will say bad luck has hampered them. Like here. Flower's shot for 2-0 takes a wicked deflection off Ogilvie. Then Lawther charges Mike Williams when he takes a long-range effort. The linesman flags that he's crossed the line.											
36	A	WREXHAM		7	D	2-2	2-0	Lawther 8, 23	Smith	Hampton	Burgin	Pickering	Nicholl	Robertson	Flower	Massie	Lawther	Shawcross	McCarthy	
	12/4		*3,443*	*13*	45			*Tinnion 52, Griffiths 80* Ref: R Kirkpatrick	*Reeves*	*Bermingham*	*Mason*	*Bradbury*	*May*	*Griffiths*	*Moir*	*Beanland*	*Smith*	*Tinnion*	*Kinsey*	
									The ref threatens to abandon this game because of the strong wind. The elements make it a real game of two halves. With the wind, Lawther's two headers give Town a cushion. It isn't enough as Wrexham claw it back. Town live on their nerves in the last twenty minutes but hold out.											
37	H	GRIMSBY		7	D	0-0	0-0		Smith	Hampton	Burgin	Pickering	Nicholl	Robertson	Flower	Massie	Lawther	Shawcross	McCarthy	
	15/4		6,492	*23*	46			Ref: A Morrissey	*Wainman*	*Worthington*	*Duncliffe*	*Campbell*	*Rathbone*	*Jobling*	*Brace*	*Boylen*	*Hickman*	*Ross*	*Housley*	
									Halifax Town chairman Alan Maden praises the supporters for turning out in numbers. They expect to see their side walk over the struggling Mariners. Town actually do, having 90% of the play, but only Massie goes close. He hits the post and has another effort scrambled off the line.											
38	H	NEWPORT		6	W	3-0	1-0	Massie 41, 62, 69	Smith	Hampton	Burgin	Pickering	Nicholl	Robertson	Flower	Massie	Lawther	Shawcross	McCarthy	
	19/4		6,445	*21*	48			Ref: R Barker	*Miles*	*McLaughlin*	*King*	*Deacy*	*Wood*	*Rowland*	*Jones B*	*Cooper*	*McClelland*	*Hill*	*Hamilton*	
									Like Grimsby, Bobby Ferguson's Newport are struggling at the wrong end of the table. A goal down, they cause Halifax a few problems until Massie crashes the ball into the roof of the net to kill off their challenge. Massie scores his fourth career hat-trick and second against Newport.											
39	A	COLCHESTER		6	D	0-0	0-0		Smith	Hampton	Burgin	Pickering	Nicholl	Robertson	Flower	Massie	Lawther	Shawcross	McCarthy	
	21/4		*7,429*	*2*	49			Ref: R Spittle	*Macedo*	*Mochan*	*Hall*	*Honeywood*	*Bickles*	*Wood*	*Brown*	*Oliver*	*Light*	*Gibbs*	*Prince*	
									A terrific defensive performance gains Town a point and prevents Dick Graham's side from scoring at home for the first time since August. Alex Smith is in fine form and the only time he is beaten, Hampton manages to clear off the line. The whistle-happy ref awards 38 free-kicks.											
40	A	EXETER		6	L	1-2	0-2	Flower	Smith	Hampton	Burgin	Pickering	Nicholl	Robertson*	Flower	Massie	Lawther	Shawcross	McCarthy	Wallace
	24/4		*6,432*	*14*	49			*Banks, Binney* Ref: L Callaghan	*Shearing*	*Crawford*	*Blain*	*Curtis*	*Newman*	*Balson*	*Corr*	*Banks*	*Wingate*	*Binney*	*Pleat*	
									Town pay the penalty for a slack first-half performance. They allow Allan Banks and Fred Binney to put Exeter firmly in control. Flower pulls one back with a shot that rebounds into play off the back stanchion. Peter Shearing's fantastic save from Nicholl's header denies Town a point.											
41	H	BRENTFORD		5	W	2-0	1-0	Flower 16, Lawther 73	Smith	Hampton*	Burgin	Pickering	Nicholl	Wallace	Flower	Massie	Lawther	Shawcross	McCarthy	Robertson
	28/4		6,948	*17*	51			Ref: S Kayley	*Phillips*	*Jones*	*Renwick*	*Nelmes*	*Gelson*	*Higginson*	*Dobson**	*Richardson*	*Ross*	*Fenton*	*Mansley*	*Neilson*
									The Shaymen get their promotion surge back on track. Chris Nicholl, who is catching the eye of bigger clubs, uses his head to set up both goals for Flower and Lawther. Lowly Brentford have a lucky let-off when Lawther amazingly balances the ball on his head before hitting the post.											
42	A	ROCHDALE		5	L	0-1	0-1		Smith	Burgin	Meagan	Pickering	Nicholl	Wallace	Flower*	Massie	Lawther	Shawcross	McCarthy	Robertson
	30/4		***13,266***	*2*	51			*Butler 30* Ref: G Jones	*Harker*	*Smith*	*Ryder*	*Leech*	*Parry*	*Radcliffe*	*Whitehead*	*Rudd*	*Melledew*	*Jenkins*	*Butler*	
									This game attracts Dale's biggest crowd of the season. It's gripping stuff, won by Dennis Butler's goal that goes in off the post. Town deserve a draw. Wallace and Shawcross both hit the post and they are denied a penalty for hands. They end with ten men when Wallace is carried off.											
43	H	ALDERSHOT		4	W	1-0	1-0	Lawther 20	Smith	Burgin	Meagan	Pickering	Nicholl	Wallace	Flower	Massie	Lawther	Shawcross	McCarthy	
	3/5		6,596	*13*	53			Ref: D Turner	*Dickie*	*Walden*	*Lloyd*	*Newman*	*Rafferty*	*Walker*	*Walton*	*Priscott*	*Howarth*	*Melia*	*Gowans*	
									Despite having former Liverpool and England schemer Jimmy Melia in their side, Aldershot slip to their tenth defeat in 13 games. It's a headed goal by Lawther that keeps Town in the promotion frame. Massie later hits the bar. Smith has to be at his best to keep out Melia and Gowans.											
44	A	YORK		3	D	0-0	0-0		Smith	Burgin	Meagan	Pickering	Nicholl	Wallace	Flower*	Massie	Lawther	Shawcross	McCarthy	Robertson
	5/5		*3,829*	*21*	54			Ref: R Harper/W Johnston	*Andrews*	*Sibbald*	*Kelly*	*Carr*	*Jackson*	*Topping*	*Taylor**	*Hodgson*	*MacDougall*	*Hewitt*	*Boyer*	*Pennick*
									While the point here nudges Town a little nearer to Division Three, the tragic death of referee Roy Harper puts things into perspective. After only eight minutes he collapses and dies later in the dressing room. The game is held up for six minutes. Linesman Bill Johnston takes over.											
45	H	ROCHDALE		2	W	1-0	0-0	Massie 76	Smith	Burgin	Meagan	Pickering	Nicholl	Wallace	Robertson	Massie	Lawther	Shawcross	McCarthy	
	8/5		**17,186**	*3*	56			Ref: J Hunting	*Harker*	*Smith*	*Ryder*	*Leech*	*Parry*	*Ashworth*	*Whitehead*	*Rudd**	*Melledew*	*Jenkins*	*Butler*	*Buck*
									The Shaymen are promoted! Les Massie's header, meeting McCarthy's cross beyond the far post, breaks the deadlock. It is a defining moment and the Shay erupts. At times the tension is unbearable, so the game is no classic. On the final whistle, boss Alan Ball leads the celebrations.											
46	A	BRADFORD PA		2	D	0-0	0-0		Smith	Hampton	Burgin	Meagan	Pickering	Wallace	Flower	Massie	Lawther	Shawcross*	McCarthy	Pearson
	12/5		*6,112*	*24*	57			Ref: J Thacker	*Hardie*	*Hudson*	*Singleton*	*Atkinson*	*Hawkins*	*Dolan*	*Clancy*	*Robinson*	*Andrews*	*Henderson*	*Saville*	
	Home		Away						A case of after the Lord Mayor's Show. The Avenue were long condemned to bottom spot – they will lose their League status next year – and the Shaymen can't raise their game. Bradford's Trevor Atkinson provides the game's highlight – an overhead kick that bounces onto the bar.											
Average	5,684		6,023																	

LEAGUE DIVISION 4 (CUP-TIES) Manager: Alan Ball (Snr) SEASON 1968-69

League Cup						F-A	H-T	Scorers, Times, and Referees	1	2	3	4	5	6	7	8	9	10	11	12 sub used
1	H	HULL			L	0-3	0-1		Smith	Russell	Hampton	Meagan	Pickering	Shawcross	Ryden	Massie	Morris*	Wallace	McCarthy	Buxton
14/8			4,493	*2:*				*Wagstaffe 37, Chilton 80, Wilkinson 87*	*McKechnie*	*Greenwood*	*Beardsley*	*Jarvis*	*Simkin*	*Pettit*	*Wilkinson*	*Wagstaffe*	*Chilton*	*Houghton*	*Butler I*	
								Ref: R Darlington	Dave Wagstaffe cost Hull £40,000 four years ago. He's been a good investment. He breaks clear for the first goal, but the Tigers can't just rely on him. Town have chances to level it, but the tie goes away from them with Chris Chilton's lob. Late on Wagstaffe crosses for Bill Wilkinson.											

FA Cup																				
1	A	BILSTON		10	W	3-1	0-0	Massie 60, Flower 78, Lawther 81	Smith	Hampton	Buxton	Pickering	Nicholl	Meagan	Flower	Massie	Lawther	Shawcross	McCarthy	
16/11			*4,300*	*WML*				*Silwood 61p*	*Barnsley*	*Price*	*Dowen*	*Dyke*	*Davies*	*Webb*	*Haywood*	*Silwood*	*Foggartly*	*Duckhouse*	*Wright*	
								Ref: R Barker	Plucky Bilston elected to keep this game at their Queen Street ground. Silwood's penalty for hands cuts short Town's celebrations after Massie scores the opener. This makes things interesting but fitness tells in the end. Flower scores from ten yards, then Lawther heads under Barnsley.											
2	H	CREWE		9	D	1-1	0-1	Wallace 81	Smith	Hampton	Buxton	Pickering	Nicholl	Meagan	Flower	Massie	Lawther	Shawcross	McCarthy*	Wallace
7/12			6,636	*3:22*				*Hallett 3*	*Mailey*	*Lowry*	*Leigh*	*Stott*	*Barnes*	*Gannon*	*Ratcliffe*	*McHale*	*Hallett*	*Inglis*	*Tarbuck*	
								Ref: R Tinkler	Crewe are struggling in Division Three but Ball says that only Town's best will do. Maybe, but it only earns them a replay. Hallett breaks through early on, but when Town lose McCarthy before half-time it isn't such bad news. Substitute Wallace equalises after Flower's fine run.											
2R	A	CREWE		*9*	W	3-1	0-1	Shawcross 88p, 100, Massie 101	Smith	Hampton	Buxton	Pickering	Nicholl	Meagan*	Flower	Massie	Lawther	Shawcross	Lee	Pearson
11/12			*7,625*	*3:22*		*aet*		*Hallett 13*	*Mailey*	*Lowry*	*Leigh*	*Stott*	*Barnes*	*Gannon*	*Ratcliffe*	*McHale*	*Hallett**	*Inglis*	*Tarbuck*	*Bradshaw*
								Ref: R Tinkler	Town do it the hard way. Meagan's misplaced pass allows Keith Stott to set up Hallett for the opener. Town get a lifeline when Kevin McHale handles late on. Shawcross nets the penalty, and in extra-time two goals in a minute from Shawcross, again, and Massie seal a memorable win.											
3	A	SWANSEA		5	W	1-0	0-0	Massie 70	Smith	Hampton	Burgin	Pickering	Nicholl	Wallace	Flower	Massie	Lawther	Shawcross	McCarthy	
4/1			*9,726*	*11*					*John*	*Lawrence*	*Gomersall*	*Thomas*	*Williams A*	*Slee*	*Evans*	*Williams H*	*Biggs*	*Screen*	*Gwyther*	
								Ref: D Corbett	Billy Lucas' side should be favourites but Swansea are sadly missing skipper Mel Nurse. The pitch is heavy and greasy but as it happens Town master the conditions well. Victory actually looks easy. Les Massie decides it with a diving header at the far post from Flower's accurate cross.											
4	A	STOKE		9	D	1-1	0-0	Massie 83	Smith	Burgin	Meagan	Pickering	Nicholl	Wallace	Flower	Massie	Lawther	Shawcross	McCarthy	
25/1			*30,109*	*1:17*				*Dobing 80*	*Banks*	*Marsh*	*Elder*	*Skeels*	*Bloor*	*Bernard*	*Eastham*	*Herd*	*Conroy*	*Dobing*	*Burrows*	
								Ref: R Tinkler	This is Halifax Town's greatest away performance in years. Peter Dobing thinks he's won it for Stoke with his late goal, but McCarthy's long throw leads to Massie's equaliser. With two minutes left Massie has a clear run on goal, but Banks shows why he is England's Number One.											
4R	H	STOKE			L	0-3	0-1		Smith	Burgin	Meagan	Pickering	Nicholl	Wallace	Flower	Massie	Lawther	Shawcross	McCarthy	
28/1			24,891	*1:17*				*Burrows 27, Conroy 48, 82*	*Banks*	*Marsh*	*Elder*	*Bernard*	*Bloor*	*Skeels*	*Eastham*	*Dobing*	*Conroy*	*Herd*	*Burrows*	
								Ref: R Tinkler	Class tells and Stoke make no mistake this time. Harry Burrows sees a gap in the defensive wall and fires in a fierce low shot that gives Smith no chance. The tie is virtually over just after half-time when Terry Conroy gets free to fire in. For Town the carnival is now well and truly over											

		Home					Away					
	P	W	D	L	F	A	W	D	L	F	A	Pts
1 Doncaster	46	13	8	2	42	16	8	9	6	23	22	59
2 HALIFAX	46	15	5	3	36	18	5	12	6	17	19	57
3 Rochdale	46	14	7	2	47	11	4	13	6	21	24	56
4 Bradford C	46	11	10	2	36	18	7	10	6	29	28	56
5 Darlington	46	11	6	6	40	26	6	12	5	22	19	52
6 Colchester	46	12	8	3	31	17	8	4	11	26	36	52
7 Southend	46	15	3	5	51	21	4	10	9	27	40	51
8 Lincoln	46	13	6	4	38	19	4	11	8	16	33	51
9 Wrexham	46	13	7	3	41	22	5	7	11	20	30	50
10 Swansea T	46	11	8	4	35	20	8	3	12	23	34	49
11 Brentford	46	12	7	4	40	24	6	5	12	24	41	48
12 Workington	46	8	11	4	24	17	7	6	10	16	26	47
13 Port Vale	46	12	8	3	33	15	4	6	13	13	31	46
14 Chester	46	12	4	7	43	24	4	9	10	33	42	45
15 Aldershot	46	13	3	7	42	23	6	4	13	24	43	45
16 Scunthorpe U	46	10	5	8	28	22	8	3	12	33	38	44
17 Exeter	46	11	8	4	45	24	5	3	15	21	41	43
18 Peterborough	46	8	9	6	32	23	5	7	11	28	34	42
19 Notts Co	46	10	8	5	33	22	2	10	11	15	35	42
20 Chesterfield	46	7	7	9	24	22	6	8	9	19	28	41
21 York	46	12	8	3	36	25	2	3	18	17	50	39
22 Newport	46	9	9	5	31	26	2	5	16	18	48	36
23 Grimsby	46	5	7	11	25	31	4	8	11	22	38	33
24 Bradford PA	46	5	8	10	19	34	0	2	21	13	72	20
	1104	262	170	120	852	520	120	170	262	520	852	1104

Odds & ends

Double wins: (3) Aldershot, Notts Co, Scunthorpe.
Double losses: (0).

Won from behind: (6) Colchester (h), Exeter (h), Peterborough (h), Swansea (h), Notts Co (a), Crewe (a) (FAC).
Lost from in front: (1) Southend (a).

High spots: 17 league games unbeaten up to 21 April.
Four consecutive league victories up to 7 April.
Beating champions-elect Doncaster 4-1.
Reaching 4th Round of the FA Cup.
Drawing at 1st Division Stoke in the FA Cup.

Low spots: Consecutive defeats in August and September.
Losing 0-4 at home to Darlington and York.

Town drew 8 out of 9 games (January through to March).
Halifax's final total of 57 points set a new club record for two points for a win.
22 points were gained away from home - a club record.

Player of the Year: Phil McCarthy.
Ever-presents: (3) John Pickering, David Shawcross, Alex Smith.
Hat-tricks: Les Massie (1).
Leading scorer: Les Massie (19).

	Appearances						Goals			
	Lge	*Sub*	LC	*Sub*	FAC	*Sub*	**Lge**	LC	FAC	**Tot**
Burgin, Andy	**27**				3					
Buxton, Mick	**18**			*1*	3					
Flower, Tony	**26**				6		**5**		1	**6**
Hampton, Ivan	**34**		1		4		**1**			**1**
Lawther, Ian	**45**				6		**14**		1	**15**
Lee, Jeff	**10**	*3*			1					
McCarthy, Phil	**42**		1		5		**4**			**4**
Massie, Les	**45**		1		6		**15**		4	**19**
Meagan, Mick	**23**		1		5					
Morris, Elf	**3**		1							
Nicholl, Chris	**39**				6		**3**			**3**
Parry, David	**2**									
Pearson, Mark	**2**	*3*				*1*	**1**			**1**
Pickering, John	**46**		1		6					
Robertson, Lammie	**14**	*3*								
Russell, Malcolm	**1**		1							
Ryden, Hugh	**14**	*1*	1				**2**			**2**
Shawcross, David	**46**		1		6		**7**		2	**9**
Smith, Alex	**46**		1		6					
Wallace, Bob	**23**	*7*	1		3	*1*	**1**		1	**2**
20 players used	**506**	***17***	**11**	***1***	**66**	***2***	**53**		**9**	**62**

No	Date		Att	Pos	Pt	F-A	H-T	Scorers, Times, and Referees	1	2	3	4	5	6	7	8	9	10	11	12 sub used
1	H	SHREWSBURY			W	1-0	1-0	Shawcross 34	Smith	Wallace	Burgin	**Lennard**	Pickering	Robertson	Flower	Shawcross	Lawther	**Hill**	McCarthy	
	9/8		5,926		2				*Phillips*	*Fellows*	*Loska*	*Moore*	*Dolby*	*Clapham*	*Roberts*	*Meredith*	*Harkin*	*Hawkins**	*McLaughlin*	*Moir*
								Ref: F Nicholson	Halifax Town's return to Division Three begins with this competent, if unspectacular, display against Harry Gregg's Shrews side. The game is settled by Shawcross' chipped goal after Hill touches an indirect free-kick to him. The club shows concern over the 'disappointing' attendance.											
2	A	ORIENT		16	L	0-1	0-1		Smith	Wallace	Burgin	Lennard*	Nicholl	Robertson	Flower	Shawcross	Lawther	Hill	McCarthy	Pickering
	16/8		*6,027*	*1*	2			*Bullock 6*	*Goddard*	*Jones*	*Rofe*	*Taylor*	*Mancini*	*Harper*	*Slater*	*Bullock*	*Allen*	*Dyson*	*Brabrook*	
								Ref: J Hunting	Mickey Bullock hooks the ball into the net early on, but over the ensuing 84 minutes his side is decidedly second best. How Town fail to win is anyone's guess. Orient's young keeper, Ray Goddard, who has an outstanding match, is one reason. Hill sees him push his shot onto the post.											
3	H	BRADFORD C		11	D	0-0	0-0		Smith	Wallace	Burgin	Lennard	Nicholl	Robertson	Ryden	Shawcross	Lawther	Hill	McCarthy	
	23/8		**10,274**	*3*	3				*Liney*	*Atkins*	*Cooper*	*Stowell*	*Swallow*	*Leighton*	*Hall*	*Ham*	*Corner*	*McConnell*	*Bannister*	
								Ref: R Paine	Questions are being asked by the Shay faithful as to why the club has sold Les Massie to The Avenue. This goalless derby game adds fuel to their argument. The Bantams followed Town up into Division Three so a tight game is expected. With few chances created that is what we get.											
4	A	LUTON		11	D	1-1	1-1	Hill 28	Smith	Wallace	Burgin	Pickering	Nicholl	Robertson	Ryden*	Lennard	Lawther	Hill	McCarthy	Shawcross
	26/8		*13,759*	*1*	4			*Macdonald 5*	*Read*	*Ryan*	*Bannister*	*Keen*	*Slough*	*Moore*	*Collins*	*Macdonald*	*Lewis**	*Allen*	*French*	*Sheffield*
								Ref: R Spittle	Luton boss Harry Haslem sees his side go top. But evidently he feels his team needs strengthening. So impressed is he with the performance of Town's Chris Nicholl that he buys him after the match. This overshadows a fine Town performance. Aggrieved supporters' letters pour in.											
5	A	BRISTOL ROV		14	L	0-2	0-1		Smith	Wallace	Burgin	Lennard	Pickering	Robertson	Lee*	Hill	Lawther	Shawcross	McCarthy	Cullen
	30/8		*11,768*	*3*	4			*Jarman 17, 86p*	*Sheppard*	*Roberts*	*Parsons*	*Marsland*	*Taylor*	*Munro*	*Graydon*	*Jones W*	*Stubbs*	*Jones R*	*Jarman*	
								Ref: R Barker	Town are to lodge a complaint to British Railways after their travelling arrangements to Bristol are upset. More pressing matters concern their injury list – amateur Cullen makes the numbers up. Town are still in the hunt until Harold Jarman's second, a penalty, conceded by Robertson.											
6	H	STOCKPORT		12	W	1-0	1-0	Burgin 38	Smith	Wallace	Burgin	Lennard	Pickering	Robertson	Flower	Hill	Lawther	Shawcross	McCarthy	
	6/9		4,927	*23*	6				*Ogley*	*Haydock*	*Bebbington*	*Griffiths*	*Low*	*Goodwin*	*Hartle*	*Rowlands*	*Morton*	*Chapman*	*Elgin*	
								Ref: R Johnson	On this showing it is clear why Walter Galbraith's Stockport are struggling, but the Shaymen make hard work of it. They do manage their third league goal, although it is scored by a full-back, Andy Burgin. Some fans are drifting away when Alan Ogley saves three close-range headers.											
7	A	PLYMOUTH		14	L	0-1	0-1		Smith	Wallace	Burgin	Lennard	Pickering	Robertson	Flower	Shawcross	Lawther	Hill	McCarthy	
	13/9		*9,070*	*13*	6			*Sullivan 63*	*Dunne*	*Reeves*	*Sullivan*	*Lean*	*Molyneux*	*Hore*	*Shepherd*	*Piper*	*Burnside*	*Reynolds*	*Hutchins*	
								Ref: R Davey	This time it's Argyle's full-back Colin Sullivan who settles this one. Thirty yards out and with no one to pass to, he powers a shot at goal and startled Smith never moves. Town have chances, the best of which sees Lennard overrun the ball in the dying minutes with just Dunne to beat.											
8	H	FULHAM		16	L	**0-8**	0-4	*[Conway 45p, 60]*	Smith	Wallace	Burgin	Lennard	Pickering	Robertson	Flower	Hill	Lawther	Shawcross	McCarthy	
	16/9		5,809	*10*	6			*Earle 13, 31, 46, 61, 67, Lloyd 30,*	*Seymour*	*Brown*	*Callaghan*	*Horne*	*Matthewson*	*Richardson*	*Conway*	*Lloyd*	*Earle*	*Haynes**	*Barrett*	*Roberts*
								Ref: D Laing	Ball must know something. Before the game he says, 'When this Fulham side really gets going someone is going to get such a hiding.' But he surely never meant this. The Shay fans get to see the legendary Johnny Haynes, but it's the name of Steve Earle they won't forget in a hurry.											
9	H	DONCASTER		15	D	1-1	1-0	Lawther 3	Smith	Burgin	McCarthy	Lennard	Pickering	Robertson	Flower	Wallace	Lawther	Shawcross	Hill	
	20/9		5,875	*8*	7			*Johnson 78*	*Clarke*	*Wilcockson*	*Gray*	*Flowers*	*Robertson*	*Haselden*	*Rabjohn*	*Regan*	*Marsden**	*Johnson*	*Usher*	*Watson*
								Ref: C Robinson	Ball tells his players, 'Forget Fulham.' Hill plays Lawther in for his early goal and Wilcockson later heads Flower's pile-driver onto the bar. But keeper Alex Smith seems to be suffering a hangover. With twelve minutes left he drops a clanger – literally – and Rod Johnson equalises.											
10	A	BOURNEMOUTH		15	D	0-0	0-0		Smith	Burgin	McCarthy	Lennard	Pickering	Robertson	Ryden	Wallace	Lawther	Lee	Hill	
	27/9		*5,727*	*19*	8				*Jones*	*Gulliver*	*White*	*Summerhill*	*Stocks*	*Foote*	*Bumstead**	*Meredith*	*Hold*	*MacDougall*	*Powell*	*Rowles*
								Ref: B Daniels	Cherries boss Freddie Cox knows a thing or two. He parted with £10,000 during the close season to recruit York's goalgetter Ted MacDougall. But Town centre-half Pickering has him sewn up. Halifax work hard and almost nick it with Ian Lawther's flicked header off Ryden's corner.											
11	A	BARROW		13	W	1-0	0-0	Shawcross 90	Smith	Burgin	McCarthy	Lennard	Pickering	Robertson	Ryden	Wallace*	Lawther	Lee	Hill	Shawcross
	29/9		*3,512*	*24*	10				*Else*	*Hollis*	*Davis*	*Ellison*	*Arrowsmith*	*Hartland*	*McArthur*	*Morrin*	*Street*	*Brown*	*Garbett*	
								Ref: A Morrissey	The chances of this game being a high-scoring one are virtually nil. Town and Barrow have only scored nine league goals between them. And it appears that a scoreless draw is what we're going to get until the outstanding Hill sets up Shawcross for a simple goal – with 25 seconds left.											

No	Venue	Opponent	Att	Pos	Pt	F-A	H-T	Scorers, Times, and Referees	1	2	3	4	5	6	7	8	9	10	11	12 sub used
12	H	BURY		12	W	2-0	2-0	Robertson 13, Ryden 39	Smith	Burgin	McCarthy	**Turnbull**	Pickering	Robertson	Ryden	Lee	Lawther	Lennard	Hill	
		4/10	4,934	*18*	12				*Ramsbottom*	*Eccleshare*	*Tinney*	*Turner*	*Lyon*	*Parry*	*Farrell*	*Jones*	*Arrowsmith**	*Towers*	*Kerr*	*Grundy*
								Ref: G Lewis	Struggling Bury have recently sacked Jack Marshall and replaced him with Les Hart. He's clearly got a big job on, as Town manage to expose the frailties of his side. Except for keeper Ramsbottom, who keeps the score down. Even he can't prevent Robertson scoring his first-ever goal.											
13	H	ORIENT			D	1-1	1-1	Lawther 35	Smith	Burgin	McCarthy*	Turnbull	Pickering	Robertson	Ryden	Lee	Lawther	Lenard	Hill	Shawcross
		7/10	4,367		13			*Bullock 37*	*Bowtell*	*Jones*	*Rofe*	*Taylor*	*Mancini*	*Parmenter*	*Bullock*	*Fairbrother*	*Allen*	*Dyson*	*Brabrook**	*Plume*
								Ref: D Pugh	Jimmy Bloomfield's Orient have only lost one game out of thirteen. They will go on to win the division. Therefore Town must be happy with a point. Lawther's header gives them the lead but the O's respond through Mick Bullock within a minute after his header comes back off the bar.											
14	A	WALSALL		15	L	1-2	1-0	Lawther 25	Smith	Burgin	Lee	Turnbull	Pickering	Robertson	Ryden	Lennard	Lawther	Shawcross	Hill	
		11/10	*6,328*	*13*	13			*Jones 65, Taylor 70*	*Parkes*	*Gregg*	*Harrison*	*Atthey*	*Jones*	*Trevis*	*Morris**	*Bennett*	*Woodward*	*Train*	*Taylor*	*Crowe*
								Ref: N Graham	For the second time in five days Lawther gives Town the lead with another header, only for his side to lose it. Shawcross fluffs a chance with just Phil Parkes to beat and rues that miss when Stan Jones equalises. Colin Taylor then dispossesses Burgin and his shot slips under Smith.											
15	A	TORQUAY		13	W	1-0	0-0	Ryden 88	**Connaughton**	Wallace	Burgin	Turnbull	Pickering	Robertson	Ryden	Lennard	Lawther	Shawcross	Hill	
		18/10	*7,732*	*3*	15				*Donnelly*	*Sandercock*	*Glozier*	*Joy*	*Kitchener*	*Dunne*	*Welsh*	*Cave*	*Binney*	*Mitchinson*	*Scott*	
								Ref: K Wynn	For the first time in his career Alex Smith is dropped following a series of inept performances. 19-year-old John Connaughton comes in on loan from Man Utd and plays a blinder to keep high-flying Torquay at bay. Ryden then silences the crowd with his goal when Hill sets him up.											
16	H	MANSFIELD		15	L	1-2	1-0	Shawcross 5	Connaughton	Wallace*	Burgin	Turnbull	Pickering	Robertson	Ryden	Lennard	Lawther	Shawcross	Hill	**Verity**
		25/10	3,625	*9*	15			*Keeley 63, Jones 90*	*Hollins*	*Pate*	*Walker*	*Stenson!*	*Boam*	*Keeley*	*Hopkinson*	*Partridge*	*Jones*	*Roberts*	*Bates*	
								Ref: M Kerkhof	Referee Kerkhof is the centre of attention when he finds seven minutes of injury-time, during which Dai Jones heads the winner. What makes things worse is that a mediocre Stags side ends with only ten men, John Stenson having been sent off for tripping Wallace in the 80th minute.											
17	A	BARNSLEY		17	L	0-2	0-2		Connaughton	Wallace	Burgin	Turnbull	Pickering	Lee	Ryden*	Lennard	Lawther	Shawcross	Hill	Flower
		1/11	*13,229*	*3*	15			*Boardman 23, Pickering 28 (og)*	*Arblaster*	*Murphy*	*Booth*	*Bettany*	*Winstanley*	*Howard*	*Earnshaw*	*Boardman*	*Loyden*	*Evans*	*Hamstead*	
								Ref: R Darlington	Alan Ball receives a death-threat before the game. A letter says that he will be killed with a cyanide-tipped dart. Ball sits in the directors box, flanked by plainclothes policemen. Town see plenty of the ball but go two goals down when Pickering inadvertently turns in Earnshaw's cross.											
18	H	ROCHDALE		16	W	3-1	1-0	Lennard 23, 90, Hill 85	Smith	Burgin	McCarthy	Turnbull	Pickering	Wallace	Ryden	Lennard	Lawther	Atkins	Hill	
		8/11	6,557	*2*	17			*Buck 51*	*Harker*	*Smith*	*Ryder*	*Ashworth*	*Parry*	*Leech*	*Whitehead*	*Rudd*	*Buck*	*Jenkins*	*Butler*	
								Ref: D Corbett	Smith is recalled and Big Bill Atkins returns to the fold. Dale are lying second and looking for a ninth successive victory. With six minutes left Dennis Butler blazes over the bar. Within a minute his side is behind when Hill fires in. Lennard's second is virtually the last kick of the game.											
19	H	TRANMERE		18	D	2-2	1-0	Hill 12, Atkins 85	Smith	Burgin	McCarthy	Lennard	Pickering	Robertson	Flower	Wallace	Lawther	Atkins	Hill	
		22/11	3,727	*13*	18			*Smith 58, Beamish 68*	*Thomas*	*Storton S*	*Dempsey*	*King*	*Storton T*	*Brodie*	*Beamish*	*Scott**	*Yardley*	*Smith*	*Crossley*	*Pritchard*
								Ref: A Matthewson	Bill Atkins rescues Town a point, and, but for a daring last-minute save at the feet of Lawther by Kevin Thomas, they might have won. After Hill scores Town slump badly. Alex Smith is at fault for the equaliser, when he fails to cut out Yardley's cross from which Derek Smith scores.											
20	H	SOUTHPORT		13	W	1-0	1-0	Atkins 15	Smith	Burgin	Lee	Lennard	Pickering	Robertson	Flower	Wallace	Lawther	Atkins	Hill	
		6/12	3,028	*21*	20				*Armstrong*	*Pearson*	*Alty*	*Peat*	*Dunleavy*	*Harrison*	*McCarthy*	*Field*	*Redrobe*	*Russell A*	*Pring*	
								Ref: P Baldwin	Don McEvoy was in charge when Town were relegated in 1963. This time he will take Southport down. Atkins' strike, after Dunleavy fails to clear, is enough for Town. Lawther hits the bar, but though they deserve to win, Town are relieved to see Peat's last-gasp effort hit the post.											
21	H	PLYMOUTH		11	W	2-0	2-0	Holmes 30, Lawther 38	Smith	Burgin	Lee	Lennard	Pickering	Robertson	Holmes	Wallace	Lawther	Atkins	Hill	
		13/12	3,619	*20*	22				*Clamp*	*Piper*	*Sullivan*	*Lean*	*Foster*	*Hore*	*Davey*	*Rickard*	*Burnside*	*Bickle*	*Maher*	
								Ref: R Barker	Argyle boss Billy Bingham, also manager of the Northern Ireland national side, gives debuts to keeper Martin Clamp and Derek Rickard. But it's Town's Barry Holmes, recalled to the side after two years, who makes the biggest impact. He scores the opener in this comfortable win.											
22	A	BRADFORD C			L	1-2	0-1	Atkins 82	Smith	Burgin	Lee !	Lennard	Pickering	Robertson	Holmes	Wallace*	Lawther	Atkins	Hill	Shawcross
		26/12	*14,295*		22			*Hallett 42, Bannister 88p*	*Liney*	*Atkins*	*Cooper**	*Stowell*	*Hallett*	*McConnell*	*Hall*	*Ham*	*Corner*	*Bannister*	*Middleton*	*Bayliss*
								Ref: D Laing	It all happens in this heated derby. Smith is impeded when Hallett nets the opener. He later saves a penalty from Ian Cooper. Atkins equalises late on, but Bannister scores a penalty when Bobby Ham takes a tumble. A minute later Jeff Lee is sent off for a retaliatory tackle on Ham.											
23	H	BRISTOL ROV		16	D	1-1	0-0	Shawcross 48	Smith	Burgin	Lee	Lennard	Pickering	Robertson	Holmes*	Wallace	Lawther	Shawcross	Hill	Verity
		27/12	5,388	*8*	23			*Taylor 60*	*Sheppard*	*Ford*	*Munro*	*Marsland*	*Taylor S*	*Prince*	*Graydon**	*Jones B*	*Jones R*	*Gilbert*	*Higgins*	*Stanton*
								Ref: A Bone	Shawcross makes a welcome return to the side after eight weeks out by crashing in a free-kick. Rovers' Ray Graydon disputes the award and gets booked. But as the pitch starts to freeze over, it is Graydon who supplies the cross from which Stuart Taylor nets the deserved equaliser.											

No		Date	Att	Pos	Pt	F-A	H-T	Scorers, Times, and Referees	1	2	3	4	5	6	7	8	9	10	11	12 sub used
24	A	DONCASTER		14	W	1-0	0-0	Shawcross 66	Smith	Burgin	Lee	Lennard	Pickering	Robertson	Verity	Shawcross	Lawther	Atkins	Hill	
		10/1	6,365	9	25				Ogston	Branfoot	Clish	Flowers*	Bird	Haselden	Irvine	Gilfillan	Briggs	Johnson	Usher	Sheffield
								Ref: J Quinn	This game is in doubt thirty minutes before kick-off, as thick fog envelopes the ground. The ref elects to play and as the weather improves so too does Town's performance. They win courtesy of Shawcross' solitary headed goal. Afterwards Ball denies he has been approached by Hull.											
25	H	BOURNEMOUTH		12	W	4-1	2-0	Atkins 8, 26, Lawther 68, Pickering 76	Smith	Burgin	Lee	Lennard	Pickering	Robertson	Verity	Shawcross	Lawther	Atkins	Hill	
		17/1	3,093	20	27			Stocks 53	Tilsed	Gulliver	Foote*	Miller	Stocks	Summerhill	Longhorn	MacDougall	White	Powell	Meredith	East
								Ref: S Kayley	Despite the upsurge in Town's fortunes, attendances at the Shay appear to be going down. The stayaways miss Town's first four-goal blast this season and Pickering's first-ever goal, off Hill's corner. Atkins scores the first two and sets up Lawther's to halt a Bournemouth fightback.											
26	H	BARROW		12	W	3-0	2-0	Chadwick 18, Lawther 42, Atkins 67	Smith	Burgin	Lee	Lennard	Pickering	Robertson*	Chadwick	Shawcross	Lawther	Atkins	McCarthy	Verity
		27/1	4,345	24	29				Heyes	Dean	Cooper	Noble	Arrowsmith	Hartland	Garbett	Morrin	Ledger	Storf	Ellison*	Mulvaney
								Ref: N Graham	Former Town skipper Norman Bodell is in charge at bottom club Barrow, but reckons his side is better than the league position suggests. They show glimpses but are no match for the Shaymen. Chadwick crashes in his first on his debut. McCarthy pulls the ball back for Atkins to score.											
27	A	BURY		13	D	1-1	0-0	Verity 65	Smith	Burgin	Lee	Lennard	Pickering	Verity	Chadwick	Shawcross*	Robertson	Atkins	McCarthy	Lawther
		31/1	4,788	17	30			Grundy 58	Forrest	Tinney	Saile	McDermott	Lyon	Holt*	Hince	Arrowsmith	Jones	Kerr	Grundy	Hughes
								Ref: P Baldwin	The pitch is bumpy and keeper Alex Smith pulls a muscle. Otherwise he may have saved Brian Grundy's 25-yarder. Verity equalises, then both subs go close. With 13 minutes to go Bury's Roy Hughes heads against the upright, then Lawther has an angled shot deflected onto the post.											
28	A	STOCKPORT		10	W	1-0	1-0	Verity 25	Smith	Burgin	Lee	Lennard	Pickering	Verity	Chadwick	Robertson	Vernon	Atkins	McCarthy	
		2/2	3,428	22	32				Ogley	Haydock	Hartle	Elgin	Low	Smith J	Ryden	Goodwin	Rowland	Broadbent	Price	
								Ref: M Fussey	This pitch is waterlogged and the ref only gives the nod 35 minutes before kick-off. Ex-Shayman Ryden has one of two County efforts that hit the post. Verity's second goal in two games is a header off ex-international Roy Vernon's pass. Near the end McCarthy misses an open goal.											
29	A	READING		10	L	1-4	0-3	Shawcross 59p	Smith	Burgin	Lee	Lennard	Pickering	Verity*	Chadwick	Robertson	Vernon	Atkins	McCarthy	Shawcross
		11/2	15,160	1	32			Wagstaff B 3, 12, Chappell 45 Allen 63	Death	Dixon	Butler	Wagstaff B	Allen	Sharpe	Cumming	Chappell	Habbin	Wagstaff T	Williams	
								Ref: T Reynolds	Town will get reported to the League for handing in their team sheet after the deadline. In the game, though, they give as good as they get. The difference is in the finishing. Town only score from the spot when Dennis Butler handles. Reading go top having scored an incredible 58 goals.											
30	A	SHREWSBURY		11	L	1-3	1-2	Robertson 32	Smith	Burgin	Lee	Lennard	Pickering	Shawcross	Chadwick	Robertson	Vernon	Atkins	McCarthy*	Lawther
		14/2	3,824	13	32			McLaughlin 16, Andrews 30, Moir 78	Tooze	Gregory	Fellows	Moir	Wood	Moir	Roberts	Bridgwood*	Harkin	Andrews	McLaughlin	Hawkins
								Ref: R Kirkpatrick	Alan Ball requests that the ref abandons the game at half-time because of the icebound state of the pitch. He also knows his side is not playing well. Uncharacteristically they allow the Shrews to score three goals. Robertson's goal gives Town hope, but they are overrun and second best.											
31	A	MANSFIELD		12	D	3-3	2-0	Lawther 18, Atkins 25, Chadwick 90	Smith	Wallace	Burgin	Lennard	Pickering*	Robertson	Chadwick	Shawcross	Lawther	Atkins	McCarthy	Verity
		21/2	6,052	19	33			Partridge 68, 80, Goodfellow 86	Hollins	Pate	Walker	Quigley	Boam	Roberts	Keeley*	Stenson	Jones	Partridge	Goodfellow	Sharkey
								Ref: J Yates	Lawther makes the most of a deflection and when Atkins' glancing header goes in Halifax appear to be cruising. Late in the second half Town suffer a mad 18 minutes and appear to be heading for defeat. Chadwick saves them in injury-time, converting Robertson's indirect free-kick.											
32	H	BARNSLEY		13	L	0-2	0-2		Smith	Wallace	Burgin	Lennard	Shawcross	Robertson	Chadwick	Vernon	Lawther*	Atkins	McCarthy	Verity
		28/2	6,562	6	33			Loyden 44, Hamstead 45	Sherratt	Murphy	Booth	Brown	Winstanley	Raggett	Dean	Evans	Loyden	Boardman	Hamstead	
								Ref: P Partridge	The Shaymen slip to an unnecessary home defeat. In the 21st-minute keeper Brian Sherratt pushes away Shawcross's penalty after Dave Booth brings down Robertson. The game is lost in the minute before half-time. George Hamstead's goal is a soft one, a corner that swings straight in.											
33	H	ROTHERHAM		13	W	4-2	2-0	Verity 5, McCarthy 36, 75, Robertson 62	Smith	Wallace	Burgin	Lennard	Pickering	Robertson	Chadwick	Verity	Atkins	Shawcross	McCarthy	
		3/3	4,429		35			Warnock 57, Hague 66	Furnell	Houghton	Leigh	Hague	Watson	Hudson	Warnock	Lill	Phillips	Bentley	Mullen	
								Ref: J Thacker	Jim McAnearney's side have been going well. They have only lost two out of their last 20 matches before today. This result, therefore, was not on the cards. Rotherham go two down but never give the game up. Town's Robertson scores a screamer, returning the ball from thirty yards.											
34	A	TRANMERE		8	D	1-1	1-0	McCarthy 23	Smith	Wallace	Burgin	Lennard	Pickering	Robertson	Chadwick	Verity	Atkins	Shawcross	McCarthy	
		6/3	3,009	22	36			Beamish 80	Lane	Griffiths	Gill*	Moorcroft	Knapp	King	Kennedy	Mathias	Beamish	Pritchard	Crossley	Hinch
								Ref: F Nicholson	Town still harbour thoughts of promotion. Tranmere are fighting a relegation battle. This result does neither side any favours. The Shaymen adapt better to the gluepot pitch and take the lead through McCarthy's header. Ken Beamish equalises off a corner, then nearly nets a winner.											

No		Opponent	Att	Pos	Res	F-A	H-T	Scorers, Times, and Referees	1	2	3	4	5	6	7	8	9	10	11	12 sub used
35	A	BRIGHTON		8	L	0-4	0-1		Smith	Wallace	Burgin	Lennard	Pickering	Robertson	Chadwick	Verity	Atkins	Shawcross	McCarthy	
	11/3		*16,759*	*1*	36			*Turner 40, Gilliver 48, 54, 80*	*Powney*	*Henderson*	*Bell*	*Lawton*	*Napier J*	*Gall*	*Spearritt*	*Duffy*	*Gilliver*	*Turner*	*Napier K*	
								Ref: R Paine	Town never look like bringing off a shock result at the home of the joint league-leaders. The huge Brighton crowd watch anxiously as Town make life difficult, but when Dave Turner's shot is deflected in off Wallace it's plain sailing. Alan Gilliver is a constant thorn and bags three.											
36	H	READING		9	D	1-1	0-1	Shawcross 85	Smith	Wallace	Burgin	Lennard	Pickering	Robertson	Chadwick	Verity	Holmes	Shawcross	McCarthy	
	14/3		3,917	*5*	37			*Bell 45*	*Death*	*Dixon*	*Butler*	*Wagstaffe B*	*Allen*	*Sharpe*	*Cumming**	*Bell*	*Habbin*	*Wagstaffe T*	*Williams*	*Morgan*
								Ref: R Darlington	Ball reckons only nine of his side is fit. When Terry Bell fires home for the visitors right on half-time there are fears that the Shaymen will not respond. But promotion-chasing Reading have a habit of giving goals away and they duly oblige. Shawcross scores off McCarthy's late corner.											
37	H	GILLINGHAM		12	D	1-1	1-0	McCarthy 4	Smith	Wallace	Burgin	Lennard	Pickering	Robertson	Chadwick	Verity	**Graham**	Shawcross	McCarthy	
	17/3		3,173	*23*	38			*Bailey 82*	*Simpson*	*Machin*	*Peach*	*Bailey*	*Galvin*	*Quirke*	*Tydeman*	*Yeo*	*Green*	*Smillie*	*Pound*	
								Ref: D Laing	Alex Smith makes his 100th League appearance for Town but his blunder costs his side a point. With time running out he fails to deal with the bouncing ball off Smillie's long punt. Ray Bailey's finish is a formality. McCarthy's rising shot opens the scoring but Town fail to build on it.											
38	A	ROTHERHAM		12	D	1-1	0-0	Chadwick 48	Smith	Wallace	Burgin	Lennard	Pickering	Robertson	Chadwick	Verity	Graham*	Shawcross	McCarthy	Lee
	21/3		*7,244*	*9*	39			*Phillips 75*	*Tunks*	*Houghton*	*Leigh*	*Hague*	*Watson*	*Swift*	*Brogden**	*Phillips*	*Lill*	*Warnock*	*Mullen*	*Bentley*
								Ref: T Gill	On-loan Peter Graham plays a useful game and is involved in Town's prominent moves. He sets up Robertson but his shot hits the post. But off a free-kick Graham diverts the ball for Chadwick to score. Rotherham appear overkeen but Trevor Phillips hammers in a deserved equaliser.											
39	H	BRIGHTON		11	W	1-0	1-0	Chadwick 45	Smith	Wallace	Burgin	Lennard	Pickering	Robertson	Chadwick	Lee	Graham	Shawcross	McCarthy	
	28/3		4,006	*1*	41				*Sidebottom*	*Henderson*	*Bell*	*Lawton*	*Napier J*	*Gall*	*Spearritt**	*Duffy*	*Gilliver*	*Smith*	*Napier K*	*Stanley*
								Ref: T Dawes	Freddie Goodwin's league-leaders look a subdued lot and they rarely threaten. They've now failed to win on each of their last four visits here. Chadwick's diving header from McCarthy's cross on half-time proves enough for Town. Doing their duty Pickering and Robertson are booked.											
40	A	ROCHDALE			L	0-5	0-3	*[Riley 51]*	Smith	Wallace	Burgin	Lennard	Pickering	Robertson*	Chadwick	Lee	Graham	Shawcross	McCarthy	Verity
	30/3		*5,345*		41			*Jenkins 24, 30, 47, Whitehead 36,*	*Harker*	*Smith*	*Ryder*	*Riley**	*Parry*	*Ashworth*	*Whitehead*	*Rudd*	*Jenkins*	*Downes*	*Butler*	*Cross*
								Ref: A Morrissey	The Shaymen make too many mistakes and pay a heavy price. Home midfielders Billy Rudd and Bobby Downes boss the game, while Ross Jenkins becomes the third player to score a hat-trick against Halifax this season. It could have been more but for Alex Smith and the crossbar.											
41	H	TORQUAY		13	D	1-1	0-1	McCarthy 52	Smith	Wallace	Burgin	Lennard*	Pickering	Robertson	Chadwick	Lee	Graham	Atkins	McCarthy	Shawcross
	31/3		3,493		42			*Welsh A 42*	*Donnelly*	*Smyth*	*Glozier*	*Lucas*	*Kitchener*	*Dunne*	*Benson*	*Cave*	*Potter*	*Mitchinson*	*Welsh A*	
								Ref: R Spittle	Allan Brown's Torquay deserve a point but are thankful to McCarthy for their goal. His silly pass lets in Mitchinson, who sets up Alan Welsh. Town dig deep but are lucky when Mitchinson's shot crashes against the underside of the bar and comes out. Then McCarthy redeems himself.											
42	H	LUTON		10	D	0-0	0-0		Smith	Burgin	Lee	Shawcross	Pickering	Wallace	Chadwick	Robertson	**Brierley**	Atkins	McCarthy	
	4/4		3,482	*4*	43				*Starling*	*Ryan*	*Bannister*	*Slough*	*Branston*	*Moore*	*Collins*	*Busby*	*Macdonald*	*Keen*	*Harrison**	*Phillips*
								Ref: W Castle	None of the present top five clubs have won at the Shay this season, including now Luton. Smith foils Macdonald and Collins, but two minutes from time his counterpart Alan Starling has to dive smartly to deny Atkins. Chris Nicholl returns to the Shay, but is left out by Harry Haslam.											
43	A	SOUTHPORT		13	L	0-1	0-1		Smith	Burgin	Buxton	Shawcross	Pickering	Wallace	Chadwick	Robertson	Graham	Atkins	McCarthy	
	7/4		*3,158*	*21*	43			*Redrobe 29*	*Wraith*	*Pearson*	*Alty*	*Peat*	*Harrison*	*Russell M*	*Field*	*Russell A*	*Redrobe*	*Cheetham*	*Pring*	
								Ref: D Lyden	Southport are scrapping for their Third Division lives. This victory gives them a brief lifeline. The Shaymen have no relegation fears and find it hard to motivate themselves. McCarthy goes close but stubs his shot six yards out. Former Shay star Tony Field sets up Eric Redrobe's winner.											
44	A	FULHAM		13	L	1-2	1-0	McCarthy 10	Smith	Burgin	Buxton	Lennard	Pickering	Robertson	Chadwick	Wallace	Atkins	Shawcross	McCarthy*	Lee
	15/4		*7,072*	*7*	43			*Conway 64, Halom 71*	*Webster*	*Pentecost*	*Tranter*	*Brown*	*Matthewson*	*Moreline*	*Conway*	*Halom*	*Earle*	*Lloyd*	*Barrett*	
								Ref: J Hunting	A repeat of Fulham's 8-0 thrashing at the Shay back in September never looks likely. In fact, when McCarthy heads in early on Halifax are looking good for revenge. They fall to Conway's cracking 35-yarder and Halom's vicious volley. Fulham still have faint hopes of promotion.											
45	A	GILLINGHAM		13	L	0-2	0-1		Smith	Burgin	Lee	Buxton	Puclering	Robertson	Chadwick	Atkins	Lawther	Wallace	McCarthy	
	22/4		*4,568*		43			*Pound 37, Green 52*	*Simpson*	*Weston*	*Peach*	*Machin*	*Williams*	*Quirke*	*Tydeman*	*Bailey*	*Green*	*Yeo*	*Pound*	
								Ref: J Taylor	The Gills are desperate to get out of trouble. This win will ultimately help them. Ken Pound gives them a deserved lead when Smith drops the ball. When a suspiciously-looking offside Mike Green runs through for the second, Town boss Alan Ball is on the pitch leading the protests.											
46	H	WALSALL		18	L	0-1	0-0		Smith	Burgin	Buxton	Shawcross	Pickering	Robertson	Chadwick	Atkins	Lawther	Wallace	McCarthy	
	24/4		**1,812**	*12*	43			*Watson 53*	*Wesson*	*Gregg*	*Evans*	*Harrison*	*Cross*	*Deakin*	*Watson*	*Stephens*	*Seal*	*Baker**	*Taylor*	*Gough*
		Home	Away					Ref: H Davey	Town's campaign ends with a fourth successive defeat. But their season was over a long time ago. There is little for either side to play for, and in a drab game a goalless draw looks inevitable. Then Shawcross slices a cross, the ball falls to free-transfer Ken Watson, and he can't miss.											
Average		4,625	7,749																	

League Cup					F-A	H-T	Scorers, Times, and Referees	1	2	3	4	5	6	7	8	9	10	11	12 sub used
1 A	BARNSLEY			W	1-0	0-0	Flower 53	Smith	Wallace	Burgin	Lennard	Nicholl	Robertson	Flower	Shawcross	Lawther	Hill	McCarthy	
	13/8	*9,546*						*Arblaster*	*Murphy*	*Booth*	*Bettany*	*Robson*	*Howard*	*Earnshaw*	*Bradbury*	*Dean*	*Boardman*	*Hamstead*	
							Ref: J Thacker	Alan Ball gives credit to his own son of the same name for this victory. Ruled out of Everton's side at the weekend, Ball jnr went spying on Barnsley. His father uses his report to counteract their style and it works. Tony Flower shows good close control before scoring the only goal.											
2 A	WEST HAM		14	L	2-4	0-2	Lawther 50, Wallace 90 *[Hurst 74, 88]*	Smith	Burgin	McCarthy	Lennard	Pickering	Robertson	Ryden	Hill	Lawther	Shawcross	Flower*	Wallace
	3/9	*20,717*	*1:14*				*Lampard 14, McCarthy 30 (og),*	*Ferguson*	*Bonds*	*Lampard*	*Peters*	*Stephenson*	*Moore*	*Redknapp*	*Lindsay*	*Brooking*	*Hurst*	*Best*	
							Ref: J Osbourne	The Shaymen come face-to-face with Hammers' triumvirate – World Cup winners Moore, Hurst and Peters. With 16 minutes to go they are still in the hunt. But it's an uphill task once Lampard's shot is deflected in and McCarthy puts into his own net when challenging Clyde Best.											

FA Cup																			
1 H	CHESTER		16	D	3-3	1-2	Atkins 9, Lawther 63, Hill 67	Smith	Burgin	McCarthy	Lee	Pickering	Wallace	Ryden	Lennard	Lawther	Atkins	Hill	
	15/11	5,032	*4:10*				*Tarbuck 25, 83, Dearden 30*	*Carling*	*Cheetham*	*Birks*	*Sutton*	*Turner*	*Bradbury*	*Dearden*	*Tarbuck*	*Webber*	*Draper*	*Provan*	
							Ref: E Jolly	This game swings one way, then the other, but with seven minutes to go it looks like the Shaymen have done enough to see off the challenge of the Fourth Division side. Then keeper Alex Smith makes another blunder, allowing Alan Tarbuck's cross to sail over him and level the scores.											
1R A	CHESTER		16	L	0-1	0-0		Smith	Burgin	McCarthy	Lennard	Pickering	Wallace	Ryden	Robertson	Lawther	Atkins	Hill	
	19/11	8,352	*4:10*				*Provan 86*	*Carling*	*Cheetham*	*Birks*	*Sutton*	*Turner*	*Bradbury*	*Dearden*	*Tarbuck*	*Webber*	*Draper*	*Provan*	
							Ref: E Jolly	A few weeks ago Chester turned down Town's offer of £7,000 for winger Andy Provan. How ironic, then, that it should be he who decides this replay. Extra-time is looming when Provan stabs the ball home. Chester are more fired up than Town and victory is no more than they deserve.											

		P	W	D	L	F	A	W	D	L	F	A	Pts
			Home					Away					
1	Orient	46	16	5	2	43	15	9	7	7	24	21	62
2	Luton	46	13	8	2	46	15	10	6	7	31	28	60
3	Bristol Rov	46	15	5	3	51	26	5	11	7	29	33	56
4	Fulham	46	12	9	2	43	26	8	6	9	38	29	55
5	Brighton	46	16	4	3	37	16	7	5	11	20	27	55
6	Mansfield	46	14	4	5	46	22	7	7	9	24	27	53
7	Barnsley	46	14	6	3	43	24	5	9	9	25	35	53
8	Reading	46	16	3	4	52	29	5	8	10	35	48	53
9	Rochdale	46	11	6	6	39	24	7	4	12	30	36	46
10	Bradford C	46	11	6	6	37	22	6	6	11	20	28	46
11	Doncaster	46	13	4	6	31	19	4	8	11	21	35	46
12	Walsall	46	11	4	8	33	31	6	8	9	21	36	46
13	Torquay	46	9	9	5	36	22	5	8	10	26	37	45
14	Rotherham	46	10	8	5	36	19	5	6	12	26	35	44
15	Shrewsbury	46	10	12	1	35	17	3	6	14	27	46	44
16	Tranmere	46	10	8	5	38	29	4	8	11	18	43	44
17	Plymouth	46	10	7	6	32	23	6	4	13	24	41	43
18	HALIFAX	46	10	9	4	31	25	4	6	13	16	38	43
19	Bury	46	13	4	6	47	29	2	7	14	28	51	41
20	Gillingham	46	7	6	10	28	33	6	7	10	24	31	39
21	Bournemouth	46	8	9	6	28	27	4	6	13	20	44	39
22	Southport	46	11	5	7	31	22	3	5	15	17	44	38
23	Barrow	46	7	9	7	28	27	1	5	17	18	54	30
24	Stockport	46	4	7	12	17	30	2	4	17	10	41	23
		1104	271	157	124	888	572	124	157	271	572	888	1104

Odds & ends

Double wins: (2) Barrow, Stockport.
Double losses: (3) Barnsley, Fulham, Walsall.

Won from behind: (0).
Lost from in front: (3) Fulham (a), Mansfield (a), Walsall (a).

High spots: Going six games unbeaten up to 2 February.
Three consecutive wins in January.

Low spots: Losing 0-8 to Fulham, Town's heaviest ever home defeat.
Failing to win any of the last seven matches.
Four consecutive defeats to the end of the season.
Star player Freddie Hill missing the last three months of the season after being injured in a friendly against Sunderland.

Player of the Year: Freddie Hill.
Ever-presents: (1) Andy Burgin.
Hat-tricks: (0).
Leading scorer: Ian Lawther (9).

	Appearances						Goals			
	Lge	*Sub*	LC	*Sub*	FAC	*Sub*	**Lge**	LC	FAC	**Tot**
Atkins, Bill	**23**				2		**7**		1	**8**
Brierley, Keith	**1**									
Burgin, Andy	**46**		2		2		**1**			**1**
Buxton, Mick	**4**									
Chadwick, Dave	**21**						**4**			**4**
Connaughton, John	**3**									
Cullen, Pat		*1*								
Flower, Tony	**8**	*1*	2					1		**1**
Graham, Peter	**6**									
Hill, Freddie	**25**		2		2		**3**		1	**4**
Holmes, Barry	**4**						**1**			**1**
Lawther, Ian	**30**	*2*	2		2		**7**	1	1	**9**
Lee, Jeff	**23**	*2*			1					
Lennard, Dave	**42**		2		2		**2**			**2**
McCarthy, Phil	**36**		2		2		**6**			**6**
Nicholl, Chris	**3**		1							
Pickering, John	**43**	*1*	1		2		**1**			**1**
Robertson, Lammie	**44**		2		1		**3**			**3**
Ryden, Hugh	**11**		1		2		**2**			**2**
Shawcross, David	**32**	*6*	2				**7**			**7**
Smith, Alex	**43**		2		2					
Turnbull, Fred	**7**									
Verity, Dave	**11**	*6*					**3**			**3**
Vernon, Roy	**4**									
Wallace, Bob	**36**		1	*1*	2			1		**1**
25 players used	**506**	***19***	**22**	***1***	**22**		**47**	**3**	**3**	**53**

No	Date	Att	Pos	Pt	F-A	H-T	Scorers, Times, and Referees	1	2	3	4	5	6	7	8	9	10	11	12 sub used
1	A PRESTON			D	1-1	0-0	McCarthy 64	Smith	Burgin	Buxton	Robertson	Pickering	Wallace	Chadwick	Atkins	Brierley*	Lennard	McCarthy	Lawther
	15/8	*9,646*		1			*Heppolette 69*	*Kelly*	*Ross*	*McNab*	*Spark*	*Hawkins*	*Heppolette*	*Wilson*	*Lyall**	*Irvine*	*Gemmill*	*Hughes*	*Ingram*
							Ref: M Kerkhof	Kirby's first taste in management is against his mentor, Alan Ball, and his relegated Preston side. Honours are even. McCarthy makes the most of a defensive mix-up for the opener. Heppolette's reply gives Smith no chance. Atkins heads wide late on when Chadwick's shot hits the post.											
2	H WREXHAM		5	W	2-0	1-0	Atkins 41, Robertson 75p	Smith	Burgin	Buxton	Robertson	Pickering	Wallace	Chadwick	Atkins	Brierley	Lennard	McCarthy*	Lawther
	22/8	3,789	*14*	3				*Gaskell*	*Ingle*	*Mason*	*Davis*	*May*	*Vansittart*	*Moir*	*Park*	*Kinsey*	*Tinnion*	*Provan*	
							Ref: B Daniels	A disappointing crowd of less than 4,000 see a fine Town performance. Chadwick lays off a free-kick to Atkins for his goal, while Robertson scores a penalty when Wallace is impeded. The ref halts the game when one of the four movable corner pieces of the pitch becomes elevated.											
3	A GILLINGHAM		10	L	1-2	0-2	Lennard 75	Smith	Burgin	Buxton	Robertson	Pickering	Wallace	Chadwick	Atkins	Brierley	Lennard	McCarthy*	Holmes
	29/8	*5,240*	*13*	3			*Smillie 4, Green 19*	*Simpson*	*Bailey*	*Peach*	*Yeo*	*Williams*	*Quirke*	*Watson*	*Tydemann*	*Green*	*Smillie*	*Pound*	
							Ref: R Crabb	Despite defeat, Town's performance is encouraging. Lennard's misplaced pass leads to Mike Green making it 0-2 with less than 20 minutes gone. He manages to pull a goal back, and in the dying seconds brings out the best in veteran John Simpson. Sub Holmes earlier hits the post.											
4	H WALSALL		12	W	2-1	1-0	Atkins 38, Pickering 68	Smith	Burgin	Buxton	Robertson	Pickering	Wallace	Chadwick	Atkins	Brierley	Lennard	McCarthy	
	5/9	3,515	*16*	5			*Lennard 74 (og)*	*Wesson*	*Harrison*	*Evans*	*Bennett*	*Jones*	*Atthey*	*Morris*	*Penman*	*Woodward*	*Deakin*	*Taylor*	
							Ref: W Hall	16-year-old John Goldstraw, who applied for the vacant Town post, is made 'manager' for the day. Atkins and Pickering give Town the lead but when Lennard turns in Colin Taylor's cross the result is kept in doubt until the end. Goldstraw, though, leaves with a 100% success rate.											
5	A DONCASTER		2	W	2-1	0-0	Brierley 69, 90	Smith	Burgin	Buxton	Robertson	Pickering	Wallace	Chadwick	Atkins	Brierley	Lennard	McCarthy	
	11/9	*4,750*	*24*	7			*Briggs 66*	*Johnson G*	*Branfoot*	*Harris*	*Bird*	*Robertson**	*Haselden*	*Irvine*	*Marsden*	*Briggs*	*Johnson R*	*Usher*	*Rabjohn*
							Ref: W Johnson	Town go second overnight after this Friday evening fixture. A torrential downpour spoils the first half, while Briggs' goal upsets Town in the second. But their response is swift. Chadwick heads the ball across for Brierley's first, and his second, the winner, comes deep into injury-time.											
6	H BRIGHTON		10	L	0-1	0-0		Smith	Burgin	Buxton*	Robertson	Pickering	Wallace	Chadwick	Atkins	Brierley	Lennard	McCarthy	Lee
	19/9	3,424	*11*	7			*Gilliver 46*	*Sidebotham*	*Henderson*	*Templeman*	*Lawton**	*Napier J*	*Gall*	*Duffy*	*Spearitt*	*Gilliver*	*Turner*	*O'Sullivan*	*Napier K*
							Ref: E Jolly	A defensive blunder by Pickering gives Pat Saward's side the points. His return pass-back to Smith lets in Alan Gilliver to net the only goal. In the 36th minute, Atkins is denied by Sidebotham, playing his first game this season, when he pushes his cross-shot onto the inside of the post.											
7	H PLYMOUTH		4	W	4-1	2-0	Burgin 12, Chadwick 30, Brierley 56,	Smith	Burgin	Buxton	Robertson	Pickering	Wallace	Chadwick	Atkins	Brierley	Lennard	McCarthy	
	22/9	**3,112**		9			*Molyneux 79* [Atkins 57]	*Dunne*	*Wooldridge*	*Sullivan*	*Hore*	*Molyneux*	*Saxton*	*Rickard*	*Burnside*	*Allen*	*Bickle*	*Hutchins*	
							Ref: C Robinson	This spectacular win heeds a warning to the rest of the promotion-chasing sides. Argyle had only conceded five goals beforehand, yet keeper Pat Dunne, the ex-Irish international, has to be at his best to keep the Shaymen's score down. Atkins' header hits both posts before going in.											
8	A BARNSLEY		8	D	2-2	0-1	Brierley 60, 82	Smith	Burgin	Buxton	Robertson	Pickering	Wallace	Chadwick	Atkins	Brierley	Lennard	McCarthy*	Lee
	26/9	*9,439*	*17*	10			*Evans 38, 54*	*Arblaster*	*Murphy*	*Booth*	*McPhee*	*Winstanley*	*Howard*	*Lea*	*Evans*	*Loyden*	*Brown*	*Sharp*	
							Ref: A Morrissey	The Yorkshire TV cameras capture a fine Town fightback. Brierley claims both their goals, but his second is surrounded in confusion. The ref claims that Lennard's header has gone over the line before Murphy hooks clear, but Brierley makes sure before Lennard's effort is awarded.											
9	H ROTHERHAM			L	1-3	0-2	Atkins 55	Smith	Burgin	Buxton	Robertson	Pickering	Wallace	Chadwick	Atkins	Brierley*	Lennard	McCarthy	Lawther
	29/9	5,891		10			*Phillips 17, Brogden 41, 87*	*Tunks*	*Houghton*	*Leigh*	*Bettany**	*Swift*	*Hague*	*Brogden*	*Hill*	*Phillips*	*Bentley*	*Mullen*	*Hudson*
							Ref: P Baldwin	George Kirby pleads with the fans to 'have confidence and be tolerant' after this heavy home defeat. He feels the Millers deserve to win, and few would disagree. Town are searching for an equaliser when Rotherham break, and Lee Brogden makes the game safe with a ferocious shot.											
10	H SHREWSBURY		10	W	2-0	2-0	Atkins 26, McCarthy 37	Smith	Burgin	Lee	Robertson	Pickering	Wallace	Chadwick	Atkins	Brierley	Lennard	McCarthy	
	3/10	3,322	*14*	12				*Tooze*	*Gregory*	*Fellows*	*Moore*	*Wood*	*McLaughlin*	*Roberts**	*Bridgwood*	*Andrews*	*Chapman*	*Harkin*	*Bevan*
							Ref: R Lee	The Shrews are the division's leading scorers – they've scored 23 so far. But they hardly look like adding to their tally. Only Alf Wood's early header onto the bar causes Town any anxieties. The Shaymen win thanks to Atkins' cracking 35-yarder, and McCarthy's close-range effort.											
11	A CHESTERFIELD		11	L	**0-5**	0-3	*[Randall]*	Smith	Burgin	Lee	Robertson	Pickering	Wallace	Chadwick*	Atkins	Brierley	Lennard	McCarthy	Lawther
	10/10	*8,251*	*12*	12			*Bell 6, Phelan 35, Wright 42, 60,*	*Stevenson*	*Tiler*	*Lumsden*	*Phelan*	*Bell*	*Stott*	*Randall*	*Moss*	*Wright*	*Archer*	*Pugh*	
							Ref: C Nicholls	A series of tactical and individual blunders cost Town dearly. Too many passes go astray and it all becomes a bit too easy for Jim McGuigan's Spireites. Ex-Huddersfield player John Archer orchestrates most of his side's best moves, and the Shaymen's offside trap is constantly sprung.											

No	Date	Venue	Opponent	Att	Pos	Res	Pts	F-A	H-T	Scorers, Times, and Referees	1	2	3	4	5	6	7	8	9	10	11	subs used
12		H	PRESTON		9	W		1-0	1-0	Atkins 45	Smith	Burgin	Buxton	Robertson	Pickering	Wallace	Chadwick	Atkins	Brierley	Lennard	McCarthy	
	17/10			5,922	*8*		14				*Kelly*	*Ross*	*McMahon*	*Spark*	*Hawkins*	*Spavin*	*Wilson*	*Irvine*	*Ingram*	*Heppolette*	*Hughes**	*Lee*
										Ref: H Davey	On his first return to the Shay, Alan Ball claims this is 'just another game'. Preston lie second but Town are in determined mood. Atkins scores a spectacular free-kick that ripples one of the new nylon goal nets. Preston pile on the pressure and in injury-time Heppolette grazes the bar.											
13		A	BURY			D		1-1	0-1	Brierley 81	Smith	Burgin	Buxton	Robertson*	Pickering	Wallace	Chadwick	Atkins	Brierley	Lennard	McCarthy	Lawther
	20/10			*2,708*			15			*O'Connor 45*	*Ramsbottom*	*Eccleshare*	*Tinney*	*Lyon*	*Allen*	*Holt*	*O'Connor*	*Cassell*	*Jones*	*Tinsley*	*Connelly*	
										Ref: V Batty	The attendance here sets a new all-time low for a league game at Gigg Lane. Bury take the lead through Jim O'Connor, who actually looks a mile offside. Town dominate the second-half and Brierley equalises when Neil Ramsbottom allows McCarthy's cross to go under his body.											
14		A	FULHAM		12	L		1-3	0-2	Brierley 88	Smith	Burgin	Buxton	Robertson	Pickering	Wallace	Chadwick	Atkins	Brierley	Lennard	McCarthy	
	24/10			*10,749*	*1*		15			*Morton 16, Lloyd 25, Earle 49*	*Webster*	*Pentecost*	*Callaghan*	*Brown*	*Richardson*	*Dunne*	*Morton**	*Halom*	*Earle*	*Lloyd*	*Barrett*	*Matthewson*
										Ref: T Reynolds	League-leaders Fulham have scored in every game. Town don't need to gift them goals, but do so anyway. The third, scored by Steve Earle, is a typical error. They allow a harmless cross to reach him unmarked. Brierley, however, scores the best goal, a header off Robertson's cross.											
15		H	BRADFORD C		12	L		1-2	0-0	Atkins 66	Smith	Burgin	Buxton	Robertson	Pickering	Wallace	Chadwick	Atkins	Brierley	Lennard	McCarthy*	Lawther
	31/10			5,615	*11*		15			*Bannister 57, 69*	*Liney*	*Podd**	*Cooper*	*Stowell*	*Hallett*	*McConnell*	*Hall J*	*Bannister*	*Corner*	*O'Neill*	*Middleton*	*Owen*
										Ref: J Taylor	World Cup ref Jack Taylor cuts a controversial figure in this derby. He only allows Atkins's equaliser after consulting a linesman, as City claim handball. But the visitors are happy with him as he allows Bannister's second, when he uses his hand, without consulting the linesman.											
16		A	MANSFIELD		14	L		2-3	2-1	Lennard 27, Atkins 44	Smith	Burgin	Lee	Robertson	Pickering	Wallace	Chadwick	Atkins	Brierley	Lennard	McCarthy	
	7/11			*5,549*	*6*		15			*Stenson 23, Roberts R 75, Boam 85*	*Herriot*	*Pate*	*Walker*	*Roberts R*	*Boam*	*Waller*	*Thompson*	*Stenson*	*Roberts D*	*Quigley*	*Goodfellow*	
										Ref: G Lewis	The Shaymen might live to regret this third consecutive defeat come the end of the season. Things look good at half-time, but a glaring miss by McCarthy in the 55th minute seems to be the turning point. Mansfield get two in ten minutes, with Stuart Boam's winner going in off his chest.											
17		A	TRANMERE			W		1-0	1-0	Robertson	Smith	Burgin	Lee	Robertson	Pickering	Wallace	Chadwick	Atkins	Brierley	Lennard	McCarthy	
	9/11			*3,638*			17				*Lane*	*Joy*	*Mathias*	*King*	*Moorcroft*	*Brodie*	*Crossley*	*Rowe*	*Moore*	*Hinch**	*Gill*	*Storton*
										Ref: I Smith	Halifax's response is to inflict on Tranmere their first league defeat of the season. The scouts are out checking on Rovers' Jimmy Hinch, but he is subdued by Pickering and substituted after 62 minutes. Atkins hits a post before Robertson scores the game's only goal from 28 yards.											
18		H	ASTON VILLA		10	W		2-1	2-0	Atkins 5, 22	Smith	Burgin	Lee	Robertson	Pickering	Wallace	Chadwick	Atkins	Brierley	Lennard	McCarthy	
	14/11			5,845	*3*		19			*Turnbull 77*	*Dunn*	*Bradley*	*Aitken*	*Godfrey*	*Chatterley*	*Turnbull*	*McMahon*	*Tiler*	*Gregory*	*Hamilton*	*Anderson*	
										Ref: B Holmwood	Vic Crowe's Aston Villa are in Division 3 for the first time. Their reputation goes before them, but on the day Town more than match them. Atkins's second goal goes in off the post, but it gives Villa a mountain to climb. Turnbull's header off Anderson's corner sets up a tense finish.											
19		H	PORT VALE		9	W		2-0	2-0	Burgin 20, Chadwick 23	Smith	Burgin	Lee	Wallace	Pickering	**Rhodes**	Chadwick	Atkins	Brierley*	Lennard	Holmes	Lawther
	28/11			3,404	*16*		21				*Ball*	*Hopkinson*	*Wilson*	*Boulton*	*Cross*	*Green*	*Morris*	*Lacey*	*James*	*McLaren**	*Morgan*	*Gough*
										Ref: R Johnson	Tony Rhodes, signed from Derby two weeks ago, makes his debut and on this showing will be a keen asset. The Shaymen never look in any danger, and win the game in a three-minute spell. Burgin scores with a low 25-yarder, and Chadwick prospers from Atkins' left-wing cross.											
20		A	BRISTOL ROV		11	L		0-1	0-1		Smith	Burgin	Lee	Wallace	Pickering	Rhodes*	Chadwick	Atkins	Brierley	Lennard	Holmes	Lawther
	5/12			*12,289*	*1*		21			*Jones B 12p*	*Sheppard*	*Roberts*	*Parsons*	*Prince*	*Taylor S*	*Megson*	*Graydon*	*Gilbert*	*Stubbs*	*Jones B*	*Jarman*	
										Ref: P Capey	Confidence is high in the Shay camp as they make the long journey to Eastville. In the end, only Bryn Jones's early penalty, conceded when Burgin handles Harry Jarman's shot, separates the sides. Town create chances, but Stubbs comes closest to making it 2-0 with two minutes left.											
21		H	DONCASTER		9	W		**4-0**	2-0	Lennard 28, Rhodes 43, Atkins 65, [Brierley 90]	Smith	Burgin	Lee	Wallace	Pickering	Rhodes	Chadwick	Atkins	Brierley	Lennard	Holmes	
	12/12			3,175	*20*		23				*Johnson G*	*Adamson*	*Clish*	*Flowers*	*Robertson*	*Haselden*	*Irvine*	*Kitchen*	*Briggs**	*Rabjohn*	*Watson*	*Regan*
										Ref: F Nicholson	The fear of power cuts means a 2.30 kick-off. Lennard enjoys the afternoon, driving home the opener, and putting Brierley clear to close the scoring. Rhodes scores his first Town goal, a low shot following Holmes's corner. Doncaster are unlucky, though, as the score flatters Town.											
22		A	WREXHAM		9	D		2-2	1-2	Atkins 2, Burgin 75	Smith	Burgin	Lee	Wallace	Pickering	Rhodes	Chadwick	Atkins	Brierley	Lennard	McCarthy	
	19/12			*6,021*	*10*		24			*Ashcroft 11, May 26*	*Gaskell*	*Ingle*	*Mason*	*Davis*	*May*	*Vansittart*	*Moir*	*Evans*	*Ashcroft*	*Kinsey*	*Griffiths*	
										Ref: P Walters	Bill Atkins converts Lennard's cross to give Town an early lead, but when May scores Wrexham go in front. Four minutes later Gaskell saves Wallace's first-ever penalty. But Town won't be denied, and their equaliser arrives when Burgin turns in Chadwick's shot that was going wide.											
23		H	ROCHDALE		9	L		1-4	1-2	Brierley 17	Smith	Burgin	Lee	Wallace	Pickering	Rhodes	Chadwick	Atkins	Brierley	Lennard	McCarthy*	Lawther
	26/12			5,584	*23*		24			*Butler 35, 62, 70, Cross 38*	*Tenant*	*Smith*	*Ryder*	*Riley*	*Parry*	*Ashworth*	*Whitehead*	*Blair*	*Cross*	*Downes*	*Butler*	
										Ref: A Bone	Dick Connor's strugglers cause a sensation with this win. Brierley scores following McCarthy's long throw, but there Town's joy ends. Toast of the afternoon is left-winger Dennis Butler, who grabs his first hat-trick. He also has the shot that leads to David Cross giving Dale the lead.											

LEAGUE DIVISION 3

Manager: George Kirby

SEASON 1970-71

No	Date		Att	Pos	Pt	F-A	H-T	Scorers, Times, and Referees	1	2	3	4	5	6	7	8	9	10	11	12 sub used
24	A	PLYMOUTH		10	D	1-1	1-1	Atkins 32	Smith	Burgin	Lee	Wallace	Pickering	Rhodes	Chadwick	Atkins	Brierley*	Lennard	McCarthy	Robertson
	2/1		*6,218*	*14*	25			*Bickle 40*	*Furnell*	*Dowling*	*Sullivan*	*Hore*	*Saxton*	*Lean*	*Davey*	*Rickard*	*Allen*	*Bickle*	*Hutchins*	
								Ref: M Sinclair	The ref only passes the bone-hard pitch playable an hour before kick-off. Town put the Rochdale setback behind them and look the better side. Atkins rounds off a Chadwick-Brierley move to put them ahead, whilst Mick Bickle's equaliser comes off one of the home side's rare attacks.											
25	A	ROTHERHAM		9	D	2-2	1-2	Atkins 36, Wallace 60	Smith	Burgin	Lee	Wallace	Pickering	Rhodes	Chadwick	Atkins	Brierley	Lennard	Holmes	
	9/1		*7,446*	*8*	26			*Leigh 22p, Johnson 45*	*Tunks*	*Houghton*	*Leigh*	*Johnson*	*Hague*	*Swift*	*Warnock*	*Womble*	*Fantham*	*Bentley**	*Mullen*	*Hudson*
								Ref: K Sweet	Major decisions go against Town to deprive them of victory. Wallace plays the ball when Fantham goes down, but the ref gives the penalty. He then goes on to award a harsh indirect free-kick inside the box from which Rod Johnson scores. Atkins plays his 300th league game and scores.											
26	H	TORQUAY		7	W	2-0	1-0	Lawther 8, Pickering 80	Smith	Burgin	Lee	Wallace	Pickering	Rhodes	Chadwick	Atkins	Lawther	Lennard	Holmes	
	11/1		4,022	*6*	27				*Donnelly*	*Smyth*	*Potter*	*Lucas*	*Edwards*	*Young*	*Cave*	*Barnard*	*Rudge*	*Mitchinson*	*Jackson**	*Welsh A*
								Ref: G Hill	The Shaymen get an early fillip when the recalled Ian Lawther heads in Atkins' cross. Torquay have their own promotion ambitions and press hard for the equaliser. But they have nothing to offer once John Pickering nods an Atkins header past Andrew Donnelly off Chadwick's corner.											
27	H	BURY		6	W	3-0	0-0	Holmes 51, Lennard 80, 88	Smith	Burgin	Lee	Wallace	Pickering	Rhodes	Chadwick	Atkins	Lawther	Lennard	Holmes	
	16/1		5,089	*21*	30				*Ramsbottom*	*Eccleshare*	*Tinney*	*Robson*	*Lyon*	*Tinsley*	*Connelly*	*Rudd*	*Jones*	*White*	*Grundy*	
								Ref: J Yates	The Shakers, despite their lowly position, arrive at the Shay as the most improved side in the division. However, they are up against a Halifax team that's running into form. Holmes gives them the lead, but the game isn't made safe until the last ten minutes. Lennard's first is a header.											
28	H	READING		4	W	4-0	1-0	Wallace 45, Atkins 47, Lennard 63, [Chadwick 76]	Smith	Burgin	Lee	Wallace	Pickering	Rhodes	Chadwick	Atkins	Lawther	Lennard	Holmes	
	23/1		4,617	*13*	32				*Death*	*Dixon*	*Butler DM*	*Swain*	*Sharpe*	*Wagstaff B*	*Cumming*	*Chappell**	*Bell*	*Habbin*	*Flannigan*	*Harley*
								Ref: D Turner	The only surprise is that it takes Town almost until half-time to open the scoring. Then Bob Wallace whips Chadwick's through ball into the net. Chadwick scores the pick of the goals, controlling the ball well before firing in a low left-foot shot. Town also have three goals ruled out.											
29	A	PORT VALE		5	W	1-0	0-0	Burgin 71	Smith	Burgin	Lee	Wallace	Pickering	Rhodes	Chadwick	Atkins	Lawther	Lennard	Holmes	
	30/1		*4,059*	*16*	34				*Sharratt*	*Brodie*	*Lacey*	*Boulton*	*Cross*	*Green*	*Morris*	*Gough*	*Morgan**	*Horton*	*James*	*McLaren*
								Ref: H New	Gordon Lee's Port Vale came up from Division 4 last season. On the treacherous muddy ground they look an accomplished side, but its Town who have all the answers. They frustrate the home crowd by defending in numbers, then silence them when Burgin's angled 25-yarder flies in.											
30	H	BRISTOL ROV		5	D	0-0	0-0		Smith	Burgin	Lee	Wallace	Pickering	Rhodes	Chadwick	Atkins	Lawther	Lennard	Holmes	
	6/2		7,716	*3*	35				*Shepperd*	*Roberts*	*Parsons*	*Prince*	*Tatlor S*	*Megson*	*Graydon*	*Jones R*	*Stubbs*	*Gilbert*	*Jarman*	
								Ref: K Howley	Town launch a half-time penalty competition for the fans. Brian Barrand wins £1 for scoring one of three penalties past reserve keeper Barry White. It's the only goal of the afternoon, as the division's two highest scorers play out this stalemate, though Bill Atkins has two ruled out.											
31	A	READING		5	D	1-1	0-0	Lennard 66	Smith	Burgin	Lee	Wallace	Pickering	Rhodes	Chadwick	Atkins	Lawther	Lennard	Holmes*	Brierley
	13/2		*5,210*	*14*	36			*Bell 84*	*Death*	*Dixon*	*Flannigan*	*Swain*	*Sharpe*	*Wagstaff B*	*Cumming*	*Bell*	*Habbin*	*Wagstaff T*	*Mellows*	
								Ref: W Hall	The home side have 60% of the play, but it's the Shaymen who come closest to winning. Lennard scores off a free-kick, though he looks off-side. Terry Bell's headed equaliser is the first goal conceded by Alex Smith in 580 minutes. Steve Death makes a great save to deny Holmes.											
32	H	TRANMERE		4	W	4-3	2-1	Wallace 28p, Rhodes 36, McCarthy 56p, [Lawther 84]	Smith	Burgin	Lee	Wallace	Pickering	Rhodes	Chadwick	Atkins*	Lawther	Lennard	Holmes	McCarthy
	20/2		4,243	*20*	38			*Moore 6, Gill 55, Dempsey,*	*Lane*	*Mathias*	*Farrimond*	*Moorcroft*	*Molyneux*	*Dempsey*	*Crossley*	*Moore*	*Beamish*	*King*	*Gill*	
								Ref: H Davey	Rovers are a resilient bunch, and don't know when to give up. Town finally get the better of them when Lawther's goal off Chadwick's neat pass, gives Tranmere little time to respond. Town are awarded two penalties, scored by Wallace, then sub McCarthy, the regular penalty taker.											
33	A	BRADFORD C		3	W	1-0	0-0	Lawther 55	Smith	Burgin	McCarthy	Wallace	Pickering	Rhodes	Chadwick	Lawther	Brierley	Lennard	Holmes	
	27/2		*9,420*	*13*	40				*Liney*	*Harney*	*Fretwell*	*Stowell*	*Corner**	*Cooper*	*Owen*	*Bannister*	*Oates*	*O'Neill*	*Hall*	*Turbitt*
								Ref: Pugh	After this victory, George Kirby is named Bell's Manager of the Month. City's Graham Oates was married only two hours before the game and may have other things on his mind. He fails to clear and Lawther scores. Wallace and McCarthy pick up Town's only bookings of the season.											
34	H	FULHAM		3	W	2-1	0-1	Wallace 71, Holmes 78	Smith	Burgin	McCarthy	Wallace	Pickering	Rhodes	Chadwick	Atkins*	Lawther	Lennard	Holmes	Robertson
	6/3		8,019	*2*	42			*Johnston 27*	*Webster*	*Brown*	*Moreline*	*Callaghan*	*Matthewson*	*Dunne*	*Conway*	*Johnston*	*Earle*	*Lloyd*	*Barrett*	
								Ref: W Johnson	For an hour Fulham show why they are the league-leaders. George Johnston's goal looks like being good enough for them. But the huge Shay crowd gets behind their team as never before. Wallace fires in from 20 yards, and Holmes's header across Webster seals a memorable victory.											

No / Date	H/A	Opponent / Att	Div / Pos	Res / Pts	F-A	H-T	Scorers, Times, Referees	1	2	3	4	5	6	7	8	9	10	11	12
35	A	ASTON VILLA	3	D	1-1	0-1	Chadwick 62	Smith	Lee	Buxton	Wallace	Pickering	Rhodes	Chadwick	Atkins	Lawther	Lennard	Holmes	
13/3		*33,522*	*4*	43			*Turnbull 31*	*Dunn*	*Bradley*	*Aitken*	*Godfrey**	*Turnbull*	*Tiler*	*McMahon*	*Vowden*	*Lochhead*	*Hamilton*	*Anderson*	*Rioch*
							Ref: P Oliver	Villa's side cost £300,000 to assemble. Town's is worth £34,000. On the day it matters not. Again, it's Turnbull who gets Villa's goal, after Smith misjudges Hamilton's flighted ball, but Chadwick's left-footer equalises. Atkins then actually misses a chance to win this massive game.											
36	H	SWANSEA	3	D	2-2	1-2	Chadwick 38, Lennard 65	Smith	Burgin	Lee	Wallace	Pickering*	Rhodes	Chadwick	Atkins	Lawther	Lennard	Holmes	Robertson
16/3		8,153	*11*	44			*Gwyther 19, Thomas 44*	*Millington*	*Slee*	*Lawrence*	*Williams A*	*Rosser*	*Hole*	*Slattery*	*Thomas*	*Screen W*	*Gwyther*	*Evans B*	
							Ref: R Capey	Roy Bentley's Swansea side upsets the formbook. They are, nevertheless, worth a draw. Dave Gwyther causes problems all evening, heading the game's opener, then having a hand in Geoff Thomas's goal. But in the last minute, Holmes's header onto the post almost wins it for Town.											
37	H	MANSFIELD	4	L	0-1	0-0		Smith	Burgin	Lee	Wallace	Pickering	Rhodes	Chadwick	Atkins	Lawther	Lennard	Holmes	
20/3		6,667	*7*	44			*Roberts D 61*	*Arnold*	*Pate*	*Walker*	*Stenson*	*Boam*	*Saunders*	*Thompson*	*Roberts R*	*Roberts D*	*Jarvis**	*Jones*	*Derrick*
							Ref: T Baldwin	This defeat not only puts a big dent in Town's promotion hopes. It also means Bill Atkins will have to get his hair cut. He vowed not to have it cropped until Town lost again. The Stags' Dudley Roberts heads in Dave Thompson's corner to ensure Atkins' appointment with the barber.											
38	A	WALSALL	4	D	0-0	0-0		Smith	Burgin	Lee	Wallace	Pickering	Rhodes	Chadwick	Atkins	Brierley	Lennard	Holmes	
27/3		*3,824*	*22*	45				*Wesson*	*Harrison*	*Evans*	*Penman**	*Jones*	*Atthey*	*Morris*	*Woodward*	*Seal*	*Bennett*	*Taylor*	*Deakin*
							Ref: A Morrissey	Walsall, under Bill Moore, are fighting a relegation battle. This point might just save them, but it isn't what Town require. Another concern for George Kirby is that his side fail to score again, and never look likely to. Kirby can't explain it, but pleads with the fans, 'Don't desert us.'											
39	H	GILLINGHAM	3	W	2-1	0-1	Pickering 53, Wallace 66p	Smith	Burgin	Lee	Wallace	Pickering	Rhodes	Chadwick	Atkins*	Brierley	Lennard	Holmes	Lawther
3/4		4,026	*24*	47			*Green 27*	*Simpson*	*McVeigh*	*Peach*	*Tydemann*	*Williams*	*Quirke*	*Kent**	*Yeo*	*Green*	*Darrell*	*Watson*	*Bailey*
							Ref: I Smith	Bottom club Gillingham look like pulling off one of the shocks of the season when Mike Green makes the most of a defensive error. But Town step up a gear after the break. Pickering heads the equaliser, and when Kent pushes Wallace, the Town player himself converts the penalty.											
40	A	ROCHDALE	3	W	3-0	3-0	Rhodes 27, Lennard 34, Atkins 45	Smith	Burgin	Lee	Wallace	Pickering	Rhodes	Chadwick	Atkins	Robertson	Lennard	Holmes	
10/4		*5,756*	*17*	49				*Godfrey*	*Smith*	*Ryder*	*Riley*	*Parry*	*Blair*	*Whitehead*	*Jenkins*	*Cross*	*Gowans*	*Butler*	
							Ref: E Wallace	Other results go Town's way. Promotion is still on. Town have also got an eye on next season's Watney Cup, designed for the each division's top scorers. Their three goals win this game before the break. Lennard scores and makes one, while Chadwick's lovely chip sets up Rhodes.											
41	A	SHREWSBURY	3	D	2-2	1-1	Atkins 8, Lennard 75	Smith	Burgin	Lee	Wallace	Pickering	Rhodes	Chadwick	Atkins	Robertson	Lennard	Holmes	
14/4		*5,046*		50			*Groves 16, 81*	*Mulhearn*	*Gregory*	*Fellows*	*Matthias*	*Wood*	*Bridgwood*	*Roberts*	*Moir*	*Andrews*	*McLaughlin*	*Groves*	
							Ref: C Fallon	Questions are now being asked whether the Shaymen really want to go up. Lennard's header over Ken Mulhearn should have given Town both points, but Shrewsbury's £3,500 signing Alan Groves is allowed a second equaliser. In the last minute, though, Atkins's header nearly wins it.											
42	H	CHESTERFIELD	3	W	1-0	1-0	Lennard 17	Smith	Burgin	Lee	Wallace	Pickering	Rhodes	Chadwick	Atkins	Robertson	Lennard	Holmes	
17/4		6,609	*6*	52				*Stevenson*	*Holmes*	*Tiler*	*Fenoughty*	*Stott*	*Phelan*	*Cliff*	*Moss*	*Randall*	*Archer*	*Pugh*	
							Ref: R Matthewson	The dream is still alive. But Town must hope that Preston and Fulham, who have still to play each other, will slip up. The Shaymen avenge their FA Cup defeat when Robertson puts Lennard through for a decisive early goal. Chesterfield's ten-match unbeaten run comes to an end.											
43	A	BRIGHTON	3	W	2-0	1-0	Chadwick 23, Robertson 86	Smith	Burgin	Lee	Wallace	Pickering	Rhodes	Chadwick	Atkins	Robertson	Lennard	Holmes	
24/4		*10,671*	*16*	54				*Powney*	*Henderson*	*Spearitt*	*Templemann*	*Napier J*	*Gall*	*Murray*	*Napier K*	*Irvine*	*Turner**	*O'Sullivan*	*Duffy*
							Ref: D Corbett	Lammie Robertson is Town's hero. He dispossesses Templeman on the edge of the box to set up Chadwick's goal, then scores a low drive late on to secure the points. Brighton are full of ideas but can't find a way through. Town defend sternly, and Alex Smith's handling is impeccable.											
44	A	TORQUAY	3	L	0-2	0-1		Smith	Verity	Lee	Wallace	Pickering	Rhodes	Chadwick	Atkins*	Robertson	Lennard	Holmes	Lawther
28/4		*3,244*	*12*	54			*Rudge 44, 63*	*Donnelly*	*Twitchin*	*Kitchener*	*Lucas*	*Harrison*	*Edwards*	*Welsh E**	*Welsh A*	*Rudge*	*Mitchinson*	*Jackson*	*Stuckey*
							Ref: H New	The breaks go against Town and the dream is all but over. John Rudge's hopeful 25-yarder bounces over Smith and goes in. In the 47th minute Robertson gets through, but his shot cannons off the bar. When Smith pushes Eric Welsh's low cross onto the post, Rudge sews the game up.											
45	H	BARNSLEY	3	W	4-1	3-0	Chadwick, Atkins , Holmes 24, [Wallace 85p]	Smith	Verity	Lee	Wallace	Pickering	Rhodes	Chadwick	Atkins	Robertson	Lennard	Holmes	
1/5		6,332		56			*Lea p*	*Arblaster*	*Murphy*	*Chambers*	*Boardman*	*Raggett*	*Howard*	*Lea*	*Booth*	*Winstanley*	*Miller*	*Sharp**	*Boughan*
							Ref: K Howley	Preston's win at Fulham ensures Town will remain in Division 3 next season. They go for goals, though, and book a place in the Watney Cup. They roll Barnsley over with three goals in the first 24 minutes, and add a fourth after Les Lea's penalty, when Rhodes impedes Winstanley.											
46	A	SWANSEA	3	L	1-3	0-1	Rhodes 72	Smith	Burgin	Lee*	Wallace	Pickering	Rhodes	Chadwick	Atkins	Robertson	Lennard	Holmes	Lawther
4/5		*3,789*	*11*	56			*Evans B 24, Holme 49, Gwyther*	*Millington*	*Morgan*	*Screen A*	*Evans K**	*Williams H*	*Screen W*	*Sullivan*	*Thomas*	*Holme*	*Gwyther*	*Evans B*	*Williams A*
Average	Home 5,134	Away 7,673					Ref: P Walters	The Shaymen end on a disappointing note as Swansea's teenage defence gives them much to think about. Brian Evans heads in a free-kick and his side hardly looks back. Rhodes is off the pitch when Gwyther makes it 3-0 with his 27th of the season, but he returns to score a consolation.											

LEAGUE DIVISION 3 (CUP-TIES)

Manager: George Kirby

SEASON 1970-71

League Cup					F-A	H-T	Scorers, Times, and Referees	1	2	3	4	5	6	7	8	9	10	11	12 sub used
1	H	BRADFORD C		W	3-2	2-0	Brierley 25, Burgin 35, Atkins 86	Smith	Burgin	Buxton	Robertson	Pickering	Wallace	Chadwick	Atkins	Brierley	Lennard	McCarthy	
	19/8	6,146					*Owen 54, Ham 71*	*Roberts*	*Atkins*	*Cooper*	*Stowell*	*Hallett*	*McConnell*	*Hall J*	*Ham*	*Hall C*	*Owen*	*O'Neill*	
							Ref: C Fallon	An all-ticket crowd sees Town cruise to a 2-0 half-time lead. Terry Owen pulls one back when John Hall's shot comes back off the bar and the course of the game is altered. Ham's equaliser surprises no one, but when Atkins reads Les O'Neill's backpass, the tie swings Halifax's way.											
2	A	DERBY	12	L	1-3	1-2	McCarthy 26	Smith	Burgin	Buxton	Robertson	Pickering	Wallace	Chadwick	Atkins	Brierley	Lennard	McCarthy*	Holmes
	8/9	*20,029*	*1:8*				*Durban 19, 68, Hector 45*	*Green*	*Webster*	*Robson*	*Durban*	*McFarland**	*Rhodes*	*Wignall*	*Carlin*	*O'Hare*	*Hector*	*Hinton*	*Daniel*
							Ref: P Partridge	Former Shay favourite Willie Carlin is made Derby captain for the evening by boss Brian Clough. His side does enough but Town never give it up. McCarthy heads the equaliser for Town, before Hector restores Derby's lead right on half-time. Late on, Atkins hits the inside of the post.											

FA Cup								1	2	3	4	5	6	7	8	9	10	11	12 sub used
1	A	CHESTERFIELD	10	L	0-2	0-1		Smith	Burgin	Lee	Robertson	Lawther	Wallace*	Chadwick	Atkins	Brierley	Lennard	McCarthy	Buxton
	21/11	*11,596*	*9*				*Moss 44, 51*	*Stevenson*	*Holmes*	*Phelan*	*Fenoughty*	*Bell*	*Stott*	*Randall*	*Moss*	*Wright*	*Archer*	*Pugh*	
							Ref: C Robinson	Town lost 0-5 here in the league, and are second-best again. Ernie Moss's goals either side of half-time settle the issue. Smith is expecting a cross when Moss fires in off the angle for his second. Lennard goes close for Town, being thwarted firstly by Stevenson, and then the post.											

		Home					Away					
	P	W	D	L	F	A	W	D	L	F	A	Pts
1 Preston	46	15	8	0	42	16	7	9	7	21	23	61
2 Fulham	46	15	6	2	39	12	9	6	8	29	29	60
3 HALIFAX	46	16	2	5	46	22	6	10	7	28	33	56
4 Aston Villa	46	13	7	3	27	13	6	8	9	27	33	53
5 Chesterfield	46	13	8	2	45	12	4	9	10	21	26	51
6 Bristol Rov	46	11	5	7	38	24	8	8	7	31	26	51
7 Mansfield	46	13	7	3	44	28	5	8	10	20	34	51
8 Rotherham	46	12	10	1	38	19	5	6	12	26	41	50
9 Wrexham	46	12	8	3	43	25	6	5	12	29	40	49
10 Torquay	46	12	6	5	37	26	7	5	11	17	31	49
11 Swansea	46	11	5	7	41	25	4	11	8	18	31	46
12 Barnsley	46	12	6	5	30	19	5	5	13	19	33	45
13 Shrewsbury	46	11	6	6	37	28	5	7	11	21	34	45
14 Brighton	46	8	10	5	28	20	6	6	11	22	27	44
15 Plymouth	46	6	12	5	39	33	6	7	10	24	30	43
16 Rochdale	46	8	8	7	29	26	6	7	10	32	42	43
17 Port Vale	46	11	6	6	29	18	4	6	13	23	41	42
18 Tranmere	46	8	11	4	27	18	2	11	10	18	37	42
19 Bradford C	46	7	6	10	23	25	6	8	9	26	37	40
20 Walsall	46	10	1	12	30	27	4	10	9	21	30	39
21 Reading	46	10	7	6	32	33	4	4	15	16	52	39
22 Bury	46	7	9	7	30	23	5	4	14	22	37	37
23 Doncaster	46	8	5	10	28	27	5	4	14	17	39	35
24 Gillingham	46	6	9	8	22	29	4	4	15	20	38	33
	1104	255	168	129	824	548	129	168	255	548	824	1104

Odds & ends

Double wins: (3) Doncaster, Port Vale, Tranmere.
Double losses: (1) Mansfield.

Won from behind: (4) Fulham (h), Gillingham (h), Tranmere (h), Doncaster (a).
Lost from in front: (2) Rochdale (h), Mansfield (a).

High spots: 13 games unbeaten up to 20 March.
Beating the two promoted sides, Fulham and Preston, at the Shay.
Four consecutive wins in January.
George Kirby being voted Manager of the Month for February.

Low spots: Losing three consecutive games up to 7 November.
Losing 0-5 at Chesterfield.
Losing at home to Mansfield in the promotion run-in.

Halifax scored 74 goals in the League, the highest in the division.
Only 16 players were used, the lowest in the club's history.

Player of the Year: Dave Chadwick.
Ever-presents: (4) Dave Chadwick, Dave Lennard, John Pickering, Alex Smith.
Hat-tricks: (0).
Leading scorer: Bill Atkins (19).

	Appearances						Goals			
	Lge	*Sub*	LC	*Sub*	FAC	*Sub*	Lge	LC	FAC	Tot
Atkins, Bill	**45**		2		1		**18**	1		**19**
Brierley, Keith	**28**	*1*	2		1		**9**	1		**10**
Burgin, Andy	**43**		2		1		**4**	1		**5**
Buxton, Mick	**14**		2			*1*				
Chadwick, Dave	**46**		2		1		**7**			**7**
Holmes, Barry	**25**	*1*		*1*			**3**			**3**
Lawther, Ian	**12**	*12*			1		**3**			**3**
Lee, Jeff	**31**	*2*			1					
Lennard, Dave	**46**		2		1		**11**			**11**
McCarthy, Phil	**23**	*1*	2		1		**3**	1		**4**
Pickering, John	**46**		2				**3**			**3**
Rhodes, Tony	**28**						**4**			**4**
Robertson, Lammie	**25**	*3*	2		1		**3**			**3**
Smith, Alex	**46**		2		1					
Verity, David	**2**									
Wallace, Bob	**46**		2		1		**6**			**6**
16 players used	**506**	***20***	**22**	***1***	**11**	***1***	**74**	**4**		**78**

LEAGUE DIVISION 3   Manager: Ray Henderson   SEASON 1971-72

No	Date		Att	Pos	Pt	F-A	H-T	Scorers, Times, and Referees	1	2	3	4	5	6	7	8	9	10	11	12 sub used
1	A	MANSFIELD			D	0-0	0-0		Smith	Burgin	Lee	Wallace	Pickering	Rhodes	Chadwick	Atkins	Robertson	Lennard	Holmes	
	14/8		*5,801*		1				*Brown*	*Pate*	*Walker*	*Roberts R*	*Harford*	*Waller*	*Thompson*	*Stenson*	*Roberts D*	*Jarvis*	*Harrington*	
								Ref: N Paget	Boss Ray Henderson only took over four days ago and doesn't really know his players. But he vows to keep the accent on attack, and his team do create a host of chances. But they are almost undone on 77 minutes when the Stags' Bobby Roberts smashes a 25-yarder against the post.											
2	H	YORK		2	W	3-1	2-1	Lennard 3, 43, Atkins 85	Smith	Burgin	Lee	Wallace	Pickering	Rhodes	Chadwick	Atkins	Verity	Lennard	Holmes*	Robertson
	21/8		4,930	*20*	3			*McMahon 4*	*Hillyard*	*Mackin*	*Burrows*	*Galloway*	*Swallow*	*Topping*	*Chambers*	*Hewitt*	*McMahon*	*Aimson*	*Henderson*	
								Ref: S Kayley	The YTV cameras capture this action-crammed match against promoted York. It's a sensational start, with Kevin McMahon equalising while the home supporters are still applauding Lennard's opener. York are searching for a second equaliser when Atkins' shot goes in off the post.											
3	A	BRADFORD C		13	L	1-2	0-1	Robertson 78	Smith	Burgin	Lee	Wallace	Pickering	Rhodes	Chadwick	Atkins	Robertson	Lennard	Holmes	
	28/8		*6,053*	*21*	3			*Pickering 29 (og), Owen 88*	*Liney*	*Howell*	*Podd*	*Stowell*	*Oates*	*Cooper*	*Hall J*	*Bannister*	*Owen*	*Middleton*	*Hall C**	*O'Neill*
								Ref: P Partridge	John Pickering heads Bruce Bannister's free-kick into his own net, but Town dominate the second half. Holmes has a goal disallowed before Robertson gets the equaliser. Seconds after Holmes missed a glorious chance, City's Terry Owen wins a race for the ball to score the winner.											
4	H	BOURNEMOUTH		10	W	1-0	1-0	Wallace 17	Smith	Burgin	Lee	Wallace	Pickering	Rhodes	Chadwick	Atkins	Robertson	Lennard	Holmes	
	4/9		4,778	*3*	5				*Davies*	*Benson*	*Stocks*	*Jones*	*Kitchener*	*Powell*	*Cave*	*MacDougall*	*Boyer*	*Miller*	*Sainty**	*Davidson*
								Ref: E Jolly	League-leaders Bournemouth have spent £130,000 on players this year, but their talent is rarely expressed in this game. Ted MacDougall, who scored 41 goals last season, fluffs his one good chance, so Wallace's goal, after the Cherries failed to clear a corner, is good enough for Town.											
5	A	BARNSLEY		8	W	2-1	1-1	Lennard 29, Robertson 77	Smith	Burgin	Lee	Wallace	Pickering	Rhodes	Chadwick	Atkins	Robertson	Lennard	Holmes*	Verity
	11/9		*5,751*	*22*	7			*Lea 17*	*Barker*	*Murphy*	*Booth*	*Boardman*	*Winstanley*	*Howard*	*Earnshaw*	*Lea*	*Seal*	*Millar*	*Sharp*	
								Ref: D Lyden	The Shaymen come from behind to join the early leaders. Lennard's equaliser is remarkable, returning Barker's poor goal-kick. Robertson fires in the winner from 15 yards. The ref denies Town a late penalty when Barker hauls Chadwick down as he's about to score, and gives a corner.											
6	H	ASTON VILLA		11	L	0-1	0-0		Smith	Burgin	Lee	Wallace	Pickering	Rhodes	Chadwick	Atkins	Robertson	Lennard	Verity	
	18/9		**7,462**	*6*	7			*Graydon 82*	*Hughes*	*Bradley*	*Aitken*	*Rioch B*	*Turnbull**	*Tiley*	*Graydon*	*Vowden*	*Lochhead*	*Hamilton*	*Anderson*	*Beard*
								Ref: C Fallon	Villa show championship form. They are distinctly second best all afternoon, then nick the game. Wallace goes desperately close for Town, then four minutes later the visitors score. Willie Anderson breaks down the right, and when Smith fails to hold his shot, Ray Graydon nips in.											
7	A	PORT VALE		14	L	0-1	0-0		Smith	Burgin*	Lee	Wallace	Pickering	Rhodes	Chadwick	Atkins	Robertson	Lennard	**Farley**	Brierley
	25/9		*3,724*	*9*	7			*Gough 78*	*Bell*	*Boulton*	*Lacey*	*Flowers*	*Cross*	*Summerscales*	*Morris**	*Horton*	*Gough*	*Morgan*	*McLaren*	*Mountford*
								Ref: D Smith	Again Town are the better side, yet end up with nothing. They create a number of chances, and on-loan John Farley hits the post. Victory for Gordon Lee's side looks remote until Bob Mountford forces Smith to fist a high centre away. Lacey returns the ball and Bob Gough can't miss.											
8	A	BOLTON			D	1-1	0-0	Atkins 46	Smith	Brierley	Lee	Wallace	Pickering	Rhodes	Chadwick	Atkins	Robertson	Lennard	Farley*	Verity
	29/9		*9,304*		8			*Greaves 70*	*Wright*	*Ritson*	*Mowbray*	*Nicholson*	*Hulme*	*Rimmer*	*Jones P**	*Hunt*	*Jones G*	*Greaves*	*Byrom*	*Rowe*
								Ref: V Batty	Bolton are in Division 3 for the first time, but have since appointed ex-England skipper Jimmy Armfield as manager. World Cup winner Roger Hunt is in their side, but it's his failure to clear his lines that leads to Atkins' goal. Greaves levels it after Smith collides with John Byrom.											
9	H	TRANMERE		12	W	3-2	2-2	Farley 10, 15, Brierley 81	Smith	Brierley	Lee*	Wallace	Pickering	Rhodes	Chadwick	Atkins	Robertson	Lennard	Farley	Verity
	2/10		4,234	*17*	10			*Beamish 32, Coyne 35*	*Lawrence*	*Mathias*	*Dempsey*	*Moorcroft*	*Molyneux*	*Brodie*	*Russell*	*Coyne*	*Crossley*	*Beamish*	*Storton**	*Moore M*
								Ref: T Dawes	Tommy Lawrence, signed from Liverpool yesterday, is caught out by Brierley's header that wins the game. He expects the ball to go over the bar, but it dips late. Town had raced into a two-goal lead, before allowing the visitors to claw it back with headers from Beamish and Coyne.											
10	A	OLDHAM		13	D	0-0	0-0		Smith	Burgin	Lee	Wallace	Pickering	Rhodes	Chadwick	Atkins	Robertson	Brierley	Farley	
	9/10		*9,526*	*7*	11				*Dowd*	*Wood*	*Whittle*	*Cranston*	*Mulvaney*	*Bowie*	*Heath*	*Shaw*	*Garwood*	*Bryceland*	*Bebbington*	
								Ref: T Reynolds	After the shock record transfer of utility man Dave Lennard to Blackpool, the Town players look subdued. The game is not helped by some erratic refereeing, but Town are awarded a 57th-minute penalty. Harry Dowd brings down Brierley, but easily saves Wallace's apologetic kick.											
11	H	MANSFIELD		12	D	1-1	0-0	Wallace 53p	Smith	Burgin	Lee	Wallace	Pickering	Rhodes	Chadwick	Atkins	Robertson*	Brierley	Farley	**Johnston**
	16/10		3,864	*24*	12			*Fairbrother 66*	*Brown*	*Pate*	*Walker*	*Stenson*	*Saunders*	*Waller*	*Thompson*	*Roberts R*	*Roberts D**	*Jarvis*	*Fairbrother*	*Jones*
								Ref: G Jones	Bottom of the table Mansfield earn a point, but mystery surrounds the identity of their scorer. Fairbrother's corner appears to go straight in, but Bobby Roberts and Stenson also claim it. Whoever, it cancels out Wallace's penalty when Walker prevents Chadwick from getting to the ball.											

No	Date	Venue	Opponent	Att	Pos	Opp Pos	Res	Pts	F-A	H-T	Scorers, Times, and Referees	1	2	3	4	5	6	7	8	9	10	11	Subs used
12	19/10	H	ROCHDALE	3,288			D	13	2-2	1-0	Brierley 30, Farley 50	Smith	Burgin	Lee	Wallace	Pickering	Robertson !	Chadwick	Atkins	Johnston	Brierley	Farley	
											Kinsella 61, 71	*Godfrey*	*Smith*	*Ryder*	*Gowans*	*Blair*	*Ashworth*	*Whitehead*	*Darling*	*Buck*	*Kinsella*	*Butler*	
											Ref: J Thacker	Heavy rain brings all sorts of problems. The visitors' dressing room is flooded hours before kick-off. The waterlogged pitch makes it difficult for the players and three are booked. But it isn't responsible for Robertson's 81st-minute sending-off, for an off-the-ball incident with Darling.											
13	23/10	H	CHESTERFIELD	4,667	8	*10*	W	15	2-0	0-0	Pickering 74, Johnston 88	Smith	Burgin	Lee	Wallace	Pickering	Rhodes	Chadwick	Atkins	Robertson	Brierley	Johnston	
												Stevenson	*Moyes*	*Tiler*	*Pugh*	*Stott*	*Phelan*	*Wright*	*Moss*	*Randall*	*Archer*	*McHale*	
											Ref: C Robinson	Town bring an end to the Spireites four-game unbeaten run. With 16 minutes left a draw looks likely. Then Pickering, who later earns a second successive booking, spectacularly heads in off a free-kick. Chesterfield are still in the hunt when on-loan Johnny Johnston whips in the second.											
14	30/10	A	WREXHAM	*7,150*	12	*13*	L	15	0-2	0-1		Smith	Burgin	Lee	Wallace	Pickering	Rhodes	Chadwick	Atkins	Robertson	Brierley	Johnston*	Verity
											Kinsey 8, Provan 88	*Lloyd*	*Mason*	*Vansittart*	*Evans*	*Ashcroft*	*May*	*Moir*	*Whittle*	*McBurney*	*Kinsey*	*Provan*	
											Ref: C Howell	Wrexham are on a roll, too. This is their fifth consecutive win, and has taken them from 22nd to 13th. They are full value for this victory, as Town create only one decent chance. Kinsey intercepts Robertson's cross-field pass for his goal. Provan's effort comes off McBurney's cross.											
15	6/11	H	ROTHERHAM	5,409	11	*4*	D	16	1-1	1-1	Brogan 30	Smith	Burgin	Lee	Wallace	Pickering	Rhodes	Chadwick	Atkins	Robertson	Brierley	Brogan	
											Ham 38	*Tunks*	*Houghton*	*Leigh*	*Quinn*	*Mielczarek*	*Swift*	*Bentley*	*Gilbert*	*Ham*	*Johnson*	*Mullen*	
											Ref: P Baldwin	The Shaymen have now drawn five of their last eight games. Worse, the Shay is no longer a fortress. The appearance of new signing Brogan puts the gate up. He makes a pleasing debut and scores from outside the box. Gilbert looks offside when he sets up Ham for the equaliser.											
16	13/11	A	BRIGHTON	*9,896*	16	*6*	L	16	1-2	0-1	Brogan 52	Smith	Burgin	Lee	Wallace	Pickering	Rhodes	Chadwick	Atkins	Verity	Brierley	Brogan	
											O'Sullivan 27, Irvine 84	*Powney*	*Henderson*	*Spearitt*	*Templeman*	*Napier J*	*Gall*	*Murray*	*Napier K*	*Irvine*	*Turner*	*O'Sullivan*	
											Ref: C Nicholls	Wallace is left to rue a twice-taken penalty. He scores with his first kick, but the ref orders a retake for encroachment. Powney saves his second effort, and two minutes later O'Sullivan scores. Brogan's swerving shot levels it, but Rhodes' 30-yard backpass lets in Irvine for a late winner.											
17	15/11	H	PLYMOUTH	2,832			L	16	0-1	0-0		Smith	Burgin	Lee	Wallace	Pickering	Rhodes	Chadwick	Atkins	Verity	Brierley	Brogan*	Holmes
											Hinch 65	*Furnell*	*Davey*	*Harris*	*Hore*	*Saxton*	*Latchman*	*Reed*	*Allen*	*Hinch*	*Rickard*	*Hutchins*	
											Ref: J Wrennall	Disaster strikes twice for the Shaymen. Recent £4,000 buy Brogan fractures an ankle after a tackle by Steve Davey in the 13th minute. He will be out for the rest of the season. Argyle go on to score a fortunate goal. Rhodes deflects the ball past Smith, who had Jim Hinch's shot covered.											
18	27/11	A	SWANSEA	*5,288*	16	*4*	L	16	0-3	0-1		Smith	Burgin	Lee	Verity	Pickering	Rhodes	Chadwick	Shanahan	Brierley	Waddle	Holmes	
											Gwyther 30, 61, Davies 78	*Millington*	*Jones*	*Screen A*	*Williams A*	*Williams H*	*Hole*	*Holme*	*Thomas G*	*Davies*	*Gwyther*	*Sullivan*	
											Ref: A Oliver	The Vetch Field resembles a mudbath, and the game is delayed by 16 minutes. But Swansea still manage to notch up their sixth consecutive home win. How Town could do with someone like Dave Gwyther, who scores two, and crosses for Glen Davies to get the third with a header.											
19	4/12	H	WALSALL	3,421	*12*	*21*	W	18	3-1	0-1	Chadwick 50, Shanahan 82, Wallace 85p	Smith	Burgin	Lee	Kemp	Pickering	Rhodes	Chadwick	Shanahan	Brierley	Wallace	Verity	
											Jones 43	*Wesson*	*Gregg*	*Harrison*	*Penman*	*Jones S*	*Bennett*	*Taylor B**	*Wright*	*Woodward*	*Atthey*	*Train*	*Morris*
											Ref: A Jones	This much-needed win temporarily halts Town's slide down the table. Record signing Fred Kemp makes a favourable debut, while another new boy, Shanahan, calmly slides the ball home to give Town the lead for the first time. Stan Bennett trips Chadwick for Wallace's penalty.											
20	18/12	A	BOURNEMOUTH	*10,853*	15	*2*	L	18	1-3	0-0	Chadwick 46	Smith	Burgin	Lee	Wallace	Pickering	Rhodes	Chadwick	Atkins	Brierley	Kemp	Verity	
											Scott 53, Kitchener 82, Jones 86	*Davies*	*Machin*	*Miller*	*Benson*	*Kitchener*	*Powell*	*Cave**	*MacDougall*	*Boyer*	*De Garis*	*Scott*	*Jones*
											Ref: I Jones	Bournemouth keep up their title challenge with the help of a couple of controversial goals. Scott is offside when MacDougall's shot hits him and goes in. MacDougall appears to push Smith when Kitchener gives the Cherries the lead. Burgin's 60-yard run sets up Chadwick's opener.											
21	27/12	H	BLACKBURN	7,218	16	*19*	L	18	0-1	0-0		Smith	Burgin	Lee	Wallace	Pickering	Rhodes	Chadwick	Atkins	Shanahan	Kemp	Verity*	Robertson
											McNamee 60	*Jones*	*Heaton*	*Wood*	*Bradford*	*McNamee*	*Fazackerley*	*Arentoft*	*Garbutt*	*Endean*	*Parks*	*Field*	
											Ref: V Batty	Seven minutes into the second half, the floodlights go out and the game is held up for 20 minutes. Eight minutes after the restart, Tony Field, to whom Halifax gave a free transfer in 1966, takes the free-kick from which John McNamee scores. Two minutes later Kemp's effort hits the bar.											
22	1/1	A	ASTON VILLA	***32,749***	19	*3*	L	18	0-1	0-0		Smith	Burgin	Lee	Wallace	Pickering	Rhodes	Chadwick	Robertson	Shanahan	Kemp*	Verity	Atkins
											Graydon 46	*Cumbes*	*Wright*	*Aitken*	*Rioch B*	*Curtis*	*Turnbull*	*Graydon*	*Brown*	*Lochhead*	*Vowden**	*Anderson*	*Hamilton*
											Ref: S Kayley	In front of the second highest attendance in the division this season, Town's best is not good enough. Chadwick, Kemp and Shanahan all waste first-half opportunities. As at the Shay, it is Ray Graydon who snatches it, 25 seconds into the second half after a Town move is broken up.											
23	8/1	H	BRADFORD C	4,867	16	*18*	W	20	2-1	2-0	Robertson 15, Shanahan 33	Smith	Burgin	Lee	Wallace	Pickering	Rhodes	Chadwick	Robertson	Shanahan	Kemp	Verity	
											Owen 75	*Oldfield*	*McHale*	*Howell*	*Stowell*	*Cooke*	*Cooper*	*Hall J*	*Hall C*	*Owen*	*O'Neill*	*Middleton*	
											Ref: V James	Halifax Town's recent five-day break in Majorca pays dividends. Robertson heads the opener, then Smith makes a great double save before Shanahan's goal makes it 2-0. City contest it, claiming that Robertson impeded Oldfield. Owen's goal makes for an interesting last 15 minutes.											

No	Date		Att	Pos	Pt	F-A	H-T	Scorers, Times, and Referees	1	2	3	4	5	6	7	8	9	10	11	12 sub used
24	H	BOLTON		19	L	0-1	0-0		Smith	Burgin	Lee	Wallace	Pickering	Rhodes	Chadwick	Robertson	Shanahan	Kemp	Atkins	
	22/1		3,919	*16*	20			*Hunt 49*	*Wright*	*Ritson*	*McAllister*	*Waldron*	*Jones P*	*Hulme*	*Jones G*	*Hunt*	*Greaves*	*Seddon*	*Byrom*	
								Ref: K Baker	Bolton record their first victory in over three months. Roger Hunt's goal, his 264th of his league career, is preventable. Pickering's challenge on Byrom isn't enough and the ball runs free to Hunt. Town now look in trouble, but the board gives Henderson another vote of confidence.											
25	A	ROCHDALE		19	L	2-3	1-1	Atkins 32, Wallace 79	Smith	Burgin	Lee	Wallace	Pickering	Rhodes	Chadwick	Atkins*	Robertson	Kemp	Shanahan	Holmes
	29/1		*3,124*	*16*	20			*Parry 22, Howarth 66, 90*	*Godfrey*	*Smith*	*Ryder*	*Marsh*	*Parry*	*Kinsella*	*Whitehead*	*Gowans*	*Howarth*	*Darling*	*Butler*	
								Ref: A Morrissey	It isn't just the biting wind and cold that makes this an uncomfortable afternoon for the Shaymen. Defeat leaves them just three points clear of the relegation zone. Town recover from the loss of Atkins to draw level a second time, but in the last minute Howarth whips in Dale's winner.											
26	H	BRISTOL ROV		18	W	2-1	1-0	Kemp 45, Chadwick 77	Smith	Burgin	Lee	Wallace	Pickering	Rhodes*	Chadwick	Kemp	Robertson	Holmes	Shanahan	Verity
	5/2		**2,021**	*9*	22			*Bannister 74*	*Sheppard*	*Roberts*	*Parsons*	*Godfrey*	*Taylor*	*Prince*	*Stephens*	*Jones W*	*Stubbs*	*Bannister**	*Higgins*	*Jarman*
								Ref: D Laing	The Shay pitch is thick mud in places, but the ref gives the game the go-ahead. He also plays a good advantage for Robertson to set up Kemp for the opener. Stephens sets up Bannister and Rovers look good for a point, but Chadwick side-foots home Town's winner following a corner.											
27	A	CHESTERFIELD		18	L	1-2	0-1	Wallace 73p	Smith	Burgin	Lee	Wallace	Pickering	Verity	Chadwick	Kemp	Robertson	Holmes	Shanahan	
	12/2		*6,477*	*8*	22			*McHale 12, Moss 64*	*Mellor*	*Holmes*	*Tiler*	*Pugh*	*Bell*	*Stott*	*Wilson*	*Moss*	*Randall*	*Phelan*	*McHale*	
								Ref: R Toseland	Following advice from a fan, Henderson takes his players to the Yorkshire TV studios to watch re-runs of games from last season. The players, however, are not inspired. Even their goal has to be a penalty, when Chadwick's corner is handled. Chadwick later gets his first-ever booking.											
28	H	WREXHAM		16	W	**4-1**	2-0	Robertson 11, Kemp 29, Atkins 66, [Chadwick 71]	Smith	Burgin	Lee	Wallace	Pickering	Verity	Chadwick	Kemp	Robertson	Atkins	Shanahan*	Holmes
	19/2		2,478	*18*	24			*Mostyn 74*	*Gaskell*	*Mason*	*Ingle*	*Ashcroft*	*May*	*Evans*	*Moir**	*Tinnion*	*Mostyn*	*Park*	*Whittle*	*Smith*
								Ref: K Burns	The Town management held a 'talk-in' with the fans during the week. The side responds to the critics in fine style. The Wrexham forwards try roughing up Alex Smith, but it's Town's forwards who do the damage. Robertson rifles in the first whilst Chadwick deservedly gets the fourth.											
29	A	ROTHERHAM		18	L	2-3	2-1	Robertson 3,15	Smith	Burgin	Lee	Wallace	Pickering	Verity	Holmes	Kemp	Robertson	Atkins	Shanahan	
	26/2		*7,595*	*5*	24			*Gilbert 21, Mielczarek 88, Phillips 89*	*Tunks*	*Houghton*	*Leng*	*Quinn*	*Mielczarek*	*Swift*	*Bentley**	*Ham*	*Gilbert*	*Johnson*	*Mullen*	*Phillips*
								Ref: I Smith	Chadwick has been sold to Bournemouth for 'peanuts'. Without him Town race into a two-goal lead. Gilbert reduces the arrears, then his side turns the game with two goals in 30 seconds. Trevor Phillips seals it, but the Shaymen are left fuming, claiming that Smith already had the ball.											
30	H	BRIGHTON		19	L	**0-5**	0-3	*[Templeman 85, 90]*	Smith	Burgin	Lee	Wallace	Pickering	Verity	Brierley	Kemp	Robertson	Atkins	Shanahan*	Waddle
	4/3		2,432	*3*	24			*Irvine 8, Murray 30, Napier K 43,*	*Powney*	*Henderson*	*Spearitt*	*Templeman*	*Napier J*	*Gall*	*Murray*	*Napier K*	*Irvine*	*Bromley*	*O'Sullivan*	
								Ref: J Hunting	The pressure is on Henderson now. This game is over by half-time. Worse, several of the Town players look uninterested. Willie Irvine starts the rout. Verity deflects Murray's shot out of Smith's reach for 0-2. The second half is a lacklustre affair until Templeman's two late strikes.											
31	H	OLDHAM		19	D	0-0	0-0		Smith	Burgin	Lee	Verity	Pickering	Rhodes	Holmes	Kemp	Robertson	Atkins	Shanahan	
	11/3		3,404	*11*	25				*Dowd*	*Wood*	*Whittle*	*Bowie*	*Mulvaney*	*Cranston*	*Bebbington*	*Shaw*	*Robins*	*McNeill*	*Clements*	
								Ref: D Biddle	A stiff crosswind and a heavy pitch make things difficult, but Town do enough to restore some pride. Jimmy Frizzell's Oldham scored six in their last home match, but can't score here. Ian Wood thinks he has in the 68th minute, until he sees the linesman flagging David Shaw offside.											
32	H	TORQUAY		18	D	0-0	0-0		Smith	Burgin	Lee	Verity*	Pickering	Rhodes	Holmes	Kemp	Robertson	Atkins	Wallace	Shanahan
	14/3		2,080	*24*	26				*Connaughton*	*Boulton*	*Stocks*	*Lucas*	*Edwards*	*Hill BW*	*Twitchin*	*Welsh*	*Jackson*	*Sandercock K*	*Skirton*	
								Ref: W Hall	The Shaymen dominate this game, but can't fashion a goal against the division's bottom side. Torquay are now three points adrift. The familiar Connaughton twice denies Atkins. Skirton fluffs the game's best chance in the 68th minute. He goes through, hesitates, then puts the ball wide.											
33	A	YORK		18	D	1-1	1-1	Kemp 3	Smith	Burgin	Lee	Shanahan	Pickering	Rhodes	Holmes	Kemp	Robertson	Atkins	Wallace	
	18/3		3,943	*19*	27			*Mackin 41p*	*Crawford*	*Mackin*	*Burrows*	*Woodward*	*Swallow*	*Topping*	*Henderson*	*Rowles*	*Aimson*	*Galloway*	*Wann*	
								Ref: R Capey	York won their last home game 5-0, but both sides look tentative here. Kemp shoots low past Crawford to give Town something to hang on to, but the home side reply with Mackin's penalty when Rowles is checked. The ref finds seven minutes injury-time after four players are treated.											
34	A	TORQUAY		20	L	0-2	0-1		**White**	Burgin	Lee	Shanahan	Pickering	Rhodes	Holmes	Verity	Robertson	Atkins	Wallace	
	22/3		*4,147*	*24*	27			*Skirton 2, Twitchin 77*	*Connaughton*	*Boulton*	*Stocks*	*Twitchin*	*Edwards*	*Hill BW*	*Skirton**	*Welsh*	*Stubbs*	*Sandercock K*	*Jackson*	*Stuckey*
								Ref: T Reynolds	Ref Tom Reynolds comes under fire, and Town will report him over his 'general control'. He ignores the linesman's flag for a push on Rhodes when Skirton scores. Welsh looks well offside when Twitchin chases the keeper's long clearance for his goal. Town have four players booked.											

No	Date	Opponent	Att	Pos	Pts	F-A	H-T	Scorers, Times, and Referees	1	2	3	4	5	6	7	8	9	10	11	12 sub used
35	H	BARNSLEY		19	W	2-0	0-0	Wallace 51p, Atkins 54	White	Burgin	Lee	Wallace*	Pickering	Verity	Holmes	Kemp	Robertson	Atkins	Shanahan	Waddle
	25/3		2,702	*23*	29				*Stewart*	*Murphy*	*Booth*	*Greenwood*	*Winstanley*	*Brown*	*Boardman*	*Lea**	*Mahoney*	*Seal*	*Sharp*	*Millar*
								Ref: A Wynn	The Shaymen do themselves a favour by pushing Barnsley into deeper trouble. The visitors are a cynical lot, but pay for their misdemeanours when Eric Winstanley pushes Atkins in the box. Wallace cracks home the penalty. Three minutes later, Atkins fires in a centre from Shanahan.											
36	A	TRANMERE		19	W	3-2	1-2	Waddle 3, Atkins 72, Shanahan 81	White	Wallace	Lee	Kemp	Pickering	Verity	Holmes	Waddle	Robertson	Atkins	Shanahan	
	31/3		*5,125*	*21*	31			*King 4, Storton 43*	*Lawrence*	*Mathias*	*Farrimond*	*Molyneux*	*Yates*	*King*	*Russell*	*Crossley*	*Moore M*	*Storton*	*Maher*	
								Ref: D Corbett	A goal for either side in the opening four minutes sets the tone for this pulsating match, which swings one way, then the other. The Shaymen are behind when Holmes' shot takes a lucky deflection off Atkins' head. Shanahan finally settles it when he steers a low shot past Lawrence.											
37	H	PORT VALE		16	W	2-0	0-0	Holmes 65, Kemp 71	White	Burgin	Lee*	Wallace	Pickering	Verity	Kemp	Waddle	Robertson	Atkins	Shanahan	Holmes
	4/4		3,629	*14*	33				*Sharratt*	*Brodie*	*Loska*	*Summerscales*	*Cross*	*Flowers*	*Morris*	*Lacey*	*James*	*Morgan*	*Mountford*	
								Ref: W Johnson	Port Vale make life difficult for Town, but their back is finally broken with two spectacular goals in a six-minute spell. Following a corner, sub Holmes fires in a 30-yarder. Vale's Morgan misses a sitter, and 60 seconds later Shanahan reaches the by-line and crosses for Kemp to score.											
38	A	BRISTOL ROV		17	L	0-1	0-1		White	Burgin	Holmes	Wallace	Pickering	Verity	Kemp	Waddle	Robertson	Atkins	Shanahan	
	8/4		*5,642*		33			*John 40*	*Crabtree*	*Roberts*	*Parsons*	*Prince*	*Taylor*	*Green*	*Jones W*	*Jones R*	*Rudge*	*Jones B*	*John*	
								Ref: K Burns	Despite defeat, Town's performance is encouraging. On a windswept afternoon, a suspiciously looking offside Malcolm John heads the only goal when Bryn Jones' shot comes back off the post. In the last five minutes, Town come close to equalising but miss three good chances.											
39	A	NOTTS CO		17	L	1-3	0-2	Atkins 67	White	Burgin	Lee	Wallace	Pickering	Verity	Kemp	Waddle*	Robertson	Atkins	Rhodes	Shanahan
	12/4		*14,979*	*4*	33			*Cozens 15, 16, Carter 90*	*Brown*	*Brindley*	*Worthington*	*Jones*	*Needham*	*Stubbs*	*Nixon*	*Cozens*	*Bradd*	*Masson*	*Carter*	
								Ref: E Jolly	Town hope to pick up a point here, but after 15 minutes they have to alter their tactics when John Cozens scores two goals in a minute. After Atkins pulls one back, County winger Steve Carter thwarts Town at one end, then pops up at the other end to beat White with a spectacular lob.											
40	H	SWANSEA		19	L	0-1	0-1		White	Burgin	Lee	Wallace*	Pickering	Verity	Kemp	Holmes	Robertson	Atkins	Shanahan	Waddle
	15/4		2,620		33			*Gwyther 19*	*Millington*	*Fury*	*Morgan*	*Williams A*	*Thomas G*	*Ingram*	*Davies*	*Rees*	*Holme*	*Gwyther*	*Evans B*	
								Ref: W Castle	Not for the first time, Dave Gwyther is the scourge of the Shaymen. When Pickering attempts the pass, Verity lets the ball run, and Gwyther nips in. White helps keep the score down, and in the last minute Atkins has a goal chalked off for an infringement on Wales keeper Millington.											
41	H	NOTTS CO		18	W	3-1	1-0	Atkins 17, Holmes 50, Wallace 63	Smith	Burgin	Lee	Wallace	Pickering	Rhodes	Holmes	Kemp	Robertson	Atkins	Shanahan	
	18/4		3,943		35			*Bradd 75*	*Brown*	*Brindley*	*Worthington*	*Jones*	*Needham*	*Stubbs*	*Nixon*	*Cozens**	*Bradd*	*Masson*	*Carter*	*Cooper*
								Ref: R Lee	Henderson prepares his players by having a light meal at Bradley Hall Golf Club. A full and frank exchange of views is held, and Town might like to repeat the exercise. County could have gone second, but they are swept aside. Holmes is the star man and scores a belter from 25 yards.											
42	A	WALSALL		17	D	0-0	0-0		Smith	Burgin	Lee	Wallace	Pickering	Rhodes	Holmes	Kemp	Robertson	Atkins	Shanahan	
	21/4		*6,096*	*8*	36				*Wesson*	*Gregg*	*Evans*	*Harrison*	*Jones S*	*Atthey*	*Taylor B*	*Shinton*	*Jones C*	*Gough*	*Morris*	
								Ref: K Sweet	Fellows Park is a tough place to come and get goals right now. Walsall have only conceded 13 here all season. But Andy Burgin thinks he's got one when he fires home after carrying the ball forward. But the linesman flags Shanahan offside, though he is hardly interfering with play.											
43	A	PLYMOUTH		17	D	1-1	0-1	Atkins 54	Smith	Burgin	Lee	Wallace	Pickering	Rhodes	Holmes	Kemp	Robertson	Atkins	Shanahan	
	25/4		*7,756*		37			*Provan 22p*	*Balac*	*Harris*	*Sullivan*	*Hore*	*Provan*	*Hague*	*Allen*	*Hinch*	*Davey*	*Saxton*	*Latchman**	*Brown*
								Ref: T Spencer	Town's league position looks marginally better after this merited draw. Shanahan handles Allen's shot and Dave Provan nets the penalty, but Atkins heads the equaliser off Wallace's free-kick. Robertson gets his third booking in ten games, but victim Saxton is prepared to defend him.											
44	H	SHREWSBURY			D	0-0	0-0		Smith	Burgin	Lee	Wallace	Pickering	Rhodes	Holmes	Kemp	Robertson	Atkins	Shanahan	
	29/4		2,405		38				*Mulhearn*	*Bevan*	*Roberts I*	*Moore*	*Holton*	*Bridgwood*	*Roberts D*	*Andrews*	*Wood*	*Moir R*	*Groves*	
								Ref: J Wrennall	Shrewsbury boss Harry Gregg gives a debut at left-back to 16-year-old Ian Roberts. He looks one of the most assured players on view, but is hardly bothered by the Shaymen. Despite a terrible performance in a drab match, Town can celebrate. Their point means relegation is avoided.											
45	A	SHREWSBURY			L	0-3	0-1		Smith	Burgin	Lee	Wallace	Pickering	Rhodes	Holmes	Kemp	Robertson	Atkins	Shanahan	
	3/5		***2,329***		38			*Wood 20, 85, 88p*	*Mulhearn*	*Bevan*	*Roberts I*	*Moore*	*Holton*	*Bridgwood*	*Roberts D*	*Moir R*	*Wood*	*Andrews*	*Groves*	
								Ref: G Hill	How strange that Town should play much better in this swift return, yet concede three goals. They hit the woodwork twice, but are undone by Alf Wood's hat-trick. His penalty, when Pickering brought down Bevan, completes it, but two goals in the last five minutes flatter the Shrews.											
46	A	BLACKBURN		17	L	0-2	0-2		Smith	Burgin	Lee	Wallace	Pickering	Rhodes	Holmes	Kemp	Robertson	Brierley*	Shanahan	Waddle
	8/5		*6,499*	*10*	38			*Field 14, 26*	*Jones*	*Heaton*	*Farrell*	*Bradford*	*Martin*	*Fazackerley*	*Price*	*Garbett*	*Eccles**	*Parkes*	*Field*	*Endean*
		Home	Away					Ref: J Williams	Tony Field again helps bring down his former club by scoring both goals. The first is from eight yards, while the second is a beauty, blasting in from a difficult angle. Town fail to score again, but one feels Ray Henderson's fate was sealed awhile back. Eight days later he will be sacked.											
Average		3,852	7,818																	

League Cup

No	Date	Venue	Opponent	Att	Pos	Res	F-A	H-T	Scorers, Times, and Referees	1	2	3	4	5	6	7	8	9	10	11	12 sub used
1	18/8	H	ROCHDALE	5,195		D	1-1	1-1	Lennard 17	Smith	Burgin	Lee	Wallace	Pickering	Rhodes	Chadwick	Atkins	Robertson	Lennard	Holmes	
									Rhodes 31 (og)	*Jones*	*Blair*	*Ryder*	*Smith*	*Parry*	*Ashworth*	*Whitehead*	*Jenkins*	*Cross*	*Downes*	*Butler*	
									Ref: R Perkin												

4th Division Rochdale earn the right to a replay despite going behind. Atkins heads the ball through for Lennard to score, but over the course of the 90 minutes Dale are the better side. Their equaliser is deserved, if a little fortunate, when Rhodes heads Jenkins's shot into his own goal.

No	Date	Venue	Opponent	Att	Pos	Res	F-A	H-T	Scorers, Times, and Referees	1	2	3	4	5	6	7	8	9	10	11	12 sub used
1R	24/8	A	ROCHDALE	*6,016*	2	D	2-2 *aet*	1-0	Chadwick 25, Atkins 50	Smith	Burgin	Lee	Wallace	Pickering	Rhodes	Chadwick	Atkins	Verity	Lennard	Holmes	
									Cross 74, 82	*Jones*	*Blair**	*Ryder*	*Smith*	*Clarke*	*Ashworth*	*Whitehead*	*Jenkins*	*Cross*	*Downes*	*Butler*	*Buck*
									Ref: R Perkin												

1st Division Newcastle await the winners, and Magpies boss Joe Harvey is here to check out his opponents. Yet he doesn't know who they will be, even after the extra half-hour. Halifax appear to be cruising when David Cross scores twice, his second after Smith drops Ryder's centre.

No	Date	Venue	Opponent	Att	Pos	Res	F-A	H-T	Scorers, Times, and Referees	1	2	3	4	5	6	7	8	9	10	11	12 sub used
1 RR	31/8	H	ROCHDALE	5,718	13	W	2-0	0-0	Wallace 85, Brierley 89	Smith	Burgin	Lee	Wallace	Pickering	Rhodes	Chadwick	Atkins	Robertson	Lennard	Holmes*	Brierley
										Godfrey	*Smith*	*Ryder*	*Downes*	*Blair*	*Ashworth*	*Whitehead*	*Jenkins*	*Cross*	*Buck*	*Butler*	
									Ref: H Davey												

The odds appear to be on this five-hour marathon going into extra-time, too. Then Town score twice off set-piece moves to go through. After Blair handles, Wallace fires in off a well worked free-kick. Three minutes later Brierley touches the ball in, following Chadwick's corner.

No	Date	Venue	Opponent	Att	Pos	Res	F-A	H-T	Scorers, Times, and Referees	1	2	3	4	5	6	7	8	9	10	11	12 sub used
2	8/9	A	NEWCASTLE	*19,930 1:18*	10	L	1-2	0-2	Lennard 86	Smith	Burgin	Lee	Wallace*	Pickering	Rhodes	Chadwick	Atkins	Robertson	Lennard	Holmes	Verity
									Macdonald 15, Cassidy 17	*McFaul*	*Craig*	*Guthrie*	*Gibb*	*Burton*	*Clark*	*Cassidy*	*Taylor*	*Macdonald*	*Nattress*	*Hibbitt*	
									Ref: A Morrissey												

Town know all about Malcolm Macdonald from his Luton days. He cost Newcastle a cool £180,000, and shows his worth by firing in with his 'wrong' right foot. Cassidy's glancing header makes it 0-2. Lennard has a shot cleared off the line, but he goes on to hook in a deserved reply.

FA Cup

No	Date	Venue	Opponent	Att	Pos	Res	F-A	H-T	Scorers, Times, and Referees	1	2	3	4	5	6	7	8	9	10	11	12 sub used
1	20/11	A	WIGAN	*8,814 NPL*	16	L	1-2	0-2	Burgin 82	Smith	Burgin	Lee	Wallace*	Pickering	Rhodes	Chadwick	Atkins	Verity	**Waddle**	Holmes	**McKernan**
									Sutherland 8, Oates 45	*Reeves*	*Morris*	*Sutherland*	*Milne*	*Coutts*	*Gillibrand*	*Temple**	*Ledgard*	*Davies*	*Fleming*	*Oates*	*Koo*
									Ref: W Johnson												

No one doubts Wigan's right to be in the hat for Round 2. Inspired by Gordon Milne, they use the wind and snow in the first half to take a two-goal lead, both goals coming from set plays. Burgin's late reply isn't enough. Out of the Cup, the Town board say they are behind the manager.

		Home						Away					
	P	W	D	L	F	A	W	D	L	F	A	Pts
1 Aston Villa	46	20	1	2	45	10	12	5	6	40	22	70
2 Brighton	46	15	5	3	39	18	12	6	5	43	29	65
3 Bournemouth	46	16	6	1	43	13	7	10	6	30	24	62
4 Notts Co	46	16	3	4	42	19	9	9	5	32	25	62
5 Rotherham	46	12	8	3	46	25	8	7	8	23	27	55
6 Bristol Rov	46	17	2	4	54	26	4	10	9	21	30	54
7 Bolton	46	11	8	4	25	13	6	8	9	26	28	50
8 Plymouth	46	13	6	4	43	26	7	4	12	31	38	50
9 Walsall	46	12	8	3	38	16	3	10	10	24	41	48
10 Blackburn	46	14	4	5	39	22	5	5	13	15	35	47
11 Oldham	46	11	4	8	37	35	6	7	10	22	28	45
12 Shrewsbury	46	13	5	5	50	29	4	5	14	23	36	44
13 Chesterfield	46	10	5	8	25	23	8	3	12	32	34	44
14 Swansea	46	10	6	7	27	21	7	4	12	19	38	44
15 Port Vale	46	10	10	3	27	21	3	5	15	16	38	41
16 Wrexham	46	10	5	8	33	26	6	3	14	26	37	40
17 HALIFAX	46	11	6	6	31	22	2	6	15	17	39	38
18 Rochdale	46	11	7	5	35	26	1	6	16	22	57	37
19 York	46	8	8	7	32	22	4	4	15	25	44	36
20 Tranmere	46	9	7	7	34	30	1	9	13	16	41	36
21 Mansfield	46	5	12	6	19	26	3	8	12	22	37	36
22 Barnsley	46	6	10	7	23	30	3	8	12	9	34	36
23 Torquay	46	8	6	9	31	31	2	6	15	10	38	32
24 Bradford C	46	6	8	9	27	32	5	2	16	18	45	32
	1104	274	150	128	845	562	128	150	274	562	845	1104

Odds & ends

Double wins: (2) Barnsley, Tranmere.
Double losses: (4) Aston Villa, Blackburn, Brighton, Swansea.

Won from behind: (3) Walsall (h), Barnsley (a), Tranmere (a).
Lost from in front: (2) Bournemouth (a), Rotherham (a).

High spots: Beating First Division Manchester Utd in the Watney Cup.
Three consecutive wins up to 4 April.
Six games without defeat up to 23 October.

Low spots: Losing three consecutive matches on three occasions.
Going six games without a win up to 22 March.
Losing 0-5 at home to Brighton.
Losing at non-league Wigan in the FA Cup.
Selling star player Dave Chadwick to Bournemouth.

Player of the Year: John Pickering.
Ever-presents: (1) John Pickering.
Hat-tricks: (0).
Leading scorer: Bill Atkins (9).

	Appearances						Goals			
	Lge	*Sub*	LC	*Sub*	FAC	*Sub*	Lge	LC	FAC	Tot
Atkins, Bill	**39**	*1*	4		1		**8**	1		**9**
Brierley, Keith	**15**	*1*		*1*			**2**	1		**3**
Brogan, Frank	**3**						**2**			**2**
Burgin, Andy	**43**		4		1				1	**1**
Chadwick, Dave	**28**		4		1		**4**	1		**5**
Farley, John	**6**						**3**			**3**
Holmes, Barry	**23**	*4*	4		1		**3**			**3**
Johnston, Johnny	**3**	*1*					**1**			**1**
Kemp, Fred	**27**						**4**			**4**
Lee, Jeff	**45**		4		1					
Lennard, Dave	**9**		4				**3**	2		**5**
McKernan, Jim						*1*				
Pickering, John	**46**		4		1		**1**			**1**
Rhodes, Tony	**36**		4		1					
Robertson, Lammie	**39**	*2*	3				**6**			**6**
Shanahan, Terry	**26**	*2*					**3**			**3**
Smith, Alex	**39**		4		1					
Verity, Dave	**23**	*5*	1	*1*	1					
Waddle, Alan	**5**	*4*			1		**1**			**1**
Wallace, Bob	**44**		4		1		**7**	1		**8**
White, Barry	**7**									
21 players used	**506**	***20***	**44**	***2***	**11**	***1***	**48**	**6**	**1**	**55**

No	Date		Att	Pos	Pt	F-A	H-T	Scorers, Times, and Referees	1	2	3	4	5	6	7	8	9	10	11	12 sub used
1	A	BRENTFORD			W	1-0	0-0	Atkins 85	Smith	Burgin	Lee	**Quinn**	Pickering	Rhodes	Kemp*	Holmes	Robertson	Atkins	Brogan	Brierley
	12/8		*10,160*		2				*Priddy*	*Hawley*	*Nelmes*	*Gelson*	*Scales*	*Murray*	*Allen*	*Graham*	*Ross*	*Houston*	*Docherty*	
								Ref: H Powell	Amateur keeper Paul Priddy gets the nod over the established Gordon Phillips for Brentford, but looks suspect afternoon. The game is far from a classic, but Bill Atkins settles it, pouncing when Priddy fails to hold Robertson's cross. The Bees miss the suspended John O'Mara up front.											
2	H	BRISTOL ROV	1		W	**3-0**	0-0	Burgin 59, Brogan 66, Atkins 82	Smith	Burgin	Lee	Quinn	Pickering	Rhodes	Brierley	Holmes	Robertson	Atkins	Brogan	
	19/8		2,812	*10*	4				Sheppard	*Roberts*	*Parsons*	*Green*	*Taylor*	*Stanton*	*Stephens**	*Jones W*	*Allen*	*Bannister*	*Godfrey*	*Jones B*
								Ref: J Goggins	Town go top after Rovers are overrun, but it takes until the 59th minute for their breakthrough. Burgin makes it with a stunning 35-yarder, and Town don't look back. Brogan heads in Burgin's cross for 2-0, and Atkins finishes the job off, deflecting in Brogan's cross past Sheppard.											
3	H	WREXHAM	1		D	2-2	2-2	Burgin 12, Brogan 24p	Smith	Burgin	Lee*	Quinn	Pickering	Rhodes	Brierley	Holmes	Robertson	Atkins	Brogan	Waddle
	22/8		3,759	*2*	5			*May 27, Kinsey 41*	Lloyd	*Mason*	*Evans*	*Davis*	*May*	*Whittle*	*Tinnion*	*Sutton*	*Ashcroft*	*Kinsey*	*Thomas*	
								Ref: J Wrennall	Both sides start the day with the only 100% records in the division. Both records go, but after 24 minutes Town are looking good to maintain their's. They go 2-0 up, but Wrexham claw it back before half-time. In the end Town are thankful that Whittle's last-minute header hits the bar.											
4	A	SHREWSBURY	1		D	0-0	0-0		Smith	Burgin	Holmes	Quinn	Pickering	Rhodes	Brogan	Waddle	Robertson	Atkins	Shanahan	
	25/8		*3,458*	*6*	6				*Mulhearn*	*Bevan*	*Fellows*	*Moore*	*Holton*	*Bridgwodd*	*Roberts D*	*Moir R*	*Andrews*	*McLaughlin**	*Groves*	*Moir I*
								Ref: A Lees	Maurice Evans' Shrewsbury have made a competent start, but victory is there for the taking for the Shaymen, as they create the better chances. With three minutes left, Mulhearn makes a remarkable save from Atkins' dipping overhead kick. In a far from rough game, the ref books three.											
5	A	BOURNEMOUTH	3		L	0-1	0-0		Smith	Burgin	Holmes	Quinn	Pickering	Rhodes	Brogan	Waddle	Robertson	Atkins	Shanahan	
	29/8		*11,456*	*18*	6			*Machin 74*	*Davies*	*Machin*	*Howe*	*Gabriel*	*Jones*	*Miller*	*Redknapp*	*MacDougall*	*Boyer*	*Mitchinson*	*Powell*	
								Ref: C Nicholls	The Shaymen travel to Dean Court looking for a point. Their tactic of getting men behind the ball almost works. The Cherries' main threat of MacDougall and Boyer is stifled. But they have no answer to Mel Machin's effort, when he takes a return pass and shoots low into the corner.											
6	H	CHESTERFIELD	9		L	0-1	0-1		Smith	Burgin	Holmes	Quinn	Pickering	Rhodes	Kemp*	Brierley	Robertson	Atkins	Brogan	Shanahan
	2/9		3,784	*4*	6			*Wilson 37*	*Tingay*	*Holmes*	*Tiler*	*Barlow*	*Bell*	*Phelan*	*McHale*	*Moss*	*Downes*	*Bellamy*	*Wilson*	
								Ref: J Bent	Alex Smith's 200th league appearance for Town is not a happy one. He looks slightly out of position when Dave Wilson plays a one-two with his skipper Bellamy and fires in from 20 yards. The Spireites remain unbeaten, but the Shaymen rue missed chances before and after the goal.											
7	A	SCUNTHORPE	1		W	**3-0**	1-0	Brogan 3p, Robertson 50, 56	Smith	Burgin	Lee	Quinn	Pickering	Rhodes	Kemp	Holmes	Robertson	Atkins	Brogan	
	7/9		*4,848*	*15*	8				*Barnard*	*Foxton*	*Barker*	*Jackson*	*Deere*	*Welbourne*	*Davidson*	*Fletcher*	*Kerr*	*Heath*	*Kirk*	
								Ref: P Willis	This Friday night victory puts Town temporarily back on top. They don't look back after Welbourne handles Burgin's cross and Brogan tucks away the penalty. Robertson scores two in a six-minute spell after half-time, his first a scorcher when Frank Brogan's cross comes out to him.											
8	H	WALSALL	7		L	0-1	0-0		Smith	Burgin	Lee	Quinn	Pickering	Rhodes	Kemp*	Holmes	Robertson	Atkins	Brogan	Shanahan
	16/9		2,923	*4*	8			*Jones C 90*	*Wesson*	*Gregg*	*Evans*	*Harrison*	*Jones S*	*Atthey*	*Taylor B*	*Woodward*	*Jones C*	*Penman*	*Morris G*	
								Ref: A Gray	A depressing home trend is developing, although no one can deny Walsall their first away win of the season. But Robertson's miss, when he shoots straight at Wesson is crucial. Woodward is Walsall's danger man. He tears holes in Town's defence and lays on the goal for Cliff Jones.											
9	A	PORT VALE	11		L	1-2	0-1	Verity 70	Smith	Burgin	Lee	Quinn	Pickering	Rhodes	Kemp	Holmes	Robertson	Waddle	Brogan*	Verity
	18/9		*5,715*	*1*	8			*Morgan 33, Loska 84*	*Boswell*	*Lindsey*	*Loska*	*Summerscales*	*Cross*	*Horton*	*Morgan*	*James*	*Williams*	*Goodwin*	*Mountford**	*McLaren*
								Ref: R Kirkpatrick	Town push the league leaders in a vigorously contested match. Irish international Sammy Morgan beats Alex Smith in the air to net the opener. A minute later, Holmes' drive hits the bar. Verity scores a cracking equaliser, but Vale get a late winner when Loska's shot goes in off the post											
10	A	ROTHERHAM	10		W	1-0	1-0	Robertson 19	Smith	Burgin	Lee	Quinn	Pickering	Rhodes	Kemp	Holmes	Robertson	Waddle	Brogan*	Verity
	23/9		*6,568*	*3*	10				*Tunks*	*Houghton*	*Leng*	*Ferguson*	*Mielczarek*	*Stowell*	*Whitehead**	*Johnson*	*Gilbert*	*Ham*	*Mullen*	*Womble*
								Ref: H New	Johnny Quinn is looking forward to this game against his old club. He knows it will be a tough one, though. The Millers have won every game here so far, and scored 14 goals in the process. But Robertson makes the most of a defensive blunder, then the Shaymen go on the defensive.											
11	H	BOLTON	14		D	1-1	0-1	Robertson	Smith	Burgin	Lee	Quinn	Pickering	Rhodes	Kemp	Hholmes	Robertson	Waddle	Brogan	
	30/9		4,664	*4*	11			*Jones P*	*Wright C*	*Ritson*	*McAllister*	*Waldron**	*Jones P*	*Rimmer*	*Nicholson*	*Byrom*	*Jones G*	*Greaves*	*Phillips*	*Wright R*
								Ref: W Johnson	The Daily Mirror claims that Waddle has gone to Preston. But it's a hoax. The referee threatens to abandon the match due to bottle-throwing supporters. Paul Jones gives Bolton the lead following a corner, but Town draw level when Robertson reaches Smith's long punt downfield.											

No / Date	Venue	Opponent	Att	Pos	Res / Pts	F-A	H-T	Scorers, Times, and Referees	1	2	3	4	5	6	7	8	9	10	11	12
12	H	NOTTS CO		16	L	0-1	0-0		Smith	Burgin	Lee	Quinn	Pickering	Rhodes	Kemp	Verity	Robertson	Waddle	Brogan*	Holmes
7/10			3,233	*9*	11			*Masson 58p*	*Brown*	*Brindley*	*Worthington*	*Masson*	*Needham*	*Stubbs*	*Cozens*	*Mann*	*Randall*	*Bradd*	*Carter*	
								Ref: R Porthouse	County put their indifferent league form behind them to beat First Division Southampton in the League Cup during the week. Victory over the Shaymen is much easier. However, their only goal is Masson's penalty, unnecessarily conceded by Burgin when Bradd has his back to goal.											
13	A	ROCHDALE			D	0-0	0-0		Smith	Burgin	Lee	Quinn	Pickering	Rhodes	Kemp	Verity	Robertson	Waddle*	Holmes	Atkins
9/10			*5,425*		12				*Wainman*	*Smith*	*Renwick*	*Marsh*	*Blant*	*Kinsella*	*Brogden**	*Darling*	*Howarth*	*Gowans*	*Bebbington*	*Jenkins*
								Ref: R Capey	Ref Capey, a last-minute stand-in for Ken Burns, has a disappointing evening. He books Burgin early on, then lets worse fouls go unpunished. Town defend in numbers, and Dale can't cope with their offside trap. Smith makes two acrobatic saves which have the home fans applauding.											
14	A	TRANMERE		16	D	1-1	1-1	Atkins 17	Smith	Burgin	Lee	Quinn	Pickering	Rhodes	Kemp	Verity	Robertson	Atkins	Brogan	
13/10			*4,131*	*14*	13			*Duffy 22*	*Lawrence*	*Flood*	*Farrimond*	*Molyneux*	*Parry*	*Mathias*	*Russell*	*Duffy*	*Loyden*	*Young*	*Crossley*	
								Ref: W Castle	Mulhall is unsuccessful in bringing in a loan-player, but his injury-hit side merit this draw. Atkins glides the ball in with his head, but Rovers equalise when unchallenged Alan Duffy shoots from 20 yards. Smith is beaten again on 65 minutes, but Loyden's 35-yarder hits the post.											
15	H	GRIMSBY		18	D	1-1	1-1	Campbell 13 (og)	Smith	Burgin	Lee	Quinn	Pickering	Rhodes	Kemp*	Verity	Robertson	Atkins	Waddle	**McLachlan**
21/10			3,068	*9*	14			*Lewis 34*	*Turner*	*Campbell*	*Booth*	*Chatterley*	*Wigginton*	*Lynch*	*Brace*	*Gray*	*Lewis*	*Boylen*	*Gauden**	*Czuczman*
								Ref: J Price	Promoted Grimsby look no match early on for the Shaymen, who take the lead following Burgin's surging run. Kemp claims the goal, but the despairing Campbell gets the last touch. Jack Lewis' shock reply comes through slack marking, then the game becomes a struggle for Town.											
16	H	WATFORD			D	1-1	0-0	Robertson 69	Smith	Burgin	Holmes	Quinn	Pickering	Rhodes	Kemp	Verity	Robertson	Atkins	McLachlan*	Brogan
24/10			2,046		15			*Lindsay 80*	*Rankin*	*Butler*	*Packard**	*Keen*	*Lees*	*Franks*	*Morrissey*	*Welbourne*	*Woodfield*	*Lindsay*	*Farley*	*Wigg*
								Ref: D Richardson	The Shaymen's display matches the dismal evening. Their first goal attempt doesn't come until the 40th minute. Robertson scores when heads in Brogan's corner, but Lindsay equalises when Smith spills Woodfield's half-hit shot. In the last minute, Atkins is halted by the brave Rankin.											
17	A	PLYMOUTH		18	L	1-2	0-0	Robertson 55p	Smith	Burgin	Holmes	Quinn	Pickering	Rhodes	Kemp	Verity	Robertson	Atkins	Waddle*	**Stonehouse**
28/10			*6,910*	*19*	15			*Hinch 59, Rickard 64*	*Kearns*	*Harris*	*Sullivan*	*Hore*	*Hague*	*Provan*	*Rickard**	*Lugg*	*Hinch*	*Latchman*	*Welsh*	*Brown*
								Ref: K Walker	Tony Waiters has recently taken over at Home Park. He drafts in Eire keeper Mike Kearns on-loan, but this will be his only game for them. But it's a winning one. Two goals in five minutes mean Robertson's penalty isn't enough. John Pickering's 297th league game sets a club record.											
18	A	WREXHAM		16	D	0-0	0-0		Smith	Burgin	Lee	Quinn	Pickering	Rhodes	Stonehouse	Verity	Robertson	Atkins	Waddle*	Kemp
4/11			*4,038*	*13*	16				*Lloyd*	*Mason*	*Fogg*	*Davis*	*May*	*Evans*	*Smallman*	*Sutton*	*Ashcroft*	*Tinnion*	*Griffiths**	*McBurney*
								Ref: A Jones	Wrexham are a lively side, and the Shaymen spend most of the game defending. They do it well, though Alex Smith has to be at his best. The only time he is beaten, Jeff Lee makes a timely clearance. On-loan Stonehouse came as cover for the doubtful Pickering, but plays in midfield.											
19	H	PORT VALE		17	D	2-2	0-0	Robertson 83, 90	Smith	Burgin	Lee	Quinn	Pickering	Rhodes*	Verity	Kemp	Robertson	Atkins	Shanahan	Brogan
11/11			2,026	*3*	17			*Williams 51, Horton 65*	*Boswell*	*Brodie*	*Loska*	*Summerscales*	*Cross*	*Horton*	*Morgan*	*Tartt*	*Williams*	*Lacey*	*McLaren*	
								Ref: W Smith	An amazing finish. In the wind and rain, Port Vale are seemingly heading for a deserved win after 83 minutes, both their goals from free-kicks. Then Robertson pops up to score twice from close range, after being set up by Atkins and Brogan. Then, in injury-time, Atkins nearly wins it.											
20	H	SWANSEA		17	D	1-1	0-1	Atkins 70	White	Burgin	Lee	Quinn	Pickering	Rhodes	Verity	Kemp	Robertson*	Atkins	Holmes	Cullen
25/11			1,815	*24*	18			*Williams 18*	*Millington*	*Screen*	*Davies G*	*Curtis*	*Thomas*	*Evans W*	*Rees*	*Jones*	*Williams*	*Gwyther*	*Evans B*	
								Ref: P Baldwin	Crisis point is approaching. For the fourth successive match Town go behind, this time to a Herbie Williams goal. But they manage to equalise the moment a stray black mongrel is caught. The game is held up for four minutes, then Kemp lays the ball off to Atkins, and he guides it in.											
21	A	BLACKBURN		19	L	0-3	0-3		White	Burgin	Lee	Quinn	Pickering	Rhodes	Kemp	Verity	Shanahan	Atkins	Cullen*	Holmes
2/12			*7,402*	*16*	18			*O'Mara 9, Metcalfe 32, Price 36*	*Jones*	*Heaton*	*Arentoft*	*Metcalfe*	*McNamee*	*Fazackerley*	*Price*	*Bradford*	*O'Mara*	*Turner**	*Field*	*Martin*
								Ref: P Reeves	Pat Cullen scored twice in Jeff Lee's benefit, so he gets a place in the forward line. Despite the score Town actually play quite well. O'Mara is unmarked for the first goal, while both Metcalfe and Price have an element of fortune about theirs. Town are now just one point clear of safety.											
22	A	SOUTHEND		20	D	1-1	1-0	Brogan 42	White	Holmes	Lee	Quinn	Pickering	Rhodes	Brogan*	Kemp	Waddle	Verity	Shanahan	Cullen
22/12			*4,154*	*22*	19			*Best 50*	*Bellotti*	*Booth*	*Ternent*	*Elliott*	*Albeson*	*Woods*	*Johnson*	*Best*	*Guthrie*	*Taylor*	*Moody*	
								Ref: K Wynn	Southend's lowest crowd so far sees Town hang on for a point. Albeson hits the bar for the home side before Brogan strikes following a corner. Future England winger Peter Taylor is the creator of Southend's deserved equaliser. He goes on a jinking run, then pulls the ball back for Best.											
23	H	ROTHERHAM		20	L	0-1	0-1		White	Holmes	Lee	Quinn	Pickering	Rhodes	Brogan	Kemp	**Irvine**	Verity*	Shanahan	Waddle
26/12			3,327	*14*	19			*Ferguson 41*	*McDonagh*	*Houghton*	*Breckin*	*Ferguson*	*Mielczarek*	*Swift*	*Johnson*	*Phillips*	*Womble*	*Bentley*	*Mullen*	
								Ref: D Laing	Relegation talk follows this. It's cruel, though, that the Millers should score after Town's only real sustained spell of pressure. Johnson sends the ball over, and Ferguson dispatches it into the top corner. Rotherham reverse the September scoreline, but actually could have won by more.											

No	Date		Att	Pos	Pt	F-A	H-T	Scorers, Times, and Referees	1	2	3	4	5	6	7	8	9	10	11	12 sub used
24	A	BRISTOL ROV		21	L	**1-4**	0-2	Kemp 79 *[Prince 73]*	White	Holmes	Lee	Kemp	Pickering	Rhodes	Brogan	Verity	Irvine	Waddle*	Shanahan	Quinn
	30/12		*8,468*	*4*	19			*Jarman 10, Taylor 38, Bannister 55,*	*Sheppard*	*Roberts*	*Parsons*	*Aitken*	*Taylor*	*Prince*	*Stephens*	*Bannister*	*Rudge**	*Godfrey*	*Jarman*	*Fearnley*
								Ref: R Crabb	Thick fog makes this game hard to follow. It doesn't stop promotion-chasing Rovers finding their way to goal, though. After Jarman fires in a super volley Rovers don't look back. With the elements worsening, few see Prince touch in the winner as Halifax hope for an abandonment.											
25	H	OLDHAM		22	L	0-3	0-1		White	Burgin	Lee	Quinn	Pickering	Rhodes	Brogan	Verity	Irvine	Waddle	Shanahan	
	13/1		4,829	*3*	19			*Shaw 38, 85, Robins 75*	*Dowd*	*Wood*	*Whittle*	*Mulvaney*	*Hicks*	*Cranston*	*Lester*	*Shaw*	*McNeill*	*Garwood*	*Robins*	
								Ref: H Old	Man Utd's George Best has been linked with the Latics, but the chances of him turning out are rated as 'millions to one'. The visitors do well enough without him, although the scoreline somewhat flatters them. Town are ticking along nicely until a defensive error lets in David Shaw.											
26	H	SCUNTHORPE		23	W	1-0	1-0	Irvine 30	White	Burgin	Lee	**Hale**	Pickering	Rhodes	Verity	Brierley	Irvine	Holmes	Brogan	
	27/1		1,607	*22*	21				*Barnard*	*Markham*	*Barker*	*Welbourne*	*Deere*	*Atkin*	*Davidson*	*Fletcher*	*Heath*	*Kerr*	*Kirk*	
								Ref: A Morrissesy	At last! A home win for the first time in 23 weeks. Newly-signed Ken Hale makes his debut and makes a difference. Town live dangerously as Welbourne's shot hits the bar in the 58th minute. Willie Irvine's close-range effort comes off Brogan's cross, which Atkin should have cut out.											
27	H	ROCHDALE		21	D	0-0	0-0		Smith	Burgin	Lee	Hale	Pickering	Rhodes	Verity	Kemp	Irvine	Brierley	Brogan	
	3/2		2,411	*13*	22				*Morritt*	*Smith*	*Renwick*	*Downes*	*Blant*	*Marsh*	*Gowans*	*Darling*	*Atkins*	*Jenkins*	*Bebbington*	
								Ref: R Lee	Rochdale arrive at the Shay on the crest of a wave after beating promotion hopefuls Bournemouth during the week. They deserve to win this game, too, but it's Irvine who comes closest to winning it. For Town, the situation at the bottom of the table is becoming a very complex one.											
28	A	CHESTERFIELD		22	L	0-2	0-0		Smith	Burgin	Lee	Hale	Pickering	Rhodes	Verity	Kemp	Irvine	Brierley	**Wilkie**	
	7/2		*4,978*		22			*McHale 62, Bellamy 82*	*Brown*	*Holmes*	*Tiler*	*Barlow*	*Stott*	*Pugh*	*Cliff*	*Ferris*	*Downes*	*Bellamy*	*McHale*	
								Ref: E Spencer	Mulhall gives a debut to his new £1,000 signing from Ross County, John Wilkie. But he finds life up front very frustrating, as the supply is not forthcoming. Future Town star Ray McHale heads in Chesterfield's opener, but victory isn't secure until Bellamy's poor shot is deflected in.											
29	A	YORK		23	L	1-2	0-1	Verity 82	Smith	Burgin	Lee	Hale	Pickering	Rhodes	Brogan*	Verity	Irvine	Kemp	Brierley	Holmes
	24/2		*3,483*	*11*	22			*Rowles 20, Woodward 47*	*Crawford*	*Mackin*	*Burrows*	*Lally*	*Swallow*	*Topping*	*Pollard*	*Woodward*	*Rowles*	*Aimspn*	*Taylor*	
								Ref: W Hall	Waddle has been suspended by Mulhall for a breach of club discipline. Controversy reigns in this game. Eddie Rowles scores the opener when Smith is impeded. Two goals down, Crawford saves Brogan's penalty, but clearly moves beforehand. Verity's goal offers Town some hope.											
30	H	SHREWSBURY		23	L	0-1	0-0		Smith	Burgin	Lee	Hale	Pickering	Rhodes	Brogan	Verity	Irvine	Kemp	Holmes*	Brierley
	27/2		1,474		22			*Hughes 73*	*Mulhearn*	*Bevan*	*Roberts I*	*Mathias*	*Turner*	*Calloway*	*Roberts D*	*Moir R*	*Moir I*	*Hughes*	*Morris*	
								Ref: D Civil	The Shrews think they have obtained Stoke striker Terry Smith on loan, but the League say his registration hasn't been cleared. Kemp has a goal disallowed in the 13th minute for hands. Hughes sweeps in the winner from a corner by Dave Roberts, the game's outstanding player.											
31	A	NOTTS C		23	L	0-3	0-1		Smith	Burgin	Lee	Hale	Pickering	Rhodes	Brogan	Verity	Irvine*	Kemp	Holmes	Wilkie
	3/3		*9,820*	*3*	22			*Stubbs 44, Nixon 53, Bradd 55*	*Brown*	*Stubbs*	*Worthington*	*Masson*	*Needham*	*Mann*	*Nixon*	*Randall*	*Bradd*	*Carlin**	*Carter*	*Dyer*
								Ref: N Paget	Odds are on a home victory before kick-off. Smith has to be at his best to keep the score down. Irvine nearly gives Town a shock lead, but he takes the ball too wide. Brian Stubbs heads County's opener off Masson's free-kick. Steve Carter is instrumental in his side's last two goals.											
32	A	CHARLTON		23	L	0-1	0-0		Smith	Burgin	Lee	Hale	Pickering	Rhodes	Wilkie	Shanahan	Waddle	Kemp*	Holmes	Verity
	6/3		*3,001*	*10*	22			*Horsfield 54*	*Dunn*	*Curtis*	*Warman*	*Hunt P*	*Goldthorpe*	*Reeves*	*O'Kane*	*Flanagan**	*Rogers*	*Horsfield*	*Bowman*	*Powell*
								Ref: J Thacker	The new strike-force of Waddle, Shanahan and Wilkie creates problems and Charlton are often stretched. Defeat, therefore is hard to stomach, although few can argue with Horsfield's winner, firing home from 20 yards. Pickering later is laid out cold after colliding with his own keeper.											
33	H	TRANMERE		23	W	2-1	1-1	Kemp 19, Burgin 76	Smith	Burgin	Lee	Hale	Pickering	Rhodes	Wilkie	Shanahan	Waddle	Kemp	Verity	
	10/3		1,687	*9*	24			*Loyden 14*	*Lawrence*	*Pritchard*	*Farrimond*	*Mathias*	*Veitch*	*Fagan*	*Moore !*	*Graham*	*Loyden*	*Duffy**	*Young*	*Crossley*
								Ref: T Bond	A tangerine and blue diagonal stripe adorns Town's new shirts. This game swings Town's way in the second half. Moore is sent off for words said to the ref in the 74th minute. Two minutes later Burgin's rocket from 30 yards is allowed to stand with the linesman flagging for offside.											
34	H	YORK		23	W	1-0	0-0	Shanahan 70	Smith	Burgin	Lee	Hale	Pickering	Rhodes	Wilie	Shanahan	Waddle	Kemp	Verity	
	13/3		1,918	*12*	26				*Hillyard*	*Stone**	*Burrows*	*Lally*	*Swallow*	*Topping*	*Pollard*	*Woodward*	*Rowles*	*Seal*	*Taylor*	*Thompson*
								Ref: L Hayes	Town are not giving up the ghost. They are now just four points away from safety. York have now failed to score in their last four games, and miss Paul Aimson, sold recently to Bournemouth for £12, 000. Shanahan's close-range header is actually his first goal in the league this term.											

No	Venue / Date	Opponent	Att	Pos	Pts	Res	F-A	H-T	Scorers, Times, and Referees	1	2	3	4	5	6	7	8	9	10	11	12
35	A	GRIMSBY		23		D	0-0	0-0		Smith	Burgin	Lee	Hale	Pickering	Rhodes	Wilkie*	Shanahan	Waddle	Kemp	Verity	**Womble**
	17/3		*10,836*	*7*	27					*Turner*	*Campbell*	*Booth*	*Hickman*	*Wigginton*	*Gray*	*Brace*	*Lewis*	*Hubbard*	*Boylen*	*Gauden*	
									Ref: W Castle	A first for Lawrie McMenemy's Grimsby side. A home draw. Both sides have chances. Lee hurls himself horizontally to keep out Wigginton's header, but it's Town who nearly win the game. In the 87th minute Shanahan shoots over the bar. Earlier, Verity has a goal ruled out for hands.											
36	H	PLYMOUTH		23		W	2-1	0-0	Burgin 60, Wilkie 65	Smith	Burgin	Lee	Womble	Pickering	Rhodes	Wilkie	Shanahan	Waddle	Kemp*	Verity	Quinn
	24/3		1,893	*12*	29				*Lugg 47*	*Furnell*	*Provan*	*Sullivan*	*Hore*	*Hague*	*Darke*	*Dowling*	*Rickard**	*Hinch*	*Welsh*	*Latchman*	*Lugg*
									Ref: C Howell	Mulhall bills this as 'the match of the season', and takes his players on a four-day break in Billingham to prepare for it. They respond with a win. Argyle have only lost twice this year, once to mighty Leeds in the Cup, so Wilkie's lobbed winner ensures Town are in good company.											
37	A	WATFORD		23		L	1-2	0-0	Waddle 49	Smith	Burgin	Lee	Womble	Pickering	Rhodes	Wilkie*	Shanahan	Waddle	Kemp	Verity	Quinn
	28/3		*5,184*	*19*	29				*Keen 77, Welbourne 78*	*Rankin*	*Welbourne*	*William*	*Lees*	*Keen*	*Franks*	*Craker*	*Jennings*	*Morrissey*	*Kenning*	*Farley**	*Jenkins*
									Ref: R Perkin	The Hornets, whose manager is former Town boss George Kirby, win this crucial basement battle. He is full of praise for Town's performance but reckons his side deserved to win. Alan Waddle volleys the Shaymen in front, then Watford go in front with two goals in a 30-second spell.											
38	A	SWANSEA		23		L	0-2	0-1		Smith	Burgin*	Lee	Quinn	Pickering	Rhodes	Womble	Shanahan	Waddle	Kemp	Verity	Irvine
	31/3		***2,499***	*22*	29				*Johnson 22, Allan 59*	*Millington*	*Davies G*	*McLaughlin*	*Jones*	*Williams*	*Moore*	*Johnson*	*Evans W*	*Thomas !*	*Allan*	*Evans B*	
									Ref: J Hunting	Swansea are refused permission to put back this game until after the televised Grand National. They go on to win with goals from two players on loan, Johnson (Man City) and Allan (Bristol Rov). They are glad of their cushion, for late on Geoff Thomas is sent off for striking Irvine.											
39	H	BRENTFORD		23		W	3-2	3-0	Shanahan 7, 10, 35	Smith	Burgin	Lee	Hale	Pickering	Rhodes	Wilkie	Shanahan	Waddle	Kemp	Womble	
	4/4		**970**	*21*	31				*Webb 74, Allen 76*	*Phillips*	*Hawley*	*Gelson*	*Houston**	*Scales*	*Murray*	*Allen*	*Docherty*	*Webb*	*Cross*	*Salvage*	*Nelmes*
									Ref: R Matthewson	The ice-bound pitch means the game is in doubt, and the attendance is affected. Shanahan makes it a day to remember for those that are there, with Town's first hat-trick since Massie in the promotion year. The Bees, with the wind behind them, score twice as Town live on their nerves.											
40	H	BLACKBURN		23		D	2-2	2-1	Womble 3, Hale 36	Smith	Burgin	Lee	Hale	Pickering	Rhodes	Wilkie	Shanahan	Waddle	Kemp	Womble	
	7/4		**4,838**	*3*	32				*Fazackerley 9, Parkes 51*	*Jones*	*Heaton*	*Arentoft*	*Metcalfe*	*Wood*	*Fazackerley*	*Napier*	*Garbett*	*Endean*	*Parkes*	*Field*	
									Ref: K Baker	Rovers' away form is the best in the division, worth 20 points from as many matches. Promotion is still on their agenda, but a draw here does neither side any favours. Womble, who starts the scoring early on, and Hale score from close range, but twice Blackburn wipe out the deficit.											
41	A	OLDHAM		23		D	1-1	1-1	Wilkie 25	Smith	Verity	Lee	Hale	Pickering	Rhodes	Wilkie	Shanahan	Waddle	Kemp	Womble	
	14/4		*8,071*	*6*	33				*Lester 22*	*Dowd*	*Blair*	*Whittle*	*Cranston*	*Hicks*	*Edwards**	*McVitie*	*Lester*	*Robins*	*Wood*	*Garwood*	*McNeill*
									Ref: D Smith	Mike Lester scores the opener for the Latics when Robins' header rebounds off a post. Wilkie beats the offside and coolly slots past Dowd. In the 35th minute Hicks pulls down Waddle, but Lee hits his penalty against the post. Town's luck is out when Waddle and Womble hit the bar.											
42	A	BOLTON		23		L	0-3	0-3		Smith	Verity	Lee	Hale	Pickering	Rhodes	Wilkie	Shanahan	Waddle	Kemp	Womble	
	16/4		***20,062***	*1*	33				*Lee 5, 11, 40*	*Siddall*	*Ritson*	*McAllister*	*Rimmer*	*Jones P*	*Nicholson*	*Byrom*	*Jones G*	*Greaves*	*Lee*	*Phillips*	
									Ref: P Partridge	The last thing Town need is an away trip to Jimmy Armfield's title favourites. The game is as good as over within eleven minutes of kick-off, as defensive errors let in Stuart Lee for the first of his three goals. Alex Smith later injures his hand, and the game is held up for three minutes.											
43	H	CHARLTON		22		W	**3-0**	2-0	Waddle 10, Wilkie 22, Shanahan 57	Smith	Quinn	Lee	Hale	Pickering	Rhodes	Wilkie	Shanahan	Waddle	Kemp	Womble	
	21/4		1,573	*12*	35					*Franklin*	*Jones*	*Tumbridge*	*Hunt P*	*Shipperley*	*Reeves*	*Powell*	*Bond*	*Peacock*	*Horsfield*	*Davies P**	*Goldthorpe*
									Ref: R Garner	Charlton's first ever appearance at the Shay is not a happy one. A resurgent Town could actually have won by more. Waddle's downward header fools reserve keeper Mick Franklin. Horsfield misses a great chance at one end, then the next minute Shanahan wraps it up at the other.											
44	H	SOUTHEND		22		W	2-1	2-0	Womble 39, Shanahan 44	Smith	Quinn	Lee	Hale	Pickering	Rhodes	Wilkie	Shanahan	Waddle	Kemp	Womble	
	24/4		2,887	*14*	37				*Moore 83*	*Bellotti*	*Johnson T*	*Smith*	*Elliott*	*Albeson*	*Moody*	*Horsfall**	*Ternent*	*Moore*	*Best*	*Taylor*	*Booth*
									Ref: P Willis	Town are still alive. Two of the best goals scored at the Shay give them the edge. The first is a volley by Womble, the second from Shanahan, after he takes the ball on his chest. When the home defence hesitates, Taylor nips in to pull one back, but Town survive the last seven minutes.											
45	H	BOURNEMOUTH		21		W	2-0	1-0	Hale 35p, Quinn 52	Smith	Burgin	Lee	Hale	Pickering	Rhodes	Wilkie	Shanahan	Waddle	Kemp	Quinn	
	28/4		3,380	*7*	39					*Baker*	*Howe*	*Powell*	*Gabriel*	*Jones*	*Miller*	*Redknapp*	*Chadwick*	*Boyer*	*De Garis*	*Goddard*	
									Ref: I Smith	Mulhall has likened his side's run-in to the Grand National. Red Rum won this year's in the very last strides. Are Town about to survive in the same manner? Ex-Southampton and Everton star Jimmy Gabriel handles for Hale's penalty. Quinn doubles the lead with a shot from 20 yards.											
46	A	WALSALL		20		W	1-0	1-0	Waddle 35	Smith	Burgin	Lee	Hale	Pickering	Rhodes	Wilkie	Shanahan	Waddle	Kemp	Quinn	
	1/5		*3,989*	*17*	41					*Inger*	*Gregg*	*Atthey*	*Penman*	*Robinson*	*Harrison*	*Birch*	*Shinton*	*Jones C*	*Bennett*	*Taylor B**	
		Home	Away						Ref: F Bassett	It's do or die now. Town can send Rotherham down if they win, and Mulhall predicts they will. He's right. When Quinn floats the ball over, keeper Inger comes too late, and he is beaten by Waddle's header. After that, it is tense stuff, but Town hold out. They stay up on goal-average.											
	Average	2,736	6,724																		

League Cup					F-A	H-T	Scorers, Times, and Referees	1	2	3	4	5	6	7	8	9	10	11	12 sub used
1	H	BURY		L	1-2	1-0	Atkins 44	Smith	Burgin	Lee	Quinn	Verity	Rhodes	Brierley	Holmes	Robertson	Atkins	Brogan	
	15/8		3,309 *4:*				*Heslop 64, McDermott 65*	*Forrest*	*Embleton !*	*Saile*	*Robson*	*Heslop*	*Holt**	*Connelly*	*Rudd*	*Tinsley*	*Murray*	*McDermott*	*Williams G*
							Ref: H Davey	Fourth Division Bury lose David Holt after only ten minutes, then have Embleton sent off in the 37th, for a violent tackle on Brogan, but it's Town who crash out. Atkins scores just before half-time, but Heslop levels it, then McDermott chases a long ball down the middle to win it.											

FA Cup								1	2	3	4	5	6	7	8	9	10	11	12
1	A	BARNSLEY	17	D	1-1	0-1	Shanahan 85	White	Burgin	Lee	Quinn	Pickiering	Verity	Holmes*	Kemp	Robertson	Atkins	Brogan	Shanahan
	18/11		*4,330 4:13*				*Lea 28*	*Arblaster*	*Murphy*	*Chambers*	*Greenwood*	*Winstanley*	*Pettit*	*Sharp*	*Lea*	*Mahoney*	*Millar*	*Martin*	
							Ref: E Garner	Reserve keeper Barry White comes in for the injured Smith, but Town have him to thank for keeping them in the tie. Trailing to Les Lea's neat 20-yarder, he tips Martin's goalbound effort round the post. Sub Shanahan then equalises late on when Arblaster misjudges Kemp's pull-back.											
1R	H	BARNSLEY	17	W	2-1	1-1	Robertson 18, Kemp 54	White	Burgin	Lee	Quinn	Pickering	Verity	Brogan*	Kemp	Robertson	Atkins	Shanahan	Holmes
	21/11		2,461 *4:13*				*Kemp 8 (og)*	*Arblaster*	*Murphy*	*Chambers*	*Greenwood*	*Winstanley*	*Pettit*	*Sharp**	*Lea*	*Mahoney*	*Millar*	*Martin*	*Earnshaw*
							Ref: E Garner	Barnsley take the field in Town's away kit of green and black stripes, and take the lead when White slips, allowing Kemp's backpass to go in. But after Robertson squares the game within ten minutes, Kemp is on hand to net Town's winner, when Atkins knocks the ball down to him.											
2	A	SCUNTHORPE	19	L	2-3	1-2	Robertson 43, 55	White	Burgin	Lee	Quinn*	Pickering	Rhodes	Brogan	Kemp	Robertson	Verity	Shanahan	Brierley
	9/12		*4,037 3:21*				*Heath 22, Fletcher 24, Welbourne 69*	*Barnard*	*Foxton*	*Barker*	*Atkin*	*Deere*	*Welbourne*	*Warnock*	*McDonald*	*Fletcher*	*Heath*	*Kirk*	
							Ref: R Matthewson	The sale of Atkins on the morning of the match is a shock. On current form, not so Town's exit. The Iron take a two-goal lead, but Robertson's two headers look to have saved the day for Town. Until, that is, White punches out a corner, only for Welbourne to return the ball with interest.											

		Home						Away					
		P	W	D	L	F	A	W	D	L	F	A	Pts
1	Bolton	46	18	4	1	44	9	7	7	9	29	30	61
2	Notts Co	46	17	4	2	40	12	6	7	10	27	35	57
3	Blackburn	46	12	8	3	34	16	8	7	8	23	31	55
4	Oldham	46	12	7	4	40	18	7	9	7	32	36	54
5	Bristol Rov	46	17	4	2	55	20	3	9	11	22	36	53
6	Port Vale	46	15	6	2	41	21	6	5	12	15	48	53
7	Bournemouth	46	14	6	3	44	16	3	10	10	22	28	50
8	Plymouth	46	14	3	6	43	26	6	7	10	31	40	50
9	Grimsby	46	16	2	5	45	18	4	6	13	22	43	48
10	Tranmere	46	12	8	3	38	17	3	8	12	18	35	46
11	Charlton	46	12	7	4	46	24	5	4	14	23	43	45
12	Wrexham	46	11	9	3	39	23	3	8	12	16	31	45
13	Rochdale	46	8	8	7	22	26	6	9	8	26	28	45
14	Southend	46	13	6	4	40	14	4	4	15	21	40	44
15	Shrewsbury	46	10	10	3	31	21	5	4	14	15	33	44
16	Chesterfield	46	13	4	6	37	22	4	5	14	20	39	43
17	Walsall	46	14	3	6	37	26	4	4	15	19	40	43
18	York	46	8	10	5	24	14	5	5	13	18	32	41
19	Watford	46	11	8	4	32	23	1	9	13	11	25	41
20	HALIFAX	46	9	8	6	29	23	4	7	12	14	30	41
21	Rotherham	46	12	4	7	34	27	5	3	15	17	38	41
22	Brentford	46	12	5	6	33	18	3	2	18	18	51	37
23	Swansea	46	11	5	7	37	29	3	4	16	14	44	37
24	Scunthorpe	46	8	7	8	18	25	2	3	18	15	47	30
		1104	299	146	107	883	488	107	146	299	488	883	1104

Odds & ends

Double wins: (2) Brentford, Scunthorpe.
Double losses: (2) Chesterfield, Notts Co.

Won from behind: (3) Plymouth (h), Tranmere (h), Barnsley (FAC) (h).
Lost from in front: (3) Plymouth (a), Watford (a), Bury (LC) (h).

High spots: Being unbeaten in their first four matches and going top of the table.
Winning the last four matches to avoid relegation.

Low spots: Going 15 games without a win up to 13 January.
Five consecutive defeats up to 6 March.
Losing to Fourth Division Bury in the League Cup.
Only 970 turning up for the visit of Brentford – the lowest crowd ever at the Shay up to then.

Player of the Year: Alex Smith.
Ever-presents: (2) John Pickering, Tony Rhodes.
Hat-tricks: Terry Shanahan (1).
Leading scorer: Lammie Robertson (11).

	Appearances						Goals			
	Lge	*Sub*	LC	*Sub*	FAC	*Sub*	**Lge**	LC	FAC	**Tot**
Atkins, Bill	**16**	*1*	1		2		**4**	1		**5**
Brierley, Keith	**7**	*2*	1			*1*				
Brogan, Frank	**22**	*2*	1		3		**4**			**4**
Burgin, Andy	**39**		1		3		**4**			**4**
Cullen, Pat	**1**	*2*								
Hale, Ken	**18**						**2**			**2**
Holmes, Barry	**22**	*3*	1		1	*1*				
Irvine, Willie	**9**	*1*					**1**			**1**
Kemp, Fred	**39**	*1*			3		**2**		1	**3**
Lee, Jeff	**41**		1		3					
McLachlan, Doug	**1**	*1*								
Pickering, John	**46**				3					
Quinn, Johnny	**29**	*3*	1		3		**1**			**1**
Rhodes, Tony	**46**		1		1					
Robertson, Lammie	**20**		1		3		**8**		3	**11**
Shanahan, Terry	**23**	*2*			2	*1*	**6**		1	**7**
Smith, Alex	**39**		1							
Stonehouse, Basil	**1**	*1*								
Verity, Dave	**28**	*3*	1		3		**2**			**2**
Waddle, Alan	**28**	*2*					**3**			**3**
White, Barry	**7**				3					
Wilkie, John	**15**	*1*					**3**			**3**
Womble, Trevor	**9**	*1*					**2**			**2**
(own-goals)							**1**			**1**
23 players used	**506**	***26***	**11**		**33**	***3***	**43**	**1**	**5**	**49**

LEAGUE DIVISION 3 — Manager: George Mulhall — SEASON 1973-74

No	Date		Att	Pos	Pt	F-A	H-T	Scorers, Times, and Referees	1	2	3	4	5	6	7	8	9	10	11	12 sub used
1	H	OLDHAM			D	0-0	0-0		Smith	Burgin	Quinn	Kemp*	Pickering	Rhodes	**Jones**	**Pugh**	Shanahan	**Ford**	Hale	Cullen
	25/8		4,883		1				*Dowd*	*Wood*	*Whittle*	*Lester*	*Hicks*	*Edwards*	*McVitie*	*Jones*	*Lochhead*	*McNeill*	*Garwood*	
								Ref: P Reeves	Oldham will be a tough team to beat but Town play their part in this entertaining, yet goalless opener. Both sides are disappointed not to score. Oldham's George Jones has a second-half goal ruled out for a foul on Alex Smith. Harry Dowd pulls off a great save to keep out Andy Burgin.											
2	A	YORK		13	D	1-1	1-0	Jones 22	Smith	Burgin	Quinn	Ford	Pickering	Rhodes	Jones	Pugh	**Gwyther**	Kemp	Hale	
	1/9		*3,960*	*7*	2			*Jones 56*	*Crawford*	*Stone*	*Burrows*	*Topping*	*Swallow*	*Pollard*	*Butler*	*Holmes*	*Seal*	*Jones*	*Taylor*	
								Ref: W Hall	On the way to Bootham Crescent the Town bus gets stuck in traffic. Manager George Mulhall has to sprint half a mile to hand the teamsheet in before the 2.30 deadline. Alan Jones scores a memorable solo goal. Namesake Chris equalises. In the last minute Gwyther's header hits the bar.											
3	H	SOUTHEND		10	D	0-0	0-0		Smith	Burgin	Quinn	Kemp	Pickering	Pugh	Jones	Shanahan*	Ford	Gwyther	Hale	Wilkie
	8/9		2,604	*20*	3				*Mackay*	*Smith*	*Ford*	*Elliott**	*Townsend*	*Moody*	*Johnson T*	*Moore*	*Guthrie*	*Booth*	*Taylor*	*Johnson K*
								Ref: E Garner	Daylight robbery! Despite the fact that Town dominate from start to finish, Southend boss Arthur Rowley has his side well drilled. They repel almost everything that the Shaymen throw at them. When Town do get through, bad finishing lets them down, as when Shanahan hits the post.											
4	A	GRIMSBY		19	L	1-4	0-2	Gwyther 76 *[Barton 85]*	Smith	Burgin	Quinn	Kemp*	Pickering	Pugh	Jones	Shanahan	Ford	Gwyther	Hale	Wilkie
	11/9		*7,860*		3			*Chatterley 35p, 43, Wigginton 47,*	*Wainman*	*Beardsley*	*Booth*	*Chatterley*	*Wigginton*	*Gray*	*Barton*	*Hickman*	*Hubbard*	*Boylen*	*Sharp*	
								Ref: G Trevett	Town slump to their first defeat. They clearly miss centre-half Tony Rhodes as the Mariners score three goals from set pieces. Lew Chatterley has a happy evening, scoring twice. His second is a penalty after Quinn handles on the line. Gwyther scores when Clive Wigginton slips up.											
5	A	BRISTOL ROV		20	L	0-2	0-1		Smith	Burgin	Quinn	Pugh	Pickering	Rhodes	Jones	Wilkie*	Ford	Gwyther	Hale	Shanahan
	15/9		*7,485*	*2*	3			*Stanton 41, 79*	*Eadie*	*Jacobs*	*Parsons*	*Green*	*Taylor*	*Prince*	*Stephens*	*Stanton*	*Worboys*	*Bannister*	*Dobson*	
								Ref: A Turvey	Don Megson's Rovers are one of the title favourites. Defeat here is no disgrace. Tom Stanton scores just before the break but the game goes away from Town in the 79th minute. Gwyther misses at one end, and seconds later Stanon gets his second after Smith initially foils Bannister.											
6	H	CHARLTON		16	W	2-1	2-0	Wilkie 6, 45	Smith	Burgin	Quinn	Kemp	Pickering	Rhodes	Jones	Ford	Wilkie	Gwyther	Pugh	
	18/9		2,160		5			*Hales 75*	*Forster*	*Jones*	*Tumbridge*	*Smart*	*Shipperley*	*Bowman**	*Powell*	*Hales*	*Peacock*	*Horsfield*	*Flanagan*	*Arnold*
								Ref: J Whalley	Mulhall hands the captaincy to David Pugh, claiming John Pickering is 'too quiet'. The game is played in torrential rain but Pugh has a happy start. Wilkie gets both Town goals, his second a spectacular effort with his back almost to goal. Derek Hales' goal keeps the game interesting.											
7	H	HEREFORD		17	D	1-1	0-1	Gwyther 85	Smith	Burgin	Quinn	Kemp	Pickering	Rhodes	Jones	Ford*	Wilkie	Gwyther	Pugh	Shanahan
	22/9		2,538	*14*	6			*Mallender 25*	*Hughes*	*Carver*	*Naylor*	*McLaughlin*	*Tucker*	*Mallender*	*Evans**	*Owen*	*Redrobe*	*Gregory*	*Radford*	*Lee*
								Ref: D Richardson	Hereford, elected to the League in 1972, won promotion to Division Three at the first attempt. This is their first visit to the Shay. With five minutes to go Mallender's 30-yarder looks like being enough for them. Then Gwyther gets between two defenders to head powerfully home.											
8	A	TRANMERE		13	W	1-0	1-0	Gwyther 21	Smith	Burgin	Quinn	Kemp	Pickering	Rhodes	Jones	Ford	Wilkie	Gwyther	Pugh	
	28/9		*5,840*	*4*	8				*Johnson*	*Mathias*	*Farrimond*	*Moore*	*Yeats*	*Stevenson*	*Tynan*	*Palios*	*Loyden*	*Young*	*McAuley*	
								Ref: H Powell	Tranmere, who lost only their first game last week, under-perform here and are slow-handclapped by their own supporters. Gwyther's first-half goal rounds off a lovely Town move. Wilkie is deprived a clear run in on goal by Rovers' player-manager Ron Yeats, when he handles the ball											
9	A	CHARLTON			L	2-5	1-4	Wilkie 31, Gwyther 70	Smith	Burgin	Quinn	Kemp*	Pickering	Rhodes	Jones	Ford	Wilkie	Gwyther	Pugh	Shanahan
	2/10		*5,131*		8			*Hales 4, 35, Horsfield 15, 29, Peacock 46*	*Dunn*	*Jones*	*Warman*	*Smart*	*Goldthorpe*	*Curtis*	*Powell*	*Hales*	*Peacock*	*Horsfield*	*Flanagan*	
								Ref: J Hunting	Andy Burgin doesn't have a happy evening. His two careless backpasses lead to Charlton's opening goals. But he isn't alone when it comes to defensive errors. Kemp is dispossessed by Peacock to set up Hales' second. Hales himself and Goldthorpe make bad errors for Town's goals.											
10	H	CHESTERFIELD		13	W	2-0	1-0	Gwyther 25, Jones 72	Smith	Burgin	Quinn	Kemp	Pickering	Rhodes	Jones	Ford	Wilkie	Gwyther	Pugh	
	6/10		2,728	*10*	10				*Tingay*	*Tiler*	*Burton*	*Barlow*	*Winstanley*	*Stott*	*McHale*	*Wilson*	*Downes*	*Bellamy*	*Ferris*	
								Ref: A Porter	New Spirites boss Joe Shaw feels his side is unlucky to lose this game. Chesterfield slip to tenth but won't be as low again. After falling behind they take the game to Town and an equaliser looks imminent. Until, that is, Jones fires in past reserve keeper Phil Tingay and the game is over.											
11	A	BRIGHTON		12	W	1-0	1-0	Gwyther 36	Smith	Jones	Burgin*	Hale	Pickering	Rhodes	Shanahan	Ford	Wilkie	Gwyther	Pugh	Kemp
	13/10		*6,228*	*21*	12				*Powney*	*Howell G*	*Spearritt*	*Templeman*	*Gall*	*Piper*	*Towner*	*Beamish*	*Hilton*	*Boyle*	*O'Sullivan*	
								Ref: R Perkins	Pat Saward is manager of struggling Brighton, but he will only be in the job one more week. Chairman Mike Bamber will soon be enlisting the help of Brian Clough. Support is diminishing – this is their lowest attendance so far. They see Town nick it through Gwyther from close range.											

No	Venue	Opponent	Att	Pos	Res	Pts	F-A	H-T	Scorers, Times, and Referees	1	2	3	4	5	6	7	8	9	10	11	12
12	H	WREXHAM		14	L		1-2	1-2	Rhodes 1	Smith	Jones	Quinn	Hale	Pickering	Rhodes	Shanahan*	Ford	Wilkie	Gwyther	Pugh	Kemp
20/10			2,299	*9*		12			*Sutton 2, Tinnion 15*	*Lloyd*	*Jones*	*Fogg*	*Davis*	*May*	*Whittle*	*Tinnion*	*Sutton*	*Davies*	*Ashcroft*	*Griffiths*	
									Ref: J Hough	The Shaymen suffer their first home defeat in the league since February. Although Rhodes gives them a dream start following a short corner, Sutton replies within 30 seconds, before Brian Tinnion poaches a goal in the 15th minute – the winner. Too many Town players have off days.											
13	A	CAMBRIDGE		12	W		1-0	1-0	Gwyther 8	Smith	Worthington	Quinn	Hale	Pickering	Rhodes	Jones	Ford	Shanahan	Gwyther	Pugh	
27/10			*4,630*	*20*		14				*Vasper*	*O'Donnell*	*Akers*	*Guild*	*Eades*	*Watson*	*Ferguson*	*Foote*	*Lill**	*Greenhalgh*	*Lennard*	*Ross*
									Ref: A Lees	Bill Leivers' struggling Cambridge side have only won three games all season, but beat Port Vale 4-2 last week. George Mulhall has drafted in Dave Worthington, on loan, for a second spell, to help his side out. But Town have few problems, and Gwyther's early headed goal is enough.											
14	H	BOURNEMOUTH		15	D		1-1	1-0	Gwyther 40	Smith	Worthington	Quinn	Hale	Pickering	Rhodes	Jones	Ford*	Shanahan	Gwyther	Pugh	Kemp
3/11			2,324	*3*		15			*Howe*	*Baker*	*Machin**	*Howe*	*Benson*	*Jones D*	*Powell*	*Redknapp*	*Chadwick*	*Sainty*	*Boyer*	*Buttle*	*De Garis*
									Ref: P Willis	The Cherries are lying 3rd so Town expect - and get - a tough game. It's a thrilling encounter. Town shade the first half and Gwyther fires low into the net. The visitors come back strongly in the second and Howe heads the equaliser to stretch his side's unbeaten run to twelve matches.											
15	A	PLYMOUTH		16	D		1-1	1-1	Jones 35	Smith	Worthington	Quinn	Hale	Pickering	Rhodes*	Jones	Ford	Shanahan	Gwyther	Pugh	Kemp
10/11			*8,014*	*13*		16			*Davey 25*	*Furnell*	*Randall*	*Sullivan*	*Hore*	*Saxton*	*Hague*	*Welsh*	*Davey*	*Mariner*	*Machin*	*Rogers*	
									Ref: A Robinson	Plymouth's Colin Sullivan recently won England Under-23 honours, but he is given a roasting by Alan Jones. It is Jones who heads Town's equaliser ten minutes after Davey heads in Machin's free-kick. Late on, Gwyther, looking for his eighth goal in nine games, heads just wide.											
16	A	WATFORD			D		0-0	0-0		Smith	Worthington	Quinn	Hale	Pickering	Pugh	Jones	Ford	Shanahan	Gwyther	Kemp	
12/11			*5,358*			17				*Rankin*	*Butler*	*Williams*	*Keen*	*Lees*	*Welbourne*	*Morgan*	*Bond*	*Morrissey*	*Jennings*	*Farley*	
									Ref: A Oliver	After two poor seasons under former Town boss George Kirby, Watford have appointed Mike Keen as their eleventh post-war manager. He's made a mediocre start and here is thankful to Rankin for avoiding defeat. He saves Gwyther's 74th-minute penalty after Jones is brought down.											
17	H	PORT VALE		11	W		1-0	0-0	Pugh 61	Smith	Burgin	Quinn	Hale	Pickering	Pugh	Jones	Ford	Shanahan	Worthington	Kemp	
17/11			2,094	*17*		19				*Boswell*	*Brodie*	*Loska*	*Summerscales*	*Harris*	*Horton*	*Woodward*	*Tartt**	*McLaren*	*Lacey*	*Mountford*	*Williams*
									Ref: C Seel	This is a 2.15 kick-off due to the government's ban on the use of floodlights because of the energy crisis. Port Vale are a physical lot and have three men booked as tempers flare. But the Shaymen come out on top when skipper Pugh scores after Boswell fails to hold his original header.											
18	A	ALDERSHOT		13	L		1-2	1-0	Ford 27	Smith	Burgin	Quinn	Hale*	Pickering	Rhodes	Jones	Ford	Kemp	Gwyther	Pugh	Shanahan
8/12			*3,019*	*20*		19			*Howarth 69, Wallace 79*	*Godfrey*	*Walden*	*Walker*	*Wallace*	*Dean*	*Richardson*	*Stenson*	*Brown*	*Howarth*	*Brodie*	*Jennings*	
									Ref: D Smith	There is drama on the train heading south when Mulhall and Hale have to help an injured passenger. The train runs late and Town don't reach the ground until 1.18 – for a 2.00 start. Drama on the pitch, too, as ex-Shayman Wallace scores the winner while Hale is lying on the ground.											
19	H	TRANMERE		12	W		2-1	1-0	Pugh 25, Shanahan 85	Smith	Burgin	Quinn	Pugh	Pickering	Rhodes	Jones	Ford	Kemp	Gwyther	Shanahan	
22/12			1,844	*10*		21			*Allen 57*	*Lawrence*	*Mathias*	*Farrimond*	*Seasman*	*Stevenson*	*Moore*	*Crossley*	*Veitch*	*Tynan*	*Young*	*Allen*	
									Ref: P Baldwin	The lowest crowd so far see the Shaymen complete their first double. Pugh's 30-yard strike would be good enough to win any game, but not here. That honour goes to Shanahan who, after Ross Allen has equalised, scores a less spectacular goal when a corner isn't dealt with properly.											
20	A	HUDDERSFIELD		14	L		**0-4**	0-1		Smith	Burgin	Quinn	Pugh	Pickering	Rhodes	Jones	Ford	Kemp	Gwyther	Shanahan	
26/12			***11,514***	*6*		21			*Lawson 6, Dolan 56, Gowling 65, 76*	*Poole*	*Hutt*	*Garner*	*Smith*	*Saunders*	*Marshall*	*Hoy*	*Lawson*	*Gowling*	*Dolan*	*Chapman*	
									Ref: R Capey	Two seasons ago the Terriers were in Division 1. Consecutive relegations see them facing Halifax for the first time in the league. £65,000 buy Alan Gowling from Man Utd scores their last two goals to give his side a rather flattering scoreline. The Shaymen acually play quite well.											
21	A	SOUTHEND		10	W		2-1	2-0	Shanahan 3, 35	Smith	Burgin	Quinn	Hale	Pickering*	Rhodes	Shanahan	Ford	Kemp	Gwyther	Pugh	**McDonald**
29/12			*6,387*	*16*		23			*Guthrie 76*	*Bellotti*	*Worthington*	*Ford*	*Elliott*	*Townsend*	*Dyer*	*Moody*	*Brace*	*Guthrie*	*Coulson*	*Johnson T*	
									Ref: R Joseland	Shanahan gives the Shaymen a two-goal half-time lead but in the second half they feel the ref is not playing fair. He gives Southend a penalty for a push on Brace. However, Smith saves Brace's kick. He then allows Guthrie's direct free-kick to stand even though he awards it indirect.											
22	A	SHREWSBURY		9	W		2-0	1-0	Kemp 33p, Shanahan 59	Smith	Burgin	Quinn	Hale	Pickering	Rhodes	Shanahan	Ford	Kemp	Gwyther	Pugh	
5/1			*2,542*	*23*		25				*Mulhearn*	*Gregory*	*Calloway*	*Dolby*	*Turner*	*Durban*	*Hughes*	*Irvine*	*Marlowe*	*Tarbuck*	*Morris**	*Roberts D*
									Ref: M Kerkof	The Town bus makes it to Gay Meadow with seven minutes to spare after it had been stuck in traffic heading for the Wolves v Leeds FA Cup-tie. The players don't look affected. Kemp's penalty sets them on their way after Quinn is tripped by Shrewsbury player-boss Alan Durban.											
23	H	BRISTOL ROV		11	D		0-0	0-0		Smith	Burgin	Quinn	Hale	Pickering	Rhodes	Jones	Ford*	Kemp	Shanahan	Pugh	Wilkie
12/1			4,507	*1*		26				*Eadie*	*Jacobs*	*Parsons*	*Green*	*Taylor*	*Prince*	*Rudge*	*Stanton*	*Worboys*	*Bannister*	*Dobson*	
									Ref: K McNally	Including last season, league-leaders Rovers are unbeaten in thirty games. Town raise their game and it would have been an injustice for either side to lose. Shanahan looks to have won Town a penalty following Hale's quick free-kick – but Hale is booked for taking the kick too soon!											

No	Date		Att	Pos	Pt	F-A	H-T	Scorers, Times, and Referees	1	2	3	4	5	6	7	8	9	10	11	12 sub used
24	A	OLDHAM		11	L	2-3	1-1	Kemp 30, Shanahan 60	Smith	Burgin	Quinn	Hale	Pickering	Rhodes	Jones	Wilkie	Kemp	Shanahan	Pugh	
	19/1		*8,432*	*8*	26			*Blair 5, 72, Robins 57*	*Ogden*	*Wood*	*Whittle*	*Mulvaney*	*Hicks*	*Bailey*	*McVitie*	*McNeill*	*Jones*	*Blair*	*Robins*	
								Ref: R Tinkler	Luck goes against the Shaymen. At 1-1 Shanahan's shot hits the bar. At 2-2 Oldham's Tony Bailey commits a professional foul on Kemp, who otherwise would be clear. Oldham get a winner when Ian Robins' cross comes back off the post and falls for Ronnie Blair, and he can't miss.											
25	H	SOUTHPORT		14	D	1-1	0-0	Gwyther 74	Smith	Burgin	Quinn	Hale	Pickering	Rhodes	Ford	Shanahan	Kemp	Gwyther	Pugh	
	27/1		4,178	*22*	27			*Fryatt 79*	*Taylor*	*Sibbald*	*Ryder*	*Noble*	*Philpotts*	*Scott*	*Wright*	*Russell*	*Fryatt*	*Provan**	*Coleman*	*Molyneux*
								Ref: D Civil	Town play their first-ever game on a Sunday because of the energy crisis. The attendance is way up on the season's average. Halifax RLFC are not happy. Their game played at the same time only attracts 1,302. Southport earn a point but new boss Alan Ball fails to board the team bus.											
26	H	WALSALL		12	W	**3-1**	2-0	Jones 2, Shanahan 33, 67	Smith	Burgin	Quinn	Pugh	Pickering	Rhodes	Jones	Shanahan	Kemp	Gwyther	Ford	
	3/2		3,543	*14*	29			*Taylor 49*	*Kearns*	*Harrison*	*Fry*	*Robinson*	*Saunders*	*Atthey**	*Sloan*	*Shinton*	*Andrews*	*Buckley*	*Taylor*	*Bennett*
								Ref: I Smith	Teamwork and individual opportunism work to win this one over a Walsall side that causes a few problems. Brian Taylor pulls a goal back after half-time off a free-kick, but Town kill off the Saddlers' hopes of a point when Gwyther pulls the ball back for Shanahan to net the third.											
27	H	BRIGHTON		13	D	2-2	2-0	Shanahan 18, 41	Smith	Burgin	Quinn	Hale	Pickering	Rhodes	Pugh	Shanahan	Kemp	Gwyther*	Ford	Wilkie
	16/2		2,767	*18*	30			*Robertson 65p, Templeman 68*	*Grummitt*	*Templeman*	*Wilson*	*Welch*	*Brown*	*Piper*	*Towner*	*Spearritt*	*Bridges*	*Robertson*	*O'Sullivan*	
								Ref: J Goggins	Brighton are managed by former Derby supremo Brian Clough. He isn't happy to see Grummitt spill the ball twice for Shanahan's goals. But he is happy with his side's fightback, begun when Robertson nets a penalty against his old club. At 2-2 Spearritt's goal is ruled out for offside.											
28	A	CHESTERFIELD		13	D	1-1	1-1	Pugh 17	Smith	Burgin	Quinn	Hale	Pickering	Rhodes	Pugh	Shanahan	Kemp	Gwyther	Ford	
	23/2		*6,538*	*3*	31			*McHale 36*	*Brown*	*Holmes*	*Burton*	*McHale*	*Winstanley*	*Phelan*	*Thompson*	*Moss*	*Large*	*Bellamy*	*Wilson*	
								Ref: A Grey	Halifax Town's 2,000th League game. Johnny Quinn misses it but celebrates the birth of his daughter. Town should be celebrating victory but future Scotland keeper Jim Brown denies them in the second half. Pugh gives Town the lead but Ray McHale equalises with a vicious volley.											
29	H	HUDDERSFIELD		14	D	0-0	0-0		Smith	Burgin	Quinn	Hale	Pickering	Rhodes	Pugh	Shanahan*	Kemp	Gwyther	Ford	Wilkie
	2/3		**8,126**	*7*	32				*Poole*	*Hutt*	*Garner*	*Smith*	*Saunders*	*Marshall*	*Firth**	*Lawson*	*Gowling*	*Pugh*	*Summerill*	*Chapman*
								Ref: R Perkin	Halifax's 1,000th League game at the Shay. Near neighbours Huddersfield add spice to the occasion. But there are no goals. The Terriers' failings in front of goal in the first half are matched by Halifax's in the second. Kemp goes closest but Hutt clears his clever chip off the line.											
30	H	CAMBRIDGE		15	L	0-1	0-0		Smith	Burgin	Quinn	Pugh	Pickering	Rhodes	Wilkie	Shanahan	Kemp	Gwyther	Ford	
	10/3		2,346	*21*	32			*Lennard 48*	*Vasper*	*O'Donnell*	*Bannister*	*Guild*	*Eades*	*Batson*	*Ferguson*	*Lennard*	*Simmons**	*Lill*	*Watson*	*Ross*
								Ref: A Morrissey	The supporters come out in the rain and sleet, and endure their side's worst display of the season. Relegation-bound Cambridge conceded six during the week but do enough here to record only their second win of the season. It is former Town star Dave Lennard who pounces to score.											
31	A	HEREFORD		15	L	1-3	0-1	Wilkie 88	Smith	Burgin	Quinn	Hale	Pickering	Rhodes	Wilkie	Pugh	Kemp*	Gwyther	Ford	McDonald
	13/3		*6,170*	*20*	32			*Brown 16, 74, Redrobe 79*	*Hughes*	*Radford*	*Naylor*	*McLaughlin*	*Tucker*	*Addison*	*Redrobe*	*Tyler**	*Brown*	*Evans*	*Rudge*	*Lee*
								Ref: A Robinson	The going is tough on Hereford's heavily sanded pitch. On-loan striker Willie Brown makes his debut, scores two and claims another. But the Bulls' third is credited to Eric Redrobe, who has the last touch in a goalmouth scramble. Wilkie's goal for Town is no more than a consolation.											
32	A	WREXHAM		18	L	1-2	0-0	Smith D 64	Smith	Burgin	Quinn	Hale	Pickering	Rhodes	**Smith D**	Pugh	Kemp	Gwyther	Ford	
	16/3		*4,672*	*6*	32			*Sutton 82, Griffiths 84*	*Lloyd*	*Jones*	*Fogg*	*Evans*	*May*	*Whittle*	*Tinnion*	*Sutton*	*Davies**	*Smallman*	*Griffiths*	*Thomas*
								Ref: R Lee	The sight of a mini-pitch invasion at the Racecourse is quite perplexing. The game is only ten minutes old and there is no score. On-loan David Smith is on hand to give Town the lead. Wrexham's response is late but Griffiths' back-headed winner header sparks another pitch invasion.											
33	A	WALSALL			D	2-2	2-0	Smith D 23, Gwyther 28	Smith	Burgin	Quinn	Hale	Pickering	Rhodes	Smith D	Pugh	Kemp	Gwyther	Ford	
	19/3		*3,960*		33			*Harrison 76, 82*	*Kearns*	*Saunders*	*Fry*	*Robinson*	*Bennett*	*Atthey*	*Harrison*	*Sloan*	*Andrews*	*Buckley*	*Taylor*	
								Ref: A Porter	The pace is fast and furious. Town withstand early pressure then score two in five minutes. Gwyther's goal is a dropping header. Walsall pile it on in the second half and deservedly draw level, though Burgin will have nightmares about his backpass that leads to Colin Harrison's second.											
34	H	PLYMOUTH		16	W	1-0	0-0	Saxton 83 (og)	Smith	Burgin	Quinn	Pugh	Pickering	Rhodes	Smith D	Shanahan	Kemp	Gwyther	Ford*	McDonald
	23/3		1,715	*17*	35				*Furnell*	*Randall*	*Sullivan*	*Hore*	*Shipperley*	*Saxton*	*Reed*	*Rafferty*	*Mariner*	*Machin*	*Darke*	
								Ref: E Garner	The Shaymen end a run of six games without a win. The visit of Tony Waiters' Argyle attracts Town's lowest attendance so far. In a drab game Kemp has a goal disallowed for hands, but later his corner leads to Bobby Saxton knocking the ball over his own line to give Town the points.											

No	Venue / Date	Opponents	Att	Pos	Res / Pts	F-A	H-T	Scorers, Times, and Referees	1	2	3	4	5	6	7	8	9	10	11	12 sub used
35	H	SHREWSBURY			W	1-0	1-0	Shanahan 35	Smith	Burgin	Quinn	Pugh	Pickering	Rhodes	Smith D	Shanahan	Kemp	Gwyther*	McDonald	Wilkie
	26/3		**1,346**		37				*Mulhearn*	*King*	*Calloway*	*Durban*	*Kearney*	*Turner*	*Roberts D*	*Matthias*	*Marlowe*	*Roberts L*	*Tarbuck*	
								Ref: E Jolly	Gwyther damages his knee and Town are left with only ten fit men after this. Mulhall will ask the League to postpone Town's next game. He expresses concern, too, over the low attendance. The only bit of good news is Shanahan's winner, when Mulhearn fails to hold Burgin's cross.											
36	A	SOUTHPORT		15	D	1-1	1-0	Kemp 16	Smith	Burgin	Quinn	Pugh	Pickering	Rhodes	Smith D	Shanahan	Kemp	Gwyther	McDonald	
	1/4		*1,083*	*22*	38			*Moore 55*	*Taylor*	*Sibbald*	*Ross*	*Wright*	*Noble*	*O'Neil*	*Moore*	*Hughes*	*Fryatt*	*Provan*	*Russell*	
								Ref: T Bosi	Four of Town's players are still not fully fit. The game is spoilt by the wind. Kemp gives Town the lead when he fires in from 18 yards. The home side's shock equaliser comes when Provan's shot hits the bar and falls nicely for Mick Moore. Late on, Jim Fryatt misses a one-on-one.											
37	H	WATFORD		16	D	0-0	0-0		Smith	Burgin	Quinn	Hale	Pickering	Pugh	Smith D	Shanahan	Kemp	Gwyther	Ford*	Wilkie
	6/4		1,866	*8*	39				*Rankin*	*Butler*	*Williams*	*Morrissey*	*Lees*	*Keen*	*Farley*	*Bond*	*Jenkins**	*Scullion*	*Jennings*	*Craker*
								Ref: A Jones	Tony Rhodes is out of action. Working on his car he scolded his face removing the car radiator cap. On the pitch David Ford retires after only 13 minutes. This is a typical mid-table clash. Mulhall admits it's hard to motivate the players. Elton John, Watford director, attends the match.											
38	H	GRIMSBY			L	1-2	1-1	Smith D 29p	Smith	Burgin	Quinn	Hale	Pickering	Rhodes	Smith D	Shanahan	Kemp	Gwyther	Pugh	
	9/4		1,624		39			*Hubbard 20, Lumby 75*	*Wainman*	*Beardsley*	*Booth*	*Hubbard*	*Wright*	*Czuczman*	*Barton*	*Hickman*	*Lewis*	*Lumby*	*Boylen*	
								Ref: H Davey	Town deserve, but don't get, something from this game. They fall behind to Hubbard's well-struck shot from 18 yards. David Smith levels it with a retaken penalty – Wainman, who moves, saves Hale's first effort. Defensive errors lead to Boylan chipping over for Lumby to head in.											
39	A	PORT VALE		15	D	1-1	0-0	Kemp 78	Smith	Burgin	Quinn	Hale	Pugh	Rhodes	Smith D	Shanahan	Kemp	Gwyther	McDonald	
	13/4		*2,707*	*19*	40			*McLaren 75*	*Boswell*	*Brodie*	*Griffiths*	*Tartt*	*Harris**	*Horton*	*Mountford*	*Lacey*	*Woodward*	*Williams*	*McLaren*	*Gough*
								Ref: J Whalley	John Pickering's pulled thigh muscle means he misses his first game after 190 consecutive appearances. David Smith has the chance to win the game when Town are awarded a penalty when Tartt pulls back Shanahan. But Boswell saves his kick, Town's fourth penalty miss this season.											
40	A	BLACKBURN		16	D	1-1	0-1	Shanahan 55	Smith	Burgin	Quinn	Hale	Pugh	Rhodes	Wilkie	Shanahan	Kemp	Gwyther	McDonald	
	15/4		*4,788*	*11*	41			*Endean 3*	*Bradshaw*	*Heaton*	*Arentoft*	*Hird*	*Waddington**	*Fazackerley*	*Martin*	*Hutchins*	*Parkes*	*Endean*	*Kenyon*	*Turner*
								Ref: J Williams	Any lingering relegation fears are wiped away as Town do more than enough to win a point in this Easter Monday fixture. Gordon Lee's side are disappointing and offer little after Endean's early goal. Shanahan beats Arentoft to the ball to fire low past Bradshaw for Town's equaliser.											
41	H	BLACKBURN		15	D	1-1	0-1	Wilkie 58	White	Burgin	Quinn	Hale	Pugh	Rhodes	Wilkie	Shanahan	Kemp	Gwyther	McDonald	
	16/4		2,446	*10*	42			*Martin 37*	*Bradshaw*	*Heaton*	*Arentoft*	*Metcalfe*	*Wood*	*Fazackerley*	*Kenyon*	*Hird*	*Martin*	*Parkes*	*Wright*	
								Ref: C Newsome	Reserve keeper Barry White gets his chance in this swift return. He makes a super 84th-minute save when he pushes Metcalfe's 25-yarder onto the post. He has little chance, though, with Don Martin's fizzing first-time effort. Wilkie gets onto Gwyther's flick to net a deserved equaliser.											
42	H	ALDERSHOT		14	D	0-0	0-0		White	Burgin	Quinn	Hale*	Pugh	Rhodes	Wilkie	Shanahan	Kemp	Gwyther	McDonald	Smith D
	20/4		1,552	*10*	43				*Johnson*	*Walden*	*Jopling*	*Walker*	*Richardson*	*Wallace*	*Bell**	*Brown*	*Howarth*	*Joslyn*	*Brodie*	*Stenson*
								Ref: J Rice	Tom McAnearney's Aldershot put six past Cambridge last week. Jack Howarth, who scored a hat-trick, gets special attention from the Town defence. Smith misses a golden chance with six minutes left, but a goal would have been an injustice. Mulhall, away scouting, misses nothing.											
43	H	ROCHDALE		13	W	1-0	0-0	Shanahan 88	Smith	Burgin	Smith D	Hale	Pugh	Rhodes	Quinn	Shanahan	Kemp	Gwyther	McDonald	
	22/4		1,431	*24*	45				*Poole*	*Fielding*	*Seddon*	*Horne*	*Hanvey*	*Tobin*	*Taylor*	*Gowans**	*Brennan*	*Carrick*	*Downes*	*Arnold*
								Ref: R Clay	Walter Joyce's first season in charge at Rochdale ends in relegation. His side is already condemned. It's a funny game which only comes to life in the last seven minutes. A goalless draw looks likely until Shanahan heads home Gwyther's cross - and ends up in the net with the ball, too.											
44	A	BOURNEMOUTH		12	D	1-1	1-0	Smith D 44	White	Burgin	Quinn	Hale	Pugh	Rhodes	Smith D	Shanahan	Kemp	Gwyther	McDonald	
	24/4		*4,475*	*9*	46			*Goddard 58*	*Charlton*	*Payne*	*Miller*	*Howe*	*Jones D*	*Powell*	*Goddard*	*Welsh*	*Greenhalgh**	*Cave*	*O'Rourke*	*Jones G*
								Ref: B Homewood	16-year-old Howard Goddard catches the eye, and scores his first league goal with a close-range volley to level the scores. David Smith beats two defenders to put Town ahead. Cherries' recent £40,000 signing Brian Greenhalgh is marked out of the game by Quinn, and is substituted.											
45	A	ROCHDALE		11	D	1-1	1-1	Smith D 40	White	Burgin	Quinn	Hale	Pugh	Rhodes	Smith D	Shanahan	Kemp	Gwyther	McDonald	
	27/4		*1,320*	*24*	47			*Skeete 6*	*Poole*	*Fielding*	*Seddon*	*Horne*	*Hanvey*	*Tobin*	*Taylor*	*Skeete*	*Brennan*	*Carrick*	*Downes*	
								Ref: E Wallace	A predictable end-of-season game that could have offered more after Leo Skeete's early goal. David Smith keeps up his good scoring record for the Shaymen. Dale's Keith Hanvey nearly wins it, whipping the ball against the bar, but his side go down and won't play at this level again.											
46	H	YORK		9	W	2-1	0-1	Hale 63, Shanahan 85	White	Burgin	Quinn	Hale	Pugh	Rhodes	Smith D	Shanahan	Kemp	Gwyther	McDonald	
	30/4		4,275	*3*	49			*Hunter 20*	*Crawford*	*Hunter*	*Burrows*	*Holmes*	*Swallow*	*Topping*	*Lyons*	*Woodward*	*Seal*	*Jones*	*Butler*	
		Home	Away					Ref: J Hunting	Gordon Hunter gives promoted York the lead with a memorable goal – a 50-yard free-kick that finds its way in. In an exciting finale, Halifax draw level, then Shanahan scores a controversial late winner. Crawford says he is impeded and Burrows reckons he cleared the ball on the line.											
Average		2,835	5,309																	

League Cup

League Cup			F-A	H-T	Scorers, Times, and Referees	1	2	3	4	5	6	7	8	9	10	11	12 sub used
1 H BARNSLEY		D	1-1	1-1	Rhodes 36	Smith	Burgin	Quinn	Kemp	Pickering	Rhodes	Jones	Pugh	Shanahan	Ford	Hale	
28/8	2,768				*Mahoney 7*	*Arblaster*	*Murphy*	*Chambers*	*Pettit*	*Cole*	*Greenwood*	*Doyle*	*Mahoney*	*Butler*	*Millar*	*Lea*	
					Ref: J Goggins	Barnsley surprise the Shaymen with an early goal from Mahoney after Smith fails to gather Doyle's cross. Rhodes' header from a corner levels it, then Town step up a gear. Chances go begging, with Kemp guilty of the worst miss when Arblaster fists out his penalty after he felled Jones.											
1R A BARNSLEY	13	W	1-0	1-0	Rhodes 10	Smith	Burgin	Quinn	Kemp	Pickering	Rhodes	Jones	Pugh	Ford	Gwyther	Hale	
4/9	*4,168 4:24*					*Arblaster*	*Murphy*	*Chambers*	*Brown*	*Boyle*	*Greenwood*	*Doyle*	*Butler*	*Mahoney**	*Millar*	*Lea*	*O'Connor*
					Ref: J Goggins	A home tie with the mighty Wolves is awaiting the winners, so the incentive is there. Tony Rhodes is the hero on the night as he scores early on following Hale's corner. He then plays his part in the defence as Town keep Barnsley at bay. It's nerve-wracking stuff, but Halifax hold out.											
2 H WOLVES	13	L	0-3	0-1		Smith	Burgin	Quinn	Kemp*	Pickering	Rhodes	Jones	Ford	Wilkie	Gwyther	Pugh	Shanahan
8/10	8,222 *1:19*				*Sunderland 36, Dougan 60, Richards 82*	*Parkes*	*Palmer*	*Taylor*	*Bailey*	*Munro*	*McAlle*	*McCalliog*	*Sunderland*	*Richards*	*Dougan*	*Wagstaffe**	*Daley*
					Ref: R Lee	Town have First Division Wolves worried until Alan Sunderland beats the offside to score. Six minutes into the second half Kemp is left to rue his penalty miss when Gerry Taylor brings down Jones. Wolves take control, win the match, then actually go on to win the League Cup itself.											

FA Cup

FA Cup			F-A	H-T	Scorers, Times, and Referees	1	2	3	4	5	6	7	8	9	10	11	12 sub used
1 H FRICKLEY COL	11	W	6-1	3-0	Gwyther 8, 27, 71, Ford 17, Hale p,	Smith	Burgin	Quinn	Hale	Pickering	Rhodes	Jones	Kemp	Ford	Gwyther	Pugh	
24/11	3,560 *ML*				*Moran 70* [Rhodes]	*Chapman*	*Green*	*Jones*	*Maloney*	*Parsons**	*Millward*	*Taylor*	*Moran*	*Whiteley*	*Levitt*	*Scothorne*	*Spence*
					Ref: J Butcher	Dave Gwyther claims a unique record as he scores his third headed hat-trick of his career, and his fourth in the FA Cup – all against non-league opposition. Frickley, who have in their side former Town winger Archie Taylor, are a colourful lot and enjoy the day, but they are outclassed.											
2 H OLDHAM	13	L	0-1	0-0		Smith	Burgin	Quinn	Hale	Pickering	Rhodes	Jones	Ford	Kemp	Gwyther	Pugh	
15/12	*3:4*				*McVitie 70*	*Dowd*	*Wood*	*Whittle*	*Mulvaney*	*Hicks*	*Edwards*	*McVitie*	*Jones*	*Garwood*	*Blair*	*Robins*	
					Ref: R Tinkler	Town go out but only have themselves to blame. On a hard, snow-covered pitch, they miss several chances, notably from Gwyther who puts wide twice from close range. Oldham dominate after the break and score when McVitie fires in from 25 yards. Town's gallant fight is in vain.											

		Home						Away					
	P	W	D	L	F	A	W	D	L	F	A	Pts
1 Oldham	46	13	6	4	50	23	12	6	5	33	24	62
2 Bristol Rov	46	15	6	2	37	15	7	11	5	28	18	61
3 York	46	13	8	2	37	15	8	11	4	30	23	61
4 Wrexham	46	15	6	2	44	15	7	6	10	19	28	56
5 Chesterfield	46	14	6	3	31	16	7	8	8	24	26	56
6 Grimsby	46	14	6	3	48	21	4	9	10	19	29	51
7 Watford	46	12	6	5	34	21	7	6	10	30	35	50
8 Aldershot	46	13	6	4	47	22	6	5	12	18	30	49
9 HALIFAX	46	9	11	3	23	15	5	10	8	25	36	49
10 Huddersfield	46	14	5	4	37	16	3	8	12	19	39	47
11 Bournemouth	46	11	5	7	25	23	5	10	8	29	35	47
12 Southend	46	10	7	6	40	30	6	7	10	22	32	46
13 Blackburn	46	13	4	6	38	21	5	6	12	24	43	46
14 Charlton	46	13	5	5	43	29	6	3	14	23	44	46
15 Walsall	46	11	7	5	37	19	5	6	12	20	29	45
16 Tranmere	46	10	8	5	31	15	5	7	11	19	29	45
17 Plymouth	46	13	6	4	37	17	4	4	15	22	37	44
18 Hereford	46	10	5	8	31	25	4	10	9	22	32	43
19 Brighton	46	10	3	10	31	31	6	8	9	21	27	43
20 Port Vale	46	12	6	5	37	23	2	8	13	15	35	42
21 Cambridge	46	11	7	5	36	27	2	2	19	12	54	35
22 Shrewsbury	46	7	7	9	24	24	3	4	16	17	38	31
23 Southport	46	4	14	5	19	20	2	2	19	16	62	28
24 Rochdale	46	1	12	10	24	38	1	5	17	14	56	21
	1104	268	162	122	841	521	122	162	268	521	841	1104

Odds & ends

Double wins: (2) Shrewsbury, Tranmere.
Double losses: (2) Grimsby, Wrexham.

Won from behind: (1) York (h).
Lost from in front: (3) Wrexham (h & a), Aldershot (a).

High spots: Winning two consecutive matches on three occasions.
Scoring six against Frickley for the first time since 1967.
Ending the season with eight unbeaten matches.
Finishing above Huddersfield for the first time.

Low spots: Seven games without a win up to 20 April.
Three consecutive defeats in March.
Losing 0-4 at Huddersfield.

Halifax drew 21 matches – a club record up to then.

Player of the Year: Johnny Quinn.
Ever-presents: (1) David Pugh.
Hat-tricks: Dave Gwyther (FA Cup).
Leading scorers: Dave Gwyther & Terry Shanahan (13).

	Appearances						Goals			
	Lge	*Sub*	LC	*Sub*	FAC	*Sub*	Lge	LC	FAC	Tot
Burgin, Andy	**41**		3		2					
Cullen, Pat		*1*								
Ford, David	**34**		3		2		**1**		1	**2**
Gwyther, Dave	**42**		2		2		**10**		3	**13**
Hale, Ken	**34**		2		2		**2**		1	**3**
Jones, Alan	**23**		3		2		**4**			**4**
Kemp, Fred	**40**	*4*	3		2		**3**			**3**
McDonald, Gerry	**10**	*3*								
Pickering, John	**38**		3		2					
Pugh, David	**46**		3		2		**3**			**3**
Quinn, Johnny	**45**		3		2					
Rhodes, Tony	**41**		3		2		**1**	2	1	**4**
Shanahan, Terry	**35**	*4*	1	*1*			**13**			**13**
Smith, Alex	**41**		3		2					
Smith, David	**12**	*1*					**5**			**5**
White, Barry	**5**									
Wilkie, John	**14**	*7*	1				**5**			**5**
Worthington, Dave	**5**									
(own-goals)							**1**			**1**
18 players used	**506**	***20***	**33**	***1***	**22**		**48**	**2**	**6**	**56**

LEAGUE DIVISION 3

Manager: Mulhall ⇨ Johnny Quinn

SEASON 1974-75

No	Date		Att	Pos	Pt	F-A	H-T	Scorers, Times, and Referees	1	2	3	4	5	6	7	8	9	10	11	12 sub used
1	H	CHARLTON			D	2-2	1-0	Downes 9, 87	Smith A	Burgin	**Collins**	Quinn	Rhodes	Pugh	Jones	**Moir**	**Downes**	Gwyther	Ford	
	17/8		2,513		1			*Curtis 66p, Hales 78*	*Dunn*	*Curtis*	*Warman*	*Bowman*	*Horsfield*	*Young*	*Powell*	*Hales*	*Davies**	*Dunphy*	*Peacock*	*Hunt*
								Ref: N Ashley	George Mulhall reckons Town will be a force to be reckoned with. Downes gets them off to a flyer, but then misses a first-half penalty. Curtis nets a penalty when Moir brings down Powell, and Hales breaks away to give Charlton the lead. Downes gets to Jones' cross to save the game.											
2	A	WALSALL		10	D	1-1	0-1	Shanahan 88p	Smith A	Burgin	Collins	Quinn	Rhodes	Pugh	Jones	Shanahan	Downes	Moir	Ford	
	24/8		*3,280*	*15*	2			*Robinson 26*	*Kearns*	*Saunders*	*Fry*	*Robinson*	*Bennett*	*Atthey*	*Harrison*	*Andrews**	*Wright*	*Buckley*	*Taylor*	*Sloan*
								Ref: J Hough	Like the Shaymen, Doug Fraser's Walsall opened with a 2-2 draw. Here, they look to be heading for victory thanks to Dave Robinson's strike from 20 yards. But, with two minutes remaining, Moir takes a tumble. Shanahan keeps his cool to send Kearns the wrong way from the spot.											
3	H	CRYS PALACE		5	W	3-1	2-1	Downes 13, 66, Gwyther 38	Smith A	Burgin	Collins	Pugh	Rhodes	**Lowe**	Jones	Shanahan	Downes	Gwyther	Ford	
	31/8		3,295	*21*	4			*Whittle 34*	*Hammond*	*Barry*	*Jump*	*Jeffries*	*Blyth*	*Johnson J*	*Whittle*	*Lindsay*	*Davies**	*Chatterton*	*Taylor*	*Swindlehurst*
								Ref: E Garner	Palace beat Watford 5-1 in midweek, but they are no match for a lively Halifax side. Wyn 'The Leap' Davies is in their side, but it's the Town forwards who show the way. Downes' second is a dipping shot from outside the box. Palace boss Malcolm Allison criticises the Shay facilities.											
4	A	SOUTHEND			L	**0-4**	0-1		Smith A	Burgin	Collins	Pugh*	Rhodes	Lowe	Jones	Shanahan	Downes	Gwyther	Ford !	Moir
	2/9		*7,973*		4			*Brace 8, Guthrie 67, 73, 87*	*Cawston*	*Dyer*	*Worthington R*	*Elliott*	*Townsend*	*Moody*	*Coulson**	*Brace*	*Guthrie*	*Taylor*	*Cunningham*	*Worthington D*
								Ref: B Stevens	The Shaymen blow their chance to go top. Goalkeeper Alex Smith is out of this world and keeps the score down. Shanahan's bad backpass lets in Brace and Southend are on their way. Chris Guthrie's three goals are all headers. On the hour, Ford walks for chopping down Cunningham.											
5	A	WATFORD		8	D	2-2	0-0	Moir 49, Collins	Smith A	**Smith F**	Collins	Quinn	Rhodes	Lowe	Moir	Shanahan	Downes	Gwyther	Ford	
	7/9		*6,078*	*6*	5			*Scullion, Jenkins*	*Rankin*	*Butler**	*Williams*	*Lees*	*Keen*	*Goodeve*	*Morrissey*	*Bond*	*Jenkins*	*Scullion*	*Downes*	*McGettigan*
								Ref: K Lambert	Alex Smith is again in great form and makes world-class saves from Bond and Lees. Trialist Fred Smith is given a chasing by Scullion, who gets Watford's first. Town lead twice, with Collins' goal a fluke – a cross that goes in at the near post. He claims he saw the keeper off his line.											
6	H	BURY		13	L	0-1	0-1		Smith A	Smith F	Collins	Quinn	Rhodes	Lowe	Jones	**Luckett**	Downes	Gwyther	Ford	
	14/9		3,167	*15*	5			*Spence 43*	*Forrest*	*Hoolickin*	*Kennedy*	*Williams*	*Hulme*	*Holt*	*Buchan*	*Rudd*	*Rowland*	*Spence*	*Hamstead*	
								Ref: A Hamil	Mulhall is unhappy with this. It's unfortunate that everyone plays so badly when young Luckett makes his debut. Bury's John Forrest only has one shot to save – a thunderbolt from Jones. Derek Spence scores the game's only goal, following up when Smith can't hold Rowland's shot.											
7	H	CHESTERFIELD			L	1-3	1-2	Gwyther 41	Smith A	Smith F	Collins	Quinn	Rhodes	Lowe	Jones	**Harrold**	Downes	Gwyther	Ford	
	17/9		1,906		5			*Moss 8, 64, Kowalski 18*	*Tingay*	*Tiler*	*Burton*	*McHale*	*Winstanley*	*Barlow*	*Darling*	*Moss*	*Kowalski*	*Bellamy*	*Phelan*	
								Ref: G Trevett	The Shaymen have injury worries, so local lad Mark Harrold is called up. Ernie Moss twice exposes the frailties in the Town side, while Andy Kowalski finishes off a move involving six players. Town simply aren't good enough, and the following day, a fed-up George Mulhall resigns.											
8	A	BLACKBURN		20	L	0-1	0-1		Smith A	Luckett	Collins	Quinn	Rhodes	Lowe	Jones	Harrold	Downes	Gwyther	Ford	
	21/9		*7,884*	*6*	5			*Oates 42p*	*Jones*	*Burgin*	*Heaton*	*Metcalfe*	*Hawkins*	*Waddington*	*Beamish*	*Oates*	*Martin*	*Parkes*	*Hilton*	
								Ref: K Ridden	Johnny Quinn takes over as caretaker-manager and the Shaymen give their all against a strong Blackburn side. Smith is again outstanding, but he is beaten by Graham Oates' penalty when Beamish suspiciously tumbles in the box when Collins gives chase. Collins and Quinn say he fell.											
9	A	PETERBOROUGH		20	D	1-1	0-1	Ford 60	Smith A	Luckett	Collins	Quinn	Rhodes	Lowe	Jones	Harrold	Ford	Gwyther	White	
	25/9		*8,156*	*5*	6			*Robson 3*	*Steele*	*Bradley*	*Lee*	*Walker*	*Turner*	*Carmichael*	*Murray*	*Gregory*	*Hall**	*Hill*	*Robson*	*Nixon*
								Ref: B James	Quinn is appointed full-time manager, then immediately tries to get this game called off because of too many injuries to his squad. In the end, keeper Barry White plays as emergency sweeper. Town fall behind early on, but get a deserved point through Ford's first-timer from 18 yards.											
10	H	PORT VALE		20	D	1-1	0-0	Ford 56	Smith A	Luckett	Collins	Quinn	Rhodes	Lowe	Jones	Moir	Ford	Gwyther	White	
	28/9		1,897	*16*	7			*Bailey 57*	*Connaughton*	*Brodie*	*Griffiths*	*Chadwick*	*Harris*	*Horton*	*Lacey*	*Mountford*	*Williams*	*Bailey*	*Sharp*	
								Ref: H Robinson	White continues as an outfield player, but Quinn's best move is to play Ford up front. He gets onto Gwyther's flick to open the scoring. The lead lasts less than a minute, though. Smith drops Sharp's shot and Bailey scores. Mountford's rash challenge on White earns him a booking.											
11	A	ALDERSHOT		20	L	1-3	1-2	Jones 16	Smith	Luckett	Collins	**McHale**	Rhodes	**Phelan**	Jones	Lowe	Ford	Gwyther	White	
	2/10		***2,464***	*23*	7			*Walden 11, Howarth 20, Bell 89*	*Johnson*	*Walden*	*Jopling*	*Harley*	*Richardson*	*Walker*	*Sainty*	*Brown**	*Howarth*	*Joslyn*	*Bell*	*Wallace*
								Ref: H Powell	The Shots score a couple of beauties. Walden's is a curling shot, while Howarth's header, that restores their lead, comes off a deep cross. Ford has a goal ruled out, then hits the post, before Bell wraps the game up. Shots' Dennis Brown is substituted and throws his shirt on the floor.											

No	Venue	Opponent	Att	Pos	Res	F-A	H-T	Scorers, Times, and Referees	1	2	3	4	5	6	7	8	9	10	11	12
12	A	TRANMERE		20	L	1-3	0-3	Moir 69	Smith A	Luckett	Collins*	McHale	Rhodes	Phelan	Jones	Quinn	Ford	Gwyther	White	Moir
4/10			*2,584*	*16*	7			*Tynan 2, Coppell 38, Peplow 40*	*Johnson R*	*Webb*	*Mathias*	*Moore*	*Philpotts**	*Veitch*	*Coppell*	*Tynan*	*Young*	*Seasman*	*Peplow*	*Crossley*
								Ref: A Porter	Town pay for their generosity. They concede another early goal when Tynan is unmarked to meet Webb's free-kick. The game is as good as over by half-time. An unhappy night for Collins, who leaves the field with a temperature. His replacement, Moir, however, gets a consolation.											
13	H	SWINDON		23	D	0-0	0-0		Smith A	Luckett	Collins	McHale	Phelan	**Blair**	Jones	Downes*	Ford	Gwyther	Moir	Quinn
12/10			1,730	*7*	8				*Barton*	*Dixon*	*Trollope*	*Hubbard*	*Burrows*	*Prophett*	*Moss*	*Syrett*	*Eastoe*	*McLean**	*Butler*	*McLaughlin*
								Ref: W Johnson	Danny Williams' relegated Swindon side are handily placed for a swift return. Town find them a tough nut to crack, although they do create enough chances to win. Town appear to be lacking in confidence. Swindon's McLean comes closest to scoring, with a low drive onto the post.											
14	H	SOUTHEND		20	W	3-1	2-0	Gwyther 29, Moir 38, 56	Smith A	Luckett	Collins	McHale	Rhodes	Phelan	Jones	Blair	Ford	Gwyther	Moir	
15/10			**1,210**	*6*	10			*Brace 55*	*Webster*	*Worthington D*	*Ford*	*Dyer*	*Townsend*	*Elliott**	*Silvester*	*Brace*	*Guthrie*	*Taylor*	*Johnson*	*Love*
								Ref: C Seel	Town look a completely different side as they tear into Southend. Gwyther cracks in a 25-yarder to send them on their way. Moir dives to head in Ford's free-kick for 2-0. He crouches to nod in his second just after Brace pulled one back. Town end a run of eleven games without a win.											
15	A	HEREFORD		19	D	0-0	0-0		Smith A	Luckett	Collins	McHale	Rhodes	Phelan	Jones	Quinn	Ford	Gwyther	Moir	
19/10			*6,833*	*13*	11				*Hughes*	*Emery*	*Byrne*	*Tucker*	*Rylands*	*Rudge*	*Tyler**	*Paine*	*Redrobe*	*McNeil*	*Evans*	*Lee P*
								Ref: C White	A day before this game, Quinn tells the Welsh selectors to take a look at Gwyther. In this game, though, he hardly gets a kick, as all the action is at the other end. Town fight a successful rearguard. Hereford boss John Sillett admits, 'They played it really tight and gave nothing away.'											
16	H	COLCHESTER		20	D	1-1	1-0	Blair 31	Smith A	Luckett	Collins*	McHale	Rhodes	Phelan	Jones	Blair	Ford	Gwyther	Moir	Downes
26/10			1,935	*4*	12			*Svarc 60*	*Walker*	*Smith A*	*Smith L*	*Leslie*	*Dominey*	*Dyson*	*Thomas*	*Svarc*	*Froggatt*	*Lindsay*	*Cook**	*Bunkell*
								Ref: I Smith	Former Town wing-half Jim Smith is now manager of Colchester. Both sides have chances to win. Flanked by defenders, Walker drops a cross and Blair scores. Another goal looks likely until the ref gets in the way of Blair's cross. Svarc's equaliser is a header, and he later hits the bar.											
17	H	PRESTON		18	W	**3-0**	3-0	Moir 23, McHale 35, Blair 45	Smith A	Luckett	Collins	McHale	Rhodes	Phelan	Jones	Blair	Ford	Gwyther	Moir	
2/11			4,878	*2*	14				*Brown*	*Spark*	*Burns*	*Charlton*	*Bird*	*Sadler*	*Lamb*	*Morley**	*Elwiss*	*Holden*	*Treacy*	*Stiles*
								Ref: K Salmon	Soccer legend Bobby Charlton's first season in management ended in relegation last season. He's now back playing, and has recruited Nobby Stiles. They arrive as league-leaders, but Town are the ones showing promotion form. Ray McHale's first Town goal is a twice-taken free-kick.											
18	A	GILLINGHAM		20	L	**0-4**	0-1		Smith A	Luckett	Collins	McHale	Rhodes	Phelan	Jones	Blair	Ford	Gwyther	Moir*	Downes
9/11			*5,809*	*19*	14			*Richardson 44p, Feely 60, 67, 80*	*Hillyard*	*Wiltshire*	*Ley*	*Galvin*	*Shipperley*	*Tydeman*	*Knight*	*Jacks*	*Richardson*	*Chadwick*	*Feely*	
								Ref: T Bosi	The scoreline suggests a rout, but in reality it was never that. Town are giving as good as they get until Blair tugs Jacks' shirt and gives away a penalty on the stroke of half-time. In the second half, Peter Feely scores a hat-trick, his first goal from close range, while the others are headers.											
19	H	HUDDERSFIELD		18	W	2-1	1-1	Blair 15, Gwyther 70	Smith	Luckett	Collins	McHale	Rhodes	Phelan	Jones	Blair	Ford	Gwyther	Moir*	Downes
16/11			6,827	*19*	16			*Ellam 41*	*Poole*	*Hutt*	*Garner**	*Dolan*	*Saunders*	*Ellam*	*Smith*	*O'Neil*	*Gowling*	*Gray*	*Chapman*	*Spriggs*
								Ref: G Hesp	A cracker of a local derby. Blair's 25-yarder is deflected in, but unmarked Ray Ellam, now back from Leeds United, equalises with a header. Sub Downes puts life into Town in the second half, and their winner comes courtesy of Gwyther after Poole fails to cut out Luckett's free-kick.											
20	H	BRIGHTON		16	W	1-0	1-0	Gwyther 44	Smith A	Luckett	Collins	McHale	Rhodes	Phelan	Jones	Blair	Ford	Gwyther	Downes	
30/11			1,961	*23*	18				*Grummett*	*Tiler*	*Wilson*	*Mason*	*Rollings*	*Winstanley*	*O'Sullivan*	*Towner*	*Binney*	*Mellor*	*Walker*	
								Ref: N Saul	After Brian Clough's departure to Leeds in the summer, Peter Taylor has been left in contol at the Goldstone Ground. Here, strong winds make the game interesting. Tom Mason and Fred Binney hit the bar, before Gwyther scores the only goal, a beauty, turning in Downes' low cross.											
21	A	GRIMSBY		17	L	1-2	0-1	Gwyther 50	Smith A	Luckett	Collins	McHale	Rhodes	Phelan	Jones	Blair	Ford	Gwyther	Downes	
7/12			*4,331*	*18*	18			*Hubbard 22, Lewis 59*	*Freeman*	*Czuczman*	*Booth*	*Coyle*	*Wigginton*	*Gray*	*Barton*	*Hubbard*	*Lewis*	*Boylen*	*Beardsley*	
								Ref: E Jolly	Gwyther is hero and villain. He breaks clear to convert Ford's pass to cancel out Hubbard's opener. With two minutes remaining, he misses two great chances to save the game. Booth clears one off the line, then he blazes over. The referee is satisfied Hubbard's effort crossed the line.											
22	H	BOURNEMOUTH		17	W	3-2	2-2	McHale 25, Downes 40, Gwyther 49	Smith A	Luckett	Collins	McHale	Rhodes	Phelan	Jones	Blair	Downes	Gwyther	Moir	
21/12			1,523	*20*	20			*Payne 8, Downes 23 (og)*	*Charlton*	*Hague*	*Falconer*	*Howard*	*Merrick*	*Cunningham*	*Miller*	*Payne*	*Goddard*	*Wingate*	*Buttle**	*Rickard*
								Ref: K Dodd	After cup defeat at Stafford, Town need to win over their fans. But when Downes cuts Cunningham's centre past Smith, Town go two goals down. Town's fighting spirit gets them level before the break. Gwyther drives in just after half-time, and Town actually look good for more.											
23	A	BURY		18	L	1-4	0-0	Downes 70	Smith A	Luckett	Collins	McHale	Rhodes	Phelan	Jones	Blair	Downes	Gwyther	Moir*	Harrold
26/12			*6,260*	*15*	20			*Duffey 57, 74, 76, 90*	*Forrest*	*Hoolickin*	*Kennedy*	*Nicholson*	*Hulme*	*Thomson*	*Buchan*	*Riley*	*Spence*	*Duffey*	*Hamstead*	
								Ref: G Courtney	Bury's Chris Duffey scored eight goals in his short time at Gigg Lane. Half of them come in this game. He gets a lucky break for his first, but after Downes volleys in a smart equaliser, Duffey finishes them off. It's all a little too easy for him, as he scores three in the last 16 minutes.											

No	Date		Att	Pos	Pt	F-A	H-T	Scorers, Times, and Referees	1	2	3	4	5	6	7	8	9	10	11	12 sub used
24	H	PLYMOUTH		18	D	1-1	1-1	Blair 1	Smith A	Luckett	Collins	McHale	Rhodes	Phelan	Jones	Blair	Downes	Gwyther	Quinn	
	28/12		2,063	*3*	21			*McAuley 39*	*Furnell*	*Hore*	*Burrows P*	*Delve*	*Green*	*Saxton*	*Johnson*	*Mariner*	*Rafferty*	*Hardcastle*	*McAuley*	
								Ref: G Trevett	Quinn has to play to help out a midfield crisis, but the tempo rarely slackens in this gale-lashed game. Blair heads in Gwyther's cross within 30 seconds of the kick-off. Furnell then has to tip Collins' effort over the bar. Hugh McAuley's equaliser is also a header, off Rafferty's cross.											
25	H	GRIMSBY		18	D	1-1	0-1	Gwyther 60	Smith A	Quinn	Luckett	McHale	Rhodes	Phelan	Jones	Blair	Ford	Gwyther	Moir	
	11/1		2,063	*17*	22			*Lewis 7*	*Freeman*	*Beardsley*	*Booth*	*Coyle*	*Young*	*Czuczman*	*Barton*	*Hubbard*	*Lewis*	*Boylen**	*Brown*	*Hickman*
								Ref: D Lloyd	Grimsby boss Ron Ashman feels his side is unlucky not to win, but he will shortly be out of a job. Jack Lewis gives the Mariners an early lead, but after Gwyther's headed equaliser, it's the visitors who create the chances. Boylen hits the bar, and near the end sub Hickman goes so close.											
26	H	GILLINGHAM		20	D	1-1	0-1	McHale 90	Smith A	Quinn	Luckett	McHale	Rhodes	Phelan	Jones	Blair	Ford	Moir	**Scaife**	
	1/2		1,742	*13*	23			*Richardson 16*	*Hillyard*	*Wiltshire*	*Ley*	*Tydeman*	*Hill*	*Shipperley*	*Jacks*	*Gauden*	*Richardson*	*Chadwick*	*Feely*	
								Ref: E Garner	The Shaymen turn out in new track-suit tops provided by the Supporters Club. They don't inspire the team, but McHale's rocket shot from 18 yards saves the day with only 30 seconds left. Damien Richardson's goal is a joke. Four players are on the floor when he prods the ball home.											
27	A	WREXHAM			L	**0-4**	0-3	*[Tinnion 59]*	Smith A	Quinn	Luckett*	McHale	Rhodes	Phelan	Jones	Blair !	Ford	Moir	Downes	Scaife
	4/2		*2,532*		23			*Ashcroft 13, Smallman 16, Whittle 25,*	*Lloyd*	*Hill*	*Jones*	*Evans*	*Davis*	*Whittle*	*Tinnion*	*Sutton*	*Ashcroft*	*Smallman*	*Griffiths**	*May*
								Ref: K Walmsley	This defeat is as bad as gets. Billy Ashcroft's header bounces off the mud to start the rout. After 25 minutes the game is lost. Brian Tinnion's goal on the hour doesn't end Town's misery. On 70 minutes Blair is sent off for dissent after tangling with Tinnion. Relegation now beckons.											
28	A	PRESTON		22	L	0-1	0-0		Smith A	**Smith A**	Luckett	McHale	Rhodes	Phelan	Jones	Blair	**Campbell**	Gwyther	Scaife*	Downes
	8/2		*9,786*	*4*	23			*Holden 75*	*Tunks*	*McMahon*	*Burns*	*Spark*	*Bird*	*Sadler*	*Stiles*	*Morley*	*Elwiss*	*Holden*	*Charlton*	
								Ref: G Flint	Hope springs eternal despite defeat. Town play quite well and a draw would have been a fairer result. This actually looks likely until Rhodes, Phelan and Luckett fail to deal with Elwiss's cross. Mel Holden is the sole beneficiary, but looks embarrassed as the ball rolls in off his shin.											
29	H	WREXHAM		20	W	1-0	0-0	Gwyther 65	Smith A	Smith A	Luckett	McHale	Rhodes	Phelan	Jones	Ford	Campbell	Gwyther*	Scaife	
	15/2		2,039	*14*	25				*Lloyd*	*Hill*	*Jones*	*Evans*	*Davis*	*Whittle*	*Tinnion*	*Sutton*	*Ashcroft*	*Smallman*	*Griffiths*	
								Ref: I Smith	Victory here for the Shaymen is the platform for survival. They gain swift revenge for the hammering at the Racecourse Ground eleven days ago. A misunderstanding between Joey Jones and Mickey Evans lets in Gwyther, who runs 40 yards and beats Lloyd with a fierce cross-shot.											
30	A	CHESTERFIELD		18	D	1-1	1-0	Ford 13	Smith A	Smith A	Collins	McHale	Rhodes	Phelan	Jones	Ford	Campbell*	Gwyther	Scaife	Downes
	19/2		*4,385*	*19*	26			*Kowalski 57*	*Tingay*	*Holmes*	*Burton*	*O'Neil*	*Winstanley*	*Barlow*	*Darling*	*Moss*	*Kowalski*	*Bellamy*	*Wilson**	*Shanahan*
								Ref: R Capey	Another encouraging performance. Town could actually have won this one. Ford, latching onto Jones' crossfield pass, scores from 20 yards. Joe Shaw's Chesterfield equalise thanks to Kowalski's header after Smith, under pressure from Darling, punches away Burton's long cross.											
31	A	HUDDERSFIELD		18	W	2-1	2-1	Gwyther 17, Scaife 18	Smith A	Smith A	Collins	McHale	Rhodes	Phelan	Jones	Ford	Campbell	Gwyther	Scaife	
	22/2		*7,931*	*24*	28			*Gowling 29p*	*Taylor*	*McGifford*	*Garner*	*Gray*	*Saunders*	*Dolan*	*Fowler*	*Smith*	*Gowling*	*Fairclough*	*Maitland*	
								Ref: D Richardson	Three years ago, Huddersfield were in the 1st Division. Today they stand bottom of Division 3. The Shaymen take command with quick goals by Gwyther's header, and Scaife, a 30-yarder. They then defend resolutely after Gowling's penalty when Collins drags down Mick Fairclough.											
32	A	CRYS PALACE		17	D	1-1	1-0	Gwyther 24	Smith A	Smith A	Collins	McHale	Rhodes	Phelan	Jones	Ford	Campbell	Gwyther	Blair	
	28/2		*18,024*	*5*	29			*Swindlehurst 54*	*Burns*	*Mulligan**	*Cannon*	*Johnson J*	*Jeffries*	*Evans*	*Holder*	*Whittle*	*Hill*	*Swindlehurst*	*Taylor*	*Chatterton*
								Ref: J Taylor	At 1-1, with three minutes to go, Palace's Mick Hill crashes to the ground when challenged by Gwyther. An obvious penalty. Not according to ref Jack Taylor. Fuming Palace boss Allison says it was 'a diabolical decision.' Town go in front and over 90 minutes are deserving of a draw.											
33	H	PETERBOROUGH		15	W	2-1	2-1	Phelan 20, McHale 22	Smith A	Smith A	Collins	McHale	Rhodes	Phelan	Jones	Ford	Downes	Gwyther	Blair	
	8/3		2,322	*12*	31			*Price 41*	*Steele*	*Bradley*	*Lee**	*Walker*	*Turner*	*Carmichael*	*Murray*	*Gregory*	*Nixon*	*Price D*	*Hobson*	*Hall*
								Ref: R Lee	Noel Cantwell's Peterborough leave the Shay with nothing, despite dominating for long periods. The Shaymen score two in a 90-second spell. McHale's goal for 2-0 is a direct free-kick. The Posh deservedly pull one back through David Price, on loan from Arsenal, his first-ever goal.											
34	A	PORT VALE		18	L	1-2	0-2	Downes 59	Smith A	Smith A	Collins	McHale	Rhodes	Phelan	Jones	Ford	Downes	Gwyther	Blair	
	15/3		*3,334*	*7*	31			*Brownbill 15, Bailey 27*	*Connaughton*	*Tartt*	*Dulson*	*Cross*	*Harris*	*Bailey*	*Lacey*	*Brownbill*	*Williams*	*Woodward*	*McLaren*	
								Ref: J Goggins	The Shaymen make the big mistake of trying to play through the mud. Derek Brownbill heads the opener for Port Vale, and Terry Bailey gets their second, scooping the ball in when it loops up off Rhodes. On the hour, Downes heads in Gwyther's cross but Town can't muster a second.											

No	Venue	Opponent	Att	Pos	Pts	F-A	H-T	Scorers, Times, and Referees	1	2	3	4	5	6	7	8	9	10	11	12
35	A	CHARLTON		18	L	1-3	0-3	Downes 74	Smith A	Smith A*	Collins	McHale	Rhodes	Phelan	Jones	Ford	Downes	Gwyther	Blair	Campbell
	18/3		9,561	1	31			Hales 2, 9, 20	Tutt	Penfold	Warman	Kelly	Horsfield	Young	Powell	Hales	Hunt	Bowman	Peacock	
								Ref: T Bosi	Derek Hales is making a name for himself. His quick hat-trick takes his tally to 16. It also takes Charlton back to the top of the table. Downes' reply comes when Mark Penfold slips on the snow-covered surface. Relegation now threatens Town. 'Not if we carry on fighting,' says Quinn.											
36	H	WATFORD		18	W	2-0	0-0	Jones 46, Smith 63	Smith A	Smith A	Collins	McHale	Rhodes	Phelan	Jones	Campbell	Downes	Gwyther	Blair	
	22/3		1,872	19	33				Rankin	Butler	Walsh	Joslyn	Goodeve	Garner*	Scullion	Bond	Mayes	Greenhalgh	Downes	Mercer
								Ref: J Wrennall	The Shaymen should be four goals up at half-time. Within 30 seconds of the second half, however, Jones' blistering shot from a narrow angle flies straight in. McHale puts full-back Alex Smith away, and he makes it 2-0. Town compound Watford's relegation fears, but ease their own.											
37	A	PLYMOUTH			L	0-2	0-0		Smith A	Smith A	Collins	McHale	Rhodes	Phelan	Jones	Ford	Downes !	Campbell	Blair	
	28/3		**19,580**		33			Mariner 74, McAuley 80	Furnell	Hore	Burrows P	Saxton	Green	Delve	Randall	Johnson	Mariner	Rafferty	McAuley	
								Ref: M Sinclair	Town seem to be resisting the threat of Argyle. But in the 50th minute they press the self-destruct button. Downes chases 20 yards to head-butt Argyle skipper Mike Green and is sent off. Collins deflects Mariner's shot into his own net, and McAuley goes past four players for his goal.											
38	A	BOURNEMOUTH		18	W	1-0	1-0	Rhodes 6	Smith A	Smith A	Collins	McHale	Rhodes	Phelan	Jones	Ford	Downes	Campbell*	Blair	Moir
	29/3		5,247	22	35				Baker	Payne	Miller	Howard	Morgan	Hague*	Redknapp	Livermore	Rudge	Rickard	Buttle	Welsh
								Ref: P Walters	The Easter programme keeps Town on the South coast. John Benson is now in charge at Dean Court, but Bournemouth are in trouble. Town have Tony Rhodes to thank for victory. He heads the game's only goal off Jones' corner very early on, then is a tower of strength at the back.											
39	H	BLACKBURN		17	D	1-1	1-0	McHale 35	Smith A	Smith A	Collins	McHale	Rhodes	Phelan	Jones	Ford	Downes	Campbell	Blair	
	1/4		**8,689**	1	36			Parkes 55	Jones	Heaton	Burgin	Hickman	Hawkins	Fazackerley*	Beamish	Oates	Martin	Parkes	Hoy	Metcalfe
								Ref: P Reeves	Title-chasing Blackburn bring enough supporters to swell the gate – it's the biggest at the Shay since the visit of Man Utd. The new 160 Stand is opened and the crowd see two fine goals. McHale scores direct from a free-kick 20 yards out. Parkes' equaliser is a header from Hoy's cross.											
40	A	COLCHESTER		18	L	0-2	0-2		Smith A	Smith A	Collins	McHale	Rhodes*	Phelan	Jones	Ford	Downes	Campbell	Blair	Pugh
	4/4		3,501	10	36			Svarc 4, Rowe 30	Walker	Packer	Cook	Bunkell	Dominey	Smith L*	Lelie	Svarc	Froggatt	Lindsay	Rowe	Harford
								Ref: R Tinkler	Amazingly, the home side offer little to this game apart from their goals. Ford and goalkeeper Smith get in a tangle and Svarc's goal is a gift. Colwyn Rowe is then left free on the left to score at the second attempt. That is Colchester's last serious threat, as Town dominate thereafter.											
41	H	ALDERSHOT			W	1-0	0-0	McHale 76	Smith A	Smith A	Collins	McHale	Rhodes*	Phelan	Jones	Ford	Campbell	Gwyther	Blair	Pugh
	8/4		1,835		38				Johnson	Walden	Walker	Crosby	Dean	Richardson	Brown*	Morrissey	Brodie	McGovern	Walton	Jopling
								Ref: P Richardson	Gwyther returns to the Halifax side for this blizzard-lashed match. The Shots live dangerously, and early in the second half Alan Jones goes close when he hits the post. Ray McHale breaks the deadlock, heading in Jones' free-kick, then promptly jumps into the arms of a policeman.											
42	H	TRANMERE		18	D	0-0	0-0		Smith A	Smith A	Collins	McHale	Pugh	Phelan	Jones	Ford	Campbell	Gwyther	Blair	
	12/4		2,201	23	39				Johnson R	Mathias	Flood	Palios	Philpotts	Moore	Kenny	Mitchell	Allen	Peplow	Crossley*	Woodin
								Ref: K Baker	Part of the Shaymen's problems has been their inability to dispose of poor sides. Tranmere defend in numbers and have three players booked, but their season will end in relegation. This is an awful match, with Town short on ideas. Even Gwyther wastes a few half-decent chances.											
43	A	BRIGHTON		17	D	0-0	0-0		Smith A	Smith A	Collins	McHale	Pugh	Phelan	Jones	Ford	Campbell	Gwyther	Blair	
	16/4		10,309	19	40				Grummitt	Tiler	Wilson	Walker	Piper	Winstanley	Towner	Machin	Marlowe	Fell	O'Sullivan	
								Ref: R Toseland	The Shaymen come for a point. They stick men behind the ball and frustrate not only the Brighton players, but also the Goldstone crowd, who resort to slow-handclapping. On the muddy pitch, Collins actually carves out the game's best opening for Campbell, but he loses his balance.											
44	A	SWINDON		18	L	1-3	0-1	Downes 76	Smith A	Smith A	Collins	McHale	Pugh	Phelan	Blair	Jones	Ford*	Campbell	Blair	Harrold
	19/4		6,615	6	40			Stroud 45, Dixon 52, Eastoe 71	Allan	Dixon	Trollope	Stroud	Burrows	Prophett	Moss	McLaughlin	Eastoe	Jenkins	Anderson	
								Ref: N Ashley	On the sand-covered pitch Town are given a real chasing. John McLaughlin poses the biggest threat and makes all three goals. Right on half-time, Smith spills his cross and Stroud takes advantage. Downes, returning from a three-match suspension, scores Town's goal from ten yards.											
45	H	WALSALL		18	W	1-0	1-0	Gwyther 29	Smith A	Smith A	Collins	McHale	Rhodes	Phelan	Jones	Pugh	Downes	Gwyther	Blair	
	22/4		2,030	10	42				Kearns	Brown	Harrison	Robinson	Saunders	Atthey	Caswell	Andrews	Wright	Buckley	Birch	
								Ref: C Seel	Chairman Percy Albon pleads with the fans to come out in force for Town's last two games. They hardly respond. Those that do see this game settled by a flash of brilliance from Gwyther, who smashes in a swerving left-foot volley. Walsall's Buckley has a goal ruled out for pushing.											
46	A	HEREFORD		17	D	2-2	1-2	McHale 25p, Harrold 73	Smith A	Smith A	Luckett	McHale	Rhodes*	Phelan	Jones	Pugh	Downes	Gwyther	Blair	Harrold
	26/4		1,893	12	43			Paine 21p, Tucker 43	Hughes	Emery	Byrne	Tucker	Rylands	Walker	Paine	Carter	Galley	Deacy	Tyler	
		Home	Away					Ref; K McNally	This game is above end-of-season quality. Hereford's evergreen Terry Paine is the best player on view. He nets the game's first penalty when full-back Smith tangles with Walker. Jones is tripped by Emery for McHale's. Local lad Harrold resists two challenges before saving the game.											
Average		2,678	7,063																	

League Cup					F-A	H-T	Scorers, Times, and Referees	1	2	3	4	5	6	7	8	9	10	11	12 sub used
1 A BARNSLEY			W		1-0	1-0	Gwyther 45	Smith A	Burgin	Collins	Quinn*	Rhodes	Pugh	Jones	Moir	Downes	Gwyther	Ford	Shanahan
20/8	5,139	4:						*Stewart*	*Yates*	*Chambers*	*Doyle*	*Pickering*	*Murphy*	*Butler*	*Lea*	*Manning**	*Millar*	*Brown*	*O'Riley*
							Ref: H Davey	The first of two more cup-ties with Barnsley this season. The Tykes are clearly the better side, but Gwyther's goal, glancing in Moir's corner, gives Town something to hang on to. Pugh makes a desperate stop on the line to prevent Butler's 12-yarder. Quinn goes off with concussion.											
2 A STOKE		8	L		0-3	0-1		Smith A	Quinn	Collins	Moir	Rhodes	Lowe	Jones	Shanahan*	Downes	Gwyther	Ford	Smith F
11/9	17,805	1:4					*Conroy 42, 66, 71p*	*Farmer*	*Marsh*	*Pejic*	*Mahoney*	*Smith*	*Dodd*	*Haslegrave*	*Greenhoff*	*Hurst*	*Conroy*	*Salmons**	*Robertson*
							Ref: P Reeves	Stoke's Terry Conroy is only playing because Alan Hudson was injured in a car crash. He makes the most of his opportunity. Greenhoff hits the bar in the fourth minute before Conroy takes over. His first two are headers, and he wins the penalty from which he completes his hat-trick.											

FA Cup								1	2	3	4	5	6	7	8	9	10	11	12 sub used
1 A BARNSLEY		18	W		2-1	0-1	Jones 51, 62	Smith A	Luckett	Collins	McHale	Rhodes	Phelan	Jones	Blair*	Ford	Gwyther	Downes	Moir
23/11	5,314	4:15					*Brown 40*	*Stewart*	*Yates*	*Chambers*	*Doyle*	*Pickering*	*Murphy*	*Butler**	*Lea*	*Mahoney*	*Millar*	*Brown*	*Collingwood*
							Ref: R Lee	Halifax go through thanks to Gwyther. He doesn't score, but asks the ref to consult the linesman about Jones' winner. He says Stewart scooped away Jones' effort from behind the line. Jones beats Murphy for pace for his first, equalising Brown's goal after Doyle's shot had hit the post.											
2 A STAFFORD		17	L		1-2	1-0	Gwyther 21	Smith A	Luckett	Collins	McHale	Rhodes	Phelan	Jones	Blair	Ford	Gwyther	Downes*	Moir
14/12	5,534	NPL					*Cullerton 48, Sargeant 90*	*Arnold*	*Ritchie*	*Cooke*	*Sargeant*	*Seddon*	*Morris*	*Keyes*	*Chapman*	*Jones*	*Cullerton*	*Chadwick*	
							Ref: R Toseland	Quinn warns his players against complacency. They think victory is in the bag when Gwyther drives Ford's cross into the net. After half-time Stafford take control and Cullerton heads the equaliser. Town are hanging on for the draw, until Sargeant fires in – with just 44 seconds left.											

		Home					Away					
	P	W	D	L	F	A	W	D	L	F	A	Pts
1 Blackburn	46	15	7	1	40	16	7	9	7	28	29	60
2 Plymouth	46	16	5	2	38	19	8	6	9	41	39	59
3 Charlton	46	15	5	3	51	29	7	6	10	25	32	55
4 Swindon	46	18	3	2	43	17	3	8	12	21	41	53
5 Crys Palace	46	14	8	1	48	22	4	7	12	18	35	51
6 Port Vale	46	15	6	2	37	19	3	9	11	24	35	51
7 Peterborough	46	10	9	4	24	17	9	3	11	23	36	50
8 Walsall	46	15	5	3	46	13	3	8	12	21	39	49
9 Preston	46	16	5	2	42	19	3	6	14	21	37	49
10 Gillingham	46	14	6	3	43	23	3	8	12	22	37	48
11 Colchester	46	13	7	3	45	22	4	6	13	25	41	47
12 Hereford	46	14	6	3	42	21	2	8	13	22	45	46
13 Wrexham	46	10	8	5	41	23	5	7	11	24	32	45
14 Bury	46	13	6	4	38	17	3	6	14	15	33	44
15 Chesterfield	46	11	7	5	37	25	5	5	13	25	41	44
16 Grimsby	46	12	8	3	35	19	3	5	15	20	45	43
17 HALIFAX	46	11	10	2	33	20	2	7	14	16	45	43
18 Southend	46	11	9	3	32	17	2	7	14	14	34	42
19 Brighton	46	14	7	2	38	21	2	3	18	18	43	42
20 Aldershot*	46	13	5	5	40	21	1	6	16	13	42	38
21 Bournemouth	46	9	6	8	27	25	4	6	13	17	33	38
22 Tranmere	46	12	4	7	39	21	2	5	16	16	36	37
23 Watford	46	9	7	7	30	31	1	10	12	22	44	37
24 Huddersfield	46	9	6	8	32	29	2	4	17	15	47	32
	1104	309	155	88	921	506	88	155	309	506	921	1103

* 1 pt deducted

Odds & ends

Double wins: (2) Bournemouth, Huddersfield.
Double losses: (1) Bury.

Won from behind: (2) Bournemouth (h), Barnsley (FAC) (a).
Lost from in front: (1) Stafford (FAC) (a).

High spots: Two consecutive wins in November.
A late season rally ensuring relegation is avoided.
Doing the double over Huddersfield.

Low spots: Losing at non-league Stafford in the FA Cup.
Managing only one win in the first 13 games.
Manager George Mulhall resigning after only seven league games.
Ten games without a win up to 12 October.

Player of the Year: Dave Gwyther.
Ever-presents: (1) Alex Smith.
Hat-tricks: (0).
Leading scorer: Dave Gwyther (14).

	Appearances						Goals			
	Lge	*Sub*	LC	*Sub*	FAC	*Sub*	**Lge**	LC	FAC	**Tot**
Blair, Ken	**30**				2		**4**			**4**
Burgin, Andy	**4**		1							
Campbell, Bobby	**14**	*1*								
Collins, John	**40**		2		2		**1**			**1**
Downes, Steve	**26**	*6*	2		2		**9**			**9**
Ford, David	**39**		2		2		**3**			**3**
Gwyther, Dave	**38**		2		2		**12**	1	1	**14**
Harrold, Mark	**3**	*3*					**1**			**1**
Jones, Alan	**45**		2		2		**2**		2	**4**
Lowe, Nick	**9**		1							
Luckett, Paul	**24**				2					
McHale, Ray	**36**				2		**7**			**7**
Moir, Ricky	**16**	*3*	2			*2*	**5**			**5**
Phelan, Albert	**36**				2		**1**			**1**
Pugh, David	**9**	*2*	1							
Quinn, Johnny	**14**	*1*	2							
Rhodes, Tony	**42**		2		2		**1**			**1**
Scaife, Bobby	**5**	*1*					**1**			**1**
Shanahan, Terry	**4**		1	*1*			**1**			**1**
Smith, Alex (1)	**46**		2		2					
Smith, Alex (2)	**19**						**1**			**1**
Smith, Fred	**3**			*1*						
White, Barry	**4**									
23 players used	**506**	*17*	**22**	*2*	**22**	*2*	**49**	**1**	**3**	**53**

No	Date		Att	Pos	Pt	F-A	H-T	Scorers, Times, and Referees	1	2	3	4	5	6	7	8	9	10	11	12 sub used
1	H	MILLWALL			L	1-2	0-2	Downes 76	**Gennoe**	Smith A	Luckett*	McHale	Rhodes	Phelan	Jones A	Ford	Downes	Gwyther	Pugh	Harrold
	16/8		2,460		0			*Saul 34, Salvage 36*	*Goddard*	*Evans*	*Moore*	*Jones*	*Kitchener*	*Hazell*	*Fairbrother*	*Brisley*	*Saul*	*Summerill*	*Salvage*	
								Ref: G Flint	Relegated Millwall, with their notorious supporters, provide Town with a tough opener. The Shaymen play well, but concede two goals in as many minutes. Downes fires over Goddard, but isn't enough to prevent Halifax suffering their first home defeat on the first day since 1950.											
2	A	ALDERSHOT		12	W	2-1	1-1	McHale 43, Gwyther 80	Gennoe	Smith A	Collins	McHale	Rhodes	Phelan	Jones A	Ford	Downes	Gwyther	Pugh	
	23/8		*3,221*	*23*	2			*Howarth 21*	*Johnson*	*Walden*	*Wallace J*	*Sainty*	*Walker*	*Jopling*	*Walton*	*Morrissey*	*Howarth*	*Bell*	*Warnock**	*Crosby*
								Ref: D Biddle	Two days after turning down a player-exchange deal – Bob Wallace for Ford – Town visit the Recreation Ground and come from behind to win. Howarth heads the opener, but McHale equalises from the edge of the box. Ford, who plays, crosses for Gwyther to net the winner.											
3	H	WALSALL		7	W	2-1	1-1	Ford 25, Gwyther 80	Gennoe	Smith A	Collins	McHale	Rhodes	Phelan	Jones A	Ford*	Downes	Gwyther	Pugh	Bell
	30/8		2,076	*19*	4			*Harrison 1*	*Kearns*	*Fry*	*Harrison*	*Robinson*	*Saunders*	*Atthey*	*Dennehy*	*Andrews*	*Wright*	*Buckley*	*Spinner**	*Birch*
								Ref: J Wrennall	Colin Harrison's 35-yard drive after only 45 seconds shocks everyone. Town compose themselves and gradually take control. After Jones and Gwyther have efforts blocked, Ford whips the ball in. Gwyther again gets the winner, making the most of Jones' cross that is deflected to him.											
4	A	COLCHESTER		3	W	1-0	0-0	McHale 47p	Gennoe	Smith A	Collins	McHale	Rhodes	Phelan	Jones A	Ford	Bell	Gwyther	Pugh	
	6/9		*2,819*	*24*	6				*Walker*	*Thomas*	*Williams*	*Bunkell*	*Harrison**	*Dominey*	*Cook*	*Svarc*	*Froggatt*	*Leslie*	*Anderson*	*Dyer*
								Ref: R Lewis	New Colchester boss Bobby Roberts has got his side off to an awful start. This is their fourth defeat in as many games. They drag the Shaymen down to their level, but the visitors do get a break when Bell is tripped by sub Paul Dyer. McHale nets the resultant penalty, the first of many.											
5	H	SHREWSBURY		6	D	0-0	0-0		Gennoe	Smith A	Collins	McHale	Rhodes	Phelan	Jones A	Ford	Bell	Gwyther	Pugh*	Downes
	13/9		2,501	*3*	7				*Mulhearn*	*Collier*	*Gregory*	*Durban*	*Kearney*	*Turner*	*O'Loughlin*	*Roberts I*	*Haywood**	*Bates*	*Tarbuck*	*Duffey*
								Ref: T Farley	Promoted Shrewsbury come for a point, and get it as they constantly pull men behind the ball. McHale heads against the bar for Halifax – the game's only highlight. Quinn criticises the Shrews' tactics, but their boss, Durban, retorts, 'People want to put their own houses in order first.'											
6	A	CARDIFF		3	D	0-0	0-0		Gennoe	Smith A	Collins	McHale	Rhodes	Phelan	Jones A	Ford*	Bell	Gwyther	Pugh	**Veitch**
	20/9		*8,035*	*13*	8				*Healey*	*Attley*	*Charles*	*Dwyer*	*England*	*Larmour*	*Livermore*	*Giles*	*Reece*	*Clark*	*Evans*	
								Ref: K Ridden	Cardiff are refusing admission to unaccompanied under-17s. Town play well, and deserve a point, if not two. McHale has a penalty well saved by former Man City keeper Healey. Rhodes, making his 200th league appearance, heads against the post. Dwyer also hits the post for Cardiff.											
7	A	GRIMSBY		6	D	2-2	0-2	Bell 50, 88	Gennoe	Smith A	Collins	McHale	Rhodes	Phelan	Jones A	Veitch	Bell	**Harris**	Pugh	
	23/9		*6,130*		9			*Lewis 32, Hubbard 45*	*Wainman*	*Marley*	*Cumming*	*Barton*	*Young*	*Gray*	*Lewis*	*Booth*	*Hubbard*	*Boylen*	*Brown*	
								Ref: A Morrissey	Bell is the saviour for the Shaymen. With time running out he grabs his second goal, getting to Jones' cross to bring the game level. Hubbard turns the ball in to give the Mariners a two-goal lead right on half-time, though Town feel Gennoe is impeded when he fists away a long throw.											
8	H	CHESTER		4	W	**5-2**	3-1	Bell 16, Rhodes 25, 33, McHale 53, [Phelan 85]	Gennoe	Smith A	Collins	McHale	Rhodes	Phelan	Jones A	Veitch	Bell	Gwyther	Harris	
	27/9		2,240	*23*	11			*Owen 27, Whitehead 80*	*Watling*	*Edwards*	*Loska*	*Storton*	*Dunleavy*	*Mason*	*Whitehead*	*Pugh*	*Owen**	*Daniels*	*Lennard*	*Seddon*
								Ref: I Smith	Town go fourth, but will never be as high ever again. Bell's low left-foot shot starts the rout, and Rhodes robs former Shay star Dave Lennard for 2-0. Chester try to stay in contention, but Phelan finishes the job off, reacting first to the loose ball after Watling saves McHale's penalty.											
9	A	GILLINGHAM		5	D	1-1	0-0	Bell 60	Gennoe	Smith A	Collins	McHale	Rhodes	Phelan	Jones A	Veitch	Bell	Gwyther	Pugh	
	4/10		*5,934*	*10*	12			*Gauden 61*	*Hillyard*	*Wiltshire*	*Ley*	*Galvin**	*Shipperley*	*Tydeman*	*Jacks*	*Gauden*	*Richardson*	*Wilks*	*Feely*	*Knight*
								Ref: A Glasson	The players travel to Priestfield unaware that Gwyther has asked for a transfer. Bell heads the opening goal, but Halifax's lead lasts less than 60 seconds when Allan Gauden's shot goes in off Veitch. Town's point means they are unbeaten in their first five away games – a club record.											
10	A	SWINDON		7	L	1-3	0-1	McHale 57	Gennoe	Smith A	Collins	McHale	Rhodes	Phelan	Jones A	Veitch	Bell	Gwyther !	Pugh	
	11/10		*6,214*	*20*	12			*Anderson 25, 54, Stroud 50*	*Allan*	*Dixon*	*Trollope*	*McLaughlin*	*Burrows*	*Stroud*	*Moss*	*Butler*	*Eastoe*	*Jenkins*	*Anderson*	
								Ref: C Maskell	Town miss a number of early chances, then see their away record go. Swindon's first two goals come from corners. Anderson gets his second from a tight angle after drawing Gennoe. Gwyther sets up McHale, but any fightback diminishes when he is sent off for kicking out at Dixon.											
11	H	HEREFORD		9	L	0-1	0-1		Gennoe	Harrold	Collins	McHale	Rhodes	Phelan	Jones A	Veitch	Bell	**Blair**	Pugh	
	18/10		2,667	*2*	12			*Tyler 41*	*Charlton*	*Emery*	*Ritchie*	*Galley*	*Layton*	*Lindsay*	*Paine*	*Tyler*	*Redrobe**	*Davey*	*Silkman*	*Tucker*
								Ref: E Garner	Hereford have only lost one game so far, and look a useful side. Town are without suspended Gwyther, so McHale plays up front. But all the action is at the other end, although Hereford only score one. Tyler mis-hits the ball, but it rolls away from Gennoe and goes in off the far post.											

No	Date	Venue	Opponent	Att	Pos	Pts	F-A	H-T	Scorers, Times, and Referees	1	2	3	4	5	6	7	8	9	10	11	12 sub used
12	20/10	A	SOUTHEND	*3,089*	10	L 12	**1·4**	1·2	McHale 42 *[Little 63]*	Gennoe	Veitch	Collins	McHale	Rhodes	Phelan	Jones A	Blair	Bell	Gwyther	Pugh*	Harrold
									Nicholl 12, Parker 20, Moody 57p,	*Rafter*	*Worthington*	*Ford*	*Little*	*Townsend*	*Moody*	*Brace*	*Foggo*	*Parker*	*Lamb*	*Nicholl*	
									Ref: A Robinson	Terry Nicholl scores from Southend's first real attack, and his side rarely looks in trouble. They go two goals up before McHale gives Town some hope with a goal just before the interval. This disappears in the 57th minute, when Moody scores a penalty and Little shortly wraps it up.											
13	25/10	A	BURY	*7,516*	11 *2*	D 13	0·0	0·0		Gennoe	Smith A	Collins	McHale	Rhodes	Phelan	Jones A	Veitch	Bell	Gwyther	Blair	
										Forrest	*Hoolickin*	*Kennedy*	*Nicholson*	*Hulme*	*Bailey*	*Smith**	*Phillips*	*Rowland*	*Riley*	*Williams*	*Buchan*
									Ref: D Civil	Early pace-setters Bury can't break down the Shaymen, who continually frustrate them. New signing Malcolm Smith doesn't get a look in. In the 84th minute Bell has a header that comes back off the post. Gennoe is injured in a challenge with Buchan and spends the night in hospital.											
14	1/11	H	CRYS PALACE	3,282	16 *1*	L 13	1·3	0·2	McHale 56	Gennoe	Harrold	Collins	McHale	Rhodes	Phelan	Harris	Veitch	Bell	Gwyther	Blair	
									Cannon 13, Swindlehurst 45, Taylor 74	*Hammond*	*Wall*	*Whittle*	*Holder*	*Cannon*	*Evans*	*Chatterton*	*Johnson J*	*Kemp*	*Swindlehurst*	*Taylor*	
									Ref: K McNally	Malcolm Allison's flamboyancy rubs off on his Palace side that oozes confidence. Star man is left-footed right-winger Peter Taylor. He reads Gennoe's bad goal-kick to set up Swindlehurst for their second, then scores an angled shot to kill the game after McHale had halved the deficit.											
15	4/11	H	PRESTON	3,366	10	W 15	2·1	1·0	Bell 16, Rhodes 70	Gennoe	Harrold	Collins	McHale	Rhodes	Phelan	Harris*	Veitch	Bell	Gwyther	Blair	Pugh
									Morley 87	*Tunks*	*McMahon*	*Williams*	*Brown*	*Baxter*	*Spark*	*Bruce*	*Burns*	*Treacy*	*Elwiss*	*Morley*	
									Ref: J Sewell	Former Everton manager Harry Catterick has taken over at Preston following Bobby Charlton's shock resignation. His side is unlucky to lose as they dominate for long periods. When Rhodes deftly touches in Bell's low cross, Town go two up. Tony Morley's goal is too little, too late.											
16	8/11	A	MANSFIELD	*5,288*	11 *24*	D 16	1·1	0·0	McHale 61	Gennoe	Harrold	Collins	McHale*	Rhodes	Phelan	Pugh	Veitch	Bell	Gwyther	Blair	Ford
									Bird 88	*Evans*	*Pate*	*Foster B*	*Madden*	*Mackenzie*	*Bird*	*Matthews*	*Eccles*	*Clarke*	*Hodgson*	*McDonald*	
									Ref: P Suter	It is hard to work out whether this is a point gained, or a point dropped. Mansfield boss the game for an hour, before McHale's 20-yarder gives Town the lead. Seconds after he is carried off injured, the Stags equalise when Bird heads in McDonald's overhead kick from out on the left.											
17	15/11	H	BRIGHTON	2,201	15 *2*	L 16	1·3	1·1	Ford 39	Gennoe	Harrold	Collins	McHale	Rhodes	Phelan	Ford	Veitch	Bell	Gwyther	Blair*	Downes
									Martin 31, Binney 57, Fell 83	*Grummitt*	*Tiler*	*Wilson*	*Machin*	*Rollings*	*Burnett*	*Fell*	*Binney*	*Martin*	*O'Sullivan*	*Beal*	
									Ref: W Bond	Brighton are moving in the right direction. Martin gives them the lead with a header, but Ford replies before the interval. The game goes away from Halifax when Binney chests the ball over, and three minutes later Ford is carried off with a trapped nerve. Fell scores his from 19 yards.											
18	29/11	A	WREXHAM	*3,063*	15 *20*	D 17	1·1	0·0	McHale 55	Gennoe	Veitch	Collins	McHale	Rhodes	Phelan	Ford	Downes	Bell	Gwyther	Pugh	
									Lee 88p	*Lloyd*	*Hill*	*Fogg*	*Scott*	*May*	*Thomas*	*Tinnion*	*Sutton*	*Ashcroft**	*Dwyer*	*Lee*	*Lyons*
									Ref: A Turvey	Town are unhappy with ref Turvey. He awards Wrexham a dubious penalty for elbowing by Phelan. New boy Stuart Lee scores at the second attempt, when Turvey ruled Gennoe moved early when he put his first effort wide. McHale scores for Town, firing through the defensive wall.											
19	6/12	H	PETERBOROUGH	2,289	19 *3*	L 17	0·1	0·1		Gennoe	Veitch*	Collins	McHale	Rhodes	Phelan	Ford	Downes	Bell	Gwyther	Pugh	Harrold
									Murray 33	*Steele*	*Murray*	*Lee*	*Eustace*	*Turner*	*Carmichael*	*Nixon*	*Gregory**	*Cozens*	*Hughes*	*Robson*	*Jones*
									Ref: J Worrall	A spirited second-half fightback by the Shaymen doesn't get them their just deserts. The Posh dominate the first period and their goal comes from right-back Murray, a 25-yarder. In the 63rd minute, an excellent reflex save by Steele sees him push Ford's similar effort onto the bar.											
20	20/12	A	CHESTERFIELD	*3,703*	16 *19*	W 19	2·1	0·0	Bell 69, Gwyther 72	Gennoe	Smith A	Collins	McHale	Rhodes	Phelan	Jones A	Downes*	Bell	Gwyther	Pugh	Blair
									Shanahan 70p	*Tingay*	*O'Neill*	*Burton*	*McEwan*	*Hunter*	*Barlow*	*Kowalski*	*Moss*	*Shanahan*	*Bentley*	*Roberts*	
									Ref: E Wallace	All the drama comes in a four-minute spell in the second half. Bell beats the advancing Tingay with a low shot to give Town the lead. When Shanahan's shot hits Pugh's hand, the former Town player nets the penalty. But two minutes later, Gwyther stoops to head in from six yards.											
21	26/12	H	PORT VALE	2,959	18 *10*	L 19	1·3	1·1	Bell 19	Gennoe	Smith A	Collins	McHale	Rhodes	Phelan	Jones A	Blair	Bell	Gwyther	Pugh	
									Brownbill 31, Cullerton 71, 86	*Connaughton*	*McLaren*	*Griffiths*	*Ridley*	*Harris*	*Horton*	*Lees*	*Williams*	*Brownbill*	*Cullerton*	*Bailey*	
									Ref: B Martin	Port Vale, warned as to their future conduct after amassing over 100 disciplinary points, still manage to have Ridley booked. Town take the lead but make too many defensive blunders that prove costly. Like when Gennoe fails to hold the ball before Cullerton nips in for his second.											
22	27/12	A	ROTHERHAM	*7,614*	16 *13*	W 21	1·0	1·0	Gwyther 24	Gennoe	Smith A	Collins	McHale	Rhodes	Phelan	Jones A	Blair	Bell	Gwyther	Pugh	
										Watling	*Green*	*Breckin*	*Rhodes*	*Stancliffe*	*Spencer*	*Leng*	*Phillips*	*Finney*	*Goodfellow*	*Crawford*	
									Ref: R Chadwick	In front of Rotherham's highest crowd so far, Gennoe is kept busy early on. Town weather the storm, then score the only goal when Gwyther climbs to head Collins' cross over Barry Watling. In the second half, Town's defence holds firm. Then Bell goes down in the box – no penalty.											
23	10/1	A	WALSALL	*7,167*	18 *2*	L 21	0·2	0·2		Smith A	Smith A	Collins	McHale	Veitch	Phelan	Jones A	Blair*	Bell	Gwyther	Pugh	Luckett
									Robinson 27, Wright 42	*Kearns*	*Fry*	*Harrison*	*Robinson*	*Hynd*	*Taylor*	*Dennehy*	*Andrews*	*Wright*	*Buckley*	*Evans*	
									Ref: R Matthewson	Gennoe pulled a hip muscle in training, so there is a recall for Alex Smith. He makes great saves from Harrison and Dennehy, but is helpless with both Walsall's goals. Robinson's goes in off Bell, whilst Wright can't miss from eight yards when Phelan's pass is deflected into his path.											

No	Date		Att	Pos	Pt	F-A	H-T	Scorers, Times, and Referees	1	2	3	4	5	6	7	8	9	10	11	12 sub used
24	H	CARDIFF		18	D	1-1	0-0	Phelan 88	Smith A	Smith A*	Collins	McHale	Rhodes	Phelan	Jones A	Veitch	Bell	Gwyther	Pugh	Downes
	17/1		2,399	*6*	22			*England 60*	*Irwin*	*Dwyer*	*Charles*	*Buchanan*	*England*	*Larmour*	*Villars*	*Livermore*	*Evans*	*Alston*	*Anderson*	
								Ref: C Seel	Town's form now looks worrying. They need a late goal from Phelan, after Gwyther's header comes back off the point, to save a point. Cardiff know they should have won this one, but can't build on their only goal scored by Mike England from 20 yards, following up Alston's effort.											
25	A	SHREWSBURY		18	L	0-2	0-2		Smith A	Smith A	Luckett	McHale	Rhodes	Phelan	Jones A	Veitch	Bell	Gwyther	Pugh*	Downes
	24/1		*3,398*	*8*	22			*Bates 17, Irvine 30*	*Mulhearn*	*King*	*Leonard*	*Durban*	*Griffin*	*Turner*	*Irvine*	*Atkins*	*Kearney*	*Bates*	*McGregor*	
								Ref: G Nolan	Quinn says he will dip into the transfer market if things don't improve. They don't. On a snowbound pitch, McHale's terrible backpass lets in Bates, and Irvine doubles Shrewsbury's lead following a corner. The knives are being sharpened and Quinn is about to be stabbed in the back.											
26	A	PRESTON		21	L	1-2	0-0	McHale 71	Smith A	Smith A	Collins	McHale	Rhodes	Phelan	Jones A	Veitch	Bell	Gwyther	Blair*	Pugh
	7/2		*5,480*	*13*	22			*Elwiss 47, Doyle 55*	*Tunks*	*McMahon*	*Williams*	*Doyle*	*Sadler*	*Spark*	*Smith*	*Bruce*	*Treacy*	*Elwiss*	*Brown*	
								Ref: J Taylor	There is anger at the way Quinn was sacked, but life goes on. Alan Ball has returned to try to steady the ship, but he immediately tastes defeat. Unmarked Elwiss, and Doyle's 20-yarder, put Preston in control McHale replies with a scrambled effort. Ball, though, has 'no complaints'.											
27	H	MANSFIELD		22	L	1-2	0-0	Downes 81	Smith A	Smith A	Collins	McHale	Rhodes	Phelan	Jones A	Veitch*	Bell	Downes	Pugh	Harris
	14/2		2,378	*24*	22			*Clarke 53, Saxby 89*	*Arnold*	*Pate*	*Foster B*	*Matthews*	*Mackenzie*	*Saxby*	*Randall*	*Eccles*	*Clarke*	*Hodgson*	*McCaffrey*	
								Ref: R Lee	Ball pleads with the fans: 'Forget Quinn and I, support the players.' Then literally just before kick-off, he sells Gwyther to Rotherham. Town hardly trouble the Stags until Downes' equaliser, but Saxby rises unchallenged to give his side the points. This win will kick-start their season.											
28	A	BRIGHTON		23	L	0-1	0-0		Smith A	Smith A	Collins	McHale	Rhodes	Phelan	Jones A	**McGill***	**Bullock**	Downes	Pugh	Harris
	21/2		*13,686*	*3*	22			*Binney 73*	*Grummitt*	*Tiler*	*Wilson*	*Machin*	*Rollings*	*Burnett*	*Towner*	*Morgan*	*Binney*	*O'Sullivan*	*Mellor*	
								Ref: K Baker	The Shaymen give a good account of themselves against high-flyers Brighton. Ball has signed Jimmy McGill to add a bit of steel to the side. The defence soaks up a lot of pressure, but falls to Fred Binney's goal after a mix-up. Rhodes and Collins are booked, as is Ball, for coaching.											
29	H	GRIMSBY		23	W	2-1	1-1	Downes 19, McHale 46p	Gennoe	Smith A	Collins	McHale	Rhodes*	Phelan	Jones A	McGill	Bullock	Downes	Pugh	Harris
	24/2		2,229	*16*	24			*Czuczman 41p*	*Wainman*	*Marley**	*Booth*	*Young*	*Czuczman*	*Gray*	*Lewis*	*Barton*	*Patridge*	*Boylen*	*Cumming*	*Wigg*
								Ref: R Kirkpatrick/G Boothman	Czuczman equalises with a penalty after Phelan clears the ball with his hand. McHale's winner is a twice-taken penalty, as Wainman moves when he puts his first kick over the bar. Marley and Rhodes are both stretchered off, and an injured ref is eventually replaced by a linesman.											
30	H	BURY		23	L	0-2	0-2		Gennoe	Smith A	Collins	McHale	Veitch	Phelan	Jones A	McGill	Bullock	**Jones G**	Pugh*	Downes
	28/2		3,606	*11*	24			*Woolfall 5, Rowland 26*	*Forrest*	*Hoolickin*	*Kennedy*	*Nicholson*	*Hulme*	*Bailey*	*Woolfall*	*Phillips*	*Rowland*	*Spence**	*Williams*	*McIlwraith*
								Ref: J Moss	Despite falling to free headers from Woolfall - his first-ever goal - and Rowland, Town create a number of chances to at least gain a draw. But McHale puts wide with the goal at his mercy, and Downes fluffs a one-on-one. Up front, George Jones makes his debut, but looks out of sorts.											
31	H	SHEFFIELD WED		22	D	0-0	0-0		Gennoe	Smith A	Collins	McHale	Pugh	Phelan	Jones A	McGill	Bullock	Jones G	Harris	
	2/3		**5,876**	*20*	25				*Fox*	*Shaw*	*Quinn*	*Mullen*	*Cusack*	*O'Donnell*	*McIver*	*Wylde*	*Prendergast*	*Feely*	*Nimmo*	
								Ref: G Courtney	After Mansfield's victory last night, Town start this game bottom of the table. Len Ashurst's Wednesday are a fallen giant, and lie just one place above them. Despite the game being played at a furious pace, the first real shot at goal doesn't come until the 30th minute, from McHale.											
32	H	GILLINGHAM		23	D	1-1	0-1	Jones G 51	Smith A	Smith A	Collins	McHale	Pugh	Phelan	Jones A	McGill	Bullock	Jones G	Harris	
	9/3		1,886	*12*	26			*Knight 29*	*Hillyard*	*Knight*	*Ley*	*Wiltshire*	*Shipperley*	*Tydman*	*Jacks*	*Fogarty*	*Richardson*	*Westwood*	*Durrell*	
								Ref: R Chadwick	The Shaymen's three-day break in Southport doesn't appear to have done them much good. They struggle to get to grips with a Gills side that takes the lead when the ball falls to Knight. Town, however, do conjure up an equaliser, when George Jones keeps his cool to beat Hillyard.											
33	H	SWINDON		23	L	0-2	0-1		Smith A	Smith A*	**Flavell**	McHale	Pugh	Phelan	Jones	McGill	Bullock	Jones G	**Overton**	Harris
	13/3		1,846	*22*	26			*Syrett 26, 55*	*Barron*	*McLaughlin*	*Trollope*	*Stroud*	*Aizlewood*	*Prophett*	*Moss*	*O'Brien*	*Syrett*	*Anderson*	*Rogers*	
								Ref: N Ashley	The side is changing, but fortunes are not, as relegation fears grow. Fellow-strugglers Swindon take the lead when favourite Don Rogers, who has just returned to the club, slips Flavell and sets up Syrett. Syrett gets a break for his second, when Phelan's clearance rebounds into his path.											
34	A	HEREFORD		23	W	2-1	0-0	Jones G 63, Overton 90	Smith A	Flavell	Collins	McGill	Rhodes	Phelan	Jones A	McHale	Bullock	Jones G	Overton	
	17/3		*7,395*	*1*	28			*Galley 82*	*Charlton*	*Emery*	*Richards*	*Layton*	*Galley*	*Lindsay*	*Paine**	*Tyler*	*Davey*	*McNeil*	*Carter*	*McCafferty*
								Ref: J Hough	One of the shocks of the season. It's top versus bottom, but few can deny Town their right to victory, even if Overton's dramatic winner comes in seven minutes of injury-time. Galley thinks he's saved the game when he scoops the ball in, after George Jones had volleyed Town in front.											

No	Date	Venue	Opponents / Att	Pos	Res / Pts	F-A	H-T	Scorers, Times, and Referees	1	2	3	4	5	6	7	8	9	10	11	12
35		H	WREXHAM	24	L	0-1	0-0		Smith A	Flavell	Collins	McGill	Rhodes	Phelan	Jones A	McHale	Bullock	Jones G	Overton	
	20/3		2,970	*6*	28			*Ashcroft 67*	*Lloyd*	*Evans*	*Fogg*	*Davis A*	*May*	*Whittle*	*Tinnion*	*Sutton*	*Lee*	*Ashcroft*	*Griffiths*	
								Ref: H Davey	Quarter-finalists Wrexham went out of the Cup-Winners' Cup narrowly to Anderlecht – who will beat West Ham in the final – three days ago. A game at the Shay is a bit of an anti-climax for them, but they win nevertheless. Ashcroft rises high to head the only goal off Sutton's cross.											
36		H	SOUTHEND	19	W	1-0	0-0	Rhodes 57	Smith A	Flavell	Collins	McGill	Rhodes	Phelan	Jones A	McHale	Bullock	Jones G	Overton	
	23/3		1,450	*20*	30				*Webster*	*Banks*	*Ford*	*Little*	*Hadley*	*Moody*	*Foggo*	*Brace*	*Goodwin**	*Silvester*	*Taylor*	*Pountney*
								Ref: A Hughes	Town are hardly inspired, but fortunately Southend are worse. Alex Smith has only one save to make. It's a dour game, but a welcome victory comes courtesy of Rhodes' header off McHale's cross when the visitors failed to clear a corner. Ball now predicts Town will avoid relegation.											
37		A	PETERBOROUGH	22	L	0-1	0-1		Smith A	Flavell	Collins	McGill	Rhodes	Phelan	Jones A	McHale*	Bullock	Jones G	Overton	Pugh
	27/3		*4,933*	*9*	30			*Moss 7*	*Steele*	*Hodson*	*Lee*	*Eustace*	*Jones*	*Carmichael*	*Nixon**	*Gregory*	*Moss*	*Hughes*	*Cozens*	*Walker*
								Ref: L Burden	A month ago, Peterborough were right in among the promotion frame. Victory here, however, ends a run of eight games without a win. Ernie Moss's early header, following a corner, wins the game. Town sub Pugh is still cold when he heads over the bar when it looked easier to score.											
38		H	CHESTERFIELD	20	W	1-0	1-0	Overton 8	Smith A	Flavell	Collins	Pugh	Rhodes	Phelan	Harris	McHale	Bullock	Jones G	Overton	
	30/3		1,975	*19*	32				*Hardwick*	*O'Neill*	*Burton*	*Charlton*	*Hunter*	*Cross*	*Welch*	*Cammack*	*Fern*	*Bentley*	*Darling*	
								Ref: J Goggins	John Overton pounces to head home early on when George Jones' drive comes back off the bar. Chesterfield are a poor side and offer little, but as Halifax fail to take further chances, the tension mounts. The ref again speaks to Ball for coaching, but Town move out of the bottom four.											
39		A	MILLWALL	20	L	0-1	0-0		Smith A	Flavell	Collins	Pugh	Rhodes	Phelan	Ford	McHale	Bullock	Harris	Overton	
	3/4		*7,237*	*4*	32			*Moore 60*	*Goddard*	*Donaldson*	*Moore*	*Brisley*	*Kitchener*	*Hazell*	*McGrath*	*Shanahan*	*Summerill*	*Walker*	*Lee*	
								Ref: E Read	Millwall keeper Ray Goddard is injured in a first-half collision with teammate Kitchener, but he is rarely tested. McHale is unlucky to see a 30-yarder ruled out for offside against Bullock. The visitors score when Brisley flicks a free-kick to Moore, and he fires home from 18 yards.											
40		A	CHESTER	22	L	1-2	1-0	Overton 26	Smith A	Flavell	Collins	McGill	Overton	Pugh	Jones A	McHale	Bullock	Jones G*	Veitch	Ford
	7/4		*3,369*	*15*	32			*Storton 51, Redfern 83*	*Millington*	*Edwards*	*Loska*	*Storton*	*Dunleavy*	*Draper*	*Whitehead*	*Pugh*	*Owen*	*Mason**	*Redfern*	*Delgado*
								Ref: G Trevett	The Shaymen throw away a point, and time is running out. When Bullock flicks on a corner, Overton gives them the lead. Just after half-time, they play a kamikaze offside trap which leaves Storton free. Chester's late winner comes through Redfern off Draper's defence-splitting pass.											
41		A	CRYS PALACE	23	D	1-1	1-1	McHale 14	Smith A	Flavell	Collins	Pugh	Rhodes	Phelan	Jones A	McHale	Bullock	Bell	Overton	
	13/4		***19,175***	*5*	33			*Martin 16*	*Hammond*	*Wall*	*Cannon*	*Sansom*	*Jump*	*Evans*	*Johnson J*	*Martin*	*Whittle*	*Swindlehurst**	*Taylor*	*Kemp*
								Ref: R Crabb	Recent FA Cup semi-finalists Palace drop a valuable point in their bid for promotion. Town take the lead when McHale's shot is deflected in, but their lead lasts all but two minutes when Neil Martin rolls the ball in. Smith is Town's hero, for saving Peter Taylor's 40th-minute penalty.											
42		A	PORT VALE	23	D	1-1	1-0	Phelan 44	Smith A	Flavell	Collins	Pugh	Rhodes	Phelan	Jones A	McHale	Bullock	Bell	Overton	
	17/4		*3,169*	*13*	34			*Beech 70*	*Connaughton*	*Griffiths*	*Dulson*	*Ridley*	*Lees*	*Beech*	*McLaren*	*Tartt**	*Cullerton*	*Bailey*	*Brownbill*	*Robson*
								Ref: P Partridge	Mid-table Port Vale have little to play for, in stark contrast to the Shaymen. Phelan looks to have sent Town on their way a minute before the interval when Alan Jones' cross sneaks through to him. But, inevitably, the defence caves in, and when they fail to clear, Kenny Beech fires in.											
43		H	ROTHERHAM	24	L	0-1	0-1		Smith A	Flavell	Collins	Pugh	Rhodes	Phelan	Jones A	McHale	Downes	Bell	Overton	
	19/4		2,614	*16*	34			*Gwyther 1*	*McAllister*	*Derrett*	*Breckin*	*Rhodes*	*Stancliffe*	*Spencer*	*Finney**	*Phillips*	*Gwyther*	*Goodfellow*	*Crawford*	*Leng*
								Ref: I Smith	When these two sides met in December, Dave Gwyther scored the only goal – for Town. How ironic, then, that he should settle this game, too, and hammer a nail into his former side's coffin. He doesn't have to wait long for his goal, latching onto Flavell's backpass in the first minute.											
44		A	SHEFFIELD WED	24	L	0-1	0-1		Smith A	Flavell	Collins	Pugh	Rhodes	Phelan*	Jones A	McHale	Bullock	Bell	Overton	Downes
	20/4		*13,143*	*19*	34			*Henson 30*	*Fox*	*Walden*	*Shaw*	*Mullen*	*Cusack*	*O'Donnell*	*Henson*	*Wylde*	*Prendergast*	*Nimmo*	*Potts*	
								Ref: D Richardson	Ball reckons his side will be safe with another five points. Where they'll come from, no one knows. Phil Henson has already hit the bar before he scores the game's only goal, a lob over Smith. McHale looks for a penalty when he falls over, but the best he gets is an indirect free-kick.											
45		H	ALDERSHOT	24	L	1-3	1-1	Harris 15	Smith A	Smith A	Collins	Pugh	Rhodes	Overton	Harris	McHale*	Downes	Bell	Flavell	Veitch
	24/4		1,608	*20*	34			*Howarth 28, 71, Rhodes 69 (og)*	*Johnson*	*Howitt*	*Walker*	*Wallace R*	*Goldthorpe*	*Jopling*	*Warnock*	*Morrissey*	*Howarth*	*Crosby*	*Brodie*	
								Ref: C Newsome	Relegation is confirmed. After this wretched display it's not hard to see why. Harris's goal only prolongs the agony. Jack Howarth is a regular scorer against Town, and bags two more. Rhodes' own-goal is a disaster, heading over Smith. Ball's reaction to relegation: 'I'm not surprised.'											
46		H	COLCHESTER	24	D	1-1	0-1	Smith 70 (og)	Gennoe	Smith A	Flavell	Pugh	Rhodes	Overton	Harris	McHale	Downes	Bell	Blair	
	26/4		**856**	*22*	35			*Gough 25*	*Walker*	*Bright*	*Williams*	*Bunkell*	*Smith*	*Packer*	*Allinson*	*Gough*	*Foley*	*Dyer*	*Leslie*	
	Home		Away					Ref: A Hamil	The Shay resembles a wake as the lowest crowd in Town's history turns up for this game between two relegated sides. Town never look like winning, and after Gough hammers the ball past Gennoe, they need Lindsay Smith's leg to avoid defeat, turning in a ball that is going wide.											
Average	2,510		6,556																	

LEAGUE DIVISION 3 (CUP-TIES) Manager: Quinn ⇨ Alan Ball (Snr) SEASON 1975-76

League Cup					F-A	H-T	Scorers, Times, and Referees	1	2	3	4	5	6	7	8	9	10	11	12 sub used
1:1	H	HARTLEPOOL		W	4-1	3-0	Phelan 2, Albeson 20 (og), Bell 36, 47	Gennoe	Smith A	Collins	McHale	Rhodes	Phelan	Jones A	Ford	Downes	**Bell***	Pugh	Blair
	19/8	1,476	*4:*				*Johnson 59*	*Hope*	*Crowther*	*Smith R*	*Potter*	*Goad*	*Albeson*	*Honour**	*Smith D*	*Moore*	*McMahon*	*Johnson*	*Skillen*
							Ref: P Richardson	The first round is now played over two legs, and superior Halifax give themselves a great chance. They get off to a flyer with Phelan's early header. Albeson's header, when under no pressure, doubles Town's lead. Bell gets two, clipping in his second before anyone can reach him.											
1:2	A	HARTLEPOOL	12	L	1-2	1-0	Downes 8	Gennoe	Smith A	Collins	McHale	Rhodes	Phelan	Jones A	Ford	Downes	Gwyther	Pugh	
	25/8	*1,726*	*4:12*				*McMahon 61, Skillen 78*	*Richardson*	*Smith R*	*Crowther*	*Honour*	*Goad*	*Potter*	*Skillen*	*Smith D*	*Moore*	*McMahon*	*Johnson*	
							Ref: P Richardson (Halifax won 5-3 on aggregate)	Defeat in the second leg gives cause for concern. Downes' early goal puts Town 5-1 up on aggregate, but they can't handle Ken Hale's side in the second half. Goad beats the offside to set up McMahon's goal. Skillen's goal is a fierce header. The Pool could actually have scored more.											
2	H	SHEFFIELD UTD	3	L	2-4	1-2	Rhodes 43, Downes 82	Gennoe	Smith A*	Collins	McHale	Rhodes	Phelan	Jones	Ford	Bell	Gwyther	Pugh	Downes
	10/9	7,925	*1:22*				*Guthrie 32, 35, 52, Phelan 53 (og)*	*Brown*	*Badger*	*Hemsley*	*Eddy*	*Colquhoun*	*Franks*	*Woodward*	*Garbutt*	*Guthrie*	*Currie*	*Speight*	
							Ref: D Richardson	Town are still in the hunt at half-time against the First Division strugglers. But after a bout of lightning delays the second half, the Blades step up a gear. Guthrie completes his hat-trick with a header off a corner, whilst Phelan is unlucky to divert Woodward's rocket shot in off his head.											

FA Cup																			
1	H	ALTRINCHAM	15	W	3-1	2-0	McHale 18p, 86, Rhodes 45	Gennoe	Veitch	Collins	McHale	Rhodes	Phelan	Ford	Downes	Bell	Gwyther	Pugh	
	22/11	4,077	*NPL*				*Moore 80*	*Cavanagh*	*Allan*	*Brooke*	*Clements**	*Casey*	*Owens*	*Wain*	*Dickinson*	*Moore*	*Hughes R*	*Hughes J*	*Carrick*
							Ref: P Reeves	Town get the breaks in the first half. McHale scores a penalty after he is brought down, and right on half-time Rhodes scores a header when Cavanagh loses the ball. With ten minutes to go, Moore's clever solo goal gives Altrincham hope, until McHale fires in a blistering cross-shot.											
2	A	STAFFORD	19	W	3-1	0-0	McHale 47p, Downes 55, Gwyther 80	Gennoe	Smith A	Collins	McHale	Rhodes	Phelan	Harrold*	Downes	Bell	Gwyther	Pugh	Jones A
	13/12	*4,650*	*NPL*				*Seddon B 60*	*Arnold*	*Ritchie*	*Richards*	*Seddon D**	*Seddon B*	*Morris*	*Hutchison*	*Chapman*	*Jones*	*Lowe*	*Chadwick*	*Sargeant*
							Ref: R Lee	The freezing pitch makes this an interesting tie. McHale settles Town's nerves with another penalty when Arnold brings down Gwyther. Town lead 2-0 when Ben Seddon's glancing header kicks across the sanded area and goes in. Dave Gwyther's chipped goal ends a Stafford fightback.											
3	A	IPSWICH	16	L	1-3	1-3	McHale 23p	Gennoe	Smith A	Collins	McHale	Veitch	Phelan	Jones A	Blair	Bell*	Gwyther	Pugh	Downes
	3/1	*23,488*	*1:11*				*Lambert 2, 12, 35*	*Cooper*	*Burley*	*Beattie*	*Talbot*	*Hunter*	*Peddelty*	*Woods*	*Mills*	*Johnson**	*Whymark*	*Lambert*	*Austin*
							Ref: M Sinclair	Mick Lambert scores after only 88 seconds, and Town go two goals down after only twelve minutes. McHale's penalty, when Beattie handled Jones' corner, halves the deficit. Lambert goes on to complete his hat-trick, but Town never give up and earn praise from Alf Ramsey, no less.											

		P	W	D	L	Home F	Home A	W	D	L	Away F	Away A	Pts
1	Hereford	46	14	6	3	45	24	12	5	6	41	31	63
2	Cardiff	46	14	7	2	38	13	8	6	9	31	35	57
3	Millwall	46	16	6	1	35	14	4	10	9	19	29	56
4	Brighton	46	18	3	2	58	15	4	6	13	20	38	53
5	Crys Palace	46	7	12	4	30	20	11	5	7	31	26	53
6	Wrexham	46	13	6	4	38	21	7	6	10	28	34	52
7	Walsall	46	11	8	4	43	22	7	6	10	31	39	50
8	Preston	46	15	4	4	45	23	4	6	13	17	34	48
9	Shrewsbury	46	14	2	7	36	25	5	8	10	25	34	48
10	Peterborough	46	12	7	4	37	23	3	11	9	26	40	48
11	Mansfield	46	8	11	4	31	22	8	4	11	27	30	47
12	Port Vale	46	10	10	3	33	21	5	6	12	22	33	46
13	Bury	46	11	7	5	33	16	3	9	11	18	30	44
14	Chesterfield	46	11	5	7	45	30	6	4	13	24	39	43
15	Gillingham	46	10	8	5	38	27	2	11	10	20	41	43
16	Rotherham	46	11	6	6	35	22	4	6	13	19	43	42
17	Chester	46	13	7	3	34	19	2	5	16	9	43	42
18	Grimsby	46	13	7	3	39	21	2	3	18	23	53	40
19	Swindon	46	11	4	8	42	31	5	4	14	20	44	40
20	Sheffield Wed	46	12	6	5	34	25	0	10	13	14	34	40
21	Aldershot	46	10	8	5	34	26	3	5	15	25	49	39
22	Colchester	46	9	6	8	25	27	3	8	12	16	38	38
23	Southend	46	9	7	7	40	31	3	6	14	25	44	37
24	HALIFAX	46	6	5	12	22	32	5	8	10	19	29	35
		1104	278	158	116	890	550	116	158	278	550	890	1104

Odds & ends

Double wins: (1) Chesterfield.
Double losses: (4) Brighton, Millwall, Peterborough, Swindon.

Won from behind: (2) Walsall (h), Aldershot (a).
Lost from in front: (4) Aldershot (h), Port Vale (h), Chester (a), Hartlepool (LC) (a).

High spots: Three consecutive wins up to 6 September.
Unbeaten in the first five away games – a club record in the League.
Going eight games without defeat up to 4 October.
Beating champions-elect Hereford away from home.

Low spots: Four consecutive defeats up to 21 February.
The manner of Johnny Quinn's sacking.
Failing to win any of the last eight matches.
Finishing bottom and getting relegated.

The attendance for the last game of the season was the lowest ever at the Shay for a League game – 856.

Player of the Year: Tony Rhodes.
Ever-presents: (1) Ray McHale.
Hat-tricks: (0).
Leading scorer: Ray McHale (16).

	Appearances Lge	*Sub*	LC	*Sub*	FAC	*Sub*	Goals Lge	LC	FAC	Tot
Bell, Derek	**30**	*1*	2		3		**7**	2		**9**
Blair, Ken	**12**	*1*		*1*	1					
Bullock, Mickey	**16**									
Collins, John	**42**		3		3					
Downes, Steve	**12**	*6*	2	*1*	2	*1*	**3**	2	1	**6**
Flavell, Bobby	**14**									
Ford, David	**10**	*2*	3		1		**2**			**2**
Gennoe, Terry	**26**		3		3					
Gwyther, Dave	**24**		2		3		**4**		1	**5**
Harris, Geoff	**10**	*4*					**1**			**1**
Harrold, Mark	**5**	*3*			1					
Jones, Alan	**36**		3		1	*1*				
Jones, George	**10**						**3**			**3**
Luckett, Paul	**2**	*1*								
McGill, Jimmy	**11**									
McHale, Ray	**46**		3		3		**12**		4	**16**
Overton, John	**14**						**2**			**2**
Phelan, Albert	**43**		3		3		**3**	1		**4**
Pugh, David	**36**	*3*	3		3					
Rhodes, Tony	**40**		3		2		**3**	1	1	**5**
Smith, Alex (1)	**20**									
Smith, Alex (2)	**27**	*1*	3		2					
Veitch, Tommy	**20**	*2*			2					
(own-goals)							**1**	1		**2**
23 players used	**506**	***24***	**33**	***2***	**33**	***2***	**41**	**7**	**7**	**55**

No	Date		Att	Pos	Pt	F-A	H-T	Scorers, Times, and Referees	1	2	3	4	5	6	7	8	9	10	11	12 sub used
1	H	BOURNEMOUTH			L	2-3	1-2	Jones G 36, McHale 54	Gennoe	Flavell	**Kent**	McHale	**Trainer**	Phelan	Jones A	Johnston*	Bullock	Jones G	**Lawson**	Bell
	21/8		1,711		0			*Riley 13, Paterson 45, Buttle 78*	*Baker*	*Butler*	*Miller*	*Benson*	*Morgan*	*Barton*	*Riley*	*Johnson*	*Paterson*	*Reeves*	*Buttle*	
								Ref: D Shore	Town's return to Fourth Division football sees them attract fewer than 2,000 on the opening day for the first time. Ball needs to stimulate some interest. McHale's 25-yarder, Town's second equaliser, is the game's best goal. Buttle's lob over Gennoe turns out to be the most important.											
2	A	COLCHESTER			L	0-3	0-0		Gennoe	Flavell	Kent	McHale	Trainer	**Rylands**	Jones A	McGill*	Jones G	Bell	Lawson	Johnston
	24/8		*2,489*		0			*Allinson 75, 77, Gough 90*	*Walker*	*Dyer*	*Williams**	*Bunkell*	*Smith*	*Packer*	*Greenwood*	*Gough*	*Allinson*	*Leslie*	*Gough*	*Dowman*
								Ref: D Reeves	This game looks like petering out into a goalless bore-draw. The crowd begins to slow-handclap. Alan Jones and Mike Packer liven things up when they trade punches. Then Colchester hit Town with three late knockout blows. Gennoe claims Allinson's second never crossed the line.											
3	A	WORKINGTON		19	D	1-1	0-0	McHale 81	Gennoe	Flavell	Kent	McHale	Trainer	Rylands	Jones A	McGill*	Jones G	Lawson	Bell	Bullock
	28/8		*2,081*	*10*	1			*Ashworth 69*	*Rogan*	*Kisby*	*Ellison*	*Kavanagh*	*Dawes*	*Brown*	*Harris*	*Lowrey*	*Ashworth*	*Honour*	*Leng*	
								Ref: A Porter	Under Alan Ashman, Workington's two goals so far have been a penalty and an own-goal. The signs look ominous for them. Likewise for the Shaymen, who end the game with four up front. McHale snatches a late equaliser off Alan Jones' square pass to cancel out Ashworth's header.											
4	H	ROCHDALE		20	D	0-0	0-0		Gennoe	Flavell	Kent	McHale	Trainer	Rylands	Jones A	McGill	Jones G	Lawson	Bell	
	4/9		2,003	*6*	2				*Poole*	*Hallows*	*Lacey*	*Mulvaney**	*Summerscales*	*Hanvey*	*Helliwell*	*Melledew*	*Whelan*	*O'Loughlin*	*Tarbuck*	*Mullington*
								Ref: P Partridge	This scoreless draw ensures Town's worst start since 1966. Still, Ball reckons, 'we'll be top by Christmas.' Lawson hits the bar, George Jones blunders with just Poole to beat, and McHale's shot from 24 yards flashes just wide. But these are isolated incidents in a game of few chances.											
5	A	SOUTHEND		20	D	1-1	1-1	Bell 35	Gennoe	Flavell	Kent	Johnston	Rylands	Phelan	Jones A	Trainer	Jones G	Lawson	Bell	
	10/9		*5,143*	*7*	3			*Moody 20p*	*Freeman*	*Moody*	*Ford*	*Little*	*Townsend*	*Hadley*	*Nicholl*	*Goodwin*	*Denny*	*Pountney*	*Cunningham*	
								Ref: R Lewis	Southend boss Dave Smith is not impressed with Town's negative approach. Dull they may be, but at least they score their goal in open play. George Jones and Johnston combine to set up Bell, who flicks the ball in. Lawson upends Nicholl for Southend's penalty, scored by Moody.											
6	H	EXETER		22	L	1-2	0-0	Lawson 49p	Gennoe	Flavell	Kent	McGill	Rylands	Phelan	Johnston*	Trainer	Jones G	Lawson	Bell	Bullock
	18/9		1,424	*9*	3			*Kellow 61, Beer 90*	*Key*	*Templeman*	*Hore*	*Morrin*	*Clapham*	*Hatch*	*Jennings*	*Kellow*	*Robertson*	*Weeks*	*Beer*	
								Ref: K McNally	Town get a lucky break when the ref awards them a dubious penalty when Johnson is checked by Weeks. Lawson accepts it. But when Gennoe fails to hold a cross, Kellow scores. Then, in injury-time, Kent's back-header leaves Gennoe stranded, Beer nips in and Town's luck runs out.											
7	H	HARTLEPOOL		20	W	1-0	0-0	Bullock 54	Gennoe	Flavell	Kent	McGill	Trainer	Phelan	**Carroll**	Jones G	Bullock	Lawson	Bell	
	24/9		1,393	*23*	5				*Edgar*	*Goad*	*Luckett*	*Veitch*	*Scott*	*Rowlands*	*Scaife*	*Elliott*	*Endean*	*Prudman*	*Maggiore*	
								Ref: L Hayes	Town experiment with Friday night football, but the gate is actually down on last week's. However, Town do manage to win their first game. Bullock gets the goal, turning in Flavell's cross at the far post. McGill is booked, as is coach Farrimond, for comments made on the booking.											
8	A	WATFORD		19	D	0-0	0-0		Gennoe	Flavell	Kent	McGill	Trainer	Phelan	Carroll	Jones G*	Bullock	Lawson	Bell	Johnston
	2/10		*4,353*	*10*	6				*Rankin*	*How*	*Walsh*	*Bond*	*Eades*	*Garner*	*Craker*	*Joslyn*	*Mercer*	*Poole*	*Hayes*	
								Ref: W Harvey	The ref inspects the rain-savaged pitch under cover of a huge white umbrella before he gives the go-ahead, and the Shaymen dig deep to earn a point. They soak up all that Watford throw at them, but it's Rankin, with amazing reflexes, who makes the game's best save, denying Trainer.											
9	H	SCUNTHORPE		21	L	0-1	0-1		Gennoe	Flavell	Kent	McGill	Trainer	Phelan	Carroll	Johnston*	Bullock	Lawson	Bell	**Bradley**
	9/10		1,854	*8*	6			*Wigginton 12*	*Letheran*	*Markham**	*Peacock*	*Oates*	*Wigginton*	*Money*	*Collier*	*Pilling*	*Davidson*	*Keeley*	*Green*	*Wadsworth*
								Ref: A Challinor	Gennoe is badly at fault for Clive Wigginton's early headed goal, when he hesitates on Pilling's high centre. Seconds after the restart, Carroll misses an open goal. McGill tries a spectacular overhead kick in the 33rd minute, but Letheran saves well. After that, the Shaymen offer little.											
10	A	CREWE		21	L	1-3	1-1	McCann 8	Gennoe	Flavell*	Kent	McGill	Trainer	Phelan	Johnston	**McCann**	Bullock	Lawson	Bell	Harris
	16/10		*2,363*	*13*	6			*Abbott 13, Lugg 55p, Purdie 73*	*Crudgington*	*Lowry*	*Evans*	*Lugg*	*Nicholls*	*Mayman*	*Davies D*	*Abbott*	*Davies W*	*Purdie*	*Tully*	
								Ref: A McDonald	On-loan McCann makes a dream start for Town, but then it all goes pear-shaped. Crewe take the lead with a controversial penalty. Gennoe has hold of the ball when Wyn Davies falls over his leg. Ball says afterwards that 'the game was played by professionals and ruined by amateurs.'											
11	H	CAMBRIDGE		21	L	0-2	0-2		Gennoe	Bradley	Kent	McGill	Trainer	Phelan	Bell	McCann	Carroll	Lawson	**Hoy**	
	23/10		1,523	*3*	6			*Stringer 16, Seddon 29*	*Webster*	*Batson*	*Baldry*	*Stringer*	*Fallon*	*Howard*	*Seddon*	*Spriggs*	*Biley*	*Bowker*	*Finney*	
								Ref: G Kew	It's another unhappy game for Gennoe. First, he misjudges Dave Stringer's free-kick just inside the Town half, and the ball sails over his head. Next, he allows Ian Seddon's corner to drift just over the line. Strong winds spoil the game, but it becomes a stroll for a strong Cambridge side.											

No	Date	Att	Pos	Res	F-A	H-T	Scorers, Times, and Referees	1	2	3	4	5	6	7	8	9	10	11	subs used
12 A	BRADFORD C		21	L	0-3	0-3		Gennoe	Bradley	Kent	McGill	Trainer	Phelan	Hoy	Carroll	Bullock	Lawson	Bell*	Johnston
27/10		*7,271*	*1*	6			*Cooke 5, 45, Kent 34 (og)*	*Downsboro'*	*Hardcastle*	*Podd*	*Johnson*	*Middleton*	*Fretwell*	*Ingram*	*Watson*	*Cooke*	*Dolan*	*Hutchins*	
							Ref: P Willis	Bobby Kennedy's Bantams make the most of defensive blunders and cruise to victory. When Gennoe calls for Hutchins' corner, Trainer leaves the ball, and Cooke has a free header for his first. Ingram's zipping cross is turned in by Kent, while Cooke dispossesses Carroll for his second.											
13 H	STOCKPORT		21	W	2-1	1-1	Johnston 2, Bullock 55	Gennoe	Bradley	**Loska**	McGill	Trainer	Phelan	Hoy	Carroll	Bullock	Lawson	Johnston	
30/10		2,149	*3*	8			*Thompson 18*	*Holbrook*	*Loadwick*	*Rutter*	*Thompson*	*Lennard*	*Fogarty*	*McBeth*	*McNeill*	*Daniels*	*Johnson*	*Massey**	*Sutcliffe*
							Ref: J Wrennall	It looks like being a familiar story when County's Thompson cancels out Johnston's second-minute header. But the much-maligned Bullock pops up to head in following a short corner routine. It proves decisive, though the recently-troubled Gennoe has to show his better side late on.											
14 H	DONCASTER		19	W	**6-0**	4-0	Dunleavy 6, Hoy 13, 32, Carroll 45, [Bullock 58, Lawson 60]	Gennoe	Trainer	Loska*	McGill	**Dunleavy**	Phelan	Hoy	Carroll	Bullock	Lawson	Johnston	Bradley
2/11		2,350	*17*	10				*Peacock*	*Reed*	*Brookes*	*Binch*	*Wignall S**	*Taylor*	*Miller*	*Jones*	*O'Callaghan*	*Kitchen*	*Laidlaw*	*Robinson*
							Ref: J Worrall	Town's record League victory. New signing Dunleavy starts the rout with a powerful header. Both Hoy's goals are tap-ins. Carroll, right on half-time, and Bullock also score with headers. Lawson's cross is deflected in by Peacock. Ball doesn't care, and beams, 'It's a great feeling.'											
15 A	DARLINGTON		19	D	0-0	0-0		Gennoe	Trainer	Bradley	McGill	Dunleavy	Phelan	Hoy	Carroll	Bullock	Lawson	Johnston	
6/11		*3,392*	*13*	11				*Ogley*	*Nattress*	*Cochrane*	*Stone*	*Craig*	*Noble*	*Lyons*	*Rowles*	*Ferguson*	*Holbrook*	*Wann**	*Lees*
							Ref: C Seal	The events of midweek look to have kick-started Town's season. Darlington have won their last four home games, but Halifax surprise them. The home side have the better of things, but it's Town who come closest to winning it, when Ogley saves at Carroll's feet in the 87th minute.											
16 H	SWANSEA		18	W	1-0	0-0	Hoy 66	Gennoe	Trainer	Bradley	McGill	Dunleavy	Phelan	Hoy	Carroll	Bullock	Lawson	Johnston	
9/11		2,244	*16*	13				*Brown*	*Evans*	*Bartley*	*Bruton**	*May*	*Harris*	*Lally*	*James*	*Curtis*	*Charles*	*Chappell*	*Smith*
							Ref: M Peck	Both sides go into this game on the back of goalless draws. A similar outcome looks likely here, too. That is until Hoy scores an amazing goal. He hits over an inswinger, and the ball curls in at the far post with Graham Brown beaten by both pace and swerve. Later on, Hoy hits the post.											
17 A	NEWPORT		19	D	1-1	1-0	Lawson 21	Gennoe	Trainer	Loska	McGill	Dunleavy	Phelan	Hoy	Carroll	Bullock	Lawson	Johnston	
27/11		*2,901*	*20*	14			*Woods 71*	*Plumley*	*Woods*	*Bell*	*Emmanuel*	*Walker*	*Murray*	*Villars*	*Parsons*	*Williams**	*Clark*	*White*	*Morgan*
							Ref: M Bevan	Newport are £110,000 in the red, and will wrap up if a buyer doesn't come in before 11 December. This could be their last league game away. Lawson holds off his man to put Town in front, but Newport won't be outdone. Town don't respond to a free-kick, and Woods nips in to score.											
18 A	SOUTHPORT		19	D	0-0	0-0		Gennoe	Trainer	Loska	McGill	Dunleavy	Phelan	Hoy	Carroll	Bullock	Lawson	Johnston	
18/12		***1,164***	*21*	15				*Coates*	*Hughes*	*Snookes*	*O'Neil*	*Higham*	*Taylor*	*Sibbald*	*Wilkinson*	*Galley*	*Wilson*	*Dewsnip*	
							Ref: N Midgley	Both managers face their former clubs. Ray Henderson is now in charge at Haig Avenue. This is a dire game. Dewsnip has the only chance after two minutes when Loska miskicks, but he shoots wide. Southport have most of the possession, but Ball knows he can rely on his defence.											
19 H	HUDDERSFIELD		19	D	0-0	0-0		Gennoe	Trainer	Loska	McGill	Dunleavy	Phelan	Hoy	Carroll	Bullock	Lawson	Johnston	
27/12		**8,720**	*8*	16				*Poole*	*Hart*	*Oliver*	*Smith*	*Baines*	*Hague*	*Butler*	*Sidebottom*	*Jones**	*Maitland*	*Johnson*	*Newton*
							Ref: K Hackett	The rain doesn't prevent a bumper crowd turning out for this derby. Unfortunately, they witness a non-event. Referee Keith Hackett fails to get a grip on the game, and lets too many things go. Bullock has the best chance, but Terry Poole knocks his rising shot from 23 yards onto the bar.											
20 A	BARNSLEY			L	0-1	0-0		Gennoe	Trainer	Loska	McGill	Dunleavy	Phelan	Hoy*	Carroll	Bullock	Lawson	Johnston	Jones G
29/12		*5,528*		16			*Joicey 70*	*Springett*	*Murphy*	*Collins*	*Pugh*	*Saunders*	*Pickering*	*Warnock*	*Price*	*Joicey*	*Millar*	*Brown*	
							Ref: D Richardson	The pitch is freezing over, and the game is in doubt. Neither manager wants to play, but Barnsley's Jim Iley will happily take the points. Brian Joicey scores the only goal, a dropping header off Millar's cross. McGill is carried off, but has to return, as Town have already used their sub.											
21 A	BOURNEMOUTH		20	L	0-3	0-1		Gennoe	Trainer	Loska	McGill	Dunleavy	Phelan	Hoy	Carroll	Bullock	Lawson	Johnston*	Bell
22/1		*3,888*	*5*	16			*Paterson 22, Johnson 64, Barton 86p*	*Baker*	*Butler*	*Miller*	*Impey*	*Morgan*	*Barton*	*Johnson*	*Riley*	*Howarth*	*Paterson*	*Buttle*	
							Ref: J Roost	A controversial goal changes the course of this game. Loska is lying injured on the ground, but plays Paterson onside, and he scores. Johnson is on hand to double the lead, whilst the third goal is a dubious penalty when Dunleavy clashes with Howarth. Ball rates the ref as low as 0/10.											
22 A	BRENTFORD		20	L	1-2	1-1	Hoy 40	Gennoe	Trainer	Loska	Flavell	Dunleavy	Phelan	Hoy	Carroll	Bullock	Lawson	Johnston	
29/1		*4,520*	*22*	16			*Sweetzer 38, French 64*	*Burns*	*Salman*	*Allen*	*Riddick*	*Smith*	*Carlton*	*Fraser*	*Aylott*	*Sweetzer*	*French*	*Smillie*	
							Ref: H Robinson	To curb the wage bill, Town have put all 21 players up for sale. This won't do the morale any good, and defeat here is almost inevitable. Both Brentford goals come through basic errors in the Town defence, with Gennoe's handling looking suspect. Hoy fires in his goal from 20 yards.											
23 A	STOCKPORT			D	1-1	0-1	Flavell 87	Gennoe	Trainer	Loska	Flavell	Dunleavy	Phelan	Hoy	Carroll	Bullock	Lawson	Johnston*	Bradley
31/1		*3,004*		17			*Sutcliffe 39*	*Holbrook*	*Loadwick*	*Rutter*	*Thompson*	*Lennard*	*Edwards*	*McBeth*	*Jackson*	*Daniels*	*Massey*	*Sutcliffe*	
							Ref: J Rice	Leading by Peter Sutcliffe's goal, Stockport have the perfect chance to put the game beyond the Shaymen. Loska brings down George McBeth, but Barney Daniels' tame penalty is easily saved by Gennoe. With time running out, Flavell then saves the game with a spectacular 30-yarder.											

No	Date		Att	Pos	Pt	F-A	H-T	Scorers, Times, and Referees	1	2	3	4	5	6	7	8	9	10	11	12 sub used
24	H	WORKINGTON		19	W	6-1	3-1	J'nston 11, 82, Lawson 12, Carroll 14, 79,	Gennoe	Trainer	Loska	Flavell	Dunleavy	Bradley	Hoy	Carroll*	Bullock	Lawson	Johnston	McGill
	5/2		1,580	*24*	19			*Ashworth 20* [Flavell 55]	*Rogan*	*Leng*	*Brown*	*Kavanagh*	*Blant*	*Johnston*	*Harris**	*Donaghy*	*Moore*	*Owen*	*Ashworth*	*Williamson*
								Ref: K McNally	It's a dismal last Shay appearance for Workington, who will lose their league status at the end of the season. Town score two in a minute, then Carroll volleys in the third. Flavell and Johnston's second are 30-yard efforts. Ashworth shows neat control for the visitor's last-ever goal here.											
25	H	TORQUAY			W	2-0	0-0	Hoy 66, Flavell 82	Gennoe	Trainer	Loska	Flavell	Dunleavy	Phelan	Hoy	Carroll	Bullock	Lawson	Johnston	
	8/2		2,124		21				*Robbins*	*Twitchin*	*Sandercock**	*Chatterley*	*Kruse*	*Dunne*	*Morrall*	*Lee C*	*Boulton*	*Provan*	*Rudge*	*Kennedy*
								Ref: A Jenkins	The Shaymen are brought down to earth, and have to work hard for this victory. A draw is looking likely until Jack Trainer joins in the attack. It's he who starts the move that leads to Carroll dummying the ball and Hoy scoring from 15 yards. Flavell's strike is a memorable 25-yarder.											
26	A	ROCHDALE		19	L	1-4	1-2	Bullock 8 *[Helliwell 79, Cooper 86]*	Gennoe	Trainer	Loska*	Flavell	Dunleavy	Phelan	Hoy	Carroll	Bullock	Lawson	Johnston	Bradley
	12/2		*2,255*	*13*	21			*Summerscales 25, Mountford 40,*	*Poole*	*Hallows*	*O'Loughlin*	*Bannon*	*Summerscales*	*Boslem**	*Melledew*	*Mountford*	*Whelan*	*Cooper*	*Helliwell*	*Hamstead*
								Ref: G Kew	Bullock has all the time in the world to give Town an early lead. Summerscales equalises, and Mountford gives his side the lead when the ball comes back off a post. The second half is a disaster, as Town give away two more goals and Gennoe breaks a finger in a clash with Mountford.											
27	H	DARLINGTON			W	2-1	0-1	Bullock 54, Johnston 85	**Leonard**	Trainer	Loska	Flavell	Dunleavy	Phelan	Hoy	Carroll	Bullock	Lawson	Johnston	
	14/2		1,720		23			*Seal 18*	*Ogley*	*Crosson**	*Cochrane*	*Nattress*	*Craig*	*Stone*	*Lyons*	*Rowles*	*Seal*	*Holbrook*	*Wann*	*Ferguson*
								Ref: K Walmsley	Mick Leonard is drafted in for his debut, but has little to do, apart from picking the ball out of the net when Seal forces the ball in following a corner. Darlington's goal comes against the run of play, but Bullock, swivelling to score, and Johnston's powerful strike, redress the balance.											
28	H	SOUTHEND		17	W	3-1	1-1	Hoy 23, Johnston 55, Bradley 82	Leonard	Trainer	Loska*	Flavell	Dunleavy	Phelan	Hoy	Carroll	Vullock	Lawson	Johnston	Bradley
	19/2		1,994	*4*	25			*Parker D 45*	*Freeman*	*Banks*	*Ford*	*Laverick*	*Moody*	*Young*	*Morris*	*Goodwin*	*Parker D*	*Hadley**	*Little*	*Cunningham*
								Ref: D Turner	Referee Turner threatens to abandon the match if the rain continues. He plays a good advantage when Johnston restores Town's lead. Leonard makes a point-blank save to keep Town in front, then Bradley's angled 20-yarder ensures Southend's 14-match unbeaten run comes to an end.											
29	A	EXETER		17	L	0-1	0-0		Leonard	Trainer	Bradley	Flavell !	Dunleavy	Phelan	Hoy	Carroll	Bullock	Lawson !	Johnston	
	26/2		*5,995*	*6*	25			*Beer 53*	*Key*	*Templeman*	*Hore*	*Weeks*	*Saxton*	*Hatch*	*Hodge*	*Kellow*	*Robertson*	*Beer*	*Jennings*	
								Ref: D Biddle	Flavell hasn't calmed down from a booking four minutes earlier, when his rash tackle on Jennings sees him walk after only 36 minutes. Beer is left clear from Dunleavy's back-pass to score. Hopes of a Town fightback disappear when Lawson is also sent off after a flare-up with Hodge.											
30	A	HARTLEPOOL		18	L	0-1	0-0		Leonard	Trainer	Loska	McGill*	Dunleavy	Phelan	Hoy	Carroll	Bullock	**Ferguson**	Johnston	Bell
	5/3		*1,651*	*20*	25			*Bielby 65*	*Edgar*	*Creamer*	*Wiggett*	*Elliott**	*Goad*	*Simpkin*	*Scaife*	*McMordie*	*Endean*	*Poskett*	*O'Donnell*	*Bielby*
								Ref: W Johnson	The Town bus gets lost in the centre of Middlesbrough en route, and doesn't reach the ground until just before the 2.30 deadline. The players seem unaffected in the first half, but they lose their way after the break. They fall to a goal from Bielby, who's only been on the field seconds.											
31	H	COLCHESTER			L	1-2	1-1	Lawson 44p	Leonard	Trainer	Loska	Flavell	Dunleavy	Phelan	Hoy	Carroll	Bullock	Lawson	Johnston	
	8/3		2,097		25			*Packer 36, Leslie 88*	*Walker*	*Cook*	*Williams*	*Leslie*	*Smith*	*Dowman*	*Foley*	*Gough*	*Froggatt*	*Packer*	*Dyer*	
								Ref: N Glover	Promotion-chasing Colchester leave it late, but nick both points when Leslie meets Froggatt's cross with a diving header. Froggatt also makes Packer's opener, but Town get back into the game when Walker hauls down Lawson. Town's most effective player nets the resultant penalty.											
32	H	WATFORD		18	D	1-1	1-0	Bullock 33	Leonard	Trainer	Loska	Ferguson	Dunleavy	Phelan	Hoy	Bell	Bullock	Lawson	Johnston	
	12/3		1,902	*9*	26			*Downes 61*	*Rankin*	*Geidmintis*	*Pritchett*	*Bond**	*Horsfield*	*Garner*	*Downes*	*Joslyn*	*Mercer*	*Hayes*	*Jenkins*	*Walsh*
								Ref: R Kirkpatrick	Leonard is the star of the show. He pulls off two amazing saves, the second in the last minute at Joslyn's feet, to deny Watford. Bell draws the keeper before setting up Bullock for Town's goal. But Town give away a silly free-kick, and Leonard is helpless to stop Downes' 20-yarder.											
33	A	SCUNTHORPE		19	L	1-2	1-1	Dunleavy 16	Leonard	Trainer	Loska	Flavell	Dunleavy	Phelan	Carroll	Bell	Bullock	Lawson	Johnston	
	19/3		*2,902*	*17*	26			*Lumby 45, Keeley 79*	*O'Meara*	*Peacock*	*Pilling*	*Oates*	*Wigginton*	*Money*	*Czuczman*	*Kilmore*	*Keeley*	*Lumby*	*Lee*	
								Ref: T Farley	Town are second best to a mediocre Iron side, but now lie only four points clear of safety. Dunleavy shoots high into the net to give Town the lead. Lumby has plenty of time to get the equaliser right on half-time. The home side grab the winner when Keeley's header goes in off the bar.											
34	H	ALDERSHOT		18	W	2-0	0-0	Bullock 75, 79	Leonard	Trainer	Loska	Flavell	Dunleavy	Bradley	Hoy	Carroll	Bullock	Lawson	Johnston*	Bell
	22/3		1,341	*15*	28				*Johnson*	*Howitt*	*Wallace J*	*Crossley*	*Wiltshire*	*Wooler*	*Hilton*	*Morrissey*	*Bell*	*Walton*	*McGregor*	
								Ref: K Ridden	This is a dreary game, and only the result will be remembered. Tom McAnearney's Aldershot are hanging on for a goalless draw, when they are undone twice by Bullock in a four-minute spell. He fires in off Loska's pass for the first, then gets his second with a header at the far post.											

No	Venue	Date	Opponents	Att	Pos	Res	F-A	H-T	Scorers, Times, Referees	1	2	3	4	5	6	7	8	9	10	11	12
35	H	26/3	CREWE	1,589	18 / *12*	W / 30	3-0	1-0	Carroll 20, Hoy 56, Dunleavy 80	Leonard	Trainer	Loska	Flavell	Dunleavy	Bradley	Hoy	Carroll	Bullock	Lawson	Johnston	
										Brand	*Lowry*	*Roberts*	*Lugg*	*Bowles*	*Bevan*	*Humphreys*	*Mayman*	*Purdie*	*Rimmer*	*Tully*	
									Ref: J Wrennall	The Shaymen plough through the mud to gain victory and give hope to the fans that re-election will not be necessary. Carroll strokes home the first, then beats Brand for the second, only to see Hoy touch the ball over the line. Hoy makes the third for Dunleavy, following a short corner.											
36	A	1/4	CAMBRIDGE	*4,376*	18 / *1*	L / 30	**0-4**	0-1		Leonard	Trainer	Loska	Flavell	Dunleavy*	Bradley	Hoy	Carroll	Bullock	Lawson	Johnston	Bell
									Spriggs 33, Hall 55, 75, Finney 72	*Webster*	*Batson*	*Harper*	*Stringer*	*Fallon*	*Howard*	*Watson**	*Spriggs*	*Hall*	*Finney*	*Biley*	*O'Neill*
									Ref: T Bune	Mike Ferguson is recalled to act as manager with Ball and coach Farrimond down with flu. He can't inspire Town against the league-leaders. The game is all but over in the 55th minute when Dunleavy pulls a hamstring. Immediately after he goes off, Hall hooks in his side's second.											
37	A	5/4	HUDDERSFIELD	***7,591***		L / 30	0-1	0-0		Leonard	Trainer	Loska	Flavell	Phelan	Bradley	Hoy	Carroll	Bullock	Lawson	Johnston	
									Smith 90	*Starling*	*Sweeney*	*Oliver*	*Fowler*	*Baines*	*Hart*	*Gray*	*Smith*	*Eccles*	*Johnson*	*Butler*	
									Ref: R Chadwick	A miserable evening. With the wind already spoiling things, five players are booked, and the game is held up for more than a minute with fans fighting on the pitch. The ref is looking at his watch when Steve Smith scores a lucky winner, a skidding cross that hits the far post and goes in.											
38	H	9/4	BARNSLEY	3,529	20 / *4*	L / 30	0-1	0-1		Leonard	Trainer	Loska	Flavell	Phelan	Bradley	Hoy	Carroll*	Bullock	Lawson	Johnston	Bell
									Peachey 1	*Springett*	*Murphy*	*Chambers*	*Pugh*	*Saunders*	*Pickering*	*Warnock*	*Joicey*	*Peachey*	*Millar*	*Brown*	
									Ref: R Capey	Former England Under-23 international keeper Peter Springett will never have an easier time. He only has two saves to make as Town put on a wretched display. Peachey scores in the first minute following a free-kick, and but for their poor finishing, Barnsley could have won by more.											
39	A	12/4	DONCASTER	*4,840*	20	L / 30	0-3	0-1		**Chmilowsky**	Trainer	Loska	Flavell	Phelan	Bradley	Hoy	Bell	Bullock*	Lawson	Johnston	Carroll
									Kitchen 26, Miller 52, Laidlaw 76	*Peacock*	*Brookes*	*Reed*	*Robinson*	*Olney*	*Taylor*	*Miller*	*Snodin*	*O'Callaghan*	*Kitchen*	*Laidlaw*	
									Ref: R Matthewson	Both Leonard, at the last minute, and Gennoe are ruled out, so trialist Chmilowsky makes a shock debut. Trainer Brian Hendy gets him to the ground with just 40 minutes to spare. He is at fault for the first goal, failing to hold Snodin's cross, but he can't take all the blame for defeat.											
40	H	16/4	BRADFORD C	6,402	18 / *2*	W / 32	2-1	1-0	Johnston 31, Bell 73	Leonard	Trainer	Loska	Flavell	Phelan	Bradley	Hoy*	Bell	Bullock	Lawson	Johnston	Carroll
									Watson 57	*Downsboro'*	*Middleton*	*Podd*	*Hall*	*Nicholls*	*Fretwell*	*Watson*	*Dolan*	*Cooke*	*Wright*	*Hutchins*	
									Ref: J Worrall	Bullock opens the scoring, but City level it through Watson's diving header. Bell's first goal for 16 months, however, eases re-election fears. He pounces to beat Downsborough with a low shot into the corner. It sets up a nail-biting finish as promotion-seeking City pile on the pressure.											
41	H	19/4	BRENTFORD	1,464	19	D / 33	0-0	0-0		Leonard	Dunleavy	Loska	Flavell	Phelan	Bradley	Carroll	Bell	Bullock	Lawson	Trainer	
										Priddy	*Fraser*	*Allen*	*Smith*	*Kruse*	*Shrubb*	*Bain*	*McCulloch*	*Glover*	*Carlton*	*Phillips*	
									Ref: A Porter	With injuries and suspensions, Town have to play Trainer in an unaccustomed midfield role. He looks out of place, but Town dig in for a point. Brentford extend their unbeaten run to eight games, but clearly miss 19-goal leading scorer Gordon Sweetzer, and can't do much without him.											
42	A	23/4	SWANSEA	*7,344*	19 / *6*	L / 33	1-2	1-1	Carroll 35	Leonard	Dunleavy	Loska	Flavell	Phelan	Bradley	Carroll	Bell	Bullock	Lawson	Trainer	
									James 22, 83	*Potter*	*Evans*	*Bartley*	*Smith*	*May*	*Bruton*	*Lally*	*James*	*Curtis*	*Charles*	*Chappell*	
									Ref: E Hughes	Harry Griffiths' side have one eye on Division 3, but they are lucky to win this one, though. Carroll scores off Bullock's nod down, but Robbie James' second headed goal gives Town little time to reply. Then Trainer meets a corner, only to see Potter clear the ball with the help of a post.											
43	H	30/4	NEWPORT	**1,299**	20 / *21*	D / 34	0-0	0-0		Leonard	Dunleavy	Loska	Flavell	Phelan	Bradley	Hoy*	Bell	Bullock	Lawson	Johnston	Trainer
										Plumley	*Derrett*	*Bell*	*Emanuel*	*Walker*	*Jones R*	*Preece*	*Woods*	*Clark**	*Relish*	*Byrne*	*Murray*
									Ref: J Hough	A drab, featureless game between two struggling sides. Alan Ball is taunted throughout, and responds by shouting out the names of Northern Premier League clubs to his players. Town may live to regret not winning this one. Newport lie six points behind but have two games in hand.											
44	A	4/5	ALDERSHOT	*2,359*	20	D / 35	0-0	0-0		Leonard	Dunleavy	Loska	Flavell	Phelan	Bradley	Carroll	Johnston	Bullock	Lawson	Trainer	
										Johnson	*Howitt*	*Butler*	*Crosby*	*Wooler*	*Jopling*	*Needham*	*Morrissey*	*Bell*	*Earls*	*McGregor*	
									Ref: R Challice	Ball changes the system and plays Trainer as a sweeper. His ploy works, as Town play out for a draw. It's boring and frustrating for the home fans, and Aldershot boss McAnearney is not happy. But the point is vital for Town, and a content Ball says, 'We came for a draw and got one.'											
45	A	7/5	TORQUAY	*2,574*	20 / *17*	L / 35	2-3	0-1	Trainer 74, Bullock 90	Leonard	Dunleavy	Loska	Flavell	Phelan	Bradley	Carroll	Johnston	Bullock	Bell	Trainer	
									Dunne 27, Vassallo 67, Morrall 89	*Lee T*	*Lynch*	*Sandercock*	*Vassallo*	*Dunne*	*Boulton*	*Morrall*	*Lee C*	*Rudge*	*Brown*	*Twitchin*	
									Ref: J Bente	Town's fate is still in their own hands – just. When Vassallo's shot skids under Leonard, Town go two goals down. Trainer starts a fightback but it's in vain. Morrall's volley is worth going miles to see, but preferably not here. Bullock is sprawled on the deck when he puts the ball in.											
46	H	14/5	SOUTHPORT	1,364	20 / *23*	D / 36	1-1	1-1	Dunleavy 40	Leonard	Dunleavy	Loska	Flavell	Phelan	Bradley	Carroll	Bell	Bullock	Johnston	Trainer	
			Home	Away					*Brookes 21*	*Harrison*	*Higham*	*Snookes*	*O'Neil*	*Brookes*	*Birchall*	*Dewsnip*	*Fisher*	*Jones*	*Smith*	*Wilson*	
Average			2,338	3,912					Ref: G Nolan	Brookes scores against the run of play but Dunleavy gets the equaliser. Two minutes after the break Town have the perfect chance to go ahead. Carroll goes down in the box, but Flavell smashes his penalty against the bar. Failure to win means Town's destiny now depends on Newport.											

League Cup	Att	Pos	Res	F-A	H-T	Scorers, Times, and Referees	1	2	3	4	5	6	7	8	9	10	11	12 sub used
1:1 H DARLINGTON			D	0-0	0-0		Gennoe	Flavell	Kent	McHale	**Trainer**	Phelan	Jones A	Johnston	Bullock	Jones G*	Lawson	Bell
14/8	1,750						*Ogley*	*Nattress*	*Cochrane*	*Crosson*	*Craig*	*Noble*	*Lyons*	*Sinclair*	*Ferguson**	*Rowles*	*Stone*	*Holbrook*
						Ref: A Morrissey	Alan Ball likes a challenge. Now he's got one. Failure to beat Peter Madden's physical Darlington side means Town face an uphill task in the second leg. They look poor up front, but do carve out a couple of chances, not least than when Phelan has a header cleared away by Nattress.											
1:2 A DARLINGTON			D	1-1	1-1	Jones G 14	Gennoe	Flavell	Kent	McHale	Trainer	Phelan	Jones A	Johnston*	Bullock	Jones G	Lawson	Bell
18/8	2,911					*Rowles 23*	*Ogley*	*Nattress*	*Cochrane*	*Crosson*	*Craig*	*Noble*	*Lyons*	*Sinclair*	*Ferguson*	*Rowles*	*Stone*	
						Ref: H Hackney (Halifax drew 1-1 on aggregate)	This improved performance isn't quite enough. George Jones is hero and villain, as he gives Town the lead off namesake Alan's corner, then, late on, puts wide when a goal would surely have clinched it. Eddie Rowles levels things, nipping in to head over Gennoe, also from a corner.											
1R H DARLINGTON		19	L	1-2	1-1	Lawson 44	Gennoe	Flavell	Kent	McHale	Trainer	Rylands	Jones A	McGill*	Jones G	Lawson	Bell	Bullock
30/8	1,818	*16*		*aet*		*Craig 19, 99*	*Owens*	*Nattress*	*Cochrane*	*Crosson*	*Craig*	*Noble*	*Lyons*	*Sinclair*	*Ferguson*	*Rowles**	*Stone*	*Wann*
						Ref: G Nolan	The pressure is on Ball already. Town dominate the game, force 16 corners, score the best goal off a five-man move, but bow out. Derek Craig gets both Darlington's goals, his first a header. His extra-time winner is an untidy affair from eight yards. In a rough game, seven are booked.											

FA Cup	Att	Pos	Res	F-A	H-T	Scorers, Times, and Referees	1	2	3	4	5	6	7	8	9	10	11	12 sub used
1 A STAFFORD		19	D	0-0	0-0		Gennoe	Trainer	Bradley	McGill	Dunleavy	Phelan	Hoy	Carroll	Bullock	Lawson	Johnston	
20/11	4,482	*NPL*					*Arnold*	*Morris*	*Seddon B*	*Sargeant*	*Seddon A*	*Richards*	*Allner*	*Chapman*	*Hardman*	*Lowe*	*Chadwick*	
						Ref: A Morrissey	For the third successive season, these two clubs draw each other. Alan Ball knows it will be tough. Stafford are unbeaten in eight. This one's not a great game. Chadwick hits the bar early on, but there are few other chances. Town give the ball away too much, but are not punished.											
1R H STAFFORD		19	W	1-0	1-0	Phelan 19	Gennoe	Trainer	Loska	McGill	Dunleavy	Phelan	Hoy	Carroll	Bullock	Lawson	Johnston	
23/11	3,877	*NPL*					*Arnold*	*Morris*	*Seddon B*	*Sargeant*	*Seddon A*	*Richards*	*Allner*	*Chapman*	*Hardman*	*Lowe*	*Chadwick*	
						Ref: A Morrissey	Stafford boss Reg Berks is confident his side will win here. Town just about prove him wrong. Phelan's scrappy goal epitomises the rest of the match. He heads in, with Morris desperately trying to clear, after a couple of efforts are blocked. Unhappy Sargeant is booked after the game.											
2 H PRESTON		19	W	1-0	0-0	Lawson 63	Gennoe	Trainer	Loska	McGill	Dunleavy	Phelan	Hoy	Carroll	Bullock	Lawson	Johnston	
14/12	5,219	*3:5*					*Tunks*	*McMahon*	*Williams*	*Burns*	*Sadler*	*Lawrenson*	*Coleman*	*Brown*	*Smith**	*Elwiss*	*Bruce*	*Mitchell*
						Ref: K Baker	A shock result over 3rd Division Preston, who are otherwise going well. It's nailbiting stuff, though, as Town hang on in the last 20 minutes. Lawson's lovely goal comes off a well-rehearsed free-kick. Trainer then clears off the line and Gennoe twice saves at the feet of John Smith.											
3 H LUTON		19	L	0-1	0-1		Gennoe	Trainer	Loska	Bradley	Dunleavy	Phelan	Hoy	Carroll	Bullock*	Lawson	Johnston	Jones G
8/1	5,519	*2:12*				*Aston 22*	*Aleksic*	*Price*	*Buckley*	*Chambers*	*Faulkner*	*Futcher P*	*Husband*	*West*	*Futcher R*	*Fuccillo*	*Aston*	
						Ref: J Yates	England manager Don Revie is in the crowd eyeing up Luton's centre-back Paul Futcher. He is probably not overly impressed with any Town player, but they give their all, anyway. A swift breakaway goal settles the game. Aston scores when Gennoe can't hold Chambers' strong shot.											

		P	W	D	L	F	A	W	D	L	F	A	Pts
			Home					Away					
1	Cambridge	46	16	5	2	57	18	10	8	5	30	22	65
2	Exeter	46	17	5	1	40	13	8	7	8	30	33	62
3	Colchester	46	19	2	2	51	14	6	7	10	26	29	59
4	Bradford C	46	16	7	0	51	18	7	6	10	27	33	59
5	Swansea	46	18	3	2	60	30	7	5	11	32	38	58
6	Barnsley	46	16	5	2	45	18	7	4	12	17	21	55
7	Watford	46	15	7	1	46	13	3	8	12	21	37	51
8	Doncaster	46	16	2	5	47	25	5	7	11	24	40	51
9	Huddersfield	46	15	5	3	36	15	4	7	12	24	34	50
10	Southend	46	11	9	3	35	19	4	10	9	17	26	49
11	Darlington	46	13	5	5	37	25	5	8	10	22	39	49
12	Crewe	46	16	6	1	36	15	3	5	15	11	45	49
13	Bournemouth	46	13	8	2	39	13	2	10	11	15	31	48
14	Stockport	46	10	10	3	29	19	3	9	11	24	38	45
15	Brentford	46	14	3	6	48	27	4	4	15	29	49	43
16	Torquay	46	12	5	6	33	22	5	4	14	26	45	43
17	Aldershot	46	10	8	5	29	19	6	3	14	20	40	43
18	Rochdale	46	8	7	8	32	25	5	5	13	18	34	38
19	Newport	46	11	6	6	33	21	3	4	16	9	37	38
20	Scunthorpe	46	11	6	6	32	24	2	5	16	17	49	37
21	HALIFAX	46	11	6	6	36	18	0	8	15	11	40	36
22	Hartlepool	46	8	9	6	30	20	2	3	18	17	53	32
23	Southport	46	3	12	8	17	28	0	7	16	16	49	25
24	Workington	46	3	7	13	23	42	1	4	18	18	60	19
		1104	302	148	102	922	501	102	148	302	501	922	1104

Odds & ends

Double wins: (0).
Double losses: (6) Barnsley, Bournemouth, Cambridge, Colchester, Exeter, Scunthorpe.

Won from behind: (1) Darlington (h).
Lost from in front: (4) Exeter (h), Crewe (a), Rochdale (a), Scunthorpe (a).

High spots: Two consecutive wins on three occasions.
Scoring six goals against both Doncaster and Workington.
Beating 3rd Division Preston to reach the 3rd Round of the FA Cup.

Low spots: Failing to win any of their first six matches.
Failing to score in four consecutive matches up to 22 January.
Going seven games without a win up to 31January.
Dropping into the re-election zone after completing their fixtures.

Town's 6-0 victory over Doncaster equalled their record League win set in 1955 when they beat Bradford by the same score.

Player of the Year: Jimmy Lawson.
Ever-presents: (0).
Hat-tricks: (0).
Leading scorer: Mickey Bullock (9).

	Appearances						Goals			
	Lge	*Sub*	LC	*Sub*	FAC	*Sub*	**Lge**	LC	FAC	**Tot**
Bell, Derek	**20**	*6*	1	*2*			**2**			**2**
Bradley, Lee	**20**	*5*			2		**1**			**1**
Bullock, Mickey	**40**	*2*	2	*1*	4		**9**			**9**
Carroll, Joe	**35**	*2*			4		**5**			**5**
Chmilowsky, Roman	**1**									
Dunleavy, Chris	**29**				4		**4**			**4**
Ferguson, Mike	**2**									
Flavell, Bobby	**33**		3				**3**			**3**
Gennoe, Terry	**26**		3		4					
Harris, Geoff		*1*								
Hoy, Bobby	**30**				4		**7**			**7**
Johnston, Johnny	**37**	*3*	2		4		**6**			**6**
Jones, Alan	**5**		3							
Jones, George	**8**	*1*	3			*1*	**1**	1		**2**
Kent, Paul	**12**		3							
Lawson, Jimmy	**43**		3		4		**5**	1	1	**7**
Leonard, Mick	**19**									
Loska, Tony	**31**				3					
McCann, Jim	**2**						**1**			**1**
McGill, Jimmy	**20**	*1*	1		3					
McHale, Ray	**4**		3				**2**			**2**
Phelan, Albert	**39**		2		4				1	**1**
Rylands, Dave	**5**		1							
Trainer, Jack	**45**	*1*	3		4		**1**			**1**
24 players used	**506**	***22***	**33**	***3***	**44**	***1***	**47**	**2**	**2**	**51**

No	Date		Opponent	Att	Pos	Pt	F-A	H-T	Scorers, Times, and Referees	1	2	3	4	5	6	7	8	9	10	11	12 sub used
1		A	WIMBLEDON			D	3-3	1-0	Carroll 40, 55, Bell 87	Gennoe	Flavell	Loska	**Smith**	Dunleavy	Bradley	Carroll	Johnston	Bullock	Bell	Horsfall	
	20/8			*4,616*		1			*Bryant 51, Leslie 70, Connell 86*	*Guy*	*Bryant*	*Galvin*	*Donaldson*	*Aitken*	*Davies*	*Galliers*	*Smith*	*Connell*	*Holmes*	*Leslie*	
									Ref: D Smith	Workington have been voted out and Wimbledon join the League. Sport On Two covers a cracking opener. Carroll pounces on Donaldson's poor throw-out to put Town ahead. But with four minutes left, Connell's 25-yarder gives the Dons a 3-2 lead. Then Bell's cross floats in.											
2		H	HARTLEPOOL		2	W	**3-0**	2-0	Carroll 10, Bullock 42, 56	Gennoe	Flavell	Loska	Smith	Dunleavy	Bradley	Carroll	Lawson	Bullock	Bell	Horsfall	
	23/8			1,614		3				*Edgar*	*Malone*	*Wiggett*	*Gibb*	*Ayre*	*Simpkin*	*McMordie*	*Goad*	*Downing*	*Poskett*	*Scaife*	
									Ref: R Bridges	Pool, like Town, were re-elected in the summer. On this showing, boss Billy Horner has got his work cut out to avoid successive bottom-four finishes. Halifax coast to victory after Carroll gets onto the end of Horsfall's flick-on. Bullock's second from 18 yards is his 100th league goal.											
3		H	NORTHAMPTON		6	L	0-1	0-0		Gennoe	Flavell	Loska	Smith	Dunleavy	Bradley	Carroll	Bell	Bullock	Lawson	Horsfall	
	27/8			1,869	*9*	3			*Bryant 72*	*Garnham*	*Tucker*	*Bryant*	*Liddle*	*Robertson*	*Best*	*Farrington*	*Williams*	*Reilly*	*Haywood**	*Christie*	*McGowan*
									Ref: D Owen	John Petts is trying his hand at management, and his Cobblers side brings the Shaymen down to earth with their first win of the season. They could actually have scored long before Bryant's 72nd-minute winner. He blasts in Farrington's corner, with Loska vainly attempting to clear.											
4		A	READING		11	L	1-2	1-1	Carroll 32	Gennoe	Flavell	Loska	Smith	Dunleavy	Bradley	Carroll	Bell	Bullock	Lawson	**Gregoire**	
	3/9			*3,242*	*14*	3			*Earles 39, 90*	*Death*	*Peters*	*Lewis*	*Bowman*	*Hetzke*	*Moreline*	*Earles*	*Murray*	*Nelson*	*Bennett*	*Britten*	
									Ref: D Reeves	The Shaymen take the lead when Gregoire pulls the ball back for Carroll, then Pat Earles equalises. He is later on hand to score the winner and secure Reading's first win of the season. He leaves it late. There are only ten seconds left when he runs in Gary Peters' 25-yard daisy-cutter.											
5		H	CREWE		13	D	1-1	0-1	Flavell 62	Gennoe	Loska	Flavell	Smith	Dunleavy	Bradley	Carroll	Bell	Gregoire	Lawson	Horsfall*	Bullock
	10/9			1,128	*18*	4			*Purdie 16*	*Crudgington*	*Collier*	*Roberts*	*Rimmer*	*Bowles*	*Bevan*	*Davies D*	*Tully*	*Purdie*	*Coyne*	*McGinley*	
									Ref: A Saunders	Crewe come out of a rut. They lost at home at the weekend 4-6 to Brentford, their third straight defeat. They are the better side at the Shay and deserve more than a point. Town's shaky defence is only punished once, then Bullock comes off the bench to help set up Flavell's leveller.											
6		A	DARLINGTON			L	1-2	1-0	Bullock 15	Gennoe	Loska	Flavell	Smith	**Alcock**	Dunleavy	Carroll	Bell	Bullock	Lawson	Gregoire*	Trainer
	13/9			*1,863*		4			*Wann 47, Rowles 67*	*Burleigh*	*Crosson*	*Cochrane*	*Hague*	*Craig*	*Nattress*	*Young**	*Rowles*	*Ferguson*	*Seal*	*Wann*	*Maitland*
									Ref: C Seel	Darlington are bottom of the pile, but Town can't bring an end to their miserable away form. It now stretches 32 games without a win. Bullock beats Burleigh to the ball to give Town the lead, but Lloyd Maitland comes on at half-time and changes the game, making both his side's goals.											
7		A	BOURNEMOUTH		13	D	0-0	0-0		Gennoe	Loska*	Flavell	Smith	Alcock	Dunleavy	Carroll	Bell	Bullock	Lawson	Horsfall	Trainer
	17/9			*3,282*	*18*	5				*Baker*	*Cunningham*	*Butler*	*Miller*	*Phill-Masters*	*Barton*	*Johnson*	*Riley*	*Showers*	*Cave*	*Lennard*	
									Ref: D Hutchinson	John Benson's Cherries side have made a poor start to the season, winning only their first game at the fifth attempt during the week. Former Town star Dave Lennard has since signed for them, and he makes his debut. Gennoe saves Town a point, denying Barton in the last minute.											
8		H	SOUTHEND		17	L	0-1	0-1		Gennoe	Flavell	Loska	Smith	Alcock	Dunleavy	Carroll	Bell	Bullock	Lawson	Horsfall*	Johnston
	24/9			1,537	*1*	5			*Townsend 19*	*Freeman*	*Moody*	*Banks*	*Laverick*	*Townsend*	*Young*	*Morris*	*Goodwin*	*Parker*	*Hadley*	*Foggon*	
									Ref: C Napthine	Although Southend are the league leaders, Town are always in with a chance of a point. Neil Townsend breaks from defence to start and finish the move that gives his side the lead. The Shaymen press hard to avoid defeat, but it's in vain. Alcock marks his home debut by being booked.											
9		H	BARNSLEY			D	1-1	0-1	Carroll 54	Leonard	Loska	Flavell	Smith	Alcock	Dunleavy	Carroll	Bell	Bullock	Lawson	Johnston	
	27/9			2,728		6			*Collier ??*	*Springett*	*Murphy*	*Collins*	*Pugh*	*Saunders*	*McCarthy*	*Warnock*	*Price*	*Wigg*	*Little**	*Collier*	*Joicey*
									Ref: G Nolan	Barnsley are among the early pace-setters, but on home soil Town raise their game. Although Collier scores for the visitors, and Dunleavy later has to head off the line, the Shaymen dominate the second half. Carroll scores a deserved equaliser, albeit with the aid of a wicked deflection.											
10		A	BRENTFORD		22	L	1-4	0-1	Bullock 51	Leonard	Flavell	Loska	Smith	Alcock	Dunleavy	Carroll	Bell	Bullock	Lawson	Trainer	
	1/10			*6,240*	*3*	6			*Phillips 40, 50p, Graham J 85, [Lloyd 88]*	*Bond*	*Fraser*	*Allen*	*Lloyd*	*Salman*	*Shrubb*	*Carlton*	*Graham J*	*Sweetzer*	*McCulloch*	*Phillips*	
									Ref: L Burton	Brentford boss Bill Dodgin is kind to Town. 'I was thankful to get two points. It was just one of those games,' he says afterwards. Phillips gets his first when McCulloch's header comes back off the post. Alcock fouls McCulloch for the penalty. At 1-2, Carroll has a goal ruled offside.											
11		A	ROCHDALE		22	L	1-3	1-1	Alcock 24	Gennoe	Falvell	Bradley	Smith	Alcock	Dunleavy	Carroll	Gregoire	Bullock	Lawson	Trainer	
	4/10			***1,201***	*24*	6			*Owen 16, Melledew 59, 90*	*Shyne*	*Hallows*	*Oliver*	*O'Loughlin*	*Scott*	*Bannon*	*Owen*	*Seddon*	*Melledew*	*Esser*	*Tarbuck*	
									Ref: J Sewell	Town feel they are unlucky to lose as Rochdale record only their second win. Lawson scores off an indirect free-kick given inside the box, but the ref orders a retake. After Alcock equalises, Gregoire hits the post just before half-time. Melledew's first is a cross that floats over Gennoe.											

No		Opponent	Att	Pos	Res	F-A	H-T	Scorers, Times, Referees	1	2	3	4	5	6	7	8	9	10	11	12
12	H	HUDDERSFIELD		23	D	0·0	0·0		Gennoe	Flavell	Bradley	Smith	Alcock	Dunleavy	Carroll	Gregoire	Bullock	Lawson*	Johnston	Bell
8/10			**4,956**	*14*	7				*Taylor*	*Brown*	*Sandercock*	*Hart*	*Baines*	*Sidebottom*	*Armstrong*	*Gray*	*Eccles*	*Johnson*	*Butler**	*McCaffrey*
								Ref: N Ashley	Ball is quite frank. 'I don't know what to do for the best,' he says. Seemingly, neither do his players, as Halifax extend their run to ten games without a win. This is an awful, scrappy derby. Only Huddersfield's Eccles goes close, when his shot almost squeezes through Gennoe's legs.											
13	H	TORQUAY		23	D	0·0	0·0		Gennoe	Flavell	Bradley	Smith	Alcock	Dunleavy	Carroll	Bell	Bullock	Horsfall	Johnston	
15/10			**1,077**	*15*	8				*Lee T*	*Twitchin*	*Parsons*	*Vassallo*	*Green*	*Boulton*	*Tomlin*	*Dunne*	*Lawrence*	*Brown*	*Raper*	
								Ref: D Clarke	'I am helpless sat in the stand,' says Ball, and off he goes to cast his eye over a player at a Central League game. He misses little as Town play out another bore draw. Things could have been worse, and would have been had Gennoe not plucked Willie Brown's late effort out of the air.											
14	A	SOUTHPORT		21	W	2·1	2·1	Horsfall 22, Powell 30	Gennoe	Flavell	Bradley	Smith	Alcock	Dunleavy*	Carroll	Bell	**Powell**	Horsfall	Johnston	Bullock
21/10			*2,225*	*20*	10			*Gay 23*	*Harrison*	*Kisby**	*Snookes*	*O'Neil*	*Brookes*	*Fisher*	*Higham*	*Wilson*	*Ashworth*	*Jones*	*Gay*	*Brookfield*
								Ref: D Turner	On-loan Wayne Powell (Bristol Rovers) is Town's hero. His looping header over Harrison rounds off an eight-minute scoring spree and gives Town their first away win in 36 attempts. Horsfall's opener is the best goal when he dummies his man, then shoots on the turn from 18 yards.											
15	A	SCUNTHORPE		23	L	0·2	0·1		Gennoe	Flavell	Bradley	Smith	Alcock	Dunleavy	Carroll	Bell	Powell	Horsfall*	Johnston	Bullock
29/10			*2,420*	*18*	10			*Lumby 5p, Keeley 54*	*Crawford*	*Czuczman*	*Peacock*	*Kavanagh*	*Money*	*Bridges*	*Oates*	*Kilmore*	*Keeley*	*Lumby*	*Wigg*	
								Ref: G Flint	Scunthorpe take the lead after only five minutes through Lumby's penalty, when Bradley clumsily challenges Kilmore. Three minutes later, the Shaymen get a penalty when Bridges handles on the line, but Carroll blasts wide. The Iron ride their luck, then Keeley prods home the second.											
16	H	DONCASTER		23	L	0·1	0·0		Gennoe	Flavell	Bradley	Smith	Alcock	Dunleavy	Powell	Bell	Bullock	Horsfall	Johnston	
5/11			1,757	*16*	10			*Jones C 75*	*Peacock*	*Robinson*	*Olney*	*Laidlaw*	*Owen*	*Taylor*	*Miller*	*Bowden**	*O'Callaghan*	*Jones C*	*Habbin*	*Snodin*
								Ref: G Owen	The despair on Alan Ball's face says it all. He has a new chairman to try to please in Andrew Delaney, but he is nowhere near solving things on the pitch. Alcock has to clear Habbin's effort off the line before Rovers get their goal. Chris Jones scores it, after Town fail to clear three times.											
17	A	NEWPORT		23	L	0·2	0·2		Gennoe	Flavell	Bradley	Smith	Alcock	Dunleavy	Johnston	Bell	Powell	Laswon	Horsfall	
12/11			*3,992*	*5*	10			*Guscott 15, Woods 30*	*Plumley*	*Derrett*	*Byrne*	*Emmanuel*	*Walker R*	*Aizlewood*	*Walker S*	*Woods**	*Goddard*	*Relish*	*Guscott*	*Williams*
								Ref: A Hamil	Ball has had a two-hour talk with his players and wrongly believes the tide is about to turn. In this rain-affected match, his side is stretched to the full by a useful Newport side. Ray Guscott and Eddie Woods score first-half goals, and only the brilliance of Gennoe keeps the score down.											
18	H	ALDERSHOT		22	W	2·1	1·1	Trainer 26, Flavell 70	Gennoe	Flavell	Loska	Smith	Trainer	Dunleavy	Johnston	Carroll	Bullock	Lawson	Bell	
19/11			1,093	*2*	12			*Crosby 23*	*Rockett*	*Howitt*	*Wooler*	*Crosby*	*Youlden*	*Jopling**	*Hooper*	*Brodie*	*Needham*	*Dungworth*	*McGregor*	*Butler*
								Ref: G Tyson	After admitting his job is on the line, Alan Ball is proved correct by being dismissed. Jimmy Lawson is asked to provisionally take charge. The players respond and dominate the game, despite going behind. Trainer heads the equaliser, then Flavell cracks home the winner off a free-kick.											
19	A	WATFORD		21	D	1·1	1·0	Smith 18	Gennoe	Flavell	Loska	Johnston	Dunleavy	Trainer	Smith	Carroll	Bullock	Lawson	Bell	
3/12			*9,429*	*1*	13			*Garner 73*	*Sherwood*	*Joslyn*	*Prtichett*	*Booth*	*Ellis*	*Garner*	*Downes*	*Mercer*	*Jenkins*	*Bolton*	*Pollard*	
								Ref: R Lewis	Graham Taylor's Watford, the league-leaders, are lucky here. Town, with Lawson now appointed on a permanent basis, take the lead, but then find the ref doing them no favours. The sight of chairman Elton John with Taylor on the touchline is the cue for Garner's scrambled equaliser.											
20	H	SWANSEA		21	W	3·1	0·0	Carroll 51, Bullock 65, May 90 (og)	Gennoe	Flavell	Loska	Johnston	Dunleavy	Trainer	Smith	Carroll	Bullock	Lawson	Bell	
10/12			1,722	*10*	15			*James R 90*	*Barber*	*Evans*	*Bartley*	*Burton*	*May*	*Gray**	*Moore K*	*James R*	*Curtis*	*Moore G*	*Conway*	*Griffiths*
								Ref: T Farley	'Jimmy Lawson is magic,' chant the Shay supporters, as the player-manager leads by example. Swansea are no pushovers, but they are swept aside after the break. Carroll opens the scoring, then later has the shot which May turns into his own net. Gennoe breaks his nose, but plays on.											
21	H	ROCHDALE		18	W	3·1	1·1	Bullock 34, Flavell 76, Johnston 79	Gennoe	Flavell	Loska	Johnston	Dunleavy	Trainer	Smith	Carroll	Bullock	Lawson	Bell	
17/12			1,918	*24*	17			*Scott 4*	*Poole*	*Hallows*	*Green*	*Morrin*	*Scott!*	*Boslem*	*Owen*	*Scaife*	*Melledew*	*O'Loughlin*	*Hoy*	
								Ref: W Butcher	Bobby Hoy signed for Rochdale during the week, and makes his debut against his old club. It's a memorable evening for their defender Bob Scott. He volleys his side in front, then is later sent off for punching Johnston. Flavell scores from the resultant free-kick to put Town in front.											
22	A	GRIMSBY			D	0·0	0·0		Gennoe	Flavell	Loska	Johnston*	Dunleavy	Trainer	Smith	Carroll	Bullock	Lawson	Bell	Bradley
26/12			*6,051*		18				*Wainman*	*Mawer*	*Moore K*	*Waters*	*Barker*	*Hanvey*	*Lester*	*Liddell**	*Donovan*	*Partridge*	*Brolly*	*Drinkell*
								Ref: P Richardson	It's now five matches unbeaten since Lawson took over. They don't have to work too hard to gain a point as John Newman's side don't look as if they want to win. It's a poor game, epitomised by Partridge's last-minute shot that drifts into the stand, to be met with catcalls from the fans.											
23	H	STOCKPORT		19	D	1·1	1·0	Horsfall 44	Gennoe	Flavell	Loska	Smith	Dunleavy	Trainer	Horsfall	Carroll	Bullock	Lawson*	Bell	Bradley
27/12			4,036	*7*	19			*Summerbee 90*	*Rogan*	*Lawler*	*Rutter*	*Fletcher*	*Loadwick*	*Smith*	*Summerbee*	*Halford*	*Park*	*Prudham*	*Massey**	*McBeth*
								Ref: K Redfern	Referee Ken Redfern should have got a new watch for Christmas. He somehow finds five minutes of injury-time, during which Stockport nick a point. Horsfall rises to head in Smith's corner to give Town a lead they look like hanging on to. Until Summerbee stabs in Prudham's cross.											

No	Date		Att	Pos	Pt	F-A	H-T	Scorers, Times, and Referees	1	2	3	4	5	6	7	8	9	10	11	12 sub used
24	A	DONCASTER		19	D	1-1	1-1	Carroll 19	Gennoe	Flavell	Loska	Smith	Dunleavy	Trainer	Horsfall	Carroll	Bullock	Lawson	Bell	
	31/12		*3,918*	*11*	20			*Habbin 27*	*Peacock*	*Olney*	*Wignall*	*Laidlaw*	*Owen*	*Reed*	*Miller*	*Snodin*	*O'Callaghan*	*Habbin*	*Bentley**	*Bowden*
								Ref: A Morrissey	£10, 000 Dick Habbin was signed by Doncaster following his match-winning display in a reserve match for Rotherham at the Shay back in September. He is on hand to head their equaliser playing against Town's first-string. Carroll's rocket-shot gives Town the lead from 18 yards.											
25	H	YORK		17	W	2-0	0-0	Bullock 77, Bell 84	Gennoe	Flavell	Loska	Smith	Dunleavy	Trainer	Horsfall	Carroll	Bullock	Lawson*	Bell	Bradley
	2/1		3,774	*20*	22				*Brown*	*Clements*	*Hutt*	*Scott*	*Topping*	*James*	*Novacki*	*Young !*	*Randall*	*McDonald*	*Staniforth*	
								Ref: G Courtney	The game only goes ahead after eight bulbs in the floodlights are replaced. The ref will report Halifax for their inadequate lighting. York have Tony Young sent off in the 39th minute, but still create chances. Town don't play well, but Bullock scores when the ball comes back off a post.											
26	H	WIMBLEDON		20	L	1-2	1-0	Bullock 10	Gennoe	Flavell	Loska	Smith	Dunleavy	Trainer	Horsfall*	Carroll	Bullock	Lawson	Bell	Bradley
	14/1		2,770	*21*	22			*Bryant 56, Denny 84*	*Guy*	*Bryant*	*Galvin*	*Donaldson*	*Edwards*	*Bassett*	*Galliers*	*Bithell**	*Summerill*	*Parsons*	*Denny*	*Tilley*
								Ref: M Scott	The league's newest club have the newest manager. Dario Gradi replaced Allen Batsford only three days ago. He gets off to a winning start as Lawson's eight-match unbeaten run comes to an end. Bullock swivels to put Town ahead, but Denny pounces to give a poor Dons side victory.											
27	A	HARTLEPOOL		20	D	1-1	0-0	Alcock 64	Gennoe	Flavell	Loska	Johnston	Dunleavy	Alcock	**Firth**	Carroll	Bullock	Lawson	Bell	
	7/2		*3,475*	*23*	23			*Downing 63*	*Edgar*	*Malone*	*Downing*	*Gibb*	*Ayre*	*Smith G*	*Creamer*	*McMordie*	*Newton*	*Foggon*	*Bielby*	
								Ref: A Jenkins	Town return to action after having three games postponed. Hartlepool are lying next to bottom and sold Malcolm Poskett to Brighton last week for a record £65,000. Downing gives them the lead, and the crowd are still applauding when Alcock's header off Loska's free-kick powers in.											
28	A	SOUTHEND		20	L	**0-5**	0-3	*[Polycarpou]*	Gennoe	Flavell	Loska	Johnston	Dunleavy	Alcock	Firth	Carroll	Bullock	Lawson	Bell*	Smith
	17/2		*6,128*	*2*	23			*Morris, Moody, Laverick (2),*	*Burridge*	*Banks*	*Yates*	*Laverick*	*Hadley*	*Moody*	*Morris*	*Pountney*	*Parker*	*Abbott*	*Polycarpou*	
								Ref: M Taylor	Terry Venables' Crystal Palace have offered Town £25,000 for keeper Terry Gennoe. Town are considering it when Southend put five goals past him. In the crowd is Southampton boss Lawrie McMenemy. Despite the scoreline, Gennoe impresses and goes to the Dell – for £30,000.											
29	A	CREWE		19	D	0-0	0-0		Leonard	Flavell	Loska	Johnston	Dunleavy	Trainer	Firth	Smith	Bullock	Lawson	Bell	
	22/2		*1,462*	*18*	24				*Crudgington*	*Bevan*	*Roberts*	*Lugg*	*Bowles*	*Rimmer*	*Davies D*	*Cheetham*	*Purdie*	*Coyne**	*Tully*	*Spence*
								Ref: A McDonald	Crewe haven't won at home since 5 November. Over the 90 minutes, they are second best, but both sides have great chances. On a very heavy pitch Jimmy Lawson has to clear two shots off the line, whilst at the other end Bell races away, only to put his shot onto the inside of the post.											
30	H	BRENTFORD		19	D	1-1	1-1	Smith 13	Leonard	Flavell	Loska	Johnston	Dunleavy	Trainer	Firth	Smith	Bullock	Lawson*	Bell	Carroll
	25/2		1,764	*8*	25			*Carlton 1*	*Bond*	*Salman*	*Tucker*	*Shrubb*	*Kruse*	*Carlton*	*Graham W*	*Sweetzer*	*Allder*	*McCulloch*	*Phillips*	
								Ref: P Willis	David Carlton scores a bizarre first-minute goal when Trainer's attempted clearance ricochets off his nose. It's Brentford's 52nd goal of the season. Smith is on hand to equalise, but in the 52nd minute Johnston has his penalty saved by Len Bond following Salman's push on Bullock.											
31	H	BOURNEMOUTH		19	D	0-0	0-0		Leonard	Flavell	Loska	Johnston	Dunleavy	Trainer	Firth	Carroll	Bullock	Lawson	Bell	
	28/2		1,632	*14*	26				*Baker*	*Cunningham*	*Miller*	*Impey*	*Brown*	*Butler*	*Paterson*	*Showers*	*Finnigan**	*Shanahan*	*Riley*	*Wallbridge*
								Ref: K McNally	Bournemouth's Mick Cave has gone to seek fame and fortune in the States. This fixture doesn't promise many goals, and in the end doesn't deliver any. Town only manage two shots on goal. Bell's last-minute effort has Baker saving at full stretch, the game's most exciting moment.											
32	A	HUDDERSFIELD		20	D	2-2	1-2	Trainer 23, Dunleavy 86	Leonard	Flavell	Loska	Johnston	Dunleavy	Trainer	Firth	Carroll	Bullock	Lawson	Bell	
	4/3		*6,571*	*10*	27			*Johnson 19p, 44*	*Starling*	*Banagan*	*Sandercock*	*Armstrong*	*Baines*	*Sidebottom*	*Butler*	*Hart*	*Mountford*	*Johnson*	*Gray*	
								Ref: J Worrall	The powerful sun makes life difficult for Leonard in the first half, but dies down after half-time. Kevin Johnson twice puts the Terriers in front, off a penalty for hands on the line by Flavell and a free-kick. Dunleavy preserves local pride, hammering home when Starling spills Bell's shot.											
33	H	DARLINGTON			L	0-2	0-1		Leonard	Bradley	Loska	Johnston	Dunleavy	Trainer	Flavell	Carroll	Bullock	Lawson*	Bell	Firth
	7/3		1,619		27			*Young 26, Lyons 67p*	*Burleigh*	*Crosson*	*Cochrane*	*Hague*	*Craig*	*Stone*	*Young*	*Maitland*	*Lyons*	*Ferguson*	*Seal*	
								Ref: G Flint	Town fans with short memories tell the Town player-boss, 'You're rubbish, Lawson.' Halifax fall to a side that has lost its last three matches. Controversy surrounds the award of Lyons' twice-taken penalty. It's given for a foul on Ferguson by Leonard, who had already caught the ball.											
34	A	TORQUAY		21	D	2-2	0-1	Carroll 58, Mountford 60	Leonard	Trainer	Loska	Johnston	**Burke**	Dunleavy	Firth	Carroll	**Mountford**	Flavell	Bradley	
	11/3		*2,948*	*11*	28			*Twitchin 7, Brown 85*	*Lee T*	*Twitchin*	*Parsons*	*Raper*	*Green*	*Darke**	*Tomlin*	*Cooper*	*Dunne*	*Brown*	*Coffill*	*Boulton*
								Ref: D Nippard	Lawson has his side more organised. Torquay include recent £5,000-buy Peter Coffill (Watford). Loska is booked for protesting about the free-kick award that leads to Twitchin's 25-yarder. Carroll equalises, then Mountford, on his debut, blasts in for 2-1. But victory is denied Town.											

No		Opponent	Att	Pos	Res	F-A	H-T	Scorers, Times, and Referees	1	2	3	4	5	6	7	8	9	10	11	subs used
35	A	NORTHAMPTON		18	W	2-1	1-0	Mountford 18, Bell 70	Leonard	Bradley	Loska	Johnston	Burke	Dunleavy	Smith	Carroll	Mountford	Flavell	Bell	
	14/3		*2,278*	*17*	30			*Farrington 48*	*Jayes*	*Geidminits*	*Mead**	*Best*	*Robertson*	*Bryant*	*Farrington*	*Liddle*	*Hall*	*Reilly*	*Christie*	*Martin*
								Ref: T Reynolds	Town's best performances seem to be coming away from home. This is a re-election battle, and Town's win is crucial. Mountford heads them in front off Bradley's corner. The home side come back strongly after the break, but, after Farrington's equaliser, Bell glances in the winner.											
36	H	SOUTHPORT		17	W	2-1	2-1	Flavell 16, Smith 21	Leonard	Bradley	Loska	Johnston	Burke	Dunleavy	Smith	Carroll	Mountford	Flavell	Bell	
	18/3		1,680	*23*	32			*Cooper 44*	*Cumbes*	*Kisby*	*Snookes*	*O'Neil*	*Brookes*	*Fisher*	*Hilton*	*Wilson*	*Howarth*	*Cooper*	*Gay*	
								Ref: A Hamil	Southport, under player-boss Hugh Fisher (ex-Southampton), have only won three games all season. Lawson pleads with the fans to be patient. Though far from convincing, Town get two more vital points. Smith ghosts in to flick home their second to put the game beyond the visitors.											
37	A	STOCKPORT		16	W	3-1	1-0	Bell 13, 79, Mountford 88	Leonard	Trainer	Bradley	Smith	Burke	Dunleavy	Firth	Johnston	Mountford	Lawson	Bell	
	25/3		*2,168*	*11*	34			*Fletcher 90*	*Rogan**	*Smith*	*Rutter*	*Thompson*	*Fogarty*	*Massey*	*Jackson*	*Halford*	*Fletcher*	*Park*	*Howard*	*Lawler*
								Ref: G Courtney	A monsoon-type burst of rain just before kick-off leaves the pitch resembling a paddy field. Bell revels in it, though, and is in irresistible form. In the 62nd minute, County lose keeper Rogan with a leg injury. Former Liverpool defender Chris Lawler takes his place, but lets in two goals.											
38	H	GRIMSBY			D	0-0	0-0		Leonard	Trainer	Bradley	Smith	Burke	Dunleavy	Firth	Johnston	Mountford	Lawson	Bell	
	27/3		2,481		35				*Wainman*	*Waters*	*Booth*	*Lester*	*Barker**	*Hanvey*	*Ford*	*Liddell*	*Donovan*	*Moore K*	*Brolly*	*Drinkell*
								Ref: W Johnson	Halifax Town have asked for volunteers to help prepare the pitch that is about to stage two games in two days. This game is scrappy, with only a few chances. Donovan hits the bar just before half-time. In the 80th minute, Burke is celebrating, but the ref rules out his goal for obstruction.											
39	H	SCUNTHORPE			D	2-2	1-0	Burke 36, Bell 50	Leonard	Trainer !	Bradley	Smith	Burke	Dunleavy	Firth	Flavell	Mountford	Lawson	Bell	
	28/3		2,215		36			*Lumby 51p, Grimes 81*	*Crawford*	*O'Donnell*	*Pilling*	*Oates*	*Deere*	*Czuczman*	*Grimes*	*Kilmore*	*Keeley*	*Lumby*	*Wigg*	
								Ref: K Walmsley	The ref feels the wrath of the partisan Shay supporters after this game. Within a minute of Town going 2-0 up, he awards the visitors a dubious penalty when Wigg takes a tumble. On the hour, he sends off Trainer for an ordinary-looking foul on Kilmore, and Scunthorpe take advantage.											
40	A	YORK		15	D	1-1	1-0	Bell 15	Leonard	Bradley	Loska	Smith	Burke	Dunleavy	Firth	Flavell	Mountford	Lawson	Bell	
	31/3		*1,526*	*21*	37			*Novacki 89*	*Brown*	*Clements*	*Hutt*	*Scott*	*Topping*	*Bainbridge*	*Novacki*	*Hunter*	*Randall*	*McDonald**	*Staniforth*	*Taylor*
								Ref: D Chadwick	'The lads realise the position and know that it is a very tight situation,' says Lawson before the visit to Bootham Crescent. His side look to be heading for a smash and grab win after Bell's cool finish. Town hold out until 100 seconds from the end when Novacki stabs the ball home.											
41	A	BARNSLEY		15	L	2-3	0-2	Bullock 76, Lawson 83p	Leonard	Bradley	Loska	Smith	Burke	Trainer	Firth	Flavell	Bullock	Lawson	Bell	
	4/4		*6,150*	*5*	37			*Joicey 20p, Prendergast 35, Warnock 88*	*Springett*	*Murphy*	*Collins**	*Pugh*	*Saunders*	*McCarthy*	*Warnock*	*Prendergast*	*Joicey*	*Little*	*Millar*	*Nixon*
								Ref: N Midgley	Lawson's penalty which levels the score, given for handball against Murphy on the line, is more clearcut that Joicey's which opens the scoring. Bullock claims the ball hit his knee, but the ref reckons it was his hand. Town's fightback looks complete, until Warnock prods in the winner.											
42	H	NEWPORT		14	W	3-1	0-0	Lawson 53, 77, Dunleavy 72	Leonard	Trainer	Loska	Smith	Burke	Dunleavy	Firth	Flavell	Bullock	Lawson	Bell	
	8/4		1,653	*11*	39			*Goddard 80p*	*Turner*	*Steel*	*Relish*	*Emanuel*	*Walker R*	*Aizlewood*	*Guscott**	*Goddard*	*Clark*	*McLaughlin*	*Williams*	*Jones*
								Ref: G Nolan	Both trainers are called into action when ball-boy Paul Berry is hit in the face by the ball and the ref slips on the speedway track when going to his aid. Lawson's second goal is the highlight of the season. He kills the ball on his chest, slips his marker, beats two men, then fires home.											
43	A	ALDERSHOT		16	D	0-0	0-0		Leonard	Trainer	Loska	Smith	Burke	Dunleavy	Firth	Flavell	Bullock	Lawson	Bell	
	15/4		*3,727*	*5*	40				*Johnson*	*Dixon*	*Wooler*	*Crosby*	*Youlden*	*Jopling*	*Longhorn*	*Brodie*	*Needham*	*Dungworth*	*McGregor*	
								Ref: A Glasson	John Dungworth, 19 goals to his credit, is kept under wraps by the Town defence, as Halifax become the first team to prevent Aldershot from scoring at home. Town are slow-handclapped, but it's they who almost score when Flavell hits the post and Bell fires the rebound over the bar.											
44	H	READING			L	2-4	2-2	Smith 10, Bell 18	Leonard	Trainer	Loska	Smith	Burke	Dunleavy*	Firth	Flavell	Mountford	Lawson	Bell	Bullock
	18/4		1,632		40			*Lewis 23, Earles 41p, 50, Kearney 73*	*Turner*	*Peters*	*White*	*Bowman*	*Hicks*	*Bennett*	*Earles*	*Kearney*	*Nelson*	*Lewis*	*Davies*	
								Ref: A Hughes	Halifax race into a two-goal lead, then Dunleavy is caught in the face by Nelson's boot. Before sub Bullock can get on, Lewis pulls one back. Flavell uses his hand when smothering the ball to concede the penalty. Pat Earles' second, following a corner, swings the game Reading's way.											
45	H	WATFORD		18	D	1-1	1-1	Bell 45	Leonard	Bradley*	Loska	Smith	Burke	Trainer	Firth	Flavell	Mountford	Lawson	Bell	Bullock
	22/4		3,542	*1*	41			*How 15*	*Rankin*	*How*	*Pritchett*	*Booth*	*McClenaghan*	*Garner*	*Downes*	*Mayes*	*Mercer*	*Joslyn**	*Bond*	*Blissett*
								Ref: R Perkin	Watford chairman Elton John returns from the USA, via Paris, to see this brutal Shay encounter. Burke, Lawson and Bradley all receive facial injuries. Graham Taylor's side have long been crowned champions. Bell's acrobatic bicycle-kick gains the point that ensures Town's safety.											
46	A	SWANSEA		20	L	0-2	0-0		Leonard	Bradley	Loska	Smith	Burke	Trainer	Firth	Flavell	Mountford	Lawson	Bell	
	29/4		***16,130***	*3*	41			*Toshack 68, Curtis 86*	*Barber*	*Evans*	*Morris*	*Bruton*	*May*	*Bartley*	*Moore K*	*James R*	*Curtis*	*Toshack*	*Charles*	
	Home		Away					Ref: M Baker	Ex-Liverpool star John Toshack, who took over at Swansea in February, guides his side into Division 3 with this win. But in the first half, it's Town who look promotion contenders. Toshack's deflected shot, however, followed by Curtis's 33rd goal, means Swansea's party can begin.											
Average	2,182		4,393																	

LEAGUE DIVISION 4 (CUP-TIES) Manager: Ball ⇨ Jimmy Lawson SEASON 1977-78

League Cup					F-A	H-T	Scorers, Times, and Referees	1	2	3	4	5	6	7	8	9	10	11	12 sub used
1:1	A	ROCHDALE		D	1-1	0-0	Horsfall 56	Leonard	Trainer	Loska	Bradley	Dunleavy	Johnston	Carroll	Flavell	Bullock	Lawson !	**Horsfall**	
13/8			*1,512*				*Tarbuck 90*	*Poole*	*Hallows**	*O'Loughlin*	*Morrin*	*Scott*	*Bannon*	*Melledew*	*Seddon*	*Mountford*	*Esser !*	*Tarbuck*	*Boslem*
							Ref: J Hough	Rochdale's Seddon goes to hospital for treatment to a head injury after three minutes. He returns in the 47th minute. Both sides have had a player sent off for fighting. Town go in front, but Dale equalise when Leonard punches the ball into Tarbuck's face, only to see it rebound in.											
1:2	H	ROCHDALE		L	1-2	0-1	Lawson 85	Leonard	Trainer	Loska	Bradley*	Dunleavy	Johnston	Carroll	Flavell	Bullock	Lawson	Horsfall	Bell
16/8			1,784				*Esser 18, Mountford 47*	*Poole*	*Hallows*	*O'Loughlin*	*Morrin*	*Scott*	*Bannon*	*Melledew*	*Seddon*	*Mountford*	*Esser*	*Tarbuck*	
							Ref: P Richardson (Halifax lost 2-3 on aggregate)	It's a disappointing Shay start. Esser, sent off on Saturday, races in to put the visitors in front. Just after half-time, Mountford ghosts in to head a simple goal. Lawson, also sent off on Saturday, pulls one back with a shot that goes in off the underside of the bar. But the Shaymen go out.											

FA Cup																			
1	A	CHESTERFIELD	22		0-1	0-0		Gennoe	Flavell	Loska	Johnston	Dunleavy	Trainer	Smith	Carroll	Bullock	Lawson	Bell	
26/11			*4,948 3:15*				*Fern*	*Tingay*	*Badger*	*Burton*	*Kowalski*	*Cottam*	*O'Neill*	*Cammack*	*Fern*	*Simpson*	*Tartt*	*Heppolette*	
								Town battle but never look like winning this tie. They don't win their first corner until the 85th minute. Rodney Fern, who played in the 1969 Cup Final for Leicester, settles the game with a piece of magic. Receiving the ball with his back to goal, he turns, then scores from 25 yards.											

		Home					Away					
	P	W	D	L	F	A	W	D	L	F	A	Pts
1 Watford	46	18	4	1	44	14	12	7	4	41	24	71
2 Southend	46	15	5	3	46	18	10	5	8	20	21	60
3 Swansea	46	16	5	2	54	17	7	5	11	33	30	56
4 Brentford	46	15	6	2	50	17	6	8	9	36	37	56
5 Aldershot	46	15	8	0	45	16	4	8	11	22	31	54
6 Grimsby	46	14	6	3	30	15	7	5	11	27	36	53
7 Barnsley	46	15	4	4	44	20	3	10	10	17	29	50
8 Reading	46	12	7	4	33	23	6	7	10	22	29	50
9 Torquay	46	12	6	5	43	25	4	9	10	14	31	47
10 Northampton	46	9	8	6	32	30	8	5	10	31	38	47
11 Huddersfield	46	13	5	5	41	21	2	10	11	22	34	45
12 Doncaster	46	11	8	4	37	26	3	9	11	15	39	45
13 Wimbledon	46	8	11	4	39	26	6	5	12	27	41	44
14 Scunthorpe	46	12	6	5	31	14	2	10	11	19	41	44
15 Crewe	46	11	8	4	34	25	4	6	13	16	44	44
16 Newport	46	14	6	3	43	22	2	5	16	22	51	43
17 Bournemouth	46	12	6	5	28	20	2	9	12	13	31	43
18 Stockport	46	14	4	5	41	19	2	6	15	15	37	42
19 Darlington	46	10	8	5	31	22	4	5	14	21	37	41
20 HALIFAX	46	7	10	6	28	23	3	11	9	24	39	41
21 Hartlepool	46	12	4	7	34	29	3	3	17	17	55	37
22 York	46	8	7	8	27	31	4	5	14	23	38	36
23 Southport	46	5	13	5	30	32	1	6	16	22	44	31
24 Rochdale	46	8	6	9	29	28	0	2	21	14	57	24
	1104	286	161	105	894	533	105	161	286	533	894	1104

Odds & ends

Double wins: (1) Southport.
Double losses: (3) Darlington, Reading, Southend.

Won from behind: (2) Aldershot (h), Rochdale (h).
Lost from in front: (4) Reading (h & a), Wimbledon (h), Darlington (a).

High spots: Eight games unbeaten up to 2 January.
Two consecutive wins in December.
Drawing twice with eventual champions Watford.

Low spots: Eleven games without a win up to 15 October.
Nine games without a win up to 11 March.
Losing 0-5 at Southend.

Player of the Year: Derek Bell.
Ever-presents: (0).
Hat-tricks: (0).
Leading scorers: Derek Bell & Mickey Bullock (9).

	Appearances						Goals			
	Lge	*Sub*	LC	*Sub*	FAC	*Sub*	**Lge**	LC	FAC	**Tot**
Alcock, Terry	**14**						**2**			**2**
Bell, Derek	**43**	*1*		*1*	1		**9**			**9**
Bradley, Lee	**23**	*4*	2							
Bullock, Mickey	**32**	*5*	2		1		**9**			**9**
Burke, Peter	**13**						**1**			**1**
Carroll, Joe	**32**	*1*	2		1		**8**			**8**
Dunleavy, Chris	**43**		2		1		**2**			**2**
Firth, Francis	**17**	*1*								
Flavell, Bobby	**44**		2		1		**4**			**4**
Gennoe, Terry	**26**				1					
Gregoire, Roland	**5**									
Horsfall, Tommy	**15**	*1*	2				**2**	1		**3**
Johnston, Johnny	**25**	*1*	2		1		**1**			**1**
Lawson, Jimmy	**38**		2		1		**3**	1		**4**
Leonard, Mick	**20**		2							
Loska, Tony	**36**		2		1					
Mountford, Bob	**10**						**3**			**3**
Powell, Wayne	**4**						**1**			**1**
Smith, Steve	**40**	*1*			1		**4**			**4**
Trainer, Jack	**26**	*3*	2		1		**2**			**2**
(own-goals)							**1**			**1**
20 players used	**506**	***18***	**22**	***1***	**11**		**52**	**2**		**54**

No	Date	Opponent	Att	Pos	Pt	F-A	H-T	Scorers, Times, and Referees	1	2	3	4	5	6	7	8	9	10	11	12 sub used
1	A	BARNSLEY			L	2-4	0-1	Burke 51, Bell 60	Leonard	Trainer	Loska	Smith	Burke	Dunleavy	Nixon	Johnston	Bullock	Lawson	Bell	
	19/8		*5,634*		0			*Joicey 27, 87, 90, Little 72*	*Springett*	*Collins*	*Chambers*	*Pugh*	*Saunders*	*McCarthy*	*Little*	*Clarke*	*Joicey*	*Millar**	*Peachey*	*Riley*
								Ref: K Butcher	The ref awards Barnsley a controversial penalty for pushing and Joicey follows up when Leonard saves his original shot. However, Town take a deserved lead in the second half. With three minutes left a draw looks likely, then Joicey volleys home and the game slips away from Town.											
2	H	STOCKPORT			W	2-1	0-1	Bell 46, Bullock 83	Leonard	Trainer	Loska	Smith	Burke	Dunleavy	Nixon	Johnston	Bullock	Lawson	Bell	
	22/8		2,253		2			*Lee 34*	*Rogan*	*Thorpe*	*Rutter*	*Thompson*	*Park*	*Fogarty*	*Summerbee*	*Goodfellow**	*Bradd*	*Loadwick*	*Lee*	*Halford*
								Ref: B Martin	Bullock's headed winner should provide Town with some confidence, even if the performance doesn't. Stockport are the better side, and Stuart Lee has already hit the bar before he pounces to open the scoring. Smith catches the visitors cold, and sets up Bell ten seconds after the break.											
3	H	GRIMSBY		17	L	1-2	1-1	Bullock 39	Leonard	Trainer	**Hutt**	Smith	Burke	Dunleavy	Nixon	Johnston	Bullock	Lawson	Bell	
	26/8		2,055	*6*	2			*Donovan 36, Ford 60*	*Batch*	*Mawer*	*Moore K*	*Waters*	*Barker*	*Crombie*	*Ford*	*Donovan*	*Lester*	*Mitchell*	*Brolly*	
								Ref: K Redfern	Town create few chances, and the signs are looking ominous already. Nixon's terrible back-pass lets in Donovan for Grimsby's first. Bullock's sharp reply is his third headed goal so far. Ford makes and scores his side's winning goal after he runs 40 yards unchallenged with the ball.											
4	A	ALDERSHOT		19	L	0-1	0-0		Leonard	Trainer	Hutt	Smith	Burke	Dunleavy	Nixon	Johnson	Bullock	Lawson	Bell	
	2/9		*2,884*	*6*	2			*Edwards 90*	*Johnson*	*Edwards*	*Wooler*	*Dixon*	*Youlden*	*Jopling*	*Longhorn*	*Brodie*	*Needham*	*Dungworth*	*McGregor*	
								Ref: B Hill	Mick Leonard puts on a wonder show to keep Aldershot at bay. Even the Shots manager Tom McAnearney is full of praise for him. It looks as if he has earned his side a point, until Nigel Edwards powers in a header off McGregor's curling free-kick as the match moves into injury-time.											
5	A	TORQUAY		22	L	0-2	0-1		Leonard	Trainer	Hutt	Smith	Burke	Dunleavy	Firth	Johnston	Bullock	Lawson	Bell	
	9/9		*2,048*	*15*	2			*Lawrence 34, 88*	*Turner*	*Twitchin*	*Darke*	*Davies*	*Green*	*Dunn*	*Wilson*	*Lawrence*	*Cooper*	*Murphy*	*Raper*	
								Ref: W Bombroff	It's now Town's worst start in twelve seasons. They create few openings, then Trainer is guilty of missing an open goal in the 53rd minute. Les Lawrence gets both the goals for the Gulls, his first a soaring header, his second, a cool finish after slipping Trainer. Cooper also hits the bar.											
6	H	YORK			L	0-1	0-0		Leonard	Trainer	Hutt	Smith	Burke	Dunleavy	Firth	Johnson	Mountford	Lawson	Bell*	Bullock
	12/9		1,701		2			*Randall 49*	*Needham*	*Scott*	*Kay*	*Stronach*	*Bainbridge*	*Clements*	*Young*	*Randall*	*Loggie*	*McDonald*	*Staniforth*	
								Ref: J Hough	Halifax will be beaten by better teams than Charlie Wright's York. Lawson can point to a 12th-minute injury to Bell that disrupts his side, but the plain fact is, they aren't good enough. Stronach resists three challenges before starting the move that leads to Kevin Randall heading home.											
7	H	DARLINGTON		23	L	0-2	0-0		Leonard	Bradley	Loska	Johnston	Burke	Dunleavy	Firth	Mountford	Bullock*	Johnson	Nixon	Carroll
	16/9		1,203	*17*	2			*Stone 54, Seal 67*	*Burleigh*	*Nattress*	*Cochrane*	*Hague*	*Craig*	*Stone*	*Maitland*	*Probert*	*Ferguson*	*Seal*	*Wann*	
								Ref: D Clarke	Lawson leaves himself out to see where things are going wrong. Johnson goes close in a goalless first half, but inevitably, it's the visitors who break the deadlock. Stone prods in skipper Wann's free-kick, and Seal doubles the lead following a corner. The gate drops alarmingly by 498.											
8	A	HARTLEPOOL		23	L	1-3	0-0	Lawson 53	Leonard	Bradley	Loska	Trainer	Dunleavy	Johnson	Firth	Carroll	Bullock	Lawson	Bell !	
	23/9		*3,947*	*7*	2			*Houchen 46, Newton 47p, Goldthorpe 88*	*Platt*	*Smith G*	*Gorry*	*Hogan*	*Brookes*	*Ayre*	*Linacre*	*Goldthorpe*	*Newton*	*Houchen**	*Lawrence*	*Crumplin*
								Ref: R Chadwick	Town look more dangerous when reduced to ten men. Bell goes on the hour for a second bookable offence. Pool get two in as many minutes just after the break, the second Newton's penalty after Trainer brings him down. Town go close on several occasions until Goldthorpe strikes.											
9	A	BRADFORD C		24	L	0-3	0-0		Leonard	Bradley	Loska	Trainer	Dunleavy	Johnson	Firth	Carroll	Bullock	Lawson	Johnston*	**Kennedy**
	27/9		*4,115*	*14*	2			*Baines 63, Cooke 79, Jackson D 89*	*Downsboro'*	*Podd*	*Watson*	*Bates*	*Baines*	*Middleton*	*Johnson*	*Jackson D*	*Cooke*	*Szabo*	*McNiven*	
								Ref: N Midgley	Town hit rock bottom, and the gifts they hand out have City thinking Christmas has come early. Trainer gives away a silly corner, and Baines scores. Cooke makes it 2-0 when Leonard fluffs a goal-kick, and Jackson completes the rout, hammering home with Town all over the place.											
10	H	CREWE		23	D	0-0	0-0		Leonard	Bradley	Loska	Trainer	Dunleavy	Johnson	Firth	Carroll	Mountford	Lawson	Bell	
	30/9		**985**	*20*	3				*Caswell*	*Bevan*	*Roberts*	*Rimmer*	*Bowles*	*Wilshaw*	*Davies*	*Purdie*	*Nelson*	*Tully*	*Robertson*	
								Ref: F Jenkins	The Shaymen pick up their first points in eight games. Crewe have former Scotland international Jimmy Robertson in their side, but he won't have played in front of a lower crowd. The local paper runs its own 'Spot the crowd'. Johnson goes close, but Bowles scrambles the ball away.											
11	A	ROCHDALE		23	D	1-1	1-0	Bell 32	Leonard	Bradley	Loska	Johnson	Burke	Dunleavy	Firth	Carroll	Mountford*	Lawson	Bell	Smith
	7/10		*1,579*	*24*	4			*Hoy 65*	*Felgate*	*Hallows*	*Snookes*	*Hart*	*Scott*	*Scaife*	*Owen*	*Hoy*	*Esser*	*Mullington**	*O'Loughlin*	*Hilditch*
								Ref: D Shaw	Rochdale, under former Town player Mike Ferguson, are still looking for their first win. Town have the upper hand when Bell scores out of the blue, his 23-yard shot hitting both posts before going in. But ex-Shaymen Scaife and Hoy combine for the latter to steer the ball past Leonard.											

No	Venue / Date	Opponent / Att	Div / Pos	Res / Pts	FT	HT	Scorers, Times, and Referees	1	2	3	4	5	6	7	8	9	10	11	subs used
12	H	PORT VALE	24	L	**0-3**	0-1		Leonard	Bradley	Loska	Smith	Burke	Dunleavy	Firth	Johnson	Mountford	Kennedy	Bell	
	14/10	1,591	*13*	4			*Wright 37, 58, Tully 69*	*Connaughton*	*Keenan*	*Bentley*	*Ridley*	*Sproson*	*Hawkins*	*Sutcliffe*	*Todd*	*Wright*	*Chamberlain*	*Healy**	*Tully*
							Ref: A Morrissey	Port Vale have not won for five games. They stroll to victory here, though. Leonard has to make his first notable save in the very first minute. Wright's opener comes as no surprise. Dunleavy and Loska miss the ball when he gets his second. Tully was here a fortnight ago with Crewe.											
13	A	WIGAN	24	L	0-1	0-1		Leonard	Hutt	Loska	Smith	Burke	Dunleavy	Firth	Carroll	Bullock	Lawson	Johnson	
	18/10	*5,216*		4			*Hinnigan 6*	*Brown*	*Smart*	*Hinnigan*	*Gore*	*Ward*	*Fretwell*	*Corrigan*	*Wright*	*Moore**	*Brownbill*	*Purdie*	*Houghton*
							Ref: D Lloyd	The league's newest club, elected in the summer, didn't record their first win until their sixth match. Alan McNeill's side have started to pick up now, and look for all the world stronger than Town do. Hinnigan's early vicious 15-yarder is enough, as Halifax have four players booked.											
14	A	PORTSMOUTH	24	L	1-3	0-1	Firth 47	Leonard	Trainer	Loska	Smith	Burke	Dunleavy	Carroll	Johnson	Bullock	Lawson*	Bell	Firth
	21/10	***12,365***	*5*	4			*Garwood 12, 85p, Denyer 76*	*Mellor*	*Ellis*	*Viney*	*Denyer*	*Foster*	*Piper*	*Hemmerman**	*Lathan*	*Garwood*	*McIlwraith*	*Pullar*	*Davey*
							Ref: L Burden	Pompey legend Jimmy Dickinson took his beloved side into Division 4 last season. They prove too strong for Town, although Firth does score the best goal of the game, running away to chip Mellor. Denyer restores Pompey's lead. Trainer up-ends Jimmy McIlwraith for the penalty.											
15	H	BOURNEMOUTH	24	L	0-2	0-1		Leonard	Hutt	Loska	Smith	Trainer	Dunleavy	Firth	**Prendergast**	Campbell	**Sidebottom**	Johnson*	Johnston
	28/10	1,184	*10*	4			*Massey 29, 62*	*Allen*	*Cunningham*	*Miller*	*Impey*	*Brown R*	*Barton*	*Borthwick*	*Johnson*	*Butler*	*Massey*	*Brown K*	
							Ref: A Saunders	Bell has gone to Barnsley for £30,000. Lawson includes three new players, including Campbell who's been here before, but his side slips to its fifth home defeat. Massey celebrates his return to the Bournemouth side by netting both their goals. Time has run out for Lawson the manager.											
16	A	HEREFORD	24	D	2-2	2-1	Mountford 9, Dunleavy 32	Leonard	Hutt	Loska	Smith*	Burke	Dunleavy	Prendergast	Mountford	Campbell	Sidebottom	Johnson	Firth
	4/11	*3,616*	*13*	5			*Jones 16, Gould 47*	*Hughes*	*Price*	*Burrows*	*Cornes*	*Leyton*	*Bailey*	*Stephens**	*Emery*	*Jones*	*Gould*	*Spiring*	*Holmes*
							Ref: A McDonald	George Kirby is back at the helm, and is delighted that his 'new' team avoids defeat. Town lead twice, with Mountford and Dunleavy both scoring headed goals. Hereford take charge in the second half, but the Shaymen feel they are unlucky with two efforts that hit the woodwork.											
17	H	ALDERSHOT	24	D	1-1	1-1	Mountford 36	Leonard	Hutt	Loska	Smith	Burke	Dunleavy	Prendergast	Mountford	Campbell	Sidebottom*	Johnson	Nixon
	11/11	1,438	*6*	6			*Dungworth 25*	*Johnson*	*Edwards*	*Wooler*	*Dixon*	*Youlden*	*Jopling*	*Longhorn*	*Brodie*	*Needham*	*Dungworth*	*McGregor*	
							Ref: M Baker	Aldershot manage to extend their unbeaten run to eight games, but have keeper Johnson to thank for that. He is outstanding in the second half, and makes one world-class save from Mountford. John Dungworth actually gives the visitors the lead, but Mountford provides the equaliser.											
18	A	GRIMSBY	24	L	1-2	1-0	Prendergast 3	Leonard	Hutt	Loska	Smith	Burke	Dunleavy	Prendergast	Mountford	Campbell	Sidebottom*	Johnson	Nixon
	18/11	*4,128*	*5*	6			*Cumming 78, Moore K 89*	*Batch*	*Moore D*	*Moore K*	*Waters*	*Barker*	*Crombie*	*Brolly*	*Partridge **	*Drinkell*	*Cumming*	*Mitchell*	*Ford*
							Ref: T Earley	Luck goes against Town. After taking an early lead, they lose Sidebottom to a wreckless challenge from Partridge, then have a second goal in the 49th minute by Prendergast given offside. After Cumming's unlikely equaliser, Kevin Moore steals in to score Grimsby's cruel winner.											
19	A	WIMBLEDON	24	L	1-2	0-1	Campbell 84	Leonard	Hutt	Loska	Smith	Burke*	Dunleavy	Nixon	Mountford	Campbell	Sidebottom	Johnson	Kennedy
	2/12	*2,374*	*1*	6			*Cork 4, 76*	*Goddad*	*Perkins*	*Haverson*	*Galliers*	*Galvin*	*Donaldson*	*Leslie*	*Briley*	*Denny*	*Cork*	*Parsons*	
							Ref: T Spencer	The Dons start this game suggesting they will run up a cricket score. Town are all over the place when Cork scores the opener. They are in the game, though, until Cork pops up with a second. However, after Campbell pulls one back, Haverson has to clear off the line in the last minute.											
20	H	READING	24	D	0-0	0-0		Leonard	Hutt	Loska	Smith	Sidebottom	Dunleavy	Nixon	Mountford	Campbell	Kennedy	Johnson	
	9/12	1,401	*2*	7				*Death*	*Peters*	*White*	*Bowman*	*Hicks*	*Bennett*	*Alexander*	*Earles*	*Kearney*	*Sanchez*	*Lewis*	
							Ref: P Partridge	For the second week running, Town show they can compete with the best. Although Earles misses a sitter from two yards in the 10th minute, Maurice Evans' side don't have things all their own way. Town winger Jon Nixon is a constant thorn, and brings out the best in Steve Death.											
21	H	WIGAN	24	L	1-2	0-2	Carroll 65	Leonard	Hutt	Loska	Smith	Sidebottom	Dunleavy	Nixon	Mountford	Campbell*	Kennedy	Johnson	Carroll
	16/12	2,437	*7*	7			*Moore 18, Purdie 44*	*Grew*	*Smart*	*Hinnigan*	*Gore*	*Davids*	*Fretwell*	*Corrigan*	*Wright*	*Moore*	*Brownbill*	*Purdie*	
							Ref: G Courtney	Wigan, on their first-ever visit to the Shay, look good for their two-goal first-half lead, thanks to Mickey Moore's angled 20-yarder and Ian Purdie's bullet header. But the game changes after the break, with the introduction of Joe Carroll, but constant pressure only brings one goal.											
22	A	HUDDERSFIELD	24	L	0-2	0-1		Leonard	Bradley	Hutt	Smith	Sidebottom	Dunleavy	Nixon	Carroll	Mountford *	Kennedy	Loska	Campbell
	26/12	*5,341*	*16*	7			*Robins 30, Fletcher 72*	*Starling*	*Brown*	*Branagan*	*Gray*	*Topping*	*Sutton*	*Fletcher*	*Hart*	*Cowling*	*Robins*	*Bielby*	
							Ref: A Challinor	Five of Halifax's twelve men are former Huddersfield players. They should feel at home. The Shaymen are playing well when tragedy strikes. Mick Leonard slips when taking a goal-kick, and presents Robins with an open goal. The game is out of reach when Fletcher heads in for 2-0.											
23	A	NORTHAMPTON	24	L	1-2	1-1	Nixon 31	Leonard	Bradley	Hutt	Smith	Sidebottom	Dunleavy	Nixon	Kennedy	Campbell	Loska	**Stafford ***	Mountford
	30/12	*2,208*	*18*	7			*Reilly 28, McCaffrey 67*	*Jayes*	*Walker**	*Mead*	*Geidmintis*	*Robertson*	*Bryant*	*Farrington*	*Williams*	*Froggatt*	*Reilly*	*McCaffrey*	*Brown*
							Ref: D Hutchinson	Mick Kennedy is Town's star player, and a brighter future beckons for him. Town slip to yet another defeat, the price they are paying for too many missed chances. Like Bradley's penalty in the dying minutes, which is well saved by Jayes. McCaffrey's winner is real route-one stuff.											

No	Date		Att	Pos	Pt	F-A	H-T	Scorers, Times, and Referees	1	2	3	4	5	6	7	8	9	10	11	12 sub used
24	A	CREWE		24	L	0-1	0-1		Leonard	Bradley	Dunleavy	Smith	Sidebottom	Burke	Firth	Kennedy	Mountford	Loska	Stafford*	Johnson
	10/2		*1,594*	*22*	7			*Warnock 13*	*Baswell*	*Purdie*	*Pulson*	*Nicholls*	*Bowles*	*Bevan*	*Davies*	*Roberts*	*Nelson*	*Warnock**	*Robertson*	*Wilkinson*
								Ref: M Scott	The winter weather is playing havoc with the football programme. This is Town's first game for six weeks. Town pile on the pressure late on, but can't cancel out Warnock's untidy goal off Robertson's corner. Town are now six points adrift of Rochdale, and twelve away from safety.											
25	A	PORT VALE		24	W	1-0	1-0	Bentley 34 (og)	Leonard	Bradley	Dunleavy	Smith	Sidebottom	Burke	Firth	Kennedy	Mountford*	Loska	Johnson	Campbell
	24/2		*3,117*	*15*	9				*Connaughton*	*Keenan*	*Bentley*	*Beach*	*Delgado !*	*Hawkins*	*Bramage**	*Sinclair*	*Wright*	*Todd*	*Farrell*	*Chamberlain*
								Ref: C Newsome	Town get the breaks as they record only their second victory of the season. The first comes when Johnson's corner touches the head of Bentley and goes in. The second is the sending off of Delgado for punching Kennedy. The third is Leonards's jaw, broken following a hefty challenge.											
26	A	DARLINGTON		24	L	1-2	0-1	Mountford 71	**Kilner**	Bradley	Dunleavy	Smith	Sidebottom*	Burke	Firth	Kennedy	Mountford	Loska	Johnson	Campbell
	27/2		***1,403***	*20*	9			*Seal 36, Nattress 81*	*Burleigh*	*Crosson*	*Nattress*	*Cochrane*	*Craig*	*Stone*	*Probert**	*Wann*	*Walsh*	*Ferguson*	*Seal*	*Maitland*
								Ref: N Glover	Preston reserve keeper Kilner comes in to help out Town. He was recommended by Alex Smith. Town are down to ten men when necessary sub Campbell himself has to retire. Darlington win following a controversial free-kick. Kilner can only carry Nattress's volley over the line.											
27	H	PORTSMOUTH		24	W	**2-0**	2-0	Ellis 29 (og), Johnson 35	Kilner	Bradley	Dunleavy	Smith	Trainer	Burke	Firth	Kennedy	Mountford	Loska	Johnson	
	3/3		1,741	*5*	11				*Mellor*	*Ellis*	*Wilson*	*Denyer*	*Foster*	*Davey*	*Hemmerman*	*Lathan*	*Showers**	*Barnard*	*Pullar*	*Garwood*
								Ref: G Owen	In their first home game for three months, Town put a huge dent in Pompey's promotion hopes. They get lucky when Johnson's free-kick takes a wicked deflection off Ellis. Johnson scores the second from 23 yards. In the second half Town dig deep to defend a novelty – a two-goal lead.											
28	H	DONCASTER		24	D	0-0	0-0		Kilner	Bradley	Dunleavy	Smith	Trainer	Burke	Firth	Kennedy	Mountford	Loska	Johnson	
	6/3		1,658	*15*	12				*Peacock*	*Hemsley*	*Snodin*	*Flanagan*	*Bradley*	*Olney*	*Laidlaw*	*Owen*	*French*	*Lally**	*Pugh*	*Cox*
								Ref: J Hough	Former Leeds ace Billy Bremner is now in charge of Rovers. His side is lying in mid-table at the moment, but won't be for long. This game is their fourth without a goal, but at least it ends a run of three straight defeats. Town have the busier keeper, with Kilner twice denying Laidlaw.											
29	A	BOURNEMOUTH		24	L	0-1	0-0		Kilner	Bradley	Dunleavy	Smith	Trainer	Burke	Firth	Kennedy	Mountford	Loska*	Johnson	Hutt
	10/3		*3,078*	*10*	12			*MacDougall 66*	*Allen*	*Cunningham*	*Miller*	*Impey*	*Brown*	*Holder*	*Borthwick*	*MacDougall*	*Scott*	*Lennard*	*Johnson*	
								Ref: J Martin	Ted MacDougall is back for a second spell at Dean Court. His career has seen him take in, amongst others, Man Utd, West Ham, Norwich and Southampton. Played in thick mud, Supermac finds himself stuck in the right place to score the only goal when the ball comes back off the bar.											
30	A	YORK		24	L	0-2	0-1		Kilner	Hutt	Dunleavy	Smith	Trainer	Burke	Firth	Kennedy	Nixon	Johnson	Bradley*	Loska
	13/3		*2,196*	*16*	12			*Loggie 39, Staniforth 72*	*Neenan*	*Kay*	*Walsh*	*Pugh*	*Faulkner*	*Clements*	*Ford*	*Randall*	*Loggie*	*McDonald*	*Staniforth*	
								Ref: J Worrall	Results elsewhere go for them, such as Grimsby's win at Rochdale, but Town can't take advantage. Yet this is a game they look like winning, until they fall to set-piece goals. Loggie heads in a corner, while Staniforth's goal comes at a time when a Town equaliser looks more likely.											
31	A	STOCKPORT		24	W	2-1	0-0	Johnson 80, Campbell 84	Kilner	Hutt	Dunleavy	Smith	Trainer	Sidebottom	Firth	Kennedy	Campbell	Johnson	Loska*	Nixon
	23/3		*3,033*	*9*	14			*Bradd 76*	*Lawson*	*Thorpe*	*Rutter*	*Edwards*	*Connor*	*Smith**	*Henson*	*Summerbee*	*Bradd*	*Halford*	*Lee*	*Seddon*
								Ref: T Farley	In a game punctuated by 33 free-kicks, all the goals come in the last 16 minutes. Town amazingly come from behind to claim their first double. Bradd gives County the lead off Summerbee's corner. Johnson swoops to equalise, then Campbell gets to the ball to head over David Lawson.											
32	H	BARNSLEY		24	L	0-2	0-0		Kilner	Hutt	Dunleavy	Smith	Trainer	Sidebottom	Firth	Kennedy	Campbell	Johnson	Loska*	Nixon
	27/3		**5,654**	*5*	14			*Graham 52, Bell 67p*	*Springett*	*Collins*	*Chambers*	*Pugh*	*Saunders*	*McCarthy*	*Little*	*Riley*	*Graham*	*Millar*	*Bell*	
								Ref: D Richardson	Another former Leeds star, Allan Clarke, is the player-manager at Division 3-bound Barnsley. He is injured for this game, so he leaves it to future and former Town players to do the damage. Tommy Graham heads in the first, and Bell scores a penalty when Hutt brings down Riley.											
33	A	NEWPORT		24	L	0-2	0-1		Kilner	Hutt	Dunleavy	Smith	Trainer	Sidebottom	Firth	Kennedy	Campbell	Johnson	Loska	
	31/3		*3,927*	*7*	14			*Bruton 44, Vaughan 80*	*Plumley*	*Walden*	*Relish*	*Davies*	*Oakes*	*Bruton*	*Bailey*	*Lowndes**	*Goddard*	*Tynan*	*Moore*	*Vaughan*
								Ref: B Stevens	Town have two goals disallowed, then they slip to their 23rd defeat in 33 matches. Bruton's glancing header gives Len Ashurst's side the lead just before the break, and Vaughan hammers home the loose ball to seal the win. Kennedy is lucky to stay on the field after kicking Plumley.											
34	H	TORQUAY		24	W	1-0	0-0	Trainer 68	Kilner	Hutt	Dunleavy	Smith	Trainer	Sidebottom	Firth	Kennedy	Campbell*	Johnson	Loska	Mountford
	3/4		1,112	*9*	16				*Turner*	*Twitchin*	*Ritchie*	*Green*	*Darke**	*Dunne*	*Davies*	*Lawrence*	*Cooper*	*Wilson*	*Coffill*	*Murphy*
								Ref: R Chadwick	Entertainment is kept to the minimum as the players play out this game in a blizzard. Jack Trainer is the Shaymen's unlikely hero when he fires in from eight yards off Johnson's corner that skims into the box. However, Kilner still has to react in time to keep out Les Lawrence late on.											

No	H/A	Date/Opponent	Att	Pos	Pts	F-A	H-T	Scorers, Times, Referees	1	2	3	4	5	6	7	8	9	10	11	12
35	H	WIMBLEDON		24	W	2-1	2-1	Trainer 20, Johnson 24	Kilner	Hutt	Dunleavy	Smith	Trainer	Sidebottom	Firth	Kennedy	Mountford	Johnson*	Loska	Nixon
	7/4		1,576	*6*	18			*Ketteridge 41*	*Goddard*	*Perkins !*	*Haverson*	*Briley*	*Galvin*	*Cunningham*	*Galliers*	*Denny**	*Knowles*	*Cork*	*Ketteridge*	*Parsons*
								Ref: A Porter	Trainer heads in the game's opener off Johnson's corner, and Johnson squeezes in a second. Ketteridge's reply makes for an interesting second half. The Dons are clearly the better side, but having Steve Perkins' sent-off in the 78th minute for striking Kennedy doesn't help their cause.											
36	H	HUDDERSFIELD		24	L	2-3	0-1	Mountford 78, Sidebottom 90	Kilner	Hutt	Dunleavy	Smith	Trainer	Sidebottom	Firth	Kennedy	Mountford	Johnson*	Loska	Nixon
	14/4		4,027	*12*	18			*Fletcher 12, 53, Holmes 54*	*Starling*	*Brown*	*Sandercock*	*Holmes*	*Hanvey*	*Sutton*	*Fletcher**	*Hart*	*Armstrong*	*Robins*	*Bielby*	*Branagan*
								Ref: K Baker	The Shaymen are three down after 54 minutes, so the scoreline hints at a fightback. But Sidebottom's astonishing 35-yard shot, mistimed by Starling, comes too late to change the result. Fletcher volleys the Terriers' first goal, whilst Brown provides identical crosses for the other two.											
37	A	SCUNTHORPE		24	L	0-1	0-0		Kilner	Dunleavy	Hutt	Smith	Burke	Sidebottom	Firth	Kennedy	Mountford*	Nixon	Loska	Johnson
	16/4		*1,624*	*15*	18			*Earl 60*	*Crawford*	*Czuczman*	*Peacock*	*Oates*	*Deere*	*Hall*	*Grimes*	*Kilmore*	*Earl**	*Kavanagh*	*Gibson*	*Couch*
								Ref: A Saunders	Ron Ashman's Scunthorpe side hardly look world beaters, so after this defeat Halifax boss George Kirby must be asking questions about his players. The defence does well, but their one lapse allows Steve Earl, unmarked, to score the only goal. The Iron's Kilmore looks promising.											
38	A	DONCASTER		24	D	1-1	1-1	Sidebottom 29	Kilner	Dunleavy	Hutt	Smith	Burke	Trainer	Firth	Kennedy	Campbell	Sidebottom	Johnson	
	17/4		*2,227*	*18*	19			*Cox 24*	*Peacock*	*Lister*	*Snodin G*	*Meagan*	*Cannell*	*Olney**	*Ustin*	*Packer*	*Cox*	*Lewis*	*Flanagan*	*Pugh*
								Ref: J Bray	Billy Bremner puts out a side that contains only three players aged over 20. They look lively, but Town prove to be a match for them. After Burke's blunder that lets in Cox, Sidebottom equalises when set up by Campbell. Kilner later fists away outside the box and is rightly booked.											
39	H	NORTHAMPTON		24	D	2-2	1-2	Geidmintis 31 (og), Johnson 62	Kilner	Hutt	Dunleavy	Smith	Burke	Trainer	Firth	Kennedy	Campbell	Sidebottom*	Johnson	Nixon
	21/4		1,172	*15*	20			*McCaffrey 11, Froggatt 18*	*Jayes*	*Geidmintis*	*Mead*	*Saunders*	*Robertson*	*Farrington*	*Williams*	*Matthews*	*McCaffrey*	*Reilly*	*Froggatt*	
								Ref: D Shaw	Jim McCaffrey and John Froggatt cash in on defensive errors to put the Cobblers well in control after only 18 minutes. A Geidmintis own-goal – his second in consecutive matches – puts Town back in the picture. An equaliser is on, and comes courtesy of Johnson's deflected free-kick.											
40	H	BRADFORD C		24	W	**2-0**	2-0	Campbell 8, Dunleavy 13	Kilner	Hutt	Dunleavy	Smith	Burke	Trainer	Firth	Kennedy	Campbell	Carroll	Loska	
	26/4		2,343	*17*	22				*Smith*	*Podd*	*Watson*	*Middleton*	*Baines*	*Wood*	*Johnson*	*Dolan*	*Szabo*	*McNiven**	*Hutchins*	*Martinez*
								Ref: K Styles	George Mulhall has taken on the mantle of Bantams' boss. But he finds his former side well geared up for this derby. The Shaymen have the game won as early as the 13th minute. Campbell, from close range, and Dunleavy's header off a corner give Town something to hang on to.											
41	A	READING		24	L	0-1	0-1		Kilner	Hutt	Dunleavy	Smith	Burke	Trainer	Firth	Kennedy	Campbell	Carroll	Loska*	Stafford
	28/4		*7,408*	*1*	22			*Hetzke 38*	*Death*	*Peters*	*Withe*	*Bowman*	*Hicks*	*Bennett*	*Earles*	*Alexander**	*Hetzke*	*Shipley*	*Sanchez*	*Kearns*
								Ref: D Beevers	The Shaymen drink champagne after this defeat, though they have nothing to celebrate. It is provided by the home side, who, thanks to Steve Hetzke's volley from eight yards, have clinched promotion. For Town, the world's worst kept secret is out – re-election is now unavoidable.											
42	H	NEWPORT		24	L	1-2	0-1	Burke 64	Kilner	Dunleavy	Hutt	Smith	Burke	Trainer	Firth	Kennedy	Campbell	Johnson	Stafford	
	5/5		1,007	*7*	22			*Goddard 22, 65p*	*Plumley*	*Walden*	*Thompson*	*Cosslett*	*Oakes*	*Bruton*	*Bailey*	*Lowndes*	*Goddard*	*Tynan*	*Moore*	
								Ref: D Owen	Peter Burke is a central figure in this game. He equalises following a corner for a goal Town don't deserve, then 30 seconds later redresses the balance by bringing down Moore from behind to concede a penalty. Goddard's opener is a header off Moore's cross that goes in off the post.											
43	H	ROCHDALE		24	W	2-1	2-0	Johnson 23p, Bradley 40	Kilner	Hutt	Dunleavy	Bradley	Burke	Trainer	Firth	Kennedy	Campbell	Johnson	Stafford	
	7/5		2,150	*21*	24			*Hilditch 69*	*Felgate*	*Hart*	*Snookes*	*Oliver**	*Bannon*	*Taylor*	*Hoy*	*Owen*	*Jones*	*O'Loughlin*	*Esser*	*Hilditch*
								Ref: G Flint	Five consecutive victories will help Doug Collins' Rochdale haul themselves out of trouble. But Town win this tense derby. Johnson's penalty, after Snookes handles, has to be taken three times. Bradley scores from fully 30 yards, but Hilditch's effort from similar range is just as good.											
44	H	HEREFORD		23	W	1-0	0-0	Johnson 51	Kilner	Hutt	Dunleavy	Bradley	Burke	Trainer*	Firth	Kennedy	Campbell	Johnson	Stafford	Mountford
	9/5		1,036	*12*	26				*Knight**	*Emery*	*Thomas*	*Cornes*	*Layton*	*Felley*	*Spiring*	*Hendry*	*McGrellis*	*Jones*	*White*	*Holmes*
								Ref: G Tyson	'Anchors Aweigh!' proclaims the Halifax Courier. Johnson's powerful close-range header is enough to take Town off the bottom for the first time since 14 October. Hereford lose their keeper, Knight, with a broken nose after only six minutes, but stand-in Holmes is rarely troubled.											
45	H	HARTLEPOOL		23	L	2-4	1-3	Firth 29, Johnson 90p	Kilner	Dunleavy	Hutt	Bradley	Burke*	Trainer	Firth	Kennedy	Mountford	Johnson	Stafford	Smith
	14/5		1,012	*15*	26			*Lawrence 19, 25, 45, 86*	*Watson*	*Goldthorpe*	*Gorry*	*Smith*	*Brookes*	*Ayre*	*Linacre*	*Lawrence*	*Houchen*	*Harding*	*Loadwick*	
								Ref: C Seel	Les Lawrence almost repeats the feat of Fulham's Steve Earle nearly ten years ago. Three of his goals are gifts, especially the first when Kilner comes out to head clear, but misses the ball completely. Johnson's last-minute penalty means he's Town's top scorer with a paltry seven goals.											
46	H	SCUNTHORPE		23	L	2-3	0-1	Bradley 68, 90	Kilner	Hutt	Dunleavy	Smith	Trainer	Bradley	Firth	Kennedy	Mountford	Johnson	Stafford*	Johnston
	18/5		1,037	*12*	26			*Couch 29, Grimes 60, Gibson 73*	*Crawford*	*Davy*	*Peacock*	*Oates*	*Deere*	*Hall*	*Grimes*	*Kilmore*	*Couch*	*Kavanagh*	*Gibson*	
		Home	Away					Ref: D Clarke	Halifax are not the worst team in the League. Crewe's eighth consecutive defeat - by Rochdale gives them that distinction. The Iron don't have to work too hard for victory. Bradley, who is being released by Town, signs off with both their goals. A mini demonstration follows the game.											
Average		1,816	3,698																	

LEAGUE DIVISION 4 (CUP-TIES)

Manager: Lawson ⇨ George Kirby

SEASON 1978-79

League Cup				F-A	H-T	Scorers, Times, and Referees	1	2	3	4	5	6	7	8	9	10	11	12 sub used
1:1 A WALSALL			L	1-2	1-1	Bullock 24	Leonard	Trainer	Loska	Smith	Burke	Dunleavy	**Nixon**	Lawson	Bullock	**Johnson***	Carroll	Bradley
12/8	*4,589*	*3:*				*Buckley 13, Birch 47*	*Kearns*	*Paul*	*Caswell**	*Harrison*	*Serella*	*Macken*	*Birch*	*King*	*Austin*	*Buckley*	*Kelly*	*Clarke*
						Ref: R Bridges	Favourite Bell has been injured in a car crash, and record signing Kevin Johnson suffers a fractured ankle debut after only 46 minutes. Seconds after he goes off, Alan Birch grabs Walsall's winner, off Kelly's cross. Bullock's earlier equaliser was neatly scored with the outside of his foot.											
1:2 H WALSALL			L	0-2	0-0		Leonard	Trainer	Loska	Smith	Burke*	Dunleavy	Nixon	Johnston	Bullock	Lawson	Bell	Bradley
15/8	2,276	*3:*				*Paul 49, Buckley 76*	*Kearns*	*Paul*	*Caswell*	*Harrison*	*Serella*	*King*	*Birch*	*Macken*	*Austin*	*Buckley*	*Kelly*	
						Ref: N Glover (Halifax lost 1-4 on aggregate)	The Shaymen run out in their brand new all-white strip, but the result is an all-too familiar one. They fall to Ian Paul's angled free-kick, and a lovely-worked goal from ace marksman Alan Buckley. Walsall, under new boss Alan Ashman, expected a hard second leg, but don't get one.											

FA Cup				F-A	H-T	Scorers, Times, and Referees	1	2	3	4	5	6	7	8	9	10	11	12 sub used
1 A CARLISLE		24	L	0-1	0-0		Leonard	Hutt	Loska	Smith	Burke	Dunleavy	Prendergast	Mountford	Campbell	Sidebottom*	Johnson	Carroll
25/11	*5,238*	*3:7*				*Lumby 85*	*Swinburne*	*Hoolickin*	*McCartney*	*Bonnyman*	*Tait*	*Parker*	*McVitie*	*Ludlam*	*Kemp*	*Lumby*	*Hamilton*	
						Ref: K Walmsley	Bobby Moncur's Carlisle side maybe in the 3rd Division promotion race, but they make hard work of defeating the Shaymen. Town's battling performance looks like earning them a welcome replay, until five minutes from time. Jim Lumby then dispatches the ball from ten yards out.											

		Home					Away					
	P	W	D	L	F	A	W	D	L	F	A	Pts
1 Reading	46	19	3	1	49	8	7	10	6	27	27	65
2 Grimsby	46	15	5	3	51	23	11	4	8	31	26	61
3 Wimbledon	46	18	3	2	50	20	7	8	8	28	26	61
4 Barnsley	46	15	5	3	47	23	9	8	6	26	19	61
5 Aldershot	46	16	5	2	38	14	4	12	7	25	33	57
6 Wigan	46	14	5	4	40	24	7	8	8	23	24	55
7 Portsmouth	46	13	7	3	35	12	7	5	11	27	36	52
8 Newport	46	12	5	6	39	28	9	5	9	27	27	52
9 Huddersfield	46	13	8	2	32	15	5	3	15	25	38	47
10 York	46	11	6	6	33	24	7	5	11	18	31	47
11 Torquay	46	14	4	5	38	24	5	4	14	20	41	46
12 Scunthorpe	46	12	3	8	33	30	5	8	10	21	30	45
13 Hartlepool	46	7	12	4	35	28	6	6	11	22	38	44
14 Hereford	46	12	8	3	35	18	3	5	15	18	35	43
15 Bradford C	46	11	5	7	38	26	6	4	13	24	42	43
16 Port Vale	46	8	10	5	29	28	6	4	13	28	42	42
17 Stockport	46	11	5	7	33	21	3	7	13	25	39	40
18 Bournemouth	46	11	6	6	34	19	3	5	15	13	29	39
19 Northampton	46	12	4	7	40	30	3	5	15	24	46	39
20 Rochdale	46	11	4	8	25	26	4	5	14	22	38	39
21 Darlington	46	8	8	7	25	21	3	7	13	24	45	37
22 Doncaster	46	8	8	7	25	22	5	3	15	25	51	37
23 HALIFAX	46	7	5	11	24	32	2	3	18	15	40	26
24 Crewe	46	3	7	13	24	41	3	7	13	19	49	26
	1104	281	141	130	852	557	130	141	281	557	852	1104

Odds & ends

Double wins: (1) Stockport.
Double losses: (10) Barnsley, Bournemouth, Darlington, Grimsby, Hartlepool, Huddersfield, Newport, Scunthorpe, Wigan, York.

Won from behind: (2) Stockport (h & a).
Lost from in front: (2) Barnsley (a), Grimsby (a).

High spots: Two consecutive wins in April and May.
Beating Hereford with two games left to get off the bottom of the table.

Low spots: 22 games without a win up to 10 February.
Seven consecutive defeats up to 27 September.
Having to apply for re-election.

Town didn't play any games in January, but played eight in April and five in May.

Player of the Year: Kevin Johnson.
Ever-presents: (1) Chris Dunleavy.
Hat-tricks: (0).
Leading scorer: Kevin Johnson (7).

	Appearances						Goals			
	Lge	*Sub*	LC	*Sub*	FAC	*Sub*	Lge	LC	FAC	Tot
Bell, Derek	**11**		1				**3**			**3**
Bradley, Lee	**19**	*1*		*2*			**3**			**3**
Bullock, Mickey	**10**	*1*	2				**2**	1		**3**
Burke, Peter	**31**		2		1		**2**			**2**
Campbell, Bobby	**19**	*3*			1		**3**			**3**
Carroll, Joe	**9**	*3*	1			*1*	**1**			**1**
Dunleavy, Chris	**46**		2		1		**2**			**2**
Firth, Francis	**33**	*2*					**2**			**2**
Hutt, Geoff	**31**	*1*			1					
Johnson, Kevin	**37**	*2*	1		1		**7**			**7**
Johnston, Johnny	**5**	*2*	1							
Kennedy, Mick	**28**	*2*								
Kilner, John	**21**									
Lawson, Jimmy	**12**		2				**1**			**1**
Leonard, Mick	**25**		2		1					
Loska, Tony	**34**	*1*	2		1					
Mountford, Bob	**23**	*3*			1		**4**			**4**
Nixon, Jon	**12**	*7*	2				**1**			**1**
Prendergast, Mick	**4**				1		**1**			**1**
Sidebottom, Arnold	**21**				1		**2**			**2**
Smith, Steve	**38**	*2*	2		1					
Stafford, Andy	**7**	*1*								
Trainer, Jack	**30**		2				**2**			**2**
(own-goals)							**3**			**3**
23 players used	**506**	***31***	**22**	***2***	**11**	***1***	**39**	**1**		**40**

No	Date		Att	Pos	Pt	F-A	H-T	Scorers, Times, and Referees	1	2	3	4	5	6	7	8	9	10	11	12 sub used
1	A	TRANMERE			L	0-2	0-1		Leonard	Dunleavy	Hutt	Evans	Harris	Hendrie	Firth	Kennedy	Mountford	Johnson	Stafford*	Burke
	18/8		*2,650*		0			*Craven 33, Kerr 64*	*Johnson*	*Mathias*	*Flood*	*Bramhall*	*Edwards*	*O'Neil*	*Peplow*	*Craven*	*Kerr*	*Evans*	*Lumby*	
								Ref: M Heath	Kirby is trying to build a side that will be challenging for promotion next season. On this showing he has a lot of work to do. His side manages only four shots on goal. Craven gives the home side the lead when Lumby's effort rebounds off the post. O'Neil pounces to set up Kerr's goal.											
2	H	DONCASTER			D	1-1	1-1	Harris 34	Leonard	Dunleavy	Hutt	Evans	Harris	Hendrie	Firth	Kennedy	Mountford	Johnson	**Geidmintis**	
	21/8		2,501		1			*Warboys 27*	*Peacock*	*Russell*	*Riley*	*Cork**	*Bradley*	*Dowd*	*Pugh*	*Nimmo*	*Warboys*	*Dowie*	*Bentley*	*Lewis*
								Ref: D Shaw	Halifax Harriers stage two races around the speedway track. Winner of the Boys' 800m during the interval is Rotherham's Peter Elliott. In the game, Warboys, back at his first club, hooks in Rovers' goal. New-boy Harris provides Town's quick equaliser, heading in Kennedy's corner.											
3	A	PETERBOROUGH		20	L	1-2	1-1	Johnson 45	Leonard	Dunleavy	Hutt	Evans	Harris	Hendrie	Firth	Kennedy	Mountford*	Johnson	Geidmintis	Burke
	25/8		*4,014*	*9*	1			*Kellock 3, Chard 55*	*Waugh*	*Carmichael*	*Collins*	*Heppolette*	*McVay*	*Foster*	*Gynn*	*Kellock*	*Guy*	*Robson**	*Lambert*	*Chard*
								Ref: G Flint	The Posh have spent £25,000 on Billy Kellock from Kettering. He gets his fourth goal of the season, escaping his marker to head in. Town play their part in an entertaining game. Johnson scrambles in the equaliser just on half-time. But indecision costs them as Chard shoots home.											
4	H	CREWE		15	W	3-1	3-0	Burke14, Johnson 36p, 45	Leonard	Dunleavy	Hutt	Evans	Harris	Hendrie	Firth	Kennedy	Burke	Johnson	Geidmintis	
	1/9		1,418	*23*	3			*Hunter 67*	*Phillips*	*Wilkinson*	*Bowers*	*Hunter*	*Scott*	*Bowles*	*Davies*	*Purdie*	*Nelson*	*Lewis*	*Ashworth**	*Dulson*
								Ref: D Richardson	Mountford is injured, so Burke gets to play up front. He's an instant success, heading in the first goal off Kennedy's corner. Johnson wins his penalty when Phillips, the former Chelsea keeper, brings him down. Town have this game won by half-time, though Crewe never give it up.											
5	A	NORTHAMPTON		15	D	0-0	0-0		Leonard	Dunleavy	Hutt	Evans	Harris	Hendrie	Firth*	Kennedy	Burke	Johnson	Geidmintis	Mountford
	7/9		*2,759*	*20*	4				*Jayes*	*Walker*	*Saunders*	*Farmer*	*Waldock*	*Ward*	*Denyer*	*Sargent*	*McCaffrey*	*Reilly*	*Bowen*	
								Ref: M Bidmead	Clive Walker's Cobblers have yet to win in the league. They never look like breaking their duck in this game. Town, for their part, offer little, and seem happy with a point. Kevin Johnson epitomises their approach with a back-pass to his keeper from the Northampton half of the field.											
6	H	HEREFORD		12	W	1-0	1-0	Mountford 34	**Hough**	Dunleavy	Hutt	Evans	Harris	Hendrie	Firth*	Kennedy	Mountford	Johnson	Burke	Stafford
	15/9		1,500	*10*	6				*Hughes*	*Price*	*Burrows*	*Hunt*	*Layton*	*Emery*	*Cunningham*	*Feeley*	*McGrellis*	*Gould*	*White**	*Comes*
								Ref: R Banks	Mick Leonard has gone to Notts County, so Town return to Preston for Kilner. But his registration is not cleared in time, so local league lad Johnny Hough is called up. He makes the save of the match from Price's 30-yarder. Mountford heads in the winner off Kennedy's long throw.											
7	H	ROCHDALE		9	W	1-0	0-0	Stafford 64	Kilner	Dunleavy	Hutt	Evans	Harris	Hendrie	Stafford	Kennedy	Mountford	Johnson	Burke	
	18/9		2,390	*21*	8				*Watson*	*Hart*	*Snookes*	*Weir*	*Bannon*	*Taylor*	*Oliver**	*Scaife*	*Hilditch*	*Wann*	*Esser*	*Jones*
								Ref: A Saunders	Andy Stafford hails from Littleborough, on the outskirts of Rochdale. He will enjoy this moment. Johnson releases him and he races on to net the only goal, his first-ever in senior football. Johnson could have made the game safer, but when Bannon handles, Watson saves his penalty.											
8	A	BOURNEMOUTH		9	W	1-0	1-0	Moore 31 (og)	Kilner	Dunleavy	Hutt	Evans	Harris	Hendrie	Stafford	Kennedy	Mountford	Johnson	Burke	
	22/9		*3,233*	*16*	10				*Allen*	*Bryant*	*Moore*	*Impey*	*Ferns*	*Chambers*	*Holder*	*Thomas**	*Borthwick*	*Heffernan*	*Evanson*	*Butler*
								Ref: D Vickers	A dull game punctuated only by a couple of magic moments by Town's Johnson. After a mazy run, he sees his shot hit the angle of bar and post. But the next minute it is his low cross that is turned into his own net by Jon Moore. On the hour, Kilner gets down at Bryant's feet to save.											
9	H	HARTLEPOOL		6	W	2-1	0-0	Mountford 61, Dunleavy 78	Kilner	Dunleavy	Hutt	Evans	Harris	Hendrie	Stafford	Kennedy	Mountford	Johnson*	Burke	**Whiteley**
	29/9		2,293	*15*	12			*Newton 55*	*Watson*	*Sweeney*	*Normanton*	*Smith*	*Brookes*	*Ayre*	*Lawrence*	*Houchen*	*Newton*	*Harding**	*Loadwick*	*Larkin*
								Ref: A Dobson	Pool's Bob Newton shows no mercy to former teammate Johnson when he breaks his leg in the 48th minute. He then rubs salt in the wound by putting his side ahead. But Town re-group and Mountford, who later hits both post and bar, levels the game, before Dunleavy's headed winner.											
10	A	ROCHDALE			D	2-2	2-2	Hendrie 25, Burke 28	Kilner	Dunleavy	Hutt	Evans	Harris	Hendrie	Stafford*	Kennedy	Mountford	Whiteley	Burke	**Goodman**
	2/10		*2,359*		13			*Scaife 30, Hoy 45p*	*Watson*	*Hart*	*Cliff*	*Weir*	*Bannon*	*Taylor*	*Hoy*	*Esser*	*Hilditch*	*Scaife*	*Jones*	
								Ref: C Seel	The Shaymen race into a two-goal lead, then lose it in silly fashion. Former Shayman Scaife scores from close range, before Stafford does Dale a big favour. His woeful return from a goal-kick leads to Kilner hauling down Esser for a penalty, converted by Hoy – a former Shayman.											
11	H	NEWPORT		5	W	2-1	2-1	Mountford 16p, Dunleavy 30	Kilner	Dunleavy	Hutt	Evans	Harris	Hendrie*	**Thomas**	Kennedy	Mountford	Whiteley	Burke	Geidmintis
	6/10		2,540	*10*	15			*Goddard 45*	*Plumley*	*Walden*	*Warriner*	*Davies*	*Oakes*	*Bailey**	*Vaughan*	*Lowndes*	*Goddard*	*Tynan*	*Moore*	*Aldridge*
								Ref: J Lovatt	George Kirby is hailed as September's 4th Division Manager of the Month. His team joins the promotion race. Mountford's penalty is awarded for a foul on Hendrie. Goddard's goal keeps the game on edge until the very last kick – an injury-time penalty from Goddard, saved by Kilner.											

No	Date	Venue	Opponent	Att	Pos	Res	Pts	F-A	H-T	Scorers, Times, and Referees	1	2	3	4	5	6	7	8	9	10	11	12
12	9/10	A	DONCASTER	*3,551*	7	L	15	1-2	0-1	Whiteley 83	Kilner	Dunleavy	Hutt	Evans	Harris	Geidmintis*	Thomas	Kennedy	Mountford	Whiteley	Burke	Goodman
					12					*Lister 10, 66* / Ref: N Glover	*Shipley*	*Russell*	*Snodin G*	*Lister*	*Dowd*	*Lally*	*Pugh*	*Nimmo*	*Warboys*	*Lewis*	*Bentley**	*Flanagan*
											Steve Lister sweeps Rovers into a tenth minute lead, then grabs his second when Lewis cleverly steps over Russell's centre. Rovers are looking for a third when Whiteley chips in – literally – with his first Town goal. But no one needs telling Kirby that his squad needs strengthening.											
13	13/10	A	DARLINGTON	*1,670*	7	D	16	1-1	1-0	Burke 26	Kilner	Goodman	Hutt	Evans	Harris	Hendrie	Thomas	Kennedy	Mountford	Firth*	Burke	Stafford
					16					*Walsh 61p* / Ref: G Tyson	*Owers*	*Coleman*	*Cochrane*	*Ball*	*Bainbridge*	*Smith*	*McLean*	*Charlton*	*Ferguson*	*Ellis*	*Walsh*	
											Ref George Tyson awards a mystifying penalty to the home side. Kilner is impeded, but Tyson has seen a push by Mountford. Walsh scores to cancel out Burke's angled 12-yarder. Kirby, who is to comment on refereeing standards to the FA, sees Hendrie pick up Town's 18th booking.											
14	20/10	H	WALSALL	3,184	7	W	18	2-1	1-0	Kennedy 2, Firth 60	Kilner	Dunleavy	Hutt	Evans*	Harris	Hendrie	Thomas	Kennedy	Mountford	Firth	Burke	Goodman
					4					*Penn 77* / Ref: N Midgley	*Green*	*Mackin*	*Mower*	*Sbragia*	*Serella*	*Paul*	*Penn*	*Waddington*	*McDonough*	*Buckley**	*Caswell*	*Williams*
											Alan Buckley, now Walsall's player-manager, brings his side to the Shay as the League's last unbeaten team, a run of 13 games. It comes to an end thanks to Kennedy's speculative 30-yarder, and Firth's volley from just outside the box. Penn's goal gives them hope, but Town hang on.											
15	23/10	H	BRADFORD C	7,012	9	L	18	0-1	0-1		Kilner	Dunleavy	Hutt	Evans	Harris	Hendrie	Thomas	Kennedy	Mountford*	Firth	Burke	Goodman
					3					*Gallagher 35* / Ref: T Farley	*Smith*	*Podd*	*Watson*	*Wood*	*Baines*	*Cooper*	*Bates*	*Dolan*	*Staniforth*	*Gallagher*	*Jones*	
											A bumper crowd for this promotion derby sees Town's unbeaten home record go. They lose the injured Mountford after only six minutes, but Town still dominate. However, when Hutt slips, Barry Gallagher is free to score. Dolan's 80th minute goal-line clearance protects their lead.											
16	27/10	A	TORQUAY	*3,340*	11	L	18	0-3	0-2		Kilner	Dunleavy	Hutt	Evans	Harris	Hendrie	Geidminitis*	Kennedy	Goodman	Firth	Burke	Stafford
					6					*Lawrence 36, Davies 43, Sermanni 68* / Ref: T Glasson	*Turner*	*Pethard*	*Ritchie*	*Larmour*	*Bourne*	*Sermanni*	*Davies*	*Lawrence*	*Coffill*	*Twitchin*	*Murphy*	
											Torquay are a surprise package, with defeat during the week ending an unbeaten run of nine games. This evening fixture gives them the chance to start another run. Lawrence puts them in front following Dunleavy's weak back-pass. Davies' diving header is a 'Match of the Day' special.											
17	3/11	H	TRANMERE	2,181	11	D	19	0-0	0-0		Kilner	Dunleavy	Hutt	Goodman	Harris	Hendrie	Firth	Kennedy	Mountford	Geidmintis	Burke	
					13					Ref: K Redfern	*Johnson*	*Mathias*	*Flood*	*Bramhall*	*Edwards*	*Evans*	*O'Neil*	*Craven*	*Kerr*	*Kelly*	*Peplow*	
											Kirby has been granted £60,000 to spend. He needs a forward on this showing. Town's main threat comes from midfield, when Hendrie causes Dickie Johnson to tip his 25-yarder over the bar. At the other end, Kilner makes a wonder-save when John Kerr heads towards an 'open' goal.											
18	7/11	A	BRADFORD C	*4,439*	11	L	19	0-2	0-1		Kilner	Dunleavy	Hutt	Evans	Harris !	Hendrie*	**Smith**	Kennedy	Mountford	Geidmintis	Stafford	Burke
					3					*Martinez 30, McNiven 70* / Ref: D Owen	*Smith*	*Podd*	*Watson*	*Robertson*	*Baines*	*Wood*	*Bates*	*Dolan*	*Staniforth*	*McNiven*	*Martinez*	
											This is a niggly derby, but with more composure Town could have gained a point. Instead, they fall behind to a Martinez goal off Podd's free-kick. Former Leeds striker David McNiven converts a low cross, then eight minutes later he is involved in Harris' sending off for kicking out.											
19	10/11	H	PORT VALE	1,798	11	D	20	0-0	0-0		Kilner	Dunleavy	Hut	Evans	Goodman	Hendrie	Smith	Kennedy	Mountford	Geidmintis*	Stafford	Burke
					22					Ref: R Chadwick	*Dance*	*Keenan*	*Griffiths*	*Beech*	*Bowles*	*Sproson*	*Woolfall*	*Farrell*	*Wright*	*Jones*	*Bentley*	
											Struggling Port Vale have handed the job of steering them to safety to Alan Bloor and Gordon Banks. They will only be in the job two months. In difficult conditions, though, their side provides the one gleaning moment in the 26th minute when Kilner pushes Wright's shot onto the post.											
20	17/11	A	ALDERSHOT	*3,352*	11	L	20	1-3	0-2	Burke 90	Kilner	Geidmintis	Goodman*	Evans	Harris	Hendrie	Firth	Kennedy	**Dryhurst**	Smith	Burke	Whiteley
					8					*Needham 31, Brodie 43, 66* / Ref: M Taylor	*Johnson*	*Scott*	*Wooler*	*Dixon*	*Bennett*	*Jopling*	*Crosby*	*Brodie*	*French*	*Needham*	*McGregor*	
											Dave Evans' 13th-minute free-kick causes the home side some anxieties, but by half-time these have been allayed. Needham pounces to put the Shots in front, and Brodie's powerful header doubles the lead. Brodie looks offside for his second, and Burke's late reply is inconsequential.											
21	1/12	A	PORTSMOUTH	***14,087***	12	L	20	1-3	0-1	Firth 73	Kilner	Dunleavy	Hutt	Evans	Harris	Goodman*	Firth	Kennedy	Burke	Smith	Stafford	Dryhurst
					1					*Brisley 29, Garwood 58, Laidlaw 69* / Ref: C Maskell	*Mellor*	*Ellis*	*Viney*	*Brisley*	*Aizlewood*	*Davey*	*Garwood*	*Laidlaw*	*Hemmerman*	*Bryant*	*Rogers*	
											Frank Burrows has taken over at Fratton Park and taken Pompey to the top of the table. Their win in front of the TV cameras is a comfortable one. Brisley scores unmarked off a corner. The league's top scorer, Garwood, scores his 17th of the season – then talks about a move to Exeter.											
22	8/12	H	LINCOLN	1,991	11	W	22	1-0	0-0	Hendrie 63	Kilner	Dunleavy	Hutt	Evans	Harris	Hendrie	Firth	Kennedy	**Allatt**	Burke	Stafford*	Smith
					9					Ref: N Ashley	*Grotier*	*Thompson*	*Neale*	*Watson*	*Saunders*	*Peake*	*Hobson*	*Carr*	*Harford*	*Bell*	*Ball**	*Cunningham*
											Former Shay favourite 'Dinger' Bell has been in trouble for allegedly hitting his wife. This has not escaped the attention of the Town fans, who are quick to remind him Kirby has bought a forward, Allatt, a coal miner, but it's Hendrie who settles the game, heading in Harris' knockdown.											
23	21/12	A	SCUNTHORPE	***1,473***	12	L	22	0-1	0-1		Kilner	Dunleavy	Goodman*	Evans	Harris	Hendrie	Smith	Kennedy	Mountford	Allatt	Burke	Geidmintis
					21					*Cammack 22* / Ref: P Willis	*Gordon*	*Davy*	*Peacock*	*Dall*	*Deere*	*Oates*	*Green**	*Cammack*	*Pilling*	*Partridge*	*Stewart*	*Cowling*
											Town reach the halfway stage with 22 points – only four less than their total last season. On a ground that gradually freezes, Town look a mere shadow of the side that has played two draws with Walsall in the Cup. A further point is out of reach when Steve Cammack scores off a corner.											

LEAGUE DIVISION 4 — Manager: George Kirby — SEASON 1979-80

No	Date		Att	Pos	Pt	F-A	H-T	Scorers, Times, and Referees	1	2	3	4	5	6	7	8	9	10	11	12 sub used
24	H	HUDDERSFIELD		10	W	2-1	1-0	Kennedy 40, Burke 77	Kilner	Dunleavy	Hutt	Evans	Harris	Hendrie	Firth	Kennedy	Burke	Smith	Stafford	
	26/12		**10,061**	3	24			Dunleavy 71 (og)	Rankin	Brown	Robinson	Stanton	Sutton	Hanvey	Laverick	Hart	Fletcher	Robins*	Cowling	Kindon
								Ref: J Worrall	A dramatic, action-packed derby. A five-figure gate sees Kennedy opens the scoring with a scorching left-foot half-volley. Huddersfield bring on new signing Kindon. His first touch is a cross turned in by Dunleavy. But Burke dives through a mass of bodies to head home the winner.											
25	H	PETERBOROUGH		11	D	0-0	0-0		Kilner	Dunleavy	Hutt	Evans	Harris	Hendrie	Firth	Kenedy	Burke	Smith	Stafford	
	29/12		3,639	12	25				Waugh	Carmichael	Phillips	Gay	Slough	Foster	Quow	Kellock	Cliss	Syrett	Robson	
								Ref: D Richardson	One contributory factor for the relatively high attendance for the visit of Peter Morris's side could be that Town are handing out vouchers for the forthcoming Man City cup-tie. After needing three games to see off Walsall, Town look tired. The heavy mud and a blizzard don't help.											
26	A	CREWE		13	L	1-2	0-0	Firth 70	Kilner	Dunleavy	Hutt	Evans	Harris	Hendrie	Firth	Kennedy	Mountford*	Smith	Stafford	Burke
	12/1		2,579	24	25			Scott 55, Hunter 80	Grobbelaar	Lewis	Bowers	Hunter	Scott	Prophett	McMahon	Guy	Conroy	Palios	Ashworth*	Davies
								Ref: M Robinson	A week is a long time in football. Seven days ago, Town, with the same line-up, were beating 1st Division Man City in the FA Cup. Here, they are brought down to earth with a big bang. Debutante Terry Conroy has tormented Town before, and does so again, making Hunter's winner.											
27	A	HEREFORD		16	L	0-2	0-0		Kilner	Dunleavy	Hutt	Evans	Harris	Hendrie*	Allatt	Kennedy	Burke	Goodman	Stafford	Smith
	2/2		2,814	18	25			Marshall 70, Binney 90	Hughes	Price	Burrows	Spiring	Layton	Thomas	McGrellis	Marshall	Binney	Jones	White	
								Ref: J Sewell	The cup run is over, and Town find it hard to re-adapt to the realities of Division 4 soccer. Hereford far from dominate, but get the goals. The first is a volley from Julian Marshall. The second, in injury-time, is highly controversial, when Fred Binney charges Kilner's kick-out to score.											
28	H	BOURNEMOUTH		16	W	2-0	1-0	Smith 3, Dunleavy 80	Kilner	Dunleavy	Hutt	Evans	Harris	Goodman	Firth	Kennedy	Allatt	Smith	Stafford*	Whiteley
	9/2		1,939	10	27				Smoulders	Bryant	Ferns	Heffernan	Moore	Chambers	Elliott	MacDougall	Butler	Evanson	Miller	
								Ref: K Walmsley	Town's first home game since the City cup win attracts a disappointing attendance. How quickly people forget. Town at least return to winning ways in the league. Smith reaches Evans' cross to head in early on, and Dunleavy wraps up the points when he pops up to smack in the ball.											
29	A	YORK		15	D	2-2	1-0	Harris 27, Evans 74	Kilner	Dunleavy	Hutt	Evans	Harris	Hendrie	Firth	Kennedy	Allatt	Goodman	Smith	
	12/2		2,124	19	28			Faulkner 63, 79	Crawford	Hood	Walsh	Pugh	Faulkner	Clements	Ferebee	Lorimer	Eccles	McDonald	McGhie	
								Ref: A Challinor	York have enlisted the help this season of former Leeds and Scotland ace Peter Lorimer. They are struggling now, but will end up above Town, who actually should have won. Crawford drops the ball for Harris to score. Town lead 2-1 before Faulkner gets his second goal from a corner.											
30	A	HARTLEPOOL		13	W	2-1	0-0	Harris 75, Firth 88	Kilner	Dunleavy	Hutt	Evans	Harris	Hendrie	Firth	Kennedy	Allatt*	Smith	Whiteley	Dryhurst
	16/2		3,392	16	30			Newton 83	Burleigh	Sweeney	Carr	Lawrence	Fagan	Ayre	Linacre	Harding*	Newton	Gorry	Hampton	Houchen
								Ref: R Banks	Town record only their second double. All the goals come in the last 15 minutes. Harris starts the flourish of goals, heading in Kennedy's free-kick, then Newton – villain at the Shay – equalises. Firth's winner is a shot that deceives Burleigh and bounces over him on the hard ground.											
31	H	DARLINGTON		14	D	1-1	0-0	Evans 51p	Kilner	Dunleavy	Hutt	Evans	Harris	Hendrie	Firth	Kennedy	Dryhurst	Goodman	Smith	
	23/2		2,129	20	31			Hamilton 85	Owers	Nattress	Cochrane	Ball	Craig	Smith	McLean	Charlton	Stalker	Hamilton	Walsh	
								Ref: R Heath	Town should be beating struggling sides like Billy Elliott's Darlington. But they fail to capitalise on Evans' penalty for a push by any one of three defenders on Harris. Ian Hamilton glances in a corner to send the visitors away happier. Twice in the first half a stray dog holds up play.											
32	A	WALSALL		15	L	0-2	0-1		Kilner	Dunleavy	Hutt	Evans	Harris	Hendrie*	Firth	Kennedy	Dryhurst	Goodman	Stafford	Burke
	1/3		5,859	1	31			McDonough 6, Buckley 90	Green	Macken	Mower	Sbragia	Serella*	Paul	Penn	Waddington	McDonough	Buckley	Caswell	Williams
								Ref: G Owen	The Saddlers go five points clear at the top after this. They will view that as more important than gaining revenge over their cup conquerors. Roy McDonough's header gives his side an early lead, but Dryhurst misses a sitter from six yards before Alan Buckley pounces in injury-time.											
33	H	NORTHAMPTON		11	W	2-1	2-0	Smith 5, 45	Kilner	Dunleavy	Hutt	Evans	Harris	Goodman	Firth	Kennedy	Burke	Whiteley*	Smith	Dryhurst
	4/3		1,377	10	33			Byatt 67	Poole	Walker	Sandercock	Byatt	Gage	Farrington	Denyer	Sandy	McCaffrey	Bowen	Sargent	
								Ref: K McNally	It is the result that matters. Smith's brace, the second of which comes crucially at half-time, gives Town a cushion, which they are grateful for. The Cobblers throw everything at Town after the break, manage to pull one back through Byatt's 30-yarder, but find that second goal elusive.											
34	A	NEWPORT		15	L	2-5	0-1	Smith 80, 88 [Aldridge 85]	Kilner	Dunleavy	Hutt	Evans	Harris	Hendrie*	Firth	Kennedy	Burke	Goodman	Smith	Allatt
	14/3		4,777	5	33			Gwyther 23, 52, Vaughan 46p, 70,	Plumley	Walden	Relish	Oakes	Davies	Bruton	Vaughan	Lowndes	Gwyther	Aldridge	Moore	
								Ref: B Stevens	A stray black and white mongrel delays kick-off. It reappears after 25 minutes, so the ref takes the teams off the pitch. In the game, Town are taken apart. Former Shayman Gwyther grabs two, whilst Hutt flattens Moore for the penalty. Smith's second successive 'double' is in vain.											

No	Date	Opponent	Att	Pos	Pt	Res	F-A	H-T	Scorers, Times, and Referees	1	2	3	4	5	6	7	8	9	10	11	12
35	H	WIGAN		13		D	0-0	0-0		Kilner	Dunleavy	Hutt	Evans	Harris	Goodman	Firth	Kennedy	Allatt	Burke	Smith	
	19/3		1,406	*9*	34					*Brown*	*Fretwell*	*Whittle*	*Gore*	*Methven*	*Davids*	*Corrigan*	*Wright*	*Houghton*	*Shearer*	*Urquhart*	
									Ref: M Scott	This fixture was postponed yesterday. The ref gives it the go-ahead this time around, despite sub-zero temperatures and blizzards. Still, it's an entertaining game, despite no scoring, with Wigan just about on top. But it's Kennedy who fluffs the best chance when only eight yards out.											
36	A	PORT VALE		15		L	0-1	0-0		Kilner	Dunleavy	Hutt	Evans	Harris	Goodman*	Firth	Kennedy	Allatt	Burke	Smith	Stafford
	22/3		*2,993*	*20*	34				*Smith 53 (og)*	*Dance*	*Keenan*	*Griffiths*	*Elsby*	*Harwood*	*Sproson*	*Beech*	*Chamberlain N*	*Fleming*	*Sealy*	*Bentley*	
									Ref: D Owen	Suddenly the pressure is on Town. They now need at least six points to avoid finishing in the re-election zone. New Vale boss John McGrath is struggling to turn around his side's fortunes, too. So he is grateful for the points after Town's Smith inadvertently turns in Chamberlain's cross.											
37	H	ALDERSHOT		14		W	1-0	0-0	Kennedy 58	Kilner	Dunleavy	Hutt	Evans	Harris	Burke	Firth	Kennedy	Allatt*	Smith	Stafford	Dryhurst
	29/3		1,202	*10*	36					*Johnson*	*Edwards*	*Wooler*	*Briley*	*Bennett**	*Youlden*	*Green*	*Brodie*	*Garwood*	*French*	*McGregor*	*Crosby*
									Ref: A Hamil	Aldershot include in their side recent expensive signings Briley (£45,000 from Wimbledon) and Garwood (£54,000 from Portsmouth). Halifax know they won't be easy to beat. But they work hard and hang on to Kennedy's 25-yard wind-assisted strike, after Briley misses his tackle.											
38	A	HUDDERSFIELD		14		L	**0-5**	0-0		Kilner	Dunleavy	Hutt*	Evans	Harris	Hendrie	Firth	Kennedy	Allatt	Smith	Burke	Mountford
	5/4		*10,580*	*2*	36				*Robins 49, 73, Kindon 66, 81p, Sutton 70*	*Rankin*	*Brown*	*Purdie*	*Stanton*	*Sutton*	*Topping*	*Laverick*	*Hart*	*Kindon*	*Robins*	*Cowling**	*Fletcher*
									Ref: G Nolan	A goal down, George Kirby gambles by taking off a defender for a striker, then watches Mick Buxton's Huddersfield tear his side apart. Chief architect is Kindon, who careers through to double the lead a minute after Kirby's switch. Buxton takes off Cowling, a target for the boo-boys.											
39	H	YORK		14		D	1-1	1-1	Firth 38	Kilner	Dunleavy	Hutt	Evans	Harris	Hendrie	Firth	Kennedy	Burke	Smith	Stafford*	Mountford
	7/4		1,778	*17*	37				*Pugh 25*	*Crawford*	*Hood*	*Kay*	*Ford*	*Faulkner*	*Clements*	*Wellings*	*Pugh*	*Eccles*	*McDonald*	*Walsh*	
									Ref: R Bridges	Pugh scores his first goal for York, in almost two seasons, against his former club. He moves in to shoot past Kilner off Ian McDonald's low cross. Town want to put the hammering at Leeds Road behind them, and go some way to doing so when Firth robs Kay and advances to score.											
40	H	SCUNTHORPE		14		D	2-2	1-2	Burke 34, Mountford 51	Kilner	Dunleavy	Hutt	Evans	Harris	Hendrie	Firth	Kennedy	Burke	Mountford	Smith	
	8/4		1,660	*19*	38				*Oates 2, Cammack 33*	*Gordon*	*O'Donnell*	*Peacock*	*Oates*	*Deere*	*Dall*	*Pugh*	*Cammack*	*Pilling*	*Partridge*	*Stewart**	*Cowling*
									Ref: N Ashley	England cricketer Ian Botham is not included in Scunthorpe's twelve. Also missing this evening is FIFA referee Pat Partridge, due to a family bereavement. Town claw back a two-goal deficit, then miss a chance to go in front when Jimmy Gordon saves Kennedy's 73rd-minute penalty.											
41	A	WIGAN		15		L	1-3	0-1	Smith 60	Kilner	Dunleavy	Hutt	Evans	Burke	Smith	Firth	Kennedy	Dryhurst	Mountford	Stafford*	Whiteley
	12/4		*5,076*	*8*	38				*Quinn M 32, Davids 61, Houghton 76*	*Brown*	*Fretchley*	*Whittle*	*Gore*	*Methven*	*Davids*	*Corrigan*	*Wright*	*Quinn M*	*Houghton*	*Urquhart*	
									Ref: A Seville	John Smith comes off the bench to score a historic goal. His chip over Brown is Town's 3,000th in League football. It also ties the game up. But not for long. In the next minute, unmarked Davids heads in to restore Wigan's lead, and Houghton's close-range header finishes off Town.											
42	H	PORTSMOUTH		18		L	1-2	0-1	Hendrie 57	Kilner	Dunleavy	Hutt	Evans	Harris*	Hendrie	Firth	Kennedy	Mountford	Burke	Smith	Allatt
	19/4		2,950	*4*	38				*Hemmerman 14, Gregory 51*	*Mellor*	*McLaughlin*	*Bryant*	*Brisley*	*Ellis*	*Davey*	*Hemmerman*	*Laidlaw*	*Gregory*	*Brown*	*Rogers*	
									Ref: C Seel	Town lose, but hear good news. Other results go their way, so they now know that a re-election bid will not have to be made. Pompey have promotion on their mind. David Gregory's angled drive puts them well in control. A hobbling Hendrie halves the deficit with Mellor stranded.											
43	H	STOCKPORT		18		L	1-3	0-2	Firth 84	Kilner	Burke	Hutt	Evans	Harris	Smith	Firth	Kennedy	Mountford	Allatt	Stafford	
	22/4		1,233	*19*	38				*Booth 21, Sword 24p, Uzelac 63*	*Lawson*	*Rutter*	*Sherlock*	*Thorpe*	*Sword*	*Uzelac*	*Williams*	*Bradd*	*Prudham*	*Galvin*	*Booth*	
									Ref: B Martin	Kirby concedes, 'We can compete with the best, but only with all our players fit.' Which they aren't. Stockport aren't even one of the best. But they have an ally in Brian Martin. He awards them a penalty for hands, then overrules a flagging linesman to allow Uzelac to run away for 0-3.											
44	A	LINCOLN		18		L	0-4	0-2	*[Harford 89]*	Kilner	Dunleavy	Hutt	Evans	Harris	Burke	Smith	Kennedy	Mountford	Allatt	Stafford	
	25/4		*2,696*	*7*	38				*Shipley 12, 84, Cunningham 24,*	*Fox*	*Thompson*	*Keeley*	*Shipley*	*Peake*	*Carr*	*Hobson*	*Hughes*	*Harford*	*Cunningham*	*Turner*	
									Ref: D Hutchinson	Colin Murphy's Imps side extend their unbeaten home run to 22 games. It's almost too easy for them, as Kilner works overtime. Hit-man Mick Harford knocks down for George Shipley to score the first from close range, then rounds off the scoring late on with a blistering 35-yard shot.											
45	H	TORQUAY		18		D	3-3	1-2	Firth 28, 55, Evans 89	Kilner	Dunleavy	Hutt	Evans	Harris	Goodman	Firth	Kennedy	Allatt	Burke	Smith	
	29/4		**1,022**	*9*	39				*Lawrence 19, Cox 36, 66,*	*O'Keefe*	*Pethard*	*Ritchie*	*Twitchin*	*Wilson*	*Larmour*	*Coffill*	*Lawrence*	*Cox*	*Levy*	*Marmon*	
									Ref: K Baker	Town are lucky to still be in the hunt at half-time, and they get a roasting from Kirby. Firth lashes home a second equaliser, but Torquay go in front again when Cox heads in. Town then pile on the pressure, and deservedly level it a third time when Evans heads in off Kilner's long kick.											
46	A	STOCKPORT		18		L	1-4	0-3	Kennedy 83	Kilner	Dunleavy	Hutt	Evans	Harris	Goodman	Firth	Kennedy	Allatt	Burke*	Smith	Stafford
	2/5		*1,979*	*16*	39				*Prudham 14, 37, 72, Booth 30*	*Lawson*	*Rutter*	*Sherlock*	*Thorpe*	*Sword*	*Uzelac*	*Williams*	*Bradd*	*Prudham*	*Galvin*	*Booth*	
		Home	Away						Ref: A Saunders	County's free-scoring Eddie Prudham was given a free transfer just before the kick-off. He signs off with a hat-trick. His second, for 0-3, looks offside, but it ends the game as a contest. His third is a header. Kennedy is Town's best player, and his 25-yarder is just reward for his efforts.											
Average		2,574	3,991																		

League Cup		F-A	H-T	Scorers, Times, and Referees	1	2	3	4	5	6	7	8	9	10	11	12 sub used
1:1 H SHREWSBURY	D	2-2	1-1	Johnson 2, Mountford 55	Leonard	Dunleavy	Hutt	**Evans**	**Harris**	**Hendrie**	Firth	Kennedy	Mountford	Johnson	Stafford	
11/8 1,904 *3*				*Turner 30, Maguire 70*	*Mulhearn*	*King*	*Leonard*	*Turner*	*Griffin*	*Keay*	*Maguire*	*Atkins*	*Tong*	*Biggins*	*Mann*	
				Ref: P Willis	The fans get full value for their money. George Kirby wants a quick goal. He gets one, when, after only two minutes, Johnson heads in off a corner. Town lead 2-1 when Evans gives away a penalty for pushing. Leonard saves Atkins' kick, but Maguire reacts quickest to the loose ball.											
1:2 A SHREWSBURY	L	0-1	0-0		Leonard	Dunleavy	Hutt*	Evans	Harris	Hendrie	Firth	Kennedy	Mountford	Johnson	Stafford	Burke
14/8 *4,820*				*Atkins 75*	*Mulhearn*	*King*	*Leonard*	*Turner*	*Griffin*	*Keay*	*Maguire*	*Atkins*	*Tong*	*Biggins*	*Mann*	
				Ref: R Bridges (Halifax lost 2-3 on aggregate)	Graham Turner's Division 3 side are made to work hard for victory. Town create few chances, but they frustrate their opponents. The Shrews make the breakthrough and go through, courtesy of Atkins' header following Maguire's cross. The ref books Johnson and Biggins for fighting.											

FA Cup		F-A	H-T	Scorers, Times, and Referees	1	2	3	4	5	6	7	8	9	10	11	12 sub used
1 H SCARBOROUGH 11	W	2-0	2-0	Burke 5, Stafford 45	Kilner	Dunleavy	Hutt	Evans	Harris	Hendrie	Firth	Kennedy	Burke	Smith	Stafford	
24/11 3,778 *APL*					*Livsey*	*Murphy*	*Fountain*	*Dunn H*	*Dixey*	*Marshall*	*Dunn HA*	*Donoghue**	*Gauden*	*Sellers*	*Boylan*	*Abbey*
				Ref: A Saunders	Victory for the Shaymen does more than put them in the next round. It ends a run of six games without a win. Burke is in support to give them the perfect start, turning in Smith's pass. Stafford cuts in and scores a cracker from 25 yards. Boro's £50,000-rated Bob Gauden is contained.											
2 A WALSALL 11	D	1-1	0-0	Kennedy 62	Kilner	Dunleavy	Hutt	Evans	Harris	Hendrie	Firth	Kennedy	Burke	Smith	Stafford	
15/12 *4,651 2*				*Buckley 52p*	*Green*	*Macken*	*Mower*	*Sbragia*	*Serella*	*Paul*	*Penn*	*Waddington*	*McDonouh**	*Buckley*	*Caswell*	*Williams*
				Ref: D Webb	Mick Kennedy scored against Walsall in the league at the Shay earlier this season. He scores his second Town goal, a low shot from 18 yards, to earn Town a replay on a cold, wet and windswept afternoon. Walsall go ahead through Buckley's penalty, when Firth brings down Caswell.											
2R H WALSALL 11	D	1-1 *aet*	1-0	Harris 33	Kilner	Dunleavy	Hutt	Evans	Harris	Hendrie	Firth	Kennedy	Burke	Smith	Stafford*	Mountford
18/12 3,641 *2*				*Buckley 60*	*Green*	*Macken*	*Mower*	*Sbragia*	*Serella**	*Paul*	*Penn*	*Waddington*	*McDonough*	*Buckley*	*Caswell*	*Williams*
				Ref: D Webb	A home tie with 1st Division Man City awaits the winners. It is they who should be worried. There is little to choose between these two sides, even after extra-time. Harris gives Town the lead, heading in when Dunleavy returns the ball. Buckley scores the equaliser from close range.											
2 H WALSALL 12	W	2-0 *aet*	0-0	Burke 93, Smith 102	Kilner	Dunleavy	Hutt	Evans	Harris	Hendrie	Firth	Kennedy	Burke	Smith	Stafford	
RR 24/12 6,530 *1*					*Green*	*Macken*	*Mower*	*Sbragia*	*Williams*	*Paul*	*Penn*	*Waddington*	*McDonough**	*Buckley*	*Caswell*	*Rees*
				Ref: N Midgley	Despite the freezing weather, a bumper Shay crowd is treated to an early Christmas cracker. Roy McDonough misses a golden 75th-minute chance when he hesitates with only Kilner to beat. He regrets it in extra-time as Burke prods Town in front, and then Smith hooks in a second.											
3 H MANCHESTER C	W	1-0	0-0	Hendrie 75	Kilner	Dunleavy	Hutt	Evans	Harris	Hendrie	Firth	Kennedy	Mountford	Smith	Stafford	
5/1 12,599 *1:15*					*Corrigan*	*Ranson*	*Power*	*Reid*	*Caton*	*Bennett*	*Henry*	*Daley*	*Robinson*	*Viljoen*	*Shinton*	
				Ref: M Lowe	The floodlights don't suit the TV cameras, so it's a 2.00 kick-off. The pitch is a mudbath, but proves to be great leveller. Hypnotist Romark has put a curse on City boss Malcolm Allison, whose side create chances. But Kilner is in great form. Hendrie's winner will go down in folklore.											
4 A BOLTON	L	0-2	0-1		Kilner	Dunleavy	Hutt	Evans	Goodman	Hendrie	Firth	Kennedy	Burke	Smith	Stafford	
26/1 *21,085 1:22*				*Greaves 32, Whatmore 90*	*McDonagh*	*Nicholson*	*Burke*	*Greaves*	*Allardyce*	*Walsh*	*Morgan*	*Whatmore*	*Carter*	*McNab*	*Reid*	
				Ref: T Farley	A travelling army of 6,000 Town supporters sees their team compete well, but there is no repeat Cup shock. The Shaymen are still in the hunt until Whatmore scrambles in Walsh's late cross. Despite the win, relegation-haunted Bolton will sack their manager Ian Greaves on Monday.											

		Home						Away					
		P	W	D	L	F	A	W	D	L	F	A	Pts
1	Huddersfield	46	16	5	2	61	18	11	7	5	40	30	66
2	Walsall	46	12	9	2	43	23	11	9	3	32	24	64
3	Newport	46	16	5	2	47	22	11	2	10	36	28	61
4	Portsmouth	46	15	5	3	62	23	9	7	7	29	26	60
5	Bradford C	46	14	6	3	44	14	10	6	7	33	36	60
6	Wigan	46	13	5	5	42	26	8	8	7	34	35	55
7	Lincoln	46	14	8	1	43	12	4	9	10	21	30	53
8	Peterborough	46	14	3	6	39	22	7	7	9	19	25	52
9	Torquay	46	13	7	3	47	25	2	10	11	23	44	47
10	Aldershot	46	10	7	6	35	23	6	6	11	27	30	45
11	Bournemouth	46	8	9	6	32	25	5	9	9	20	26	44
12	Doncaster	46	11	6	6	37	27	4	8	11	25	36	44
13	Northampton	46	14	5	4	33	16	2	7	14	18	50	44
14	Scunthorpe	46	11	9	3	37	23	3	6	14	21	52	43
15	Tranmere	46	10	4	9	32	24	4	9	10	18	32	41
16	Stockport	46	9	7	7	30	31	5	5	13	18	41	40
17	York	46	9	6	8	35	34	5	5	13	30	48	39
18	HALIFAX	46	11	9	3	29	20	2	4	17	17	52	39
19	Hartlepool	46	10	7	6	36	28	4	3	16	23	36	38
20	Port Vale	46	8	6	9	34	24	4	6	13	22	46	36
21	Hereford	46	8	7	8	22	21	3	7	13	16	31	36
22	Darlington	46	7	11	5	33	26	2	6	15	17	48	35
23	Crewe	46	10	6	7	25	27	1	7	15	10	41	35
24	Rochdale	46	6	7	10	20	28	1	6	16	13	51	27
		1104	269	159	124	898	562	124	159	269	562	898	1104

Odds & ends

Double wins: (2) Bournemouth, Hartlepool.
Double losses: (3) Bradford C, Portsmouth, Stockport.

Won from behind: (1) Hartlepool (h).
Lost from in front: (0).

High spots: Eight games without defeat up to 6 October.
Four consecutive wins up to 29 September.
George Kirby being awarded the division's Manager of the Month for September, repeating his feat of February 1971.
Beating 1st Division Man City to reach 4th Round of the FA Cup.
Beating eventual champions Huddersfield at home on Boxing Day.

Low spots: Failing to win last 9 matches including 4 consecutive defeats.
Kevin Johnson breaking his leg in September.

Town's Boxing Day clash with neighbours Huddersfield attracted the last five-figure gate for a League match at the Shay.
Town conceded only nine goals at home in the first 18 League matches and eleven in their last five.

Player of the Year: Paul Hendrie.
Ever-presents: (1) Mick Kennedy.
Hat-tricks: (0).
Leading scorers: Peter Burke & Francis Firth (8).

	Appearances						Goals			
	Lge	*Sub*	LC	*Sub*	FAC	*Sub*	Lge	LC	FAC	Tot
Allatt, Vernon	**14**	*2*								
Burke, Peter	**35**	*6*		*1*	5		**6**		2	**8**
Dryhurst, Carl	**4**	*4*								
Dunleavy, Chris	**43**		2		6		**3**			**3**
Evans, David	**45**		2		6		**3**			**3**
Firth, Francis	**35**		2		6		**8**			**8**
Geidmintis, Tony	**10**	*2*								
Goodman, Malcolm	**18**	*4*			1					
Harris, David	**44**		2		5		**3**		1	**4**
Hendrie, Paul	**34**		2		6		**3**		1	**4**
Hough, John	**1**									
Hutt, Geoff	**44**		2		6					
Johnson, Kevin	**9**		2				**3**	1		**4**
Kennedy, Mick	**46**		2		6		**4**		1	**5**
Kilner, John	**40**				6					
Leonard, Mick	**5**		2							
Mountford, Bob	**23**	*3*	2		1	*1*	**4**	1		**5**
Smith, John	**26**	*2*			6		**6**		1	**7**
Stafford, Andy	**20**	*5*	2		6		**1**		1	**2**
Thomas, John	**5**									
Whiteley, Andy	**5**	*4*					**1**			**1**
(own-goals)							**1**			**1**
21 players used	**506**	***32***	**22**	***1***	**66**	***1***	**46**	**2**	**7**	**55**

No	Date		Att	Pos	Pt	F-A	H-T	Scorers, Times, and Referees	1	2	3	4	5	6	7	8	9	10	11	12 sub used
1	H	MANSFIELD			L	0-2	0-0		Kilner	Nattress	Dunleavy	Evans	Harris*	Goodman	Firth	Hendrie	Allatt	Ward	**O'Neil**	Stafford
	16/8		1,682		0			*Austin 65, 66*	*Arnold*	*Dawkins*	*Mann*	*Bird*	*McClelland*	*Burrows*	*Phillips*	*Caldwell*	*Austin*	*Parkinson*	*Pollard*	
								Ref: D Owen	The lowest opening day Shay crowd sees Kirby reshuffle his side after only 27 minutes. Allatt squanders a golden chance just after half-time, when he hesitates eight yards out. £200,000-rated Terry Austin kills the game with two quick goals, his second a dipping 25-yader over Kilner.											
2	A	PETERBOROUGH			D	2-2	0-0	Ward 52, Firth 61	Kilner	Nattress	Dunleavy	Evans	Harris	Goodman	Firth	Hendrie	Allatt	Ward	O'Neil	
	20/8		*3,885*		1			*Cooke 55, Kellock 88p*	*Waugh*	*McVay*	*Phillips*	*Hodgson*	*Foster*	*Slack*	*Quow*	*Kellock*	*Cooke*	*Syrett**	*Cliss*	*Gallagher*
								Ref: A Hamil	Controversy reigns at London Road. Town are two minutes away from a deserved victory when the linesman views Nattress' foul on Quow as inside the box, when the referee has initially given it outside. The expensive Kellock steps up to score the penalty, and save his side a point.											
3	H	BURY			W	**4-2**	3-1	Firth 5, 38, Dunleavy 10, Allatt ??	Kilner	Nattress*	Dunleavy	Evans	Harris	Goodman	Firth	Hendrie	Allatt	Ward	O'Neil	**Burton**
	23/8		1,861		3			*Whitehead 20, Johnson 89*	*Forrest*	*Howard*	*Kennedy*	*Halford*	*Whitehead*	*Waddington*	*Mullen**	*Butler*	*Johnson*	*Waldron*	*Madden*	*Halton*
								Ref: J Bray	The Shaymen gain revenge for their League Cup defeat. They do it in style, with even Allatt hooking in his first goal for the club. Firth looks irresistible and scores his first goal from 19 yards out. The most spectacular goal is reserved for Johnson, a stinging daisy-cutter from 35 yards.											
4	A	STOCKPORT		8	D	1-1	0-0	Firth 73	Kilner	Nattress	Dunleavy	Evans	Harris	Goodman	Firth	Hendrie	Allatt	Ward !	O'Neil	
	29/8		*2,487*	*9*	4			*Sword 80*	*Lawson*	*Sherlock*	*Rutter*	*Fowler*	*Sword*	*Uzelac*	*Williams*	*Sunley*	*Bradd*	*Galvin*	*Coyle*	
								Ref: N Glover	The Shaymen play over half the march with only ten men after Steve Ward's sending off for a tackle from behind on John Rutter. They battle on, and take a shock lead when Firth races through to blast home from eight yards. Sword saves County's blushes with a headed equaliser.											
5	A	LINCOLN		15	L	0-3	0-0		Kilner	Nattress	Dunleavy	Evans	Goodman	Harris	Firth	Hendrie	Allatt	Burton	O'Neil	
	6/9		*3,720*	*1*	4			*Hobson 63, 72, Thompson S 78*	*Felgate*	*Thompson T*	*Keeley*	*Thompson S*	*Peake*	*Carr*	*Turner*	*Harford*	*Hobson*	*Hughes*	*Shipley*	
								Ref: J Deakin	Lincon take advantage of Town's indiscipline to go top.Gordon Hobson has all the time he needs to open the scoring, and lack of cover allows him his second goal. Burton loses the ball to Trevor Thompson, who sets up namesake Steve for the third. Card-happy ref Deakin books seven.											
6	H	SCUNTHORPE		14	W	1-0	1-0	Firth 10	Kilner	Nattress	Burton	Evans	Harris	Dunleavy	Firth	Hendrie	Allatt	Ward	O'Neil	
	13/9		1,226	*22*	6				*Neenan*	*Pugh*	*Pilling*	*Grimes*	*Dall*	*Oates*	*Ashworth*	*Cammack*	*Lambert**	*Partridge*	*Stewart*	*O'Berg*
								Ref: K Redfern	Scunthorpe are without a win so far, but they make Town work hard. Firth scores when Allatt flicks Ward's cross into his path. The margin of victory could have been more but for Neenan's penalty save from O'Neil after Firth is fouled. The attendance is the lowest in the League so far.											
7	H	WIGAN		15	L	0-1	0-0		Kilner	Nattress	Burton	Evans	Harris	Dunleavy	Firth	Hendrie	Allatt	Ward	O'Neil	
	16/9		2,052	*14*	6			*Quinn 88*	*Brown*	*Curtis*	*Kettle*	*Gore*	*Methven*	*Davids*	*McMullan*	*Wright*	*Hutchinson*	*Quinn T*	*Corrigan*	
								Ref: B Martin	Bobby Charlton returns to the Shay as a Wigan director. His side doesn't provide stiff opposition, but Town can't score. Firth misses in first-half injury-time, faced by a limping Brown, hurt in a collision with Harris. The game boils over, then near the end Quinn heads the winner.											
8	A	CREWE		19	L	1-2	1-1	Nattress 8	Kilner	Nattress	Burton	Evans*	Harris	Dunleavy	Firth	Hendrie	Allatt	Ward	O'Neil	Stafford
	20/9		*2,102*	*17*	6			*McMahon 11, Conroy 59*	*Mulhearn*	*McMahon*	*Lewis*	*Hunter*	*Scott*	*Prophett*	*Davies*	*Coyne*	*Conroy*	*Palios*	*Bowers**	*Wilkinson*
								Ref: D Allinson	This is Crewe's first home win. They have to come from behind, with Terry Conroy, scorer of many goals against the Shaymen over the years, getting the winner from eight yards. Nattress's first goal for Town is deflected. Kirby experiences a third successive defeat for the first time.											
9	H	WIMBLEDON		23	L	0-1	0-0		Kilner	Nattress	Burton	Ward	Harris	Dunleavy	Firth	Hendrie	Allatt	Johnson	O'Neil	
	27/9		1,407	*9*	6			*Leslie 73*	*Beasant*	*Brown*	*Perkins*	*Galliers*	*Smith*	*Cunningham*	*Davies*	*Downes*	*Leslie*	*Cork*	*Hubbick**	*Hodges*
								Ref: R Bridges	John Leslie turned down a £50,000 move to the Shay during the close season. He shows the Town fans what he is about by heading smoothly into the net to score the decisive goal. After a year out, Kevin Johnson makes a welcome return to the Town side, but can't inspire his team.											
10	A	WIGAN		24	L	1-4	0-2	Firth 87	Kilner	Nattress	Burton	Ward	Harris	Dunleavy	Firth	Hendrie	Allatt	Johnson*	O'Neil	Goodman
	1/10		*4,247*	*11*	6			*Quinn 43, 54, Kettle 45, Urquhart 80*	*Ward*	*Curtis*	*Kettle*	*Gore*	*Methven*	*Davids*	*Urquhart*	*Wright*	*Hutchinson*	*Quinn M*	*Corrigan*	
								Ref: A Seville	Town hit rock bottom, but Kirby says, 'It is not the end of the world.' They look like holding out for a goalless first half, then Quinn beats the offside, and Kettle is left free as Wigan take a two-goal half-time lead. The rest is inevitable, as much as Firth's consolation is unexpected.											
11	A	TORQUAY		24	L	0-1	0-0		Kilner	Nattress	Burton	Ward*	Harris	Dunleavy	Firth	Hendrie	Allatt	Goodman	Stafford	Whiteley
	4/10		*1,849*	*10*	6			*Wilson 47*	*O'Keefe*	*Pethard*	*Cochrane*	*Jones*	*Wilson*	*Hayes*	*Fell**	*Cox*	*Cooper*	*Bowker*	*Weston*	*Lawrence*
								Ref: R Lewis	Kirby is away on a player-hunting mission as his side slip to a fifth consecutive defeat. In a rare venture forward, Goodman breaks through just before half-time, but shoots tamely at O'Keefe. Town pack the defence, but they can't prevent Brian Wilson's header from Gerry Fell's corner.											

No	Venue	Opponent	Pos	Res	F-A	H-T	Scorers, Times, and Referees	1	2	3	4	5	6	7	8	9	10	11	12 sub used
12	H	YORK	22	W	3-1	1-0	Nattress 31, Hendrie 64, O'Neil 69	Kilner	Nattress	Burton	Evans	Harris	Hendrie	Firth	Allatt	**Graham**	O'Neil	**McIlwraith**	
7/10		1,088	*18*	8			*Smith 77*	*Blackburn*	*Hood**	*Kay*	*Smith*	*Clements*	*Craig*	*Ford*	*Byrne*	*Eccles*	*Millar*	*McDonald*	*Walsh*
							Ref: K McNally	Town include new signings Graham and McIlwraith. Heavy rain affects the attendance, but most go away well pleased. Hendrie's left-foot 20-yarder is the pick of the goals. O'Neil says in the club programme that he never scores, then he does when Allatt's shot comes back off the bar.											
13	H	SOUTHEND	24	L	**1-5**	0-2	O'Neil 86 *[Gray 71, 73]*	Kilner	Nattress	Burton	Evans	Harris	Hendrie	Firth	Allatt	Graham	O'Neil	McIlwraith*	Johnson
11/10		1,609	*1*	8			*Spence 19, Moody 25, Cusack 50,*	*Cawston*	*Dudley*	*Yates*	*Hadley*	*Moody*	*Cusack*	*Gray*	*Pountney*	*Spence*	*Mercer*	*Otulakowski*	
							Ref: M Peck	Dave Smith's side are the league leaders, but that is no excuse for this Shay sham. Town simply give in, and the visitors hardly have to break sweat. Elementary defensive errors lead to all five of Southend's goals, such as Harris's back-header for Cusack's. Kirby – 'I can't believe it.'											
14	A	DONCASTER	24	D	0-0	0-0		Kilner	Nattress	Dunleavy	Evans	Goodman	Hendrie	Firth	Graham	McIlwraith*	O'Neil	Stafford	Ward
18/10		*4,044*	*6*	9				*Boyd*	*Rusell*	*Dowie*	*Lister*	*Harle*	*Dowd*	*Pugh**	*Nimmo*	*Warboys*	*Flanagan*	*Little*	*Snodin I*
							Ref: C Maskell	The Shaymen set about repairing the damage. They hardly set the world alight, but with Rovers on the fringe of the promotion places, they have to play a cautious game. The home side dominates, but Town hold out. Warboys comes closest to scoring with a header that hits the bar.											
15	A	TRANMERE	24	L	0-2	0-0		Kilner	Nattress	Dunleavy	Evans	Goodman	Hendrie	Firth	Graham	McIlwraith	O'Neil	Ward*	Whiteley
20/10		*2,314*	*5*	9			*Lumby 57, Mungall 65*	*Johnson*	*Mathias*	*Flood*	*Williams*	*Parry*	*Evans*	*Peplow*	*Mungall*	*Lumby*	*Beamish*	*Hamilton*	
							Ref: J Hough	Despite playing better than at Doncaster, Town end up with nothing to show for their efforts. Bryan Hamilton's side has a ten-minute purple patch and score twice. Steve Mungall's goal is a peach, after playing a one-two with Lumby. Never a dirty game, the ref awards 43 free-kicks.											
16	H	HEREFORD	24	D	0-0	0-0		Kilner	Nattress*	Dunleavy	Evans	Harris	Goodman	Firth	Graham	Hendrie	McIlwraith	O'Neil	Whiteley
25/10		1,288	*22*	10				*Brand*	*Spiring*	*Bartley*	*Cornes*	*Dobson*	*Hunt*	*Thomas*	*Strong*	*Price*	*Jones*	*White*	
							Ref: P Partridge	While the 92 Football League chairmen are holding a summit meeting to discuss the future of the game, Town need to address their own short-term problems. Two poor sides create few openings. Firth goes close for Town early on, while Jones heads wide for the Bulls on the half-hour.											
17	H	BRADFORD C	23	W	2-0	1-0	Graham 30, Hendrie 56	Kilner	Dunleavy	Goodman	Evans	Harris	Hendrie	Firth	Graham	Johnson*	McIlwraith	O'Neil	Whiteley
28/10		2,365	*15*	12				*Smith*	*Podd*	*Watson*	*Ingham*	*Jackson*	*Wood*	*Chapman*	*Staniforth*	*Campbell*	*McNiven*	*Hutchins*	
							Ref: N Midgley	Town are becoming the Jekyll and Hyde of Division 4. They are unrecognisable from the side that drew with Hereford. This is a cracker of a local derby, with Town in determined mood. Hendrie is the star, and scores a memorable 35-yarder, after Graham's header gets them going.											
18	A	NORTHAMPTON	23	L	1-2	1-1	McIlwraith 29p	Kilner	Dunleavy	Burton	Evans	Goodman*	Hendrie	Firth	Graham	Nattress	McIlwraith	O'Neil	Whiteley
31/10		*2,226*	*12*	12			*Phillips 30, 60*	*Poole*	*Saxby*	*Sandercock*	*Waldock*	*Gage*	*Heeley*	*Carlton*	*Denyer*	*Phillips*	*Williams*	*Farmer*	
							Ref: C Downey	Goodman shows courage by continuing to play on with a badly gashed head, but retires after Steve Phillips scores his second goal – his 13th of the season. The Cobblers conceded eight at Lincoln last week, but only one this time, McIlwraith's penalty after Denyer brings down Graham.											
19	A	YORK	23	D	1-1	0-0	Evans 82	Kilner	Dunleavy	Goodman	Evans	Harris	Hendrie	Firth*	Graham	McIlwraith	O'Neil	Stafford	Whiteley
4/11		*1,837*	*19*	13			*Eccles 56*	*Blackburn*	*Hood*	*Kay*	*Ford*	*Clements*	*Craig*	*Walsh*	*Byrne*	*Eccles*	*McDonald*	*Richards*	
							Ref: A Saunders	For the first time this season Town fall behind and come back to earn a point away from home. They actually look the better side, and Eccles' goal for York comes out of the blue. But Town fight back and deservedly draw level when Evans' low drive off a free-kick finds its way in.											
20	H	HARTLEPOOL	23	L	1-2	0-1	Goodman 65	Kilner	Dunleavy*	Goodman	Evans	Harris	Hendrie	Johnson	Graham	McIlwraith	O'Neil	Stafford	Whiteley
8/11		1,692	*4*	13			*Hampton 10, Hogan 60*	*Burleigh*	*Sweeney*	*Brown*	*Hogan*	*Bird*	*Linacre*	*Kerr*	*Lawrence*	*Newton*	*Houchen*	*Hampton*	
							Ref: M Robinson	Hartlepool are having a good time of things of late, but they need the help of Kilner to get them going here. He slips as Hampton shoots from 30 yards, and the ball trickles over the line. Town claim a handball when Pool get the second, and Kirby is ticked off by the ref for telling him.											
21	H	PETERBOROUGH	23	L	2-3	1-2	Nattress 10, McIlwraith 82p	Kilner	Nattress	Goodman*	Evans	Harris	Hendrie	Johnson	Graham	McIlwraith	O'Neil	**Bullock**	Ward
11/11		1,151	*6*	13			*Cooke 22, Gynn 44, Kellock 79*	*Waugh*	*McVay*	*Phillips*	*Gynn*	*Slack*	*Slough*	*Quow*	*Kellock*	*Cooke*	*Hodgson*	*Robson*	
							Ref: R Banks	Nattress's 30-yarder gives Town a dream start, and McIlwraith nets a late penalty after Phillips brings him down. But in between, Halifax gift three goals. Cooke is unmarked to head in McVay's free-kick, Kellock waltzes through to set up Gynn, then curls in another free-kick for 1-3.											
22	A	MANSFIELD	23	W	1-0	0-0	McIlwraith 47p	Kilner	Nattress	Burton	Evans	Goodman	Hendrie	Ward	Graham	McIlwraith	Bullock	Stafford	
15/11		*2,561*	*6*	15				*Arnold*	*McJannet*	*Foster*	*Hamilton*	*McClelland*	*Bird*	*Allen*	*Mann*	*Austin**	*Parkinson*	*Thomson*	*Caldwell*
							Ref: D Vickers	The ref is the centre of attention. He rightly awards Town a penalty when Arnold takes Bullock's legs. But Mansfield feel he is too harsh when he disallows Parkinson's free-kick after Hendrie breaks from the wall. A disappointing Terry Austin is booed off at half-time, and later subbed.											
23	H	BOURNEMOUTH	23	L	1-2	0-1	Bullock 90	Kilner	Nattress	Burton	Evans	Goodman	O'Neil	Firth	Graham	McIlwraith	Bullock	Ward*	Johnson
29/11		**987**	*14*	15			*Morgan 34, 72*	*Allen*	*Cunningham*	*Moore*	*Impey*	*Compton*	*Heffernan*	*Spackman*	*McGrath*	*Morgan*	*Massey*	*Fern*	
							Ref: H Taylor	After defeat in the FA Cup last week, Town can now concentrate on the League. On a cold afternoon, many supporters choose to stay at home. Those that do turn up begin to drift away when Morgan flicks in his second, and there aren't many left to see Bullock head his first Town goal.											

LEAGUE DIVISION 4 — Manager: George Kirby — SEASON 1980-81

No	Date		Att	Pos	Pt	F-A	H-T	Scorers, Times, and Referees	1	2	3	4	5	6	7	8	9	10	11	12 sub used
24	A	ALDERSHOT		23	L	1-2	0-1	Burton 90	Kilner	O'Neil	Burton	Evans	Goodman	Whiteley	Firth	Graham	McIlwraith	Dunleavy	Stafford*	Bullock
	6/12		*2,335*	*5*	15			*Robinson 23, Sanford 58*	*Johnson*	*Edwards*	*Wooler*	*Briley*	*Youlden*	*Jopling*	*Tomlin*	*Sanford*	*Garwood*	*Crosby*	*Robinson*	
								Ref: H King	After this, Town are now five points adrift of safety. Stuart Robinson takes advantage of a deflection to score the Shots' first goal, whilst Mark Sandford's cool finish doubles the lead. Kirby is heartened by the fact that his side never gives up. Burton's goal is the last kick of the match.											
25	H	PORT VALE		24	D	2-2	2-2	Dunleavy 7, Nattress 41	Kilner	O'Neil	Burton	Evans	Goodman	Dunleavy	Firth	Nattress	McIlwraith	Allatt	Bullock*	Johnson
	20/12		1,215	*21*	16			*Dunleavy 14 (og), Woolfall*	*Cherry*	*Brissett*	*Miller**	*Beech*	*Bowles*	*Sproson*	*Farrell*	*Bennett*	*Chamberlain N*	*Woolfall*	*Bromage*	*Elsby*
								Ref: G Flint	Don Robinson and his non-league Scarborough want to swap places with Town. It's all paper talk. Town end a run of three defeats, but drop to bottom place. Dunleavy is leaving for Australia, and signs off by scoring for both sides, turning in Bromage's centre to cancel out his opener.											
26	A	ROCHDALE		23	D	1-1	0-1	Nattress 70	Kilner	O'Neil	Burton	Evans	Goodman	Hendrie	Firth	Nattress	McIlwraith	Allatt*	Bullock	Graham
	26/12		*2,623*	*9*	17			*Wann 16p*	*Crawford*	*Weir*	*Snookes*	*Esser**	*Burke*	*Taylor*	*Wann*	*O'Loughlin*	*Hilditch*	*Wellings*	*Martinez*	*Jones*
								Ref: D Shaw	Kirby reckoned his side would win here. They don't but it's not for the lack of trying. Kilner will feel aggrieved that the referee orders Wann's penalty to be retaken after he saves the first kick. Sleet and snow make conditions difficult, but don't stop Nattress nipping in for the equaliser.											
27	H	DARLINGTON		23	L	1-2	0-2	Graham 65	Kilner	O'Neil	Burton	Evans	Goodman	Ward	Firth	Nattress	McIlwraith*	Graham	Bullock	Johnson
	27/12		1,805	*10*	17			*Walsh 10, Skipper 35*	*Cuff*	*Kamara*	*Wilson*	*Smith*	*Skipper*	*Speedie*	*Hawker*	*McLean !*	*Stalker*	*Hamilton*	*Walsh*	
								Ref: A Dobson	The Shaymen pay for more missed chances. Billy Elliott's Darlington run up a two-goal lead. Skipper's soft shot rolls apologetically into the net off a post. Graham's header gives Town hope, but the visitors hold out after having captain McLean sent off in the 85th minute for arguing.											
28	H	TRANMERE		23	D	1-1	1-0	Graham 30	Kilner	Ward	Burton	Goodman	**Ayre**	Hendrie	Firth	Graham	McIlwraith	Flavell	Bullock	
	10/1		1,268	*17*	18			*Kelly 48*	*Johnson*	*Edwards*	*Flood*	*Bramhall*	*Parry*	*Evans*	*Kelly*	*Hamilton*	*Craven*	*Kerr*	*Griffiths*	
								Ref: A Porter	An old favourite reappears. Bobby Flavell's arrival is as surprising as his mysterious impending departure will be. But he can't help Town win, as Rovers end a run of six consecutive defeats. Graham pounces to score when Johnson spills the ball, but Kelly equalises off Craven's cross.											
29	A	BOURNEMOUTH		23	L	1-2	0-2	Firth 72p	Kilner	Ward	Burton	Goodman	Ayre	Hendrie	Firth	Graham	McIlwraith*	Nattress	Bullock	Harris
	17/1		*2,413*	*12*	18			*Morgan 16, Ferns 30*	*Allen*	*Cunningham*	*Moore**	*Smith*	*Compton*	*Heffernan*	*Spackman*	*Morgan*	*Mooney*	*Massey*	*Ferns*	*Chambers*
								Ref: D Letts	McIlwraith misses a simple header, then Morgan puts the Cherries in front, heading in Cunningham's free-kick. Phil Ferns' fluke makes it 0-2, when his corner is blown straight into goal. Firth pulls one back from the spot, but Town fail to take full advantage with the wind at their backs.											
30	H	STOCKPORT		22	W	2-0	1-0	Allatt 16, Graham 58	**Turner**	O'Neil	Ward	Evans	Ayre	Hendrie	Firth	Graham	Allatt	Goodman	Nattress	
	24/1		3,286	*21*	20				*Lawson*	*Rutter*	*Sherlock*	*Fowler*	*Thorpe*	*Bradd*	*Williams*	*Sunley*	*Power**	*Galvin*	*Coyle*	*Booth*
								Ref: R Chadwick	Sam Rorke has just been appointed new chairman. He allows 1,000 schoolboys in free, and the players kick footballs into the stand. Then the action on the pitch begins. The Shaymen put on a wonder show. Allatt runs onto the ball to score from 18 yards, then sets up Graham for 2-0.											
31	A	BURY		22	D	0-0	0-0		Turner	O'Neil	Ward	Evans	Ayre	Hendrie	Firth	Graham	Allatt	Goodman	Nattress	
	31/1		*3,144*	*20*	21				*Southall*	*Howard*	*Kennedy*	*Gore*	*Hilton*	*Whitehead*	*Mullen**	*Butler*	*Johnson*	*Jakub*	*Farley*	*Cruickshank*
								Ref: M Warner	1976 FA Cup winner Ian Turner, on loan from Walsall, kept a clean sheet last week, and does so here. But he is made to work for it. With the game 37 minutes old, he saves Johnson's penalty after Ayre upends him. Three minutes earlier, Neville Southall had to save at the feet of Firth.											
32	A	SCUNTHORPE		22	D	2-2	1-2	Ayre 2, Hendrie 71	Turner	O'Neil	Ward	Evans	Ayre	Hendrie	Firth	Graham	Allatt	Goodman	Nattress	
	7/2		*2,023*	*17*	22			*Stewart 28, Grimes 31*	*Neenan*	*Davy*	*Jarvis*	*Grimes*	*Boxall*	*Oates*	*O'Berg*	*Cammack*	*Green*	*Pugh*	*Stewart*	
								Ref: K Salmon	Town put in a worthwhile display, though they have some anxious moments. After going in front through Ayre's header, they find themselves behind at the break. O'Berg hits the post before Scunthorpe twice make the most of poor defending. Hendrie rescues the game from 20 yards.											
33	A	BRADFORD C		23	D	0-0	0-0		Turner	O'Neil	Ward	Evans	Ayre	Hendrie	Firth	Graham	Allatt	Goodman	Nattress	
	11/2		*3,056*		23				*Ramsbottom*	*Robertson*	*Hebditch*	*Ingham*	*Jackson*	*Watson*	*Chapman*	*Staniforth**	*Campbell*	*Gallagher*	*Black*	*McNiven*
								Ref: P Richardson	Bantams' boss George Mulhall is full of admiration for his old side's battling qualities in this local derby. There is not much entertainment, and Town restrict former Shayman Bobby Campbell to a 30-yarder. Allatt rounds the keeper in Town's best moment, but finds the angle too tight.											
34	H	LINCOLN		23	L	1-3	0-1	Firth 75p	Turner	O'Neil	Ward	Evans	Ayre	Hendrie	Firth	Graham	Allatt	Goodman	Nattress	
	14/2		**4,444**	*2*	23			*Hobson 40, 69, Shipley 55p*	*Felgate*	*Thompson*	*Keeley*	*Hughes*	*Peake*	*Carr*	*Neale*	*Turner*	*Hobson*	*Cunningham*	*Shipley*	
								Ref: G Tyson	Lincoln are on a roll, but though it isn't exactly a St Valentine's Day Massacre, it's they who take the points. Gordon Hobson's opener comes against the run of play, but Lincoln don't look back after Ward upends Hobson for Shipley's penalty. Firth's penalty is conceded by Keeley.											

No	H/A	Opponent / Date	Att	Pos	Res / Pts	FT	HT	Scorers, Times, and Referees	1	2	3	4	5	6	7	8	9	10	11	12
35	A	WIMBLEDON		23	L	0-3	0-2		Kilner	Ward	Burton	Evans	Ayre	Hendrie	Firth	Graham	Allatt*	McIlwraith	Nattress	Goodman
		21/2	2,501	9	23			Galliers 18, Downes 30, Cork 80	Beasant	Jones	Armstrong	Galliers	Smith	Cunningham	Ketteridge*	Hodges	Leslie	Cork	Downes	Joseph
								Ref: J Martin	Dons manager Dave Bassett admits after the game, 'We were never three goals better than them.' Beasant is forced to handle outside the box to prevent Hendrie in the fourth minute. The linesman is flagging for offside when Galliers opens the scoring. Town reckon the ref is a 'homer'.											
36	H	TORQUAY		23	W	2-1	1-0	Graham 31, 86	Kilner	Ward	Burton	Harris	Ayre	Hendrie	Firth	Graham	**Chambers**	Nattress	McIlwraith	
		7/3	2,008	12	25			Fell 84	O'Keefe	Jones	Pethard	Coffill	Hayes	Twitchin	Fell	Lawrence*	Bowker	Sermanni	Weston	Cox
								Ref: M Scott	Torquay defender Brian Wilson, having travelled up with the team, takes a taxi back home to be with his wife Anne, of the Nolans pop group, who has gone into labour. Tommy Graham is Town's hero, scoring with a looped header, then chipping over O'Keefe to win the game late on.											
37	A	SOUTHEND		23	L	**1-5**	0-2	Graham 85 [Pountney 72, Gray 74]	Kilner	Ward	Burton	Harris	Ayre	Hendrie	Firth	Graham	Chambers	Nattress	McIlwraith	
		13/3	**5,542**	1	25			Cusack 30p, Moody 38, Spence 63,	Cawston	Stead	Yates	Hadley	Moody	Cusack	Gray	Pountney	Spence	Mercer	Otulakowski	
								Ref: C White	Town are no match for the league leaders, who won 5-1 at the Shay. Kirby has four players out through suspension, which doesn't help. His side is holding out until Ayre fists out a cross, and Cusack's penalty starts the rout. Despite the hammering, Town keeper Kilner is outstanding.											
38	H	DONCASTER		23	L	0-3	0-2		Kilner	Evans	Ward	O'Neil*	Ayre	Hendrie	Firth	Graham	Chambers	Allatt	Nattress	Harris
		21/3	3,762	3	25			Saunders 23, Dawson 26, Nimmo 60	Boyd	Russell	Dawson	Snodin I	Saunders	Lally	Pugh	Nimmo*	Warboys	Snodin G	Little	Lister
								Ref: C Seel	Luck goes against Town against high-flying Rovers. They lose the injured O'Neil and Hendrie, and play the second half with only ten men. O'Neil is on the pitch when he deflects Ian Snodin's shot into Dawson's path for Rovers' second. In the 74th minute, Graham hits the post.											
39	H	CREWE		23	W	1-0	1-0	McIlwraith 16p	Kilner	Ward	Harris	Evans	Ayre	Chambers	Firth	Graham	Allatt	McIlwraith	Nattress	
		24/3	2,266	15	27				Mulhearn	McMahon	Lewis	Hunter	Scott	Prophett	Nelson	Davies	Chesters	Palios	Bowers*	Coyne
								Ref: G Courtney	Crewe boss Tony Waddington criticises the ref's decision to play the game. Heavy rain the previous day means the pitch cuts up badly. Still, it doesn't stop Town providing plenty of excitement, although their only goal is McIlwraith's penalty, conceded by Bob Scott for a foul on Allatt.											
40	A	HEREFORD		22	W	1-0	1-0	Allatt 6	Kilner	Ward	Harris	Evans	Ayre	Chambers	Firth	Graham	Allatt	Nattress	McIlwraith	
		28/3	2,588	24	29				Cashley	Price	Pejic	Hicks	Cornes	Bartley	Harvey	Laidlaw	Showers	McGrellis*	White	Spiring
								Ref: M Bidmead	For the first time in 18 months, Town record a second successive victory. It's a vital one as well, for Frank Lord's Hereford are struggling as well. Kirby has set a survival target of 38 points, and Allatt's astonishing goal, scored from the edge of the centre-circle, keeps the season alive.											
41	H	NORTHAMPTON		22	L	0-1	0-1		Kilner	Ward	Harris	Evans	Ayre	Chambers	Firth	Graham	Allatt	Nattress	McIlwraith	
		4/4	1,996	13	29			Phillips 32	Poole	Saxby	Gage	Farmer	Saunders	Denyer	Carlton*	Williams	Phillips	Bowen	Heeley	Sandy
								Ref: D Webb	Bill Dodgin's Cobblers side have nothing to play for. They are comfortably placed in mid-table, and, one would expect, an easy victim for the Shaymen. Graham is denied a penalty after only four minutes, but Phillips sweeps in the game's only goal as Northampton stroll to victory.											
42	A	HARTLEPOOL		23	L	0-3	0-2		Kilner	Ward	Harris*	Evans	Ayre	Chambers	Firth	Burton	Allatt	Nattress	McIlwraith	Graham
		11/4	**1,576**	10	29			Hogan 4, Houchen 44, Lawrence 80	Richardson	Linacre	Stimpson	Lawrence	Bird	Brown	Kerr	Linigan	Howard	Houchen	Hogan	
								Ref: J Lovatt	The odds are on Town applying for re-election after this. Mathematically, they can still escape, but it's looking unlikely. Hartlepool include six teenagers in their side, one of whom is Howard, who helps make Hogan's early goal. Evans' woeful back-pass lets in Lawrence for the third.											
43	A	DARLINGTON		24	L	1-3	0-3	McIlwraith 60p	Kilner	Ward	Burton	Evans	Ayre	Chambers	Firth	Graham	Allatt	Whiteley	McIlwraith	
		18/4	2,015	8	29			Stalker 2, Walsh 23, 26	Cuff	Wilson	McLean	Smith	Skipper	Speedie	Hawker	Stell	Stalker	Hamilton	Walsh	
								Ref: D Owens	Re-election is a certainty if Town lose here. The players begin as if their fate has already been sealed. Darlington's John Stalker hits the post before he scores a second-minute opener. After 26 minutes, Town are 0-3 down. McIlwraith's penalty, after Wilson fouls Graham, is academic.											
44	H	ROCHDALE			W	2-0	0-0	Graham 60, 72	Kilner	Ward	Burton	Evans	Ayre	Chambers !	Firth	Graham	Allatt	Whiteley	McIlwraith	
		20/4	2,278		31				Crawford	Jones	Snookes	Seal	Burke	Weir	Wann	O'Loughlin	Hilditch	Wellings	Martinez	
								Ref: B Newsome	Town are playing for pride now, particularly in this Easter Monday local derby. Brian Chambers is involved in both the moves which lead to Graham's two goals. But he spoils his afternoon's work by getting sent off late on for head-butting Eugene Martinez, a nuisance all afternoon.											
45	A	PORT VALE		23	D	0-0	0-0		Kilner	Ward	Harris	Evans	Ayre	Whiteley	Firth	Burton	Allatt	Graham	McIlwraith	
		26/4	2,301	20	32				Lloyd	Brissett	Bromage	Beech*	Bowles	Sproson	Miller	Armstrong	Chamberlain N	Chamberlain M	Bennett	Farrell
								Ref: J Bray	Port Vale's season has been marginally better than Town's. At least they will finish above the re-election zone. The Shaymen feel it will help their re-election bid if they avoid defeat, which is what they set out to do. In this Sunday fixture, Vale dominate, but can't find a way through.											
46	H	ALDERSHOT		23	W	1-0	1-0	Jopling 28 (og)	Kilner	Ward	Burton	Evans	Ayre	Chambers	Firth	Graham	Allatt	Whiteley	McIlwraith	
		2/5	1,587	6	34				Johnson	Edwards	Wooler	Scott*	Bennett	Jopling	Lucas	Crosby	Sanford	Brodie	Briley	McGregor
		Home	Away					Ref: K Walmsley	Town want to avoid finishing bottom, and may do so, although both York and Hereford have midweek games. Officially it's an own-goal that settles it, but a ballboy insists Chambers' shot was over the line before Jopling touched it. Kirby doesn't care – 'We got the result we needed.'											
Average		1,927	2,756																	

League Cup

No	Venue	Opponent	Att/Pos	Res	F-A	H-T	Scorers, Times, and Referees	1	2	3	4	5	6	7	8	9	10	11	12 sub used
1:1	A	BURY		D	2-2	1-2	Firth 28, Evans 54	Kilner	**Nattress**	**Burton**	Evans	Goodman*	Dunleavy	Firth	Hendrie	Allatt	**Ward**	Stafford	Harris
9/8			*3,029 4:*				*Butler 19, Johnson 27*	*Forrest*	*Howard*	*Kennedy*	*Halford*	*Whitehead*	*Waddington*	*Mullen*	*Butler*	*Johnson*	*Madden*	*Farley*	
							Ref: V Callow	Bury were relegated to Division 4 last season, and have a new man in Jim Iley as their new boss. They are expected to prove a stern test for Kirby's men. Johnson's goal gives Bury a 2-0 lead, but within a minute Firth nips in to halve the deficit, then Evans' vicious volley ties it up.											
1:2	H	BURY		L	0-1	0-0		Kilner	Nattress	Dunleavy	Evans	Harris	Goodman	Firth	Hendrie	Allatt	Ward	Stafford	
12/8			2,268 *4:*				*Johnson 70*	*Forrest*	*Howard*	*Kennedy*	*Halford*	*Whitehead*	*Waddington*	*Mullen*	*Butler*	*Johnson*	*Waldron*	*Madden*	
							Ref: T Farley (Halifax lost 2-3 on aggregate)	The hard work was seemingly done at Gigg Lane. But though Evans' 16-yarder hits the post with Forrest claiming the rebound, and Kennedy has to clear Firth's cross off the line, overall Bury are the better side. Johnson scores his second goal of the tie, heading in a cross from Mullen.											

FA Cup

No	Venue	Opponent	Att/Pos	Res	F-A	H-T	Scorers, Times, and Referees	1	2	3	4	5	6	7	8	9	10	11	12 sub used
1	A	HULL	23	L	1-2	0-0	Firth 68	Kilner	Nattress	Burton	Evans	Goodman	Hendrie*	Ward	Graham	Firth	Bullock	Stafford	O'Neil
22/11			*4,024 3:24*				*Edwards 48, 75*	*Norman*	*Nisbet*	*Horswill*	*Roberts G*	*Roberts J*	*Roberts D*	*Marwood*	*Norrie*	*Edwards*	*McClaren*	*Deacy**	*Flounders*
							Ref: K Redfern	3rd Division Hull are expected to win, but Town make it tough for them. Goal machine Keith Edwards converts Brian Marwood's cross for his first, but Firth pounces off Graham's flick-on to equalise. Then Edwards sticks out a leg to touch in Nisbet's 30-yarder, and Hull go through.											

		Home					Away					
	P	W	D	L	F	A	W	D	L	F	A	Pts
1 Southend	46	19	4	0	47	6	11	3	9	32	25	67
2 Lincoln	46	15	7	1	44	11	10	8	5	22	14	65
3 Doncaster	46	15	4	4	36	20	7	8	8	23	29	56
4 Wimbledon	46	15	4	4	42	17	8	5	10	22	29	55
5 Peterborough	46	11	8	4	37	21	6	10	7	31	33	52
6 Aldershot	46	12	9	2	28	11	6	5	12	15	30	50
7 Mansfield	46	13	5	5	36	15	7	4	12	22	29	49
8 Darlington	46	13	6	4	43	23	6	5	12	22	36	49
9 Hartlepool	46	14	3	6	42	22	6	6	11	22	39	49
10 Northampton	46	11	7	5	42	26	7	6	10	23	41	49
11 Wigan	46	13	4	6	29	16	5	7	11	22	39	47
12 Bury	46	10	8	5	38	21	7	3	13	32	41	45
13 Bournemouth	46	9	8	6	30	21	7	5	11	17	27	45
14 Bradford C	46	9	9	5	30	24	5	7	11	23	36	44
15 Rochdale	46	11	6	6	33	25	3	9	11	27	45	43
16 Scunthorpe	46	8	12	3	40	31	3	8	12	20	38	42
17 Torquay	46	13	2	8	38	26	5	3	15	17	37	41
18 Crewe	46	10	7	6	28	20	3	7	13	20	41	40
19 Port Vale	46	10	8	5	40	23	2	7	14	17	47	39
20 Stockport	46	10	5	8	29	25	6	2	15	15	32	39
21 Tranmere	46	12	5	6	41	24	1	5	17	18	49	36
22 Hereford	46	8	8	7	29	20	3	5	15	9	42	35
23 HALIFAX	46	9	3	11	28	32	2	9	12	16	39	34
24 York	46	10	2	11	31	23	2	7	14	16	43	33
	1104	280	144	128	861	503	128	144	280	503	861	1104

Odds & ends

Double wins: (0).
Double losses: (8) Bournemouth, Darlington, Hartlepool, Lincoln, Northampton, Southend, Wigan, Wimbledon.

Won from behind: (0).
Lost from in front: (3) Peterborough (h), Crewe (a), Northampton (a).

High spots: Two consecutive wins in March.
Four games without defeat up to 11 February.

Low spots: Five consecutive defeats up to 4 October.
Seven games without a win up to 17 January.
Losing 1-5 to Southend home and away.
Having to apply for re-election.

Player of the Year: Paul Hendrie.
Ever-presents: (0).
Hat-tricks: (0).
Leading scorer: Francis Firth (10).

	Appearances						Goals			
	Lge	*Sub*	LC	*Sub*	FAC	*Sub*	Lge	LC	FAC	Tot
Allatt, Vernon	**30**		2				**3**			**3**
Ayre, Billy	**19**						**1**			**1**
Bullock, Simon	**8**	*1*			1		**1**			**1**
Burton, Ken	**26**	*1*	1		1		**1**			**1**
Chambers, Brian	**10**									
Dunleavy, Chris	**20**		2				**2**			**2**
Evans, David	**39**		2		1		**1**	1		**2**
Firth, Francis	**43**		2		1		**8**	1	1	**10**
Flavell, Bobby	**1**									
Goodman, Malcolm	**27**	*2*	2		1		**1**			**1**
Graham, Tommy	**32**	*2*			1		**9**			**9**
Harris, David	**25**	*2*	1	*1*						
Hendrie, Paul	**34**		2		1		**3**			**3**
Johnson, Kevin	**5**	*4*								
Kilner, John	**41**		2		1					
McIlwraith, Jimmy	**29**						**5**			**5**
Nattress, Clive	**37**		2		1		**5**			**5**
O'Neil, Tommy	**31**					*1*	**2**			**2**
Stafford, Andy	**6**	*2*	2		1					
Turner, Ian	**5**									
Ward, Steve	**33**	*2*	2		1		**1**			**1**
Whiteley, Andy	**5**	*7*								
(own-goals)							**1**			**1**
22 players used	**506**	***23***	**22**	***1***	**11**	***1***	**44**	**2**	**1**	**47**

No	Date	Att	Pos	Pt	F-A	H-T	Scorers, Times, and Referees	1	2	3	4	5	6	7	8	9	10	11	12 sub used
1 A	PORT VALE			D	0-0	0-0		Kilner	Ward	**Carr**	Evans	Ayre	Hendrie	Graham	**Davison**	Allatt	**Chamberlain**	McIlwraith	
	29/8	*3,883*		1				*Harrison*	*Keenan*	*Dzakin*	*Huntre*	*Bowles*	*Sproson*	*Greenhoff*	*Moss*	*Chamberlain N*	*Bromage*	*Chamberlain M*	
							Ref: K Barrett	For the first time since 1977, Town kick off without an away defeat. Port Vale include in their forward line the experienced Jimmy Greenhoff (ex Stoke and Man Utd) and Ernie Moss. Town's £20,000 recruit, Davison, goes closest to scoring, but Sproson clears his header off the line.											
2 H	PETERBOROUGH			D	1-1	0-0	Davison 55	Kilner	Ward	Carr	Evans	Ayre	Hendrie	Firth	Davison	Graham	Chamberlain	McIlwraith	
	5/9	1,805		2			*Cooke 87*	*Smelt*	*Winters*	*Collins*	*Gynn*	*Slack*	*Rodaway*	*Quow*	*Kellock*	*Cooke*	*Hodgson*	*Clarke**	*Chard*
							Ref: K Walmsley	Daylight robbery! Mickey Bullock has got Town playing attacking football and they dominate this game. Davison's header gives his side the lead, but Town pay the price for missing too many chances. With time running out, Robbie Cooke's overhead kick means his side steal a point.											
3 A	ALDERSHOT	19		L	1-3	1-1	Graham 9	Kilner	Ward	Carr	Evans	Ayre	Hendrie !	Firth	Davison*	Graham	Chamberlain	McIlwraith	Allatt
	12/9	*1,733*	*11*	2			*Sanford 32, Wanklyn 65, Lucas 76*	*Johnson*	*Scott*	*Wooler*	*Wanklyn*	*Bennett*	*Jopling*	*Lucas*	*Sanford*	*Garwood*	*Crosby*	*Robinson*	
							Ref: J Moules	Aldershot record their first win, while Town suffer their first defeat. It's a thrilling tussle, but it swings the home side's way after the sending-off of Hendrie for fouling Sandford, who had cancelled out Graham's header. Wanklyn scores on his debut, and the Shots take the initiative.											
4 H	BOURNEMOUTH	18		D	1-1	1-0	Davison 23	Kilner	Ward	Carr	Evans	Ayre	Hendrie	Firth	Davison	Allatt*	Chamberlain	Graham	McIlwraith
	19/9	1,588	*1*	3			*Funnell 82*	*Allen*	*Heffernan*	*Sulley*	*Smith*	*Compton*	*Impey*	*Kelly**	*Dawtry*	*Mooney*	*Morgan*	*Williams*	*Funnell*
							Ref: B Martin	Déjà vu? This mirrors the Peterborough game, for though the Shaymen are well on top, they find that one goal isn't enough. Davison cracks in Town's goal from eight yards, but heads wide from similar range a minute before £5,000-buy Funnell preserves Bournemouth's unbeaten start.											
5 H	TRANMERE	21		L	0-2	0-2		Kilner	Ward	Carr	Evans	Ayre	Hendrie	Firth	Davison	Allatt*	Chamberlain	Graham	McIlwraith
	22/9	1,943	*19*	3			*Bramhall 23, Brown 27*	*Endersby*	*Mungall*	*Burgess*	*Mountfield*	*Bramhall*	*Williams*	*Kelly*	*Hamilton*	*Kerr*	*Brown*	*Griffiths*	
							Ref: R Chadwick	Bramhall's header already has Town in trouble when Town keeper Kilner commits the schoolboy error of not playing to the whistle. When the linesman flags for offside, Kilner places the ball to take the kick. But the ref hasn't blown, Brown nips in, and puts the ball into the empty net.											
6 A	HARTLEPOOL	21		L	2-3	2-1	Davison 28, McIlwraith 31	Kilner	Ward	Carr	Evans	Ayre	Whiteley	Graham	Davison	Allatt	Chamberlain	McIlwraith*	Firth
	26/9	*1,800*	*11*	3			*Hampton 6, Linacre 65, Houchen 66*	*Burleigh*	*Sweeney*	*Stimpson*	*Hogan**	*Bird*	*Linighan A*	*Linacre J*	*Newton*	*Hampton*	*Houchen*	*Johnson*	*Brown*
							Ref: D Allison	After this defeat Bullock is concerned enough to take drastic action. He places Kilner, Firth, Allatt and McIlwraith on the transfer list. 'They have not been doing it for me,' he says. Town actually come from behind to lead 2-1, but are eventually undone by Keith Houchen's 25-yarder.											
7 A	BLACKPOOL	23		L	**1-7**	0-2	Davison 48 *[Noble 73, Harrison 80]*	Kilner	Ward	Carr	Evans	Ayre	Hendrie	Whiteley*	Davison	Graham	Chamberlain	Bullock	O'Neil
	30/9	*5,084*		3			*Hock' 30, Bamber 31, 56, 65, Sim' 52,*	*Hesford*	*Simmonite*	*Pashley*	*Blair**	*Hart*	*McEwen*	*Morris*	*Noble*	*Bamber*	*Hockaday*	*Harrison*	*Wann*
							Ref: D Owen	Allan Brown's relegated Blackpool won't have an easier time in Division 4. Kilner keeps his place in the Town goal, but wishes he hadn't. Just after half-time, Davison's header gives the Shaymen hope, but Blackpool's five goals in 29 minutes are pretty decisive, and pretty humiliating.											
8 H	BURY	20		W	2-1	1-0	Allatt 23, Graham 61	**Smelt**	O'Neil	Carr	Evans	Ayre	Hendrie	Ward	Davison	Allatt	Chamberlain	Graham	
	3/10	2,420	*5*	6			*Madden 59*	*Platt*	*Constantine*	*Kennedy*	*Gore*	*Hilton P*	*Howard*	*Mullen**	*Butler*	*Madden*	*Jakub*	*Cruikshank*	*Hilton M*
							Ref: M Heath	Lee Smelt joins Town on loan from Forest, where he is England keeper Peter Shilton's understudy. Town break their duck in style. Allatt soars to head them in front. The prolific Madden equalises, but Town's response is almost immediate. Afterwards, Bullock opens the champagne.											
9 A	HEREFORD	20		D	2-2	1-1	Davison 27, Graham 58	Smelt	O'Neil	Carr	Evans	Ayre	Hendrie	Ward	Davison	Allatt	Chamberlain	Graham	
	10/10	*2,359*	*13*	7			*Dungworth 45, Binney 70*	*Hughes*	*Price*	*Bray*	*Hicks*	*Cornes*	*Dobson*	*Harvey*	*Laidlaw*	*Phillips**	*Dungworth*	*White*	*Binney*
							Ref: R Milford	Edgar Street has proved to be a happy hunting ground for Town. They earn another point, but have Lee Smelt to thank for making a string of 'world-class' saves. With six minutes to go, Davison is celebrating a likely winner, but the linesman rules that Ward's cross drifted out of play.											
10 H	ROCHDALE	21		D	0-0	0-0		Smelt	O'Neil	Carr	Evans	Ayre	Hendrie	Ward	Davison	Allatt	Chamberlain	Bullock	
	17/10	2,140	*22*	8				*Poole*	*Cooper*	*Snookes*	*Dolan*	*Burke*	*Taylor*	*Goodwin*	*O'Loughlin*	*Hilditch*	*Wellings*	*Martinez*	
							Ref: A Saunders	Peter Madden's Rochdale are struggling to find the net. They've only scored five goals so far this season. In this game, there is little to choose between the sides. Both appeal for penalties. Hendrie is impeded in the 69th minute, then Hilditch is tackled from behind by Evans in the 81st.											
11 A	DARLINGTON	21		D	1-1	0-0	Graham 30	Smelt	O'Neil	Carr	Evans*	Ayre	Hendrie	Ward	Davison	Allatt	Chamberlain	Graham	Whiteley
	20/10	*1,642*		9			*Hamilton 15*	*Cuff*	*McLean*	*Wilson*	*Smith*	*Skipper*	*Kamara*	*Hawker*	*Speedie*	*Mitchell**	*Hamilton*	*Walsh*	*Stalker*
							Ref: P Richardson	Town gain another away point, but it's not pretty stuff. David Speedie is the architect of Hamilton's goal for Darlington, whilst Graham, with a looping header, nets Town's equaliser. Darlington have now won only one in 13, but manager Billy Elliott is offered a new five-year contract.											

No	Date	Opponent	Att	Pos	Pt	F-A	H-T	Scorers, Times, and Referees	1	2	3	4	5	6	7	8	9	10	11	12
12	H	COLCHESTER		22	L	0-2	0-1		Smelt	O'Neil	Carr	Evans	Ayre	Hendrie	Ward	Davison	Allatt	Chamberlain	Graham	
	24/10		1,374	*3*	9			*Allinson 2p, McDonough 47*	*Walker*	*Cook*	*Coleman*	*Leslie*	*Wignall*	*Wright*	*Adcock**	*Bremner*	*Osborne*	*McDonough*	*Allinson*	*Longhorn*
								Ref: D Webb	Town are already one goal down when a 'phantom whistler' in the crowd confuses the players. McDonough makes it 2-0 after the ref awards a drop-ball. Smelt brings down Ian Allinson for his early penalty. Colchester's defence is well organised, and catches Town offside 23 times.											
13	A	CREWE		19	W	1-0	0-0	Allatt 90	Smelt	O'Neil	Carr	Evans	Ayre	Hendrie	Ward*	Davison	Allatt	Chamberlain	Graham	Firth
	31/10		*2,291*	*24*	12				*Mulhearn*	*Lewis*	*Bowers*	*Salathiel*	*Scott*	*Keighley*	*Hanlon*	*Callaghan*	*Chesters*	*Palios*	*Williams*	
								Ref: B Stevens	Bottom-of-the-table Crewe have enlisted the help of former Liverpool and England winger Ian Callaghan. But he can't do it on his own, and it's Town's Vernon Allatt who takes the plaudits. He goes close on three occasions, before getting onto Carr's cross for a last-gasp winner.											
14	H	TORQUAY		20	L	1-2	0-0	Graham 50	Smelt	O'Neil	Carr	Evans	Ayre	Hendrie	Ward	Davison	Allatt	Chamberlain	Graham*	Firth
	3/11		1,523	*7*	12			*Brown 69, Bourne 80*	*O'Keefe*	*Jones*	*Pethard*	*Brown*	*Wilson*	*Larmour*	*Sermanni*	*Cox**	*Cooper*	*Rioch*	*Young*	*Bourne*
								Ref: N Ashley	Bullock regards Town's performance as 'our best show yet'. But every mistake they make is being punished. Graham fires his side ahead, but Evan's error leads to Tony 'Bomber' Brown, ex-West Brom, equalising. Bourne comes off the bench to score the winner with his first touch.											
15	H	MANSFIELD		18	W	2-1	2-0	Evans 38, Allatt 45	Smelt	O'Neil*	Carr	Evans	Ayre	Hendrie	Ward	Davison	Allatt	Chamberlain	Graham	Whiteley
	7/11		1,447	*21*	15			*Caldwell 56*	*Arnold*	*McJannet*	*Wood*	*Bell*	*Burrows*	*Bird*	*Thomson**	*Morgan*	*Mann*	*Caldwell*	*Parkinson*	*Nicholson*
								Ref: J Lovatt	Town move out of the bottom four, but the sweetness of victory is soured by O'Neil's broken leg, following a challenge by Dave Caldwell that goes unpunished. Caldwell's next telling contribution is his side's goal that halves the lead given to Town by Evans, with a header, and Allatt.											
16	A	STOCKPORT		19	L	1-2	1-1	Allatt 4	Smelt	Ward	Carr	Evans	Ayre	Hendrie	Whiteley	Davison	Allatt	Chamberlain*	Graham	**Walker**
	13/11		*2,493*	*11*	15			*Power 2, Sherlock 52*	*Lloyd*	*Rutter*	*Dwyer*	*Fowler*	*Thorpe*	*Sword*	*Williams*	*Power*	*Coyle*	*Park*	*Sherlock*	
								Ref: J Bray	Stockport have their former Wales keeper Brian Lloyd, as well as Steve Sherlock, to thank for victory. He is in inspired form to keep dominant Town at bay. The game starts in sensational style. Sherlock's eventual winner is a 20-yarder that goes in off the bar. Seven players are booked.											
17	H	SCUNTHORPE		21	L	1-2	1-1	Graham 27	Smelt	Whiteley	Carr	Evans	Ayre	Hendrie	Ward	Davison	Graham	Chamberlain	Firth	
	28/11		1,396	*22*	15			*Cowling 35, Moss 75*	*Neenan*	*Davy*	*Pilling*	*Keeley*	*Arins*	*Oates*	*Grimes*	*O'Berg*	*Cowling*	*Moss*	*Stewart*	
								Ref: P Willis	'Match of the Day' run a feature on Halifax Town, but chairman Sam Rorke feels the club is not portrayed in a great light. On the field, the poor marking is exposed. O'Berg nips round Carr to set up Cowling's equaliser, and Evans' poor pass leads to Moss crashing home the winner.											
18	A	WIGAN		21	L	0-2	0-0		Smelt	Chamberlain	Carr	Evans	Ayre	Hendrie	Ward	Davison	Graham*	**Spooner**	Firth	Whiteley
	5/12		*4,022*	*7*	15			*Houghton 50, Bradd 52*	*Tunks*	*McMahon*	*Glenn*	*Wignall*	*Bradd*	*Methven*	*Sheldon*	*Barrow*	*Quinn*	*Houghton**	*Evans*	*Wright*
								Ref: F Roberts	Wigan, under player-boss Larry Lloyd, the former Liverpool legend, pushed League Champions Aston Villa all the way before going down 1-2 in the League Cup in midweek. Here, the Shaymen make them look second best, but they are caught out by two goals in a two-minute spell.											
19	A	SHEFFIELD UTD		21	D	2-2	0-1	Ward 71, 84	Smelt	Chamberlain	Whiteley	Evans	Ayre	Hendrie	Ward	Daavison	Graham	Spooner	Bullock*	Firth
	2/1		***11,623***	*2*	16			*Hatton 8, Kenworthy 65p*	*Waugh*	*Ryan*	*Garner*	*Richardson !*	*Houston*	*Kenworthy*	*Neville*	*Broddle*	*Edwards*	*Hatton*	*Charles*	
								Ref: V Callow	Chairman Sam Rorke has called a public meeting to discuss whether there is a future for soccer at the Shay. On this performance, the players at least think there is. The high-flying Blades go 2-0 up when Kenworthy nets a penalty, but Ward pops up with a late brace for an unlikely draw.											
20	A	ROCHDALE		19	W	1-0	1-0	Davison 2	Smelt	Chamberlain	Whiteley	Evans	Ayre	Hendrie	Ward	Davison*	Allatt	Spooner	Graham	Firth
	13/1		***1,122***	*20*	19				*Poole*	*Cooper*	*Weir*	*Dolan*	*Burke*	*Taylor*	*Goodwin*	*Esser*	*Hilditch**	*Wellings*	*Martinez*	*Hamilton*
								Ref: G Napthine	The club plods along thanks to donations from supporters. There's only around 70 of them who make the short journey over the Pennines on a bitterly cold night. On a snow-covered pitch, Davison races away in the second minute to settle this game, and end his nine-game goal famine.											
21	H	PORT VALE		17	D	1-1	0-1	Ward 62	Smelt	Chamberlain	Whiteley	Evans	Ayre	Hendrie	Ward	Davison	Allatt*	Spooner	Graham	Firth
	22/1		2,965	*8*	20			*Chamberlain N 39*	*Harrison*	*Tartt*	*Bromage*	*Hunter*	*Sproson*	*Bowles*	*Chamberlain N*	*Moss*	*Greenhoff**	*Armstrong*	*Chamberlain M*	*Farrell*
								Ref: R Bridges	Town are experimenting with Friday night football. Despite heavy rain beforehand, the attendance is encouraging. Not so Town's performance and they need a scrambled Ward equaliser to avoid defeat. Neville Chamberlain's goal helps Vale extend their unbeaten run to twelve games.											
22	A	PETERBOROUGH		18	D	0-0	0-0		Smelt	Chamberlain	Whiteley	Evans	Ayre	Hendrie	Ward*	Davison	Allatt	Spooner	Graham	Firth
	26/1		*3,016*	*7*	21				*Freeman*	*Butler*	*Collins*	*Gynn*	*Smith*	*Rodaway*	*Chard*	*Kellock*	*Cooke*	*Hodgson*	*Massey**	*Clarke*
								Ref: D Civil	Sam Rorke takes exception to a story run by Halifax Courier reporter Ian Rushworth, and bans him from travelling on the team bus. He makes his own way to promotion-seeking Peterborough to see Allatt go closest to bringing off a shock result with a shot off the post in a drab game.											
23	A	BOURNEMOUTH		18	D	1-1	1-0	Ward 41	Smelt	Chamberlain	Whiteley	Evans	Ayre	Hendrie	Ward	Davison	Allatt*	Spooner	Graham	Firth
	30/1		*4,690*	*7*	22			*Funnell 90*	*Leigh*	*Heffernan*	*Sulley*	*Dawtry*	*Brignull*	*Impey*	*Spackman*	*Crawford**	*Funnell*	*Goddard*	*Williams*	*Dawkins*
								Ref: A Ward	Both Bullock and Bournemouth manager David Webb are united in their condemnation of referee Tony Ward. He awards a staggering 62 free-kicks, and books eight players. Funnell scored a late equaliser at the Shay, and does so again, with Town's Graham lying injured in the box.											

No	Date		Att	Pos	Pt	F-A	H-T	Scorers, Times, and Referees	1	2	3	4	5	6	7	8	9	10	11	12 sub used
24	H	ALDERSHOT		18	D	2-2	2-1	Ayre 14, Davison 43	Smelt	Ward	**Kendall**	Evans	Ayre	Hendrie	Firth	Davison	Bullock	Spooner	Carr*	McIlwraith
	6/2		1,754	*11*	23			*French 9, Bennett 87*	*Johnson*	*Edwards*	*Wooler*	*Wanklyn*	*Bennett*	*Jopling*	*Lucas*	*McDonald*	*Sanford**	*French*	*Robinson*	*Brodie*
								Ref: K Walmsley	Bullock wishes games only lasted 85 minutes. Bennett is on hand to net Aldershot's equaliser with three minutes to go when McDonald's free-kick comes back off the bar. His side had recovered from conceding a shock early goal to lead through Ayre's left-footer and Davison's curler.											
25	A	TRANMERE		18	D	1-1	0-0	Ayre 51	Smelt	Chamberlain	Kendall	Evans	Ayre	Hendrie	Ward	Davison	Allatt*	Spooner	Firth	Bullock
	9/2		*1,454*	*12*	24			*Bramhall 90*	*Endersby*	*Mungall*	*Burgess*	*Parry*	*Bramhall*	*Williams*	*Hamilton*	*Mountfield**	*Kerr*	*Morley*	*Powell*	*Ferguson*
								Ref: R Banks	Victory is snatched from Town again in the last seconds. Bullock stands in disbelief when the ref blows for time the moment Town restart the match following Bramhall's equalising header that just crosses the line. Ayre fired Town into the lead, then Davison's 30-yard chip hit the bar.											
26	A	BURY		18	D	1-1	0-1	Ward 55	Smelt	Chamberlain	Kendall	Evans	Ayre	Hendrie	Ward	Davison	Bullock	Spooner	Firth	
	13/2		*3,590*	*7*	25			*Madden 25*	*Brown*	*Howard*	*Kennedy*	*Gore*	*Hilton*	*Baines*	*Mullen*	*Butler*	*Madden*	*Jakub*	*Cruickshank**	*Bradley*
								Ref: M Baker	Bury have an impressive home record. Only Hull (who won) and Hartlepool have taken any points here. Halifax, therefore, join an exclusive club. They get a slice of luck, though, when Spooner's shot deflects into Ward's path for his equaliser. Madden's goal is his 26th this season.											
27	H	BLACKPOOL		20	D	0-0	0-0		Smelt	Kendall*	Chamberlain	Evans	Ayre	Hendrie	Ward	Davison	Bullock	Spooner	Firth	Carr
	20/2		2,245	*9*	26				*Hesford*	*Gardner*	*Brockbank*	*Blair*	*Wann**	*McEwan*	*Deary*	*Noble*	*Hockaday*	*Pashley*	*Entwistle*	*Stewart*
								Ref: J Hunting	Town clock up the club's longest unbeaten run for eleven seasons. There is cause for concern, though. It is their seventh successive draw, and too many points are being dropped. In a disappointing match, Blackpool look a shadow of the side that put seven past Town back in October.											
28	H	HEREFORD		20	L	1-2	1-1	Davison 20	Smelt	Kendall*	Chamberlain	Evans	Ayre	Hendrie	Ward	Davison	Allatt	Spooner	Firth	Carr
	27/2		2,098	*15*	26			*Showers 29, Harvey 52*	*Brand*	*Price*	*Pejic*	*Hicks*	*Dobson*	*Musial*	*Harvey*	*Laidlaw*	*Phillips*	*Showers*	*White*	
								Ref: N Glover	Hereford include in their side Poland international Adam Musial, and he helps his side end Town's nine-match unbeaten run. Winston White is a constant threat, and makes both their goals. McIlwraith has gone public saying he earns £350 a week, and his team-mates look clearly upset.											
29	A	HULL		20	L	0-2	0-0		Smelt	Kendall*	Chamberlain	Evans	Ayre	Hendrie	Ward	Davison	Allatt	Spooner	Firth	Carr
	2/3		*6,952*	*14*	26			*Davis 47, Mutrie 61p*	*Norman*	*Swann*	*Thompson*	*Roberts D**	*Horswill*	*Davis*	*Marwood*	*McClaren*	*Flounders*	*Mutrie*	*Deacy*	*Eccleston*
								Ref: G Courtney	Two clubs in crisis meet. Sam Rorke put the entire playing staff up for sale yesterday. Hull, with debts of £350,000, called in the receiver last week. In the league, the Tigers are going well. This is their third consecutive victory. Les Mutrie's penalty, after he is tripped by Ayre, seals it.											
30	H	DARLINGTON			D	3-3	0-2	Davison 52, 78, Ayre 85	Smelt	Chamberlain	Carr	Evans	Ayre	Hendrie	Ward	Davison	Allatt	Spooner	Firth	
	9/3		1,508		27			*Stalker 42, 45, Speedie 90*	*Cuff*	*Kamara*	*Wilson*	*Smith*	*Skipper*	*Speedie*	*Stalker*	*McLean*	*Hawker*	*Hamilton*	*Walsh*	
								Ref: P Richardson	The ref ignores the linesman's flag and allows the offside Stalker to go through and curl in the opener. On half-time, he scores again. With the driving wind and rain behind them, Town pull it back, then go in front. But with the last kick of the game, Speedie provides the sting in the tail.											
31	A	COLCHESTER		21	D	1-1	1-1	Ayre 30	Smelt	Chamberlain	Carr	Evans	Ayre	Hendrie	Ward	Davison	Allatt	Spooner	Firth	
	12/3		*2,464*	*7*	28			*Bremner 5*	*Walker*	*Cook*	*Coleman*	*Lyons*	*Wignall*	*Wright*	*Cotton*	*Bremner*	*Osborne*	*McDonough*	*Allinson*	
								Ref: D Reeves	Hard-up Halifax give up their normal overnight hotel stay, and plump for a 500-mile round-trip. Bremner's header seemingly sets promotion-chasing Colchester on the road to victory. But Ayre fires in the equaliser, and the Town players eat their post-match snack back on the coach.											
32	H	CREWE		20	W	2-1	1-0	Spooner 45, Ward 82	Smelt	Chamberlain	Carr	Evans	Ayre	Hendrie	Ward	Davison	**Keys**	Spooner	Firth*	Graham
	20/3		2,128	*24*	31			*Palios 48*	*Mulhearn*	*Lewis*	*Griffiths*	*Salathiel*	*Scott*	*Palios*	*Haslegrave*	*Callaghan**	*Chesters*	*Howat*	*Williams*	*Heath*
								Ref: G Tyson	Today, Sam Rorke is allowing the fans to 'pay what you can afford', in the hope of getting more through the turnstiles. Only 150 pay less than normal. Ward's close-range effort finally sees off the challenge of the league's worst club. Palios' goal for Crewe is only their 18th this season.											
33	H	BRADFORD C		21	D	0-0	0-0		Kilner	Chamberlain	Carr	Evans	Ayre	Hendrie	Ward	Davison	Graham	Spooner	Firth	
	23/3		5,926	*3*	32				*Ramsbottom*	*Podd*	*Watson*	*Ingham*	*Cooke*	*McFarland*	*Lester*	*Gallagher*	*Campbell*	*McNiven*	*Chapman*	
								Ref: N Midgley	Keeper John Kilner comes in from the cold to halt City's promotion bid. In his last game, he conceded seven at Blackpool, and has been in the reserves since. Smelt has a fractured knuckle, but Kilner shows his best form to deny Barry Gallagher and Bobby Campbell with flying saves.											
34	A	MANSFIELD		22	L	2-3	1-1	Davison 16, 57	Kilner	Chamberlain	Carr	Whiteley*	Ayre	Hendrie	Ward	Davison	Graham	Spooner	Firth	Keys
	27/3		*2,197*	*17*	32			*Caldwell 12, 64, Cannell 63*	*Arnold*	*Bird*	*Foster*	*Bell*	*Burrows*	*Wood*	*Mann*	*Cannell*	*Lumby*	*Nicholson*	*Caldwell*	
								Ref: A Hamil	Bullock points the finger at his defence for allowing this game to slip away from Town. His side has come from behind to lead 2-1, when Dave Caldwell gets the better of Whiteley to set up Paul Cannell's equaliser. A minute later, Caldwell finds himself unmarked to head in a free-kick.											

No	H/A Date	Opponent	Att	Pos	Res Pts	F-A	H-T	Scorers, Times, Referees	1	2	3	4	5	6	7	8	9	10	11	12
35	H	STOCKPORT		18	W	**4-1**	2-0	Firth 11, Davison 17, 77, Spooner 48	Kilner	Chamberlain	Carr	Evans	Ayre	Hendrie	Ward	Davison	Graham	Spooner	Firth	
	2/4		2,135	*17*	35			*Williams 90*	*Lloyd*	*Rutter*	*Sherlock*	*Emerson*	*Thorpe*	*Smith*	*Williams*	*Phillips*	*Sunley*	*Park*	*Stafford*	
								Ref: R Chadwick	Town climb out of the bottom four with their first four-goal blast since beating Workington five years ago. Davison sets up Firth for his first goal this season. Davison's first for 2-0 comes when Lloyd drops the ball. Spooner scores from 30 yards when Ward taps a free-kick to him.											
36	A	BRADFORD C		22	L	2-5	0-2	Davison 53, Graham [McNiven]	Kilner	Chamberlain	Carr	Evans	Ayre	Hendrie	Ward*	Davison	Graham	Spooner	Firth	Allatt
	10/4		*5,179*	*3*	35			*Gallagher 10p, ??, Cooke 16, Campbell 52,*	*Ramsbottom*	*Podd*	*Watson*	*Lester*	*Cooke*	*McFarland*	*Gallagher*	*Staniforth*	*Campbell*	*McNiven*	*Chapman*	
								Ref: G Napthine	The ref appears to be on City's side. He gives a penalty for hands against Chamberlain, who appears to have been pushed. He then fails to give Town blatant free-kicks before McNiven and Gallagher, with his second, score their goals. In an ill-tempered game, Ayre is kicked in the face.											
37	H	SHEFFIELD UTD		23	L	1-5	1-1	Hendrie 1 [Edwards ??, ??]	Kilner	Goodman*	Carr	Evans	Ayre	Hendrie	Firth	Davison	Graham	Spooner	Bullock	Whiteley
	12/4		**8,077**	*2*	35			*Kenworthy 35p, ??, Charles 57,*	*Waugh*	*Casey*	*Garner*	*Matthews*	*McPhail*	*Kenworthy*	*Morris*	*Trusson*	*Edwards*	*Hatton*	*Charles*	
								Ref: B Newsome	Hendrie fires Town into the lead after only 45 seconds, then it all goes wrong. Carr pushes Edwards for Kenworthy's penalty and United take control. A wall collapses in the Skircoat Shed that has been given to the away supporters, then the ref orders Mickey Bullock from the dug-out.											
38	H	WIGAN		23	D	0-0	0-0		Smelt	Goodman	Carr	Evans	Ayre	Hendrie	Firth	Davison	Graham	Spooner	Ward*	Kendall
	17/4		3,660	*1*	36				*Tunks*	*McMahon*	*Glenn*	*Cribley*	*Lloyd*	*Methven*	*O'Keefe*	*Barrow*	*Bradd*	*Houghton*	*Weston*	
								Ref: A Saunders	Wigan are the league leaders and arrive at the Shay on the back of four straight wins. Town's performance, therefore, is all the more creditable. They restrict them to a couple of long-range efforts from record £65,000 buy Eamon O'Keefe (Everton) in a game where defences hold sway.											
39	A	NORTHAMPTON		19	W	1-0	0-0	Graham 54p	Smelt	Goodman	Carr	Evans	Ayre*	Hendrie	Firth	Davison	Graham	Spooner	Ward !	Kendall
	20/4		*1,935*	*22*	39				*Poole*	*Carlton*	*Saxby*	*Gage*	*Brady*	*Buchanan**	*Saunders*	*Coffill*	*Massey*	*Sandy*	*Bryant*	*Muir*
								Ref: A Gunn	With both sides starting the day in the re-election zone, this game is a real six-pointer. Tommy Graham scores the decisive goal from the spot after Davison is tripped. Ward later misses an open goal, then three minutes from time is sent off – a bad day for the former Cobblers player.											
40	A	SCUNTHORPE		21	D	0-0	0-0		Smelt	Goodman	Carr	Evans	Ayre	Hendrie	Firth	Davison	Graham	Spooner	Ward*	Kendall
	24/4		*1,643*	*23*	40				*Neenan*	*Grimes*	*Keeley*	*Boyd**	*Cowling*	*Thompson*	*Stewart*	*Telfer*	*Cammack*	*Moss*	*Goodlass*	*Duncan*
								Ref: L Robinson	Scunthorpe, under John Duncan, are in trouble too. Despite picking up a valuable point, the Shaymen drop back into the bottom four, as other results go against them. In a dull game, Davison has the chance to win it, but with an open goal, he floats the ball over the bar from 25 yards.											
41	A	TORQUAY		21	D	2-2	1-2	Davison 16, 57	Smelt	Goodman	Carr	Evans	Ayre	Hendrie	Firth	Davison	Graham	Spooner	Ward	
	27/4		*1,331*		41			*Brown 22, Jones 44*	*O'Keefe*	*Smith*	*Wilson*	*Jones*	*Lawrence*	*Rioch*	*Brown*	*Cox*	*Cooper*	*Tainton*	*Sermanni*	
								Ref: D Letts	Davison strikes twice to keep Town alive. His first goal is a contender for Town's goal of the season, a volley that rounds off a six-man move and puts Town ahead. Graham Jones' 30-yarder that puts Torquay ahead just before half-time will probably qualify as their goal of the season.											
42	H	HARTLEPOOL		19	W	2-0	1-0	Evans 14, Ward 72	Smelt	Goodman	Carr	Evans	Ayre	Hendrie	Firth	Davison	Graham	Spooner	Ward	
	1/5		**1,305**	*17*	44				*Watson*	*Sweeney*	*Stimpson*	*Lawrence*	*Bird*	*Brown*	*Linacre J*	*Lowe**	*Newton*	*Linacre P*	*Hampton*	*Clarke*
								Ref: T Fitzharris	Everything goes for Town. As well as winning in fine style, other struggling teams lose, and they move out of the re-election zone. Evans' rocket free-kick puts Town in control. Ward scores a spectacular second, holding off Sweeney for fully 35 yards, before blasting the ball home.											
43	H	NORTHAMPTON		18	W	2-1	0-1	Davison 50, 52	Smelt	Goodman	Carr	Evans	Ayre	Hendrie	Firth	Davison	Graham	Spooner	Kendall	
	4/5		1,730		47			*Sandy 2*	*Poole*	*Carlton*	*Bryant*	*Kruse*	*Gage*	*Heeley**	*Coffill*	*Buchanan*	*Saxby*	*Sandy*	*Massey*	*Brady*
								Ref: R Nixon	The Shaymen go a goal down after only two minutes when Adam Sandy's shot is deflected in, but Davison's two goals in as many minutes after the break means Town are just one win away from safety. Manager Bullock wonders whether to have his first day off since taking over.											
44	A	YORK		20	L	0-4	0-1	[Hood 82p]	Smelt	Goodman	Carr	Evans*	Ayre	Hendrie	Firth	Davison	Graham	Spooner	Ward	Kendall
	7/5		*2,423*	*18*	47			*Davison 24 (og), Walwyn 58, Byrne 66,*	*Blackburn*	*Dawson*	*Kay*	*Hood*	*Czuczman*	*Aitken*	*Pollard*	*Byrne*	*Walwyn*	*Ford*	*Laverick*	
								Ref: A Challinor	Davison's 35-yard backpass sails over Smelt to send York on their way. They are now virtually safe. Both Evans and Ayre come off second best in challenges with striker Keith Walwyn, and Town play the last half-hour with only ten men. Hendrie handles to concede a late penalty.											
45	H	YORK		19	D	0-0	0-0		Smelt	Ward	Kendall	Evans	Goodman	Hendrie	Firth	Davison	Graham	Spooner	Carr	
	11/5		1,903		48				*Atbury*	*Dawson*	*Kay*	*Hood*	*Czuczman*	*Aitken*	*Pollard*	*Byrne*	*Walwyn*	*Ford*	*Laverick*	
								Ref: C Seel	Rochdale, the last team that could have overhauled Halifax, lost over the weekend, so Town are safe. York, who are managed temporarily by director Barry Swallow, are also safe, and contribute little in a drab match. Walwyn gets special treatment from Town players and supporters.											
46	H	HULL		19	D	2-2	1-1	Davison 12, Hendrie 62	Smelt	Kendall*	Carr	Evans	Goodman	Hendrie	Firth	Davison	Graham	Spooner	Ward	Whiteley
	14/5		2,293	*8*	49			*Marwood 43, 58*	*Davies*	*Davis*	*Booth*	*Roberts D*	*Roberts G*	*Thompson*	*Marwood*	*Kynman*	*Whitehurst*	*Mutrie*	*Richards*	
		Home	Away					Ref: M Peck	Town go into the record books with this 22nd draw – it equals the league record set by Aldershot in 1971-72. Paul Hendrie's dipping 25-yarder secures it after the Tigers had roared into a 2-1 lead. Bobby Davison's 20th league goal, a 30-yarder which opens the scoring, is just as good.											
Average		2,407	3,258																	

League Cup			F-A	H-T	Scorers, Times, and Referees	1	2	3	4	5	6	7	8	9	10	11	12 sub used
1:1 H PRESTON		L	1-2	0-2	Davison 52	Kilner	Ward	Carr	Evans	Ayre	Hendrie	Firth	Davison	Graham	Chamberlain	McIlwraith	
1/9	2,719 *3:*				*Clark 4, Naughton 18*	*Litchfield*	*Coleman*	*Westwell*	*Clark*	*O'Riordan*	*Blackley*	*Houston*	*Doyle*	*Elliott**	*Bruce*	*Naughton*	*Walsh*
					Ref: K Redfern	Preston are managed by the colourful Tommy Docherty, formerly in charge of Chelsea, Man Utd and Scotland. He won't last long here. His side takes a first-leg lead thanks to two goals off similar free-kick moves, but only a fool would write off Town thanks to Davison's first goal.											
1:2 A PRESTON	19	D	0-0	0-0		Kilner	Ward	Carr	Evans	Ayre	Hendrie	Firth	Davison	Allatt	Chamberlain	Graham	
15/9	*4,090 3:18*					*Litchfield*	*Westwell*	*McAteer*	*Clark*	*O'Riordan*	*Bell J*	*Walsh*	*Bell G*	*Bruce*	*Coleman*	*McGee*	
					Ref: B Newsome (Halifax lost 1-2 on aggregate)	Bullock consigns League Cup defeat to 'history', but it's tough on his team. Preston, in Division 2 last season, are expected to win, but Town push them all the way. The game could have gone into extra-time but the referee saw an 88th-minute foul on Davison inside the box as outside.											

FA Cup			F-A	H-T	Scorers, Times, and Referees	1	2	3	4	5	6	7	8	9	10	11	12 sub used
1 H PETERBOROUGH	19	L	0-3	0-0		Smelt	Ward	Carr	Evans	Ayre	Hendrie	Whiteley	Davison	Allatt	Chamberlain	Graham	
21/11	2,614 *6*				*Cooke 75, 78, Syrett 82*	*Freeman*	*Butler*	*Collins*	*Gynn*	*Smith*	*Phillips*	*Syrett*	*Kellock*	*Cooke*	*Hodgson*	*Chard*	
					Ref: M Scott	The way this game is going, the best that Town can hope for is a replay. Then Cooke, who scored a late equaliser here in September, gets two in three minutes, then sets up Dave Syrett for the third. It is Town's worst FA Cup defeat since Stoke in 1969 – but they were in Division One.											

		Home						Away					
		P	W	D	L	F	A	W	D	L	F	A	Pts
1	Sheffield Utd	46	15	8	0	53	15	12	7	4	41	26	96
2	Bradford C	46	14	7	2	52	23	12	6	5	36	22	91
3	Wigan	46	17	5	1	47	18	9	8	6	33	28	91
4	Bournemouth	46	12	10	1	37	15	11	9	3	25	15	88
5	Peterborough	46	16	3	4	46	22	8	7	8	25	35	82
6	Colchester	46	12	6	5	47	23	8	6	9	35	34	72
7	Port Vale	46	9	12	2	26	17	9	4	10	30	32	70
8	Hull	46	14	3	6	36	23	5	9	9	34	38	69
9	Bury	46	13	7	3	53	26	4	10	9	27	33	68
10	Hereford	46	10	9	4	36	25	6	10	7	28	33	67
11	Tranmere	46	7	9	7	27	25	7	9	7	24	31	60
12	Blackpool	46	11	5	7	40	26	4	8	11	26	34	58
13	Darlington	46	10	5	8	36	28	5	8	10	25	34	58
14	Hartlepool	46	9	8	6	39	34	4	8	11	34	50	55
15	Torquay	46	9	8	6	30	25	5	5	13	17	34	55
16	Aldershot	46	8	7	8	34	29	5	8	10	23	39	54
17	York	46	9	5	9	45	37	5	3	15	24	54	50
18	Stockport	46	10	5	8	34	28	2	8	13	14	39	49
19	HALIFAX	46	6	11	6	28	30	3	11	9	23	42	49
20	Mansfield*	46	8	6	9	39	39	5	4	14	24	42	47
21	Rochdale	46	7	9	7	26	22	3	7	13	24	40	46
22	Northampton	46	9	5	9	32	27	2	4	17	25	57	42
23	Scunthorpe	46	7	9	7	26	35	2	6	15	17	44	42
24	Crewe	46	3	6	14	19	32	3	3	17	10	52	27
		1104	245	168	139	888	624	139	168	245	624	888	1486

* 2 pts deducted

Odds & ends

Double wins: (2) Crewe, Northampton.
Double losses: (0).

Won from behind: (1) Northampton (h).
Lost from in front: (7) Hereford (h), Scunthorpe (h) Sheffield Utd (h), Torquay (h), Aldershot (a), Hartlepool (a), Mansfield (a).

High spots: Nine games without defeat up to 20 February.
Two consecutive wins win May.
Not having to apply for re-election.

Low spots: Failing to win any of the first seven games.
Three consecutive defeats in September.
11 games without a win up to 12 March.
Losing 1-7 at Blackpool.
Conceding five goals in consecutive games in April.

Halifax drew 22 of their 4th Division matches – a new club record.
Halifax drew 7 consecutive matches up to 20 February.

Player of the Year: Bobby Davison.
Ever-presents: (2) Bobby Davison, David Evans.
Hat-tricks: (0).
Leading scorer: Bobby Davison (21).

	Appearances						Goals			
	Lge	*Sub*	LC	*Sub*	FAC	*Sub*	**Lge**	LC	FAC	**Tot**
Allatt, Vernon	**22**	*2*	1		1		**4**			**4**
Ayre, Billy	**44**		2		1		**4**			**4**
Bullock, Simon	**7**	*1*								
Carr, Everton	**35**	*3*	2		1					
Chamberlain, Glyn	**35**		2		1					
Davison, Bobby	**46**		2		1		**20**	1		**21**
Evans, David	**46**		2		1		**2**			**2**
Firth, Francis	**29**	*8*	2				**1**			**1**
Goodman, Malcolm	**10**									
Graham, Tommy	**36**	*1*	2		1		**8**			**8**
Hendrie, Paul	**45**		2		1		**2**			**2**
Kendall, Paul	**9**	*4*								
Keys, Paul	**1**	*1*								
Kilner, John	**12**		2							
McIlwraith, Jimmy	**4**	*3*	1				**1**			**1**
O'Neil, Tommy	**8**	*1*								
Smelt, Lee	**34**				1					
Spooner, Steve	**29**						**2**			**2**
Walker, Steve		*1*								
Ward, Steve	**44**		2		1		**7**			**7**
Whiteley, Andy	**10**	*5*			1					
21 players used	**506**	***30***	**22**		**11**		**51**	**1**		**52**

No	Date	Att	Pos	Pt	F-A	H-T	Scorers, Times, and Referees	1	2	3	4	5	6	7	8	9	10	11	12 sub used
1	A COLCHESTER			L	0-1	0-0		Smelt	**Nobbs**	Carr	Evans	Goodman	**Wood**	**Hallybone**	Davison	**Staniforth**	Spooner	Ward	
	28/8	2,610		0			*McDonough 47*	*Walker*	*Cook*	*Coleman*	*Groves*	*Wignall*	*Hunter*	*Allinson*	*Osborne*	*Lyons*	*McDonough**	*Leslie*	*Bremner*
							Ref: R Lewis	As if an opening-day trip to Layer Road wasn't difficult enough, Town play without the suspended Hendrie and Smith. Colchester look as if they could score at will, yet their only goal is a highly controversial one, when Roy McDonough appears to kick the ball out of Smelt's hands.											
2	H MANSFIELD		20	D	0-0	0-0		Smelt	Nobbs	Carr	Evans	Smith	Hendrie	Hallybone	Davison	Spooner	Staniforth	Ward	
	3/9	2,225	8	1				*Arnold*	*Bell*	*Kennedy*	*Day*	*Ayre*	*Bird*	*Matthews*	*Caaldwell**	*Waddle*	*Dungworth*	*Laidlaw*	*Nicholson*
							Ref: R Nixon	Halifax have elected to play a number of Friday games, the first of which is this one. But it's a frustrating evening for the Shaymen, who do everything but score in the second half. Mansfield's main threat comes from the head of recently signed Alan Waddle, a former Town player.											
3	H DARLINGTON		11	W	2-0	2-0	Hendrie 23, Spooner 40	Smelt	Nobbs	Carr	Evans	Smith	Hendrie	Hallybone	Davison	Spooner	Staniforth	Ward	
	7/9	1,891	2	4				*Cuff*	*Brissett*	*Wilson*	*Smith*	*Kamara*	*Gilbert*	*Wicks**	*McLean*	*Dunn*	*Walsh*	*McFadden*	*Hawker*
							Ref: K Baker	Darlington have scored eight goals in their opening two games. They hardly get out of their own half here, though. Town dominate from start to finish, and should have won by more. Ward is provider of both goals, stinging efforts by Hendrie and Spooner, both from outside the box.											
4	A SWINDON		5	W	1-0	0-0	Davison 90	Smelt	Nobbs	Carr	Wood	Smith	Hendrie	Hallybone	Davison	Spooner	Staniforth	Ward	
	11/9	3,450	10	7				*Allen*	*Baverstock*	*Baddeley*	*Emmanuel**	*Lewis*	*Graham*	*Carter*	*Hughes*	*Rideout*	*Rowland*	*Barnard*	*Quinn*
							Ref: T Holbrook	The Shaymen watch the film 'Rocky' on the coach going down to Swindon. On the pitch, they resist all that John Trollope's side, relegated last season, can throw at them. Then, in injury-time, Davison delivers the killer punch, racing into space to head Nobbs' cross over keeper Allan.											
5	H ALDERSHOT		9	L	1-3	0-1	Davison	Smelt	Nobbs	Wood	Evans	Smith	Hendrie	Hallybone	Davison	Spooner	Staniforth	Carr*	**Nuttall**
	18/9	2,243	3	7			*Brodie 8, Wood (og), Banton 69*	*Johnson*	*Scott*	*Gillard*	*Sanford*	*Wood*	*Jopling*	*Shrubb*	*Banton*	*Goddard*	*McDonald*	*Brodie*	
							Ref: R Bridges	Town could go top, but events transpire that they don't. Several players play with stomach bugs, Town play the last 40 minutes with ten men after Hendrie goes off, and Smelt cracks a finger. Gillard's cross goes in off Wood's chest. Davison rounds the keeper to keep the game alive.											
6	A BURY		15	L	0-2	0-2		**Butcher**	Nobbs	Wood	Evans	Smith	Nuttall*	Hallybone	Davison	Spooner	Staniforth	Ward	Kendall
	25/9	2,244	2	7			*Potts 37, Johnson 44*	*Brown*	*Gardner*	*Kenworthy*	*Gore*	*Hilton*	*Bramhall*	*Potts*	*Madden*	*Johnson*	*Jakub*	*Firth**	*Cruickshank*
							Ref: M Peck	Bullock feels his side played some of their best football so far this season, and is at a loss to explain this defeat. He locks his players away for 40 minutes afterwards. Former Shayman Firth sets up Potts' goal, and Johnson doubles the lead when he pounces onto Smith's weak backpass.											
7	A YORK		16	L	2-3	0-0	Davison 48, 63	Butcher	Nobbs	Carr	Evans	Smith	Wood	Hallybone	Davison	Spooner	Staniforth	Ward	
	28/9	1,772	13	7			*Laverick 59, Ford 67, Busby 79*	*Jones*	*Evans*	*Hay*	*Sbragia*	*Crosby*	*Hood*	*Pollard*	*Ford*	*Walwyn*	*Byrne**	*Laverick*	*Busby*
							Ref: A Saunders	A goalless first half gives no indication of the drama that lies in the second. Davison races clear to open the scoring, then he wins a 50-50 with the keeper to give Town a 2-1 lead. York can afford to see on-loan Butcher save Ford's penalty. Busby comes off the bench to win the game.											
8	H CHESTER		17	D	0-0	0-0		Butcher	Nobbs	Carr	Evans	Smith	Wood	Hallybone	Davison	Spooner	Staniforth*	Ward	Nuttall
	1/10	1,925	8	8				*Millington*	*Edwards*	*Lane*	*Storton*	*Zelem*	*Dean*	*Sloan*	*Kinsey*	*Thomas*	*Ludlam*	*Wilson*	
							Ref: R Banks	Mickey Bullock's after-match briefing this time lasts an hour. He is concerned that his players are relying too much on the long ball, with little success. Last week, John Sear's side hammered five goals past Hereford, but their contribution to this drab game is just three attempts on goal.											
9	A BLACKPOOL		18	D	0-0	0-0		Butcher	Nobbs	Carr	Evans	Smith	Wood	Hallybone	Davison	Spooner*	Nuttall	Ward	Goodman
	9/10	4,150	11	9				*Hesford*	*Simmonite*	*Hart*	*Jeffrey*	*Deary*	*Greenall*	*Hockaday*	*Stewart**	*Bamber*	*Pashley*	*Downes*	*Noble*
							Ref: N Ashley	After this hard-earned point, Town are down to just ten fit men. Already without Hendrie, Smelt, Staniforth and Kendall, Spooner and Evans are the latest casualties. Blackpool's Dave Bamber scored a hat-trick in the corresponding fixture a year ago, but is well marshalled this time.											
10	H PORT VALE		17	L	0-2	0-1		Butcher	Nobbs	Carr	Evans	Smith	Wood*	Hallybone	Davison	Goodman	Nuttall	Ward	Kendall
	15/10	2,009	4	9			*Moss 9, Cegielski 75*	*Siddall*	*Tartt*	*Bromage*	*Hunter*	*Sproson*	*Cegielski*	*Lawrence**	*Moss*	*Newton*	*Ridley*	*Armstrong*	*Earle*
							Ref: N Wilson	Vale's boss John McGrath was an uncompromising stopper in his playing days. He has instilled this into his players, and they intimidate the Shaymen. Unmarked Moss heads their opener. Cegielski's killer headed goal comes off a free-kick. The Shaymen will report for extra training.											
11	H BRISTOL CITY		19	D	2-2	2-1	Davison 27, 35	Smelt	Nobbs	Goodman	Evans	Smith	Hendrie	Wood*	Davison	Spooner	Nuttall	Ward	Hallybone
	19/10	1,465	23	10			*Ritchie 41, Newman 49*	*Shaw*	*Newman*	*Johnson*	*Nicholls*	*Boyle*	*Riley*	*Cooper*	*Ritchie*	*Chandler*	*Williams*	*Crawford*	
							Ref: M Scott	Only three seasons ago, City were in the First Division. Their fall from grace looks complete when Town race into a two-goal lead. It's Nuttall who makes both for Davison, threading the ball through for his first. But Evans' weak headed backpass lets in Ritchie, to start City's fightback											

No/Date	H/A	Opponent/Att	Pos	Res/Pts	Score	H-T	Scorers, Times, and Referees	1	2	3	4	5	6	7	8	9	10	11	12
12	A	ROCHDALE	17	D	2-2	2-0	Spooner 30, Keenan 41 (og)	Smelt	Nobbs	Goodman	Evans	Smith	Hendrie*	Wood	Davison	Spooner	Nuttall	Ward	Hallybone
23/10		*1,765*	*20*	11			*Hilditch 60, Thompson D 81*	*Pearce*	*Keenan*	*Snookes*	*Farrell*	*Garner*	*Williams*	*Thompson D*	*Comstive*	*French**	*Wellings*	*Hilditch*	*Martinez*
							Ref: A Seville	Bullock sees his side again throw away a two-goal lead. After Spooner opens the scoring, Dale's Gerry Keenan, scores an own-goal, lobbing Pearce form 20 yards when under no pressure. Hilditch controls the ball well before scoring his goal, and the rest is becoming all-too familiar.											
13	H	CREWE		L	0-3	0-1		Smelt	Nobbs	Goodman	Evans	Smith	Wood	Nuttall*	Davison	Spooner	Staniforth	Ward	Hallybone
29/10		1,726		11			*Sutton 13, Scott 61, Smith 70 (og)*	*Smith*	*Purdie*	*Bowers*	*Salathiel*	*Scott*	*Hanlon*	*Haslegrave*	*Sutton*	*Waller*	*Evans*	*Craven*	
							Ref: N Glover	It doesn't get much grimmer than this. The fans are walking out with 20 minutes to go, and Bullock feels humiliated at his side's performance. Crewe had only taken one point from the last 24 on offer, but make this look easy. Smith's own-goal is a carbon copy of Keenan's at Rochdale.											
14	A	PETERBOROUGH	22	L	1-2	0-1	Nobbs 46	Smelt	Nobbs	Goodman*	Evans	Smith	Hendrie	Ward	Davison	Allatt	Spooner	Ward	Carr
3/11		*2,038*	*17*	11			*Firm 5, Small 68*	*Seaman*	*Rayment*	*Imlach*	*Gynn*	*Firm*	*Slack*	*Clark*	*Quow*	*Collins*	*Benjamin*	*Chard**	*Small*
							Ref: I Borrett	This defeat leaves Town joint bottom on points with Hereford and Tranmere. Nobbs has a mixed evening. It's he who deflects in 6' 3" Neil Firm's strong header, who somehow arrived unnoticed, then equalises just after half-time with a 25-yarder. Small's winner was on the cards.											
15	H	HEREFORD	22	D	2-2	1-1	Spooner 10, Smith 87	Smelt	Nobbs	Carr	Evans	Smith	Hendrie	Ward*	Davison	Allatt	Spooner	Ward	Goodman
5/11		1,065	*23*	12			*White 18p, McNeil 50*	*Plumley*	*Price*	*Bray*	*Hicks*	*Pejic*	*Ross*	*Lane*	*Crabbe*	*Showers**	*McNeil*	*White*	*Bartley*
							Ref: P Willis	Hereford look like gaining their first away win until Smith pops up with a late equaliser following a free-kick for hands against veteran forward McNeil. McNeil had given his side the lead, after White's equalising penalty when Smelt collided with Lane. Town are often slow-hanclapped.											
16	A	WIMBLEDON	20	W	4-2	1-0	Davison 42, 52, 68, Allatt 53	Smelt	Nobbs	Wood	Evans	Smith	Hendrie	Staniforth	Davison	Allatt	Spooner	Goodman	
13/11		*2,104*	*6*	15			*Entwhistle 56, Thomas 79p*	*Beasant*	*Peters*	*Thomas*	*Dibble*	*Tagg*	*Morris*	*Belfield*	*Entwhistle*	*Leslie**	*Downes*	*Hodges*	*Gage*
							Ref: K Barratt	After eleven games and two months without a win, Town provide one of the shocks of the season against Harry Bassett's promotion-chargers. Davison's first-time strike sends Town on their way, and he goes on to score his first league hat-trick. Town get two in a minute to go 3-0 up.											
17	A	HARTLEPOOL	18	W	2-1	0-1	Wood 48, Staniforth 55	Smelt	Nobbs	Wood	Evans	Smith	Hendrie	Staniforth	Davison	Allatt*	Spooner	Goodman	Ward
27/11		*1,367*	*16*	18			*Linighan A 4*	*Wright*	*Brown*	*Stimpson*	*Hogan*	*Barker*	*Linighan A*	*Staff*	*Dobson*	*Linacre*	*Lawrence**	*Hamilton*	*Johnson*
							Ref: C Seel	This is Town's response to Cup defeat by non-league North Shields – a second successive away win. Things look bleak when Linighan heads the home side in front. But after a roasting from Bullock at half-time, Town respond, with Staniforth, showing neat contol to net the winner.											
18	H	TRANMERE	20	L	1-2	0-1	Hamilton 82 (og)	Smelt	Nobbs	Goodman	Evans	Smith	Hendrie	Ward	Spooner	Allatt	Staniforth*	Wood	Nuttall
17/12		**912**	*16*	18			*Ferguson 17, ??*	*Endersby*	*Mungall*	*Burgess*	*Mooney*	*Hamilton*	*Williams*	*Ferguson*	*Aspinall*	*Kerr*	*Brown*	*Griffiths*	
							Ref: G Napthine	Mark Ferguson, a British Rail joiner, scores with Tranmere's only two shots of the night. Without Davison, now at Derby, the Shaymen leave it to Rovers to score their goal, player-boss Bryan Hamilton turning in Hendrie's cross. The bitterly cold night ensures a pathetic attendance.											
19	A	HULL	21	D	1-1	0-0	Staniforth 86	Smelt	Nobbs	Goodman*	Evans	Smith	Hendrie	Ward	Spooner	Allatt	Nuttall	Wood	Staniforth
27/12		***10,042***	*3*	19			*Skipper 55*	*Norman*	*Swann*	*Askew*	*Roberts D*	*Skipper*	*Booth*	*Hawley*	*McClaren*	*Flounders*	*Mutrie*	*Roberts G*	
							Ref: M Heath	Hull chairman Don Robinson, the formerly at Scarborough, provides dancing girls, and leads the carol-singing at half-time. When Skipper taps in a simple goal, Hull are all set to start their Christmas celebrations. Until Town sub Staniforth spoils the party with a late brave diving header.											
20	H	SCUNTHORPE	21	W	3-1	2-0	Spooner 4, Staniforth 11, Nuttall 70	Smelt	Nobbs	Wood	Evans	Smith	Hendrie	Ward	Spooner	Allatt	Nuttall	Staniforth	
28/12		2,270	*5*	22			*Parkinson 61p*	*Neenan*	*Ooates*	*Pointon*	*Fowler*	*Baines*	*Hunter*	*O'Berg*	*Cammack*	*Cowling*	*Angus*	*Parkinson*	
							Ref: J Hough	The Shaymen take the field wearing new pin-stripe shirts, then put on a five-star performance. Spooner puts Town ahead when Nuttall's shot comes back off the keeper. Nuttall goes on to score a memorable solo goal to make it 3-1, so ending Scunthorpe's hopes of salvaging a point.											
21	A	STOCKPORT	20	L	2-4	0-1	Allatt 55, Spooner 90p	Smelt	Nobbs	Wood	Evans !	Smith	Hendrie*	Ward	Spooner	Allatt	Nuttall	Staniforth	Goodman
1/1		*2,871*	*11*	22			*Quinn 30, 64, 79, Emerson 70*	*Lloyd*	*Rutter*	*Sherlock*	*Emerson*	*Sword*	*Thorpe*	*Smith*	*Phillips*	*Quinn*	*Power*	*Coyle*	
							Ref: D Richardson	Mick Quinn is Stockport's hero, as he grabs a hat-trick. Town feel he is lucky to stay on the field after he poleaxes Smelt in the 68th minute. In the end, it is Evans who goes for an early bath for words said to the referee. Quinn's second goal for 1-2 is the killer, and Town don't recover.											
22	H	TORQUAY	18	W	3-0	1-0	Spooner 45p, Nuttall 77, Allatt 82	Smelt	Nobbs	Wood	Evans	Smith	Hendrie	Ward	Spooner	Allatt	Nuttall	Staniforth	
3/1		1,776	*8*	25				*Horn*	*Doyle*	*Wilson*	*Sheridan*	*Little*	*Hughes*	*Young*	*O'Donnell*	*Cooper*	*Anderson*	*Gallagher*	
							Ref: G Courtney	Torquay boss Bruce Rioch reckons that on this showing, Town are the best team he has seen. Spooner's penalty for a needless push on Allatt right on half-time gets them going. Nuttall's looping header makes it 2-0, then it is his shot that sticks in the mud that allows Allatt to score.											
23	A	MANSFIELD	14	W	2-1	1-0	Nuttall 20, 72	Smelt	Nobbs	Wood	Evans	Smith	Hendrie	Ward	Spooner	Allatt	Nuttall	Staniforth	
8/1		*2,398*	*9*	28			*Dungworth 80*	*Arnold*	*Blackhall**	*Kennedy*	*Bell*	*Ayre*	*Calderwood*	*Matthews*	*Hutchinson*	*Dungworth*	*Caldwell*	*Nicholson*	*Woodhead*
							Ref: D Lloyd	The Shaymen respond magnificently to recent criticism. The team bus arrives just before the 2.30 deadline, but the players seem unaffected. Nuttall is the talk of the Town. He shows neat close control for his first goal. Smelt saves Dungworth's penalty, but can't stop his follow-up.											

LEAGUE DIVISION 4

Manager: Mickey Bullock

SEASON 1982-83

No	Date		Att	Pos	Pt	F-A	H-T	Scorers, Times, and Referees	1	2	3	4	5	6	7	8	9	10	11	12 sub used
24	H	COLCHESTER			W	**4-0**	2-0	Nuttall 30, Staniforth 32, 80, 83	Smelt	Nobbs	Wood	Evans	Smith	Hendrie	Ward	Spooner	Allatt	Nuttall	Staniforth	
	14/1		1,863		31				*Chamberlain*	*Cook*	*Ward*	*Longhorn*	*Wignall*	*Coleman*	*Allinson*	*Osborne*	*Linford*	*Adcock*	*Hull*	
								Ref: R Guy	Player-coach Staniforth was fined by the club during the week after a booking for dissent. He leaves the Shay with a £40 match ball after his first-ever senior hat-trick. Nuttall's opener goes in off the post, then Staniforth takes over. His first two are headers, his third a deflected shot.											
25	A	DARLINGTON		12	W	2-1	1-1	Staniforth 7, 50	Smelt	Nobbs	Wood	Goodman	Smith	Hendrie	Ward	Spooner	Allatt*	Nuttall	Staniforth	Kendall
	22/1		*1,175*	*22*	34			*McFadden 19*	*Cuff*	*Liddle*	*Wilson*	*Smith*	*Rhodes*	*Kamara*	*Gilbert*	*McLean*	*Honour*	*Walsh*	*McFadden*	
								Ref: D Shaw	Staniforth takes the honours with two more goals as the Shaymen record their fifth away success. His first is a header off Spooner's corner. His second, the winner, is a comic-cut goal, when Cuff completely misses Ward's cross. The home fans call for manager Billy Elliott to be sacked.											
26	H	NORTHAMPTON		10	W	2-0	1-0	Ward 26, Staniforth 75	Smelt	Nobbs	Wood	Goodman	Smith	Hendrie	Ward	Spooner	Kendall	Nuttall	Staniforth	
	1/2		1,927	*13*	37				*Kendall*	*Tucker*	*Phillips*	*Gage*	*Burrows*	*Coffill*	*Saunders**	*Patching*	*Buchanan*	*Syrett*	*Massey*	*Denyer*
								Ref: J Worrall	This original fixture was abandoned after 78 minutes due to fog back in December, with Town leading 3-2. The often-criticised Ward ensures the Cobblers don't get a second chance. He scores the first from 15 yards, then whips over the cross for Staniforth to head powerfully home.											
27	H	BURY		8	W	1-0	0-0	Evans 83	Smelt	Nobbs	Wood	Evans	Smith	Hendrie	Ward	Spooner	Allatt	Nuttall	Staniforth	
	5/2		4,021	*3*	40				*Brown*	*Gardner*	*Davis*	*Gore*	*Bramhall*	*Halliday*	*Firth*	*Madden*	*Parker*	*Jakub*	*Potts**	*Johnson*
								Ref: V Callow	Bullock is expecting champagne from Hull chairman Don Robinson, who's promised him a crate of bubbly for every top-four side Town beat. Bury provide tough opposition, but Evans' header off Spooner's corner gives Halifax their sixth consecutive win for the first time since 1964.											
28	A	CHESTER		9	L	0-2	0-1		Smelt	Nobbs	Wood	Evans	Smith	Hendrie	Ward	Spooner*	Allatt	Nuttall	Staniforth	Kendall
	12/2		*1,907*	*11*	40			*Zelem 21, Williams 77*	*Harrington*	*Needham*	*Lane*	*Blackwell*	*Zelem*	*Williams*	*Sloan*	*Simpson*	*Thomas*	*Workman*	*Wilson L*	
								Ref: N Midgley	Town fail to emulate the class of '64 – seven straight wins – but have the chances to bury Chester out of sight. Nuttall squanders the first after only 15 seconds. Ward side-foots the easiest over the bar. Zelem's 25-yarder gives Chester an undeserved lead. Williams heads the killer goal.											
29	A	BRISTOL CITY		9	L	0-3	0-2		Smelt	Nobbs	Wood	Evans	Smith	Hendrie	Ward	Kendall*	Allatt	Nuttall	Staniforth	Goodman
	15/2		*3,169*		40			*Ritchie, Cooper, Economou*	*Shaw*	*Newman*	*Williams*	*Nicholls*	*Phill-Masters*	*Riley**	*Cooper*	*Ritchie*	*Economou*	*Musker*	*Crawford*	*Chandler*
								Ref: B Daniels	The pitch isn't the only thing that is frozen. Town's defence is at a standstill, and Terry Cooper's side take advantage. Tom Ritchie scores their first goal, then tries to claim a second when Cooper's cross sails in. Cooper plays in Economou for his goal as Town hope for an abandonment.											
30	H	BLACKPOOL		9	W	2-0	0-0	Spooner 61p, Allatt 77	Smelt	Nobbs	Wood*	Evans	Smith	Hendrie	Ward	Spooner	Allatt	Nuttall	Staniforth	Goodman
	18/2		2,366	*18*	43				*Hesford*	*Bardsley*	*Pritchett*	*Deary*	*Hetzke*	*Greenall*	*Hockaday*	*Jeffrey*	*Stewart*	*Noble**	*Pashley*	*Serella*
								Ref: T Jones	A collection, taken at half-time for the Lord Mayor of Blackpool's Appeal Fund, after four people drowned earlier in the year, raises £250. On the pitch, Town return to winning ways. Spooner returns from injury to slam home a penalty for handball. Allatt makes it 2-0 with a low drive.											
31	A	PORT VALE		9	L	1-2	1-0	Spooner 40	Smelt	Nobbs	Wood*	Evans	Smith	Hendrie	Ward	Spooner	Allatt	Nuttall	Staniforth	Goodman
	26/2		*5,163*	*1*	43			*Sproson 48, Hunter 67*	*Southall*	*Tartt*	*Bromage*	*Hunter*	*Sproson*	*Cegielski*	*Fox*	*Lawrence*	*Newton*	*Ridley*	*Armstrong*	
								Ref: K Walmsley	Vale's Neville Southall kept goal for Wales against England at Wembley during the week. He follows that up by throwing the ball straight to Spooner to score Town's goal. Sproson provides Vale's equaliser, then Geoff Hunter runs 30 yards unchallenged before scoring the winner.											
32	H	PETERBOROUGH		9	L	1-2	1-1	Staniforth 27	Smelt	Nobbs	Kendall	Evans	Smith	Hendrie*	Ward	Spooner	Allatt	Nuttall	Staniforth	Goodman
	1/3		2,002	*10*	43			*Ippolito 25, 46*	*Naylor*	*Winters*	*Collins*	*Gynn*	*Firm*	*Slack*	*Clarke*	*Rodaway*	*Chard*	*Benjamin*	*Ippolito*	
								Ref: M Peck	The Posh recover from the shock resignation of manager Martin Wilknson less than 24 hours earlier to end Town's six-game home winning streak. Diminutive Mario Ippolito is their hero, scoring the winner, with a looping shot 30 seconds after the break, then hopes for a contract.											
33	H	ROCHDALE		9	D	0-0	0-0		Smelt	Nobbs	Carr	Goodman	Smith	Hallybone	**Wilkes**	Spooner	Allatt	Ward	Kendall	
	4/3		2,128	*21*	44				*Pearce*	*Williams*	*Snookes*	*Greaves*	*McElhinney*	*Taylor*	*Thompson D*	*Thompson S*	*French*	*Hilditch*	*Compstive*	
								Ref: H Taylor	Town's squad has been depleted through injury. Therefore, Carr and Hallybone are recalled, whilst Spooner and Nobbs defy doctor's orders to play. Town are fortunate that their opponents are lowly Rochdale. Even so, there are no goals. Spooner's hopeful 35-yarder misses by as much.											
34	A	CREWE		11	D	1-1	0-0	Staniforth 56	Smelt	Nobbs	Carr	Evans	Smith	**Skivington**	Wilkes	Spooner	Allatt	Ward	Staniforth	
	11/3		*2,518*	*23*	45			*Waller 85*	*Smith*	*Brady*	*Bowers*	*Edwards*	*Scott*	*Hart*	*Craven*	*Bancroft**	*Waller*	*Walker*	*Cliss*	*Haslegrave*
								Ref: R Chadwick	A tale of woe for centre-backs Nigel Hart and David Evans. Hart slips to allow Staniforth to go through to put Town ahead. The Shaymen are looking good for a sixth away win when Evans swings out his boot but fails to clear the ball, leaving Waller free to net Crewe's late equaliser.											

No	H/A	Opponent	Att	Pos	Res	F-A	H-T	Scorers, Times, and Referees												
35	H	SWINDON		9	W	1·0	0·0	Nuttall 47	Smelt	Nobbs	Carr	Evans	Smith	Wilkes	Skivington	Spooner	Nuttall	Ward*	Staniforth	Hallybone
	15/3		1,806	*8*	48				*Allan*	*Bailie*	*Baddeley*	*Emmanuel*	*Lewis*	*Graham*	*Pritchard*	*Batty*	*Rideout*	*Rowland*	*Barnard*	
								Ref: D Allison	At the end of December, Swindon looked certainties for promotion. This defeat, however, their fourth on the trot, means they've slipped off the pace. Nuttall only plays because Allattt has tonsillitis, but scores a gem. He takes the ball on the edge of the box, then lobs the stranded keeper.											
36	A	HEREFORD		9	L	0·2	0·1		Smelt	Nobbs	Carr	Evans*	Smith	Skivington	Wilkes	Spooner	Nuttall	Ward	Staniforth	Hallybone
	19/3		*2,006*	*24*	48			*Harvey 30, Phillips 83*	*Wilmot*	*Price*	*Bartley*	*Hicks*	*Pejic*	*Maddy*	*Harvey*	*Lane*	*Phillips*	*Carter*	*White*	
								Ref: B Hill	Bottom club Hereford end a run of seven games without a win. Keeper Rhys Wilmot, on loan from Arsenal, receives special dispensation from the League to play with Kevin Rose serving a two-match suspension. Town become disorganised when Evans goes off after only 15 minutes.											
37	A	SCUNTHORPE			L	0·2	0·1		Smelt	Nobbs	Wood	Evans	Smith	Hendrie	**Gallagher**	Skivington*	Allatt	Ward	Staniforth	Spooner
	1/4		*3,775*		48			*Lester 32, Cammack 80*	*Neenan*	*Keeley*	*Pointon*	*Boxall*	*Baines*	*Hunter*	*Graham*	*Cammack*	*Cowling**	*Lester*	*Leman*	*Oates*
								Ref: J Lovatt	Victory for Allan Clarke's Scunthorpe comes easily. Town keeper Lee Smelt has to be at his best to prevent them scoring long before Lester heads the opener. Town don't win their first corner until the 68th minute, but Cammack's close-range goal follows a corner at the other end.											
38	H	HULL			L	1·2	0·1	Nuttall 54	Smelt	Nobbs	Wood	Evabs	Smith	Hendrie*	Gallagher	Spooner	Nuttall	Ward	Staniforth	Allatt
	4/4		**5,011**		48			*Woof 45, Marwood 66*	*Norman*	*Hughes*	*Thompson*	*Roberts D*	*Skipper*	*Swann*	*Marwood*	*McClaren*	*Woof*	*Mutrie*	*Roberts G*	
								Ref: A Hamil	Former Liverpool and England defender Emlyn Hughes has signed for Hull in a bid to keep their promotion bid on course. He's a big attraction at the Shay, but it's pint-sized Brian Marwood who takes the honours. He scores the winner, after Nuttall had equalised, with a super solo goal.											
39	A	NORTHAMPTON		13	L	1·3	0·0	Staniforth 89	Smelt	Nobbs	Spooner	Evans	Smith	Hendrie	Gallagher*	Allatt	Nuttall	Ward	Staniforth	Goodman
	10/4		*2,208*	*17*	48			*Buchanan 65, 74, Jeffrey 77*	*Gleasure*	*Tucker*	*Phillips*	*Burrows*	*Gage*	*Muir**	*Coffill*	*Jeffrey*	*Buchanan*	*Syrett*	*Massey*	*Heeley*
								Ref: M James	A freak storm just before kick-off means parts of the pitch becomes a quagmire, but Bullock won't use this as an excuse for defeat. His team looks well in control for the first 65 minutes, but collapses alarmingly once Buchanan scores the first of his two goals from outside the area.											
40	H	YORK		13	D	2·2	1·0	Allatt 32, 67	Smelt	Nobbs	Wood	Evans	Goodman	Hendrie	Gallagher	Nuttall*	Allatt	Ward	Staniforth	Kendall
	15/4		2,117	*7*	49			*Pollard 86p, Sbragia 88*	*Jones*	*Evans*	*Hay*	*Sbragia*	*McPhail*	*Hood*	*Busby*	*Senior**	*Walwyn*	*Byrne*	*Pollard*	*King*
								Ref: F Roberts	Bullock doesn't mind so much that his players let slip a two-goal lead in the last four minutes. He's more pleased that they have played with some pride. Allatt's brace is his first for the club. Walwyn is fouled by Goodman for Pollard's penalty, then Sbragia nets a dramatic equaliser.											
41	A	TRANMERE		14	W	2·1	1·1	Spooner 17, 64p	Smelt	Nobbs	Wood	Evans	Smith	Hendrie	Gallagher	Spooner	Allatt	Ward	Staniforth	
	23/4		*1,401*	*19*	52			*Kerr 1*	*Endersby*	*Mathias*	*Burgess*	*Mungall*	*Leonard*	*Palios*	*Ferguson*	*Kerr*	*Wellings*	*Brown*	*Griffiths**	*Powell*
								Ref: T Fitzharris	The Shaymen go behind to Kerr's goal in the first minute following Ferguson's corner. Spooner's equaliser is a freak. His 30-yard daisy-cutter hits a divot and the ball flies up into the top-net off the underside of the bar. His winner is a penalty after Mungall handles Gallagher's cross.											
42	H	HARTLEPOOL			D	1·1	1·0	Staniforth 10	Smelt	Goodman	Wood	Evans	Smith	Nobbs	Gallagher	Spooner	Allatt	Ward	Staniforth	
	29/4		1,245		53			*Dobson 67*	*Blackburn*	*Smithies*	*Stimpson*	*Brown*	*Bird*	*Linighan*	*Hogan*	*Stewart*	*Dobson*	*Staff*	*Robinson*	
								Ref: N Ashley	Hartlepool's players are on the verge of a mutiny over a pay wrangle, but it doesn't prevent them from becoming the fifth club from the bottom six to get points at the Shay. Nobbs' cross beats Linighan for Staniforth to give Town a dream start. Dobson, however, sidefoots the equaliser.											
43	A	TORQUAY		11	W	3·1	1·1	Wood 45, Allatt 55, Smith 62	Smelt	Nobbs	Wood	Evans	Smith	Hendrie	Gallagher	Spooner	Allatt	Ward	Staniforth	
	2/5		*1,558*	*9*	56			*Anderson 8*	*Horn*	*Smith*	*Pluckrose*	*James*	*Little*	*Jones*	*Shreidan**	*Carter*	*Cooper*	*Anderson*	*Doyle*	*Gallagher*
								Ref: D Letts	As at Tranmere, the Shaymen come from behind to win. The margin of eventual victory could have been much more. Wood's looping header right on half-time gets Town back in the game. Smith's header completes the scoring. 'It's the best performance since I took over,' – Bullock.											
44	A	ALDERSHOT		13	L	**1·6**	1·2	Staniforth 20	Smelt	Nobbs	Wood	Evans	Smith	Hendrie	Gallagher	Spooner	Nuttall*	Ward	Staniforth	Goodman
	7/5		*1,701*	*16*	56			*Banton 16, 23, 65, 72, 78, Robinson 54*	*Johnson*	*Scott*	*Shrubb*	*Briley*	*Whitlock**	*Gillard*	*Lucas*	*Banton*	*Senior*	*McDonald*	*Robinson*	*Fielder*
								Ref: M Taylor	Dale Banton's nap-hand is the main feature of this game, as Town are humiliated. He also scored a hat-trick a fortnight ago as Aldershot beat Rochdale 6-4. He completes his hat-trick here with a shot that goes in off the post. His fifth goal is a powerful shot that completes the scoring.											
45	H	WIMBLEDON			D	1·1	1·0	Spooner 10	Smelt	Nobbs	Wood	Evans	Smith	Hendrie	Gallagher	Spooner	Kendall	Ward	Staniforth	
	10/5		1,233		57			*Fishenden 88*	*Beasant*	*Peters*	*Sparrow*	*Thomas*	*Morris*	*Hatter*	*Evans*	*Fishenden*	*Leslie*	*Downes*	*Gage**	*Hodges*
								Ref: K Redfern	Wimbledon clinched the Fourth Division title three days ago. They arrive on the back of an unbeaten run stretching 20 games, but are thankful to Fishenden, whose late volley extends their run. Keeper Dave Beasant also plays a blinder after Spooner's early strike, as Halifax dominate.											
46	H	STOCKPORT		11	W	1·0	1·0	Staniforth 17	Smelt	Nobbs	Wood	Evans	Smith	Hendrie	Gallagher	Spooner	Allatt	Ward*	Staniforth	Goodman
	13/5		1,522	*16*	60				*Lloyd*	*Rutter*	*Thorpe*	*Emerson*	*Sword*	*Bowles**	*Smith*	*Wardrobe*	*Quinn*	*Phillips*	*Coyle*	*Leigh*
	Home	Away						Ref: J Hunting	Dave Staniforth celebrates being voted Town's Player of the Season by scoring his 16th goal of the campaign to ensure Town end the season with a win. He times his run to slam the ball home following Wood's free-kick. Sword comes closest to equalising with a header onto the bar.											
Average	2,033	2,756																		

Milk Cup			F-A	H-T	Scorers, Times, and Referees	1	2	3	4	5	6	7	8	9	10	11	12 sub used
1:1 H DERBY		W	2-1	0-0	Davison 80, Staniforth 89	Smelt	Nobbs	Carr	Evans*	Smith	Hendrie	Hallybone	Davison	Spooner	Staniforth	Ward	Wood
31/8	2,820 *2:*				*Swindlehurst 85*	*Banovic*	*Barton*	*Attley*	*Powell*	*Foster*	*McAlle*	*Brolly*	*Skivington*	*Wilson**	*Swindlehurst*	*Reid*	*Emson*
					Ref: D Shaw	The Shaymen raise their game to topple Second Division Derby. All the goals come in a frantic last ten minutes, with Staniforth side-footing home the winner with two minutes left. He has swapped his unlucky Number 9 shirt for the Number 10 of Spooner, a former Derby player.											
1:2 A DERBY	5	L	2-5	0-2	Davison 65, 72 *[Wilson 118]*	Smelt	Nobbs	Carr*	Evans	Smith	Hendrie	Hallybone	Davison	Spooner	Staniforth	Ward	Wood
15/9	*8,534 2:16*		*aet*		*Skivington 6, Hill 39, Buckley 84, 97p,*	*Banovic*	*Barton*	*Buckley*	*Skivington*	*Foster*	*McAlle*	*Brolly*	*Attley*	*Hill*	*Swindlehurst*	*Dalziel**	*Wilson*
					Ref: B Callow (Halifax lost 4-6 on aggregate)	'I've been in the game along time, but never cried before,' admits a proud Bullock, after his side forces extra-time. Skivington's early goal sets the tone for a pulsating match. Derby lead 3-2 after 90 minutes. The fans won't forget this game in a hurry, and Derby take note of Davison.											

FA Cup			F-A	H-T	Scorers, Times, and Referees	1	2	3	4	5	6	7	8	9	10	11	12 sub used
1 H NORTH SHIELDS	20	L	0-1	0-0		Smelt	Nobbs*	Wood	Evans	Smith	Hendrie	Staniforth	Davison	Allatt	Spooner	Goodman	Ward
20/11	2,277 *NL:15*				*McCaffrey 50*	*Harrison*	*Waterson*	*Dickson*	*Varty**	*Harmison*	*Young*	*Smith*	*Doig*	*Ross*	*Donaldson*	*McCaffrey*	*Cassidy*
					Ref: T Fitzharris	After providing a shock last week by defeating Wimbledon, Town are on the receiving end against this Northern League outfit, whose weekly wage bill is £230. The Shaymen become more anxious the longer the game goes on, then McCaffrey strikes with a 30-yard bolt out of the blue.											

		Home					Away					
	P	W	D	L	F	A	W	D	L	F	A	Pts
1 Wimbledon	46	17	4	2	57	23	12	7	4	39	22	98
2 Hull	46	14	8	1	48	14	11	7	5	27	20	90
3 Port Vale	46	15	4	4	37	16	11	6	6	30	18	88
4 Scunthorpe	46	13	7	3	41	17	10	7	6	30	25	83
5 Bury	46	15	4	4	43	20	8	8	7	31	26	81
6 Colchester	46	17	5	1	51	19	7	4	12	24	36	81
7 York	46	18	4	1	59	19	4	9	10	29	39	79
8 Swindon	46	14	3	6	45	27	5	8	10	16	27	68
9 Peterborough	46	13	6	4	38	23	4	7	12	20	29	64
10 Mansfield	46	11	6	6	32	26	5	7	11	29	44	61
11 HALIFAX	46	9	8	6	31	23	7	4	12	28	43	60
12 Torquay	46	12	3	8	38	30	5	4	14	18	35	58
13 Chester	46	8	6	9	28	24	7	5	11	27	36	56
14 Bristol City	46	10	8	5	32	25	3	9	11	27	45	56
15 Northampton	46	10	8	5	43	29	4	4	15	22	46	54
16 Stockport	46	11	8	4	41	31	3	4	16	19	48	54
17 Darlington	46	8	5	10	27	30	5	8	10	34	41	52
18 Aldershot	46	11	5	7	40	35	1	10	12	21	47	51
19 Tranmere	46	8	8	7	30	29	5	3	15	19	42	50
20 Rochdale	46	11	8	4	38	25	0	8	15	17	48	49
21 Blackpool*	46	10	8	5	32	23	3	4	16	23	51	49
22 Hartlepool	46	11	5	7	30	24	2	4	17	16	52	48
23 Crewe	46	9	5	9	35	32	2	3	18	18	39	41
24 Hereford	46	8	6	9	19	23	3	2	18	23	56	41
	1104	283	142	127	915	587	127	142	283	587	915	1512

* 2 pts deducted

Odds & ends

Double wins: (3) Darlington, Swindon, Torquay.
Double losses: (3) Aldershot, Peterborough, Port Vale.

Won from behind: (3) Hartlepool (a), Torquay (a), Tranmere (a).
Lost from in front: (2) Port Vale (a), York (a).

High spots: Six consecutive wins up to 5 February.
Winning 4-2 at eventual champions Wimbledon.
Taking 2nd Division Derby to extra-time in the Milk Cup.

Low spots: 11 games without a win up to 5 November.
Losing at home to non-league North Shields in the FA Cup.
Losing 1-6 at Aldershot.
Losing 0-3 at home to Crewe.

Player of the Year: Dave Staniforth.
Ever-presents: (1) Keith Nobbs.
Hat-tricks: Bobby Davison (1), Dave Staniforth (1).
Leading scorer: Dave Staniforth (16).

	Appearances						Goals			
	Lge	*Sub*	LC	*Sub*	FAC	*Sub*	Lge	LC	FAC	Tot
Allatt, Vernon	**27**	*1*			1		**7**			**7**
Butcher, John	**5**									
Carr, Everton	**14**	*1*	2							
Davison, Bobby	**17**		2		1		**9**	3		**12**
Evans, David	**42**		2		1		**1**			**1**
Gallagher, Barry	**10**									
Goodman, Malcolm	**15**	*10*			1					
Hallybone, Jimmy	**11**	*5*	2							
Hendrie, Paul	**34**		2		1		**1**			**1**
Kendall, Paul	**5**	*5*								
Nobbs, Keith	**46**		2		1		**1**			**1**
Nuttall, Martin	**26**	*3*					**7**			**7**
Skivington, Glen	**4**									
Smelt, Lee	**41**		2		1					
Smith, Tony	**44**		2		1		**2**			**2**
Spooner, Steve	**42**	*1*	2		1		**11**			**11**
Staniforth, Dave	**38**	*1*	2		1		**15**	1		**16**
Ward, Steve	**43**	*1*	2			*1*	**1**			**1**
Wilkes, David	**4**									
Wood, Mick	**38**			*2*	1		**2**			**2**
(own-goals)							**2**			**2**
20 players used	**506**	***28***	**22**	***2***	**11**	***1***	**59**	**4**		**63**

No	Date		Att	Pos	Pt	F-A	H-T	Scorers, Times, and Referees	1	2	3	4	5	6	7	8	9	10	11	12 sub used
1	H	TORQUAY			D	2-2	1-1	Cook 28, Hendrie 63	Smelt	Nobbs	Wood	Evans	Smith	Hendrie	Ward	**Cook**	**Mell***	**Hanson**	Staniforth	Kendall
	27/8		1,448		1			*Bishop 26, Hughes 85*	*Turner*	*Collins*	*Holmes*	*Impey*	*Little*	*Carr*	*Hughes*	*Carter*	*Bishop*	*Sims*	*Anderson*	
								Ref: J Ashworth	Halifax Town look to be heading for their first opening-day victory since 1972 when Hendrie sends in a looping header from outside the box to give them the lead for the first time. But Torquay aren't finished, and in the closing minutes Brian Hughes equalises with a bending free-kick.											
2	A	HEREFORD		17	D	0-0	0-0		Smelt	Nobbs	Wood	Evans	Smith	Hendrie	Gallagher B	Cook	Ward	Kendall	Staniforth	
	3/9		*3,188*	*4*	2				*Rose*	*Emery*	*Leonard*	*Hicks*	*Pejic*	*Delve*	*Harvey*	*Beacock**	*Phillips*	*Black*	*Dalziel*	*Kearns*
								Ref: J Deakin	Mickey Bullock is aiming for a top-six place, and this sort of performance augurs well. Hereford won 4-1 at Aldershot on the opening day, but can't break down Town's solid defence. In fact, Town almost clinch victory, but Leonard clears Smith's header off the line in the last minute.											
3	A	SWINDON		5	W	3-2	2-0	Kendall 9, Staniforth 45, Cook 70	Smelt	Nobbs	Wood	Evans	Smith	Hendrie	Gallagher B*	Cook	Ward	Kendall	Staniforth	Mell
	6/9		*3,635*	*15*	5			*Hockaday 46, Rowland 50*	*Allan*	*Henry**	*Bailie*	*Emmanuel*	*Gray*	*Graham*	*Hockaday*	*Richardson*	*Rowland*	*Mayes*	*Nelson*	*Quinn*
								Ref: J Moules	The Shaymen stun the home crowd into silence with a first-half performance that Bullock reckons is the finest he's seen since he took over. But within five minutes of the second half the scores are level. Cook turns on a sixpence to net Town's winner, and earn his team-mates a day off.											
4	H	MANSFIELD		12	D	0-0	0-0		Smelt	Nobbs	Wood	Evans	Smith	Hendrie	Gallagher B	Cook	Ward*	Kendall	Staniforth	Mell
	9/9		1,725	*24*	6				*Arnold*	*Whitworth*	*Kearney*	*Lowery*	*Foster*	*Calderwood*	*Matthews*	*Hutchinson*	*Dungworth*	*Caldwell*	*Nicholson**	*Barrowclough*
								Ref: R Guy	Ian Greaves' Stags side have lost their opening three matches. The two goals they have scored have been own-goals. This draw is a step in the right direction for them, but leaves Town still waiting for their first home win. Hendrie goes closest, but his chip over Rod Arnold hits the bar.											
5	A	BURY		15	L	0-3	0-2		Smelt	Nobbs	Wood	Evans	Smith	Hendrie	Gallagher B	Cook*	Ward	Kendall	Staniforth	Nuttall
	18/9		*3,258*	*3*	6			*Potts 4, Evans 31 (og), Hilton 88*	*Brown*	*Gardner*	*Pashley*	*Coleman*	*Hilton*	*Bramhall*	*Potts*	*Madden*	*Entwistle*	*Jakub*	*Deacy*	
								Ref: N Ashley	Bullock hopes to delve into the transfer market after his side is given a Sunday roasting by Bury. Despite spending time in training defending near-post corners, Smelt is beaten by Eric Potts' inswinger. Evans turns in Potts' cross for 0-2 when Smelt comes but doesn't call for the ball.											
6	H	HARTLEPOOL		11	W	3-2	1-2	Mell 16, 49, Staniforth 68	Smelt	Nobbs	Wood	Evans	Smith	Hendrie	Gallagher B	Mell	Staniforth	Kendall	Ward	
	23/9		1,416	*21*	9			*Waddle 40, Lowe 41*	*Blackburn*	*Brown*	*Wilson*	*Buckley*	*Linighan A*	*Weir*	*Staff*	*Whitfield*	*Waddle*	*Lowe**	*Robinson !*	*Linighan D*
								Ref: J Lovatt	Referee John Lovatt missed Dave Caldwell's leg-breaking challenge on Tommy O'Neil two years ago. But he's on the spot to send off Pool's Mark Robinson for a challenge on Hendrie - with only six minutes gone. Town go on to record their first home win, but make hard work of it.											
7	H	NORTHAMPTON		12	D	2-2	0-1	Staniforth 56, Mell 73	Smelt	Nobbs	Wood	Evans	Smith	Hendrie	Gallagher B	Mell	Staniforth	Kendall	Ward	
	27/9		1,519	*8*	10			*Jeffrey 21, Syrett 64*	*Gleasure*	*Forster*	*Tucker*	*Mundee*	*Lewis*	*Burrows*	*Jeffrey*	*O'Neill*	*Syrett*	*Belfon*	*Austin*	
								Ref: C Seel	Stewart Mell scores Town's second equaliser, then begins celebrating a likely 83rd-minute winner. But ref Colin Seel isn't fooled. He's seen him use his hand, and promptly books him. Northampton miss injured 6'4" defender Wakeley Gage: Town's two legitimate goals are headers.											
8	A	WREXHAM		16	L	0-1	0-0		Smelt	Nobbs	Wood	Evans	Smith	Hendrie	Gallagher B	Mell	Staniforth	Kendall	Ward*	Cook
	1/10		*5,472*	*8*	10			*Hunt 76*	*Wardle*	*King*	*Cunnington*	*Hunt*	*Coleman*	*Keay*	*Wright*	*Arkwright*	*Buxton**	*Gregory*	*Heath*	*Edwards*
								Ref: H King	Wrexham begin their new drive to get more youngsters to their home games and let hundreds in for free. There is little for them to cheer about, except perhaps Simon Hunt's winner. His boss Bobby Roberts describes it as a real individual goal. Bullock puts the blame on poor defending.											
9	A	BRISTOL CITY		19	L	0-3	0-3		Smelt	Nobbs	Wood	Evans*	Smith !	Hendrie	Nuttall	Mell	Staniforth	Kendall	Ward	Cook
	8/10		*6,739*	*2*	10			*Riley 1, Crawford 14, Kerr 42*	*Shaw*	*Stevens*	*Williams*	*Halliday*	*Phill-Masters*	*Riley*	*Pritchard*	*Ritchie*	*Kerr*	*Economou**	*Crawford*	*Cooper*
								Ref: J Martin	Terry Cooper's Robins side get off to a dream start with Riley's goal after only 45 seconds. They have the game sewn up by half-time. After the break, Town lose Smith, who is sent off for a 54th-minute professional foul on Riley, then Evans, after a clash of heads, 13 minutes later.											
10	H	PETERBOROUGH		14	W	2-1	1-0	Mell 10, Nuttall 57	Smelt	Nobbs	Wood	Evans	Smith	Hendrie	Nuttall	Mell	Cook	Kendall*	Ward	Gallagher B
	15/10		1,079	*9*	13			*Benjamin 52*	*Seaman*	*Chard*	*Imlach*	*Benjamin*	*Wile*	*Slack*	*Buchanan*	*Pike*	*Linton*	*Quow**	*Clarke*	*Firm*
								Ref: P Willis	Mickey Bullock gives his players whisky before they take the field. He may repeat the dosage after this impressive victory. On a cold and wet day, Mell heads the opener, then, after Benjamin's equaliser, he rounds keeper David Seaman 40 yards out before setting up Nuttall's winner.											
11	H	CREWE		8	W	1-0	0-0	Ward 90	Smelt	Nobbs	Wood	Evans	Smith	Hendrie	Nuttall*	Mell	Cook	Kendall	Ward	Gallagher B
	18/10		1,352	*18*	16				*Naylor*	*Edwards*	*Brady*	*King*	*Scott*	*Hart*	*Cliss*	*Spittle*	*Waller*	*Newell*	*Pullar*	
								Ref: G Courtney	Crewe arrive at the Shay on the back of a 0-5 hammering at Reading. They are within seconds of earning a morale-boosting draw when Town score. Mystery initially surrounds the identity of the scorer, but Ward claims it despite the fact that the ball hits Hart and Scott before going in.											

No	Venue	Opponent	Att	Pos	Res	Pts	F-A	H-T	Scorers, Times, and Referees	1	2	3	4	5	6	7	8	9	10	11	12
12	A	DONCASTER		11	L		2-3	0-3	Staniforth 69, Cook 78p	Smelt	Nobbs	Wood	Evans	Smith	Hendrie	Nuttall*	Mell	Cook	Kendall	Ward	Staniforth
	21/10		3,299	2		16			Snodin G 3, 10, Russell 35	Boyd	Russell	Breckin	Snodin I	Lister	Humphries	Miller*	Moss	Douglas	Kowalski	Snodin G	Harle
									Ref: M Robinson	A game of two halves. Glyn Snodin scores two in the opening ten minutes, then hits the post. Russell scrambles in the third following a corner. Staniforth pulls one back with a shot on the turn, then Cook's penalty, for a trip on ex-Rovers player Mell, makes for an exciting finish.											
13	H	ALDERSHOT		12	W		1-0	1-0	Gallagher B	Smelt	Nobbs	Wood	Evans	**Gallagher J**	Hendrie	Gallagher B	Mell	Staniforth	Cook	Ward	
	29/10		1,242	17		19				Coles	Shrubb	Mazzon	Day	Wooler !	Jopling	Lucas	Banton	Burvill	McDonald	O'Sullivan	
									Ref: N Glover	Burnley's former England B international Joe Gallagher has joined Town on loan. But it's his namesake Barry who makes the headlines. He heads in the only goal off Wood's cross. Aldershot's cause is not helped by Wooler's first-ever sending off, for a tackle from behind on Mell.											
14	A	CHESTER		12	D		1-1	0-0	Cook 90p	Smelt	Nobbs	Wood	Evans	Gallagher J	Hendrie	Gallagher B	Mell*	Staniforth	Cook	Ward	Nuttall
	2/11		1,211	23		20			Parker 79	Harrington	Williams	Lane	Elliott	Storton	Holden	Manns	Zelem	Bulmer	Parker	Wann	
									Ref: D Allison	Joe Gallagher is penalised for calling 'let it run' – the ball – to concede the free-kick from which Stuart Parker heads Chester in front. Smelt cracks his head trying to make the save. Barry Gallagher takes over in goal. Cook scores a late penalty equaliser for Storton's foul on Hendrie.											
15	H	TRANMERE		13	L		1-2	1-2	Hendrie 15	**Vesey**	Nobbs	Wood	Evans	Gallagher J	Hendrie	Gallagher B	Mell	Cook	Smith*	Ward	Nuttall
	4/11		1,735	5		20			Philpotts 2, Williams G 22	Davies	McMahon	Burgess	Higgins*	Palios	Philpotts	Ferguson	Aspinall	Allen	Brown	Williams G	Mathias
									Ref: H Taylor	With Smelt injured, Rochdale college boy Kieron Vesey, a member of Town's Northern Intermediate side, comes in for his debut. Though he lets in two goals, he receives praise from Wrexham's Dai Davies. It is the 35-year-old former Wales international who is actually the busier.											
16	A	STOCKPORT		17	L		0-4	0-1		Smelt	Smith	Wood	Evans	Gallagher J	Hendrie	Gallagher B	Mell	Nuttall	Kendall	Ward	
	11/11		2,034	16		20			Quinn 26, 62, Sword 51, 75	Salmon	Rutter	Sherlock	Smith	Bowles	Thorpe	White	Jones	Quinn	Sword	Coyle	
									Ref: A Seville	Eric Webster's Stockport cut the Town defence to shreds, with Mick Quinn and Tommy Sword bagging a brace apiece. Town's only effort of note is Nuttall's 40-yard lob, touched onto the bar by Salmon. Next week's cup foes Whitby, who are represented here, will have little to fear.											
17	H	DARLINGTON		20	L		0-2	0-1		Smelt	Nobbs	Wood	Evans	Smith	Hendrie	Gallagher B*	**Little**	Cook	Kendall	Ward	Hanson
	25/11		1,018	19		20			Walsh 39, 82	Barber	Craggs	Johnson	Honour	Smith	Barton	Cartwright	Todd	Davies*	Walsh	McLean	Young
									Ref: M Scott	After last week's cup defeat by Whitby, things don't appear to be getting any better. The fans are on the back of Bullock, but Darlington boss Cyril Knowles reckons he's the best Town will get. Walsh is the difference between the sides. He takes his career tally to 94 – a club record.											
18	A	READING		21	L		0-1	0-0		Smelt	Nobbs	Wood	Evans	Smith	Hendrie	Ward	Little	Cook*	Mell	**Greenway**	Kendall
	2/12		3,930	6		20			Crown 74	Judge	Williams	Richardson	Beavon	Hicks	Wood	Duncan	Horrix*	Senior	Sanchez	Crown	Price
									Ref: T Spencer	Town are within 16 minutes of becoming the first side to prevent Reading from scoring at Elm Park. They frustrate Maurice Evans' promotion hopefuls before David Crown's 25-yarder skids under Smelt. Town come close to an 83rd-minute equaliser when Kendall's drive hits the post.											
19	A	COLCHESTER		21	L		1-4	0-2	Greenway 54	Smelt	Nobbs	Wood	Evans	Smith	Hendrie	Greenway*	Little	Nuttall	Kendall	Ward	Cook
	17/12		1,866	3		20			Houston 5, Adcock 33, Bowen 67, 88	Chamberlain	Cook !	Phillips	Hadley	Wignall	Houston	Groves	Osborne	Bowen	Adcock*	Leslie	Hubbick
									Ref: A Buksh	In a crazy game, Town contribute much and might even have won. Despite falling to Houston's early headed goal, they create many chances. Greenway scores his first senior goal, then celebrates another soon after. The ref disallows it, but sends off Cook for an off-the-ball incident.											
20	H	YORK		21	L		1-2	1-1	Little 25	Smelt	Nobbs	Wood	Evans	Smith	Hendrie	Greenway*	Little !	**Cooper**	Kendall	Ward	Cook
	26/12		**2,457**	1		20			Walwyn 7, 71	Jones	Senior	Hay	Sbragia	MacPhail	Hood*	Ford	Crosby	Walwyn	Byrne	Pollard	Chippendale
									Ref: A Challinor	Keith Walwyn has proved a handful for Town in the past, and continues to do so. He squeezes in his first, then restores his side's lead, when he climbs high to head home. Little crashes in Town's equaliser, but doesn't see out the last six minutes, sent off for a second bookable offence.											
21	A	ROCHDALE		22	D		1-1	0-1	Cook 87	Smelt	Nobbs	Wood	Evans	Smith	Hendrie	Kendall	Little	Cooper*	Cook	Ward	Greenway
	27/12		1,896	21		21			Higgins 20	Conroy	Oates	Chapman	O'Connor	Williams	Higgins	Thompson D	Hamilton	Johnson*	Allatt	Griffiths	Thompson S
									Ref: M Heath	The Shaymen end a depressing run of seven league and cup defeats with Cook's scrambled equaliser just three minutes from time. The game matches the miserable weather, but Dale are on course for victory when Andy Higgins heads home a well-rehearsed move following a corner.											
22	H	BLACKPOOL		19	W		1-0	0-0	Little 51p	Smelt	Nobbs	Greenway	Evans	Smith*	Hendrie	Nuttall	Little	Cooper	Staniforth	Ward	Kendall
	31/12		1,958	4		24				Pierce	Moore	Ferns	Rodaway	Hetzke	Greenall	Britton	Mercer	Stewart	Windridge	McNiven*	Dyer
									Ref: T Holbrook	Young Mark Greenway is the star as Town record a memorable victory over Sam Ellis's high-flyers. It's his pass that leads to Pierce bringing down Nuttall for Little's penalty. Then at the other end, he hacks the ball off the line in the 65th minute when Stewart's header hit the post.											
23	A	CHESTERFIELD		18	D		0-0	0-0		Smelt	Nobbs	Greenway	Evans	Kendall	Hendrie	Nuttall	Little	Cooper	Staniforth	Ward	
	2/1		2,298	16		25				Brown	O'Neill	Stimpson	Kendal	Baines	Bellamy	Bell	Spooner	Newton	Walker	Scrimgeour	
									Ref: J Hough	Chesterfield include in their side former Shaymen Derek Bell and Steve Spooner, and Town find them in charitable mood, as firstly Bell fluffs a one-on-one, then Spooner slices wide with the goal gaping. Town defend into a gale in the first half, then find it dies down after the break.											

No	Date			Att	Pos	Pt	F-A	H-T	Scorers, Times, and Referees	1	2	3	4	5	6	7	8	9	10	11	12 sub used
24		H	HEREFORD		16	W	2-1	2-0	Cooper 9, Little 21	Smelt	Nobbs	Greenway	Evans	Kendall	Hendrie	Nuttall	Little	Cooper	Staniforth	Ward	
	7/1			1,037	*21*	28			*Harvey 49*	*Rose*	*Price**	*Leonard*	*Hicks*	*Pejic*	*Larkin*	*Francis*	*Harvey*	*Phillips*	*Beacock*	*Dalziel !*	*Emery*
									Ref: N Wilson	Hereford slip to their twelfth game without a win and fifth consecutive defeat. Town make hard work of it, even after on-loan Steve Cooper's header floats over Rose early on – his first league goal. The Bulls have Ian Dalziel sent off for a nasty challenge on Hendrie before the break.											
25		A	TORQUAY		17	D	1-1	0-1	Nuttall 77	Smelt	Nobbs	Greenway	Evans	Smith	Hendrie	Nuttall	Kendall	Cooper*	Staniforth	Ward	Wood
	14/1			*1,369*	*14*	29			*Curle 45*	*Turner*	*Pugh*	*Wharton*	*Impey*	*Hughes*	*Carr*	*Lennox*	*Curle*	*Cooper*	*Sims*	*Barnes*	
									Ref: C Downey	Torquay boss Bruce Rioch resigns before the game, fed up at having to run the team single-handedly. Snow greets the Town players, but they plunder a point when Nuttall heads in Nobbs' cross. Smelt keeps Town in the game, but can't stop Keith Curle's 25-yard free-kick that flies in.											
26		H	BURY		17	D	0-0	0-0		Smelt	Nobbs	Greenway	Evans	Kendall	Wood	Nuttall	Gallagher B	Cooper *	Staniforth	Ward	Mell
	21/1			1,728	*11*	30				*Butcher*	*Gardner*	*Pashley*	*Park*	*Hilton*	*Bramhall*	*White*	*Madden*	*Entwistle*	*Jakub*	*Deacy*	
									Ref: G Tyson	Keeper John Butcher had a loan spell at the Shay last season. He's now helping out Bury, and does it in style to keep out Town. On the snow-covered pitch, he makes a string of crucial saves, not least a reflex effort from Staniforth's bullet header. Smelt plays his 100th league game.											
27		H	WREXHAM		17	D	1-1	0-1	Smith 90	Smelt	Nobbs	Greenway	Evans	Kendall	Wood	Nuttall*	Gallagher B	Mell	Staniforth	Ward	Smith
	4/2			1,184	*18*	31			*Gregory 45*	*Millington*	*King*	*Cunnington*	*Hunt*	*Keay*	*Wright*	*Arkwright*	*Gregory*	*Salathiel*	*Steel*	*Heath*	
									Ref: J Worrall	Gregory's stylish finish, to put Wrexham ahead right on half-time, means he has scored all his side's goals in the last four matches. It's another poor Town performance, but Smith saves them in injury time. After clashing heads with Steel, Evans plays on with his shirt soaked in blood.											
28		A	HARTLEPOOL		17	L	0-3	0-1		Smelt	Nobbs	Wood	Evans	Smith	Kendall	Gallagher B	Little	Mell	Staniforth	Ward*	Nuttall
	11/2			*1,658*	*23*	31			*Linacre 36, Kennedy 60, Smithies 74*	*Blackburn*	*Smithies*	*Barker*	*Hogan*	*Linighan A*	*Linighan D*	*Kennedy*	*Lowe*	*Linacre*	*Dobson*	*Staff*	
									Ref: M Peck	Bullock orders his players in for another Sunday training session after this inept showing. Phil Linacre scored Whitby's winner in the cup and curls in the first. Ray Kennedy, ex Arsenal, Liverpool and England, and scorer of the second, will soon be diagnosed with Parkinson's Disease.											
29		H	CHESTER		17	D	2-2	0-2	Gallagher B 37, Thornber 74	Smelt	Nobbs	Greenway	Evans	Kendall	Hendrie	Gallagher B	Little	Staniforth	Wood	Ward*	**Thornber**
	14/2			**911**	*24*	32			*Elliott 15, Holden 35*	*Harrington*	*Bulmer*	*Lane*	*Elliott*	*Zelem*	*Hildersley*	*Brett*	*Sanderson*	*Holden*	*Blackwell*	*Allen*	
									Ref: R Banks	Chester, now managed by John McGrath, look to be heading for only their third win of the season when they go two goals up. After Gallagher pulls one back, Steve Thornber comes off the bench and drives in the equaliser from 25 yards. It's his first touch of the ball in League football.											
30		A	ALDERSHOT		18	L	2-5	1-4	Staniforth 44, Gallagher B 65p	Smelt	Nobbs	Wood	Evans	Kendall	Hendrie	Gallagher B	Little	Staniforth	Thornber	Ward	
	18/2			*2,382*	*3*	32			*Banton 12, 68, L'rence 21, 31, McD'd 40p*	*Coles*	*Shrubb*	*Gillard*	*Briley*	*Souter*	*Jopling*	*Burvill*	*Banton*	*Lawrence*	*McDonald*	*Mazzon*	
									Ref: E Scales	With the score at 2-4, Town are fuming when Staniforth scores his second, only for the ref to rule it out for offside. Three minutes later Banton makes it 2-5. Kendall twice leaves Lawrence free to score. Evans concedes the penalty which ultimately puts the game out of Halifax's reach.											
31		H	DONCASTER		21	L	1-2	1-2	Harle 37 (og)	Smelt	Nobbs	Wood	Evans	Kendall	Hendrie	Gallagher B	Little	Cook*	Thornber	Ward	Smith
	25/2			2,408	*2*	32			*Woods 9, Snodin I 19*	*Peacock*	*Russell*	*Yates*	*Snodin I*	*Lister*	*Humphries*	*Harle*	*Moss*	*Douglas*	*Woods*	*Snodin G*	
									Ref: K Redfern	Halifax fan David Dibb runs ten laps of the speedway track before kick-off. He's raising money for a diatherapy machine for the treatment room. On the pitch, high-flying Rovers then show Town the way in finishing – at both ends. David Harle heads Ward's cross into his own net.											
32		A	CREWE		21	L	1-6	0-2	Gallagher B 68p *[Pullar 51]*	Smelt	Nobbs	Wood	Evans	Smith	Hendrie	Gallagher B	Little	Staniforth	Thornber*	Ward	Cook
	3/3			*2,050*	*9*	32			*Williams 1, Waller 28, 84, 87 Leonard 50,*	*Naylor*	*Edwards*	*Bowers*	*Cliss*	*Scott*	*Hart*	*Pullar*	*Crabbe*	*Waller*	*Leonard*	*Williams*	
									Ref: V Callow	Town come off the rails at Crewe. This match is a disaster from start to finish. Williams puts the home side ahead after only 38 seconds. Cook comes on after half-time, then Smith is stretchered off three minutes later. A sympathetic ref awards Town a penalty for a foul outside the box.											
33		A	TRANMERE		21	L	2-3	0-2	Staniforth 62, Cook 82	Smelt	Kendall	Wood	Evans	Smith	Hendrie	Gallagher B	Little	Staniforth*	Cook	Ward	Mell
	5/3			*1,486*		32			*Hutchinson 25, Palios 33, Aspinall 61*	*Davies*	*Higgins*	*Burgess*	*Philpotts*	*Williams*	*Palios*	*Ferguson**	*Aspinall*	*Mungall*	*Hutchinson*	*Goodlass*	*Brown*
									Ref: N Midgley	Former Everton winger Ronnie Goodlass is a constant threat to Town, and his free-kick and cross lead to Tranmere's first two goals. Cook has the chance to halve the deficit, but the referee blocks his route to goal. Town's fightback at 0-3 is admirable, but inevitably it proves in vain.											
34		H	STOCKPORT		20	W	2-0	2-0	Gallagher B 13, 26	Smelt	Kendall	Wood	Evans	Smith	Hendrie	Gallagher B	Little	Mell*	Cook	Ward	Staniforth
	9/3			1,261	*11*	35				*Salmon*	*Jones*	*Rutter*	*Emerson*	*Bowles*	*Thorpe*	*Smith**	*Evans*	*Kerr*	*Sword*	*Coyle*	*Sutcliffe*
									Ref: N Glover	The Shaymen climb out of the bottom four thanks to a scintillating first-half performance. Gallagher stabs home his first goal, then doubles his tally with a Brazilian-style free-kick. Smith also hits the bar, and Gallagher has a valid penalty appeal turned down – all in the opening period.											

No	Date	Opponent / Att	Pos	Res	F-A	H-T	Scorers, Times, and Referees	1	2	3	4	5	6	7	8	9	10	11	12
35	H	BRISTOL CITY	21	L	1-2	0-0	Evans 89	Smelt	Kendall	Wood	Evans	Smith	Hendrie	Gallagher B	Little	Staniforth	Cook*	Ward	Mell
	17/3	1,204	*4*	35			*Pritchard 48, Riley 76*	*Shaw*	*Stevens*	*Newman*	*Halliday*	*Phill-Masters*	*Stroud*	*Pritchard*	*Ritchie*	*Riley*	*Morgan*	*Curle*	
							Ref: J Lovatt	A machine breakdown means that only 350 of 1,200 match programmes are available. City notch up only their third away win of the season, but it will help them out of Division 4. A poor game is punctuated by quality strikes from Pritchard and Riley. Evans' late shot is deflected in.											
36	A	PETERBOROUGH	21	L	0-4	0-1	*[Chard 89]*	Smelt	Nobbs	Wood	Evans	Smith	Hendrie	Gallagher B	Little	Staniforth	Kendall	Ward	
	24/3	*2,304*	*8*	35			*Benjamin 15, Worrall 57, Kelly 64,*	*Seaman*	*Chard*	*Imlach*	*Beech*	*Slack*	*Firm*	*Benjamin*	*Tydeman*	*Waddle**	*Kelly*	*Worrall*	*Buchanan*
							Ref: I Borrett	Peterborough unleash Errington Kelly, on loan from Coventry, on the Shaymen. He's meant to be the fastest player ever at London Road. A blunder by Smelt, when he drops the ball, lets in Benjamin to start the rout. Posh player-manager Wile admits, 'It was a little bit easy for us.'											
37	H	SWINDON	20	W	2-1	1-0	Kendall 44, Gallagher B 54	Smelt	Evans	Wood	Kendall	Smith	Nobbs	Gallagher B*	Little	Staniforth	Cook	Ward	Mell
	30/3	1,008	*14*	38			*Quinn 89*	*Endersby*	*Bailie*	*Baddeley*	*Batty*	*Gibson*	*Graham*	*Hockaday*	*Emmanuel*	*Rowland*	*Mayes**	*Nelson*	*Quinn*
							Ref: A Saunders	With re-election looking a distinct possibility, Bullock asks his players to play as if their lives depended on it. Kendall responds by making a spectacular goal-line clearance, then scoring with a sweet half-volley. Gallagher's neat finish gives Town some much-needed breathing space.											
38	A	NORTHAMPTON	21	D	1-1	0-0	Evans 82	Smelt	Evans	Wood	Kendall	Smith	Nobbs	Gallagher B	Little	Staniforth	Cook	Ward*	Mell
	7/4	*1,356*	*16*	39			*Hayes 79*	*Gleasure*	*Lewis*	*Forster*	*Gage**	*Burrows*	*Hayes*	*Jeffrey*	*O'Neill*	*Austin*	*Belfon*	*Martinez*	*Tucker*
							Ref: L Shapter	Cobblers' boss Clive Walker reckons his team 'got away with murder.' Bullock reckons Town could have won 5-0. They have to settle for a point, and games are running out. Hayes cuts in to give the home side the lead, but Evans gets Town a deserved equaliser from outside the box.											
39	A	MANSFIELD	21	L	**1-7**	0-1	Foster 54 (og) *[Matthews 73, C'well 88]*	Vesey	Evans	Wood	Kendall	Smith	Nobbs	Gallagher B	Little	Staniforth	Cook*	Ward	Mell
	10/4	*1,696*	*22*	39			*B'clough 7, Juryeff 60, 72, 79, Lowery 68,*	*Hitchcock*	*Woodhead*	*Whitworth*	*Lowery*	*Calderwood*	*Foster*	*Barrowclough*	*Matthews*	*Juryeff*	*Caldwell*	*Keegan*	
							Ref: G Courtney	Smelt is injured, so Vesey comes in again. Unfortunately, nothing goes right in the second half. When Foster heads Cook's cross into his own net, Town draw level. Then Mansfield tear them apart. On-loan Juryeff scores a 19-minute hat-trick. 'My pride has been hurt,' admits Bullock.											
40	H	READING	22	L	0-1	0-1		Smelt	Evans	Wood	Kendall	Smith	Hendrie	Nuttall	Little*	Staniforth	Nobbs	Ward	Gallagher B
	13/4	1,113	*4*	39			*Sanchez 13*	*Judge*	*Williams*	*Richardson*	*Price*	*Hicks*	*Wood*	*White*	*Horrix*	*Senior*	*Sanchez*	*Crown*	
							Ref: D Shaw	Bullock has set a safety target of 50 points, but on this performance it will be hard to reach. Town have plenty of possession, but rarely trouble Judge. Lawrie Sanchez will one day score an FA Cup Final winner. His early goal settles this game, latching on to Richardson's flick to score.											
41	A	YORK	22	L	1-4	0-3	Mell 69	Smelt	Evans	Wood	Kendall	Smith	Hendrie	Nobbs	Little	Gallagher B	Mell	Ward	
	20/4	***7,123***	*1*	39			*Byrne 10, 35, 72, Walwyn 28*	*Jones*	*Evans*	*Hay*	*Sbragia*	*MacPhail*	*Hood*	*Ford*	*Haslegrave**	*Walwyn*	*Byrne*	*Pollard*	*Houchen*
							Ref: M Scott	Town know all about the potent strike force of Byrne and Walwyn, but don't know how to stop them. Evans has already hit a 35-yard backpass against his own post before Byrne opens the scoring. Mell reacts quickly for Town's goal. Chants of 'Bullock out' clearly hurt the Town boss.											
42	H	ROCHDALE	20	W	**5-0**	2-0	Mell 15, Gallagher B 34, 53, 82, 85	Smelt	Nobbs	Wood	Evans	Smith	Hendrie	Cook*	Little	Gallagher B	Mell	Ward	Nuttall
	23/4	1,422	*21*	42				*Conroy*	*Oates*	*Chapman*	*Reid**	*McMahon*	*Doyle*	*McCluskie*	*Hamilton*	*Thompson S*	*Allatt*	*Griffiths*	*Heaton*
							Ref: R Nixon	Town flourish in the Easter sunshine, and Gallagher nets Town's first four-goal haul since Des Frost in 1951. Mell races away to put Town in front. Rochdale include ex-Man City defender Mick Doyle in their side, but it's his awful backpass that allows Gallagher to walk in his fourth.											
43	A	DARLINGTON	21	L	2-3	1-0	Ward 40, Nuttall 88	Smelt	Nobbs	Wood	Evans	Smith	Hendrie	Cook	Little	Gallagher B	Mell*	Ward	Nuttall
	28/4	***1,161***	*17*	42			*Forster 75, Angus 81, 89*	*Barber*	*Craggs*	*Johnson*	*Honour**	*Smith*	*Lloyd*	*Todd*	*Cartwright*	*Forster*	*Angus*	*McLean*	*Hannah*
							Ref: I Hendrick	Halifax are relieved that prolific Darlington striker Walsh is out injured. The home side manage without him. Ward's cross finds its way in to give Town the lead. Nuttall thinks he's salvaged a point, until Angus prods in the winner following an indirect free-kick given inside the area.											
44	H	CHESTERFIELD	21	W	2-1	1-0	Mell 44, Gallagher B 66p	Smelt	Nobbs	Wood	Evans	Smith	Hendrie	Cook	Little	Gallagher B	Mell	Ward	
	4/5	1,001		45			*O'Neill 88*	*Brown J*	*Bellamy*	*Brown N*	*Kendal*	*Baines*	*Hunter*	*Brown P*	*Scrimgeour*	*Newton*	*Klug*	*O'Neill*	
							Ref: R Guy	Lion-hearted Alan Little leaves the pitch in the first half to have a dislocated toe put back in place. He returns to help Town to a crucial victory. Mell clips in their first and Gallagher's penalty is given for handball against Phil Brown. O'Neill's 25-yarder gives Town the jitters at the end.											
45	A	BLACKPOOL	21	L	0-4	0-1		Smelt	Kendall	Wood	Evans	Smith	Hendrie	Cook*	Little	Gallagher B	Mell	Ward	Nuttall
	7/5	*2,324*	*6*	45			*Britton 41, 48, 78, Stonehouse 86*	*Brand*	*Moore*	*Walsh*	*Rodaway*	*Hetzke*	*Greenall*	*Britton*	*Davies*	*Stewart*	*Walker*	*Stonehouse*	
							Ref: R Bridges	The Shaymen can muster only one shot on goal all afternoon, and Blackpool's margin of victory could have been more. The game is virtually over when Britton, ex-Chelsea, volleys the opener. He races clear to set up Stonehouse for his goal, then shrugs off Smith to score his third.											
46	H	COLCHESTER	20	W	4-1	2-0	Ward 11, Gallagher B 45, 60, Mell 83	Smelt	Kendall	Wood	Evans	Smith	Hendrie	Nobbs	Little	Gallagher B*	Mell	Ward	Nuttall
	11/5	1,248	*8*	48			*Mutrie 90*	*Chamberlain*	*Hadley*	*Phillips*	*Farrell*	*Wignall*	*Houston*	*Groves**	*Osborne*	*Bowen*	*Adcock*	*Hull*	*Mutrie*
	Home	Away					Ref: D Owen	This terrific win means Wrexham must now take seven points from their final three matches to overhaul the Shaymen in the table and avoid re-election. Ward's clinical finish starts the ball rolling. Gallagher's two goals are headers, whilst Mell cuts inside before sweeping in the fourth.											
Average	1,412	2,771																	

Milk Cup							F-A	H-T	Scorers, Times, and Referees	1	2	3	4	5	6	7	8	9	10	11	12 sub used
1:1	H	DARLINGTON			L		0-1	0-0		Smelt	Nobbs	Wood	Evans	Smith	Hendrie	Gallagher B	Cook	Mell*	Hanson	Staniforth	Nuttall
30/8			1,331						*Honour 77*	*Barber*	*Craggs*	*Gilbert*	*McLean*	*Smith*	*Barton*	*Cartwright*	*Ross*	*Lee*	*Walsh*	*Honour*	
									Ref: R Nixon	Former Spurs favourite Cyril Knowles has taken over at Darlington, and his team of hard-tacklers makes life uncomfortable for the Shaymen. Honour volleys the only goal to give his side a first-leg advantage. Town striker Mell is given a midfield role, but is taken off after 58 minutes.											
1:2	A	DARLINGTON		12	L		2-3	1-0	Kendall 40, Staniforth 60	Smelt	Nobbs	Wood	Evans	Smith	Hendrie	Gallagher B	Cook*	Ward	Kendall	Staniforth	Mell
13/9			*1,793*	*9*					*Pugh 69, Walsh 83, 87*	*Barber*	*Craggs*	*Gilbert*	*McLean*	*Smith*	*Barton*	*Cartwright*	*Ross**	*Lee*	*Walsh*	*Honour*	*Pugh*
									Ref: K Walmsley (Halifax lost 2-4 on aggregate)	For an hour, there looks to be only one team in this tie, and when Staniforth scores from a narrow angle Town are sitting pretty at 2-0. But they collapse alarmingly. Pugh levels the score on aggregate before Walsh hammers in two crosses late on to give Darlington a passage to Round 2.											

FA Cup																					
1	H	WHITBY		17	L		2-3	1-0	Ward 43, Evans 58	Smelt	Nobbs	Wood	Evans	Gallagher J	Hendrie	Gallagher B	Cook	Nuttall*	Kendall	Ward	Mell
19/11			2,588	*NL:1*					*Hampton 61, Sills 65, Linacre 70*	*Coleby D*	*Granycome*	*Walker*	*Smith*	*Coleby S*	*Gollogly*	*Lilley*	*Lawrence*	*Linacre*	*Sills*	*Hampton*	
									Ref: C Seel	Bullock refuses to resign after this humiliation by Tony Lee's Northern League side. Defeat, however, looks unlikely when Evans heads in for 2-0, but Hampton's angled drive gets Whitby back into the game. Town visibly crumble, and Linacre runs through to score Whitby's winner.											

		Home						Away					
	P	W	D	L	F	A	W	D	L	F	A	Pts
1 York	46	18	4	1	58	16	13	4	6	38	23	101
2 Doncaster	46	15	6	2	46	22	9	7	7	36	32	85
3 Reading	46	17	6	0	51	14	5	10	8	33	42	82
4 Bristol City	46	18	3	2	51	17	6	7	10	19	27	82
5 Aldershot	46	14	6	3	49	29	8	3	12	27	40	75
6 Blackpool	46	15	4	4	47	19	6	5	12	23	33	72
7 Peterborough	46	15	5	3	52	16	3	9	11	20	32	68
8 Colchester	46	14	7	2	45	14	3	9	11	24	39	67
9 Torquay	46	13	7	3	32	18	5	6	12	27	46	67
10 Tranmere	46	11	5	7	33	26	6	10	7	20	27	66
11 Hereford	46	11	6	6	31	21	5	9	9	23	32	63
12 Stockport	46	12	5	6	34	25	5	6	12	26	39	62
13 Chesterfield	46	10	11	2	34	24	5	4	14	25	37	60
14 Darlington	46	13	4	6	31	19	4	4	15	18	31	59
15 Bury	46	9	7	7	34	32	6	7	10	27	32	59
16 Crewe	46	10	8	5	35	27	6	3	14	21	40	59
17 Swindon	46	11	7	5	34	23	4	6	13	24	33	58
18 Northampton	46	10	8	5	32	32	3	6	14	21	46	53
19 Mansfield	46	9	7	7	44	27	4	6	13	22	43	52
20 Wrexham	46	7	6	10	34	33	4	9	10	25	41	48
21 HALIFAX	46	11	6	6	36	25	1	6	16	19	64	48
22 Rochdale	46	8	9	6	35	31	3	4	16	17	49	46
23 Hartlepool	46	7	8	8	31	28	3	2	18	16	57	40
24 Chester	46	7	5	11	23	35	0	8	15	22	47	34
	1104	285	150	117	932	573	117	150	285	573	932	1506

Odds & ends

Double wins: (1) Swindon.
Double losses: (6) Bristol C, Darlington, Doncaster, Reading, Tranmere, York.

Won from behind: (1) Hartlepool (h).
Lost from in front: (3) Darlington (a), Darlington (MC) (a), Whitby (FAC) (h).

High spots: Unbeaten in the first four games.
Unbeaten in seven games up to 4 February.
Beating Rochdale 5-0, with Barry Gallagher scoring four.

Low spots: Losing at home to non-league Whitby in the FA Cup.
Six consecutive defeats up to 26 December.
Four consecutive defeats up to 5 March.
Losing 1-7 at Mansfield.
Losing 1-6 at Crewe.
Having to apply for re-election after Wrexham overhauled them in their last game of the season.

Player of the Year: Barry Gallagher.
Ever-presents: (2) David Evans, Steve Ward.
Hat-tricks: Barry Gallagher (1).
Leading scorer: Barry Gallagher (14).

	Appearances						Goals			
	Lge	*Sub*	LC	*Sub*	FAC	*Sub*	Lge	LC	FAC	Tot
Cook, Jeff	**25**	*5*	2		1		**6**			**6**
Cooper, Steve	**7**						**1**			**1**
Evans, David	**46**		2		1		**2**		1	**3**
Gallagher, Barry	**32**	*3*	2		1		**14**			**14**
Gallagher, Joe	**4**				1					
Greenway, Mark	**10**	*1*					**1**			**1**
Hanson, Neil	**1**	*1*	1							
Hendrie, Paul	**40**		2		1		**2**			**2**
Kendall, Paul	**36**	*3*	1		1		**2**	1		**3**
Little, Alan	**27**						**3**			**3**
Mell, Stewart	**22**	*8*	1	*1*		*1*	**8**			**8**
Nobbs, Keith	**41**		2		1					
Nuttall, Martin	**13**	*8*		*1*	1		**3**			**3**
Smelt, Lee	**44**		2		1					
Smith, Tony	**37**	*2*	2				**1**			**1**
Staniforth, Dave	**28**	*2*	2				**6**	1		**7**
Thornber, Steve	**3**	*1*					**1**			**1**
Vesey, Keiron	**2**									
Ward, Steve	**46**		1		1		**3**		1	**4**
Wood, Mick	**42**	*1*	2		1					
(own-goals)							**2**			**2**
20 players used	**506**	***35***	**22**	***2***	**11**	***1***	**55**	**2**	**2**	**59**

CANON LEAGUE DIVISION 4 — Manager: Mickey Bullock ⇨ Mick Jones — SEASON 1984-85

No		Date	Att	Pos	Pt	F-A	H-T	Scorers, Times, and Referees	1	2	3	4	5	6	7	8	9	10	11	12 sub used
1	H	BLACKPOOL			L	0-2	0-0		**Roche**	**Podd**	**Watson**	**Moyses***	Kendall	**Knill**	**Sanderson**	Little	**Lowe**	Gallagher	Ward	Thornber
		25/8	1,870		0			*Stonehouse 51p, 87*	*O'Rourke*	*Moore*	*Ferns*	*Conroy*	*Hetzke*	*Greenall*	*Britton*	*Stonehouse*	*Stewart*	*Deary*	*Dyer*	
								Ref: J Lovatt	Bullock includes seven new signings, but his team are decidedly second best, and the signs look ominous. Sam Ellis' well-organised Blackpool side, though, need Stonehouse's penalty, when Knill trips Stewart, to break the deadlock. His late header crosses the line before Ward clears.											
2	A	BURY			L	0-3	0-1		Roche	Podd	Watson	Kendall	Ayre	Knill	Sanderson*	Little	Lowe	Gallagher	Ward	Cook
		1/9	*1,717*		0			*Ross 40, Bramhall 50, Young 77*	*Brown*	*Hill*	*Young*	*Ross*	*Bramhall*	*Dobson*	*White*	*Madden*	*Entwistle*	*Jakub*	*James*	
								Ref: C Seel	Bury's star-studded line-up includes ex-internationals Martin Dobson and Leighton James. Needless to say, they prove too hot for Town. Former Arsenal and Everton midfielder Trevor Ross opens the scoring following a disputed indirect free-kick inside the box conceded by Ayre.											
3	H	ALDERSHOT			L	1-2	0-0	Little 77	Roche	Podd	Watson	Kendall	Ayre	Knill	Cook	Little	Lowe*	Gallagher	Ward	Sanderson
		8/9	1,004		0			*Foley 87, Foyle 90*	*Coles*	*Day**	*Gillard*	*Shrubb*	*Peters*	*Massey*	*Burvill*	*Banton*	*Foyle*	*McDonald*	*Mazzon*	*Foley*
								Ref: K Redfern	Town look set to avert the possibility of a third consecutive league defeat when Little finishes off a breakaway move 13 minutes from the end. But the Shots have other ideas. Not content with £20,000 striker Peter Foley's equaliser, they grab an injury-time winner through Martin Foyle.											
4	A	NORTHAMPTON		21	W	1-0	0-0	Thornber 86	Roche	Podd	Watson	Kendall	Ayre	Knill	Cook	Little	Sanderson*	Gallagher	Moyses	Thornber
		15/9	*1,437*	*24*	3				*Gleasure*	*Lewis*	*Mundee*	*Gage*	*Barnes**	*Train*	*Cavener*	*Benjamin*	*Lee*	*Shirtliff*	*Hayes*	*Belfon*
								Ref: R Groves	This is a lifeless game, but Town are up and running thanks to sub Thornber's late sliding strike. Cobblers' boss Tony Barton was in charge of Aston Villa when they lifted the European Cup in 1982. In charge here since July, his new side have now lost all their opening league games.											
5	A	TRANMERE		21	L	0-1	0-1		Roche	Podd	Greenway	Kendall*	Ayre	Knill	Cook	Little	Sanderson	Gallagher	Thornber	Moyses
		17/9	*1,432*	*5*	3			*Clayton 43*	*Adkins*	*Imlach*	*Burgess*	*Higgins*	*Rodaway*	*Williams*	*Woods*	*Aspinall**	*Clarke*	*Clayton*	*Anderson*	*Heath*
								Ref: K Walmsley	This season will be Tranmere manager Bryan Hamilton's last throw of the dice. His side have made a promising start, but he knows that they have been given a run for their money here. Town do create chances, but when Clayton's header goes in off the bar, the rest is all too familiar.											
6	H	SOUTHEND		16	W	1-0	0-0	Gallagher 54	Roche	Podd	Watson	Kendall	Ayre	Knill	Cook	Little	Lowe	Gallagher	Thornber	
		21/9	1,120	*22*	6				*Stannard*	*Stead*	*Pennyfather*	*Clark*	*Hadley*	*Ellis*	*Fuccillo*	*Pountney*	*Whymark**	*Phillips*	*Rogers*	*Shepherd*
								Ref: G Courtney	Former England skipper Bobby Moore is relatively new to soccer management. His first season with Southend, however, ended in relegation. He may view this defeat as one of the lowest points in his career. Gallagher nets the only goal when Cook back-heels Little's free-kick to him.											
7	A	SCUNTHORPE		20	L	**0-4**	0-3	*[Matthews 56]*	Roche	Podd	Watson	Kendall	Ayre	Knill	Thornber	Little	Lowe	Gallagher	Ward*	Sanderson
		28/9	*1,929*	*23*	6			*Broddle 11, Cowling 22, Brolly 34,*	*Neenan*	*Longden*	*Pointon*	*Matthews*	*Webster*	*Green*	*Brolly*	*Graham**	*Broddle*	*Lester*	*Cowling*	*Lees*
								Ref: H Taylor	After enjoying the high life with the two Spurs Milk Cup games, the Shaymen come crashing back down to earth. What makes it worse is that that is the Iron's first win. Broddle's cross, that sails over Roche, starts the rout. Roche ends up in the net when Cowling heads in the second.											
8	A	CHESTER		21	L	0-2	0-0		Roche	Podd	Greenway	Kendall	Ayre	Knill	Thornber	Little	Lowe	Gallagher	Ward	
		6/10	*1,412*	*13*	6			*Zelem 70p, Fox 88*	*Butcher*	*Dixon*	*Bulmer*	*Holden*	*Zelem*	*Higgins*	*Fox*	*Walker*	*Brown*	*Speight**	*Brett*	*Sayer*
								Ref: I Hendrick	Gallagher has an unhappy afternoon. When Town are awarded a 7th-minute penalty for a foul on Lowe, he puts his kick against the post. Later, he hits the post again when it looked easier to score. Zelem shows him the way with his penalty, then Fox beats the offside to finish off Town.											
9	H	CHESTERFIELD		23	L	1-3	0-2	Gallagher 54	Roche	Podd	Greenway	Kendall	Ayre	Knill	Thornber	Little	Sanderson*	Gallagher	Ward	Moyses
		13/10	1,592	*2*	6			*Moss 5, 30, Newton 88*	*Marples*	*Bellamy*	*O'Neill*	*Matthews*	*Baines*	*Hunter*	*Brown*	*Moss*	*Newton*	*Spooner*	*Kendal*	
								Ref: D Allinson	Town are already taking solace in the fact that other struggling teams have also lost. Matthews has already hit the post before Ernie Moss nets his 200th league goal after only five minutes. Gallagher dives low to give Town hope, but Newton makes it 1-3 after Roche saves his penalty.											
10	H	DARLINGTON		24	L	0-1	0-0		Roche	Podd	Watson	Kendall	Ayre	Knill	Thornber	Little	Lowe	Gallagher	Ward	
		19/10	1,224	*5*	6			*Todd 80*	*Barber*	*Craggs**	*Johnson*	*Tupling*	*Smith*	*Lloyd*	*Cook*	*Todd*	*Airey*	*Forster*	*McLean*	*Aldred*
								Ref: N Ashley	Town hit rock bottom. Mickey Bullock asks for 'pride and passion' from his players. They put in the effort, but fall to Kevin Todd's scrambled headed goal ten minutes from time. The fans have had enough, and so too have the directors. Three days later, they will elect to sack Bullock.											
11	A	PETERBOROUGH		24	L	0-2	0-2		Roche	Podd*	Watson	Kendall	Ayre	Knill	Moyses	Little	Lowe	Gallagher	Ward	Thornber
		24/10	*3,770*	*4*	6			*Cassidy 12, Kelly 30*	*Turner*	*Chard*	*Pike*	*Cassidy*	*Wile*	*Slack*	*Johnson*	*Klug*	*Kelly*	*Quow*	*Worrall*	
								Ref: A Ward	Centre-half Billy Ayre is given temporary charge of the team, but it's a case of as you were. Town show plenty of fight in the second half, but don't get the breaks. They are unfortunate when the referee doesn't play the advantage when Little goes through before firing in from 30 yards.											

No	Venue	Opponent	Att	Pos	Res / Pts	F-A	H-T	Scorers, Times, and Referees	1	2	3	4	5	6	7	8	9	10	11	subs used
12	A	COLCHESTER		22	W	3-1	1-1	Lowe 10, Ayre 67, Gallagher 86	Roche	Moyses	Watson	Kendall	Ayre	Knill	Thornber	Cook	Lowe	Gallagher	Ward	
	26/10		*2,295*	*10*	9			*Adcock 9*	*Chamberlain*	*Farrell*	*Phillips*	*Parkinson*	*Day*	*Houston*	*Groves*	*Osborne**	*Bowen*	*Adcock*	*Hull*	*Irving*
								Ref: T Bune	It's an expensive night for coach drivers Geoff Turner and Brian Hoyle. They promised the players a fish and chip supper if they won. Victory is unexpected, but not unmerited. After falling behind, they come back strongly. Ayre, who will bid for manager, heads his side into the lead.											
13	A	TORQUAY		24	D	1-1	1-0	Lowe 5	Roche	Podd	Watson	Kendall	Ayre	Knill	Cook	Little	Lowe	Gallagher	Ward*	Thornber
	6/11		*1,153*	*18*	10			*Mooney 75*	*Allen*	*Dawkins*	*Anderson*	*Pugh S*	*Fowler*	*Impey*	*Best*	*Mooney*	*Pugh G**	*Currie*	*Hall*	*Chambers*
								Ref: B Stevens	After the home game with Exeter was postponed, Town drop back to bottom. They stay there despite this worthwhile showing. Lowe's superb individual goal gives them a dream start. Torquay have ex-England star Tony Currie in their side, and he's glad to see Mooney's header go in.											
14	H	MANSFIELD		22	W	1-0	1-0	Cook 3	Roche	Podd	Watson	Kendall	Ayre	Knill	Cook	Little	Lowe	Gallagher	Ward	
	10/11		1,237	*13*	13				*Hitchcock*	*Woodhead*	*Kearney*	*Pollard*	*Foster*	*Logan*	*Lowery*	*Luke*	*Vinter*	*Caldwell*	*Calderwood*	
								Ref: G Tyson	A mixed day for Ayre. He leads Town to their third unbeaten match, then finds that the directors have chosen a former Mansfield manager in Mick Jones as Bullock's replacement. Cook is on the line to head in early on, but Gallagher sees his 74th-minute penalty saved by Hitchcock.											
15	A	CREWE		20	W	1-0	1-0	Ward 37	Roche	Podd	Watson*	Thornber	Ayre	Knill	Cook	Little	Lowe	Gallagher	Ward	Moyses
	23/11		*1,920*	*6*	16				*Naylor*	*Pullar*	*Aldridge*	*Thomas*	*Davis*	*Hart*	*Blissett*	*Crabbe*	*Waller*	*Allatt*	*Cliss*	
								Ref: H King	The Shaymen lose Watson after 30 minutes when his jaw is broken in a flare-up with former Shayman Vernon Allatt. Justice is served when Ward rounds off a lovely move to net the only goal. Roche ensures this with a 75th-minute penalty save from Crabbe after Ayre fouled Waller.											
16	H	PORT VALE		17	W	2-1	0-0	Lowe 57, 84	Roche	Podd	Greenway	Thornber	Ayre	Knill	Cook	Moyses	Lowe	Gallagher	Ward	
	30/11		1,688	*11*	19			*Hunter 78*	*Pearce*	*Webb*	*Bromage*	*Hunter*	*Sproson*	*Ridley*	*Williams !*	*Earle*	*Brown*	*O'Keefe*	*Griffiths*	
								Ref: A Robinson	The 37th-minute sending off of Vale's Oshor Williams for retaliation against Greenway only adds spice to a thrilling contest. A Lowe flying header puts Town ahead, but ten-man Port Vale hit back. But Lowe finds the winner, and is on his seat when the ball rolls off the post and in.											
17	A	HEREFORD		17	L	0-3	0-1		Roche	Podd	Shaw	Thornber	Ayre	Knill	Cook*	Moyses	Lowe	Gallagher	Ward	**Chippendale**
	15/12		*5,148*	*3*	19			*Kearns 1, 70, Shaw 55 (og)*	*Rose*	*Price*	*Bray*	*Hicks*	*Pejic*	*Emery**	*Harvey*	*Delve*	*Phillips*	*Kearns*	*Tester*	*Dalziel*
								Ref: T Spencer	Things are going well for John Newman's side. Not only are they in the promotion frame, they've also received a plum home-tie with Arsenal in the Cup. Ollie Kearns scores after only 31 seconds, and their lead is doubled when on-loan Shaw diverts Hick's simple header past Roche.											
18	A	SWINDON		18	L	1-2	0-1	Ward 83	Roche	Podd	Shaw	Moyses	Ayre	Knill	Chippendale*	Little	Lowe	Gallagher	Ward	Sanderson
	22/12		*2,414*	*11*	19			*Barnard 43, Batty 64*	*Endersby*	*Ramsey*	*Bailie*	*Barnard*	*Gray*	*Rowland*	*Hockaday*	*Coyne*	*Gordon*	*Batty*	*Nelson*	
								Ref: M Cotton	It's the season of goodwill, so Roche punches Barnard's corner into his own net. Swindon, now managed by former Man Utd star Lou Macari, receive another present when Batty's long-range effort takes two deflections. Ward, easily Town's best player, is on hand to score their goal.											
19	H	HARTLEPOOL		20	L	2-3	2-2	Ayre 30, Gallagher 34	Roche	Podd	Shaw	Moyses	Ayre	Knill	Sanderson	Little	Lowe	Gallagher	Ward	
	26/12		1,409	*6*	19			*Dixon K 19, 84, Linighan 21*	*Stevenson*	*Brownlie*	*Stimpson*	*Hedley*	*Smith*	*Linighan*	*Brown*	*Dixon*	*Wardrobe*	*Hogan*	*Taylor*	
								Ref: T Jones	Tony Smith, a former Town player, is made skipper for the day and helps sink his old club. His cross enables Dixon to score his side's opener. Town go two down, but hit back with Ayre's header and Gallagher's scrambled goal. Dixon's winner from six yards is embarrassingly simple.											
20	A	ROCHDALE		21	L	0-2	0-1		Roche	Thornber	Shaw	Moyses	Ayre	Knill	Cook	Little	Lowe*	Gallagher	Ward	Sanderson
	1/1		*1,671*	*18*	19			*Gamble 26, Taylor 76*	*Malcolm*	*Cavanagh*	*Chapman*	*McMahon*	*Cooke*	*Williams*	*Thompson*	*Diamond*	*Taylor*	*Reid*	*Gamble*	
								Ref: T Holbrook	Town have been hit by a flu bug, but that can't excuse this shabby performance. Vic Halom's side are a mediocre lot, but they are clearly a cut above the Shaymen. Roche is beaten by the bounce off Gamble's free-kick. Taylor reacts first when Diamond's header comes back off the bar.											
21	A	BLACKPOOL		21	D	1-1	0-0	Knill 69	Roche	Podd	Watson	Shaw	Ayre	Knill	Cook	Little	Lowe	Gallagher*	Ward	Sanderson
	5/1		***5,184***	*2*	20			*Stonehouse 60*	*O'Rourke*	*Moore*	*Walsh*	*Conroy*	*Hetzke*	*Greenall*	*Britton*	*Deary**	*Stewart*	*Stonehouse*	*Dyer*	*Ferns*
								Ref: F Roberts	A more forceful Town team takes the field at Bloomfield Road. Blackpool are looking to create a new club record with an eighth consecutive win, but Stonehouse's powerful header doesn't secure it. He misses a sitter before Knill pops up at the other end to head a surprise equaliser.											
22	H	BURY		19	W	**4-1**	1-1	Lowe 39, 52, 90, Gallagher 84	Roche	Podd	Watson	Shaw	Ayre	Knill	Cook	Little	Lowe	Gallagher	Ward	
	12/1		**2,584**	*1*	23			*Madden 23*	*Brown*	*Hill*	*Buckley*	*Ross*	*Bramhall*	*Dobson*	*White*	*Madden*	*Entwistle*	*Jakub*	*James*	
								Ref: K Redfern	Town's 2,500th League game is one of their most memorable. On a snow-bound pitch, Bury, the league-leaders, go in front, but are then swept aside. Lowe's first comes against the run of play, but Town take control after the break. Gallagher unselfishly allows Lowe his hat-trick goal.											
23	H	SCUNTHORPE		22	L	1-2	1-0	Lowe 20	Roche	Podd	Watson	Shaw*	Ayre	Knill	Cook	Little	Lowe	Gallagher	Ward	Sanderson
	1/2		1,317	*14*	23			*Whitehead 56, Broddle 68*	*Gregory*	*Lees*	*Pointon*	*Matthews*	*Whitehead*	*Green*	*Broddle*	*Hill*	*Graham*	*Cowling*	*Lester*	
								Ref: N Wilson	Lowe looks to have set Town up for a second successive victory, but subsequent injuries to Shaw, Ayre and Gallagher hamper the Shaymen's chances. Whitehead levels it with a far-post header, and then Broddle makes it a miserable evening for Town with a volley that is deflected in.											

No	Date		Att	Pos	Pt	F-A	H-T	Scorers, Times, and Referees	1	2	3	4	5	6	7	8	9	10	11	12 sub used
24	A	SOUTHEND		20	L	1-2	1-1	Ward 10	Roche	Moyses	Watson	Podd	Knill	Thornber	Cook*	Little	Lowe	Gallagher	Ward	Sanderson
	8/2		*1,362*	*17*	23			*Phillips 40, Clark 56*	*O'Brien*	*Stead*	*Seaden*	*Phillips*	*May*	*Clark*	*Pountney*	*Owers*	*Hadley*	*Engwell*	*Rogers*	
								Ref: A Buksh	Bobby Moore says he is still reeling from his side's two recent five-goal hammerings. He's thankful for Clark's headed winner here. Town boss Mick Jones slams his players for a lack of discipline. Things looked rosier when Ward fired in a spectacular volley to put Town in front.											
25	H	TRANMERE		19	W	2-1	1-0	Lowe 30, Cook 85	Roche	Podd	Greenway	Thornber	Kendall	Knill	Cook	Little	Lowe	Gallagher*	Ward	Sanderson
	12/2		914	*9*	26			*Palios 66*	*Adkins*	*Edwards*	*Burgess*	*Williams*	*Mungall*	*Williams S*	*Palios*	*Rodaway*	*Clarke*	*Clayton*	*Anderson*	
								Ref: C Seel	Mark Palios is a chartered accountant, and he thinks he's balanced the figures when he arrives in the box to score Tranmere's equaliser. Barry Gallagher is already suffering a thigh injury before he goes off with concussion. Sub Sanderson comes on and crosses for Cook's late winner.											
26	H	WREXHAM		21	L	1-2	1-1	Thornber 38	Roche	Podd	Shaw	Thornber	Kendall	Knill	Cook	Little	Lowe	Gallagher*	Ward	Sanderson
	16/2		1,119	*23*	26			*Keay 4, Horne 80*	*Hooper*	*Williams*	*Comstive*	*Keay*	*Cunnington*	*Wright*	*Edwards*	*Horne*	*Steel*	*Charles*	*Rogers*	
								Ref: A Robinson	Wrexham's second away win moves them off the bottom of the table. Roche is stranded when Keay heads over him, but his penalty save from Charles keeps Town in the game. Thornber volleys an equaliser, but when Shaw fails to cut out the ball, Horne runs through for the winner.											
27	A	EXETER		21	L	0-1	0-1		Roche	Podd	Watson	Kendall	Shaw	Knill	Cook*	Little	Lowe	Gallagher	Ward	Sanderson
	23/2		*2,549*	*16*	26			*Ling 20*	*Wood*	*Kirkup*	*Viney*	*O'Shea*	*Marker*	*King*	*Ling*	*Burgher*	*Morgan*	*Pratt*	*Barnard*	
								Ref: K Barrett	Jim Iley's Exeter stretch their unbeaten run to five games, including four wins. Margin of victory could have been far greater had it not been for the heroics of Town keeper Roche. But he can't do anything about 17-year-old Martin Ling's shot after the defence fails to clear the ball.											
28	H	NORTHAMPTON		18	W	1-0	0-0	Little 59p	Roche	Podd	Thornber	Kendall	Shaw	Knill	Sanderson*	Little	Lowe	Gallagher	Ward	**Francis**
	26/2		1,009	*24*	29				*Gleasure*	*Shirtliff*	*Mundee*	*Lewis*	*Barnes*	*Train*	*Scott*	*Mann**	*Bancroft*	*Benjamin*	*Cavener*	*Hutchinson*
								Ref: R Guy	Despite victory, Town are far from convincing. They need Little's penalty to secure it after Shirtliff handles the ball. As at the County Ground, it's a dull game with few chances. Frustrated Cobblers' boss Tony Barton shouts instructions from the touchline, and is ticked off by the ref.											
29	H	COLCHESTER		18	D	0-0	0-0		Roche	Podd	Thornber	Kendall	Moyses	Knill	Sanderson	Little	Lowe	Gallagher	Ward	
	1/3		1,022	*6*	30				*Chamberlain*	*Hedman*	*Phillips*	*Parkinson*	*Day*	*Houston*	*Groves*	*Osborne*	*Bowen*	*Irving*	*English*	
								Ref: M Peck	Thickening fog makes it hard to follow the play. Cyril Lea's side have promotion thoughts, but if Town had enough firepower, they might have nicked the points. Sanderson is guilty of two glaring misses. Jones is more happy with the fact his side has kept two consecutive clean sheets.											
30	H	PETERBOROUGH		18	D	0-0	0-0		Roche	Podd	Thornber	Kendall	Moyses	Knill	Sanderson	Little	Lowe	Gallagher	Ward	
	5/3		1,071	*7*	31				*Turner*	*La Ronda*	*Pike*	*Beech*	*Wile*	*Slack*	*Shepherd*	*Klug*	*Kelly*	*Cassidy*	*Worrall*	
								Ref: P Willis	Morale is pretty low in the Shay camp after a 0-7 thrashing defeat at Darlington on Sunday in the Freight Rover Trophy. This goalless draw at least restores some pride. The Posh come closest to scoring when Kendall has to clear Shephard's header off the line and Cassidy fires wide.											
31	A	DARLINGTON		19	L	0-2	0-2		Roche	Podd !	Thornber	Kendall*	Moyses	Knill !	Sanderson	Little	Lowe	Gallagher	**Brookes**	Francis
	9/3		*3,690*	*1*	31			*Cook 32, McLean 42p*	*Barber*	*Atkinson*	*Johnson*	*Tupling*	*MacDonald*	*Lloyd*	*Haire*	*Forster**	*Airey*	*Cook*	*McLean*	*McMahon*
								Ref: D Shaw	Town go a goal down, then lose injured Kendall three minutes later. Podd uses his hand to concede the penalty. Roche then falls heavily, and doesn't appear after the break. Little goes in goal and Town end the game with eight men after the dismissals of Knill (65 mins) and Podd (75).											
32	A	WREXHAM		18	W	1-0	0-0	Thornber 60	**Hunt**	Podd	Thornber	Brookes	Moyses	Knill	Cook	Little	Lowe	Gallagher	Ward	
	12/3		***1,025***	*22*	34				*Hooper*	*Cunnington*	*Comstive*	*Keay*	*Gregory**	*Wright*	*Edwards*	*Horne*	*Steel*	*Charles*	*Rogers*	*Williams*
								Ref: J Lovatt	Former Garforth Miners' keeper Robert Hunt comes in for his debut and plays a blinder to help Town to this crucial victory. His double save from Steel and Charles is his crowning moment. Full-back Thornber races forward to convert Ward's low cross. His goal is greeted by silence.											
33	A	CHESTERFIELD		20	L	0-3	0-1		Hunt	Podd	Thornber	Brookes	Moyses	Knill	Cook*	Little	Lowe	Gallagher	Ward	Francis
	16/3		*2,870*	*3*	34			*Spooner 38, Moss 53, Newton 67*	*Marples*	*Ferguson*	*O'Neill*	*Matthews*	*Baines*	*Hunter*	*Spooner*	*Moss**	*Newton*	*Henderson*	*Kendal*	*Brown*
								Ref: M Robinson	Hunt again plays well, but the high-flying Spireites are a better side than Wrexham. Steve Spooner sends his former side on the way to defeat with a sweetly-struck volley. Moss poaches his goal, while the third goal is the only blemish on Hunt's performance when he flaps at a corner.											
34	H	CHESTER		20	L	**0-4**	0-3	*[Sayer 80]*	Hunt	Podd	Thornber	Brookes	Moyses	Knill	Cook*	Little	Lowe	Francis	Ward	Sanderson
	22/3		1,014	*19*	34			*Greenhough 6, Speight 27, Bulmer 43,*	*Butcher*	*Dixon*	*Lane*	*Holden*	*Coy*	*Bulmer*	*Rimmer*	*Walker*	*Greenhough*	*Sayer*	*Speight**	*Kitchen*
								Ref: D Allinson	Former Leeds striker David McNiven signs for Town, then watches from the stands as his new team press the self-destruct button. A comedy of errors enables the visitors to run up a three-goal half-time lead. New Chester player-boss Mick Speight can't believe his 25-yarder crept in.											

No	Date	Opponent	Att	Pos	Res	F-A	H-T	Scorers, Times, and Referees												
35	H	EXETER		20	L	2-3	2-1	McNiven 10, Gallagher 42	Roche	Gallagher	Watson	Kendall	Moyses	Brookes	Cook	Little	Lowe	**McNiven**	Thornber*	Sanderson
	26/3		1,011	*17*	34			*Watson 24 (og), McNicholl 51, P-Masters 67*	*Smelt*	*Kirkup*	*Viney*	*McNicholl*	*Marker*	*Ling*	*O'Shea*	*Morgan*	*Smith*	*Burgher*	*Phill-Masters*	
								Ref: R Bridges	McNiven quickly marks his debut with a lob that goes in off the post. Watson turns the ball past a stranded Roche for Exeter's first. Gallagher curls in a free-kick for 2-1, but the Grecians level again before Phillipson-Masters heads them in front. Ex-Town keeper Smelt is at his best.											
36	H	TORQUAY		21	L	0-1	0-0		Roche	Gallagher	Watson	Kendall	Moyses	Brookes	Cook	Shaw	Lowe	McNiven	Sanderson*	Ward
	30/3		**890**	*22*	34			*Durham 56*	*Allan*	*Jarvis*	*Hall*	*O'Dell*	*Dawkins*	*McCaffrey*	*Loram*	*Durham*	*Walsh*	*Perry*	*Pugh*	
								Ref: R Nixon	This re-election clash attracts the lowest Shay crowd since 1976. The small band of Town fans are mystified over the award of the free-kick that leads to Torquay's goal. Ref Robert Nixon appears to give it originally to Town, then changes his mind. Durham is left free to score easily.											
37	A	ALDERSHOT		21	L	0-2	0-2		Roche	Podd	Watson	Brookes	Moyses*	Knill	Gallagher	Shaw	Lowe	McNiven	Ward	Sanderson
	2/4		*1,523*	*18*	34			*Staff 29, McDonald 45*	*Cox*	*Blankley*	*Smith*	*Mazzon*	*Coleman*	*Shrubb*	*Staff*	*Langley*	*Fielder*	*McCulloch*	*McDonald*	
								Ref: V Callow	Aldershot move away from the danger zone, but leave Town in trouble. Paul Staff goes through unchallenged for the first goal. Aldershot's second, in first-half injury-time, comes after the ref has to speak to Lowe for an off-the-ball incident, which manager Jones blasts him for.											
38	A	HARTLEPOOL		21	W	1-0	0-0	McNiven 47	Roche	Podd	Moyses	Shaw	Brookes	Knill	Gallagher	Little	Lowe	McNiven	Ward*	Sanderson
	6/4		*1,640*	*15*	37				*Stevenson*	*Robinson*	*Stimpson*	*Gollogly*	*Smith*	*Brown*	*Taylor*	*Borthwick*	*Dobson*	*Farnaby**	*Gavin*	*Proudlock*
								Ref: J Hough	Centre-back Steve Brookes returns to one of his own stomping grounds, and is a rock in the heart of the defence. He fractures his cheekbone in the first half, but soldiers on. McNiven gives Town some breathing space, chesting down Ward's cross before firing the ball high into the net.											
39	H	ROCHDALE		22	L	0-2	0-1		Roche	Watson*	Moyses	Shaw	Brookes	Knill	Gallagher	Little	Lowe	McNiven	Sanderson	Thornber
	8/4		1,706	*20*	37			*Gamble 3, McMahon 65*	*Redfern*	*Heaton*	*Grant*	*McMahon*	*Cooke**	*Dwyer*	*Thompson*	*Diamond*	*Taylor*	*Chapman*	*Gamble*	*Robinson*
								Ref: M Scott	Rochdale leap over Town in the table, and time is fast running out for the Shaymen. Roche drops Grant's corner and Gamble volleys in to give his side a dream start. Town see plenty of the ball but create little. McMahon makes them pay for it when he scores following a breakaway.											
40	A	MANSFIELD		23	L	1-2	1-0	Little 16	Roche	Podd	Thornber	Shaw*	Brookes	Knill	Gallagher	Little	Lowe	McNiven	Sanderson	Moyses
	13/4		*1,928*	*14*	37			*Luke 52, Whatmore 58*	*Hitchcock*	*Whitworth*	*Foster N**	*Garner*	*Foster G*	*Calderwood*	*Lowery*	*Whatmore*	*Luke*	*Halloway*	*Woodhead*	*Pollard*
								Ref: J Bray	Ian Greaves' side record their first home win since the beginning of March. They come from behind to take the points as Town disintegrate in the second half. Little had given Town the lead with a fine opportunist effort whilst the Mansfield players are engaged in arguing with the ref.											
41	H	CREWE		23	D	1-1	0-0	Gallagher 89	Roche	Podd*	Thornber	Shaw	Brookes	Knill	Gallagher	Little	Lowe	McNiven	Sanderson	Ward
	19/4		1,416	*9*	38			*Waller 81*	*Longley*	*Pemberton*	*Armstrong*	*Thomas*	*Davis*	*Hart*	*Platt*	*Crabbe*	*Waller*	*Blissett*	*Cliss**	*Allatt*
								Ref: T Fitzharris	John Crowther takes over the chairmanship, and hopes to instil some enthusiasm at a crucial time. 345 schoolchildren are let in for free. They are still urging Town on when Gallagher's glancing header 70 seconds from time secures a point. It cancels out Dave Waller's late simple goal.											
42	H	STOCKPORT		22	W	2-1	1-1	Lowe 21, Ward 76	Roche	Podd	Thornber	Shaw*	Brookes	Knill	Gallagher	Little	Lowe	McNiven	Sanderson	Ward
	23/4		1,291	*18*	41			*Sword 41p*	*Salmon*	*Rutter*	*Sherlock*	*Emerson*	*Smith*	*Thorpe*	*Evans*	*Hendrie*	*Leonard*	*Sword**	*Coyle*	*Buxton*
								Ref: A Saunders	Despite this win, other results mean only one point separates the bottom five teams, three of which have games in hand. Lowe's opener ends a personal goal drought of 16 games. Sword falls under Thornber to win a dodgy penalty. Ward comes off the bench to silence his many critics.											
43	A	PORT VALE		23	L	1-3	0-1	McNiven 58	Roche	Podd	Thornber	Shaw	Brookes !	Knill	Gallagher	Little	Lowe	McNiven	Sanderson*	Ward
	27/4		*2,029*	*13*	41			*Brown 24, Earle 76, Williams 79*	*Pearce*	*Webb*	*Bromage*	*Hunter*	*Sproson*	*Ridley*	*Williams*	*Earle*	*Brown*	*Ebanks**	*Smith*	*Tartt*
								Ref: K Cooper	When McNiven flashes in the equaliser, Town are looking good for a point. But in the 67th minute, Brookes is sent off for a second clumsy challenge. Vale reclaim the lead through Earle with Town appealing for a foul on Roche. A driving blizzard arrives after Vale score a third.											
44	H	HEREFORD		23	W	2-1	1-0	McNiven 8, Lowe 56	Roche	Podd	Ward	Shaw	Brookes	Knill	Gallagher	Little	Lowe	McNiven	Sanderson	
	3/5		1,629	*5*	44			*Kearns 49*	*Rose*	*Price*	*Leonard*	*Hicks*	*Pejic*	*Emery*	*Carter*	*Dalziel*	*Phillips*	*Kearns*	*Butler*	
								Ref: J Worrall	Defeat for Hereford dents their promotion challenge. In a pulsating match, McNiven volleys in early on. In the second half, Kearns turns in the Bulls' equaliser, but Lowe lobs in the winner. Had Town twice not been denied by the bar, the last half-hour would not have been so nervy.											
45	A	STOCKPORT		21	W	3-0	0-0	Lowe 49, Gallagher 65, Shaw 77	Roche	Podd	Ward	Shaw	Brookes	Knill	Gallagher	Little	Lowe	McNiven	Sanderson*	Cook
	6/5		*1,480*	*23*	47				*Salmon*	*Rutter*	*Sherlock*	*Emerson**	*Thorpe*	*Smith*	*Evans*	*Hendrie*	*Leonard*	*Sword*	*Lodge*	*Buxton*
								Ref: G Tyson	The best players from Stockport are the Silver Band who perform before kick-off. Town give themselves a lifeline by sweeping County aside with a rousing second-half showing. Lowe and Shaw get headed goals, whilst Gallagher scores when McNiven's shot comes back off the post.											
46	H	SWINDON		19	W	2-1	1-0	Cook 19, Sanderson 73	Roche	Podd	Ward	Shaw	Brookes	Knill	Gallagher	Little	Cook	McNiven	Sanderson	
	10/5		2,307	*8*	50			*Coyne 68*	*Endersby*	*Ramsey*	*Bailie*	*Mayes*	*Rowland*	*Cole*	*Coyne*	*Hockaday*	*Gordon*	*Barnard*	*Nelson*	
		Home	Away					Ref: M Heath	Sanderson has spent all week receiving treatment on a pulled hamstring. Thankfully, he is passed fit, and with the game tied at 1-1, he scores a screamer. He volleys home Shaw's cross to win the game. Hundreds of fans celebrate victory on the pitch, thinking that the Shaymen are safe.											
Average		1,367	2,243																	

Milk Cup					F-A	H-T	Scorers, Times, and Referees	1	2	3	4	5	6	7	8	9	10	11	12 sub used
1:1	H	CHESTERFIELD		D	1-1	1-0	Lowe 17	Roche	Podd	Watson	Moyses	Kendall	Knill	Sanderson*	Little	Lowe	Gallagher	Ward	Cook
28/8			1,174				*Newton 90*	*Brown J*	*Bellamy*	*O'Neill*	*Matthews*	*Baines*	*Hunter*	*Brown P*	*Moss*	*Newton*	*Scrimgeour**	*Kendal*	*Spooner*
							Ref: T Fitzharris	Moyses is a long-throw specialist, and it's from one of these that Lowe heads in his first Town career goal. It's an improved performance by the Shaymen from the weekend's home defeat by Blackpool, but they allow Newton an injury-time equaliser. 'Don't write us off.' – Bullock.											
1:2	A	CHESTERFIELD		W	2-1	1-0	Little 24, Lowe 52	Roche	Podd	Watson	Kendall	Ayre	Knill	Cook	Little	Lowe	Gallagher	Ward	
4/9			*2,976*				*Newton 87*	*Brown J*	*Bellamy*	*O'Neill*	*Matthews*	*Baines*	*Hunter*	*Brown P**	*Moss*	*Newton*	*Spooner*	*Kendal*	*Scrimgeour*
							Ref: D Brazier (Halifax won 3-2 on aggregate)	Bullock is annoyed with the Halifax Courier who, he feels, have been over-critical of his team. This is their perfect response. Skipper Alan Little leads the way with a spectacular shot from outside the box. Lowe nips in to give Town a cushion. This time Newton's goal isn't enough.											
2:1	H	TOTTENHAM	16	L	1-5	0-1	Gallagher 77	Roche	Podd	Watson	Kendall	Ayre	Knill	Cook	Little	Lowe	Gallagher	Thornber	
26/9			7,027 *1:1*				*Falco 25, 56, Crooks 68, 78, 83*	*Clemence*	*Thomas*	*Hughton*	*Stevens*	*Miller*	*Perryman*	*Chiedozie*	*Falco*	*Galvin*	*Mabbutt*	*Crooks*	
							Ref: M Scott	The BBC Sportsnight cameras are here, hoping to see Town bring off a shock against the First Division leaders. They have a couple of half-chances before Falco puts Spurs ahead. Clemence thinks Gallagher's header for 1-3 is going wide. Crooks holds off Watson for his third goal.											
2:2	A	TOTTENHAM	21	L	0-4	0-2		Roche	Podd	Greenway	Kendall	Ayre	Knill	Thornber	Little	Sanderson	Gallagher*	Ward	Watson
9/10			*14,802* *1:3*				*Hazard 8, 77, Hughton 36, Crooks 67*	*Clemence*	*Stevens*	*Hughton*	*Roberts*	*Miller*	*Perryman**	*Chiedozie*	*Falco*	*Galvin*	*Hazard*	*Crooks*	*Mabbutt*
							Ref: B Hill (Halifax lost 1-9 on aggregate)	Halifax are determined to make the most of the return leg, but it's still a little too easy for Spurs. Their manager, Peter Shreeve, praises Town for battling till the end. Paddy Roche is the star of the show, and keeps the score down. Town will net around £30,000 from the two matches.											

FA Cup																			
1	H	GOOLE	22	W	2-0	1-0	Gallagher 42, Cook 86	Roche	Podd	Watson	Kendall*	Ayre	Knill	Cook	Little	Lowe	Gallagher	Ward	Thornber
17/11			1,847 *NPL*					*Hinchliffe*	*Milner*	*Rogers*	*Levesley*	*Worsfold*	*Shutt*	*Brattan*	*Pugh*	*Hanson*	*Hamilton*	*Black*	
							Ref: I Hendrick	Former Shay favourite David Pugh is player-manager at Goole, and his side pushes Town all the way. Jones admits, 'We took a few liberties.' Town lose Kendall with a broken leg, before Gallagher's cool finish settles a few nerves. Mark Hamilton hits the post before Cook's late goal.											
2	A	BURNLEY	17	L	1-3	1-1	Gallagher 37	Roche	Podd	Greenway*	Thornber	Ayre	Knill	Cook	Moyses	Lowe	Gallagher	Ward	**Shaw**
8/12			*5,548* *3:17*				*Hird 25, Devine 60, Biggins 81*	*Hansbury*	*Palmer*	*Hampton*	*Phelan*	*Overson*	*Hird*	*Grewcock*	*Powell*	*Devine*	*Biggins*	*Hutchison*	
							Ref: M Peck	The first-ever peacetime meeting between these two near-neighbours goes Burnley's way. Ayre concedes a needless free-kick for which Hird is grateful. Lowe sets up Gallagher for a memorable equaliser. Tommy Hutchinson, 37, who scored at both ends in the 81 Final, makes the third.											

		Home					Away					
	P	W	D	L	F	A	W	D	L	F	A	Pts
1 Chesterfield	46	16	6	1	40	13	10	7	6	24	22	91
2 Blackpool	46	15	7	1	42	15	9	7	7	31	24	86
3 Darlington	46	16	4	3	41	22	8	9	6	25	27	85
4 Bury	46	15	6	2	46	20	9	6	8	30	30	84
5 Hereford	46	16	2	5	38	21	6	9	8	27	26	77
6 Tranmere	46	17	1	5	50	21	7	2	14	33	45	75
7 Colcheste	46	13	7	3	49	29	7	7	9	38	36	74
8 Swindon	46	16	4	3	42	21	5	5	13	20	37	72
9 Scunthorpe	46	14	6	3	61	33	5	8	10	22	29	71
10 Crewe	46	10	7	6	32	28	8	5	10	33	41	66
11 Peterborough	46	11	7	5	29	21	5	7	11	25	32	62
12 Port Vale	46	11	8	4	39	24	3	10	10	22	35	60
13 Aldershot	46	11	6	6	33	20	6	2	15	23	43	59
14 Mansfield	46	10	8	5	25	15	3	10	10	16	23	57
15 Wrexham	46	10	6	7	39	27	5	3	15	28	43	54
16 Chester	46	11	3	9	35	30	4	6	13	25	42	54
17 Rochdale	46	8	7	8	33	30	5	7	11	22	39	53
18 Exeter	46	9	7	7	30	27	4	7	12	27	52	53
19 Hartlepool	46	10	6	7	34	29	4	4	15	20	38	52
20 Southend	46	8	8	7	30	34	5	3	15	28	49	50
21 HALIFAX	46	9	3	11	26	32	6	2	15	16	37	50
22 Stockport	46	11	5	7	40	26	2	3	18	18	53	47
23 Northampton	46	10	1	12	32	32	4	4	15	21	42	47
24 Torquay	46	5	11	7	18	24	4	3	16	20	39	41
	1104	282	136	134	884	594	134	136	282	594	884	1520

Odds & ends

Double wins: (2) Northampton, Stockport.
Double losses: (7) Aldershot, Chester, Chesterfield, Darlington, Exeter, Rochdale, Scunthorpe.

Won from behind: (2) Bury (h), Colchetser (a).
Lost from in front: (5) Aldershot (h), Exeter (h), Scunthorpe (h), Mansfield (a), Southend (a).

High spots: Being featured on BBC TV's Sportsnight for the Spurs Milk Cup-tie at the Shay.
Three consecutive wins in a run of five unbeaten games in October and November.
Winning the last three matches.

Low spots: Losing the first three games.
Five consecutive defeats up to 24 October.
Losing 0-7 in the 2nd leg of the Freight Rover Trophy at Darlington after holding a 4-1 lead from the 1st leg.

Player of the Year: Paddy Roche.
Ever-presents: (0).
Hat-tricks: Simon Lowe (1).
Leading scorer: Simon Lowe (14).

	Appearances						Goals			
	Lge	*Sub*	LC	*Sub*	FAC	*Sub*	Lge	LC	FAC	Tot
Ayre, Billy	**22**		3		2		**2**			**2**
Brookes, Steve	**16**									
Chippendale, Brian	**1**	*1*								
Cook, Jeff	**24**	*2*	2	*1*	2		**3**		1	**4**
Francis, John	**1**	*3*								
Gallagher, Barry	**45**		4		2		**8**	1	2	**11**
Greenway, Mark	**5**		1		1					
Hunt, Robert	**3**									
Kendall, Paul	**23**		4		1					
Knill, Alan	**44**		4		2		**3**	1		**4**
Little, Alan	**41**		4		1		**1**			**1**
Lowe, Simon	**42**		3		2		**12**	2		**14**
McNiven, David	**12**						**4**			**4**
Moyses, Chris	**21**	*4*	1		1					
Podd, Cec	**41**		4		2					
Roche, Paddy	**43**		4		2					
Sanderson, Paul	**19**	*14*	2				**1**			**1**
Shaw, Adrian	**21**					*1*	**1**			**1**
Thornber, Steve	**26**	*5*	2		1	*1*	**3**			**3**
Ward, Steve	**35**	*4*	3		2		**4**			**4**
Watson, Garry	**21**		3	*1*	1					
21 players used	**506**	***33***	**44**	***2***	**22**	***2***	**42**	**4**	**3**	**49**

No	Date	Opponent	Att	Pos	Pt	F-A	H-T	Scorers, Times, and Referees	1	2	3	4	5	6	7	8	9	10	11	12 sub used
1	A	CHESTER			D	1-1	0-1	Ward 71	Roche	Brown	Ward	Shaw	Kendall	Knill	Gallagher	Kellock	Lowe	Longhurst*	Nicholson	Podd
	17/8		1,750		1			Rimmer 34	Butcher	Glenn	Lane	Holden	Gage	Coy	Speight	Graham*	Rimmer	Fox	Brett	Harley
								Ref: T Holbrook	A 66th-minute injury to new signing Longhurst sends Ward up front. Within five minutes, he has blasted Gallagher's pull-back high into the net. Stuart Rimmer, 14 goals last season, is a handful for the Town defence all afternoon. He opens this season's account after Kendall's slip.											
2	H	SCUNTHORPE			W	2-1	0-1	Graham 47 (og), Lowe 85	Roche	Brown	Ward	Shaw	Kendall	Ayre	Gallagher	Kellock	Lowe	Longhurst	Nicholson*	Podd
	23/8		1,094		4			Cammack 44p	Gregory	Russell	Pointon	Lister	Whitehead	Green	Brolly	Cammack	Broddle	Graham	Hill	
								Ref: K Green	All seating areas of the Shay have been closed off following the Bradford City fire disaster. When Brown handles, Cammack's penalty gives the Iron the lead. Ex-Shayman Graham heads into his own net, then with five minutes to go, Lowe scores a classic winner with a low header.											
3	A	MANSFIELD		12	L	0-2	0-1		Roche	Brown	Podd	Shaw	Kendall	Ayre	Gallagher	Kellock	Lowe	Longhurst	Ward	
	27/8		3,299	2	4			Vinter 12, Chamberlain 61	Hitchcock	Galloway*	Logan	Lowery	Foster	Pollard	Chamberlain	Whatmore	Cassells	Vinter	Kearney	Luke
								Ref: I Hemley	The Stags have yet to concede a goal in the league, and they are hardly put to the test here. The crosswind spoils the game, but it doesn't halt the home side cruising to victory. Vinter rounds Roche and squeezes in the first. Chamberlain seals the game with a spectacular 25-yard effort											
4	H	PRESTON		6	W	2-1	0-0	Longhurst 65, 75	Roche	Brown	Ward	Shaw	Kendall	Ayre	Gallagher	Kellock	Lowe	Longhurst	Nicholson*	Podd
	30/8		2,011	23	7			Greenwood 88	Platt	Jones	McAteer*	Atkins	Twentyman	Clark	Keen	Foster	Thomas	Rudge	Brazil	Greenwood
								Ref: J Lloyd	Both sides are still searching for their first league victory. The game swings the Shaymen's way when Longhurst directs a header over Platt. His goal comes two minutes after Kellock's penalty miss. His second is a class piece of finishing. Greenwood's goal sets up a nailbiting finish.											
5	A	COLCHESTER		12	L	1-3	0-2	Gallagher 59	Roche	Brown	Ward	Shaw	Kendall	Ayre	Gallagher	Kellock	Lowe	Longhurst*	Nicholson	Podd
	6/9		2,023	6	7			Adcock 1, 19, Bowen 55	Chamberlain	Farrell	Phillips	Reeves	Day	Hedman	Groves	Parkinson	Bowen	Adcock	English	
								Ref: M Cotton	Town are up against it after only 22 seconds. The linesman rules Adcock's curling shot off the post has crossed the line. They could have been three down within the first minute, but wait until Bowen reacts first to Parkinson's free-kick that hits the bar. Gallagher ghosts in for his goal.											
6	H	ORIENT		10	W	2-1	0-0	Nicholson 71, Longhurst 82	Roche	Brown	Ward	Shaw	Kendall	Ayre	Gallagher	Kellock	Lowe	Longhurst	Nicholson	
	13/9		1,243	9	10			Shinners 69	Wells	Hales	Dickenson	Sussex	Sitton	Cornwell	Cunningham	Brooks	Shinners	Corbett	Jones	
								Ref: R Guy	Jones says of Town's two goals that turn this game around, 'You can go anywhere in the country but you will not see goals better than those.' Nicholson's is a curling volley, to cancel out Paul Shinners' strike, and Longhurst's is a looping effort from a tight angle after he rounds Wells.											
7	H	SOUTHEND		11	L	2-3	0-2	Longhurst 53, Kendall 67	Roche	Brown	Ward	Shaw	Kendall	Ayre	Gallagher*	Kellock	Lowe	Longhurst	Nicholson	Podd
	17/9		1,514	1	10			O'Shea 21, Cadette 23, Phillips 84	Stannard	Stead	Lampard*	O'Shea	Westley	Hatter	Clark	Silkman	Cadette	Phillips	Pennyfather	McDonough
								Ref: K Redfern	A bruising encounter ends with Town going down to Phillips' free header after they had clawed back a two-goal deficit. Jones describes his side's performance as the best of the season. Southend lose ex-international Lampard, who has two teeth knocked out in a collision with Shaw.											
8	A	PORT VALE		15	L	2-3	1-2	Kellock 25, 82	Roche	Brown	Ward	Shaw	Kendall	Podd	Sanderson	Kellock	Lowe*	Longhurst	Nicholson	Thornber
	21/9		2,754	11	10			Hunter 7, 62, Maguire 42	Arnold	Banks	Bromage	Hunter	Jones	Williams J	Williams O	Earle	Brown	Johnson	Maguire	
								Ref: M Reed	Town's Billy Kellock never appeared on the losing side in twelve games for Vale last season. He scores two headers on his return, but Town slip to defeat. His first comes down off the bar with the linesman ruling it over the line. His second starts a fightback which comes too late.											
9	H	CAMBRIDGE		15	D	1-1	0-1	Kellock 66	Roche	Brown	Ward	Shaw	Kendall	Ayre	Hotte	Kellock	Sanderson	Longhurst	Nicholson	
	27/9		1,409	22	11			Crown 43	Hansbury	Clark	Bennett	Finney	Moyes	Scott	Sinton	Spriggs	Massey	Comfort	Crown	
								Ref: C Trussell	Town play out a disappointing draw, but manager Jones says, 'If the players aren't motivated it's my fault.' But he praises the diminutive Tim Hotte, who almost wins the game. Crown has already hit the post before he scores his goal. Kellock hits the bar before he slips in the equaliser.											
10	A	TORQUAY		18	L	0-2	0-0		Roche	Brown	Ward	Shaw	Kendall	Ayre	Sanderson	Kellock	Hotte	Longhurst	Nicholson	
	1/10		1,131	23	11			Kelly 58, Pugh 90	Fowler T	Fowler D	Dawkins	Kelly	Crowe	Wright	Crabbe	Pugh	Loram	Smith	West	
								Ref: V Callow	The Shaymen fall to a team that has just installed a new manager. This is Stuart Morgan's first game in charge and his half-time team-talk pays off. Up until then, Town were on top. Kelly, a double-winner with Arsenal, bundles in the first, and Pugh's angled volley comes in injury-time.											
11	H	ALDERSHOT		18	D	1-1	1-1	Kellock 37p	Roche	Brown	Ward	Shaw	Kendall	Ayre	Gallagher*	Kellock	Lowe	Longhurst	Nicholson	Hotte
	5/10		1,066	22	12			Johnson 40	Coles	Mazzon	Gillard	Smith	Morris	Shrubb	Johnson	Duncan	Foyle	McDonald	Fielder	
								Ref: T Fitzharris	After another disappointing performance, Jones tells his players: 'Work together or leave.' They need Kellock's penalty to put them ahead after Longhurst is brought down when in full flow. Aldershot look as bad as Town, but need only three minutes to draw level through Gary Johnson.											

No	Date	Opponent	Att	Pos	Pt	F-A	H-T	Scorers, Times, and Referees	1	2	3	4	5	6	7	8	9	10	11	12
12	A	WREXHAM		18	L	1-1	1-2	Gallagher 15	Roche	Podd	Ward	Shaw*	Kendall	Brown	Gallagher	Kellock	Lowe	Longhurst	Nicholson	Sanderson
	12/10		*1,609*	*10*	12			*Charles 10, Cunnington 44*	*Hooper*	*Salathiel**	*Comstive*	*Williams*	*Keay*	*Cunnington*	*Hencher*	*Horne*	*Edwards*	*Charles*	*Gregory*	*Muldoon*
								Ref: G Ashby	Shaw's weak backpass lets in Shaun Cunnington just before half-time. This epitomises the standard of play from both sides as passes go astray all afternoon. Wrexham go in front when Gregory's header comes back off the bar. Gallagher's response is a curling free-kick around the wall.											
13	H	TRANMERE		19	L	1-2	0-1	Gallagher 50	Roche	Podd	Ward	Shaw	Kendall	Brown	Gallagher	Kellock	Lowe	Longhurst	Nicholson*	Hotte
	18/10		1,412	*15*	12			*Anderson 1, Muir 52*	*Siddall*	*Mungall*	*Burgess*	*Hughes*	*Miller*	*Edwards*	*Morrissey*	*Rodaway*	*Worthington*	*Muir*	*Anderson*	
								Ref: K Lupton	Halifax-born Frank Worthington is now player-manager of Tranmere. Amazingly, this is his first ever league game at the Shay. It's from his flick that Anderson fires Rovers into a first-minute lead. Gallagher scores another free-kick, but Muir's fierce shot means his joy is short-lived.											
14	A	EXETER		20	L	0-1	0-0		Roche	Podd	Ward	Shaw	Knill	Brown	Gallagher	Kellock*	Lowe	Longhurst	Sanderson	Kendall
	23/10		*1,719*	*15*	12			*Kellow 48p*	*Shaw*	*Harrower*	*Viney*	*McNichol*	*Impey*	*Marker*	*Ling*	*Jackson*	*Kellow*	*Gale*	*Crawford*	
								Ref: B Stevens	Veteran Tony Kellow's penalty, after Ward brings down Jackson, is the one real feature of this match. Town are on top after the goal, but their shooting is as wayward as Phil Brown's in the 29th minute. He fires over and smashes an upstairs window of a house overlooking the ground.											
15	H	BURNLEY		23	D	2-2	0-1	Kellock 54, Lowe 55	Roche	Podd	Ward	Shaw	Knill	Brown	Sanderson	Kellock	Lowe	Longhurst	Nicholson	
	26/10		**2,334**	*16*	13			*Parker 19, Grewcock 86*	*Peacock*	*Hampton*	*Heesom*	*Hird**	*Heggarty*	*Deakin*	*Robinson*	*Malley*	*Taylor*	*Parker*	*Devine*	*Grewcock*
								Ref: J Worrall	After relegation, Burnley are in the 4th Division for the first time. This first league meeting is a cracker. Grewcock comes off the bench to fire an equaliser from 25 yards. Simon Lowe is unlucky in injury-time when his header, that would have won the game, hits the inside of the post.											
16	A	CREWE		23	D	2-2	1-2	Longhurst 16, 84	Roche	Podd	Ward	Shaw	Knill	Brown	Sanderson	Kellock*	Lowe	Longhurst	Nicholson	Gallagher
	2/11		*1,493*	*15*	14			*Waller 4, Platt 22*	*Parkin*	*Pemberton*	*Johnson**	*Thomas*	*Davis*	*Anderson*	*Platt*	*Edwards*	*Waller*	*Pullar*	*Power*	*Blissett*
								Ref: G Napthine	Longhurst scores two contrasting goals to earn Town a point. His first is one he knows little about, as the ball goes in off his knee. His second is an exquisite volley when Knill heads on a free-kick. Phil Power thinks he's won the game for Crewe, but a linesman is flagging for offside.											
17	A	STOCKPORT		23	L	1-2	1-1	Gallagher 3	Roche	Podd	Ward	Shaw	Knill	Brown	Sanderson	Longhurst	Lowe	Gallagher	Nicholson	
	4/11		*1,673*	*14*	14			*Chapman 23, Mossman 47*	*Salmon*	*Rutter*	*Sherlock*	*Chapman*	*Williams*	*Matthewson*	*Hodkinson*	*Hendrie*	*Leonard*	*Sword*	*Mossman**	*Evans*
								Ref: F Roberts	Mick Jones tried to sign Tommy Sword in the close season. In the end he stayed at Edgeley Park, and plays his part in Town's downfall. Town take an early lead before the ball bobbles off Sword's legs for Chapman to score. Mossman scores the winner after Sword challenges Roche.											
18	H	PETERBOROUGH		21	D	1-1	1-1	Gallagher 20p	Roche	Podd	Ward	Shaw	Knill	Brown*	Sanderson	Thornber	Lowe	Gallagher	Nicholson	Kendall
	9/11		1,007	*16*	15			*Worrall 4*	*Turner*	*Paris*	*Pike*	*Quow*	*Slack*	*Holmes*	*Cassidy*	*Fucillo*	*Gallagher*	*Rees*	*Worrall*	
								Ref: M Heath	At 2.30, Longhurst is sent home with a stomach bug. By 3.05, Town are a goal down. 25 minutes later, Brown limps out of the game. The low crowd means the atmosphere at the Shay resembles a wake, even after Gallagher's equaliser from the spot following Pike's handball offence.											
19	A	NORTHAMPTON		23	L	**0-4**	0-2	*[Schiavi 71]*	Roche	Podd	Thornber	Shaw	Knill	Gallagher	Sanderson*	Kellock	Lowe	Longhurst	Nicholson	Kendall
	23/11		*1,514*	*14*	15			*Chard 1p, Benjamin 12, Morley 48,*	*Gleasure*	*Reed*	*Mundee*	*Chard*	*Lewis*	*Nebbeling*	*Donald*	*Benjamin*	*Hill*	*Morley*	*Schiavi*	
								Ref: R Lewis	Including last week's cup defeat, it's now 14 games without a win. Town's plans for this game are in tatters after only 19 seconds, when Podd bundles over Schiavi for Chard's penalty. Roche does his best to keep the score down, and saves a second Chard penalty in the 54th minute.											
20	H	HEREFORD		23	W	1-0	0-0	Lowe 55	Roche	Brown	Ward	Shaw	Knill	Kendall	Gallagher	Kellock	Lowe	Longhurst	Nicholson	
	3/12		1,015	*9*	18				*Ross*	*Price*	*Halliday**	*Pejic*	*Cagielski*	*Maddy*	*Rodgerson*	*Delve*	*Wells*	*Kearns*	*Carter*	*Beacock*
								Ref: I Hendrick	The Shaymen belie their lowly position and play Hereford off the park. The wonder is that they only manage the one goal. Bulls' keeper Kevin Rose saves all that Town throw at him, but when Brown has a go from 30 yards, he fails to hold the ball, and Lowe nips in to net the winner.											
21	A	SWINDON		22	L	2-3	1-1	Coleman 41 (og), Kellock 49	Roche	Brown	Ward	Thornber	Knill	Kendall	Gallagher	Kellock	Lowe	Longhurst	Nicholson	
	14/12		***4,516***	*2*	18			*Coleman 36p, 52p, Henry 61*	*Allen*	*Ramsey*	*Coleman*	*Barnard*	*Cole*	*Calderwood*	*Bamber*	*Henry*	*Gordon*	*Wade*	*Hockaday*	
								Ref: T Ward	Swindon's on-loan Dave Bamber is making a habit of winning penalties. The two he claims – and gets – make it five in the last three home games. Coleman scores a hat-trick – the two penalties, and Town's first when he deflects in Nicholson's free-kick. Henry heads in the winner.											
22	A	SCUNTHORPE		22	D	3-3	3-1	Brown 7, 36, Kendall 21	Roche	Brown	Ward	Thornber	Knill	Kendall	Gallagher	Kellock*	Lowe	Longhurst	Nicholson	**Robinson**
	22/12		*2,285*	*21*	19			*Hawley 43, 47p, 77*	*Gregory*	*Russell*	*Longden*	*Matthews**	*Whitehead*	*Money*	*Barnes*	*Hawley*	*Broddle*	*Lester*	*Hill*	*Lister*
								Ref: J Bray	Phil Brown's two long-range drives, and a goal from unmarked Kendall, look set to send Town on their way to a memorable victory. But John Hawley has other ideas. He pulls one back before the break, and goes on to complete a hat-trick. Jones claims his first two were 'miles offside'.											
23	H	ROCHDALE		22	D	1-1	0-0	Kellock 85	Roche	Brown	Ward	Thornber	Knill	Kendall	Gallagher	Kellock	Lowe	Longhurst	Nicholson	
	26/12		2,253	*9*	20			*Taylor 68*	*Redfern*	*Heaton**	*Grant*	*McMahon*	*Cooke*	*Hicks*	*Thompson*	*Taylor*	*Moore*	*Seasman*	*Towner*	*Johnson*
								Ref: A Saunders	An 11.00 am kick-off pulls in Town's second-best attendance of the season. Rochdale, going well in the league, have in Steve Taylor a striker who is on fire. His goal off a corner is his eighth in his last seven games. Heaton may have got the last touch but Kellock claims his side's goal.											

No	Date	Opponent	Att	Pos	Pt	F-A	H-T	Scorers, Times, and Referees	1	2	3	4	5	6	7	8	9	10	11	12 sub used
24	A	HARTLEPOOL		22	L	0-3	0-2		Roche	Brown	Podd !	Thornber	Knill	Kendall	Gallagher	Kellock	Ward	Longhurst	Nicholson*	Robinson
	1/1		*3,392*	4	20			*Shoulder 26, 30, Dixon 69*	*Blackburn*	*Nobbs*	*Chambers*	*Hogan*	*Smith*	*Linighan*	*Honour*	*Shoulder*	*Dixon*	*Walker*	*Robinson*	
								Ref: M Scott	Alan Shoulder was a target for Jones last season. But he was put off by Carlisle's £7,000 asking price. He's now at Hartlepool, and shows what Town are missing. He scores twice, his first a diving header. He's also behind Podd's 59th-minute sending-off for halting him in his tracks.											
25	H	CREWE		21	W	1-0	0-0	Lowe 60	Roche	Brown	Ward	Thornber	Knill	Robinson	Gallagher	Kellock	Lowe	Longhurst	Nicholson	
	4/1		1,031	*23*	23				*Parkin*	*Pullar*	*Booth*	*Pemberton*	*Davis*	*Hart*	*Platt*	*Taylor**	*Waller*	*Farrell*	*Blissett*	*Saunders*
								Ref: C Seel	Dario Gradi will one day transform Crewe, but it's only his second season at Gresty Road and his team, like Town, are struggling. At the Shay, the pitch is like an ice-rink and is often played at pedestrian pace Lowe scores the crucial goal, then is told by his manager to be more selfish.											
26	A	PRESTON		21	W	1-0	1-0	Kellock 41	Roche	Brown	Ward	Thornber	Knill	Robinson	Gallagher	Kellock	Lowe	Longhurst	Nicholson	
	11/1		*3,184*	*23*	26				*Platt*	*McNeil*	*Jones**	*Atkins*	*Twentyman*	*Martin*	*McAteer*	*Gray*	*Thomas*	*Allatt*	*Brazil*	*Cooper*
								Ref: P Vanes	Mick Jones sets off on his solo sponsored walk to Deepdale in an effort to raise money for players and the Martin House Appeal, a home being built in Boston Spa for the terminally ill. He donates £250 of his own money, and gets to the ground in time to see Kellock's headed winner.											
27	H	CHESTER		20	L	1-2	0-1	Kellock 75p	Roche	Brown	Ward	Thornber	Knill	Robinson	Gallagher	Kellock	Lowe	Longhurst	Nicholson	
	17/1		1,473	*1*	26			*Houghton 42, 51*	*Butcher*	*Glenn*	*Lane*	*Greenhough*	*Able*	*Coy*	*Kelly*	*Butler*	*Richardson*	*Houghton*	*Bennett*	
								Ref: A Banks	Up the road, the rugby club is staking a claim for the championship. At the Shay, Chester are staking a claim for their own. Few would argue with the result, although Chester create few chances, but score twice through Peter Houghton. Town have to rely on Kellock's penalty goal.											
28	H	COLCHESTER		21	D	2-2	0-1	Sanderson 69, Kellock 73	Roche	Brown	Ward	Thornber	Knill	Galloway	Sanderson	Kellock	Lowe	Longhurst	Nicholson	
	31/1		**989**	*12*	27			*Baker 36, Adcock 60*	*Chamberlain*	*Hedman*	*English A*	*Osborne*	*Baker*	*Game*	*Burman*	*Parkinson*	*Groves*	*Adcock*	*Irving*	
								Ref: G Aplin	Paul Sanderson has asked to go on the transfer list, but plays his part in Town's rescue after they go two goals down. He hammers home a 25-yard drive to halve the deficit. Kellock equalises when Nicholson's volley comes back off the post. Norwich City take a look at Longhurst.											
29	H	EXETER		21	W	1-0	0-0	Longhurst 62	Roche	Brown	Ward	Thornber	Knill	**Galloway**	Sanderson	Kellock*	**Diamond**	Longhurst	Nicholson	Lowe
	4/2		1,004	*17*	30				*Shaw*	*Harrower*	*Viney*	*McNichol*	*Impey*	*McCaffrey*	*Ling*	*Keough*	*Gale*	*Pratt*	*King**	*Jackson*
								Ref: N Ashley	Longhurst continues to be the centre of attention at the Shay, and recently Town turned down a £18,000 offer from Swindon. With low gates, Town certainly need the money. But they also need Longhurst to get them out of trouble. New-boy Diamond sends over the cross for his goal.											
30	A	TRANMERE		16	W	3-0	3-0	Diamond 5, 38, Nicholson 22	Roche	Brown	**Fleming**	Thornber	Knill	Galloway	Sanderson	Kellock	Diamond	Longhurst	Nicholson	
	7/2		*1,357*	*12*	33				*Adkins*	*Mungall*	*Williams*	*Hughes*	*Rodaway*	*Edwards*	*Morrissey*	*Train**	*Hilditch*	*Muir*	*Anderson*	*Worthington*
								Ref: D Allison	Barry Diamond helps his team-mates pick up their first bonus thanks to a scheme which pays nothing while the side is in the bottom eight. His two headed goals lift Town to ninth bottom. Nicholson scores with a controlled half-volley in a scintillating performance from the Shaymen.											
31	A	SOUTHEND		20	L	1-2	1-1	Diamond 20	Roche	Brown	Fleming	Shaw	Knill	Galloway	Sanderson	Longhurst*	Diamond	Thornber	Nicholson	Kellock
	5/3		***1,006***	*8*	33			*Lampard 13, O'Shea 82*	*Stannard*	*May*	*Pennyfather*	*O'Shea*	*Hatter*	*Lampard*	*Clark*	*McDonough*	*Cadette*	*Neal*	*Rogers*	
								Ref: J Ball	The attendance is Southend's lowest for a league match. Frank Lampard's volleyed goal is his first for the Shrimpers, and his 19th and last in a career that saw him make 551 league appearances for West Ham. As O'Shea's looping header goes in, Jones points a finger at Town's defence.											
32	A	ALDERSHOT		19	W	2-1	0-1	Kellock 65, Longhurst 70	Roche	Brown	Fleming	Shaw	Knill	Galloway	Sanderson	Thornber*	Diamond !	Longhurst	Nicholson	Kellock
	8/3		*1,314*	*18*	36			*Staff 15*	*Coles*	*Blankley*	*Ferns*	*Massey*	*Mazzon*	*Coleman !*	*Shrubb*	*Johnson*	*Duncan*	*Staff*	*McDonald**	*Fadida*
								Ref: D Axcell	As the players go in at half-time, Barry Diamond and Phil Coleman square up to one another. The ref dismisses them, but refuses to let the club announcer inform the crowd. Halifax turn the game around after trailing to Staff's goal. He's only playing because McNeill's car broke down.											
33	H	WREXHAM		17	W	**5-2**	3-2	Kellock 31p, 77, 80, Knill 37, Sand'son 40	Roche	Fleming	Brown	Shaw	Knill	Galloway	Sanderson	Kellock	Diamond	Longhurst	Nicholson*	Ward
	14/3		1,268	*11*	39			*Charles 35, Steel 45*	*Ferguson*	*Salathiel*	*Cunnington*	*Jones*	*Williams*	*Comstive*	*Edwards*	*Horne*	*Steel*	*Charles*	*Weetman**	*Emery*
								Ref: K Redfern	Kellock missed all his penalties in practice. But when Town are awarded one for a foul on Diamond, Kellock sticks it way. It sets him on the way to a hat-trick, which he completes following a second penalty award. Ferguson saves his kick, but Kellock reacts first to net the rebound.											
34	A	BURNLEY		17	W	3-1	2-1	Nicholson 18, Lowe 27, Longhurst 80	Roche	Brown	Fleming	Shaw	Knill	Galloway	Sanderson	Kellock	Lowe	Longhurst	Nicholson	
	22/3		*3,321*	*12*	42			*Hampton 13*	*Neenan*	*Hird*	*Hampton*	*Malley*	*Overson*	*Heggarty*	*Grewcock*	*Deakin*	*Taylor**	*Lawrence*	*Hoskin*	*Devine*
								Ref: M Peck	Longhurst is the star of the show as Town record a famous win. After going behind to Hampton's strike, he is involved in both the goals that give Town a half-time lead. Ten minutes from time, Longhurst delivers the coup de grace with a stunning individual goal begun near halfway.											

35	H	HARTLEPOOL	16	W	3-2	2-1	Longhurst 2, Kellock 11p, Lowe 78	Roche	Brown	Fleming*	Shaw	Knill	Galloway	Sanderson	Kellock	Lowe	Longhurst	Nicholson	Ward
	28/3	2,064	*5*	45			*Shoulder 17, 66p*	*Blackburn*	*Nobbs*	*Chambers*	*Hogan*	*Smith*	*Linighan*	*Honour*	*Shoulder*	*Borthwick*	*Walker*	*Carney*	
							Ref: M Robinson	When Roche and Fleming have a clash of heads, physio Alan Sutton races on to treat them before the ball goes out play. From the resultant drop-ball, Shoulder pulls a goal back after Town had taken a 2-0 lead. His penalty levels the game, before Lowe's header wins it for Town.											
36	A	ROCHDALE	18	L	0-1	0-0		Roche	Brown	Fleming*	Shaw	Knill	Galloway	Sanderson	Kellock	Diamond	Longhurst	Nicholson	Ward
	31/3	*1,931*	*14*	45			*Moore 85*	*Redfern*	*Johnson*	*Grant*	*Heaton*	*Cooke*	*Measham*	*Thompson*	*Taylor*	*Moore*	*Hildersley*	*McCluskie*	
							Ref: R Bridges	After four consecutive wins, Jones is a candidate for the Manager of the Month award. But his chances disappear down the drain after his side slips to defeat on a pitch made up of mud and pools of water. Moore, who has a goal ruled out after only 20 seconds, sidefoots a late winner.											
37	H	STOCKPORT	18	D	0-0	0-0		Roche	Brown	Fleming	Shaw	Knill	Galloway	Sanderson	Kellock	Diamond	Longhurst	Nicholson	
	4/4	1,836	*5*	46				*Walker*	*Evans*	*Sherlock*	*Chapman*	*Sword*	*Thorpe*	*Wroe*	*Hendrie*	*Leonard*	*Newton*	*Mossman*	
							Ref: I Hendrick	The Shaymen give their all, and show promotion-chasing County that they can compete with the best in the division. Unfortunately, there are few moments of excitement, and Jones says sorry to the fans after the game. County player-boss Les Chapman almost wins it right at the death.											
38	A	CAMBRIDGE	19	L	**0-4**	0-2		Roche	Brown	Fleming	Shaw	Knill	Galloway	Sanderson	Kellock	Diamond*	Lowe	Nicholson	Ward
	8/4	*1,909*		46			*Crown 14, 69, 90p, Finney 27*	*Branagan*	*Clark*	*Mundee*	*Beattie*	*Dowman*	*Finney*	*Butler*	*Richards G*	*Crown*	*Towner*	*Cooper*	
							Ref: G Downey	Re-election is still a possibilty for Town. Yet, they have the chances to bury Chris Turner's struggling Cambridge, and the final scoreline is a bad reflection on the game. David Crown is the home side's hero, completeing his hat-trick with a penalty after a certain Peter Butler is fouled.											
39	A	PETERBOROUGH	19	D	1-1	1-1	Knill 19	Roche	Brown	Ward	Shaw	Knill	Galloway	Sanderson	Kellock	Diamond	Longhurst	Nicholson	
	12/4	*2,260*	*18*	47			*Slack 29*	*McManus*	*Paris*	*Pike*	*Collins*	*Slack*	*Gage*	*Kowalski*	*Gallagher**	*Shepherd*	*Quow*	*Cavener*	*Kelly*
							Ref: N Wilson	This is a six-pointer. Knill's powerful header from Longhurst's cross is cancelled out ten minutes later by Trevor Slack, who has all the time in the world to score. A point at this stage helps neither team, but the home side are left cursing Paddy Roche, who denies them maximum points.											
40	H	TORQUAY	19	D	0-0	0-0		Roche	Brown	Ward	Shaw	Knill	Galloway	Sanderson	Kellock	Diamond*	Longhurst	Nicholson	Lowe
	14/4	1,062	*24*	48				*Fry*	*Dawkins*	*Pugh*	*Wright*	*Compton*	*Crowe*	*Crabbe*	*Walsh*	*Phillips*	*Loram*	*Webber*	
							Ref: F Roberts	A goalless draw against the league's bottom club leaves Halifax two points clear of the re-election places. Stuart Morgan's side carve out two half-chances, as Town boss Mick Jones aptly sums up a disappointing game by saying, 'Dead night, dead pitch, dead crowd, and a dead game.'											
41	H	NORTHAMPTON	18	W	2-0	2-0	Longhurst 20, 40	Roche	Brown	Ward	Thornber	Knill	Galloway	Sanderson	Kellock	Diamond	Longhurst	Nicholson	
	18/4	1,105	*7*	51				*Gleasure*	*Curtis*	*Friar**	*Donald*	*Lewis*	*McPherson*	*Schiavi*	*Benjamin*	*Chard*	*Morley*	*Hill*	*Sugrue*
							Ref: R Nixon	This win eases re-election fears. Typically, it's Longhurst who supplies the goals. Sheer determination helps him get his first, as his slight 5'8" frame gets between two tall defenders to head in Nicholson's cross. When Gleasure spills Diamond's effort, Longhurst nips in for his second.											
42	A	ORIENT	20	L	0-1	0-1		Roche	Brown	Ward	Thornber	Knill	Galloway	Gallagher*	Kellock	Diamond	Longhurst	Nicholson	Lowe
	22/4	*1,443*		51			*Godfrey 7*	*Wells*	*John*	*Dickenson*	*Jones*	*Foster*	*Cornwell*	*Godfrey*	*Brooks*	*Juryeff*	*Castle*	*Comfort*	
							Ref: D Hedges	Frank Clarke's side were on the periphery of the promotion race until four recent consecutive defeats set them back somewhat. They look quite dangerous here though, and Kevin Godfrey had already hit the bar before his goal. Halifax don't force Wells into action until the 83rd minute.											
43	A	HEREFORD	21	L	1-2	0-0	Kellock 83	Roche	Brown	Fleming	Shaw	Knill	Galloway	Sanderson*	Kellock	Lowe	Longhurst	Nicholson	Gallagher
	26/4	*2,212*	*9*	51			*Maddy 79, Carter 82*	*Rose*	*Price*	*Pejic*	*Halliday*	*Cegielski*	*Delve*	*Harvey*	*Maddy*	*Dalziel**	*Kearns*	*Carter*	*Beacock*
							Ref: E Scales	On the way to Edgar Street, Town's coach breaks down, and the players are over an hour late for their pre-match meal. On the pitch, they look like providing a shock until Maddy's rocket shot flies in. Then Carter's unchallenged header wins the game and sends Town back into trouble.											
44	H	PORT VALE	18	W	2-0	0-0	Longhurst 50, Kellock 84p	Roche	Brown*	Fleming	Shaw	Knill	Galloway	Sanderson	Kellock	Lowe	Longhurst	Nicholson	Ward
	29/4	1,389	*3*	54				*Arnold*	*Webb*	*Banks*	*Hunter*	*Sproson*	*Williams*	*Biggins**	*Earle*	*Jones*	*Bowden*	*Maguire*	*Bromage*
							Ref: T Fitzharris	John Rudge's Port Vale have already clinched promotion, and arrive at the Shay unbeaten in their last 18 games. But Town are still fighting for their lives and they raise their game. When Ward's shot is handled on the line, Kellock can't wait to tuck away the penalty against his old club.											
45	H	SWINDON	18	L	1-3	0-1	Lowe 72	Roche	Brown*	Fleming	Shaw	Knill	Galloway	Sanderson	Kellock	Lowe	Longhurst	Nicholson	Ward
	2/5	1,626	*1*	54			*Henry 22, 50, 65*	*Allen*	*Hockaday*	*Ramsey*	*Barnard*	*Cole*	*Calderwood*	*Bamber*	*Henry*	*Coyne*	*Hall*	*Kamara*	
							Ref: J Worrall	Full-back Charlie Henry is now playing in midfield because his manager Lou Macari reckons he used to foul too much. With this hat-trick, he doubles his career tally. Mick Jones admits, 'We were beaten by champions, and it showed.' Town's fate will now be decided on the final day.											
46	H	MANSFIELD	19	L	1-2	0-0	Longhurst 90	Roche	Brown	Fleming	Thornber	Knill	Galloway	Sanderson	Kellock	Lowe	Longhurst	Nicholson	
	5/5	1,414	*3*	54			*Kent 56, Whatmore 84*	*Hitchcock*	*Graham*	*Garner*	*Robinson*	*Foster*	*Kenworthy**	*McKernon*	*Whatmore*	*Kent*	*Cassells*	*Kearney*	*Stringfellow*
	Home	Away					Ref: N Glover	Exeter's home defeat by Crewe means Town don't have to apply for re-election. But it was mightily close. Longhurst's injury-time goal means that the Shaymen finish above Exeter, who can still be overhauled by Rochdale, on goal-difference. Promoted Mansfield prolong the agony.											
Average	1,418	2,135																	

Milk Cup				F-A	H-T	Scorers, Times, and Referees	1	2	3	4	5	6	7	8	9	10	11	12 sub used
1:1 H HULL			D	1-1	1-1	Shaw 6	Roche	Brown	Ward	Shaw	Kendall	Ayre	Gallagher	Kellock	Lowe	Longhurst	Nicholson	
20/8	820	*2:*				*Flounders 37*	*Norman*	*Jobson*	*Pearson*	*Swann*	*Skipper*	*McEwan*	*Williams*	*Bunn*	*Flounders*	*Askew*	*Roberts*	
						Ref: M Pike	Town run out in blue and white shirts for the first time since 1950 and give Brian Horton's 2nd Division Hull side a real run for their money. Aidie Shaw gives them a dream start, firing in from 18 yards. Town create three more good opportunities, then watch when Flounders pounces.											
1:2 A HULL		6	L	0-3	0-3		Roche	Brown	Ward	Shaw	Kendall	Knill*	Gallagher	Kellock	Lowe	Longhurst	Nicholson	Podd
3/9	*3,299*	*2:17*				*Bunn 22, 42, Whitehurst 33p*	*Norman*	*Jobson*	*Pearson*	*Doyle*	*Skipper*	*McEwan*	*Swann*	*Bunn*	*Whitehurst*	*Askew**	*Roberts*	*Ring*
						Ref: G Tyson (Halifax lost 1-4 on aggregate)	Town are already trailing on the night when Brown nicks the ball away from £40,000 signing Bunn (Luton). But the ref awards a penalty, and Whitehurst scores. Roche saves an even more dubious penalty in the second half. Bunn bundles in his second goal to virtually end the contest.											

FA Cup				F-A	H-T	Scorers, Times, and Referees	1	2	3	4	5	6	7	8	9	10	11	12 sub used
1 H SCUNTHORPE		21	L	1-3	1-1	Kendall 3	Roche	Brown	Ward	Shaw	Knill	Kendall	Sanderson	Thornber	Gallagher	Longhurst*	Nicholson	Lowe
16/11	1,501	*20*				*Hill 8, Broddle 47, Lister 86*	*Gregory*	*Russell*	*Longden*	*Lister*	*Whitehead*	*Money*	*Brolly*	*Cammack*	*Broddle*	*Lester*	*Hill*	
						Ref: G Courtney	Town's season is all but over after this Cup defeat. Kendall stoops to score early on, but within five minutes Julian Broddle beats the offside to level the scores. After going behind, Town waste at least seven glorious chances, before Steve Lister walks through the defence to seal victory.											

	Home						Away					
	P	W	D	L	F	A	W	D	L	F	A	Pts
1 Swindon	46	20	2	1	52	19	12	4	7	30	24	102
2 Chester	46	15	5	3	44	16	8	10	5	39	34	84
3 Mansfield	46	13	8	2	43	17	10	4	9	31	30	81
4 Port Vale	46	13	9	1	42	11	8	7	8	25	26	79
5 Orient	46	11	6	6	39	21	9	6	8	40	43	72
6 Colchester	46	12	6	5	51	22	7	7	9	37	41	70
7 Hartlepool	46	15	6	2	41	20	5	4	14	27	47	70
8 Northampton	46	9	7	7	44	29	9	3	11	35	29	64
9 Southend	46	13	4	6	43	27	5	6	12	26	40	64
10 Hereford	46	15	6	2	55	30	3	4	16	19	43	64
11 Stockport	46	9	9	5	35	28	8	4	11	28	43	64
12 Crewe	46	10	6	7	35	26	8	3	12	19	35	63
13 Wrexham	46	11	5	7	34	24	6	4	13	34	56	60
14 Burnley	46	11	3	9	35	30	5	8	10	25	35	59
15 Scunthorpe	46	11	7	5	33	23	4	7	12	17	32	59
16 Aldershot	46	12	5	6	45	25	5	2	16	21	49	58
17 Peterborough	46	9	11	3	31	19	4	6	13	21	45	56
18 Rochdale	46	12	7	4	41	29	2	6	15	16	48	55
19 Tranmere	46	9	1	13	46	41	6	8	9	28	32	54
20 HALIFAX	46	10	8	5	35	27	4	4	15	25	44	54
21 Exeter	46	10	4	9	26	25	3	11	9	21	34	54
22 Cambridge	46	12	2	9	45	38	3	7	13	20	42	54
23 Preston	46	7	4	12	32	41	4	6	13	22	48	43
24 Torquay	46	8	5	10	29	32	1	5	17	14	56	37
	1104	277	136	139	956	620	139	136	277	620	956	1520

Odds & ends

Double wins: (1) Preston.
Double losses: (3) Mansfield, Southend, Swindon.

Won from behind: (4) Orient (h), Scunthorpe (h), Aldershot (a), Burnley (a).
Lost from in front: (3) Stockport (a), Swindon (a), Scunthorpe (FAC) (h).

High spots: Winning six out of seven games, four consecutively, during February and March.
Beating Burnley 3-1 away.
Scoring five goals against Wrexham.

Low spots: 13 games without a win up to 23 November.
A crowd of only 820 for the first home game of the season against Hull in the Milk Cup.
Only 989 turning up for the visit of Colchester.

Player of the Year: David Longhurst.
Ever-presents: (1) Paddy Roche.
Hat-tricks: Billy Kellock (1).
Leading scorer: Billy Kellock (17).

	Appearances						Goals			
	Lge	*Sub*	LC	*Sub*	FAC	*Sub*	**Lge**	LC	FAC	**Tot**
Ayre, Billy	**10**		1							
Brown, Phil	**45**		2		1		**2**			**2**
Diamond, Barry	**12**						**3**			**3**
Fleming, Paul	**13**									
Gallagher, Barry	**23**	*2*	2		1		**5**			**5**
Galloway, Mick	**19**									
Hotte, Tim	**2**	*2*								
Kellock, Billy	**41**	*2*	2				**17**			**17**
Kendall, Paul	**18**	*3*	2		1		**2**		1	**3**
Knill, Alan	**33**		1		1		**2**			**2**
Longhurst, David	**44**		2		1		**14**			**14**
Lowe, Simon	**32**	*3*	2			*1*	**7**			**7**
Nicholson, Gary	**44**		2		1		**3**			**3**
Podd, Cec	**11**	*5*		*1*						
Robinson, Peter	**3**	*2*								
Roche, Paddy	**46**		2		1					
Sanderson, Paul	**27**	*1*			1		**2**			**2**
Shaw, Adrian	**34**		2		1			1		**1**
Thornber, Steve	**17**	*1*			1					
Ward, Steve	**32**	*6*	2		1		**1**			**1**
(own-goals)							**2**			**2**
20 players used	**506**	***27***	**22**	***1***	**11**	***1***	**60**	**1**	**1**	**62**

No	Date		Att	Pos	Pt	F-A	H-T	Scorers, Times, and Referees	1	2	3	4	5	6	7	8	9	10	11	12 sub used
1	H	ALDERSHOT			W	1-0	1-0	Black 3	Roche	Brown	Fleming	**Robinson**	Knill	Galloway	Sanderson	**Black**	Diamond	Longhurst	Nicholson	
	23/8		1,020		3				*Lange*	*Shrubb*	*Friar*	*Burvill*	*Anderson*	*Mazzon*	*Ring*	*Foyle*	*Fielder*	*McDonald*	*Langley*	
								Ref: J Ireland	John Madeley, of Madeley's DIY, has been installed as the new chairman, and his company is now sponsoring the team. On the pitch, it's an opening day victory for the first time since 1972. Fleming provides the cross from which Black scores the fastest 4th Division goal of the day.											
2	A	CAMBRIDGE		11	L	0-1	0-0		Roche	Brown	Fleming	Robinson	Knill	Galloway	Sanderson	Black	Diamond	Longhurst	Nicholson	
	30/8		*2,261*	*1*	3			*Beck 84*	*Branagan*	*Measham*	*Mundee*	*Beattie*	*Smith*	*Beck*	*Littlejohns*	*Spriggs*	*Cooper*	*Crown*	*Towner*	
								Ref: A Buksh	Cambridge, after defeating relegated Wolves on the opening day, are the early leaders after this second win. They leave it late, but score their goal from a controversial free-kick. Knill is penalised for a push on Cooper, and debutant John Beck curls the resulting free-kick into the net.											
3	H	SOUTHEND		16	L	0-1	0-0		Roche	Brown	Fleming	Shaw	Knill	Galloway	Sanderson	Thornber	Black	Longhurst	Nicholson*	Diamond
	5/9		1,060	*13*	3			*Gymer 71*	*Stannard*	*Roberts*	*Johnson*	*O'Shea*	*Martin*	*Hall*	*Clark*	*Pennyfather*	*Cadette*	*Neal*	*Gymer*	
								Ref: R Hart	Southend are up and running. This win will be their first of many. But they hardly look interested as Town dominate the game, but fail to find a way through. Jones reckoned, 'They were there for the taking,' and is annoyed that his team should fall to a soft goal like that scored by Gymer.											
4	A	WREXHAM		20	L	1-3	1-2	Brown 23p	Roche	Brown	Fleming	Shaw	Knill	Galloway	Sanderson	Thornber	Black*	Longhurst	Robinson	Diamond
	12/9		*2,250*	*8*	3			*Horne 15, Charles 17, Steel 81*	*Pearce*	*Salathiel*	*Cunnington*	*Williams*	*Cooke*	*Conroy*	*Massey**	*Horne*	*Steel*	*Charles*	*Emson*	*Buxton*
								Ref: A Robinson	Town need new players, but have no money to buy. Wrexham keeper Chris Pearce is virtually a spectator, Phil Brown's penalty apart. That comes when Cooke uses a hand in the box. Town hope they can nick a point, but know the game is up when Steel rams home Salathiel's cross.											
5	A	PRESTON		22	L	2-3	2-0	Knill 2, Longhurst 14	Roche	Brown	Robinson*	Shaw	Knill	Galloway	Sanderson	Thornber	Diamond	Longhurst	Black	Nicholson
	16/9		*5,259*	*1*	3			*Thomas 68, 82, 86*	*Brown*	*Bennett*	*McAteer*	*Chapman*	*Jones*	*Allardyce*	*Williams*	*Clark*	*Thomas*	*Hildersley*	*Brazil*	
								Ref: P Wright	For 70 minutes, Town make their lowly league position look as artificial as Preston's plastic pitch. Longhurst scores a superb solo goal to put Town 2-0 up. But then Preston take over, and Thomas, once on loan at the Shay, nets a remarkable hat-trick. His winner is a volley on the turn.											
6	H	STOCKPORT		24	L	0-2	0-1		Roche	Brown	Fleming	Shaw	Knill	Galloway	Sanderson	Thornber	Diamond*	Longhurst	Black	Nicholson
	19/9		1,071	*21*	3			*Hodkinson 14, Glavin 88*	*Farnworth*	*Evans*	*Matthewson*	*Glavin*	*Brannigan*	*Williams*	*Lester*	*Cockhill*	*Leonard*	*Bailey*	*Hodkinson*	
								Ref: P Harrison	After this awful performance, Mick Jones threatens he will quit unless he's given cash for new players and will tear up the contracts of players who con him. His team look like total strangers, and County hardly have to break sweat. Leonard looks menacing and makes both their goals.											
7	A	BURNLEY		24	L	0-3	0-0		**Whitehead**	Brown	Fleming	Shaw*	Knill	Galloway	Sanderson	Thornber	Black	Longhurst	**Holden**	Nicholson
	27/9		*3,240*	*5*	3			*Parker 47, 69, Hoskin 54*	*Neenan*	*Rodaway*	*Hampton*	*Britton*	*Gallagher*	*Deakin*	*Grewcock*	*Parker*	*Entwistle*	*James*	*Hoskin*	
								Ref: M Peck	Phil Whitehead - in for Roche who has a virus - and Rick Holden are shock choices in the Town team. Despite the defeat, they look players for the future. Town create many chances, and might have won. Galloway hit the bar after only 90 seconds. The game turns just after the interval.											
8	H	NORTHAMPTON		24	L	**3-6**	1-3	Brown 8, Holden 53, L'hurst 69 *(Chard 74)*	**Gregory**	Brown	Thornber	**Martin***	Knill	Galloway	Sanderson	Nicholson	Black	Longhurst	Holden	**Matthews M**
	30/9		1,034	*1*	3			*Donald 5, Benjamin 20, Hill 43, 46, 87p,*	*Gleasure*	*Reed*	*Chard*	*Donald*	*Coy*	*McPherson*	*McGoldrick*	*Benjamin*	*Gilbert*	*Morley*	*Hill*	
								Ref: K Lupton	Town's best attacking display, and their worst defensive, with on loan Paul Gregory letting in six on his debut. Donald starts the scoring with a 30-yarder. Brown's goal from an indirect free-kick in the box, with all the Cobblers' players on the line, gets Halifax level, but not for long.											
9	H	SWANSEA		22	W	1-0	1-0	Galloway 43	Gregory	Brown	Robinson	Matthews M	Knill	Galloway	Sanderson	Nicholson*	Black	Longhurst	Holden	Diamond
	4/10		1,003	*2*	6				*Hughes*	*Harrison*	*Phelan*	*Lewis*	*Melville*	*Emmanuel*	*Hough*	*McCarthy*	*Love*	*Williams**	*Hutchison*	*Stevenson*
								Ref: J Lloyd	Mick Jones revealed how he ordered his players pints of lager after the 3-6 defeat in order to build up their confidence. It works a treat, as the Shaymen end their seven-match losing streak. Relegated Swansea are outplayed and fall to Galloway's thunderous header just before half-time											
10	A	TORQUAY		23	L	0-1	0-0		Gregory	Brown	Robinson	Matthews M	Knill	Galloway	Sanderson	**Matthews N**	Black	Longhurst	Holden	
	11/10		***1,571***	*15*	6			*Dobson 52*	*Smeulders*	*McNichol*	*King*	*Impey*	*Crowe*	*Rowe*	*Musker*	*Kendal*	*Phillips*	*Nardiello**	*Dobson*	*Walsh*
								Ref: K Baker	Torquay end a run of five consecutive draws in the league, but they know they have been in a game. Longhurst forms a new strike partnership with Matthews and they cause problems all afternoon. Dobson's goal, scored when he is on the deck, comes completely against the run of play.											
11	H	TRANMERE		23	D	0-0	0-0		Gregory	Brown	Robinson	Matthews M	Knill	Galloway	Sanderson	Matthews N	Black	Longhurst	Holden	
	17/10		1,245	*8*	7				*O'Rourke*	*Hughes*	*Hay*	*Vickers*	*Moore*	*Williams*	*Morrissey*	*Mungall*	*Muir*	*Worthington*	*Anderson*	
								Ref: W Flood	Tranmere player-boss Frank Worthington, once of Halifax Schoolboys, returns to the Shay to make his 800th first-team appearance. But Town run his side ragged, despite not scoring. They hit the bar three times, including Brown's 65th-minute penalty when Vickers felled Longhurst.											

No / Date	Venue	Opponent	Att	Pos	Res / Pts	F-A	H-T	Scorers, Times, and Referees	1	2	3	4	5	6	7	8	9	10	11	12
12	A	WOLVES			W	2-1	2-0	Matthews N 12, Matthews M 14	Gregory	Brown	Robinson	Matthews M	Knill	Galloway	Sanderson	Matthews N	Black	Longhurst	Holden	
21/10			*4,380*		10			*Handysides 61*	*Nixon*	*Stoutt*	*Barnes*	*Streete*	*Forman*	*Zelem*	*Lockhart**	*Holmes*	*Mutch*	*Handysides*	*Edwards*	*Purdie*
								Ref: P Tyldesley	Wolves, under Sammy Chapman, are in Division 4 for the first time. After 14 minutes they find themselves two goals down. Mick Matthews claims the first after it is deflected in – he's a former Wolves player. Ian Handyside's 20-yarder halves the deficit, but the Shaymen hold out.											
13	A	CREWE		22	D	2-2	1-1	Brown 30p, Black 56	Gregory	Brown	Robinson	Matthews M	Knill	Galloway	Sanderson	Matthews N*	Black	Longhurst	Holden	Shaw
25/10			*1,666*	*12*	11			*Cutler 15, Platt 80*	*Parkin*	*Pullar*	*Pemberton*	*Jarvis**	*Wright*	*Hart*	*Platt*	*McGuinness*	*Cutler*	*Milligan*	*Blissett*	*Power*
								Ref: R Nixon	The Town bus breaks down, and the journey to Gresty Road takes three hours. Town come from behind to take the lead in terrible conditions. Brown's penalty, when Holden is brought down by the keeper, brings them level. Platt's late equaliser is one of many headed goals he'll score.											
14	H	CARDIFF		22	D	1-1	0-1	Brown 65p	Whitehead	Brown	Robinson*	Matthews M	Knill	Galloway	Sanderson	Matthews N	Black	Longhurst	Holden	Shaw
31/10			1,640	*12*	12			*Platnauer 33*	*Rees*	*Kerr**	*Ford*	*Wimbleton*	*Brignull*	*Boyle*	*Platnauer*	*Curtis*	*Wheeler*	*Vaughan*	*Marustik*	*Bartlett*
								Ref: K Walmsley	John Madeley has announced the club are £300,000 in debt. The improved attendance will not pay the weekly wage bill. Platnauer, scorer of two goals that knocked First Division Chelsea out of the Littlewoods Cup, curls in a free-kick. Knill falls down for Brown's equalising penalty.											
15	H	EXETER		19	W	2-0	1-0	Matthews N 16, Knill 88	Whitehead	Brown	Shaw	Matthews M	Knill	Galloway	Sanderson	Matthews N	Black	Longhurst	Holden	
4/11			1,390		15				*Shaw*	*Priddle**	*Viney*	*Marker*	*McCaffrey*	*Watson*	*Pugh*	*Roberts*	*Biggins*	*Keough*	*Harrower*	*O'Connell*
								Ref: D Shaw	Town go into this game knowing that it could be their last at the Shay. John Madeley runs around the track with a breadboard proclaiming that 'Halifax fans are the best'. Exeter play their part in a fast and furious game, but it's Town who win with headers by Neil Matthews and Knill.											
16	A	SCUNTHORPE		21	L	1-2	1-2	Knill 27	Whitehead	Brown	Shaw	Matthews M	Knill	Galloway	Sanderson	Matthews N	Black	Longhurst	Holden	
9/11			*2,059*	*15*	15			*Johnson 1, Lister 2*	*Green*	*Atkins**	*Longden*	*Money*	*Lister*	*Hunter*	*Richardson*	*McLean*	*Johnson*	*Broddle*	*Hill*	*Russell*
								Ref: M Scott	The BBC film what could be the demise of Halifax Town. The cameras are only just rolling when Johnson's diving header gives Scunthorpe the lead after only 40 seconds. Within a minute they have scored again. Town can't save the game, even after Knill's header finds its way in.											
17	H	ORIENT		19	W	**4-0**	0-0	Brown 58p, Longhurst 60, 90, [Foster 87 (og)]	Roche	Brown	Shaw	Matthews M	Knill	Galloway	Sanderson	Matthews N	Black	Longhurst	Holden	
21/11			1,405	*15*	18				*Wells*	*Sitton*	*Dickenson*	*Foster*	*Hales**	*Cornwell*	*Castle*	*Brooks*	*Juryeff*	*Fishenden*	*Comfort*	*Sussex*
								Ref: F Roberts	Town withstand an early onslaught, with Roche thwarting Orient on several occasions. But when Brown nets a penalty after Neil Matthews goes down under Sitton's challenge, the game swings Town's way. Foster turns a cross into his own net under pressure from Neil Matthews.											
18	A	COLCHESTER		21	L	1-3	0-1	Longhurst 83	Roche	Brown	Shaw*	Matthews M	Knill	Galloway	Sanderson	Matthews N	Black	Longhurst	Holden	Thornber
28/11			*2,567*	*4*	18			*Farrell 38, Adcock 74, Phillips 90*	*Chamberlain*	*Hinshelwood*	*Phillips*	*Grenfell*	*Day*	*Game*	*Farrell*	*Adcock*	*Hedman*	*English T*	*English A*	
								Ref: I Hemley	The home supporters taunt the Town players by saying they will be on the dole by Christmas. But it's they who are on tenterhooks when Dave Longhurst scores a near-post header to set up an exciting finish. Halifax are pressing when Colchester break for Phillips to score at the death.											
19	A	PETERBOROUGH		21	L	0-2	0-1		Roche	Brown	Farnaby	Matthews M	Knill	Galloway	Sanderson	Thornber	Black	Longhurst	Holden	
13/12			*3,135*	*12*	18			*Luke 36, 68*	*Shoemake*	*Paris*	*Collins*	*Price*	*Nightingale*	*Gage*	*Luke*	*Gunn*	*Gallagher*	*Phillips*	*Christie**	*Kelly*
								Ref: J Borrett	The rumours are rife that Mick Jones is about to leave Halifax to join Noel Cantwell at Peterborough. This fixture comes at a most inopportune time. But Jones may enjoy working with the likes of Noel Luke, who teases the Town defence, and scores both goals as well as hitting the post.											
20	H	HEREFORD		20	W	2-1	1-1	Matthews M 16, Longhurst 75	Roche	Brown	Farnaby	Matthews M	Knill	Galloway	Sanderson	**Horwood**	Black*	Longhurst	Holden	Thornber
19/12			1,005	*18*	21			*Harvey 25p*	*Rose*	*Rodgerson*	*Dalziel*	*Halliday*	*Pejic*	*Devine*	*Harvey*	*Stant**	*Phillips*	*Kearns*	*Spooner*	*Butler*
								Ref: J Worrall	Jones has left for Peterborough, and Billy Ayre is in charge for a second spell, but hopes it will be made more permanent this time. He gets off to a good start. Roche is unlucky to concede the penalty after forcing Phillips wide, but Longhurst wins it for Town with a cool chip over Rose.											
21	A	HARTLEPOOL		20	D	0-0	0-0		Roche	Brown	Shaw	Matthews M	Knill	Galloway	Sanderson	Thornber	Horwood	Longhurst	Holden	
26/12			*1,696*	*21*	22				*Blackburn*	*Gibb*	*McKinnon*	*Hogan*	*Smith*	*Nobbs*	*Dixon*	*Shoulder*	*Borthwick*	*Walker*	*Lockhart**	*Honour*
								Ref: K Redfern	John Bird has taken over as boss at another struggling club in Hartlepool. His side may just shade this game, but Town have all the answers in defence. The highlight is Galloway's juggling act on his own line before clearing. In a game of woeful passing, Ayre is happy to play Scrooge.											
22	H	ROCHDALE		18	W	3-1	0-1	Brown 62, Matthews M 74, Black 87	Roche	Brown	Shaw	Matthews M	Knill	Galloway	Sanderson	Thornber	Horwood*	Longhurst	Holden	Black
27/12			1,667	*24*	25			*Woods 25*	*Redfern*	*Johnson*	*Grant*	*Holden*	*Bramhall*	*Gibson*	*Stanton*	*Woods*	*Young**	*Reid*	*Conning*	*Mills*
								Ref: C Trussell	Rick Holden inspires a second-half revival. He sends over the corner from which Brown heads the equaliser, then goes on a jinking run to help set up Mick Matthews' goal. Rochdale boss Eddie Gray gives his side a 30-minute dressing down afterwards, before slipping away in his car.											
23	A	ORIENT		17	W	3-1	1-0	Longhurst 9, 70, Black 81	Roche	Brown	Shaw	Matthews M	Knill	Galloway	Sanderson	Thornber	Black	Longhurst	Holden	
3/1			*2,207*	*21*	28			*Castle 85*	*Wells*	*Hughton*	*Dickenson*	*Foster*	*Hales*	*Cunningham*	*Castle*	*Brooks*	*Jones**	*Godfrey*	*Comfort*	*Cornwell*
								Ref: M Reed	Suddenly, the talk on the terraces is about making the play-offs. Longhurst prompts it with a dazzling exhibition in the capital. He shrugs off an injury to score two well-taken goals. Black's goal is a curling free-kick. At the end, the home supporters demand the head of boss Frank Clark .											

TODAY LEAGUE DIVISION 4

Manager: Mick Jones ⇨ Billy Ayre

SEASON 1986-87

No	Date		Att	Pos	Pt	F-A	H-T	Scorers, Times, and Referees	1	2	3	4	5	6	7	8	9	10	11	12 sub used
24	H	WREXHAM		15	W	2-1	0-0	Longhurst 84, Brown 87	Roche	Brown	Shaw	Matthews M	Knill	Galloway	Sanderson	Thornber	Black	Longhurst	Holden	
	31/1		1,532	5	31			*Buxton 86*	*Heyes*	*Salathiel*	*Cunnington*	*Williams*	*Cooke*	*Diamond*	*Buxton*	*Horne*	*Steel*	*Charles*	*Emson*	
								Ref: I Hendrick	David Longhurst arrives ten minutes late for the pre-match meal, and will be fined. The game itself doesn't come to life till late, but he figures prominently. He scores the first goal after 84 minutes and then has the shot that enables Brown to score the winner as soon as Buxton levels it.											
25	A	SOUTHEND		11	W	3-2	0-0	Galloway 49, Westley 54 (og), Brown 68p	Roche	Brown	Shaw	Matthews M	Knill	Galloway	Sanderson*	Thornber	Black	Longhurst	Holden	Fleming
	3/2		*2,047*	4	34			*Ling 46, 61*	*Stannard*	*O'Shea*	*Roberts*	*Martin*	*Westley*	*Hall*	*Clark**	*Pennyfather*	*Cadette*	*Rogers*	*Ling*	*Gymer*
								Ref: D Hedges	Billy Ayre at long last admits, 'Yes, we can go up,' after Town come from behind to beat high-flying Southend on their own patch. The game explodes after the break. Fleming provides the cross which Westley turns into his own net, then is brought down for Brown's winning penalty.											
26	H	PRESTON		13	L	1-3	0-2	Farnaby 66	Roche	Brown	Shaw	Matthews M	Knill	Farnaby	Fleming	Thornber*	Black	Longhurst	Holden	Nicholson
	7/2		**2,968**	2	34			*Brazil 12, Swann 30, Jemson 52*	*Kelly*	*McNeill*	*Bennett*	*Atkins*	*Jones*	*Allardyce*	*Chapman*	*Swann*	*Jemson**	*Brazil*	*Miller*	*Thomas*
								Ref: J Lovatt	The Shaymen already have injury problems when Galloway twists an ankle in the pre-match warm-up. Four minutes into the game, Thornber pulls a hamstring. Halifax soldier on, but find Preston have too much class. Farnaby, a last-minute inclusion, scores a spectacular 30-yarder.											
27	A	STOCKPORT		16	L	0-2	0-0		Roche	Brown	Shaw	Matthews M	Knill	Nicholson	Sanderson	Fleming	Black	Longhurst	Holden*	Farnaby
	14/2		*1,835*	22	34			*Allatt 73p, Moss 77*	*Gorton*	*Evans*	*McKenzie*	*Edwards*	*Matthewson*	*Williams*	*Hodkinson*	*Moss*	*Allatt*	*Robinson*	*Brown*	
								Ref: R Guy	Town look like holding out for a draw when the ref adjudges Fleming has handled ex-Shayman Allatt's header on the line. Fleming argues that the ball hit his shoulder and he couldn't get out of the way. Allatt doesn't care and scores the penalty to send County on their way to victory.											
28	H	BURNLEY		16	D	2-2	0-0	Nicholson 60, Sword 63	Roche	Brown	Shaw	Matthews M	Farnaby	**Sword**	Sanderson	Fleming	Black	Longhurst	Nicholson	
	21/2		1,735	21	35			*James 62, Grewcock 82*	*Neenan*	*Leebrook*	*Heesom*	*Gallagher*	*Rodaway*	*Deakin*	*Grewcock*	*Britton*	*Caughey*	*James*	*Hoskin*	
								Ref: R Dilkes	More injury worries means Chris Conway, a college friend of Rick Holden, is an emergency sub. Just after the hour, on-loan Sword turns the ball in for the game's third goal in three minutes. It's not the winner, as Grewcock repeats his 25-yarder of last season to get Burnley a point.											
29	H	LINCOLN			L	1-2	0-1	Black 77	Whitehead	Brown	Shaw	Matthews M	Sword	Galloway	Sanderson*	Fleming	Black	Longhurst	Nicholson	Farnaby
	24/2		1,088		35			*McGinley 23, 59*	*Butler*	*Franklin*	*Buckley*	*Cooper*	*West*	*Strodder*	*Hodson*	*McLaren*	*Lund*	*McGinley*	*Mitchell*	
								Ref: J Watson	Halifax are strapped for cash, but Ayre would be willing to give the fans their money back after this. McGinley gets clear to crash a low drive past Whitehead. His scores his second with a shot that deceives Town's keeper. Black pulls one back with a chip after Butler denies Longhurst.											
30	A	NORTHAMPTON		18	L	0-1	0-0		Whitehead	Brown	Fleming	Matthews M	Sword	Galloway	Farnaby*	Martin	Black	Diamond	Nicholson	Barr R
	27/2		***6,351***	1	35			*Benjamin 83*	*Gleasure*	*Reed*	*Logan*	*Donald*	*Wilcox*	*McPherson*	*McGoldrick*	*Benjamin*	*Gilbert*	*Chard**	*Hill*	*Coy*
								Ref: D Reeves	Town travel to the County Ground minus seven regular first-teamers. Their task, therefore, is even more daunting as Graham Carr's side are 15 points clear at the top of the table. They put up a terrific fight, but are eventually sunk by Ian Benjamin's volley following Reed's knockdown.											
31	A	CARDIFF		18	D	0-0	0-0		Whitehead	Brown	Fleming	Matthews M	Sword	Galloway	Farnaby	Martin	Black	Longhurst	Nicholson*	Diamond
	3/3		*1,785*	14	36				*Moseley*	*Kerr*	*Ford*	*Wimbleton*	*Brignull*	*Boyle*	*Curtis*	*Simmons**	*Horrix*	*Platnauer*	*Rogers*	*Bartlett*
								Ref: R Hamer	Frank Burrows' Bluebirds, who have been struggling to win at home of late, deserve to win this game, but they are thwarted by Whitehead. He is outstanding all night, making his best save at the feet of Simmons. When he does drop a cross, Horrix's lob is cleared off the line by Sword.											
32	H	CREWE		19	L	0-3	0-1		Whitehead	Brown	Fleming	Matthews M	Sword	Galloway	Sanderson	Martin	Black*	Longhurst	Farnaby	Diamond
	7/3		994	16	36			*Platt 24, Brown 46 (og), Sword 56 (og)*	*Parkin*	*Goodison*	*Pemberton*	*Thomas*	*Wright*	*Gannon*	*Platt*	*Bodak**	*Pullar*	*Milligan*	*Blissett*	*Billinge*
								Ref: G Tyson	On a snow-covered pitch, the visitors hardly have to work hard for their goals. Town can't score at the right end, so try their luck at their own. Already a goal down, Brown slices Platt's cross past Whitehead 45 seconds after half-time. Sword repeats the trick, turning in Blissett's cross.											
33	A	TRANMERE		17	W	4-3	3-2	Martin 16, Matthews, 20, Brown 27,	Whitehead	Brown	**Harrison**	Matthews M	Knill	Galloway	Sanderson	Martin	Black	Longhurst	Sword	
	13/3		*1,653*	15	39			*Moore 4, Muir 42, Bell 90* [Sword 87]	*O'Rourke*	*Thorpe*	*Mungall*	*Williams*	*Moore*	*Vickers*	*Morrissey*	*Bell*	*Bullock*	*Muir*	*Anderson*	
								Ref: J Bray	A short break in Whitby works wonders. Town come from behind to storm into a 3-1 lead. Muir's goal sets up an exciting second half. Town withstand an onslaught, then seal the game with Sword's late header. Ayre slates Rovers player-boss Ronnie Moore for clattering Whitehead.											
34	H	WOLVES		17	L	3-4	0-2	Longhurst 67, Allison 76, Sanderson 87	Whitehead	Brown	Harrison	Matthews M	Knill	Galloway	Sanderson	Martin	Black	Longhurst	Sword*	**Allison**
	17/3		2,079	6	39			*Stoutt 19, Mutch 31, 58, Thompson 78*	*Kendall*	*Stoutt*	*Barnes*	*Kelly*	*Clarke*	*Robertson*	*Thompson*	*Dennison*	*Bull*	*Mutch*	*Holmes*	
								Ref: K Lupton	Allison comes off the bench and within 15 minutes has scored to narrow Wolves' lead to one goal after they had been three up. Then Galloway trips Mutch for Thompson's penalty. His kick comes back off the post but he nets the rebound with Town claiming no one else played the ball.											

No	Venue	Opponent	Att	Pos	Res	F-A	H-T	Scorers, Times, Referees	1	2	3	4	5	6	7	8	9	10	11	12
35	H	TORQUAY		19	L	2-4	1-2	Galloway 21, Allison 55	Whitehead	Brown	Harrison	Matthews M	Knill	Galloway	Sanderson	Martin	Black	Allison	Sword*	Farnaby
21/3			1,246	*22*	39			*Dobson 20, 37, 46, 51*	*Allen*	*Richards*	*Kelly*	*Camm*	*Cole*	*McLoughlin*	*Gardiner*	*Musker**	*Walsh*	*Mann*	*Dobson*	*Dawkins*
								Ref: K Breen	This is the latest match to be billed as Town's last. If it is, then Torquay's Paul Dobson makes it one to remember, scoring all his side's goals. The Gulls are battling to avoid relegation to the Conference, and amateurish home defending helps them to their first away win of the season.											
36	A	ALDERSHOT		19	L	1-4	1-2	Allison 33	Whitehead	Brown*	Fleming	Matthews M	Knill	Galloway	Sanderson	Martin	Black	Allison	Harrison	Holden
24/3			*1,911*	*7*	39			*McDonald 15, Burvill 17, Barnes 51, [Johnson 68]*	*Lange*	*Mazzon*	*Friar*	*King*	*Smith*	*Anderson*	*Barnes*	*Burvill*	*Langley*	*McDonald*	*Johnson*	
								Ref: M Dimblebee	'Men against boys,' is how Ayre describes this game, as his side concedes four goals for the third consecutive match. Aldershot will eventually go up via the play-offs, but that is no excuse. In the rain, Burvill is chief tormentor, and it's he who tees up Barnes to effectively kill the game.											
37	A	SWANSEA			W	2-0	0-0	Black 55, Sanderson 75	**Sinclair**	Brown	Harrison	Matthews M	Knill	Galloway	Sanderson	Martin*	Black	Longhurst	Holden	Allison
29/3			*3,972*		42				*Hughes*	*Harrison*	*Phelan*	*Stevenson*	*Melville*	*Emmanuel*	*Atkinson*	*McCarthy*	*Raynor**	*Pascoe*	*Hutchison*	*Hough*
								Ref: H Taylor	Town are hanging on to Longhurst and he returns to the side to help them to a sensational victory. Black smashes in the first when Martin gets a head to Sanderson's cross, and Sanderson, who never scores simple goals, gets the other. He reaches Matthews' chip to volley over Hughes.											
38	H	SCUNTHORPE		17	D	1-1	1-1	Brown 35p	Sinclair	Brown	Harrison	Matthews M	Knill	Galloway	Sanderson	Martin	Black	Longhurst	Holden*	Allison
3/4			1,232	*15*	43			*Lister 38p*	*Green*	*Russell*	*Atkins*	*Harle*	*Hunter*	*Smith*	*Money*	*Lister*	*Johnson*	*Flounders*	*Hill*	
								Ref: A Robinson	Phil Brown marks his 300th league appearance with a penalty. Longhurst wins it, but he is going away from goal when Hunter makes minimal contact. Three minutes later, Harrison is adjudged to have pulled Flounders' shirt for Lister's penalty. 'At least the ref was consistent,' – Ayre.											
39	A	EXETER		18	D	2-2	1-1	Black 25, Brown 90p	Sinclair	Brown	Harrison	Matthews M	Knill	Galloway	Sanderson	Martin	Black	Longhurst	Holden	
11/4			*1,698*	*10*	44			*Edwards 28, 86*	*Shaw*	*O'Connell*	*Viney*	*Marker*	*Pugh*	*Olsson*	*Batty*	*Edwards*	*Kellow*	*Keough*	*Roberts**	*Harrower*
								Ref: J Deakin	Calderdale Council have stepped in to save Halifax Town. Phil Brown, who broke a window here last season, steps up to earn Town a point with another penalty in the last minute after O'Connell handled. The game looked lost when Edwards hit his second just four minutes earlier.											
40	H	CAMBRIDGE		15	W	1-0	0-0	Black 59	Sinclair	Brown	Harrison	Matthews M	Knill	Galloway	Sanderson	Martin	Black	Longhurst	Holden	
14/4			1,194	*9*	47				*Branagan*	*Measham*	*Kimble A*	*Smith*	*Crowe*	*Beck*	*Butler*	*McEvoy*	*Rigby**	*Crown*	*Schiavi*	*Kimble G*
								Ref: G Courtney	Chris Turner's Cambridge look anything but play-off candidates. They contribute to a dull game, the first half of which is as poor as any half seen at the Shay this season. The winning goal is a curious affair. Black touches in Brown's free-kick, but Crowe says it went in off his chest.											
41	A	LINCOLN		16	D	0-0	0-0		Roche	Brown	Harrison	Matthews M	Knill	Galloway	Sanderson	Martin	Black	Longhurst	Holden	
18/4			*1,673*	*19*	48				*Butler*	*Daniel*	*Franklin*	*Cooper**	*West*	*Nicholson*	*McInnes*	*Lund*	*Gilligan*	*Hood*	*McGinley*	*Gamble*
								Ref: K Morton	Lincoln City arrive at the Shay in the midst of a depressing run - one win in their last eleven games - that will ultimately cost them their league place. Manager George Kerr has gone, and full-back Peter Daniel has taken over team affairs. This game is as boring as the scoreline suggests.											
42	H	HARTLEPOOL		15	W	1-0	0-0	Allison 68	Roche	Brown	Harrison	Matthews M	Knill	Galloway	Sanderson	Martin*	Black	Longhurst	Holden	Allison
20/4			1,115	*18*	51				*Blackburn*	*Nobbs*	*McKinnon*	*Hogan*	*Smith*	*McCaffrey*	*Toman*	*Shoulder*	*Dixon*	*Gibb**	*Barrett*	*Walker*
								Ref: G Ashby	Wayne Allison hasn't scored for the youth team for five matches, but when he replaces Martin after 66 minutes, he needs only two minutes to register his fourth senior goal. When Longhurst is robbed, the ball breaks for Allison, who crashes in the game's only goal from twelve yards.											
43	A	HEREFORD		15	L	0-1	0-1		Roche	Brown	Harrison	Matthews M	Knill	Galloway*	Sanderson	Martin	Black	Allison	Holden	Nicholson
26/4			*2,061*	*17*	51			*Kearns 39*	*Rose*	*Pejic*	*Devine*	*Rogers*	*Stevens*	*Rodgerson*	*Spooner*	*Carter*	*Phillips*	*Kearns*	*Leadbitter*	
								Ref: R Nixon	Halifax's fourth successive loss at Edgar Street means they are the last team in the division to lose in April. They are unlucky, however, to see Black twice hit the post, the second off a volley saved by Rose. Halifax-born Phillips heads down for Kearns to score his 19th of the season.											
44	H	COLCHESTER		15	D	0-0	0-0		Roche	Brown	Harrison	Matthews M	Knill	Galloway	Sanderson*	Martin	Black	Allison	Holden	Nicholson
29/4			**911**	*5*	52				*Chamberlain*	*English*	*Norman*	*Reeves*	*Day*	*Hedman*	*White*	*Adcock*	*Lowe*	*Hinshelwood*	*Wilkins**	*Chatterton*
								Ref: M Heath	The attendance is the lowest crowd in the league anywhere this season. Those present don't see much action, although Knill and Adcock both hit the bar. With a minute to go, Black turns the ball in, then is horrified to see the linesman flagging that Holden had earlier run it out of play.											
45	A	ROCHDALE		16	L	3-5	1-1	Black 34, Seasman 47 (og), Brown 87p	Roche	Brown	Harrison	Matthews M	Knill	Galloway	Sanderson	**Richardson***	Black	Longhurst	Holden	**Sharpe**
4/5			*2,992*	*22*	52			*S'ds 5p, B'l 50, 69, W'shaw 80, H'den 83*	*Welch*	*Johnson*	*Grant*	*Holden*	*Bramhall*	*Seasman*	*Conning*	*Simmonds*	*Parlane*	*Reid*	*Wakenshaw*	
								Ref: P Haynes	Simmonds nets a fifth-minute penalty, but when Seasman deflects in Longhurst's shot to give Town a 2-1 lead, Rochdale have one foot in the Conference. But they score four goals to change the game and their fortunes. Brown equals Town's club record of eight penalties in a season.											
46	H	PETERBOROUGH		15	W	1-0	1-0	Holden 41	Roche	Brown	Harrison	Matthews M	Knill	Galloway	Shaw	Thornber*	Black	Longhurst	Holden	Sanderson
9/5			1,004	*10*	55				*Crichton*	*Paris*	*Gunn*	*Collins*	*Price*	*Gage*	*Luke*	*Carr**	*Nuttell*	*Fife*	*Kelly*	*Butterworth*
		Home	Away					Ref: R Bridges	Mick Jones returns to the Shay, presents Rick Holden with his Player of the Year award, then watches him drive in a stunning goal off Brown's cross to win the game. Holden later volleys onto the bar, but most supporters seem more concerned with the news of Burnley's relegation fight.											
Average		1,332	2,620																	

Littlewoods Cup					F-A	H-T	Scorers, Times, and Referees	1	2	3	4	5	6	7	8	9	10	11	subs used
1:1	A	HUDDERSFIELD		L	1-3	0-1	Brown 70	Roche	Fleming	Brown	Robinson*	Knill	Galloway	Sanderson	Black	Diamond	Longhurst	Nicholson	Shaw
26/8			2,363 2:				*Cork 18, Cowling 56, Shearer 83*	*Cox*	*Brown*	*Bray*	*Doyle*	*Webster*	*Jones**	*Cooper*	*Cork*	*Shearer*	*Wilson Phil*	*Cowling*	*Winter*
							Ref: D Phillips	The Shaymen are the better team on the night, but the Terriers take their chances. Cork can't believe his luck when he is left with an open goal to score the first. Brown's free-kick through the wall puts Town back in the hunt, but Shearer pounces to make Huddersfield clear favourites.											
1:2	H	HUDDERSFIELD	11	D	2-2	2-0	Galloway 5, Thornber 32	Roche	Brown	Fleming	Robinson*	Knill	Galloway	Sanderson	Shaw^	Black	Longhurst	Nicholson	Thornber/Diamond
2/9			1,353 2:20		aet		*Cork 110, Shearer 112*	*Cox*	*Brown*	*Bray*	*Doyle*	*Webster*	*Jones*	*Raynor*	*Cork*	*Shearer*	*Wilson Phil*	*Cowling*	
							Ref: T Mills (Halifax lost 3-5 on aggregate)	Town have everything to fight for, and almost pull off an amazing win. Galloway's direct free-kick, and Thornber's volley brings Town level on aggregate. Roche, in terrific form, thinks they are through when the 90 minutes are up. But extra-time must be played, and Town bow out.											

FA Cup					F-A	H-T	Scorers, Times, and Referees	1	2	3	4	5	6	7	8	9	10	11	subs used
1	H	BOLTON	21	D	1-1	0-0	Longhurst 76	Roche	Brown	Shaw	Thornber	Knill	Galloway	Sanderson	Diamond	Black	Longhurst	Holden	
15/11			3,370 3:18				*Oghani 90*	*Farnworth*	*Scott*	*Phillips*	*Joyce*	*Came*	*Darby*	*Caldwell*	*Thompson**	*Elliott*	*Hartford*	*Gavin*	*Oghani*
							Ref: G Aplin	Bolton, managed by former Liverpool defender Phil Neal, are lucky to survive this cup-tie. Hard-up Halifax are on top for most of the match, and look set to go through when Longhurst is left free to head home. But with the seconds ticking away, sub Oghani fires in a lucky equaliser.											
1R	A	BOLTON	21	D	1-1	0-1	Brown 82	Roche	Brown	Shaw	Thornber	Knill	Galloway	Sanderson	Diamond*	Black^	Longhurst	Holden	Farnaby/Nicholson
18/11			*4,652 3:18*		aet		*Caldwell 41*	*Salmon*	*Neal*	*Phillips*	*Joyce*	*Came*	*Darby*	*Caldwell**	*Thompson*	*Elliott*	*Hartford*	*Gavin*	*Oghani*
							Ref: G Aplin	Town's display of confidence, quality and commitment gives no hint of the club's closure problems. Brown is pushed up front late on to give his side another game. In a thrilling tussle, extra-time can't separate the sides. Bolton had a goal ruled out before Caldwell's near-post header.											
1	H	BOLTON	19	L	1-3	1-1	Galloway 9	Roche	Brown	Shaw*	Thornber	Knill	Galloway	Sanderson	Diamond	Black^	Longhurst	Holden	Farnaby/Nicholson
RR 24/11			3,338 3:19				*Thompson 12, Caldwell 56, Gavin 65*	*Salmon*	*Neal*	*Phillips*	*Joyce*	*Came*	*Scott*	*Caldwell*	*Thompson*	*Elliott**	*Hartford*	*Gavin*	*Oghani*
							Ref: M Peck	After the heroics of the last two matches, Town suffer an inglorious cup exit. Galloway heads in Sanderson's corner early on, but the usually reliable defender is guilty of an horrendous backpass that leads to Caldwell putting Bolton ahead. Roche fumbles a cross for Gavin to score.											

		Home						Away					
		P	W	D	L	F	A	W	D	L	F	A	Pts
1	Northampton	46	20	2	1	56	20	10	7	6	47	33	99
2	Preston	46	16	4	3	36	18	10	8	5	36	29	90
3	Southend	46	14	4	5	43	27	11	1	11	25	28	80
4	Wolves	46	12	3	8	36	24	12	4	7	33	26	79
5	Colchester	46	15	3	5	41	20	6	4	13	23	36	70
6	Aldershot *	46	13	5	5	40	22	7	5	11	24	35	70
7	Orient	46	15	2	6	40	25	5	7	11	24	36	69
8	Scunthorpe	46	15	3	5	52	27	3	9	11	21	30	66
9	Wrexham	46	8	13	2	38	24	7	7	9	32	27	65
10	Peterborough	46	10	7	6	29	21	7	7	9	28	29	65
11	Cambridge	46	12	6	5	37	23	5	5	13	23	39	62
12	Swansea	46	13	3	7	31	21	4	8	11	25	40	62
13	Cardiff	46	6	12	5	24	18	9	4	10	24	32	61
14	Exeter	46	11	10	2	37	17	0	13	10	16	32	56
15	HALIFAX	46	10	5	8	32	32	5	5	13	27	42	55
16	Hereford	46	10	6	7	33	23	4	5	14	27	38	53
17	Crewe	46	8	9	6	38	35	5	5	13	32	37	53
18	Hartlepool	46	6	11	6	24	30	5	7	11	20	35	51
19	Stockport	46	9	6	8	25	27	4	6	13	15	42	51
20	Tranmere	46	6	10	7	32	37	5	7	11	22	35	50
21	Rochdale	46	8	8	7	31	30	3	9	11	23	43	50
22	Burnley	46	9	7	7	31	35	3	6	14	22	39	49
23	Torquay	46	8	8	7	28	29	2	10	11	28	43	48
24	Lincoln	46	8	7	8	30	27	4	5	14	15	38	43
		1104	262	154	136	844	612	136	154	262	612	844	1497

* promoted after play-offs

Odds & ends

Double wins: (2) Orient, Swansea.
Double losses: (4) Northampton, Preston, Stockport, Torquay.

Won from behind: (3) Rochdale (h), Southend (a), Tranmere (a).
Lost from in front: (3) Preston (a), Rochdale (a), Bolton (FAC) (h).

High spots: Six games unbeaten, including four consecutive wins, up to 4 February.
Beating Southend on 2 February to move in to the top half of the table.
Six games unbeaten up to 20 April.
Beating Orient 4-0.

Low spots: Seven consecutive defeats up to 30 September.
Losing at home to Stockport on 19 September and going bottom.
Losing 3-6 to Northampton, the first time Town had conceded so many goals at home since Fulham scored eight in September 1969.
Seven games without a win up to 7 March.

Player of the Year: Rick Holden.
Ever-presents: (1) Phil Brown.
Hat-tricks: (0).
Leading scorer: Phil Brown (14).

	Appearances						**Goals**			
	Lge	*Sub*	LC	*Sub*	FAC	*Sub*	**Lge**	LC	FAC	**Tot**
Allison, Wayne	**4**	*4*					**4**			**4**
Barr, Bobby		*1*								
Black, Russell	**44**	*1*	2		3		**9**			**9**
Brown, Phil	**46**		2		3		**12**	1	1	**14**
Diamond, Barry	**5**	*5*	1	*1*	3					
Farnaby, Craig	**7**	*3*				*2*	**1**			**1**
Fleming, Paul	**14**	*1*	2							
Galloway, Mick	**43**		2		3		**3**	1	1	**5**
Gregory, Paul	**6**									
Harrison, Frankie	**14**									
Holden, Rick	**31**	*1*			3		**2**			**2**
Horwood, Neil	**3**									
Knill, Alan	**41**		2		3		**3**			**3**
Longhurst, David	**41**		2		3		**10**		1	**11**
Martin, Dean	**16**						**1**			**1**
Matthews, Mick	**38**	*1*					**4**			**4**
Matthews, Neil	**9**						**2**			**2**
Nicholson, Gary	**10**	*6*	2			*2*	**1**			**1**
Richardson, Lee	**1**									
Robinson, Dave	**10**		2							
Roche, Paddy	**24**		2		3					
Sanderson, Paul	**42**	*1*	2		3		**2**			**2**
Sharpe, Phil		*1*								
Shaw, Adrian	**19**	*2*	1	*1*	3					
Sinclair, Ronnie	**4**									
Sword, Tommy	**8**						**2**			**2**
Thornber, Steve	**14**	*2*		*1*	3			1		**1**
Whitehead, Phil	**12**									
(own-goals)							**3**			**3**
28 players used	**506**	***29***	**22**	***3***	**33**	***4***	**59**	**3**	**3**	**65**

No	Date		Att	Pos	Pt	F-A	H-T	Scorers, Times, and Referees	1	2	3	4	5	6	7	8	9	10	11	subs used
1	H	DARLINGTON			D	2-2	0-1	Allison 72, Matthews N 89	Roche	Barr	Harrison	Matthews M	Robinson	Galloway	Richardson	Thornber	**Ferebee***	Black^	Holden	Matthews N/Allison
	15/8		1,342		1			MacDonald 8, Currie 73	Roberts	Hinchley*	Morgan	Hine	Robinson	McAughtrie	Outterside	Ward	MacDonald	Currie	Bell^	Stoneh'se/Worth'ton
								Ref: P Danson	The Football League are allowing two substitutes for the first time. Wayne Allison and Neil Matthews come on in the 66th minute and create a record as they both score. Roche keeps Town in the game, but it's Matthews, latching on Robinson's knockdown, who saves the game late on.											
2	A	WOLVES		4	W	1-0	0-0	Galloway 74	Roche	Brown	Harrison	Matthews M	Robinson	Galloway	Richardson	Thornber	Matthews N	Allison*	Holden	Black
	22/8		*7,223*	*18*	4				Kendall	Stoutt	Clarke	Streete	Robertson	Robinson	Dennison	Thompson	Bull	Mutch*	Downing	Gallagher
								Ref: J Rushton	Graham Turner's Wolves are title favourites. But Mick Galloway rocks them when he powers in a header in the middle of a thunderstorm to win the game. Future England international Steve Bull is earlier thwarted by Paddy Roche when he latched onto Galloway's weak backpass.											
3	H	ROCHDALE		8	L	1-2	1-0	Holden 11	Roche	Brown	Harrison	Matthews M	Robinson	Galloway	Richardson*	Thornber	Matthews N^	Allison	Holden	Black/Ferebee
	28/8		2,275	*3*	4			Simmonds 46p, 53	Welch	Lomax	Hampton	Reid	Bramhall	Smart	Seasman	Simmonds	Parlane	Coyle	Gavin	
								Ref: N Ashley	Holden causes all sorts of problems in the first half, and his opening goal from 25 yards is no more than he deserves. But Lyndon Simmonds' penalty for hands by Mick Matthews just after the break is Rochdale's spur. Town could have gone top, but Ayre freely admits, 'We blew it.'											
4	A	WREXHAM			D	2-2	0-1	Brown 68p, Black 90	Roche	Brown	Harrison	Matthews M	Robinson	Galloway	Richardson^	Thornber	Matthews N*	Black	Holden	Allison/Martin
	31/8		*1,661*		5			Cunnington 29, Steel 49	Salmon	Williams	Jones	Hinnigan	Cooke	Bowden	Buxton	Preece*	Steel^	Russell	Cunnington	Hunter/Wright
								Ref: P Vanes	Dixie McNeil's side cannot believe they let this game slip. Steel dives bravely to head in their second, and seemingly Wrexham are coasting. But the linesman flags for handball, and Brown gladly accepts Town's fortuitous penalty. In injury-time, Black's scrambled goal saves the day.											
5	H	NEWPORT		9	W	**3-1**	0-0	Holden 80, Matthews N 89, 90	Roche	Brown	Harrison	Matthews M	Shaw	Galloway	Martin^	Thornber	Ferebee*	Allison	Holden	Matthews N/**McP'ps**
	5/9		1,095	*24*	8			Collins 62	Bradshaw	Hodson	Sherlock	Thackeray	Williams	Gibbins	Giles*	Taylor	Collins	Millett	Tupling	Withers
								Ref: A Robinson	This will be Newport's last visit to the Shay in their present guise. They look like heading for victory when Galloway deflects in Collins' shot. Town would settle for a point after Holden's equaliser, but when the ball runs for Matthews, he nets the first of his brace for a sensational win.											
6	A	BOLTON		12	L	0-2	0-1		Roche	Brown	Harrison	Matthews M	Shaw	Galloway	Richardson*	Thornber	Matthews N	Allison	Holden	Black
	12/9		*4,445*	*2*	8			Henshaw 37, Brown 53 (og)	Felgate	Scott	Crombie	Thompson	Came	Sutton	Henshaw	Joyce	Morgan	Thomas	Savage	
								Ref: G Aplin	When Mick Matthews scorches in a volley, Town think they have drawn level. But Geoff Alpin has blown for half-time before the ball crosses the line. Ayre believes this poor decision costs his team. When the ball comes off Shaw, Brown can only help it over for Bolton's second goal.											
7	H	SWANSEA		9	W	**3-1**	2-0	Matthews M 4, Holden 7, Matthews N 86	Roche	Brown	Harrison	Matthews M	Martin	Shaw	Richardson	Thornber	Matthews N	Allison*	Holden	McPhillips
	16/9		1,236	*12*	11			Raynor 75	Hughes	Harrison	Coleman^	Melville	Knill	Davies	Williams	McCarthy	Raynor	Pascoe	Emmanuel*	Andrews/Hough
								Ref: J Ireland	Swansea manager Terry Yorath is the latest to join the Halifax fan club, admitting Town were the better side. But Town need another late goal from Neil Matthews to make the game safe. They are almost punished for living on a two-goal lead, started by Mick Matthews' 25-yard effort.											
8	H	TRANMERE		4	W	2-1	0-0	Matthews N 50, Brown 62	Roche	Brown	Harrison	Matthews M	Shaw	Galloway	Richardson*	Thornber	Matthews N	Allison^	Holden	Black/McPhillips
	18/9		1,754	*21*	14			McKenna 53	O'Rourke	Mungall	McCarrick	Hughes	Thorpe	Vickers	Morrissey	Williams	McKenna	Muir	Aspinall	
								Ref: B Hill	The Shaymen show their character to join the 4th Division pace-setters. They are clearly second best to John King's Tranmere side in the first half. After the break they can afford to squander their lead after Matthews' goal, as Brown heads the winner with the game's third headed goal.											
9	A	CAMBRIDGE		8	L	1-2	1-2	Holden 44	Roche	Brown	Harrison	Matthews M*	Shaw	Galloway	Richardson	Thornber	Black^	Allison	Holden	Martin/McPhillips
	26/9		*1,805*	*9*	14			Crown 25, 73	Branagan	Poole	Murray	Beattie	Smith	Beck	Butler	Clayton	Rigby	Crown	Kimble G	
								Ref: T Ward	David Crown takes his tally into double figures. He is grateful to Mick Matthews for an under-hit back-pass for his first goal, and is left totally free for his second. Holden's half-volley gives Town hope, but they ride their luck after the break when Rigby strikes the underside of the bar.											
10	A	CARDIFF		9	D	0-0	0-0		Roche	Brown	Harrison	Matthews M	Shaw	Galloway	Robinson	Thornber	Black*	Martin	Holden	McPhillips
	29/9		*3,666*	*4*	15				Moseley	Ford	Platnauer	Wimbleton	Stevenson	Boyle	Curtis	Bartlett	Gilligan	McDermott	Kelly*	Sanderson
								Ref: G Ashby	Ayre is unconcerned that Frank Burrows' side have just won their last three games, and plays an attacking formation. Galloway leads the line, but it's his colleagues at the back who earn Town a point as the three-man defence of Robinson, Shaw and Martin give nothing away all night.											
11	H	HEREFORD		7	W	2-1	1-1	Matthews N 7, Holden 67	Roche	Brown	Harrison	Matthews M^	Shaw	Galloway	Robinson	Thornber	Matthews N*	Martin	Holden	McPhillips/Barr
	3/10		1,414	*20*	18			Rodgerson 11	Rose	Jones	Dalziel*	Devine	Pejic	Spooner	Rodgerson	Bowyer	Phillips	Stevens	McLoughlin	Benbow
								Ref: P Tyldesley	Hereford boss John Newman resigned yesterday, so coach Ian Bowyer (ex-Forest) takes temporary charge. His side looks like gaining a point with a battling display when Rick Holden intercepts Benbow's back-pass, rounds Rose to score, then breaks into an ape-like celebration dance.											

No/Date	Venue	Opponent/Att	Pos	Res/Pts	F-A	H-T	Scorers, Times, and Referees	1	2	3	4	5	6	7	8	9	10	11	subs used
12	A	SCUNTHORPE	11	L	0-1	0-0		Roche	Brown	Harrison	Matthews M	Shaw	Galloway	Robinson	Thornber	Matthews N*	Martin^	Holden	McPhillips/Barr
10/10		*2,105*	*5*	18			*Johnson 61*	*Green*	*Russell*	*Atkins*	*Taylor*	*Lister*	*Money*	*Dixon*	*Harle*	*Johnson*	*Flounders*	*Hill*	
							Ref: K Redfern	Scunthorpe include in their side new £20,000 signing Kevin Taylor from Palace, and he has the perfect chance in the opening minutes to open his account, but Roche saves at his feet. Roche has to be – and is – at his best, but he is beaten by Johnson's blistering 25-yarder on the hour.											
13	H	STOCKPORT	4	W	2-0	2-0	Martin 5, 35	Roche	Brown !	Harrison	Matthews M	Robinson	Galloway	Martin	Thornber	Ferebee	McPhillips*	Holden	Barr
16/10		1,696	*21*	21				*Marples*	*Scott*	*Bailey*	*Robinson*	*Bullock*	*Williams*	*Hodkinson*	*Colville*	*Cronin**	*Burke*	*Birch^*	*Farnaby/Edwards*
							Ref: K Walmsley	This Friday night fixture enables Town to move within four points of top spot. Martin gets the both goals, the second of which is a classic after he receives a return pass from McPhillips. But victory is soured somewhat by Brown's 80th-minute sending-off for a second bookable offence.											
14	A	HARTLEPOOL		L	1-2	0-1	Matthews M 87	Roche	Brown	Harrison	Matthews M	Robinson	Galloway	Martin	Thornber	Ferebee*	Allison	Holden	McPhillips
21/10		*2,768*		21			*Toman 14, Barratt 78*	*Prudhoe*	*Barratt*	*Kennedy*	*Nobbs*	*Smith*	*Stokes*	*Honour*	*Toman*	*Baker*	*Dixon*	*McKinnon*	
							Ref: T Fitzharris	Ayre points the fingers at his strikers for failing to win this game. They miss a hatful of chances, and in the end only have Mick Matthews' late goal to show for their efforts. Pool already have the home crowd on their backs when Barratt fires in an angled drive against the run of play.											
15	H	PETERBOROUGH	13	D	0-0	0-0		Roche	Brown	Harrison	Matthews M	Robinson	Galloway	Martin	Thornber	Ferebee*	Allison	Holden	McPhillips
24/10		1,615	*5*	22				*Neenan*	*Paris*	*Gunn*	*Gooding*	*Nightingale*	*Price*	*Luke*	*Halsall*	*Lawrence*	*Carr*	*Collins*	
							Ref: K Lupton	Mick Jones returns but says Peterborough will do his old club no favours. They have won their last three games, but here Town give as good as they get in a thrilling contest. For the Posh, Lawrence misses with the goal at his mercy, whilst for Town, Holden's 30-yarder just goes wide.											
16	A	LEYTON ORIENT	15	L	**1-4**	1-3	Holden 16	Roche	Shaw	Harrison	Matthews M	Robinson	Galloway	Martin	Thornber	Matthews N^	Allison*	Holden	McPhillips/Ferebee
31/10		*3,208*	*2*	22			*Shinners 6, 15, Hales 10p, Hull 60*	*Wells*	*Howard*	*Dickenson*	*Smalley*	*Day*	*Hull*	*Hales*	*Castle*	*Shinners*	*Harvey*	*Comfort*	
							Ref: N Butler	Town find there's no way back after conceding three goals within the first 15 minutes. After Shinners' opener from close range, Shaw gives away a penalty for the slightest of pushes on Harvey. Holden's goal fails to inspire his team-mates, some of whom Ayre describes as 'homers'.											
17	H	BURNLEY	12	W	2-1	1-1	Martin 11, Matthews N 80	Roche	Brown	Harrison	Matthews M	Shaw	Galloway	Martin	Thornber	Matthews N	Allison*	Holden	Ferebee
3/11		**3,419**	*9*	25			*Taylor 23*	*Pearce*	*Daniel*	*Malley*	*James*	*Davies*	*Gardner*	*Farrell*	*Grewcock*	*Oghani*	*Comstive*	*Taylor*	
							Ref: J Lloyd	Neil Matthews has been practising overhead kicks in training, much to the amusement of his colleagues. But they are eating their words when he provides the winning goal with such an attempt. Town go in front, but Holden's poor clearance leads to Taylor equalising before the break.											
18	H	COLCHESTER	12	L	1-2	1-1	Galloway 42	Roche	Brown	Harrison*	Matthews M	Shaw	Galloway	Martin	Thornber	Matthews N	Ferebee	Holden	Allison
6/11		1,432	*1*	25			*Wilkins 7, Chatterton 84p*	*Benstead*	*Hinshelwood*	*Grenfell*	*Chatterton*	*Baker*	*Smith*	*White*	*Wilkins*	*Tempest*	*English*	*Reeves*	
							Ref: M Dimblebee	Colchester go top in controversial fashion. The game is only five minutes old when Town full-back Frankie Harrison has his leg broken after an horrendous challenge by debutant Gary Smith, who is not punished. The U's' winner is a harsh penalty given by the linesman for handball.											
19	A	SCARBOROUGH	16	D	1-1	0-1	Black 85	Roche	Brown	Fleming*	Matthews M	Robinson	Shaw	Martin^	Thornber	Matthews N	Black	Holden	Barr/Ferebee
21/11		*2,892*	*6*	26			*Lowe 12*	*McDonagh*	*Kamara*	*Thompson*	*Bennyworth*	*Richards*	*Kendall*	*Russell*	*Graham*	*McHale*	*Hamill*	*Lowe*	
							Ref: J Watson	Scarborough, with five former Town players in their side, are the League's newest club, and have made a promising start. They look good for both points when Lowe scores from a tight angle. But Holden, shadowed by Kamara, for once gets free to set up Black's undeserved equaliser.											
20	H	CREWE	16	L	1-2	0-0	McPhillips 73	Roche	Brown	McPhillips	Matthews M	Shaw	Robinson	Martin	Thornber	Matthews N	Black*	Holden	Ferebee
27/11		1,416	*11*	26			*Murphy 48, Platt 80*	*Greygoose*	*Goodison*	*Pemberton*	*Murphy*	*Billing*	*Gage*	*Platt*	*Bodak**	*Parker*	*Milligan*	*Macowat*	*Morton^/Wright*
							Ref: W Flood	A collection for Frankie Harrison raises £198. On a frozen pitch, two gift goals hand Crewe victory. Mick Matthews slips for Murphy's goal. Robinson's backheader to Roche leads to Platt's winner after McPhillips' equaliser. Crewe sub Wright replaces sub Morton in the 89th minute.											
21	A	TORQUAY	16	W	2-1	1-1	Matthews N 39, Holden 75	Roche	Brown	Barr	Matthews M	Fleming^	Shaw	Martin*	Thornber	Matthews N	Black	Holden	Ferebee/Richardson
12/12		*2,422*		29			*Loram 33*	*Allen*	*McNichol*	*Pearce*	*Haslegrave*	*Cole*	*Impey*	*Dawkins*	*Lloyd*	*Nardiello*	*Loram*	*Dobson !*	
							Ref: R Gifford	Torquay lose top scorer Paul Dobson after 18 minutes, sent off for kicking out at Dean Martin, then seem hell-bent on revenge. The first half ends with Fleming going off on a stretcher, and police intervening with the players. A superb individual goal by Holden gives Town the points.											
22	H	EXETER		W	2-0	1-0	Collins 8 (og), Heathcote 83	Roche	Brown	Barr	Matthews M	Robinson	Shaw	**Heathcote**	Thornber^	Matthews N	Black*	Holden	Allison/Richardson
18/12		1,302		32				*Shaw*	*Harrower*	*Viney*	*Carter*	*Taylor*	*Massey**	*Batty^*	*Cooper*	*Edwards*	*O'Connell*	*Collins*	*Olsson/Rowbotham*
							Ref: G Tyson	Exeter lost their manager Colin Appleton a week ago and John Delve has taken over. On a pitch that cuts up badly, the side goes behind after only eight minutes when Collins slides the ball into his own net. On-loan Heathcote heads in his first-ever goal off Mick Matthews' free-kick.											
23	H	CAMBRIDGE	14	D	1-1	1-1	Black 8	Roche	Brown	Barr	Matthews M^	Robinson	Heathcote	Martin	Thornber	Matthews N	Black*	Holden	Allison/Richardson
23/12		1,667	*13*	33			*Horwood 13*	*Branagan*	*Poole*	*Kimble*	*Smith*	*Crewe*	*Beck*	*Butler*	*Clayton*	*Benjamin*	*Horwood*	*Pugh*	
							Ref: N Midgley	The pitch is like a glue-pot, and though Cambridge are highly rated by Billy Ayre, it's his own side that create the better openings. Both Black and Horwood score first-half goals from corners. Neil Matthews fluffs a one-on-one in the 75th minute, denied by £100,000 rated Branagan.											

No	Date		Att	Pos	Pt	F-A	H-T	Scorers, Times, and Referees	1	2	3	4	5	6	7	8	9	10	11	subs used
24	A	ROCHDALE		15	D	0-0	0-0		Roche	Brown	Barr	Matthews M*	Robinson	Heathcote	Martin	Thornber	Matthews N	Black^	Holden	Richardson/Allison
	1/1		2,050	23	34				Welch	Seasman	Mycock	Reid	Bramhall	Lomax	Coyle	Simmonds	Walling*	Warren	Gavin	Holden
								Ref: F Roberts	This game is a lottery, with constant rain making worse an already soaked pitch. The players skip through the puddles as entertaining football is kept to the minimum. In the second half, Brown has a goal ruled out for pushing, then Simmonds goes through for Dale, only to hit the post.											
25	H	BOLTON		16	D	0-0	0-0		Roche	Brown	Barr	Matthews M	Robinson	Heathcote	Martin	Richardson	Matthews N	Allison	Holden	
	12/1		2,689	4	35				Felgate	Scott	Neal	Henshaw	Came	Sutton	Storey	Thompson	Stevens	Morgan	Darby	
								Ref: J Ireland	Phil Neal's side are hoping to return to Division 3 at the first attempt. They're on course, but he's relieved to leave the Shay with a point. After only 60 seconds, Allison flashes a shot just wide to herald the start of Town's dominance. Brown can't believe his ten-yard header sailed over.											
26	A	TRANMERE		16	L	0-2	0-2		Roche	Brown	Barr	Matthews M	Robinson	Heathcote	Martin	Richardson	Matthews N*	Allison^	Holden	McPhillips/Fleming
	15/1		3,317	18	35			Morrissey 22, Muir 57	Chamberlain	Higgins	McCarrick	Martindale	Moore	Vickers	Morrissey	Harvey	Steel	Muir	Mungall	
								Ref: J Deakin	Tranmere have had a disappointing first half of the season, but are showing signs of picking up on this convincing display. Morrissey plays a one-two with Muir before crashing in the first. Below par Town sees Mick Matthews hit the bar before Muir seals victory in the next minute.											
27	A	SWANSEA		16	D	1-1	1-1	Allison 19	Roche	Brown	Barr	Matthews M	Heathcote	Richardson	Martin	Thornber	Matthews N	Allison	Holden	
	23/1		5,064	10	36			Pascoe 20	Hughes	Harrison	Lewis J	Lewis D	Knill	James	Davies*	Raynor	Davey	Pascoe	Andrews	Allon
								Ref: D Hedges	Halifax are enjoying a good run in the Sherpa Van Trophy. They've just beaten Chesterfield to reach the Northern quarter-finals. Confidence is high, and Allison proves it by firing in for 1-0 although Swansea's reply is swift. Allison has a glorious chance from eight yards but puts wide.											
28	A	NEWPORT		18	L	0-1	0-0		Roche	Brown	Barr	Matthews M	Heathcote	Richardson*	Martin	Thornber	Matthews N	Black^	Holden	Fleming/McPhillips
	5/2		1,509	24	36			Mann 58	Coles	Hodson	Sherlock	Thackeray	Carr	Osborne	Jones	Gibbins	Brook	Mann	Bodmin	
								Ref: A Seville	Brian Eastick is attempting to revive Newport, who are heading out of the League. But on Comic Relief Day, the joke is on Town as they fluff a number of first-half chances, then fall to Mann's low volley just after the break. County are eight points adrift, and will not meet Town again.											
29	H	WOLVES		17	W	2-1	1-1	Holden 35, Brown 75	Roche	Brown	Barr	Matthews M	Robinson	Fleming	Martin	Thornber	Matthews N	Allison	Holden	
	16/2		2,281	1	39			Bellamy 13	Kendall	Bellamy*	Thompson	Streete	Robertson	Robinson	Purdie^	Vaughan	Bull	Mutch	Downing	Holmes/Gallagher
								Ref: A Robinson	In this all-ticket match, Town erase the memory of defeat at Newport to beat the league leaders. Wolves' strike force of Mutch and Bull, who have netted 53 goals between them, is kept in check. Town come from behind to win thanks to Holden's deflected shot and Brown's header.											
30	A	DARLINGTON		17	L	1-4	1-2	Allison 7 [Ward 78, 80]	Roche	Brown	Barr	Matthews M	Robinson	Fleming	Martin	Richardson*	Matthews N	Allison	Holden	Black
	20/2		1,824	6	39			Stonehouse 5p, MacDonald 14,	Granger	Outterside	Morgan	Robinson	Bonnyman	Hine	Roberts	Ward	MacDonald	Currie	Stonehouse	
								Ref: D Shaw	Darlington avenge Sherpa Van Trophy defeat by Town here two days earlier, but they need a linesman's help. He flags for Stonehouse's fifth-minute penalty, apparently for pulling. After Allison's swift reply, he signals MacDonald's shot had crossed the line before Brown heads clear.											
31	H	WREXHAM			W	2-0	1-0	Matthews M 6, Holden 72	Roche	Brown	Barr	Matthews M	Robinson	Fleming	Martin	Richardson	Matthews N	Allison*	Holden	McPhillips
	23/2		1,284		42				Salmon	Wright	Jones	Hinnigan	Cooke	Flynn	Preece	Hunter	Buxton	Russell	Carter	
								Ref: N Bailey	The Shaymen turn it on at home on a bitterly cold evening, with Rick Holden in top form. After Mick Matthews rams home the first goal, it's the Town winger who drives in an angled shot for a deserved goal. Short-sighted Wrexham supporters call for the sacking of Dixie McNeil.											
32	A	HEREFORD		18	L	1-2	0-2	Holden 74	Roche	Brown	Barr	Matthews M^	Robinson	Fleming	Martin	Thornber	Matthews N	McPhillips*	Holden	Black/Richardson
	27/2		1,905	16	42			Stevens 8, Spooner 11	Rose	Jones	McLoughlin	Stevens	Pejic	Spooner^	Rodgerson	Dalziel	Phillips*	Stant	Leadbitter	Benbow/Mallender
								Ref: R Groves	Hereford, like Town, are showing indifferent form. They have something to hang onto when Spooner fires in their second after only eleven minutes. Town rally strongly after the break. Holden hits the post before scoring off McPhillips' flick. Richardson almost saves it at the death.											
33	H	CARDIFF		18	L	0-1	0-0		Roche	Brown	Barr	Matthews M	Robinson	Fleming	Martin	Thornber*	Matthews N	Black	Holden^	Richardson/McPhillips
	1/3		1,128	2	42			Bartlett 73	Roberts	Bater	Kelly	Wimbleton	Stevenson	Boyle	Sanderson	Ford	Gilligan	McDermott	Bartlett	
								Ref: K Breen	The visiting fans are waving their daffodils as promotion-chasing Cardiff record a St David's Day smash-and-grab win. They create only two real chances, but score with their second. In the last minute, Town claim a penalty but the ref sees a push on Neil Matthews as outside the box.											
34	A	STOCKPORT		18	L	0-1	0-1		Roche	Brown	Barr	Matthews M	Robinson	Richardson	Martin	Thornber	Matthews N	Allison	Holden	
	4/3		2,171	22	42			Colville 36	Marples	Farnaby	McKenzie	Robinson	Thorpe	Williams	Hodkinson	Colville	Entwistle	Hartford	Willis	
								Ref: J Lloyd	Town enjoy a lot of the ball but fail to find that cutting edge. Stockport, under player-manager Asa Hartford, the former Scotland international, are next to bottom, and record only their second win in 16 outings. Bob Colville nips in to score their goal when Robinson is caught napping.											

35	H	SCUNTHORPE	17	D	2-2	2-0	Duffield 2, 10	Roche	Brown	Barr	Matthews M	Shaw	Richardson	Martin	**Blain**	Duffield	Allison	Holden	
	12/3	1,807	*4*	43			*Harle 60p, Lister 87*	*Green*	*Money*	*Longden*	*Taylor*	*Lister*	*Nichol*	*Dixon*	*Harle*	*Johnson*	*Flounders*	*Hill**	*Brown*
							Ref: P Harrison	Having lost on penalties to Burnley in the Sherpa Van semi-final, Town suffer more penalty woe when Roche saves Harle's spot-kick, only for the ref to award a re-take. Harle scores with his second kick to start the Iron fightback after on-loan Duffield had given Town a quick-fire lead.											
36	A	PETERBOROUGH	19	L	0-1	0-0		Roche	Brown	Barr*	Matthews M	Robinson	Kendall	Martin	Thornber	Duffield^	Allison	Richardson	Shaw/Matthews N
	26/3	*2,308*	*11*	43			*Gooding 90p*	*Neenan*	*Paris*	*Collins^*	*Gooding*	*Gunn*	*Price*	*Nightingale*	*Halsall**	*Phillips*	*Corner*	*Luke*	*Nuttall/Kelly*
							Ref: D Reeves	Town seem to miss Rick Holden, who has been sold to Watford. This is a disappointing game won by Peterborough after all the action is saved for the last minute. Allison fluffs a gilt-edged chance at one end before Gooding scores a penalty at the other after he was tripped by Kendall.											
37	A	COLCHESTER	19	L	1-2	1-0	Duffield 12	Roche	Brown	Matthews N	Matthews M	Robinson	Shaw	Martin*	Thornber	Duffield	Allison	Richardson	Kendall
	1/4	*1,992*	*11*	43			*Hinshelwood 60, Farrell 80*	*Forrest*	*Hedman*	*Radford*	*Hinshelwood*	*Williams**	*Hill*	*White*	*Wilkins*	*Tempest*	*English*	*Grenfell*	*Farrell*
							Ref: K Hooper	Colchester have faint hopes of reaching the play-offs, but Town find them there for the taking. However, they fail to capitalise on Duffield's early goal. Colchester equalise, then manager Roger Brown sends on Farrell, on loan from Luton, and he heads the winner with his first touch.											
38	H	SCARBOROUGH	21	D	2-2	1-0	Duffield 6, Matthews N 71	Roche	Brown	Barr	Matthews M	Robinson	Shaw	Martin	Matthews N	Duffield	Allison*	Richardson	Black
	4/4	1,747	*14*	44			*Cook 46, Graham 83*	*Ironside*	*McJannet*	*Thompson*	*Kamara*	*Short*	*Bennyworth*	*Hamill**	*Cook*	*Brook^*	*Russell*	*Graham*	*Adams/Preston*
							Ref: K Barratt	Town fail to win for the sixth consecutive match and slip to their lowest position this season. Indiscipline costs them, for though they twice go in front they can't hang onto the lead. A static Town defence watches former player Tommy Graham net the late equaliser from eight yards.											
39	A	BURNLEY	21	L	1-3	1-1	Allison 41	Roche	Brown	Blain	Kendall	Robinson^	Shaw	Martin	McPhillips	Duffield	Allison	Richardson*	Barr/Black
	8/4	*5,766*	*6*	44			*Davis 43, Comstive 58, Taylor 65*	*Pearce*	*McGory*	*Deakin*	*Britton*	*Davis*	*Gardner*	*Farrell*	*Oghani*	*Taylor*	*Comstive*	*Hoskin*	
							Ref: C Trussell	After losing here in the Sherpa Van, Halifax are looking for revenge. Allison scores first, and Town hit the bar three times as they give their all. But they are their own worst enemies. Burnley draw level, then punish Town for two wayward passes to take the game in the second half.											
40	H	LEYTON ORIENT	19	W	1-0	1-0	Black 4	Roche	Brown	Barr	Matthews M	Kendall	Shaw	Martin	McPhillips	Duffield*	Allison	Black	Willis
	14/4	1,006	*6*	47				*Wells*	*Howard*	*Stimson*	*Sitton*	*Day*	*Baker**	*Hales*	*Castle*	*Nugent*	*Juryeff*	*Comfort*	*Godfrey*
							Ref: K Walmsley	The average age of the Town team is getting lower with every game. Billy Ayre is down to just eleven fit professionals, so the latest to make his debut as a sub is 17-year-old Paul Willis. Black, who later has a goal ruled out, flicks the ball past Wells early on for the game's only goal.											
41	A	CARLISLE	19	D	1-1	0-0	McPhillips 90	Roche	Brown	Barr	Matthews M*	Kendall	Shaw	Martin	McPhillips	Duffield^	Allison	Black	Richardson/Willis
	19/4	*1,517*	*23*	48			*Fyfe 75*	*Prudhoe*	*Clark*	*Gorman*	*Saddington*	*Wright*	*Robinson*	*Bishop*	*Hutchinson*	*Poskett*	*Halpin*	*Rowell**	*Fyfe*
							Ref: R Hart	Chants of 'What a load of rubbish' can be heard from the Shay faithful who make the long journey to Brunton Park. They are hardly impressed with Terry McPhillips' injury-time equaliser. Clive Middlemass's struggling side show more passion to their cause and are unlucky not to win.											
42	H	HARTLEPOOL	18	W	**3-1**	2-1	Black 5, Brown 30, Duffield 75	Roche	Brown	Barr	Matthews M	Robinson	Kendall*	Martin	McPhillips	Duffield	Allison	Black	Shaw
	23/4	**866**	*14*	51			*Baker 3*	*Carr*	*Barratt*	*McKinnon*	*Tinkler**	*Smith*	*Haigh*	*Honour*	*Toman*	*Baker*	*Doig*	*Barthwick^*	*Nobbs/Dixon*
							Ref: D Scott	The poor attendance reflects Town's disappointing second half to the season. It's their second worst ever, and easily the lowest in the League this season. Still, despite falling behind very early on, Town put on a super show. McPhillips threads the ball through for Duffield's killer goal.											
43	H	CARLISLE	18	D	1-1	1-0	McPhillips 8	Roche	Brown	Barr	Matthews M*	Robinson	Kendall	Martin	McPhillips	Duffield	Allison	Black	Richardson
	26/4	1,002	*23*	52			*Cooke 83*	*Prudhoe*	*Robertson*	*Gorman*	*Studdington*	*Wright*	*Robinson*	*Bishop*	*Fyfe*	*Poskett*	*Clarke*	*Cooke*	
							Ref: J Timmons	The game is held up slightly so that Paddy Roche can help a linesman and ball-boy with makeshift repairs to the goal-net. Town fail to build on McPhillips' goal when Robinson's header goes in off his legs. They fail to take their chances, then allow Cooke to equalise from a tight angle.											
44	A	CREWE	18	D	0-0	0-0		Roche	Brown	Barr	Matthews M	Robinson*	Kendall	Martin	McPhillips	Duffield	Allison	Black	Richardson^/Thornber
	29/4	*1,403*	*16*	53				*Greygoose*	*Goodison*	*Edwards*	*Ritchie*	*Wright*	*Gage*	*Fishenden*	*Harris**	*Cutler*	*Doyle*	*Parker^*	*Morton/Macowat*
							Ref: R Dilkes	Halifax stretch their unbeaten run to five games, whilst Dario Gradi's Crewe notch up their fourth consecutive draw, and 19th in all. There is little action as both sets of players find it hard to raise their game. Allison has the only real chance, but Greygoose saves when he breaks free.											
45	H	TORQUAY	18	L	2-3	1-1	Duffield 36, Brown 51p	Roche	Brown	Barr	Matthews M	Kendall	McPhillips	Martin	Thornber	Duffield	Allison	Black*	Blain
	2/5	1,218	*3*	53			*Dobson 18, Impey 65, Dawkins 90*	*Allen*	*McNichol*	*Kelly*	*Haslegrave**	*Cole*	*Impey*	*Dawkins*	*Lloyd*	*Caldwell^*	*Dobson*	*Gibbins*	*Loram/Pearce*
							Ref: A Flood	Torquay still have promotion hopes after Dawkins' last-minute winner. Town are caught out, pushing forward for a throw-in which they think is theirs. Cyril Knowles joins his players on the pitch to celebrate. Things look differently when Brown scores a penalty after Allison is fouled.											
46	A	EXETER	18	W	2-1	0-1	Duffield 71, Richardson 88	Roche	Brown	Barr^	Matthews M	Robinson	Kendall	Martin*	Thornber	Duffield	McPhillips	Black !	Richardson/Shaw
	7/5	*1,602*	*22*	56			*Delve 29*	*Gwinnett*	*Harrower*	*Viney*	*Carter*	*Taylor*	*Cooper*	*Olsson*	*Delve**	*Edwards*	*O'Connell*	*Rowbotham*	*Batty*
	Home	Away					Ref: R Groves	Sub Lee Richardson makes sure Town end the season on a high note when he tucks away the late winner after Duffield laid the ball to him. It completes a second-half revival that is made harder when Black is sent off in the 61st-minute for a bad foul on Taylor, spotted by the linesman.											
Average	1,595	2,810																	

Littlewoods Cup

Littlewoods Cup			F-A	H-T	Scorers, Times, and Referees	1	2	3	4	5	6	7	8	9	10	11	subs used
1:1 H YORK		D	1-1	1-0	Allison 2	Roche	Brown	Harrison	Matthews M	Robinson	Galloway	Richardson*	Thornber	Matthews N	Allison^	Holden	Black/Ferebee
18/8	1,359 *3*				*Gabbiadini 50*	*Endersby*	*McKenzie*	*Johnson*	*Kitchen*	*Whitehead*	*Clegg*	*Butler*	*Hood*	*Gabbiadini*	*Banton*	*Canham*	
					Ref: K Breen	This game is played against the backdrop of chairman John Madeley resigning after a row with the council. Allison forgets about off-the-field traumas to put Town ahead after only 85 seconds. He could have had more, but the only other goal falls the way of Gabbiadini from 18 yards.											
1:2 A YORK		L	0-1	0-0		Roche	Brown	Harrison	Matthews M	Martin	Galloway	Richardson	Shaw*	Matthews N	Black^	Holden	Barr W/Ferebee
25/8	*2,382 3:22*				*Hood 60p*	*Endersby*	*McKenzie*	*Johnson*	*Wilson*	*Whitehead*	*Clegg*	*Butler*	*Hood*	*Gabbiadini*	*Banton*	*Canham*	
					Ref: I Hendrick (Halifax lost 1-2 on aggregate)	York boss Bobby Saxton reckons Town could be a force to be reckoned with if they can keep up this sort of form. But an unhappy Ayre locks his players away for 20 minutes after the defeat. Galloway's error costs them, as he lets the ball run then brings down Banton for the penalty.											

FA Cup

FA Cup			F-A	H-T	Scorers, Times, and Referees	1	2	3	4	5	6	7	8	9	10	11	subs used
1 A BILLINGHAM		W	4-2	1-1	Black 2, 75, Robinson 65, Matthews N 87	Roche	Brown	Fleming	Matthews M	Shaw	Robinson	Martin	Thornber	Matthews N	Black	Holden*	Ferebee
14/11	*1,153 NL*				*Allen 39, Hewitt 48*	*Davison*	*Parry*	*Strong*	*Granycome*	*Harbron*	*Coleby*	*McMullen**	*Malone*	*Hewitt*	*Whetter*	*Allen*	*Sills*
					Ref: J Penrose	Mick Galloway signed for Hearts three days before this cup-tie, switched to Hartlepool's Victoria Ground. Town race into the lead when Black seizes on a weak back-pass. Just after half-time, Town fall behind, and they need the outstretched leg of Robinson to put them back on course.											
2 A GRIMSBY		D	0-0	0-0		Roche	Brown	Barr	Matthews N	Fleming	Shaw	Martin	Thornber	Matthews N	Black	Holden	
5/12	*3,239 3:20*					*Sherwood*	*McDermott*	*Agnew*	*Turner*	*Moore*	*Robinson*	*Grocock*	*Saunders*	*North*	*O'Riordan*	*McGarvey*	
					Ref: R Dilkes	With two minutes to go, and with Town hanging on grimly, fans spill onto the pitch after a suspected fire in the stands. The game is held up for eight minutes, but Town don't lose their concentration. Shaw ends the game with blood pouring from a head injury that later required stitches.											
2R H GRIMSBY		W	2-0	1-0	Matthews M 30, Thornber 60	Roche	Brown	Barr	Matthews M	Fleming*	Shaw	Martin	Thornber	Matthews N	Black	Holden	Richardson
8/12	2,633 *3:20*					*Sherwood*	*McDermott*	*Agnew*	*Turner*	*Burgess*	*Robinson*	*Tole**	*Saunders*	*North*	*O'Riordan*	*McGarvey*	*Grocock*
					Ref: P Tyldesley	A home tie with Brian Clough's Forest side is the reward for the winners. On a pitch that freezes rapidly, Town make sure it's them. Sherwood allows Mick Matthews' 30-yarder to skid under him. Sherwood up-ends Holden but the ref allows Thornber to net the loose ball for the second.											
3 H NOTT'M FOREST		L	0-4	0-2	*[Wilkinson 83]*	Roche	Brown	Barr	Matthews M^	Robinson	Heathcote	Martin	Thornber	Matthews N	Black*	Holden	Allison/Richardson
9/1	4,013 *1:2*				*Wilson 23, Pearce 34, Plummer 70,*	*Sutton*	*Chettle*	*Pearce*	*Walker*	*Foster*	*Wilson*	*Plummer^*	*Webb*	*Glover*	*Gaynor**	*Rice*	*Fleming/Wilkinson*
					Ref: T Fitzharris	Brian Clough's 1st Division high-flyers are not put off by the Shay pitch which is covered in sand. They are a class above Town, and will go on to reach the semi-finals. England's full-back Pearce scores the second with a shot that is turned in by Barr. 'They never got a sniff' – Clough.											

		P	W	D	L	F	A	W	D	L	F	A	Pts
			Home					Away					
1	Wolves	46	15	3	5	47	19	12	6	5	35	24	90
2	Cardiff	46	15	6	2	39	14	9	7	7	27	27	85
3	Bolton	46	15	6	2	42	12	7	6	10	24	30	78
4	Scunthorpe	46	14	5	4	42	20	6	12	5	34	31	77
5	Torquay	46	10	7	6	34	16	11	7	5	32	25	77
6	Swansea ^	46	9	7	7	35	28	11	3	9	27	28	70
7	Peterborough	46	10	5	8	28	26	10	5	8	24	27	70
8	Leyton Orient	46	13	4	6	55	27	6	8	9	30	36	69
9	Colchester	46	10	5	8	23	22	9	5	9	24	29	67
10	Burnley	46	12	5	6	31	22	8	2	13	26	40	67
11	Wrexham	46	13	3	7	46	26	7	3	13	23	32	66
12	Scarborough	46	12	8	3	38	19	5	6	12	18	29	65
13	Darlington	46	13	6	4	39	25	5	5	13	32	44	65
14	Tranmere**	46	14	2	7	43	20	5	7	11	18	33	64
15	Cambridge	46	10	6	7	32	24	6	7	10	18	28	61
16	Hartlepool	46	9	7	7	25	25	6	7	10	25	32	59
17	Crewe	46	7	11	5	25	19	6	8	9	32	34	58
18	HALIFAX*	46	11	7	5	37	25	3	7	13	17	34	55
19	Hereford	46	8	7	8	25	27	6	5	12	16	32	54
20	Stockport	46	7	7	9	26	26	5	8	10	18	32	51
21	Rochdale	46	5	9	9	28	34	6	6	11	19	42	48
22	Exeter	46	8	6	9	33	29	3	7	13	20	39	46
23	Carlisle	46	9	5	9	38	33	3	3	17	19	53	44
24	Newport	46	4	5	14	19	36	2	2	19	16	69	25
		1104	253	142	157	830	574	157	142	253	574	830	1511

^ promoted after play-offs

* 1 pt deducted

** 2 pts deducted

Odds & ends

Double wins: (2) Exeter, Wolves.
Double losses: (1) Colchester.

Won from behind: (5) Hartlepool (h), Newport (h), Wolves (h), Exeter (a), Billingham (FAC) (a).
Lost from in front: (4) Rochdale (h), Torquay (h), Burnley (a), Colchester (a).

High spots: Doing the double over eventual champions Wolves.
Beating 3rd Division Grimsby in an FA Cup replay.
Two consecutive wins in September and December.
Reaching the Northern Semi-Final of the Sherpa Van Trophy.

Low spots: Eight games without a win up to 8 April.
Losing at bottom club Newport, who were eventually demoted.
Losing on penalties to Burnley in the Sherpa Van Trophy.

Town had a point deducted for fielding an ineligible player.

Player of the Year: Phil Brown.
Ever-presents: (1) Paddy Roche.
Hat-tricks: (0).
Leading scorers: Rick Holden & Neil Matthews (10).

	Appearances						Goals			
	Lge	*Sub*	LC	*Sub*	FAC	*Sub*	Lge	LC	FAC	Tot
Allison, Wayne	**29**	*6*	1			*1*	**4**	1		**5**
Barr, Billy	**25**	*5*		*1*	3					
Blain, Colin	**2**	*1*								
Black, Russell	**19**	*8*	1	*1*	4		**5**		2	**7**
Brown, Phil	**44**		2		4		**5**			**5**
Duffield, Peter	**12**						**7**			**7**
Ferebee, Stewart	**6**	*6*		*2*		*1*				
Fleming, Paul	**7**	*2*			3					
Galloway, Mick	**17**		2				**2**			**2**
Harrison, Frankie	**18**		2							
Heathcote, Mick	**7**				1		**1**			**1**
Holden, Rick	**35**		2		4		**10**			**10**
Kendall, Paul	**9**	*1*								
McPhillips, Terry	**11**	*14*					**3**			**3**
Martin, Dean	**38**	*2*	1		4		**3**			**3**
Matthews, Mick	**45**		2		4		**3**		1	**4**
Matthews, Neil	**29**	*3*	2		4		**9**		1	**10**
Richardson, Lee	**20**	*10*	2			*2*	**1**			**1**
Robinson, Dave	**32**		1		2				1	**1**
Roche, Paddy	**46**		2		4					
Shaw, Adrian	**21**	*3*	1		3					
Thornber, Steve	**34**	*1*	1		4				1	**1**
Willis, Paul		*2*								
(own-goals)							**1**			**1**
23 players used	**506**	***64***	**22**	***4***	**44**	***4***	**54**	**1**	**6**	**61**

No	Date		Att	Pos	Pt	F-A	H-T	Scorers, Times, and Referees	1	2	3	4	5	6	7	8	9	10	11	subs used
1	A	TORQUAY			W	2-0	1-0	Bramhall 42, Allison 60	Roche	Barr W	Logan	Matthews M	Bramhall	Whitehead A	Blain	Horner	Matthews N	Allison	Richardson L	
	27/8		2,769		3				*Crichton*	*Holmes*	*Kelly*	*McNichol**	*Cole*	*Joyce*	*Pugh*	*Lloyd*	*Edwards*	*Loram*	*Gibbons*	*Thompson^/Morrison*
								Ref: J Watson	Town make a terrific start in Devon, but they are helped along by Torquay keeper Paul Crichton. He allows John Bramhall's weak daisy-cutter from 30 yards to slip firstly through his hands, then through his legs. Allison's exquisite 20-yard lofted shot on the hour is a bit more stylish.											
2	H	BURNLEY		11	L	1-2	0-1	McPhillips 87	Roche	Barr W	Logan	Matthews M	Bramhall	Whitehead A	Willis*	Horner	Watson^	Allison	Richardson	Henry/McPhillips
	3/9		3,371	3	3			*Comstive 33, O'Connell 75*	*Pearce*	*Daniel*	*Deakin*	*Farrell*	*Davis*	*Gardner*	*Britton*	*Oghani*	*O'Connell*	*Comstive*	*Atkinson*	
								Ref: A Dawson	The Town supporters are annoyed that they are being housed in the visitors' end for this first home game. They are also disappointed to see the Shaymen lose to their fierce rivals. Few can argue with the result, as the Clarets are deserving winners. McPhillips' late strike flatters Town.											
3	A	EXETER		18	L	1-4	0-1	Whitehead A 70	Roche	Barr W	Logan^	Matthews M	Bramhall	Whitehead A	Martin*	Horner	McPhillips	Allison	Richardson L	Henry/Watson
	10/9		1,725	14	3			*Withey 35, 58, Neville 54, Rowbotham 75*	*Gwinnett*	*Banks*	*Withey*	*Rogers*	*Taylor*	*Cooper*	*Rowbotham*	*Hiley*	*Batty*	*Neville*	*Harrower*	
								Ref: P Durkin	Billy Ayre has his players back on the team bus within 30 minutes of the end of this game, fuming at their performance. Withey, on his debut, proves a handful for them, and he nets a brace. Alan Whitehead's header for 1-3 is only the prelude to Rowbotham's lovely curling 20-yarder.											
4	H	CARLISLE		15	D	3-3	1-3	McPhillips 9, 46, 52p	Roche	Barr W	Barr R	Watson	Bramhall	Whitehead A	Martin	Horner	McPhillips	Henry	Richardson L	
	16/9		1,546	14	4			*Marshall 2, Hetherington 5, Sendall 32*	*Prudhoe*	*Graham*	*Dalziel*	*Saddington*	*Ogley*	*Clark*	*Marshall*	*Gorman*	*Sendall*	*Hetherington**	*Walsh*	*Fyfe*
								Ref: I Hendrick	Ayre has suspended Mick and Neil Matthews and David Logan after he discovered they were drinking less than 48 hours before the Exeter game. His bold move almost backfires when the visitors go 2-0 up early on. But McPhillips completes his hat-trick from the spot for a draw.											
5	A	STOCKPORT		15	D	1-1	0-1	Martin 76p	Whitehead P	Barr W	Blain	Watson	Barr R	Whitehead A	Martin	Horner	McPhillips*	Allison	Richardson L	Henry
	19/9		2,202	9	5			*Wylde 6*	*Gorton*	*Butler*	*Hart*	*McKenzie*	*Thorpe*	*Williams*	*Wylde*	*Hendrie*	*Payne*	*Cooke*	*Howard**	*Bullock*
								Ref: A Seville	Asa Hartford's side won 4-1 at Darlington on the season's opening day but have failed to win since. They may feel they deserved to win this game after taking a sixth-minute lead. Town defend resolutely, then equalise with a penalty when Alan Whitehead is brought down by Thorpe.											
6	H	TRANMERE		20	L	2-3	1-0	Barr W 23, McPhillips 88	Whitehead P	Barr W*	Blain^	Watson	Barr R	Whitehead A	Martin	Horner	McPhillips	Allison	Richardson L	Smith/Henry
	23/9		1,662	10	5			*Muir 51, 56, Higgins 70*	*Nixon*	*Higgins*	*McCarrick*	*Bishop**	*Hughes*	*Vickers*	*Morrison*	*Harvey*	*Steel*	*Muir*	*Mungall*	*McKenna*
								Ref: R Hart	Billy Barr scores his first-ever senior goal, but comes off at half-time with an ankle injury that later needs X-ray checks in hospital. Tranmere always look dangerous, and use their experience to turn the game around. Indecision by Blain and his keeper lets in Higgins for the killer third.											
7	A	YORK		21	L	3-5	1-3	Allison 45, 50, Horner 58 *[Howlett 77]*	Whitehead P	Barr W	Blain*	Matthews M	Whitehead A	Robinson	Martin^	Horner	McPhillips	Allison	Richardson L	Matthews N/Watson
	1/10		2,238	17	5			*Butler 3, B'shaw 24, C'ham 30, B'ton 57p,*	*Marples*	*Bradshaw*	*Branagan*	*Johnson*	*Tutill*	*Fazackerley*	*Butler*	*Howlett*	*Helliwell*	*Banton*	*Canham**	*Hotte*
								Ref: F Roberts	Town are lucky to concede only three goals in the first half as York score some spectacular efforts. Allison's miscued goal right on the whistle peps some life into the Shaymen. In the second half, they twice reduce the deficit to one goal. Ayre sends on Matthews after only 30 minutes.											
8	H	WREXHAM			W	4-0	3-0	Matthews N 21, Allison 41, McPhillips 45, [Horner 55]	Roche	Hedworth	Barr W	Matthews M	Robinson	Horner	Martin	Watson	McPhillips	Allison*	Matthews N	Richardson L
	4/10		1,199		8				*Salmon*	*Salathiel*	*Wrench*	*Bowden*	*Beaumont*	*Jones*	*Preece*	*Hunter**	*Buxton*	*Russell*	*Cooper*	*Flynn*
								Ref: K Lupton	Ayre switches to a 4-2-4 formation, and it pays dividends as Wrexham are dead and buried by half-time. The restored Neil Matthews starts the rout with a goal at the second attempt. McPhillips scores the third when two defenders get in a tangle. Horner's header completes the scoring.											
9	A	CAMBRIDGE		21	L	1-2	0-0	McPhillips 56	Roche	Hedworth	Barr W	Matthews M	Bramhall	Horner	Martin	Watson	McPhillips	Richardson L	Matthews N	
	8/10		1,800	6	8			*Smith 76p, Taylor 80*	*Vaughan*	*Bailie*	*Kimble*	*Smith*	*Chapple*	*Beck*	*Clayton*	*Ryan**	*Reilly*	*Hamilton*	*Anderson*	*Taylor*
								Ref: J Moules	Ref John Moules is a central figure in this game. With Town ahead, he awards Cambridge a penalty for hands, although nobody appeals. Then, when John Taylor, a clerk in a shipping office before signing in the summer, nets the winner, he turns way the Shaymen's protests for offside.											
10	H	ROCHDALE		15	W	4-1	2-0	McPhillips 1p, 69, Barr W 15,	Roche	Hedworth	Barr W	Matthews M	Bramhall	Horner*	Martin	Watson	McPhillips	Richardson L	Matthews N	Willis
	14/10		2,553	4	11			*Smith 54* [Matthews N 47]	*Welch*	*Copeland*	*Armitage*	*Smart*	*Sutton*	*Reid*	*Harris^*	*Smith*	*Walling**	*O'Shaughn'sy*	*Frain*	*Beaumont/Edmonds*
								Ref: A Flood	Rochdale arrive at the Shay in an unaccustomed lofty 4th place, but they are blitzed by the Shaymen. McPhillips' scores two, his first a penalty after only 48 seconds when Neil Matthews' run is checked. Town have to reorganise when Horner dislocates a shoulder after only 37 minutes.											
11	A	DONCASTER		16	W	4-1	4-1	McPhillips 9, 14, Watson 10,	Roche	Hedworth	Barr W	Matthews M	Robinson	Bramhall	Martin	Watson*	McPhillips	Allison	Matthews N	Richardson L
	21/10		3,038	9	14			*Robinson R 42* [Matthews N 11]	*Malcolm*	*Douglas*	*Robinson R*	*Turnbull*	*Beattie*	*Raven*	*Robinson L*	*Daly*	*Rankine*	*Dobson**	*Kimble^*	*Raffell/Gorman*
								Ref: P Wright	The Shaymen stun not only the Belle Vue supporters, but probably their own with an amazing four-goal blast in the first 14 minutes. The game is over by then. Rovers' goal is from an indirect free-kick inside the box. McPhillips' second means he's the League's top scorer with twelve.											

No	Venue	Opponent	Att	Pos	Pt	F-A	H-T	Scorers, Times, and Referees	1	2	3	4	5	6	7	8	9	10	11	12 sub	subs used
12	H	PETERBOROUGH		9	W	**5-0**	0-0	Rich'son L 51, McPhillips 69, Watson 83,	Roche	Hedworth*	Barr W	Matthews M	Bramhall	Robinson	Martin	Watson	McPhillips	Allison	Matthews N	Richardson L
	25/10		2,248	*19*	17			[Matthews N 84, 87]	*Neenan*	*Langan*	*Gunn*	*Luke*	*McElhinney*	*Oakes*	*Andrews*	*Halsall*	*Cusack*	*Longhurst*	*Goldsmith*	
								Ref: G Tyson	Mick Jones, now in charge at Peterborough, admits to being 'scared stiff' before the game. His side survives till half-time, before Richardson's deflected effort opens the floodgates. The Halifax Courier have labelled the Shaymen's scoring feats as 'The Great Halifax Town Goal Rush'.											
13	A	GRIMSBY		13	L	2-3	1-0	Bramhall 8, Matthews M 82	Roche	Richardson L	Barr W	Matthews M	Robinson	Bramhall	Martin	Watson	McPhillips	Allison	Matthews N	
	29/10		*3,260*	*18*	17			*Saunders 55, 65, O'Kelly 57*	*Sherwood*	*Williams*	*Agnew*	*Tillson*	*Cunnington*	*Lever*	*McDermott*	*Saunders*	*O'Kelly*	*Watson*	*Alexander*	
								Ref: E Parker	Town take an early lead but can't hang on to it. Grimsby are rampant after the break, and equalise through Saunders, who pounces after Roche saves O'Kelly's penalty. They take control, but Mick Matthews's goal starts a late rally. Town are denied a penalty when Watson goes down.											
14	H	HARTLEPOOL		9	W	1-0	1-0	Allison 4	Roche	Richardson L	Barr W	Matthews M	Robinson	Bramhall	Martin !	Watson	McPhillips	Allison	Matthews N	
	4/11		2,182	*19*	20				*Muggleton*	*Barratt*	*McKinnon*	*Tinkler**	*Smith*	*Stokes*	*Honour*	*Toman*	*Allon*	*Baker*	*Haigh*	*Doig^/Grayson*
								Ref: T Fitzharris	Fireworks of all sorts at the Shay! Allison gives Town an early lead, before a fire-cracker from over the wall explodes in the penalty box. Town play with ten men after Martin's 41st-minute dismissal for querying a penalty. Roche saves Brian Honour's kick, and Town's ten men hang on.											
15	H	COLCHESTER		7	W	3-2	2-1	Martin 41, McPhillips 45p, 88	Roche	Richardson L	Barr W	Matthews M	Robinson	Bramhall	Martin	Watson	McPhillips	Allison	Matthews N	
	8/11		2,176	*23*	23			*Kelly 13, Wilkins 84*	*Walton*	*Hedman*	*Bedford*	*Kelly*	*Hicks*	*Hill**	*Wilkins*	*English*	*Tempest*	*Walsh*	*Barnett*	*Daniels*
								Ref: J Timmons	Liverpool reject Terry McPhillips, branded a flop by a Merseyside paper, responds by firing in the winner to go back to the top of the scoring charts. The U's, with only three wins behind them, shock Town, but McPhillips' penalty for hands by Bedford, brings them level at the break.											
16	A	HEREFORD		10	L	1-3	0-2	Horner 88	Roche	Hedworth^	Barr W	Matthews M	Robinson	Bramhall	Martin*	Watson	McPhillips	Allison	Richardson L	Willis/Horner
	12/11		*1,929*	*16*	23			*Narbett 15, 23, Stant 48p*	*Rose*	*Jones M*	*Crane*	*Stevens*	*Devine*	*Jones R*	*Mardenboro'*	*Narbett*	*Stant**	*Tester*	*McLoughlin*	*Maddy*
								Ref: K Cooper	The division's leading scorers are in action, but both McPhillips and Phil Stant have quiet games. Stant's penalty takes his tally to twelve, but it's on-loan Jon Narbett (Shrewsbury) who is the game's outstanding player. He waltzes through Town's defence to send Hereford their way.											
17	A	LINCOLN		13	L	1-2	1-1	Allison 7	Roche	Hedworth	Horner	Matthews M	Robinson	Bramhall	Richardson	Watson*	McPhillips	Allison	Matthews N	Barr W
	26/11		*3,479*	*5*	23			*Cumming 41, Matthewson 47*	*Wallington*	*Evans*	*Nicholson*	*Schofield*	*Matthewson*	*Bressington*	*Davis*	*Cumming*	*Hobson*	*Brown*	*Sertori*	
								Ref: D Vickers	Town are developing a worrying away trend. They go in front through McPhillips, who runs at the defence before supplying Allison, but they are lost for ideas once Cummings' 30-yarder flies in. They lose to a soft goal just after the break when the ball goes in off Matthewson's shin.											
18	H	CREWE		13	L	0-1	0-0		Roche	Hedworth	Horner	Matthews M	Robinson	Bramhall	Richardson L	Watson	Barr W*	Allison	Matthews N	Willis
	2/12		2,026	*1*	23			*Edwards 78*	*Greygoose*	*Goodison*	*Edwards^*	*Billing*	*Swain*	*Gage*	*Callaghan*	*Murphy*	*Elliott*	*Gardiner**	*Fishenden*	*Jones/Macowat*
								Ref: K Redfern	After scoring in 20 consecutive matches, Town fail to find the net. McPhillips, out with ankle trouble, is sadly missed. A goalless draw looks the likely outcome until Crewe break swiftly. Paul Edwards breaks the deadlock, meeting Gage's cross, with a header when he is on his knees.											
19	H	SCARBOROUGH		18	L	0-2	0-1		Roche	Hedworth	Horner	Richardson L	Robinson	Bramhall	Martin	Watson	Barr W	Allison	Matthews N	
	17/12		1,890	*3*	23			*Matthews 41, Norris 47*	*Ironside*	*Kamara*	*Thompson*	*Short*	*Richards*	*Bennyworth*	*Morris**	*Matthews*	*Norris^*	*Brook*	*Graham*	*Adams/Olsson*
								Ref: P Danson	A man called Ironside – Ian – keeps Town at bay and prevents them scoring at home for the second consecutive game. At the other end, Mick Matthews, making an early return to the Shay on his debut, curls in a free-kick. Steve Norris doubles the lead, proving he is lethal from a yard.											
20	A	DARLINGTON		15	W	2-0	1-0	McPhillips 13, 47	Sinclair	Barr W	Horner	Richardson L	Robinson^	Bramhall	Martin*	Watson	McPhillips	Allison	Matthews N	Blain/Whitehead A
	26/12		*2,131*	*23*	26				*Batch*	*Robinson*	*Morgan*	*McAughtrie*	*Moore**	*Willis*	*Hyde*	*McAndrew*	*Clayton^*	*Worthington*	*Emson*	*MacD'ld/Stonehouse*
								Ref: J Watson	Ronnie Sinclair starts a second loan period with the club, and helps prevent Darlington from recording their first home win. In the 12th minute he saves Worthington's penalty for a trip by Robinson. McPhillips, back after injury, scores both Town goals, his first a cool individual effort.											
21	A	ROTHERHAM		18	L	0-2	0-0		Whitehead P	Barr W	Horner	Richardson L*	Robinson	Bramhall	Martin	Watson	McPhillips	Allison	Matthews N	Blain
	31/12		*5,258*	*2*	26			*Russell 78, Buckley 85*	*O'Hanlon*	*Russell*	*Heard*	*Grealish*	*Barnsley*	*Crosby*	*Buckley*	*Dempsey**	*Williamson*	*Evans^*	*Goodwin*	*Hazell/Mendonca*
								Ref: B Hill	Ref Brian Hill took charge of last season's FA Cup Final. He plays his part in a fine match, letting the game flow. Ayre felt that the first team to score would win. When Billy Russell opens the scoring, finishing off a move started by Goodwin's back-heel, he knows the game is over.											
22	H	SCUNTHORPE		14	W	5-1	2-0	Allis'n 18, 85, Wats'n 35, Matthews N 48,	Whitehead P	Barr W	Horner	Blain*	Robinson	Bramhall	Martin	Watson	McPhillips	Allison	Matthews N	**Fleming C**
	2/1		2,650	*8*	29			*Hamilton 67* [Robinson 60]	*Musselwhite*	*Smalley*	*Longden*	*Taylor*	*Lister*	*Brown*	*Hodkinson*	*Harle*	*Daws**	*Hamilton*	*Stevenson*	*Flounders*
								Ref: N Midgley	An amazing result. Town spend a third of the game on the defensive but the difference is in the finishing. Three of Town's goals are from set pieces. Watson's volley is scored while the Iron's Tony Brown is having stitches in a head wound. Craig Fleming gets three minutes of action.											
23	A	BURNLEY		16	L	1-2	0-1	Allison 88	Whitehead P	Barr W	Horner	Richardson L	Robinson	Bramhall	Martin	Watson	Blain*	Allison	Matthews N	Fleming P
	14/1		***8,297***	*12*	29			*Oghani 8, 66*	*Pearce*	*Measham*	*Farrell*	*Britton*	*Davis*	*Gardner*	*White*	*Oghani*	*O'Connell*	*Comstive**	*James*	*Zelem*
								Ref: P Tyldesley	For 70 minutes, Town struggle to get the Cup defeat by Kettering out of their system. Bramhall makes a hash of a clearance to present Oghani his first goal. He gets his second with a powerful header to double Burnley's lead. Allison's late goal means Burnley are hanging on at the end.											

BARCLAYS LEAGUE DIVISION 4 Manager: Billy Ayre SEASON 1988-89

No	Date			Att	Pos	Pt	F-A	H-T	Scorers, Times, and Referees	1	2	3	4	5	6	7	8	9	10	11	subs used
24		H	TORQUAY		13	W	2-0	2-0	Allison 8, 12	Whitehead P	Barr W	Horner	Richardson L	Robinson	Bramhall	Martin	Watson	Fleming P*	Allison	Matthews N	**Richardson N**
	20/1			1,830	*6*	32				*Veysey*	*Holmes**	*Kelly*	*McNichol*	*Leyden*	*Loram*	*Smith*	*Lloyd*	*Edwards*	*Weston^*	*Joyce*	*Airey/Morrison*
									Ref: K Breen	The scouts are out in force at this Friday evening fixture. Most eyes are on 18-goal McPhillips, but it's his partner in crime Wayne Allison who bags a quick brace to win the game. He gets a foot to the ball to lob Veysey for his first, then holds off his marker to convert Watson's flick-on.											
25		A	CARLISLE		15	L	1-3	0-0	Bramhall 52	Whitehead P	Barr W	Horner	Richardson L	Robinson	Bramhall	Martin	Watson	Fleming P*	Allison	Matthews N	McPhillips
	28/1			*3,007*	*16*	32			*Gorman 47, Halpin 79, 90*	*McKellar*	*Graham*	*Dalziel*	*Saddington*	*Jeffels*	*Fitzpatrick*	*Walsh*	*Gorman*	*Stephens**	*Hetherington*	*Halpin*	*Fyfe*
									Ref: R Nixon	Ayre has issued a 'hands off' message for the scouts looking at his players. But none are impressed here. Whitehead lets Gorman's shot slip under his body. Bramhall's equaliser means Town are the first team this season to net 50 goals. Town fall to pieces in the last eleven minutes.											
26		H	STOCKPORT		15	D	2-2	1-0	Watson 31, McPhillips 69	Sinclair	Barr W	Horner	Richardson L	Robinson	Bramhall	Martin !	Watson	McPhillips	Fleming	Matthews N	
	4/2			1,938	*13*	33			*Cooke 54, Caldwell 77p*	*Gorton*	*Butler**	*Logan*	*Matthews*	*Thorpe*	*Wwilliams*	*Payne^*	*Colville*	*Caldwell*	*Hancock*	*Cooke*	*Angell/McKenzie*
									Ref: P Harrison	Two minutes after Caldwell's equalising penalty, Dean Martin is sent off after squaring up to Brett Angell, who'd only been on the pitch a few seconds. County claim that McPhillips' goal for 2-1 never crossed the line. Mick Matthews makes his second debut against Town this season.											
27		A	TRANMERE			L	0-2	0-0		Sinclair	Barr W	Horner	**Pullan**	Robinson	Fleming P	Martin	Watson	McPhillips	Blain	Matthews N	
	10/2			*4,674*		33			*Vickers 72, Bishop 83*	*Nixon*	*Williams*	*McCarrick*	*Bishop*	*Hughes**	*Vickers*	*Morrissey*	*Harvey*	*Steel*	*Muir*	*Mungall*	*Malkin*
									Rref: A Flood	Lee Richardson has been sold to Watford and is then awarded the Barclays Young Eagle of the Month. John King's Tranmere side extend their unbeaten run to seven games but have to work hard. Steel flicks the ball on for Vickers to score the first. Bishop seals the game from six yards.											
28		H	LEYTON ORIENT		16	D	2-2	0-0	Matthews N 62, Allison 66	Sinclair	Barr W	Horner	Pullan	Robinson	Fleming P	Martin	Watson	McPhillips	Allison	Matthews N*	Blain
	14/2			1,477	*12*	34			*Comfort 81, 84*	*Heald*	*Howard*	*Dickenson*	*Castle*	*Day*	*Sitton*	*Baker*	*Ward*	*Cooper*	*Campbell*	*Comfort*	
									Ref: I Hendrick	Orient include in their line-up Kevin Campbell, on loan from Arsenal. He sparks his side's late revival, making both goals for Alan Comfort. Dean Martin makes both Town's goals, and sets up Phil Horner for a simple header. His miss from six yards is the turning point of the match.											
29		H	CAMBRIDGE		18	D	0-0	0-0		Sinclair	Barr W	Horner	Pullan*	Robinson	Fleming P	Martin	Watson	McPhillips	Allison	Matthews N^	Blain/**Broadbent**
	17/2			1,531	*11*	35				*Vaughan*	*Beck*	*Kimble*	*Turner*	*Chapple*	*Daish*	*Clayton*	*Holmes*	*Bull**	*Taylor*	*Leadbitter*	*Croft*
									Ref: E Parker	Cambridge beat Hartlepool 6-0 in their last game, but chances here are few and far between, as Town play out their first goalless draw of the season. Local league lad Graham Broadbent gets a 25-minute run out. Cambridge striker John Taylor misses his injured partner Dion Dublin.											
30		A	PETERBOROUGH			L	1-2	0-0	Pullan 68	Sinclair	Barr W	Whitehead A	Pullan	Robinson	Bramhall	Fleming	Watson	McPhillips*	Allison	Blain	Broadbent
	1/3			*2,159*		35			*Cusack 58, Oakes 69*	*Crichton*	*Luke*	*Dunn*	*Butterworth*	*Pollard*	*Oakes*	*Andrews*	*Halsall*	*Cusack*	*Longhurst*	*Walsh*	
									Ref: P Vanes	The Shaymen create enough chances to win, but sloppy defending costs them. Barr's backpass is read by Cusack, who scores from an acute angle. Pullan levels it, but within a minute Oakes prods home when Town fail to clear. 'Peterborough did not win the game, we lost it,' – Ayre.											
31		H	DONCASTER		16	W	2-0	0-0	Watson 51, Broadbent 82	Sinclair	Barr W	Whitehead A	Pullan*	Robinson	Bramhall	Fleming P	Watson^	McPhillips	Allison	Blain	Rich'son N/Broadbent
	3/3			1,675	*20*	38				*Samways*	*Douglas^*	*Brevitt*	*Robinson R*	*Ashurst*	*Raven*	*Robinson L*	*Daly**	*Rankine*	*Turnbull*	*Gaughan*	*Kimble/Jones*
									Ref: D Phillips	Graham Broadbent receives a great roar from the Shay faithful when he comes on after 81 minutes. With his first touch, the security guard at the Halifax Building Society, fires in his first league goal. The man he replaced, Andy Watson, scored the first, turning in Bramhall's header.											
32		A	HARTLEPOOL		20	L	0-2	0-1		Sinclair	Barr W	Horner	Whitehead A*	Robinson	Bramhall	Fleming P	Blain	McPhillips^	Allison	Matthews N	Watson/Broadbent
	11/3			*1,786*	*17*	38			*Grayson 31, Toman 69*	*Moverley*	*Barratt*	*McKinnon*	*Tinkler*	*Nobbs**	*Baker*	*Honour*	*Toman*	*Borthwick*	*Grayson*	*Dalton*	*Barrass*
									Ref: A Simmons	Town have yet to win away in 1989. They never look like breaking a depressing run here. Pool's Honour and Dalton cause Town problems all day, and are both involved in Grayson's opener. Ref Alan Simmons makes some perplexing decisions, and denies Allison a clear-cut penalty.											
33		H	GRIMSBY		16	W	2-1	2-0	Allison 6, McPhillips 8	Sinclair	Barr W	Harrison	Blain	Robinson	Bramhall	Fleming P	Watson	McPhillips	Allison	Matthews N	
	14/3			1,609	*13*	41			*O'Kelly 55*	*Sherwood*	*McDermott*	*Stephenson**	*Tillson*	*Lever*	*Cunningham*	*North*	*Saunders*	*O'Kelly*	*Jobling*	*Alexander*	*Watson*
									Ref: D Hedges / S Carr	Five minutes into the second half, with Town leading through two early goals, referee Dennis Hedges pulls a hamstring. Linesman Steven Carr takes over, and local ref Andy Gee runs the line. O'Kelly pulls a goal back, but although the Mariners outplay Town, they can't turn it round.											
34		H	EXETER		20	L	0-3	0-1		Sinclair	Fleming P	Harrison	Blain	Robinson	Bramhall	Martin	Watson^	McPhillips	Allison	Matthews N*	Broadbent/Horner
	17/3			1,473	*9*	41			*Rowbotham 27, Taylor 50, Young 81*	*Walters*	*Banks*	*Dryden*	*Rogers*	*Taylor*	*McDermott*	*Rowbotham*	*Benjamin*	*Vinnicombe**	*Young*	*Hiley*	*Smith*
									Ref: D Allison	Halifax Town have a new chairman in Jim Brown, then the Shaymen use this game to put on their worst display of the season. Exeter are glad to rekindle play-off hopes. The game is all but over when Taylor rises to head in Young's flick. Blain's weak backpass allows Young to score.											

No	Date	Opponent / Att	Pos	Res / Pts	F-A	H-T	Scorers, Times, and Referees	1	2	3	4	5	6	7	8	9	10	11	subs used
35	A	SCUNTHORPE	19	D	0-0	0-0		Roche	Fleming P	Harrison	Horner	Robinson	Bramhall	Martin	Watson	McPhillips	Allison	Barr W	
	25/3	_4,591_	_3_	42				_Musselwhite_	_Smalley_	_Longden_	_Taylor_	_Nicol_	_Brown_	_Lister_	_Cowling_	_Daws_	_Flounders_	_Hamilton*_	_Hodkinson_
							Ref: J Rushton	If Scunthorpe miss out on promotion, they may look at this game as one that cost them. Town battle hard, but it's keeper Roche who does most to earn Town a point. After ten minutes, he gets down to save Lister's ten-yard drive, and lets the Iron know what kind of game they are in for.											
36	H	DARLINGTON	13	W	1-0	0-0	Barr W 64	Roche	Fleming P	Harrison	Horner	Robinson	Bramhall	Martin	Watson	McPhillips	Allison	Barr W	
	27/3	1,849	_23_	45				_Prudhoe_	_McJannet_	_Morgan^_	_Hine_	_Dyson_	_Willis_	_Hyde_	_Gidman*_	_Stephens_	_Bonnyman_	_Emson_	_Worthington/MacD'ld_
							Ref: J Penrose	Darlington, with only five wins all season, are relegation bound. They've appointed Brian Little as manager to help stem the tide. Town make heavy work of beating them. McJannet keeps the Quakers in the game, heading off the line. Billy Barr pops up to score the game's only goal.											
37	A	SCARBOROUGH	17	L	1-3	0-1	McPhillips 66	Roche	Fleming P	Harrison	Horner	Blain	Bramhall	Martin	Watson	McPhillips	Allison	Barr W*	Broadbent
	1/1	_2,365_	_5_	45			_Thompson 44p, Norris 55, Brook 59_	_Ironside_	_Kamara_	_Thompson_	_Olsson_	_Richards_	_Short Craig_	_Norris_	_Graham^_	_Dobson*_	_Brook_	_Russell_	_Adams/Cook_
							Ref: G Alpin	A mysterious penalty award just before the break alters the game's pattern. The ref says afterwards that it was for a push on Norris by Roche, who needs his hand treating before Thompson takes the kick. Norris and Brook score their goals off corners to knock the stuffing out of Town.											
38	A	LEYTON ORIENT	19	L	0-2	0-0		Roche	Fleming P	Harrison	Horner	Barr W	Bramhall	Martin !	Watson	McPhillips	Allison	Matthews N	
	4/4	_3,288_	_6_	45			_Hales 50p, 54_	_Heald_	_Howard_	_Dickenson_	_Hales_	_Day_	_Sitton_	_Baker_	_Castle_	_Harvey_	_Campbell_	_Comfort_	
							Ref: J Ashworth	On a bitterly cold evening, Orient continue their climb towards the play-offs. The game is won in five crazy minutes. Roche clips Campbell's ankles for Kevin Hales' penalty. Two minutes later, Martin is sent off for a fourth time after a rash tackle. Hales gets his second from 18 yards.											
39	H	ROTHERHAM	19	D	1-1	1-0	McPhillips 44p	Whitehead P	Fleming P	Harrison	Horner	Robinson	Bramhall	Martin	Watson	McPhillips	Allison	Matthews N	
	7/4	2,947	_2_	46			_Williamson 67_	_O'Hanlon_	_Russell_	_Scott_	_Grealish_	_Barnsley_	_Crosbie_	_Dempsey*_	_Goodwin_	_Williamson_	_Haycock_	_Hazel_	_Buckley_
							Ref: K Breen	Billy McEwan's title challengers hit the post in the second minute, and force 16 corners to Town's one, but can't get the better of the Shaymen. The Millers pile on the pressure, then Scott gives away a penalty. Williamson ghosts in for a deserved equaliser – his 23rd goal of the season.											
40	H	YORK	19	D	0-0	0-0		Roche	Fleming P	Harrison	Horner	Robinson	Bramhall	Martin	Watson	McPhillips*	Allison	Matthews N	Broadbent
	14/4	1,875	_12_	47				_Marples_	_Barratt_	_Johnson_	_Reid_	_Greenough_	_Tutill_	_Dunn_	_Spooner_	_Helliwell_	_Himsworth_	_Canham_	
							Ref: P Tyldesley	Stern defending and woeful finishing are the main features of this game. Mid-table York have little to play for, and Halifax should be winning these games. The closest we get to a goal is when Tony Canham has to clear off the line when Andy Watson's corner looks like creeping in.											
41	A	WREXHAM	20	L	0-3	0-1		Roche	Fleming P	Harrison	Horner	Barr R^	Bramhall	Barr W	Watson	McPhillips	Allison	Richards'n N*	Broadbent/**Paterson**
	21/4	_1,782_	_7_	47			_Buxton 9, 70, Preece 89_	_Salmon_	_Thackeray_	_Wright_	_Hunter_	_Williams_	_Jones J_	_Preece_	_Flynn_	_Buxton_	_Russell_	_Bowden_	
							Ref: P Danson	This is the 100th meeting between the two sides. Wrexham looked promotion contenders a month ago, but have since fallen away. They mean business here, and are ahead as early as the ninth minute when Buxton starts the scoring from eight yards, their first goal in over 360 minutes.											
42	A	ROCHDALE		D	1-1	0-0	Barr W 49	Roche	Fleming P	Harrison	Horner	Blain	Bramhall	Barr W	Watson	McPhillips	Allison	Matthews N	
	25/4	**_1,388_**		48			_Frain 73_	_Welch_	_Fothergill^_	_Armitage*_	_Smart_	_Jones_	_Copeland_	_Beaumont_	_O'Shaughn'sy_	_Taylor_	_Walling_	_Frain_	_Mycock/Edmonds_
							Ref: A Seville	Despite the point, Town are still looking over their shoulders at the bottom of the table. This is a game they might have won, after Barr scores when Welch mishandles. They have chances to wrap the game up, but pay for not doing so when Frain equalises, his shot going in off Fleming.											
43	H	LINCOLN	20	L	0-1	0-0		Roche	Fleming P	Harrison	Horner	Blain^	Bramhall*	Barr W	Watson	McPhillips	Allison	Matthews N	Broadbent/Rich'son N
	29/4	1,261	_9_	48			_Brown 88_	_Bowling_	_Casey_	_Clarke_	_Schofield_	_James^_	_Matthewson*_	_Gamble_	_Bressington_	_Sertori_	_Smith_	_Cumming_	_Brown/Davis_
							Ref: R Pawley	Colin Murphy's Imps side extend their unbeaten run to five games. For Town, it's now seven games without a win. McPhillips misses a great chance early on. Schofield then hits the post for the Imps. Lincoln take the points when Brown is in the right place at the right time to score.											
44	A	COLCHESTER	21	L	2-3	1-0	Hill 27 (og), McPhillips 54	Roche*	Fleming P	Harrison	Horner	Richardson N	Bramhall	Barr W	Watson	Broadbent	Allison	Matthews N	McPhillips
	1/5	_5,065_	_23_	48			_Wilkins 61, Warner 74, Allinson 81p_	_McAlister_	_Radford_	_Stafford_	_Taylor*_	_Hetzke_	_Hill_	_Wilkins_	_English_	_Scott^_	_Walsh_	_Allinson_	_Warner/Coleman_
							Ref: P Don	Graham Broadbent makes his first Town start, but ends up in goal when Roche is stretchered off after 30 minutes following Walsh's challenge. Despite his heroics, Town lose to Allinson's penalty when Walsh's header hit Bramhall's hand. Town had actually led 2-0 after 54 minutes.											
45	A	CREWE	21	D	2-2	0-1	Broadbent 63, Allison 70	Whitehead P	Fleming P*	Blain	Horner	Hedworth	Bramhall	Barr W^	Watson	Richardson N	Allison	Matthews N	McPhillips/Broadbent
	5/5	_3,476_	_5_	49			_Clayton 34, Gardiner 51_	_Greygoose_	_Swain_	_Edwards_	_Billing_	_Callaghan_	_Walters_	_Jasper_	_Clayton_	_Sussex_	_Gardiner_	_Fishenden*_	_Murphy_
							Ref: G Ashby	This point means Town cannot be caught by bottom club Darlington. They are unfortunate to go two goals down when Gardiner curls in a free-kick. Broadbent comes off the bench to start Town's fightback. After Allison pounces for the equaliser, Town actually look a good bet to win.											
46	H	HEREFORD	21	D	2-2	1-1	McPhillips 8p, 50	Whitehead P	Hedworth	Harrison	Horner	Richards'n N^	Bramhall*	Barr W	Watson	McPhillips	Allison	Broadbent	Matth'ws N/**Donnelly**
	13/5	**1,082**	_15_	50			_Stant 10, Narbett 56_	_Rose_	_Jones M_	_Devine_	_Jones R_	_Peacock_	_Benbow_	_Mardenboro'_	_Narbett_	_Stant_	_Tester_	_McLoughlin_	
	Home	Away					Ref: T West	McPhillips equals Les Massie's 1967-68 haul of 25 goals. His first is a penalty after Peacock bundles over Allison. His second goes in off the post. Hereford, twice behind, respond quickly both times. Rose is lucky to remain on the field after bringing down McPhillips outside the box.											
Average	1,915	2,612																	

Littlewoods Cup				F-A	H-T	Scorers, Times, and Referees	1	2	3	4	5	6	7	8	9	10	11	subs used
1:1 A SCARBOROUGH			D	1-1	0-0	Watson 86	Roche	Barr W	Logan	Willis	Barr R	Whitehead A	Watson	Horner	Matthews N*	Allison	Richardson L	McPhillips
31/8	2,196					*Brook 63*	*Blackwell*	*Kamara*	*Thompson**	*Short*	*Richards*	*Bennyworth*	*Morris*	*Cook*	*Norris*	*Brook*	*Graham*	*McJannet*
						Ref: J Watson	Andy Watson, a housing assistant with Leeds City Council, marks his debut with a crucial goal that gives Halifax a great chance in the return leg. He ghosts in four minutes from time to head home. Town look like heading for defeat when Gary Brook forces home Colin Morris's cross.											
1:2 H SCARBOROUGH		11	D	2-2	1-2	Allison 19, McPhillips 79	Roche	Barr W	Logan	Matthews M	Bramhall	Whitehead A	Martin*	Horner	McPhillips	Allison	Richardson L	Watson
6/9	1,713	*5*				*Richards 16, Cook 32p*	*Blackwell*	*Kamara*	*Thompson*	*Short*	*Richards*	*Bennyworth*	*Morris**	*Cook*	*Norris*	*Brook*	*Graham*	*Adams*
						Ref: J Penrose (Halifax lost on away goals)	Town bow out, but without losing a game. Cup winners Luton will be the other team to remain unbeaten. The crucial moment in this game is Boro's penalty award for Bramhall's slight challenge on Norris. Town could have won, but find McPhillips' shot into the corner isn't enough.											

FA Cup																		
1 H YORK		10	W	1-0	0-0	McPhillips 78	Roche	Hedworth	Horner	Matthews M	Robinson	Bramhall	Richardson L	Watson	McPhillips	Allison	Matthews N	
19/11	2,894	*21*					*Marples*	*Branagan*	*Johnson*	*Eli*	*Tutill*	*Fazackerley*	*Butler*	*Wilson*	*Helliwell*	*Dunn**	*Canham*	*Howlett*
						Ref: I Hendrick	Patience is a virtue, and Town keep their nerve to go through. They dominate the game but find John Bird's side a tough nut to crack. A replay looks the likely outcome until McPhillips latches on to Neil Matthews' pass to steer the ball home. York claim he controlled it with his hand.											
2 A ALTRINCHAM		17	W	3-0	2-0	Barr W 41, Allison 43, 76	Roche	Hedworth	Horner	Richardson L	Robinson	Bramhall	Martin	Watson	Barr W	Allison	Matthews N	
10/12	*3,967*	*VC*					*Wealands*	*Johnson*	*Knowles*	*Cuddy*	*Farrelly*	*Ellis*	*Cook*	*Phillips**	*Stewart*	*Timmons*	*Kilner^*	*Daws/Heesom*
						Ref: R Hart	This game is featured on 'Match of the Day'. Barr's acute header finds its way in, but a minute later Gary Stewart puts wide a penalty. He rues that miss when Allison rounds the keeper for his first of his brace. Commentator John Motson describes Town's performance as 'professional'.											
3 A KETTERING		14	D	1-1	1-0	Watson 6	Whitehead P	Barr W	Horner	Richardson L	Robinson	Bramhall	Martin	Watson	McPhillips	Allison	Matthews N	
7/1	*5,800*	*VC:4*				*Griffith 58*	*Lim*	*Nightingale*	*Heywood*	*Fuccillo*	*Lewis*	*Brown*	*Keast*	*Wright**	*Moss*	*Cooke*	*Griffith*	*Richardson*
						Ref: G Pooley	With the experienced Ernie Moss and Robbie Cooke in their side, Kettering put out Bristol Rovers in the last round. Halifax don't expect, nor get, an easy ride. In a pulsating game, Andy Watson's header puts Town in front, but Cohen Griffith's stunning individual goal means a replay.											
3R H KETTERING		14	L	2-3	2-2	Bramhall 16, Barr W 28	Whitehead P	Barr W	Horner	Richardson L	Robinson	Bramhall	Martin	Watson	McPhillips	Allison	Matthews N	
10/1	5,632	*VC:4*				*Lewis 4, Cooke 37, 49*	*Lim*	*Nightingale*	*Richardson*	*Fuccillo*	*Lewis*	*Brown*	*Keast*	*Wright*	*Moss*	*Cooke**	*Griffith*	*Edwards*
						Ref: G Pooley	The game captures the imagination of the fans, most of whom think a trip to Charlton in Round 4 is a formality. After Lewis's shock opener, Town keep their cup dreams alive when Barr's soft free-kick puts Town ahead. Early in the second half, Cooke's close-range goal kills them.											

		P	W	D	L	F	A	W	D	L	F	A	Pts
			Home					Away					
1	Rotherham	46	13	6	4	44	18	9	10	4	32	17	82
2	Tranmere	46	15	6	2	34	13	6	11	6	28	30	80
3	Crewe	46	13	7	3	42	24	8	8	7	25	24	78
4	Scunthorpe	46	11	9	3	40	22	10	5	8	37	35	77
5	Scarborough	46	12	7	4	33	23	9	7	7	34	29	77
6	Leyton Orient*	46	16	2	5	61	19	5	10	8	25	31	75
7	Wrexham	46	12	7	4	44	28	7	7	9	33	35	71
8	Cambridge	46	13	7	3	45	25	5	7	11	26	37	68
9	Grimsby	46	11	9	3	33	18	6	6	11	32	41	66
10	Lincoln	46	12	6	5	39	26	6	4	13	25	34	64
11	York	46	10	8	5	43	27	7	5	11	19	36	64
12	Carlisle	46	9	6	8	26	25	6	9	8	27	27	60
13	Exeter	46	14	4	5	46	23	4	2	17	19	45	60
14	Torquay	46	15	2	6	32	23	2	6	15	13	37	59
15	Hereford	46	11	8	4	40	27	3	8	12	26	45	58
16	Burnley	46	12	6	5	35	20	2	7	14	17	41	55
17	Peterborough	46	10	3	10	29	32	4	9	10	23	42	54
18	Rochdale	46	10	10	3	32	26	3	4	16	24	56	53
19	Hartlepool	46	10	6	7	33	33	4	4	15	17	45	52
20	Stockport	46	8	10	5	31	20	2	11	10	23	32	51
21	HALIFAX	46	10	7	6	42	27	3	4	16	27	48	50
22	Colchester	46	8	7	8	35	30	4	7	12	25	48	50
23	Doncaster	46	9	6	8	32	32	4	4	15	17	46	49
24	Darlington	46	3	12	8	28	38	5	6	12	25	38	42
		1104	267	161	124	899	599	124	161	267	599	899	1495

* promoted after play-offs

Odds & ends

Double wins: (3) Darlington, Doncaster, Torquay.
Double losses: (5) Burnley, Exeter, Lincoln, Scarborough, Tranmere.

Won from behind: (1) Colchester (h).
Lost from in front: (6) Tranmere (h), Cambridge (a), Colchester (a), Grimsby (a), Lincoln (a), Kettering (FAC) (h).

High spots: Three consecutive wins in October.
Town's early season goal blast at home.
Scoring in the first 21 league and cup matches.
Winning 3-0 at non-league Altrincham in the FA Cup in front of the TV cameras.

Low spots: Six games without a win up to 1 October.
Four consecutive defeats up to 17 December.
Losing to non-league Kettering in a FA Cup replay at the Shay.
Failing to win any of the last ten matches.

Player of the Year: John Bramhall.
Ever-presents: (0).
Hat-tricks: Terry McPhillips (1).
Leading scorer: Terry McPhillips (25).

	Appearances						Goals			
	Lge	*Sub*	LC	*Sub*	FAC	*Sub*	Lge	LC	FAC	Tot
Allison, Wayne	**41**		2		4		**14**	1	2	**17**
Barr, Billy	**42**	*1*	2		3		**4**		2	**6**
Barr, Bobby	**4**		1							
Blain, Colin	**16**	*4*								
Bramhall, John	**39**		1		4		**3**		1	**4**
Broadbent, Graham	**2**	*10*					**2**			**2**
Donnelly, Paul		*1*								
Fleming, Craig		*1*								
Fleming, Paul	**22**	*1*								
Harrison, Frankie	**13**									
Hedworth, Chris	**11**				2					
Henry, Liburd	**1**	*4*								
Horner, Phil	**36**	*2*	2		4		**3**			**3**
Logan, David	**3**		2							
McPhillips, Terry	**37**	*4*	1	*1*	3		**23**	1	1	**25**
Martin, Dean	**32**		1		3		**2**			**2**
Matthews, Mick	**15**		1		1		**1**			**1**
Matthews, Neil	**32**	*2*	1		4		**7**			**7**
Paterson, Toby		*1*								
Pullan, Chris	**5**						**1**			**1**
Richardson, Lee	**22**	*3*	2		4		**1**			**1**
Richardson, Nick	**4**	*3*								
Robinson, David	**30**				4		**1**			**1**
Roche, Paddy	**25**		2		2					
Sinclair, Ronnie	**10**									
Smith, Shaun		*1*								
Watson, Andy	**42**	*3*	1	*1*	4		**5**	1	1	**7**
Whitehead, Alan	**10**	*1*	2				**1**			**1**
Whitehead, Phil	**11**				2					
Willis, Paul	**1**	*3*	1							
(own-goals)							**1**			**1**
30 players used	**506**	***45***	**22**	***2***	**44**		**69**	**3**	**7**	**79**

No	Date		Att	Pos	Pt	F-A	H-T	Scorers, Times, and Referees	1	2	3	4	5	6	7	8	9	10	11	subs used
1	H	HARTLEPOOL			W	**4-0**	1-0	Watson 37, 70, Hall 58, Juryeff 81	Whitehead	Barr	**Cook**	**Hedworth**	Bramhall	Horner	Martin	Watson	Matthews*	**Butler**	**Hall**	**Juryeff**
	19/8		1,524		3				*Bowling*	*Barrass*	*McKinnon*	*Tinkler*	*Stokes*	*Stokle*	*Atkinson**	*Ogden*	*Baker*	*Grayson*	*Dalton*	*Curry*
								Ref: J Lunt	Town set a new club record with their highest ever opening-day victory with this scintillating display against a poor Hartlepool side. Watson is the star of the show, and he rounds the keeper for the first goal. New record signing Ian Juryeff comes off the bench to head in Butler's corner.											
2	A	COLCHESTER		4	D	2-2	0-0	Hicks 51 (og), Watson 69	Whitehead	Barr	Cook	Hedworth	Bramhall	Horner	Martin	Watson	Juryeff	Butler	Hall	
	26/8		*2,404*	*13*	4			*Bennett 64, Radford 89p*	*Hansbury*	*Hicks*	*Rooke^*	*English*	*Daniels*	*Radford*	*Bennett*	*Collins*	*Wilkins*	*Scott*	*Allinson**	*Kinsella/Taylor*
								Ref: R Pawley	There is drama at the end of this match. Hicks has headed into his own net, and Watson scores a tap-in for a 2-1 lead. Then, a minute from time the ref gives a dubious penalty for hands against Butler. Radford scores at the second attempt after the ref awards a re-take for encroachment.											
3	H	TORQUAY		2	W	3-1	0-0	Watson 46, Matthews 54, 89	Whitehead	Barr	Cook	Hedworth^	Bramhall	Horner	Martin	Watson*	Matthews	Butler	Hall	McPhillips/Richardson
	2/9		1,893	*23*	7			*Loram 84p*	*Veysey*	*Holmes*	*Pugh*	*Matthews*	*Davies*	*Uzzell*	*Weston^*	*Lloyd*	*Edwards*	*Airey**	*Miller*	*Loram/Joyce*
								Ref: D Allison	A rocket from Ayre at half-time pays instant dividends when Watson lifts the ball over Veysey. Town are seemingly in control when Matthews makes it 2-0, but there are a few nerves when Loram scores a late penalty. McPhillips comes on to set up Matthews, who makes the game safe.											
4	A	WREXHAM		6	L	1-2	0-1	Hall 52	Whitehead	Barr	Cook	Butler	Bramhall	Horner	Martin	Watson	Matthews	Juryeff	Hall	
	9/9		***1,700***	*9*	7			*Worthington 42, 80*	*O'Keefe*	*Thackeray*	*Wright*	*Hunter*	*Beaumont*	*Jones*	*Preece*	*Flynn*	*Buxton**	*Worthington*	*Cooper*	*Kearns*
								Ref: I Hemley	Two costly errors leave Town with nothing. The defence is static when Worthington lobs his first. Town draw level after the break when Hall tucks away the equaliser, then Watson has a goal ruled out for offside. Worthington nets the winner when he is left free following a free-kick.											
5	H	CARLISLE		6	D	1-1	0-0	Juryeff 84	**Brown**	Barr	Cook	Hedworth	Bramhall	Horner	Martin	Watson*	Matthews	Butler	Hall^	McPhillips/Juryeff
	15/9		2,121	*12*	8			*Walwyn 56*	*McKellar*	*Graham*	*Dalziel*	*Saddington*	*Jones*	*Fitzpatrick*	*Walsh*	*Miller*	*Walwyn*	*Proudlock*	*Halpin*	
								Ref: P Tyldesley	Carlisle, unbeaten in the league, almost gain revenge for the Littlewoods Cup defeat. Walwyn's goal from 10 yards looks good enough for them until Cook's cross finds Juryeff lurking at the far post. Town feel justice is done, and point to Cook's shot that beats the keeper but hits the bar.											
6	A	CAMBRIDGE		7	L	0-1	0-0		Brown	Fleming P	Cook	Hedworth	Bramhall	Horner	Martin	Watson*	Matthews	Jureff	Hall	McPhillips
	22/9		*2,220*	*18*	8			*Philpott 78*	*Vaughan*	*Bailie*	*Kimble*	*O'Shea*	*Chapple*	*Daish*	*Dennis*	*Leadbitter*	*Robinson*	*Taylor**	*Philpott*	*Dublin*
								Ref: P Danson	After only six minutes' play, the game is held up for 15 minutes because of a bomb scare. The spectators join the players on the pitch, but it's all a hoax. When the match commences, the players put on a thriller. Philpott claims the crucial goal, but it's Brown who knocks the ball in.											
7	A	SCARBOROUGH		8	W	3-2	1-0	Watson 39, 46, Juryeff 51	Brown	Fleming P	Cook	Hedworth	Bramhall	Horner	Martin	Watson*	Matthews	Juryeff	Hall	Barr
	27/9		*3,147*	*16*	11			*Norris 73, Short 84*	*Blackwell*	*Kamara*	*Clarke*	*Short*	*Richards**	*Bennyworth^*	*Saunders*	*Graham*	*Norris*	*Robinson*	*Russell*	*Olsson/Brook*
								Ref: G Alpin	David Brown is outstanding as Town rely on strong defending at one end and errors by the home side at the other to clinch victory. A mix-up in the their defence allows Juryeff to nip in to make it 3-0, but Boro peg it back to one goal. Brown has to make a last-ditch save from Russell.											
8	H	EXETER		10	L	1-2	0-0	Matthews 49	Brown	Fleming P	Cook	Hedworth	Bramhall*	Horner^	Martin	Watson	Matthews	Juryeff	Hall	Barr/McPhillips
	30/9		1,720	*4*	11			*Neville 52, Dryden 73*	*Walter*	*Hiley*	*Vinnicombe*	*Rogers*	*Taylor*	*Whitehead*	*Rowbotham*	*Bailey*	*McDermott*	*Neville**	*Dryden*	*Young*
								Ref: W Burns	Terry Cooper's Exeter show championship qualities at the Shay, coming from behind to win. Town, despite losing Bramhall with concussion before the break, go in front through Matthews, who later inadvertently sets Neville up for a quick reply. Dryden pounces to score the winner.											
9	H	GILLINGHAM		13	L	0-1	0-0		Brown	Fleming P	Cook	Hedworth^	Bramhall	Horner	Martin	Watson	Butler	Juryeff	Hall*	McPhillips/Richardson
	6/10		1,776	*9*	11			*Lovell 82*	*Hillyard*	*Haylock*	*Johnson*	*Haines*	*Walker*	*Palmer*	*Trusson*	*Eeles**	*Lovell*	*Heritage*	*Manuel*	*Gavin*
								Ref: A Wilkie	Gills boss Damien Richardson, in his first season in charge, sees his side record their second away win in a poor game. Town's McPhillips is sent on after only 35 minutes but it's the Gills who make the breakthrough when Lovell seizes on a knockdown. Gavin has time to hit the post.											
10	A	LINCOLN		14	L	1-2	1-0	Juryeff 28	Whitehead	Fleming P	Cook	Butler	Bramhall	Horner	Martin	Watson	Matthews	Juryeff	Hall	
	14/10		*4,071*	*2*	11			*Sertori 67, Waitt 68*	*Gorton*	*Casey*	*Clarke*	*Schofield*	*Thompson*	*Brown*	*Roberts*	*Bressington*	*Sertori*	*Waitt*	*Cumming*	
								Ref: M Bailey	Lincoln, under Colin Murphy, regained their League place at the first attempt after relegation to the Conference. They've made a terrific start this time, and here they punish Town for napping for a minute. When Town wake up, their lead has gone. Unmarked Waitt scores the winner.											
11	A	CHESTERFIELD		16	L	3-4	3-1	Bramhall 26, Matthews 31, Hall 45	Whitehead	Fleming P	Cook	Butler	Bramhall	Horner	Martin	Smith	Matthews	Juryeff	Hall	
	17/10		*2,998*	*9*	11			*Arnott 18, Gunn 52p, Waller 77, 90*	*Leonard*	*Gunn*	*Ryan*	*Bloomer*	*Brien*	*Hart*	*Rolphe*	*Hewitt*	*Waller*	*Arnott*	*Morris*	
								Ref: F Roberts	Town are hardly convincing, yet manage to take a 3-1 half-time lead. A dubious penalty award for a foul on Rolphe by Smith, starting his first game, prompts a Spireites' fightback. Dave Waller equalises from the eighth of twelve second-half corners, before curling in a dramatic winner.											

No	Venue	Opponent	Att	Pos	Res	F-A	H-T	Scorers, Times, and Referees	1	2	3	4	5	6	7	8	9	10	11	subs used
12	H	ROCHDALE		16	W	1-0	0-0	Juryeff 73	Whitehead	Fleming P	Cook	Hedworth	Bramhall	Horner	Martin	Butler*	Matthews	Juryeff	Hall	Broadbent
	21/10		1,864	*18*	14				*Welch*	*Goodison*	*Hill*	*Brown*	*Cole*	*Ward*	*Ainscow*	*Holmes**	*Elliott*	*Burns^*	*Johnson*	*Edmonds/Walling*
								Ref: G Singh	There is relief all around the Shay when Juryeff gets in behind the Rochdale defence and fires past Welch. His goal ensures victory, and ends a run of four consecutive league defeats, and three consecutive home defeats. Apart from that, there is little else for the supporters to cheer about											
13	A	GRIMSBY		18	D	1-1	0-0	Bramhall 56	Whitehead	Fleming P	Cook	Hedworth	Bramhall	Horner	Martin	Watson	Matthews	Juryeff	Hall	
	28/10		*4,021*	*15*	15			*Cunnington 82*	*Reece*	*McDermott*	*Stoutt^*	*Tillson*	*Lever*	*Cunnington*	*Childs*	*Gilbert*	*Birtles*	*Watson*	*Alexander**	*Hargreaves/Willis*
								Ref: A Smith	This game is played with a gale-force wind blowing, and the elements make for an interesting afternoon. Grimsby's McDermott twice takes a throw-in, only for the ball to blow back in his face. Bramhall heads Town in front, but Shaun Cunnington is left unmarked to grab an equaliser.											
14	H	HEREFORD		18	D	1-1	0-1	Matthews 56	Whitehead	Fleming P	Cook	Hedworth	Bramhall	Horner	Martin	Watson*	Matthews	Juryeff	Hall	McPhillips
	31/10		1,235	*10*	16			*Oghani 19*	*Elliott*	*Jones MA*	*Williams*	*Hemming*	*Pejic*	*Bradley*	*Jones M*	*Narbett*	*Robinson*	*Oghani**	*Tester*	*Peacock*
								Ref: R Nixon	McPhillips has only been on the field three minutes when Peacock concedes a penalty. He elects to take it, but Elliott brilliantly saves his kick. That blunder costs Town a probable three points. Matthews had earlier cancelled out Oghani's goal after latching onto Bradley's suicidal pass.											
15	A	STOCKPORT		16	W	1-0	0-0	Horner 58	Whitehead	Fleming P	Cook	Hedworth	Bramhall	Horner	Martin	Watson	Matthews	Juryeff	Hall	
	3/11		*5,490*	*2*	19				*Siddall*	*Brown*	*Bullock*	*Matthews*	*Williams B*	*Thorpe*	*McInerney*	*Payne*	*Edwards*	*Cooke*	*Angell*	
								Ref: K Breen	Billy Ayre believes his side are beginning to show their true potential. Victory over second-placed County is a notable scalp. Before the game, they were unbeaten at home having scored the most home goals. Horner pounces for the decisive goal, and Town work hard for a clean-sheet.											
16	H	SOUTHEND		18	L	1-2	0-1	Juryeff 79	Whitehead	Fleming P	Smith*	Hedworth	Bramhall	Horner	Martin	Watson	Broadbent	Juryeff	Hall^	McPhillips/Butler
	10/11		1,908	*1*	19			*Ling 30, Martin 57*	*Sansome*	*Roberts*	*Edinburgh*	*Martin*	*Tilson**	*Brush*	*Cook*	*Butler*	*Crown*	*McDonough*	*Ling*	*Clark*
								Ref: J Lloyd	John Bramhall looks sick when Sansome saves his 23rd-minute penalty, given for a foul on Watson by Roberts. A relieved Southend side then take control. Minutes later, Edinburgh creates a goal for Ling, then Martin heads in the second. Juryeff's diving header sets up a frantic finish.											
17	H	MAIDSTONE		18	L	1-2	1-0	Juryeff 8	Whitehead	Fleming P	Butler	Hedworth	Bramhall*	Horner	Martin	Watson	Matthews	Juryeff	Hall^	Broadbent/Barr
	25/11		1,353	*15*	19			*Gall 47, Golley 63*	*Beeney*	*Roast*	*Cooper*	*Berry*	*Oxbrow*	*Pearce*	*Gall**	*Galliers*	*Golley*	*Butler*	*Burton*	*Charlery*
								Ref: P Wright	For the third home game running, the Shaymen miss a penalty. This time it's Brian Butler's turn after Beeney brings down Watson. His 57th-minute kick hits the post. A draw looks the likely outcome, but then Golley's header off Cooper's corner bounces in through a ruck of players.											
18	A	ALDERSHOT		18	L	0-2	0-1		Whitehead	Fleming P	Butler	Barr	Broadbent	Horner	Martin	Watson	Matthews	Juryeff	Hall	
	2/12		*1,749*	*11*	19			*Claridge 35, 90*	*Coles*	*Brown*	*Phillips*	*Henry*	*Ogley*	*Williams*	*Claridge*	*Puckett*	*Stewart*	*Burvill*	*Randall*	
								Ref: P Foakes	Len Walker, in his second spell as Shots' manager, has picked his side up after a slow start. Ayre, meantime, is concerned that his side fails to take a host of chances. Steve Claridge shows them how. His first is an angled drive past Whitehead, his second from close range in injury-time.											
19	H	DONCASTER		20	L	0-2	0-0		Brown	Fleming P	Smith	Matthews	Bramhall	Horner	Martin	Watson^	Richardson	Harrison*	Hall	Broadbent/Hall
	15/12		**1,233**	*19*	19			*Noteman 54, Adams 65*	*Samways*	*Robinson*	*Brevett*	*Gaughan*	*Ashurst*	*Douglas*	*Adams*	*Stiles*	*Turnbull*	*Jones*	*Noteman*	
								Ref: I Cruikshanks	A much-publicised row between Ayre and Juryeff has led to Town's record signing moving to Hereford. Town are devoid of confidence after defeat by Darlington in the Cup. Fleming and Martin try to set an example. David Jones, ex-Ipswich, has a hand in both of Doncaster's goals.											
20	A	YORK		20	W	2-0	1-0	Richardson 7, 51	Whitehead	Fleming P	Smith	Hedworth	Bramhall	Horner	Martin	Barr	Richardson	Broadbent	**Naylor**	
	26/12		*3,665*	*6*	22				*Marples*	*McMillan*	*Kelly*	*Barratt*	*Tutill*	*Warburton*	*Howlett**	*Spooner*	*Helliwell*	*Canham*	*Dixon^*	*Hall/Himsworth*
								Ref: A Simmons	York are up there with the leaders, and are favourites to win this game. But the Shaymen are prepared to scrap it out, and in a game where five players are booked in the first 40 minutes, they have in Richardson a match-winner. After his early strike, he doubles the lead with a low drive.											
21	A	BURNLEY		20	L	0-1	0-1		Whitehead	Fleming P	Smith	Hedworth	Bramhall	Horner	Martin	Barr	Richardson	Broadbent*	Naylor^	Harrison/Butler
	30/12		***9,105***	12	22			*Futcher 35*	*Pearce*	*Measham*	*Hardy**	*Deary*	*Davis S*	*Farrell*	*White*	*Eli^*	*Futcher*	*Jakub*	*Davis SM*	*McKay/Bent*
								Ref: V Callow	Burnley create a number of openings, but they find Whitehead in terrific form. He keeps the score down, although he is unable to prevent the much-travelled Futcher's guided header from going in. Youth coach Gerry Brook gestures at over-critical Town fans and is later suspended.											
22	H	PETERBOROUGH		20	D	2-2	0-1	Naylor 48, McPhillips 83	Whitehead	Fleming P	Smith	Hedworth	Bramhall^	Horner	Martin	Watson*	Richardson	Butler	Naylor	McPhillips/Harrison
	1/1		1,578	*12*	23			*Harle 45p, Butterworth 47*	*Godden*	*Luke*	*Crosby*	*Halsall*	*Robinson*	*McElhinney*	*Sterling*	*Harle*	*Longhurst*	*Osborne**	*Butterworth*	*Oakes*
								Ref: J Watson	Ex-Shayman Longhurst is clattered by both Hedworth and Bramhall for the Posh's penalty right on half-time. Minutes after the break, Town go two down, but respond immediately. Naylor dives to head in his first-ever goal, then McPhillips, a 69th-minute sub, drives in the equaliser.											
23	A	SCUNTHORPE		21	D	1-1	1-1	Cowling 2 (og)	Whitehead	Fleming P	Harrison	Hedworth	Bramhall	Horner	Hall	McPhillips^	Richardson	Butler	Naylor*	Barr/Watson
	6/1		*3,051*	*11*	24			*Taylor 30*	*Musselwhite*	*Smalley*	*Longden*	*Taylor**	*Stevenson !*	*Cotton*	*Marshall*	*Hamilton*	*Lillis*	*Flounders*	*Cowling*	*Daws*
								Ref: A Ward	Scunthorpe hand Town a goal after just 90 seconds when Cowling diverts Butler's cross in off his shin. Lillis sets up the equaliser for Taylor, but the Iron are hanging on after Stevenson's 74th-minute sending off for a late tackle on Hall. Hall ends up getting booked in the 95th minute.											

No	Date		Att	Pos	Pt	F-A	H-T	Scorers, Times, and Referees	1	2	3	4	5	6	7	8	9	10	11	subs used
24	H	COLCHESTER		21	D	1-1	1-0	Hall 12	Brown	Fleming P	Harrison*	Hedworth	Bramhall	Horner	Hall	Broadbent^	Richardson	Butler	Matthews	Cook/McPhillips
	12/1		1,397	23	25			Scott 79	Barrett	Bruce	Stafford	Taylor	Daniels	English A	Collins	Ball	Wilkins	Bennett^	Radford*	Morgan/Scott
								Ref: P Jones	Town might not like to admit it, but their league status may be under threat, and will be until they learn to kill games off like this one. Hall's goal promises more, but they don't arrive. A flare-up between Fleming and English ends the first half. The U's equalise through Scott's header.											
25	A	HARTLEPOOL		21	L	0-2	0-2		Whitehead	Fleming P	Cook	Hedworth	Naylor^	Horner	Hall	Barr*	Richardson	Butler	Matthews	Watson/Harrison
	20/1		2,444	24	25			Allon 9, Smith 45	Priestley	MacDonald*	McKinnon	Tinkler	Smith	Bennyworth	Allon	Tupling	Baker	Nobbs	Dalton	Honour
								Ref: A Bennett	After this defeat by bottom club Hartlepool, only six points now separate the sides. Pool could actually have won by more had McKinnon's 30-yarder not hit the underside of the bar. The Shaymen improve in the second half, but Mick Smith's goal seconds from the break is a real killer.											
26	H	WREXHAM		20	W	4-2	3-2	Matthews 7, 41, Watson 9, Richardson 58	Whitehead	Fleming P	Cook	Hedworth	Graham	Horner	Hall	Watson*	Richardson	Fyfe	Matthews	Harrison
	26/1		1,436	23	28			Cooper 5, 44	O'Keefe	Preece	Wright	Bowden	Beaumont	Jones J	Buxton	Hunter^	Madden*	Worthington	Cooper	Armstrong/Jones R
								Ref: E Parker	Town, who include recent signings Fyfe and Graham, returning for a second spell, recover from Graham Cooper's early goal to take the lead with only nine minutes gone. There are chances galore in the first half, but it's Richardson goal off Fyfe's header that ends Wrexham's hopes.											
27	H	CAMBRIDGE		20	D	0-0	0-0		Brown	Fleming P	Cook	Hedworth	Graham	Horner	Hall	Martin	Richardson	Fyfe	Matthews	
	2/2		1,526	13	29				Vaughan	Fensome	Kimble	Daish	Chapple	Bailie	Cheetham	Leadbitter	Dublin	Taylor*	Philpott	Cook
								Ref: G Ashby	Cambridge enjoyed FA Cup glory in midweek with victory over 1st Division Millwall. This is a case of after the Lord Mayor's Show for them. Town lose Matthews temporarily in the third minute while he has a nose injury treated, the only incident of note in a dour battle in driving rain.											
28	A	CARLISLE		20	D	1-1	0-1	Matthews 57	Brown	Fleming P	Cook	Hedworth	Graham	Horner	Hall	McPhillips	Richardson	Fyfe	Matthews	
	10/2		4,844	1	30			Fitzpatrick 17	McKellar	Walsh	McCall	Graham	Jones	Fitzpatrick	Shepherd	Miller	Walwyn*	Norris^	Goldsmith	Proudlock/Sendall
								Ref: D Allison	Carlisle, the league-leaders, have won their last four home games. They didn't expect Town to put up such a fight. All is going well for them when Fitzpatrick scores after the ref plays the advantage. Town reply through Matthews into the wind when he gets up to head in Cook's cross.											
29	H	ALDERSHOT		18	W	4-1	3-0	Cook 11, Graham 21, Matthews 24,	Brown	Fleming P*	Cook	Hedworth	Graham	Horner^	Hall	McPhillips	Richardson	Fyfe	Matthews	Butler/Watson
	17/2		1,275	16	33			Coombs 85 [Richardson 58]	Coles	Brown	Phillips	Burvill	Ogley	Anderson	Coombs	Puckett	Stewart	Henry	Randall*	Banton
								Ref: I Hendrick	Halifax are dreaming of Wembley in the Leyland DAF Cup, and warm up for their northern semi-final against Doncaster with this handsome win. They discover their early season form to send the Shots packing. Cook blasts in the first, whilst Town's other three goals are all headers.											
30	A	MAIDSTONE		18	W	2-1	2-0	McPhillips 33, Richardson 35	Brown	Fleming P	Cook	**Gannon**	Graham	Martin	Hall	McPhillips*	Richardson	Fyfe	Matthews	Butler
	24/2		2,182	7	36			Golley 51	Beeney	Roast	Cooper	Berry	Oxbrow*	Golley	Gall	Lillis	Sorrell	Butler	Pearce	Charlery
								Ref: D Elleray	Keith Peacock's Maidstone are heading for the play-offs, but this defeat will hinder their chances of automatic promotion. The damage is done by Town in a two-minute spell. The Stones pull a goal back after the break, then find Brown and on-loan Gannon (Sheffield Utd) in great form.											
31	H	SCUNTHORPE		20	L	0-1	0-0		Brown	Fleming P	Cook	Gannon	Graham	Martin	Hall	McPhillips*	Richardson	Fyfe	Matthews	Watson
	3/3		1,793	12	36			Daws 76	Musselwhite	Smalley	Longden	Ward	Bramhall	Stevenson	Hodkinson	Cowling	Daws	Flounders	Hamilton	
								Ref: D Scott	Scunthorpe, under ex-Shayman Mick Buxton, make it six clean sheets in their last six matches, and extend to 549 minutes the amount of time it's been since they last conceded a goal. Town, though, find their defence rather shaky, but can't take advantage. Daws' goal then stuns them.											
32	A	EXETER		20	L	0-2	0-1		Brown	Fleming P	Cook	Hedworth	Graham	Martin	Hall^	Watson*	Richardson	Fyfe	Matthews	Harrison/Naylor
	7/3		5,528	1	36			Taylor 30, 58	Miller	Hiley	Dryden	McNichol	Taylor	Whitehead	Rowbotham	Bailey	McDermott	Neville	Batty	
								Ref: P Durkin	Exeter's Shaun Taylor plays despite having an ankle injury, and grabs his side's goals from close-range off set pieces. He is denied a hat-trick when his 44th-minute header crashes against the bar. Both managers agree, however, that the best player on view is Town's Chris Hedworth.											
33	H	SCARBOROUGH		20	L	1-2	1-2	Matthews 40	Brown	Fleming P	Cook	Hedworth	Graham*	Martin	Broadbent	Watson	Richardson	Fyfe^	Matthews	Harrison/McPhillips
	10/3		1,490	16	36			Saunders 21, Richards 26	Richardson	Short	Kamara	Wilson	Richards	Meyer	Oghani	Saunders	Russell	Dobson	MacDonald	
								Ref: A Flood	More home woe for Town and in particular Billy Ayre. Matthews' header halves the deficit and gives Halifax enough time in which to save the game, but they don't respond to their manager. They give it their all in the last five, but Richards' header for 0-2 has the game won for Boro.											
34	A	GILLINGHAM		22	L	1-3	0-2	Matthews 55	Brown	Fleming P*	Cook	Hedworth	Graham	Martin	Broadbent^	Watson	Richardson	Hall	Matthews	Barr/Fyfe
	16/3		3,825	3	36			Lovell 2p, O'Shea 38, Heritage 52	Hillyard	Haylock	Johnson	Kimble	Walker	Palmer	Lovell	O'Shea	O'Connor	Heritage^	Trusson*	Manuel/Gavin
								Ref: J Carter	Pressure is mounting on Town at the foot of the table. They are up against it as early as the second minute when a suspiciously-looking offside Trusson is brought down by Cook for Lovell's penalty. Town have no luck when Richardson hits the bar at 0-2, and Watson's goal is ruled out.											

No	Date	H/A	Opponent	Att	Pos	Pts	Res	F-A	H-T	Scorers, Times, and Referees	1	2	3	4	5	6	7	8	9	10	11	subs used
35		H	LINCOLN		22		L	0-1	0-0		Brown	Fleming P	Barr^	Martin	Graham	Horner	Broadbent*	Watson	Richardson	Hall	Matthews	Fyfe/Butler
	20/3			1,423	*4*	36				*Smith P 75*	*Wallington*	*Stoutt*	*Clarke*	*Smith N*	*Brown*	*Davis*	*Smith P*	*Bressington*	*Hobson*	*Lormor*	*Puttnam*	
										Ref: A Seville	Both sides need the points for contrasting reasons. Lincoln still hope to make the play-offs. Horner's weak back-pass proves costly, as Hobson nips in to set up Paul Smith's goal. Defeat prompts a demonstration by the home fans. Ayre, honourable to the end, leaves 'by mutual consent'.											
36		H	CHESTERFIELD		22		D	1-1	1-0	Watson 35	Brown	Fleming P	Cook	Martin	Horner	Graham	Matthews	Butler	Fyfe	Watson	Hall	
	24/3			2,363	*7*	37				*Waller 57*	*Leonard*	*Rogers*	*Hart*	*Dyche*	*Brien*	*Gunn*	*Plummer*	*Hewitt*	*Waller*	*Chedozie*	*Morris*	
										Ref: T Fitzharris	Former Scotland international Jim McCalliog, formerly head of Town's Football in the Community scheme, has taken over as caretaker-boss. Town end their sequence of five straight defeats. Watson heads over ex-Shayman Leonard, but Waller runs onto Morris's flick-on to equalise.											
37		A	TORQUAY		22		L	0-1	0-1		Brown	Fleming P	Cook	Martin !	Fleming C	Graham	Barr*	Butler	Fyfe	Watson	Richardson^	Matthews/Broadbent
	27/3			*1,911*	*15*	37				*Whiston 27*	*Veysey*	*Holmes*	*Lloyd*	*Joyce*	*Hannigan*	*Uzzell*	*Smith P*	*Whiston*	*Loram*	*Caldwell**	*Weston*	*Smith J*
										Ref: T Holbrook	Town have a tough fight ahead of them if they are to avoid the drop. They remain only three points clear of bottom club Colchester, and will lose the services for a time of Martin after a fifth sending-off in the 80th minute. Whiston's header, his first-ever goal, ensures Town's defeat.											
38		A	ROCHDALE		22		W	2-0	0-0	McPhillips 73, Watson 82	Brown	Fleming P	Cook	Martin	Fleming C	Graham	Matthews	Butler	McPhillips	Watson*	Hall	Richardson
	31/3			*2,494*	*11*	40					*Welch*	*Goodison*	*Burns*	*Brown*	*Cole*	*Hill*	*Holmes^*	*Henshaw**	*Ward*	*O'Shaughn'sy*	*Milner*	*Johnson/Elliott*
										Ref: W Burns	McPhillips, back after injury, is involved in both Town's goals as they record a crucial win at Spotland. He takes Hall's pass in his stride and lashes the ball in. He then holds the ball up before setting up Watson for the second. Jim Brown says of Jim McCalliog, 'He'll pull us clear.'											
39		H	GRIMSBY		22		D	2-2	0-1	Watson 70, Butler 84	Brown	Fleming P	Cook	Martin	Fleming C	Graham	Matthews	Butler	McPhillips	Watson	Hall	
	7/4			3,620	*2*	41				*Rees 21, Alexander 74*	*Sherwood*	*McDermott*	*Agnew*	*Birtles*	*Lever*	*Jobling*	*Childs*	*Gilbert**	*Rees*	*Cockerill*	*Alexander*	*Hargreaves*
										Ref: R Wiseman	The home fans, not for the first time, are aggrieved at being allocated the visitors' end but are heartened by their team's display. Grimsby look like extending their winning run to eight games when Butler's back-pass lets in Alexander. But he redeems himself with a volleyed equaliser.											
40		A	HEREFORD		21		W	1-0	0-0	Barr 63	Brown	Barr	Cook	Horner	Fleming C	Graham	Matthews	Butler	McPhillips	Watson	Hall	
	11/4			*1,817*		44					*Freestone*	*Pejic*	*Devine*	*Hemming*	*Peacock*	*Bradley*	*Bowyer**	*Jones M*	*Wheeler*	*Juryeff*	*Benbow*	*Tester^/Jones S*
										Ref: K Morton	McCalliog feels his players need to believe in themselves. With Colchester's defeat last night, some of the pressure is taken off them. Brown still has to be at his best to thwart Juryeff and Benbow. Barr shows confidence in beating three players before seeing his shot beat Freestone.											
41		A	PETERBOROUGH		22		L	**0-3**	0-2		Brown	Fleming P	Cook	Horner	Fleming C	Graham	Matthews	Butler	McPhillips^	Watson	Hall*	Barr/Richardson
	14/4			*4,570*	*7*	44				*Halsall 28, Riley 30, Jepson 46*	*Godden*	*Luke*	*Crosby^*	*Halsall*	*Robinson*	*McElhinney*	*Sterling*	*Hines*	*Jepson*	*Riley**	*Oakes*	*Osborne/Butterworth*
										Ref: T West	Victory for Peterborough, now under future BBC pundit Mark Lawrenson, is their third on the trot, and takes their unbeaten sequence to five. They do the damage with two goals in three minutes. Jepson's goal just after the break comes as a result of Halifax not playing to the whistle.											
42		H	YORK		21		D	2-2	2-2	Butler 31, Fleming P 37p	Brown	Fleming P	Cook	Horner	Fleming C	Graham	Matthews	Butler	McPhillips*	Watson	Hall	Richardson
	16/4			1,605	*14*	45				*Canham 5, Helliwell 25*	*Marples*	*McMillan*	*Hall*	*Howlett*	*Tutill*	*Warburton*	*Barratt*	*Spooner*	*Helliwell*	*Colville**	*Canham^*	*Dunn/Himsworth*
										Ref: G Aplin	An out-of-sorts Town find themselves two goals down after 25 minutes. Fleming's awful back-pass leads to Helliwell's goal. Town then fight back and Fleming shows character to equalise with a penalty when Watson goes down. In the second half, Town find Marples in great form.											
43		A	DONCASTER		20		W	4-3	0-3	Cook 47, Barr 66, R'dson 81, Butler 86	Brown	Fleming P	Cook	Martin	Fleming C	Graham	Barr*	Butler	Matthews	Watson	Hall^	Richardson/Broadbent
	21/4			*2,212*	*21*	48				*Turnbull 5, Muir 21, Grayson 26*	*Samways*	*Brockie*	*Brevett^*	*Harle*	*Ashurst*	*Douglas*	*Muir*	*Grayson**	*Turnbull*	*Jones*	*Noteman*	*Adams/Gaughan*
										Ref: I Hendrick	Town look down and out at half-time, trailing by three goals. McCalliog's harsh words during the interval have the desired effect, as his side turns the game around. The game evokes memories of a similar fightback against Swindon in '63. Butler drives in Cook's pass for the winner.											
44		H	BURNLEY		21		D	0-0	0-0		Brown	Fleming P	Cook	Martin	Fleming C	Graham	Matthews	Butler	Richardson	Watson*	Hall^	McPhillips/Barr
	24/4			2,556	*17*	49					*Pearce*	*Measham*	*Deakin*	*Deary*	*Farrell*	*Davis*	*Mumby**	*Eli*	*Francis*	*Jakub*	*Hardy*	*McKay*
										Ref: A Dawson	The Shaymen are practically safe now. Frank Casper's Burnley come looking for a point and pack the defence. The draw means they have not won for eight matches. Most of what chances there are come early on in the game. Town look the better side, and are disappointed not to win.											
45		A	SOUTHEND		21		L	0-2	0-1		Brown	Fleming P	Cook	Martin	Fleming C	Graham	Barr	Butler	Richardson	Matthews*	Hall	Watson
	27/4			*3,656*	*3*	49				*Ling 22, Smith P 46*	*Sansome*	*Austin*	*Edinburgh*	*Edwards*	*Butler*	*Clark*	*Ling*	*Smith P**	*Crown*	*Benjamin*	*Ansah*	*Daley*
										Ref: I Hemley	It's been a nerve-wracking end for Southend. Having just lost their last two matches, they need three points to practically guarantee promotion. They get them here. Ling prods home Benjamin's wayward shot to the relief of the home fans. Smith's goal comes 30 seconds after half-time.											
46		H	STOCKPORT		23		L	1-2	1-0	Matthews 22	Brown	Fleming P	Barr	Martin	Fleming C	Graham	Matthews	Donnelly*	Richardson	Watson^	Cook	Hall/McPhillips
	5/5			**4,744**	*4*	49				*Beaumont 73, McInerney 76*	*Barrett*	*Brown*	*Logan*	*Frain*	*Thorpe*	*Bullock*	*Knowles**	*Gannon*	*Beaumont*	*Brookman^*	*Angell*	*McInerney/Leonard*
			Home	Away						Ref: B Hill	Stockport fans run riot in the town centre and invade the pitch three times as they see their side come from behind to clinch a place in the play-offs. Matthews' strike gives Town a deserved lead, but they can't hold it. McInerney's cool finish ensures County those extra play-off games.											
Average			1,888	3,439																		

Littlewoods Cup				F-A	H-T	Scorers, Times, and Referees	1	2	3	4	5	6	7	8	9	10	11	subs used
1:1 H CARLISLE			W	3-1	1-1	Cook 12, Hall 63, Watson 77	Whitehead	Barr	Cook	Hedworth	Bramhall	Horner	Martin	Watson^	Juryeff	Butler*	Hall	Richardson/McPhillips
22/8	1,604					*Shepherd 33*	*McKellar*	*Robertson*	*Wharton*	*Saddington*	*Ogley*	*Graham*	*Shepherd !*	*Walsh*	*Walwyn*	*Proudlock**	*Halpin*	*Hetherington*
						Ref: M Reed	Town turn on the style for a handy first-leg lead. Cook's rasping drive is cancelled out by Tony Shepherd, ex-Celtic, who is sent off late on for punching Butler. Town have the game won by then, with Andy Watson capping a fine performance by rounding McKellar to net the last goal.											
1:2 A CARLISLE		4	L	0-1	0-0		Whitehead	Barr	Cook	Hedworth	Bramhall	Horner	Martin	Watson^	Broadbent*	Butler	Hall	McPhillips/Richardson
29/8	*3,045*	*7*				*Walwyn 63*	*McKellar*	*Graham*	*Dalziel*	*Saddington*	*Ogley**	*Fitzpatrick*	*Shepherd^*	*Walsh*	*Walwyn*	*Proudlock*	*Halpin*	*Fyfe/Wharton*
						Ref: J Worrall (Halifax won 3-2 on aggregate)	Ayre warns his team about an onslaught from Carlisle. That is what Halifax get, but they are up to the task. They defend sternly and make life difficult. Walwyn manages to pull one back with a header. Watson then goes clear but is hauled down by Fitzpatrick, who isn't even booked.											
2:1 A MIDDLESBROUGH		6	L	0-4	0-2		Brown	Barr*	Cook	Butler	Bramhall	Horner	Martin	Watson	Matthews	Juryeff	Hall^	Fleming P/Richardson
20/9	*10,613*	*1:10*				*Comfort 7, Slaven 39, 61, Parkinson 86*	*Poole*	*Parkinson*	*Mohan*	*Mowbray*	*Kernaghan*	*Putney*	*Slaven*	*Proctor*	*Ripley*	*Brennan*	*Comfort*	
						Ref: A Dawson	Bruce Rioch will experience some trying times as manager at Ayresome Park. This game, though, is all too easy for his side. Bernie Slaven is the star of the show and he scores two well-taken goals. He is later denied a third goal when Butler clears his downward header off the line.											
2:2 H MIDDLESBROUGH		10	L	0-1	0-0		Brown	Fleming P	Cook	Hedworth	Bramhall	Horner	Martin*	Watson	McPhillips	Juryeff	Hall^	Richardson/Butler
3/10	1,641	*1:15*				*Slaven 88*	*Poole*	*Parkinson*	*Mohan*	*Gill*	*Kernaghan*	*Putney**	*Slaven*	*Davenport*	*Burke*	*Brennan*	*Comfort*	*McGee*
						Ref: W Flood (Halifax lost 0-5 on aggregate)	With the tie all but over before kick-off, ticket sales the day before the game are reported only as 'very slowly'. Town fight to make a game of it, but are guilty of wasting too many chances. With time running out, Slaven shows them the way by heading home Parkinson's deep cross.											

FA Cup																		
1 A STAFFORD		18	W	3-2	1-1	Fleming P 43, Horner 80, 84	Whitehead	Fleming P	Butler	Hedworth	Bramhall*	Horner	Martin	Watson	Matthews	Juryeff	Hall	Broadbent
18/11	*2,508*	*VC*				*Camden 7p, 64p*	*Price*	*Simpson*	*Upton*	*Curilo*	*Essex*	*Wood*	*Wharton**	*Gill*	*Camden*	*Cavell*	*Turley*	*Campbell*
						Ref: G Aplin	With only ten minutes left, Town are lucky to still be in this game. After Camden scores his second penalty to restore Stafford's lead, he fluffs a one-on-one. Broadbent comes on and his long throw leads to the first of Horner's two headed goals that give Town an undeserved victory.											
2 A DARLINGTON		18	L	0-3	0-1		Whitehead	Fleming P	Butler	Broadbent*	Bramhall	Horner	Martin	Watson	Matthews^	Juryeff	Hall	Barr/Harrison
9/12	*4,041*	*VC:1*				*Coverdale 31, McJannet 50, Borthwick 67*	*Prudhoe*	*McJannet*	*Coverdale*	*Willis*	*Smith*	*Corner*	*Hine*	*Toman*	*Borthwick*	*Cork*	*Emson*	
						Ref: I Hendrick	Brian Little is doing a good job of restoring Darlington's pride, and his players are full of confidence. But their opening two goals are gifts as firstly Whitehead concedes an indirect free-kick for picking the ball up twice; then he can't hold Butler's backpass for McJannet's backheeler.											

		Home					Away					
	P	W	D	L	F	A	W	D	L	F	A	Pts
1 Exeter	46	20	3	0	50	14	8	2	13	33	34	89
2 Grimsby	46	14	4	5	41	20	8	9	6	29	27	79
3 Southend	46	15	3	5	35	14	7	6	10	26	34	75
4 Stockport	46	13	6	4	45	27	8	5	10	23	35	74
5 Maidstone	46	14	4	5	49	21	8	3	12	28	40	73
6 Cambridge*	46	14	3	6	45	30	7	7	9	31	36	73
7 Chesterfield	46	12	9	2	41	19	7	5	11	22	31	71
8 Carlisle	46	15	4	4	38	20	6	4	13	23	40	71
9 Peterborough	46	10	8	5	35	23	7	9	7	24	23	68
10 Lincoln	46	11	6	6	30	27	7	8	8	18	21	68
11 Scunthorpe	46	9	9	5	42	25	8	6	9	27	29	66
12 Rochdale	46	11	4	8	28	23	9	2	12	24	32	66
13 York	46	10	5	8	29	24	6	11	6	26	29	64
14 Gillingham	46	9	8	6	28	21	8	3	12	18	27	62
15 Torquay	46	12	2	9	33	29	3	10	10	20	37	57
16 Burnley	46	6	10	7	19	18	8	4	11	26	37	56
17 Hereford	46	7	4	12	31	32	8	6	9	25	30	55
18 Scarborough	46	10	5	8	35	28	5	5	13	25	45	55
19 Hartlepool	46	12	4	7	45	33	3	6	14	21	55	55
20 Doncaster	46	7	7	9	29	29	7	2	14	24	31	51
21 Wrexham	46	8	8	7	28	28	5	4	14	23	39	51
22 Aldershot	46	8	7	8	28	26	4	7	12	21	43	50
23 HALIFAX	46	5	9	9	31	29	7	4	12	26	36	49
24 Colchester	46	9	3	11	26	25	2	7	14	22	50	43
	1104	261	135	156	841	585	156	135	261	585	841	1521

* promoted after play-offs

Odds & ends

Double wins: (1) Rochdale.
Double losses: (4) Exeter, Gillingham, Lincoln, Southend.

Won from behind: (3) Wrexham (h), Doncaster (a), Stafford (FAC) (a).
Lost from in front: (5) Exeter (h), Maidstone (h), Stockport (h), Chesterfield (a), Lincoln (a).

High spots: Winning 4-3 at Doncaster after trailing 0-3 at half-time.
Beating Hartlepool 4-0 – the best opening-day win since 1926.

Low spots: Five consecutive defeats in a run of seven games without a win in March.
Losing 0-4 at 1st Division Middlesbrough in the Littlewoods Cup.
Losing 0-3 at non-league Darlington in the FA Cup.

Town won more games away than they did at home.

Player of the Year: Brian Butler.
Ever-presents: (0).
Hat-tricks: (0).
Leading scorer: Neil Matthews (12).

	Appearances						Goals			
	Lge	*Sub*	LC	*Sub*	FAC	*Sub*	Lge	LC	FAC	Tot
Barr, Billy	**15**	*8*	3			*1*	**2**			**2**
Bramhall, John	**23**		4		2		**2**			**2**
Broadbent, Graham	**8**	*5*	1		1	*1*				
Brown, David	**27**		2							
Butler, Brian	**25**	*5*	3	*1*	2		**3**			**3**
Cook, Mitch	**36**	*1*	4				**2**	1		**3**
Donnelly, Paul	**1**									
Fleming, Craig	**10**									
Fleming, Paul	**40**		1	*1*	2		**1**		1	**2**
Fyfe, Tony	**10**	*2*								
Gannon, Jim	**2**									
Graham, Tommy	**21**						**1**			**1**
Hall, Derek	**40**	*1*	4		2		**4**	1		**5**
Harrison, Frankie	**3**	*6*				*1*				
Hedworth, Chris	**27**		3		1					
Horner, Phil	**34**		4		2		**1**		2	**3**
Juryeff, Ian	**15**	*2*	3		2		**7**			**7**
McPhillips, Terry	**10**	*12*	1	*1*			**3**			**3**
Martin, Dean	**37**		4		2					
Matthews, Neil	**38**	*1*	1		2		**12**			**12**
Naylor, Dominic	**5**	*1*					**1**			**1**
Richardson, Nick	**21**	*6*		*4*			**6**			**6**
Smith, Shaun	**6**									
Watson, Andy	**33**	*5*	4		2		**10**	1		**11**
Whitehead, Phil	**19**		2		2					
(own-goals)							**2**			**2**
25 players used	**506**	***55***	**44**	***7***	**22**	***3***	**57**	**3**	**3**	**63**

BARCLAYS LEAGUE DIVISION 4

Manager: Jim McCalliog

SEASON 1990-91

No Date		Att	Pos	Pt	F-A	H-T	Scorers, Times, and Referees	1	2	3	4	5	6	7	8	9	10	11	subs used
1 H	STOCKPORT			D	0-0	0-0		Brown	Fleming P	Cook	Evans	Fleming C	**Futcher**	Butler	Graham	McPhillips	Fyfe	Hall	
25/8		2,362		1				*Cooper*	*Brown*	*Robertson*	*Bullock*	*Williams B*	*Finley*	*Payne*	*Gannon*	*Williams PA*	*Beaumont*	*Frain*	
							Ref: K Morton	McCalliog has gone for the 'Argentina look', and Town run out in light blue and white striped shirts. Stockport missed out in the play-offs last season, but in this game there is little to choose between the sides. McCalliog is off the bench protesting about Stockport's ruthless methods.											
2 A	LINCOLN		18	L	0-1	0-1		Brown	Fleming P	Cook	Evans	Fleming C	Graham	Gregory	Donnelly*	McPhillips	Fyfe	Hall	Broadbent
1/9		*2,947*	*7*	1			*Schofield 33*	*Wallington*	*Casey*	*Clarke*	*Brown*	*Nicholson*	*Davis*	*Schofield*	*Smith P*	*Lormor**	*Smith N*	*Puttnam*	*Carmichael*
							Ref: T Lund	The Town bus is caught up in traffic and doesn't reach Sincil Bank until three minutes after kick-off time. Brian Butler fails to meet the bus after his car broke down. A bad start for Town gets worse when John Schofield heads in the only goal whilst Evans is sat in the back of the net.											
3 H	DONCASTER		22	L	0-1	0-0		Brown	Fleming P	Cook	Evans	Fleming C	Futcher	Butler	Richardson	McPhillips*	Broadbent	Graham	Fyfe
8/9		2,394	*1*	1			*Jones 54*	*Crichton*	*Rankine*	*Brevett*	*Holmes*	*Ormsby*	*Douglas*	*Gormley*	*Stiles*	*Muir*	*Jones*	*Noteman*	
							Ref: I Hendrick	Billy Bremner's Rovers side keep up their 100% record with their third win. It's Frank Bruno lookalike, David Jones, who puts them there. He climbs above an off-balance keeper David Brown to head the ball in. No one needs telling McCalliog that Town have yet to score in the league.											
4 A	DARLINGTON		23	L	0-3	0-1		Brown	Fleming P	Cook*	Evans	Fleming C	Futcher	Butler	Richardson	Juryeff	Fyfe	Graham^	Gregory/Broadbent
15/9		*2,993*	*4*	1			*Cork 45, McJannet 56, Gill 75*	*Prudhoe*	*McJannet*	*Gray*	*Gill*	*Smith*	*Corner*	*Emson*	*Toman*	*Borthwick*	*Cork*	*Tait*	
							Ref: J Lloyd	A repeat of last season's FA Cup humiliation, but Darlington could actually have won by more. Poor defending lets in David Cork to score in first-half injury-time. As well as two further goals, the home side hits the woodwork twice. Town end up with ten men when Fleming goes off.											
5 A	PETERBOROUGH		24	L	0-2	0-1		Brown	Fleming P*	Hall	Evans	Fleming C	Futcher	Gregory	Butler	Juryeff	Richardson	Broadbent	Barr
18/9		*3,082*	*10*	1			*Culpin 32, Russell 64*	*Dearden*	*Luke*	*Crosby*	*Halsall*	*Russell*	*McElhinney*	*Sterling*	*Hine*	*Bremner*	*Culpin**	*Butterworth*	*Osborne*
							Ref: J Moules	Peterborough remain unbeaten, but this is actually their first win. Halifax feel hard done by, for they more than match their opponents, except in front of goal. Culpin volleys in following Brown's punch. Russell's goal is a tap-in after some calamitous defending by Futcher and Evans.											
6 H	TORQUAY		24	L	0-1	0-1		Brown	Barr	Hall*	Evans	Fleming C	Futcher	Gregory	Donnelly	Juryeff	Richardson^	Martin	Butler/Broadbent
21/9		1,447	*2*	1			*Smith 17*	*Howells*	*Whiston*	*Uzzell*	*Lloyd*	*Elliott*	*Joyce*	*Holmes*	*Smith**	*Tynan*	*Saunders*	*Loram*	*Myers*
							Ref: J Watson	How Town could do with the sort of luck that decides this game in favour of the Gulls. The veteran Tommy Tynan's shot is destined for the terracing until the ball hits Paul Smith and goes in. Torquay, unbeaten in their opening six league matches, have scored twelve to Town's none.											
7 A	NORTHAMPTON		24	L	0-1	0-0		Brown	Fleming P	Barr^	Evans	Fleming C	Futcher	Gregory	Butler	Juryeff	Richardson*	Martin	McPhillips/Donnelly
29/9		*2,977*	*3*	1			*Collins 66*	*Beresford*	*Chard*	*Wilson*	*Terry*	*Scully*	*Angus*	*Beavon*	*Wilkin^*	*Bell*	*Barnes*	*Brown**	*Berry/Collins*
							Ref: R Biggar	Town have only themselves to blame for not breaking their duck as they miss five gilt-edged chances. Juryeff is the main culprit. The home side have the perfect opportunity to go in front, but Barnes puts his penalty wide. Three minutes later, however, sub Collins scores from six yards.											
8 H	SCUNTHORPE		24	D	0-0	0-0		Brown	Fleming P	Barr	Evans	Fleming C	Futcher	Gregory	**Norris**	Juryeff	Graham	Butler	
6/10		1,468	*17*	2				*Musselwhite*	*Longden*	*Cowling**	*Ward*	*Hicks*	*Hall*	*Cox*	*Taylor*	*Daws*	*Cotton*	*Bramhall*	*Flounders*
							Ref: A Smith	It's now twelve games since Town last won at home in the league, their worst run since the 1972-73 season. McCalliog has swapped an out of sorts Fyfe for Carlisle's Steve Norris. But Town still can't score, although the Town boss insists he will keep trying to play attractive football.											
9 A	CARLISLE		24	W	3-0	3-0	Barr 10, Norris 18, Graham 37	Brown	Fleming P	Barr	Evans	Fleming C	Futcher	Gregory	Norris	Juryeff	Graham	Butler	
13/10		*3,697*	*18*	5				*Priestley*	*Miller*	*Edwards*	*Jeffels*	*Methven*	*Fitzpatrick**	*Walsh*	*Shepherd*	*Walwyn^*	*Gates*	*Proudlock*	*Owen/Fyfe*
							Ref: K Lupton	Billy Barr's tenth-minute strike from 20 yards makes headline news. It's Town's first league goal after 730 minutes of football, and earns Barr a interview on BBC's Sport on Five. Norris gets into a regular routine when he stabs home Juryeff's low cross. 'It had to come' – McCalliog.											
10 A	YORK		24	D	3-3	0-1	Norris 46, 88, Graham 76	Brown	Fleming P	Barr	Evans	Fleming C	Futcher	Gregory	Norris	Juryeff	Graham	**Ellis**	
20/10		*2,601*	*18*	6			*Helliwell 7, Howlett 67, Dunn 71*	*Marples*	*McMillan*	*Hall*	*Reid*	*Weatherhead*	*Warburton*	*Pepper*	*Howlett*	*Helliwell*	*Blackstone**	*Canham*	*Dunn*
							Ref: I Borrett	Suddenly Town can't stop scoring, but they leave it late to earn a point. York sub Iain Dunn nips in when Evans and Craig Fleming hesitate to give his side a 3-1 lead. Graham's shot takes a deflection before Norris scores a tap-in for the late equaliser to go with his earlier headed goal.											
11 H	HEREFORD		24	L	0-4	0-1		Brown	Fleming P^	Barr	Evans	Fleming C	Futcher	Gregory	Norris	Juryeff	Graham*	Ellis	McPhillips/Butler
23/10		1,762	*11*	6			*Phillips 18, 51, 74, Millar 55*	*Wood*	*Jones M*	*Tester*	*Pejic*	*Peacock*	*Bradley*	*Jones R*	*Narbett*	*Millar**	*Phillips^*	*Lowndes*	*Wheeler/Robinson*
							Ref: T Holbrook	Stuart Phillips returns to his home town to make it an unhappy afternoon for the Shaymen. Colin Addison's Hereford are no great shakes, but Phillips punishes Town on three occasions. He is replaced after 75 minutes with the job done. Millar scores his goal off the Bulls' first corner.											

No	Venue / Date	Opponent	Att	Pos	Res / Pts	F-A	H-T	Scorers, Times, and Referees	1	2	3	4	5	6	7	8	9	10	11	subs used
12	H	BLACKPOOL		24	W	5-3	2-3	Norris 25p, Ellis 43, Grah'm 49, Greg'y 51,	**Gould**	Butler	Barr	Evans	Fleming C	Futcher	Gregory	Norris	Juryeff	Graham	Ellis	
	27/10		1,945	*15*	9			*Rodwell 12, 14, Stant 28* [Juryeff 85]	*McIlhargey*	*Hedworth**	*Wright*	*Groves*	*Horner*	*Smalley^*	*Rodwell*	*Sinclair*	*Stant*	*Garner*	*Eyres*	*Gore/Davies*
								Ref: J Ashworth	Debutant Gould doesn't know what has hit him as he lets in two goals early on. Norris' penalty for Gore's foul on Juryeff gets Halifax back in the game. Town turn the game around after the break. Juryeff's first goal since his return comes when McIlhargey can't hold Graham's shot.											
13	A	ALDERSHOT		24	D	2-2	0-1	Norris 68, 73	Gould	Fleming P	Barr	Evans	Fleming C	Graham	Gregory	Norris	Juryeff	Butler*	Ellis	Martin
	2/11		*2,686*	*23*	10			*Williams 12, Randall 60*	*Sheffield*	*Brown*	*Cooper*	*Randall*	*Wignall*	*Flower*	*Whitlock*	*Puckett*	*Williams**	*Henry*	*Stewart*	*Burville*
								Ref: R Gifford	For the third time in four games, Town rally from two goals down. Norris scores both goals, weaving his way through for his second. He later has a would-be winner ruled out for offside. Randell had put Aldershot seemingly on their way to only their second win from fully 30 yards.											
14	H	GILLINGHAM		24	L	1-2	1-0	Dobson 25	Gould	Barr	Ellis	Evans	Fleming C	Futcher	Gregory*	Norris	Juryeff	**Dobson**	Donnelly	Richardson
	9/11		1,708	*15*	10			*Crown 55, Trusson 77*	*Lim*	*McDonald*	*Manuel*	*Dunne*	*Walker*	*Trusson*	*O'Connor*	*Docker*	*Lovell*	*Crown*	*Johnson*	
								Ref: C Trussell	Town blow their chance to get off the foot of the table. On-loan Dobson (Scarborough) gives them the lead with a clinical finish, but Town run out of ideas and are beaten by two magnificient goals. Crown gets away from his marker to rifle the ball home. Trusson's is a perfect chip.											
15	A	BURNLEY		24	L	1-2	0-0	Juryeff 85	Leonard	Fleming P	Barr	Evans	Fleming C	Futcher	Martin	Norris	Juryeff	Graham	Ellis*	Butler
	24/11		***6,620***	*3*	10			*Mumby 48, Francis 54*	*Pearce*	*Measham*	*Deakin*	*Deary*	*Pender**	*Davis*	*White*	*Mumby*	*Francis*	*Jakub*	*Grewcock*	*Farrell*
								Ref: J Brandwood	Mick Leonard has returned to the Shay on loan from Chesterfield. Paul Fleming had a disappointing afternoon. His two errors lead to Burnley clinching the game in a six-minute spell. Town reject Francis beats him for pace for the second. The ref awards 49 free-kicks in a niggly derby.											
16	A	WALSALL		24	L	1-3	1-2	Norris 20	Leonard	Butler	Barr	Evans	Fleming C	Futcher	Martin	Norris	Juryeff	Graham	Ellis	
	1/12		*4,153*	*10*	10			*McDonald 18, Rimmer 33, 71*	*Green*	*Hutchings*	*Singleton*	*Methven*	*Smith*	*Skipper*	*Kelly*	*Ntamark*	*Rimmer*	*Cecere*	*McDonald**	*Littlejohn*
								Ref: D Gallagher	Stuart Rimmer takes his goal tally to 16, joint top with Wolves' Steve Bull. Until he strikes, Halifax are looking good for a point after Norris races onto Butler's perfect pass to quickly cancel out McDonald's goal. Before Rimmer hits his first, Norris heads onto the inside of the post.											
17	H	CHESTERFIELD		24	W	2-1	2-0	Norris 20p, Ellis 30	Leonard	Fleming P	Barr	Evans	Fleming C	Futcher	Butler	Norris	Juryeff	Graham	Ellis	
	15/12		1,415	*21*	13			*Plummer 47*	*Allison*	*Francis*	*Albiston*	*Lemon*	*Brien*	*Gunn*	*Dyche*	*Ryan*	*Plummer*	*Cooke*	*Morris**	*Hewitt*
								Ref: B Hill	Chesterfield make it five games without a win, despite having taken Albiston, ex-Man Utd, on board. The margin of Halifax's victory doesn't reflect their superiority. Norris scores the first from the spot after Evans is pushed by Morris. Ellis scores the eventual winner from 18 yards.											
18	H	ROCHDALE		22	W	2-0	1-0	Butler 15, Martin 67	Gould	Fleming P	Barr	Evans	Fleming C	Graham	Butler	Norris	Juryeff	Cook	Ellis*	Martin
	21/12		1,831	*10*	16				*Welch*	*Norton*	*Graham*	*O'Shaughn'y**	*Burns*	*Goodison*	*Milner*	*Lee*	*Ward*	*Costello^*	*Doyle*	*Cole/Holmes*
								Ref: G Ashby	Town move off the bottom with another display that begs the question as to why they are there in the first place. Butler whacks in his first goal for eight months. Martin heads the second moments after coming on. Despairing Dale boss Terry Dolan will shortly seek better things at Hull.											
19	A	SCARBOROUGH		23	L	1-4	1-1	Norris 34	Gould	Fleming P	Barr	Evans	Fleming C	Graham*	Butler	Norris	Juryeff	Cook	Martin	Ellis
	26/12		*1,327*	*13*	16			*Mockler 37, Oghani 66, 70p, Hirst 82*	*Ironside*	*Kamara*	*Logan*	*Matthews*	*Richards*	*Hirst*	*Himsworth*	*Mockler*	*Oghani*	*Wilson*	*Carter*	
								Ref: E Parker	Galeforce winds spoil this game, but it's Town who are blown away. They fail to capitalise on their early dominance. Cook has a goal ruled out before Norris strikes. The linesman harshly flags for the penalty conceded by Fleming. Boro's 'Black Death' logo on their shirts seems apt.											
20	A	CARDIFF		23	L	0-1	0-0		Gould	Fleming P	Barr	Evans	Fleming C	Martin	Butler	Norris	Juryeff	Cook	Ellis	
	29/12		*2,903*	*12*	16			*Taylor 77*	*Hansbury*	*Fry**	*Searle*	*Blake*	*Matthews*	*De Mange^*	*Taylor*	*Griffith*	*Gibbins*	*Pike*	*Heard*	*Jones/Lewis*
								Ref: M Pearce	Cardiff, after a run of eight games without a win, now make it two wins out of two. Mark Taylor hits the post from close range, but makes no mistake a second time with a carbon-copy effort. Halifax play well but pay for missed chances, like Ellis' shot from 12 yards that hits the post.											
21	H	HARTLEPOOL		24	L	1-2	1-1	Norris 5	Gould	Fleming P	Barr	Evans	Fleming C	Martin	Butler	Norris	Juryeff	Cook	Ellis*	Richardson
	1/1		1,707	*7*	16			*Allon 18, 61*	*Cox*	*Nobbs*	*McKinnon*	*Olsson*	*MacPhail*	*Bennyworth*	*Allon*	*Tupling*	*Baker**	*Honour*	*Dalton*	*Lamb*
								Ref: G Singh	The division's leading scorers Steve Norris and Joe Allon go into the game on 14 goals apiece, but it's the former Newcastle striker who forges ahead. Norris draws first blood, firing high into the net, but Allon responds with a double-whammy. He stabs in the winner from close range.											
22	H	LINCOLN		24	D	1-1	0-1	Broadbent 76	Gould	Fleming P	Barr*	Evans	Fleming C	Graham	Butler	Norris	Broadbent	Cook	Ellis	**Cooper**
	12/1		1,447	*22*	17			*Davis 9*	*Bowling*	*Casey*	*Nicholson*	*Lormor*	*Bressington*	*Davis*	*Schofield*	*Smith*	*Dobson*	*Carmichael*	*Alexander**	*Scott*
								Ref: R Hart	Town make heavy weather of dealing with a poor Lincoln side. The visitors, however, get the upper hand after Davis touches in Casey's free-kick. Dobson hits the post a minute before Cooper comes on to pep some life into Town. Broadbent beats Davis in the air to head the equaliser.											
23	A	STOCKPORT		24	L	**1-5**	0-3	Norris 87 [Williams PA 55]	Gould	Fleming P	Barr*	Evans !	Fleming C	Graham	Butler	Norris	Juryeff	Cook	Ellis^	Broadbent/Cooper
	18/1		*4,030*	*1*	17			*Gann'n 2, Kilner 7, Brown 41p, B'mont 51,*	*Redfearn*	*Brown*	*Bullock*	*Frain*	*Williams W*	*Barras*	*Gannon^*	*Knowles*	*Williams PA*	*Beaumont*	*Kilner**	*Matthews/Thorpe*
								Ref: T West	County go clear at the top whilst Town stay bottom after little goes right. Gannon, on loan at Halifax earlier, starts the rout. Evans is sent off for a professional foul on Kilner. Brown nets the resultant penalty. Beaumont finishes off a sweeping five-man move for the game's best goal.											

No	Date		Att	Pos	Pt	F-A	H-T	Scorers, Times, and Referees	1	2	3	4	5	6	7	8	9	10	11	subs used
24	H	DARLINGTON		24	D	0-0	0-0		Gould	Fleming P	Cook	Evans	Fleming C	Graham	Donnelly	Norris	Juryeff	Martin	Ellis	
	26/1		1,658	*4*	18				*Prudhoe*	*McJannet*	*Gray*	*Willis*	*Smith*	*Coverdale*	*Trotter*	*Toman*	*Borthwick**	*Linacre*	*Tait*	*Ellison*
								Ref: P Wright	Darlington are title contenders, but provide little sparkle in this dreary game. On a frozen pitch, Town's Paul Fleming provides the game's one piece of magic in the 70th minute. He goes on a solo run, begun in his own half, but after cutting inside, sees his shot from 18 yards hit the bar.											
25	H	PETERBOROUGH		24	D	1-1	1-0	Richardson 44	Gould	Barr	Cook	Martin	Fleming C	Graham	Donnelly	Norris	Juryeff	Richardson	Ellis	
	1/2		1,133	*8*	19			*Riley 51*	*Bradshaw*	*Clayton*	*Butterworth*	*Halsall*	*Oakes*	*Crosby*	*Luke*	*Hine*	*Riley*	*Culpin**	*Sterling*	*Danzey*
								Ref: J Worrall	Richardson scores off a corner just before the break, then Riley scores a deserved equaliser. But most people leave the Shay cursing referee Joe Worrall. With 14 minutes left, Norris' clear run in on goal is halted when Posh keeper Bradshaw handles outside the box and stays on the field.											
26	A	TORQUAY		24	L	1-3	0-1	Norris 85	Gould	Barr	Cook	Martin	Fleming C	Graham	Donnelly	Norris	Juryeff	Richardson*	Hall	Ellis
	5/2		*2,233*	*4*	19			*Edwards 7, Tynan 47, Holmes M 79*	*Howells*	*Whiston*	*Uzzell*	*Saunders*	*Elliott*	*Hodges*	*Smith*	*Holmes M*	*Tynan*	*Edwards*	*Loram*	
								Ref: R Groves	Steve Norris proves to be a constant threat, but is let down by his colleagues. As well as scoring a late consolation, he has a goal ruled out, and has another effort cleared off the line. But Town ship goals at the other end. Evergreen Tommy Tynan scores his 18th goal in all competitions.											
27	H	BURNLEY		24	L	1-2	1-0	Norris 11	Gould	Fleming P	Cook	**Gore**	Fleming C	Martin	Donnelly*	Norris	Juryeff	Hall	Cooper	Richardson
	16/2		**4,755**	*4*	19			*Francis 67p, 71*	*Williams*	*Measham*	*Deakin*	*Deary*	*Pender*	*Davis*	*Farrell*	*Francis*	*Eli*	*Jakub*	*Grewcock*	
								Ref: I Cruickshanks	Kick-off is delayed 20 minutes to allow fans into the ground. Town spend most of the time defending, even after Norris' angled shot puts them ahead. A disputed penalty award for hands against Gore gives Francis the chance to score the first of his quick brace against his former club.											
28	A	GILLINGHAM		24	L	0-1	0-0		Gould	Fleming P	Cook	Evans	Fleming C	Gore	Ellis	Norris	Juryeff	Graham	Hall	
	22/2		*2,800*	*11*	19			*Crown 83*	*Lim*	*O'Shea*	*Manuel*	*Clarke*	*Walker*	*Trusson**	*O'Connor*	*Beadle*	*Lovell*	*Crown*	*Johnson*	*Kimble*
								Ref: D Axcell	It's a miserable evening for the Shaymen. It's wet and it's windy, and just when it looks as if they have done enough to earn a point, a lapse in concentration allows Crown to convert Kimble's cross. But that's probably why faltering Gillingham forked out £50,000 to Southend for him.											
29	A	MAIDSTONE		24	L	1-5	1-3	Norris 21p	Gould	Fleming P	Cook	Evans	Fleming C	Gore	Ellis	Norris	Juryeff	Graham	Hall	
	27/2		***1,020***	*18*	19			*Cooper 7, Gall 25, 38, 46, Butler 50*	*Johns*	*Sandeman*	*Henry*	*Brown*	*Oxbrow*	*Kevan*	*Storrell**	*Charlery*	*Gall*	*Butler*	*Cooper*	*Elsey*
								Ref: P Jones	The ref delays kick-off for half an hour to allow the fog to lift over Maidstone's adopted Dartford ground. Perhaps Town had wished it hadn't. Tottenham are watching Butler, but it's his teammate Mark Gall who catches the eye. Norris keeps up his scoring rate with a penalty for hands.											
30	H	WALSALL		24	W	**5-2**	1-2	Norris 43p, 61, 88, Juryeff 63, 71	Gould*	Fleming P	Barr	Evans	Fleming C	Gore	Richardson	Norris	Juryeff	Graham	Martin	Ellis
	2/3		1,464	*15*	22			*Naughton 1p, Marsh 3*	*Green*	*Hutchings*	*Mower^*	*Methven*	*Smith*	*Skipper*	*Grealish*	*Ntamark*	*Marsh*	*McDonald*	*Naughton**	*Cecere/Littlejohn*
								Ref: W Burns	An amazing game. Evans concedes a penalty after only 15 seconds. After three minutes, Town are 0-2 down. After 37 minutes Gould goes off with a facial injury caused by Mower's boot. Graham clearly enjoys his stint in goal. Norris' penalty before the break starts the transformation.											
31	A	CHESTERFIELD		24	L	1-2	1-0	Norris 23	Whitehead	Fleming P	Barr	Evans	Fleming C	Gore	Ellis	Norris	Juryeff !	Richardson	Martin	
	9/3		*3,565*	*22*	22			*Williams S 60, Turnbull 90*	*Leonard*	*Gunn*	*Ryan*	*Lemon*	*Brien*	*McGurgan*	*Rogers*	*Williams S**	*Lancaster*	*Turnbull*	*Hewitt*	*Morris*
								Ref: A Wilkie	Town are now five points adrift at the foot of the table. They are leading through Norris' customary goal when the linesman sees Juryeff elbow Brien in the 34th minute. The ref orders him off. Town's ten men battle gamely, but are eventually beaten by Turnbull's header in injury-time.											
32	A	WREXHAM		24	W	2-1	0-1	Juryeff 73, Norris 78	Whitehead	Fleming P	Barr	Evans	Fleming C	Gore	Ellis	Norris	Juryeff	Richardson*	Martin	Cooper
	12/3		*1,263*	*23*	25			*Jones L 19*	*Morris*	*Thackeray*	*Hardy*	*Hunter*	*Beaumont*	*Jones J*	*Bowden*	*Owen*	*Jones L*	*Worthington*	*O'Gorman**	*Lunt*
								Ref: T Holbrook	The gap between Town and next to bottom Wrexham is now just two points after this crucial win. Town are in trouble when Lee Jones puts the home side ahead. But on 65 minutes, former Robin - Cooper - comes on to give Town more freedom, and crosses for Norris to head the winner.											
33	H	NORTHAMPTON		23	W	2-1	2-0	Norris 20, 34	Whitehead	Fleming P	Barr	Evans	Fleming C	Gore	Ellis	Norris	Juryeff	Richardson	Martin	
	15/3		1,346	*2*	28			*Brown 50*	*Hitchcock*	*Chard*	*Wilson*	*Terry*	*Quow**	*Angus*	*Beavon*	*Thorpe^*	*Campbell*	*Barnes*	*Brown*	*Williams/Johnson*
								Ref: T Fitzharris	Norris gets out of his sick-bed to lift the Shaymen off the bottom. Barr is provider of both his goals, as he sends over the corner, then the cross from which Norris profits. High-flying Northampton make a fight of it after the break, but after Brown's goal, Town dig in to hold their lead.											
34	H	CARLISLE		23	D	1-1	1-1	Juryeff 35	Whitehead	Fleming P	Barr*	Evans	Fleming C	Gore !	Ellis	Norris	Juryeff	Richardson^	Martin	Cook/Cooper
	19/3		**1,004**		29			*Edwards 34p*	*Priestley*	*Miller*	*Edwards*	*Fitzpatrick*	*Jeffels*	*Dalziel*	*Proudlock*	*Shepherd*	*Willis**	*Edmundson*	*Halpin*	*Sendall*
								Ref: T Lunt	With the rain lashing down, the referee initially calls the match off. Norris fails to equal the club record of scoring in six consecutive matches. Whitehead concedes a penalty, but Juryeff's response is instant. Town are grateful for a point after Gore's 86th-minute sending off for kicking.											

No	Venue/Date	Opponents	Att	Pos	Pts	F-A	H-T	Scorers, Times, and Referees	1	2	3	4	5	6	7	8	9	10	11	subs used
35	A	SCUNTHORPE		24	D	4-4	1-1	Richardson 45, Norris 46, 67p, Ellis 88	Whitehead	Fleming P	Barr	Evans	Fleming C	Gore	Ellis	Norris	Cooper	Richardson	Martin	
	23/3		*3,134*	*7*	30			*F'ders 21p, Taylor 48, Hump's 57, Lillis 86*	*Musselwhite*	*Longden*	*Lillis*	*Ward**	*Hicks*	*Humphries*	*Joyce*	*Hamilton*	*Daws*	*Flounders*	*Taylor*	*Cotton*
								Ref: I Hemley	The spectators get full value for money. Flounders' penalty for hands by Ellis starts the scoring spree. Halifax equalise in first-half injury-time, and go in front seconds after the restart. Scunthorpe twice regain the lead, but Town never give up. Norris wins the penalty for his second goal.											
36	H	WREXHAM		22	W	2-0	0-0	Norris 64, 87	Whitehead	Fleming P	Barr	Evans	Fleming C	Gore	Donnelly*	Norris	Cooper	Richardson	Martin	Butler
	26/3		1,429	*24*	33				*Morris*	*Thackeray*	*Hardy*	*Hunter*	*Beaumont*	*Jones J*	*Bowden*	*Owen*	*Armstrong**	*Jones L^*	*Griffiths*	*Kelly/Lunt*
								Ref: J Watson	ITV's 'Saint and Greavsie' show are doing a feature on Norris, and film him in action here. He doesn't let them down. In typical Greaves style of old, he rounds the keeper twice to score both his goals. The Town fans sing 'We're not bottom anymore', but Brian Flynn's Wrexham are.											
37	H	SCARBOROUGH		22	L	1-2	0-1	Norris 81	Whitehead	Fleming P	Barr	Evans*	Fleming C	Gore	**Megson**	Norris	Cooper	Richardson	Martin	Butler
	30/3		1,623	*9*	33			*Foreman 45, Mooney 87*	*Ironside*	*Kamara*	*Loan*	*Matthews*	*Richards*	*Hirst*	*Carter*	*Lee C*	*Mooney*	*Foreman**	*Reed*	*Fletcher*
								Ref: K Breen	Scarborough, under former Town favourite Ray McHale, are making a late bid to make the play-offs. They deserve nothing less than victory here, but Town are close to nicking a draw. They think they've earned one when Norris scores from close range, but Mooney has the last word.											
38	A	ROCHDALE		22	D	1-1	1-0	Juryeff 8	Whitehead	Fleming P	Barr	Martin	Fleming C	Gore	Megson	Norris	Juryeff	Butler	Cooper	
	1/4		*2,040*	*15*	34			*Hilditch 64*	*Welch*	*Goodison*	*Graham*	*Cole*	*O'Shaughn'sy*	*Brown*	*Morgan**	*Doyle*	*Hilditch*	*Milner*	*Ward*	*Burns*
								Ref: P Danson	Skipper Evans sits this one out, a victim of McCalliog's new 4-4-2 formation. Ref Danson cuts a controversial figure as he fails to get a grip on the game. Juryeff puts Town ahead, then Whitehead saves Goodison's penalty six minutes later. Mark Hilditch equalises with a diving header.											
39	H	CARDIFF		22	L	1-2	0-1	Juryeff 85	Whitehead	Fleming	Barr	Evans	Fleming C	Martin	Megson	Norris	Juryeff	Richardson*	Cooper	Butler
	6/4		1,364	*11*	34			*Pike 30, Heard 74*	*Hansbury*	*Matthews*	*Searle*	*De Mange*	*Perry*	*MacDonald*	*Heath**	*Griffith*	*Gibbins*	*Pike*	*Heard*	*Barnard*
								Ref: A Flood	Man-mountain Chris Pike is the difference between the sides. He scores Cardiff's opener with a 20-yarder that goes in off the post, then rises above Whitehead, playing his last game on loan, to head on for Heard to slide in the second. Juryeff pulls one back, but Town leave it too late.											
40	A	HARTLEPOOL		22	L	1-2	0-0	Norris 89p	Gould	Fleming P	Barr	Evans	Fleming C	Martin	Megson*	Norris	Cooper	Richardson	Ellis	Butler
	13/4		*3,185*	*4*	34			*Baker 70, Allon 86*	*Poole*	*Nobbs*	*McKinnon*	*Tinkler*	*MacPhail*	*Bennyworth*	*Allon*	*Tupling^*	*Baker*	*Honour*	*Dalton**	*Gabbiadini/Olsson*
								Ref: P Tyldesley	This is the 100th League meeting between the sides. Pool are in form – this is their seventh game unbeaten. Joe Allon draws level with Norris with his 31st of the season for a 2-0 lead. Norris responds with a penalty after he is pushed by Nobbs. Then Town find there is no injury-time.											
41	H	MAIDSTONE		22	W	3-2	2-0	Ellis 14, Richardson 31, Juryeff 59	Gould	Fleming P	Barr	Evans	Fleming C	Martin	Ellis*	Norris	Juryeff	Richardson	Cooper	Paterson
	16/4		1,002	*18*	37			*Gall 50, Moore 79*	*Johns*	*Haylock*	*Rumble*	*Oxbrow*	*Davis*	*Sanderman*	*Gall*	*Osborne*	*Henry**	*Sorrell*	*Stebbing*	*Moore*
								Ref: K Morton	The Shaymen show two sides to their game. In the first half they look irresistible and go 2-0 up. When Gall cuts inside to fire home just after the break, Town retreat and are hanging on. Juryeff restores their two-goal lead when he is on his knees. Moore's goal ensures a nervy finish.											
42	H	YORK		22	W	2-1	1-1	Norris 38, Evans 56	Gould	Fleming P	**Hutchinson**	Evans	Fleming C	Martin	Ellis	Norris	Juryeff*	Richardson	Cooper	Paterson
	19/4		1,421	*21*	40			*Evans 40 (og)*	*Kiely*	*McMillan*	*Hall*	*Pepper*	*Tutill*	*Barratt*	*McCarthy^*	*Bushell*	*Naylor**	*Blackstone*	*Canham*	*Dunn/Bradshaw*
								Ref: J Parker	Dave Evans is scorer at both ends. First, he turns in Canham's shot as he tries to clear, but then restores Town's lead, given to them initially by Norris from close range, with a rocket free-kick. Town are good value for their win, despite losing Juryeff, stretchered off with an ankle injury.											
43	A	DONCASTER		21	W	2-1	1-1	Cooper 10, Norris 55p	Gould	Fleming P	Hutchinson*	Evans	Fleming C	Gore	Paterson	Norris	Cooper	Richardson	Martin	Barr
	23/4		*2,360*	*9*	43			*Ormsby 44p*	*Samways*	*Smalley**	*Noteman*	*Ashurst*	*Ormsby*	*Douglas*	*Rankine*	*Stiles*	*Whitehurst*	*Muir*	*Gormley^*	*Reddish/Jones*
								Ref: R Nixon	Defeat for Doncaster will hinder their play-off hopes. Three is no doubting they are the more positive side, but they find Gould in terrific form. Their goal is a penalty for Paul Fleming's foul on Gormley. Norris scores a penalty to put Town back in front, then things get a little heated.											
44	A	HEREFORD		22	L	0-1	0-1		Gould	Fleming P	Hutchinson*	Evans	Fleming C	Gore	Paterson^	Norris	Cooper	Richardson	Martin	Barr/Donnelly
	27/4		*1,820*	*15*	43			*Brain 10*	*Wood*	*Jones MA*	*Devine*	*Pejic*	*Bradley*	*Jones R*	*Lowndes*	*Narbett*	*Brain*	*Phillips^*	*Tester**	*Mitchell/Jones S*
								Ref: D Elleray	A mundane contest, where only Simon Brain, a £10,000 buy from Cheltenham, gets any satisfaction. He scores the game's only goal after just ten minutes, reacting first to the loose ball after Gould saves from Phillips. Hereford's former Scotland keeper George Wood has a quiet game.											
45	A	BLACKPOOL		22	L	0-2	0-0		Gould	Barr	Butler	Evans	Fleming C	Gore	Megson*	Norris	Cooper	Richardson	Ellis	Paterson
	30/4		*5,883*	*4*	43			*Rodwell 47, Groves 65*	*McIlhargey*	*Davies*	*Wright*	*Groves*	*Briggs*	*Gore*	*Rodwell*	*Horner*	*Bamber**	*Garner*	*Eyres*	*Richards*
								Ref: A Smith	Former Town boss Billy Ayre took over at Bloomfield Road in December and has guided Blackpool nicely into the play-off placings. His side are expected to win this game, but Town put up a stern fight. The writing is on the wall, though, when Rodwell is on hand score off a corner.											
46	H	ALDERSHOT		22	W	3-0	1-0	Paterson 35, Flower 62 (og), Norris 64	Gould	Fleming P*	Barr	Evans	Fleming C	**Griffiths**	Paterson	Norris	Cooper	Richardson	Ellis^	**German**/Donnelly
	11/5		1,428	*23*	46				*Coles*	*Fisher*	*Cornish*	*Ogley**	*Flower*	*Whitlock^*	*Terry*	*Puckett*	*Henry*	*Burvill*	*Joyce*	*Halbert/Tucker*
		Home	Away					Ref: R Pawley	The Shots fans turn up in fancy dress, their side includes four teenagers and two trialists, and in the end, Town have little to beat. Paterson slots in his first Town goal. Flower inadvertently knocks the ball over the line attempting to halt Cooper. Norris curls in his 35th goal of the season.											
Average		1,701	3,014																	

Rumbelows Cup

Rd		Opponent	Att	Pos	Res	F-A	H-T	Scorers, Times, and Referees	1	2	3	4	5	6	7	8	9	10	11	subs used
1:1	H	LINCOLN			W	2-0	0-0	Fyfe 60, Richardson 77	Brown	Fleming P	Cook	Evans	Fleming C	Futcher*	Butler	Richardson	McPhillips	Fyfe	Graham	**Gregory**
28/8			1,239						*Wallington*	*Casey*	*Nicholson*	*Brown*	*Stoutt**	*Davis*	*Schofield^*	*Smith P*	*Lormor*	*Smith N*	*Puttnam*	*Dixon/Carmichael*
								Ref: K Cooper	Allan Clarke took over as Lincoln boss in the summer, and evidently has told his players to impose themselves on the opposition. Town cope well with their physical approach, and manage to gain a useful two-goal cushion. Fyfe pokes in the first, Richardson perseveres for the second.											
1:2	A	LINCOLN		18	L	0-1	0-1		Brown	Fleming P	Cook	Evans	Fleming C	Futcher	Butler	Graham	Richardson	Fyfe*	Hall	Broadbent
5/9			*2,376*	*7*				*Davis 44*	*Wallington*	*Casey*	*Clarke*	*Brown*	*McNichol*	*Davis*	*Schofield*	*Smith P*	*Carmichael**	*Smith N*	*Puttnam*	*Scott*
								Ref: G Pooley (Halifax won 2-1 on aggregate)	This is the third meeting between the two sides in eight days. The Imps win this game but it's Town who go through after a backs-to-the-wall performance. Their defence is breached just the once when Davis heads in Paul Smith's corner just before the break, but the Shaymen hang on.											
2:1	H	MANCHESTER U		24	L	1-3	1-1	Evans 30	Brown	Fleming P	Cook	Evans	Fleming C	Futcher	Gregory	Butler	McPhillips	Richardson	Martin	
26/9			7,500	*1:3*				*Blackmore 25, McClair 87, Webb 88*	*Leighton*	*Irwin*	*Blackmore*	*Donaghy*	*Phelan*	*Pallister*	*Webb*	*Ince**	*McClair*	*Hughes^*	*Beardsmore*	*Martin/Robins*
								Ref: M Bailey	Town, can't score in the league, but can here. Evans' free-kick, in off the bar, cancels out one scored by Blackmore. Alex Ferguson's side leave it late to seal victory. After last season's disappointments, including for Scotland in the World Cup, Leighton plays his last game for the Reds.											
2:2	A	MANCHESTER U		24	L	1-2	0-1	Gregory 69	Brown	Fleming P	Barr	Evans	Fleming C	Futcher	Gregory	Richardson	McPhillips*	Graham	Butler^	**Paterson**/Donnelly
10/10			*22,295*	*1:5*				*Bruce 41p, Anderson 56*	*Sealey*	*Anderson*	*Blackmore**	*Bruce*	*Phelan*	*Pallister*	*Webb*	*Irwin^*	*McClair*	*Hughes*	*Martin*	*Wallace/Robins*
								Ref: K Breen (Halifax lost 2-5 on aggregate)	Town are out to enjoy the occasion, and can be proud of their performance. United have to rely on Steve Bruce's penalty, after a challenge on Martin by Fleming, for their first goal. Gregory will never forget his goal, a glancing header. Paterson comes on and makes a fool of Pallister.											

FA Cup

Rd		Opponent	Att	Pos	Res	F-A	H-T	Scorers, Times, and Referees	1	2	3	4	5	6	7	8	9	10	11	subs used
1	H	WREXHAM		24	W	3-2	1-1	Norris 2, Graham 50, Juryeff 83	Gould	Butler	Barr	Evans	Fleming C	Futcher	Martin	Norris	Juryeff	Graham	Ellis	
17/11			2,002	*21*				*Preece 25, 90*	*Morris*	*Phillips**	*Hardy*	*Hunter^*	*Beaumont*	*Jones J*	*Thackeray*	*Owens*	*O'Gorman*	*Worthington*	*Preece*	*Bowden/Armstrong*
								Ref: G Courtney	There is rumour about the safety of McCalliog's job before the game. It looks more secure after this sparkling display. Norris wastes no time and runs onto the ball for an early goal. He later misses an 18th-minute penalty, but Town show devastating form after Preece's headed goal.											
2	A	ROTHERHAM		24	D	1-1	0-1	Juryeff 51	Gould	Fleming P	Barr	Evans	Fleming C	Futcher	Butler	Norris	Juryeff	Graham	Ellis	
11/12			*2,906*	*3:24*				*Goater 19*	*Mercer*	*Forrest*	*Robinson*	*Pickering**	*Law*	*Watts*	*Goodwin*	*Dempsey*	*Goater*	*Spooner^*	*Hazel*	*Thompson/Evans*
								Ref: M Peck	The Millers are bottom of Division 3 and boss Billy McEwan will shortly be out of a job. Here, though, his side looks capable of beating Town until Juryeff, despite a gashed forehead, stuns them with a headed equaliser. With ten minutes left, Watts clears his clipped effort off the line.											
2R	H	ROTHERHAM		24	L	1-2	0-2	Norris 46	Gould	Fleming P	Barr	Evans	Fleming C	Futcher	Butler	Norris	Juryeff	Graham*	Ellis	Richardson
17/12			2,132	*3:24*				*Evans 8, Johnson 39*	*Mercer*	*Barnsley*	*Law*	*Spooner*	*Johnson*	*Forrest*	*Goodwin*	*Thompson**	*Mendonca*	*Evans*	*Hazel*	*Dempsey*
								Ref: C Trussell	Rotherham keeper Billy Mercer is outstanding in the second half as Town pile on the pressure in an attempt to save the game. Norris pulls one back off a corner, but it isn't enough. After Evans' early goal, Johnson's diving header ultimately proves enough to send the Millers through.											

		Home					Away					
	P	W	D	L	F	A	W	D	L	F	A	Pts
1 Darlington	46	13	8	2	36	14	9	9	5	32	24	83
2 Stockport	46	16	6	1	54	19	7	7	9	30	28	82
3 Hartlepool	46	15	5	3	35	15	9	5	9	32	33	82
4 Peterborough	46	13	9	1	38	15	8	8	7	29	30	80
5 Blackpool	46	17	3	3	55	17	6	7	10	23	30	79
6 Burnley	46	17	5	1	46	16	6	5	12	24	35	79
7 Torquay *	46	14	7	2	37	13	4	11	8	27	34	72
8 Scunthorpe	46	17	4	2	51	20	3	7	13	20	42	71
9 Scarborough	46	13	5	5	36	21	6	7	10	23	35	69
10 Northampton	46	14	5	4	34	21	4	8	11	23	37	67
11 Doncaster	46	12	5	6	36	22	5	9	9	20	24	65
12 Rochdale	46	10	9	4	29	22	5	8	10	21	31	62
13 Cardiff	46	10	6	7	26	23	5	9	9	17	31	60
14 Lincoln	46	10	7	6	32	27	4	10	9	18	34	59
15 Gillingham	46	9	9	5	35	27	3	9	11	22	33	54
16 Walsall	46	7	12	4	25	17	5	5	13	23	34	53
17 Hereford	46	9	10	4	32	19	4	4	15	21	39	53
18 Chesterfield	46	8	12	3	33	26	5	2	16	14	36	53
19 Maidstone	46	9	5	9	42	34	4	7	12	24	37	51
20 Carlisle	46	12	3	8	30	30	1	6	16	17	59	48
21 York	46	8	6	9	21	23	3	7	13	24	34	46
22 HALIFAX	46	9	6	8	34	29	3	4	16	25	50	46
23 Aldershot	46	8	7	8	38	43	2	4	17	23	58	41
24 Wrexham	46	8	7	8	33	34	2	3	18	15	40	40
	1104	278	161	113	868	547	113	161	278	547	868	1495

* promoted after play-offs

Odds & ends

Double wins: (0).
Double losses: (7) Burnley, Cardiff, Gillingham, Hartlepool, Hereford, Scarborough, Torquay.

Won from behind: (3) Blackpool (h), Walsall (h), Wrexham (a).
Lost from in front: (5) Burnley (h), Gillingham (h), Hartlepool (h), Chesterfield (a), Scarborough (a).

High spots: Scoring twice over 1st Division Man Utd.
Three consecutive wins in April.
Scoring five against Blackpool and Walsall.
Beating Wrexham on 26 March to get off the foot of the table.
Beating Rotherham 3-2 after extra-time at Millmoor to win the Yorkshire Cup.

Low spots: Failing to score in any of the first eight league games.
Being rooted at the bottom of the table for most of the season.
Eleven games without a win, including four consecutive defeats, up to 27 February.

Player of the Year: Steve Norris.
Ever-presents: (1) Craig Fleming.
Hat-tricks : Steve Norris (1).
Leading scorer: Steve Norris (32).

	Appearances						Goals			
	Lge	*Sub*	LC	*Sub*	FAC	*Sub*	Lge	LC	FAC	Tot
Barr, Billy	**34**	*3*	1		3		**1**			**1**
Broadbent, Graham	**3**	*4*		*1*			**1**			**1**
Brown, David	**11**		4							
Butler, Brian	**19**	*7*	4		3		**1**			**1**
Cook, Mitch	**16**	*1*	3							
Cooper, Graham	**13**	*4*					**1**			**1**
Dobson, Paul	**1**						**1**			**1**
Donnelly, Paul	**8**	*3*		*1*						
Ellis, Mark	**27**	*3*			3		**4**			**4**
Evans, David	**42**		4		3		**1**	1		**2**
Fleming, Craig	**46**		4		3					
Fleming, Paul	**39**		4		2					
Futcher, Paul	**15**		4		3					
Fyfe, Tony	**3**	*1*	2					1		**1**
German, David		*1*								
Gore, Shaun	**15**									
Gould, Jonathan	**23**				3					
Graham, Tommy	**23**		3		3		**3**		1	**4**
Gregory, Tony	**11**	*1*	2	*1*			**1**	1		**2**
Griffiths, Neil	**1**									
Hall, Derek	**8**		1							
Hutchinson, Ian	**3**									
Juryeff, Ian	**34**				3		**9**		2	**11**
Leonard, Mick	**3**									
McPhillips, Terry	**3**	*2*	3							
Martin, Dean	**26**	*2*	1		1		**1**			**1**
Megson, Kevin	**5**									
Norris, Steve	**39**				3		**30**		2	**32**
Paterson, Jamie	**3**	*3*		*1*			**1**			**1**
Richardson, Nick	**23**	*3*	4			*1*	**3**	1		**4**
Whitehead, Phil	**9**									
(own-goals)							**1**			**1**
31 players used	**506**	***38***	**44**	***4***	**33**	***1***	**59**	**4**	**5**	**68**

No	Date		Att	Pos	Pt	F-A	H-T	Scorers, Times, and Referees	1	2	3	4	5	6	7	8	9	10	11	subs used
1	H	NORTHAMPTON			L	0-1	0-0		Gould	Evans	**Kamara**	**Abbott**	**Richards**	Graham	Megson	Cooper	Juryeff	Richardson	Paterson	
	17/8		1,834		0			*Chard 62*	*Beresford*	*Chard*	*Wilson*	*Terry*	*Angus*	*Brown*	*Burnham*	*Quow*	*Adcock*	*Bell**	*Gernon*	*Campbell*
								Ref: D Shadwell	Town kick off without injured Steve Norris but create enough chances to win. Northampton score against the run of play through Phil Chard's deflected effort following a corner. Later, Cooper's shot comes down off the underside of the bar and may just have bounced over the line.											
2	A	MAIDSTONE		10	W	1-0	0-0	Juryeff 67	Gould	Evans	Kamara	Abbott	Richards	Graham	Barr	Norris	Juryeff	Richardson	Cooper	
	24/8		***1,216***	*23*	3				*Hesford*	*Haylock*	*Thompson*	*Oxbrow*	*Davis*	*Osborne*	*Gall**	*Painter*	*Donegal*	*Sandeman^*	*Rumble*	*Cuggy/Lillis*
								Ref: G Pooley	This game could have gone either way. Maidstone have £35,000 recruit Glen Donegal and strike partner Mark Gall in their side, but they are constantly thwarted by Gould, who makes three outstanding saves. Juryeff pops up with the decisive goal after Norris makes the opening.											
3	H	YORK		7	D	0-0	0-0		Gould	Evans	Kamara	Abbott	Richards	Graham	Barr	Norris	Juryeff	Richardson	Cooper	
	30/8		2,167	*11*	4				*Marples*	*McMillan*	*Crosby*	*Reid*	*Tutill*	*Atkin*	*Pepper*	*McCarthy*	*Blackstone*	*Osborne*	*Hall**	*Barratt*
								Ref: A Wilkie	Neither side serves up much for the fans. However, York, under John Bird, have a golden opportunity to take the lead when Richards pushes Steve Osborne to concede a seventh-minute penalty. Nigel Pepper's awful spot-kick, saved by Gould, sets the tone for the rest of the match.											
4	A	WALSALL		18	L	0-3	0-1	*[McDonald 88]*	Gould	Evans	Kamara	Abbott	Richards	**Bradley**	Barr*	Norris	Juryeff	Richardson	Cooper^	Megson/Graham
	7/9		*2,981*	*11*	4			*MacDonald 12, McLoughlin 51,*	*Sinclair*	*Williams*	*Statham*	*Methven*	*Hobson*	*Smith*	*MacDonald*	*Ntamark*	*McLoughlin*	*Marsh*	*McDonald*	
								Ref: K Cooper	The Shaymen are up against it once ex-Liverpool star Kevin MacDonald gives Walsall an early lead. Controversy surrounds the second goal. Ntamark appears literally to have a hand in it before Paul McLoughlin scores. Rod McDonald misses three good chances before his late strike.											
5	H	ROTHERHAM		19	L	**0-4**	0-0	*[Wilson 76]*	Gould	Evans	Kamara	Abbott	Richards	Bradley	Paterson*	Norris	Juryeff !	Richardson	Cooper^	Megson/Graham
	13/9		2,653	*1*	4			*Cun'ham 52, Goater 63, Hutchings 64,*	*Ford*	*Hutchings*	*Taylor*	*Todd*	*Johnson*	*Law*	*Wilson*	*Barrick*	*Cunningham*	*Page*	*Hazel**	*Goater*
								Ref: P Harrison	Phil Henson's Rotherham arrive at the Shay minus five regulars, but still cruise to victory. After Tony Cunningham's free header Town collapse and they are 0-3 down when Juryeff is sent off after clashing with Nigel Johnson. Two minutes later Rob Wilson whacks in the fourth.											
6	H	CARDIFF		20	D	1-1	0-1	Bradley 58	Gould	Barr	Kamara	Graham	Richards	Bradley	Paterson	Norris	Juryeff	Richardson	Cooper	
	17/9		1,041	*15*	5			*Dale 30*	*Ward*	*Jones*	*Searle*	*Gibbins*	*Abraham^*	*Perry*	*Pike**	*Lewis*	*Millar*	*Dale*	*Ramsey*	*Griffith/Heard*
								Ref: K Redfern	Town do enough to win but Cardiff keeper Gavin Ward keeps them at bay. After falling behind to Carl Dale's 15-yarder they put disaster behind them and level through Bradley from Barr's free-kick. Cardiff play the last 22 minutes with 10 men after Allan Lewis is stretchered off.											
7	H	MANSFIELD		19	L	1-3	0-1	Norris 76	Gould	Barr	Kamara	Graham*	Richards	Bradley	Paterson^	Norris	Matthews	Richardson	Cooper	Abbott/**Lucketti**
	27/9		2,026	*1*	5			*Stant 18, Fee 68, Wilkinson 87*	*Beasley*	*Fleming*	*With**	*Spooner*	*Fee*	*Foster*	*Ford*	*Holland*	*Stant*	*Wilkinson*	*Charles*	*Gray*
								Ref: J Lloyd	This is Mansfield's fourth consecutive away win. Phil Stant gives them the lead, then Norris fluffs a penalty for hands by ex-Town star Steve Spooner. At 0-2, having used both subs, Town lose injured Richards, then make a fight of it. Steve Wilkinson's late break, though, is typical.											
8	A	LINCOLN		18	D	0-0	0-0		Gould	Barr	Kamara	Evans	Graham	Bradley !	Paterson	Norris	Matthews	Richardson	Abbott*	Lucketti
	5/10		*2,092*	*16*	6				*Dickins*	*Carmichael*	*Nicholson*	*Brown*	*West G*	*Finney**	*Schofield*	*Ward*	*Lee*	*Lormor*	*Puttnam^*	*West D/Dobson*
								Ref: J Brandwood	Town have installed John McGrath as manager. He worked wonders at Port Vale and Preston and will need to do so again. This is a start and he is full of praise for Town's determination. Bradley walks for handling on the line, but Shane Nicholson's 27th-minute penalty hits the post.											
9	H	GILLINGHAM		20	L	0-3	0-1		Gould	Barr	Kamara	Evans^	Graham	Bradley	Paterson	Norris	Matthews	Richardson*	Abbott	Lucketti/Cooper
	12/10		1,435	*13*	6			*Crown 3, 63, Beadle 46*	*Branagan*	*O'Shea*	*Elsey*	*Eeles*	*Walker*	*Trusson*	*Clark*	*Crown*	*Beadle**	*Lovell*	*O'Connor*	*Arnott*
								Ref: J Watson	David Crown is yet again a thorn in Town's side. He has now scored in each of the last three meetings between the sides. His close control allows him to score the first, whilst his pace takes him clear for his second. Peter Beadle's goal 14 seconds after the interval kills the game.											
10	H	CHESTERFIELD		17	W	2-0	0-0	Norris 52p, 62	**Bracey**	Barr	Kamara	Evans	Richards	Lucketti	Richardson	Norris	Juryeff	Graham	Ellis	
	19/10		1,506	*11*	9				*Leonard*	*Dyche*	*Williams*	*Francis*	*Brien*	*Gunn*	*Turnbull*	*Cooke^*	*Lancaster*	*Hawke**	*Hewitt*	*Caldwell/Grayson*
								Ref: T Lunt	McGrath is happy with this much needed, and merited, victory. Norris, showing shades of last season, is brought down by Lee Francis for the penalty, which he scores himself. He then latches onto sub Dave Caldwell's back-pass and rounds ex-Shayman Mick Leonard for his second.											

11	A	ROCHDALE		16	L	0-1	0-1		Bracey	Barr	Kamara	Evans	Richards	**Lewis**	Richardson*	Norris	Juryeff	Graham	Ellis	Abbott^/Lucketti
	26/10		*2,323*	*6*	9			*Flounders 26*	*Gray*	*Brown M*	*Ryan**	*Brown T*	*Reeves*	*Halpin*	*Graham*	*Doyle*	*Flounders*	*Palin*	*Kinsey^*	*Bowden/Whitehall*
								Ref: K Cooper	Dave Sutton took over at Dale in February and he has got them off to a good start. Andy Flounders lovely headed goal keeps them up with the early pacesetters. Town look good at times but lack that killer instinct. Abbott replaces Richardson but is carried off on a stretcher late on.											
12	H	BURNLEY		19	L	0-2	0-0		Bracey	Barr	Kamara	Evans	Richards	Lucketti !	Graham !	Norris	Juryeff	Richardson	Ellis	
	2/11		**4,491**	*3*	9			*Deary 55, Farrell 87*	*Marriott*	*France*	*Jakub*	*Davies*	*Pender*	*Farrell*	*Harper*	*Deary*	*Francis*	*Conroy*	*Eli**	*Lancashire*
								Ref: P Danson	The controversial sending off of young Lucketti for a professional foul on sub Graham Lancashire changes this game. Deary scores from the resultant free-kick. Town regroup, then Graham goes, for a foul – on Lancashire. Andy Farrell's volleyed goal is worth the admission fee.											
13	A	HEREFORD		16	W	2-0	1-0	Juryeff 34, Norris 80	Bracey	Barr	Kamara*	Evans	Richards	Lewis	Graham	Norris	Juryeff	Richardson	Ellis	Lucketti
	6/11		*2,207*	*4*	12				*Judge*	*Pejic**	*Downs^*	*Theodosiou*	*Devine*	*Lowndes*	*Titterton*	*Wade*	*Brain*	*Heritage*	*Caffrey*	*Hall/Robinson*
								Ref: L Shafter	Former Coventry boss John Sillett is now in charge at Edgar Street, but he sees his team lose the last 100% home record. Juryeff's swirling 35-yarder deceives Alan Judge, and Norris races through for the second. The strong wind plays its part but McGrath says this result is 'no fluke'.											
14	A	BARNET		19	L	0-3	0-1		Bracey	Barr	Lucketti	Evans	Richards	Lewis	Graham*	Norris	Juryeff	Richardson	Ellis	**Hildersley**
	9/11		*4,837*	*1*	12			*Bull 9, Lowe 54, Willis 72*	*Pape*	*Poole*	*Naylor*	*Horton*	*Howell*	*Willis*	*Wilson*	*Carter**	*Bull*	*Lowe^*	*Showler*	*Hoddle/Lynch*
								Ref: P Alcock	The Underhill outfit are the League's newest club and they are adapting well. This win puts them top for the first time. Gary Bull, brother of Wolves' international Steve, combines with Roger Willis for the first goal, whilst Willis' headed effort is Barnet's 40th League goal so far.											
15	H	SCARBOROUGH		15	W	1-0	1-0	Richardson 31	Bracey	Barr	Bradley^	Lucketti	Richards	Lewis	Abbott	Norris	Juryeff	Richardson	Ellis*	Hildersley/Evans
	22/11		1,395	*16*	15				*Hughes*	*James*	*Mudd*	*Lee*	*Hirst*	*Meyer*	*Carter^*	*Mockler*	*Mooney*	*Fletcher**	*Jules*	*Foreman/Himsworth*
								Ref: T West	Boro are managed by former Shay favourite Ray McHale, and his young charges seem to know their stuff. But McGrath is trying to steady his ship, starting with the defence, and here it acquits itself well. All Town need is a goal, which comes courtesy of Richardson following a corner.											
16	A	BLACKPOOL		18	L	0-3	0-3		Bracey	Barr	Bradley	Lucketti	Richards	Lewis	Abbott*	Norris^	Juryeff	Richardson	Hildersley	Evans/Paterson
	30/1		*3,118*	*3*	15			*Groves 4, Bamber 33, 44*	*McIlhargey*	*Davies*	*Stoneman*	*Groves*	*Briggs*	*Hedworth*	*Rodwell*	*Bonner**	*Bamber*	*Sinclair^*	*Eyres*	*Taylor/Garner*
								Ref: W Burns	Blackpool, under former Town boss Billy Ayre, have this one sewn up by half time. Paul Groves heads home a free-kick, and Dave Bamber scores a simple tap-in, and then heads in David Eyres' corner. When Tony Rodwell has a goal disallowed this is only slight relief for Town.											
17	H	WREXHAM		14	W	4-3	1-1	Paterson 22, R'son 59, 62, Juryeff 76,	Bracey	Barr	Bradley	Lucketti	Richards	Lewis	Abbott	Norris*	Juryeff	Richardson	Paterson^	Cooper/Ellis
	13/12		**881**	*20*	18			*Connolly 29, 77, Davies 52*	*O'Keefe*	*Thackeray*	*Hardy*	*Beaumont*	*Thomas*	*Sertori*	*Davies*	*Owen*	*Jones L**	*Connolly*	*Kelly*	*Cross*
								Ref: C Trussell/E Wolstenholme	This is a real thriller seen by few. Juryeff, hovering at the far post, gives Town daylight, but only for a few seconds. Norris heads against the bar, while Wrexham's Lee Jones and Gordon Davies also hit the woodwork. Ref Trussell's calf strain ends his involvement after 31 minutes.											
18	H	MAIDSTONE		15	D	1-1	0-1	Cooper 73	Bracey	Barr	**Wilson**	Lucketti	Bradley	Lewis	Abbott	Cooper	Juryeff	Richardson	Hildersley	
	21/12		1,040	*21*	19			*Painter 34*	*Hesford*	*Haylock*	*Thompson*	*Smalley*	*Oxbrow*	*Davis*	*Painter*	*Stebbing*	*Sandeman*	*Ellis*	*Heney*	
								Ref: P Wright	Maidstone have financial troubles, are fighting to find a new ground and struggling in the League. Robbie Painter's stunning 18-yard volley is, therefore, a moment to cherish. But Town are worth a point and Cooper proves lethal from a little nearer after Hesford parries Juryeff's shot.											
19	A	NORTHAMPTON		16	L	**0-4**	0-4		Bracey	Barr*	Wilson	Lucketti	Bradley^	Lewis	Abbott	Cooper	Juryeff	Richardson	Evans	Kamara/Richards
	26/12		*3,147*	*14*	19			*Adcock 33, 36, Chard 44, Barnes 45*	*Richardson*	*Chard*	*Terry*	*Quow*	*Angus*	*Burnham*	*Beavon*	*Barnes*	*McClean**	*Brown*	*Adcock*	*Campbell*
								Ref: D Elleray	The Shaymen suffer a mad twelve minutes up to half-time and the contest is over. Tony Adcock plunders the first two, then returns a pass for Phil Chard to score. Evans' poor header backwards lets in Bobby Barnes for his goal. Whistle-happy Elleray awards no less than 60 free-kicks.											
20	A	YORK		16	D	1-1	0-0	Wilson 56	Bracey	Barr	Wilson	Lucketti	Bradley	Lewis	Abbott	Cooper	Juryeff	Richardson	Evans*	Hildersley
	28/12		*2,396*	*18*	20			*Hall 90*	*Marples*	*McMillan*	*Crosby*	*Reid*	*Warburton*	*Atkin*	*Pepper*	*McCarthy*	*Barratt**	*Hall*	*Canham*	*Blackstone*
								Ref: D Allison	Injuries and bad luck handicap Town, who are denied victory at the death. Wilson's low drive off a free-kick gives them the lead, then he has a shot that looks to have crossed the line before Crosby clears. The sight of Wayne Hall's toe-poke bobbling in is agonising for the Shaymen.											
21	A	DONCASTER		16	W	2-0	0-0	Norris 49, Hutchinson 76	Bracey	Barr	Hutchinson	Lucketti	Bradley	Lewis	Kamara	Cooper	Norris	Richardson	Wilson	
	1/1		*2,067*	*23*	23				*Samways*	*Douglas*	*Limber*	*Ashurst*	*Raven*	*Gormley*	*Morrow**	*Nicholson*	*Rankine*	*Muir*	*Noteman*	*McKenzie*
								Ref: M Bailey	Belle Vue is becoming a happy hunting ground for the Shaymen. This is their fourth consecutive win here. Norris, playing his first game for a month, turns in Wilson's cross. Mark Samways is helpless as Hutchinson launches himself at another Wilson cross to halt a Rovers fightback.											

No	Date		Att	Pos	Pt	F-A	H-T	Scorers, Times, and Referees	1	2	3	4	5	6	7	8	9	10	11	subs used
22	H	SCUNTHORPE		17	L	1-4	0-1	Paterson 88	Bracey	Barr*	Wilson	Lucketti	Bradley^	Lewis	Kamara	Cooper	Juryeff	Richardson	Hildersley	Evans/Paterson
	18/1		1,232	_7_	23			_White 39, 59, 72, Hamilton 51_	_Whitehead_	_Joyce_	_Hill_	_Martin_	_Hicks_	_Humphries_	_Alexander_	_Hamilton_	_Daws_	_White_	_Helliwell_	
								Ref: P Jones	Jason White scores three and makes the other for Ian Hamilton as the Irons canter to victory. Town suffer injuries and Barr is actually off the field when White heads in his first. Hildersley could have put Town ahead in the third minute, but puts his penalty wide after Cooper is pushed.											
23	A	CARLISLE		16	D	1-1	1-0	Richardson 41	Bracey	Barr	Wilson	Lucketti	Richards	Evans	Kamara	Cooper	Juryeff	Richardson	Paterson*	Hutchinson
	25/1		_2,091_	_18_	24			_Watson 71p_	_O'Hanlon_	_Graham_	_Freeman^_	_Walsh_	_Jeffels_	_Edmondson*_	_Thomas_	_Watson_	_Walling_	_Fyfe_	_Proudlock_	_Armstrong/Cransto_
								Ref: E Parker	McGrath experiments with a front pairing of Cooper and Richardson and it almost pays off. Richardson stabs home Paterson's cross while Cooper is only thwarted twice by Kelham O'Hanlon's legs. Ex-Shayman Andy Watson nets a penalty after Gwyn Thomas is chopped down.											
24	H	ROCHDALE		16	D	1-1	1-0	Cooper 41	Bracey	Barr	Wilson	Lucketti	Richards	Evans	Kamara	Juryeff	Cooper	Richardson	Gregory*	**Hardy**
	8/2		2,213	_8_	25			_Flounders 51_	_Rose_	_Brown M_	_Graham_	_Brown T_	_Butler_	_Payne_	_Doyle_	_Milner_	_Flounders_	_Bowden*_	_Kilner_	_Halpin_
								Ref: A Flood	The ref lets all manner of things go in this return derby where neither side takes any prisoners. Quality goes by the way but Halifax draw first blood when Cooper beats the offside. Dale are deserving of a draw, and get one when defensive errors leave the door open for Andy Flounders.											
25	H	BLACKPOOL		18	L	1-2	0-2	Barr 80p	Bracey	Barr	Wilson	Lucketti	Richards	Evans	Kamara*	Juryeff	Cooper	Richardson	Gregory^	Abbott/Hardy
	12/2		2,158	_2_	25			_Bamber 21, Rodwell 34_	_Kearton_	_Davies_	_Kerr_	_Groves_	_Briggs_	_Gore_	_Rodwell_	_Gouck_	_Bamber_	_Garner_	_Eyres_	
								Ref: K Lupton	High-flying Blackpool are more than matched by the Shaymen but the difference is in front of goal. The reliable Dave Bamber, with his 27th of the season and Tony Rodwell show Town the way. Gary Briggs barges Richardson and Barr's converted penalty sets up a grandstand finish.											
26	A	WREXHAM		19	L	0-2	0-0		Bracey	Barr	Wilson	Lucketti	Richards	Evans	Kamara^	Cooper*	Juryeff	Richardson	**Donovan**	Hildersley/Hardy
	15/2		_2,076_	_17_	25			_Jones L 62, Owen 72_	_O'Keefe_	_Thackeray_	_Hardy_	_Carey_	_Thomas_	_Sertori_	_Pejic_	_Flynn^_	_Connolly_	_Watkin*_	_Phillips_	_Owen/Jones L_
								Ref: A Smith	A 57th-minute double substitution by Wrexham player-boss Brian Flynn is an inspired one. Lee Jones scores easily after Phillips robs Kamara before Gareth Owen controls Mickey Thomas's corner to score the second. Bracey has to make a string of fine saves as Town rarely threaten.											
27	H	DONCASTER		19	D	0-0	0-0		**Brown**	Barr	Wilson	Lucketti	Richards	Evans	Donovan	Juryeff	Cooper	Richardson	Hildersley	
	22/2		1,285	_22_	26				_Samways_	_Douglas_	_Prindiville_	_Ashurst_	_Ormsby_	_Gormley_	_Morrow*_	_Stiles_	_Nicholson_	_Muir^_	_Noteman_	_McKenzie/Crosby_
								Ref: R Dilkes	Rovers, under Steve Beaglehole, won only their third game of the season last week. They are obviously struggling. Town regard this result as two points dropped. It's a scrappy affair. Juryeff goes close twice and that's about it. Young keeper Brown is drafted in but has little to do.											
28	A	CREWE		19	L	2-3	1-2	Wilson 4, Richardson 83	Bracey	Barr*	Wilson	Lucketti	Richards	Kamara	Donovan	Juryeff	Paterson^	Richardson	Hildersley	Bradley/Hardy
	28/2		_3,514_	_8_	26			_Evans 36, Clarkson 45, Naylor 61_	_Noble_	_Wilson_	_McKearney_	_Carr_	_Smart_	_Rose_	_Garvey*_	_Naylor_	_Evans^_	_Gardiner_	_Clarkson_	_Edwards/Sorvel_
								Ref: I Hemley	This result flatters the Shaymen. Wilson's corner somehow finds it way straight in, then Bracey has to perform heroics to keep the score down. Phil Clarkson scores at a crucial time. Tony Naylor wriggles through for the third. Richardson's angled drive doesn't worry Dario Gradi's side.											
29	A	SCUNTHORPE		19	L	0-1	0-0		Bracey	Lucketti	Wilson	Bradley	Richards	Kamara	Donovan	Juryeff	Paterson*	Richardson	Hildersley	Abbott
	3/3		_2,448_	_8_	26			_Buckley 62_	_Musselwhite_	_Joyce_	_Longden_	_Martin_	_Hicks_	_Lister_	_Alexander_	_Hamilton_	_White*_	_Buckley_	_Helliwell_	_Daws_
								Ref: D Gallagher	Up until now the Shaymen had a tidy record at Glandford Park, with one cup win and three draws. On this showing another draw looks like being the best they can hope. The Irons step up a gear after half-time and make the breakthrough when Helliwell heads down for John Buckley.											
30	H	CARLISLE		19	W	3-2	0-1	Bradley 69, Cooper 82, Wilson 85	Bracey	Lucketti	Wilson	Bradley	Richards	Kamara	Donovan	Juryeff	Cooper	Richardson	Hildersley	
	6/3		1,015	_21_	29			_Walling 39, Watson 74_	_O'Hanlon_	_Graham_	_Gallimore_	_Holmes_	_Holliday_	_Barnsley_	_Edmondson_	_Watson_	_Thomas_	_Walling_	_Proudlock_	
								Ref: I Hendrick	Carlisle look to be heading for a deserved victory until Town's late surge. Leading 2-1 Dean Walling's overhead kick crashes against the bar. Town's second equaliser is a close-range header from Cooper. Wilson's winner will long be talked about – a rising bullet shot from 18 yards.											
31	H	HEREFORD		20	L	0-2	0-0		Bracey	Lucketti	Wilson	Barr	Richards	Kamara	Donovan	Juryeff	Cooper	Richardson	Hildersley	
	11/3		918	_16_	29			_Narbett 54p, Brain 57_	_Judge_	_Jennings_	_Downs_	_Theodosiou_	_Devine_	_Titterton_	_Fry_	_Narbett_	_Robinson_	_Brain_	_Jones_	
								Ref: R Nixon	The Shaymen are their own worst enemies at times. Hereford are an uninspired outfit, yet Town look just as bad. Then Richardson hacks down Andy Theodosiou and Jon Narbett nets the penalty. Hereford surprise themselves with a second goal when Simon Brain beats the offside trap.											

32	A	BURNLEY		20	L	0-1	0-0		Bracey	Barr	Wilson	Lucketti	Bradley	Kamara	Gregory*	Juryeff	Richardson	Abbott	Hildersley	Cooper
	14/3		***10,903***	*3*	29			*Pender 70*	*Walker*	*Measham*	*Jakub*	*Farrell*	*Pender*	*Randall*	*Harper**	*Deary*	*Francis*	*Conroy*	*Lancashire*	*Monington*
								Ref: T West	Guided by Jimmy Mullen, Burnley are heading for the title. Perhaps Town sense this and they set out to make life difficult. They end up being booed off the field by the home crowd. Clarets skipper John Pender ends their frustration with a header off John Deary's floated free-kick.											
33	H	BARNET		20	W	**3-1**	0-0	Richardson 46, 62, Wilson 71p	Bracey	Barr*	Wilson	Lucketti	Bradley	Kamara	Gregory	Juryeff	Richardson	Abbott	Hildersley	Evans
	21/3		1,756	*5*	32			*Murphy 82*	*Phillips*	*Poole*	*Cooper*	*Bodley*	*Howell*	*Horton**	*Willis*	*Carter*	*Bull*	*Hoddle*	*Showler^*	*Lowe/Murphy*
								Ref: R Hart	The Shaymen at last prove that on their day they can match anyone. Richardson is their hero. His first comes after only twelve seconds of the second half. Wilson's penalty is awarded when Gary Phillips brings down Juryeff. Defeat for Barry Fry's Bees dents their promotion hopes.											
34	A	SCARBOROUGH		20	L	0-3	0-3		Bracey	Barr	Wilson	Lucketti	Bradley	Kamara	Evans	Juryeff	Richardson	Abbott	Hildersley	
	28/3		*1,363*	*12*	32			*Marshall 11, Mooney 38, Thompson 44*	*Ironside*	*Thompson*	*Mudd*	*Lee*	*Hirst*	*Curran*	*Ashdjian*	*McGee*	*Mooney^*	*Marshall**	*Jules*	*Gabbiadini/Fletcher*
								Ref: P Jones	Town put on a horror show at Seamer Road. Scarborough include three debutants. One of them, Colin Marshall, is left free to open the scoring. Tom Mooney shows neat footwork for his goal. A mix-up between Evans and Kamara presents Simon Thompson with a one-on-one situation.											
35	A	ROTHERHAM		20	L	0-1	0-0		Bracey	Barr	Wilson	Lucketti	Bradley	Kamara	Evans	Juryeff	Richardson	Abbott	Hildersley	
	31/3		*4,517*	*4*	32			*Wilson 50*	*Mercer*	*Russell*	*Hutchings^*	*Wilson*	*Johnson*	*Law*	*Goodwin*	*Richardson**	*Goater*	*Howard*	*Barrick*	*Hazel/Hathaway*
								Ref: J Rushton	Like Burnley, recently promotion-chasing Rotherham find Town a tough nut to crack. Relief is felt all around Millmoor when Robert Wilson scores after Jonathan Howard's effort is blocked. Town have chances to make the game more interesting but the forwards are found wanting.											
36	H	WALSALL		20	W	1-0	1-0	Wilson 28	Bracey	Megson	Wilson	Lucketti	Bradley	Kamara	Gregory*	Juryeff	Richardson	Abbott	Paterson	Evans
	3/4		1,006	*17*	35				*Gayle*	*Williams*	*Statham*	*Methven*	*Edwards*	*O'Hara*	*Chine*	*Ntamark*	*Marsh*	*Cecere**	*May*	*McDonald*
								Ref: P Wright	Walsall, under Kenny Hibbitt, have failed to win any of their last five games. Unconvincing Town just do enough to win. Wilson is the best player on view and fittingly gets the only goal. It comes out of nothing. He picks up a wayward pass, beats Chine and fires past Mark Gayle.											
37	A	CHESTERFIELD		20	L	**0-4**	0-0		Bracey	Megson	Wilson	Lucketti	Bradley	Kamara	Evans	Juryeff	Richardson	Abbott	Paterson	
	7/4		*1,802*	*13*	35			*Lancaster 55, 71, Norris 64, Morris 82*	*Leonard*	*Dyche*	*Hewitt*	*Francis*	*Brien*	*McGugan**	*Whitehead*	*Norris*	*Lancaster^*	*Hebbard*	*Cooke*	*Lemon/Morris*
								Ref: K Breen	It is now 457 minutes since Town last scored away from home. Paterson has three good second-half chances but he fails to break the duck. The Spireites make the most of chances that come their way, including three in 16 minutes. Former Shayman Norris swivels to score a sweet goal.											
38	A	CARDIFF		20	L	**0-4**	0-1		Bracey	Megson	Wilson	Lucketti	Bradley !	Kamara	Evans	Juryeff	Richardson	Abbott	Paterson !	
	11/4		*5,261*	*9*	35			*Ramsey 36p, Dale 65, 85, Pike 82*	*Hansbury*	*Gorman^*	*Searle*	*Gibbins*	*Bellamy*	*Perry*	*Ramsey*	*Newton*	*Millar**	*Dale*	*Blake*	*Pike/Gill*
								Ref: M Pierce	A miserable night for the Shaymen. Again they fail to score, and both Bradley, for hauling down Chris Pike, and Paterson, for elbowing Jason Perry, are sent off. Once Paul Ramsey scores a penalty, given when Kamara fells Nathan Blake, the game follows an all-too familiar pattern.											
39	H	CREWE		20	W	2-1	0-1	Barr 85, 89	Bracey	Megson	Wilson	Lucketti	Bradley	Kamara	Evans	Juryeff	Hutchinson*	Abbott	Hildersley	Barr
	14/4		1,022	*7*	38			*McKearney 9*	*Greygoose*	*Wilson*	*Smith*	*Carr*	*McKearney*	*Walters*	*Hignett*	*Naylor*	*Whitehurst*	*Callaghan*	*Clarkson*	
								Ref: M Peck	Crewe are heading for the play-offs, but they come undone here. Dave McKearney's lobbed effort looks like being enough to win it until Barr comes off the bench. His two late goals silence the slow-handclappers. Both are headers from crosses supplied firstly by Juryeff, and Megson.											
40	A	MANSFIELD		20	L	2-3	0-1	Juryeff 57, Abbott 76	Bracey	Megson	Wilson	Lucketti	Bradley	Kamara	Barr*	Juryeff	Richardson	Abbott	Hildersley	German
	21/4		*3,936*	*3*	38			*Stant 42, 65, 83*	*Pearcey*	*Fleming**	*Charles*	*Clark*	*Fee*	*Gray*	*Ford*	*Holland*	*Stant*	*Wilkinson*	*Noteman^*	*Castledine/Stringfel*
								Ref: T Lunt	Town at last score on their travels but fall to Phil Stant's first ever hat-trick. Mansfield dominate the first half, but Town get on top after the break. Abbott heads in Town's second equaliser. A draw seems likely until Wilkinson's cross deflects off Megson for Stant to score his third.											
41	H	LINCOLN		20	L	1-4	1-1	Richardson 12	Bracey	Megson	Hutchinson	Lucketti	Evans	Kamara	**Longley***	Barr	Richardson	Abbott	German	Griffiths
	25/4		1,296	*10*	38			*Lormor 26, 52, Abbott 87 (og), [Alexander 90]*	*Bowling*	*Smith*	*West*	*Carmichael*	*Dunphy*	*Brown*	*Schofield*	*Finney**	*Lee^*	*Lormor*	*Puttnam*	*Kabia/Alexander*
								Ref: M Reed	Town's last home game is one to forget, not least by Bracey, who has a rare off day. After Richardson fires in on his 100th League appearance, the keeper gifts the Imps three goals. The game is quite even until Abbott's own-goal, a screamer, whacking in Carmichael's harmless cross.											
42	A	GILLINGHAM		20	L	0-2	0-0		Bracey	Megson	Hutchinson	Lucketti	Evans	Kamara	German	Juryeff	Richardson	Abbott	Barr*	Griffiths
	2/5		*2,413*	*11*	38			*Lovell 83, 88p*	*Harrison*	*Green*	*Martin*	*O'Connor*	*Walker*	*Smith*	*Clark*	*Beagle^*	*Butler*	*Lovell*	*Thomas**	*Arnott/Osborne*
		Home	Away					Ref: C Wilkes	It's a tenth consecutive away defeat for the Shaymen as they end their programme. Barr has a 66th-minute goal ruled out for offside. Abbott almost gets another own-goal, but the ball hits the bar. Steve Lovell gets two late goals, the second a penalty when Griffiths fouls Paul Clark.											
Average		1,637	3,177																	

Rumbelows Cup						F-A	H-T	Scorers, Times, and Referees	1	2	3	4	5	6	7	8	9	10	11	subs used
1:1	H	TRANMERE			L	3-4	3-2	Norris 6p, Richardson 15, Juryeff 45	Gould	Barr	Kamara	Abbott	Richards	Graham	Megson*	Norris	Juryeff	Richardson	Cooper	Paterson
20/8			1,910	*2:*				*Irons 17, Aldridge 19, 64p, 76*	*Nixon*	*Higgins*	*Brannan*	*Irons*	*Hughes*	*Garnett*	*Morrissey*	*Aldridge*	*Steel**	*Martindale*	*Thomas*	*Malkin*
								Ref: A Flood	Town became the first side to witness John Aldridge's famous penalty shuffle in this thriller. He is hauled down by Richards and takes the kick himself for his first. His third, the winner, is even easier – a simple tap in. Norris returns and scores, also from a penalty, after Higgins handles.											
1:2	A	TRANMERE		10	L	3-4	2-1	Barr 5, 13, Cooper 51	Gould	Evans	Kamara	Abbott	Richards	Graham	Barr	Norris	Juryeff	Richardson	Cooper*	Megson
27/8			*4,285*	*2:*		*aet*		*Aldridge 11, 119, Steel 56, 105*	*Nixon*	*Higgins*	*Brannan*	*Irons*	*Hughes !*	*Garnett**	*Morrissey*	*Aldridge*	*Steel*	*Martindale*	*Thomas*	*McNab*
								Ref: G Singh (Halifax lost 6-8 on aggregate)	This game has everything. Tranmere have skipper Mark Hughes sent off for a 51st-minute professional foul on Juryeff. Aldo misses a penalty, and on 114 minutes Norris hits the post for Town. Jim Steel's tap-in gives Tranmere the edge, but David Higgins then has to clear off the line.											

FA Cup																				
1	A	WITTON		19	D	1-1	0-1	Hildersley 89	Gould	Barr	Bradley	Evans	Richards	Lewis	Abbott*	Norris	Juryeff	Richardson	Ellis	Hildersley
16/11			*2,002*	*VC*				*Thomas 30*	*Zelem*	*Stewart*	*Coathup*	*McNellis*	*Connor Jim*	*Anderson*	*Thomas*	*Hooton*	*Lutkevitch**	*Grimshaw*	*Connor Joe*	*Dyson*
								Ref: I Hendrick	Witton have in their side Karl Thomas, who scored 47 goals last season. When Bradley heads out a corner Thomas drills in his eighth of the current campaign. Town are deserving of a draw, but they leave it very late. Super-sub Hildersley's 30-yard chip will be talked about for years.											
1R	H	WITTON		15	L	1-2	0-0	Richardson 119	Gould	Barr	Bradley	Lucketti	Richards	Evans	Abbott	Norris	Juryeff	Richardson	Ellis*	Hildersley
27/11			2,172	*VC*		*aet*		*Thomas 97, Grimshaw 122*	*Zelem*	*Coathup*	*Hooton*	*McNellis*	*Connor Jim*	*Anderson**	*Thomas*	*Cuddy*	*Lutkevitch^*	*Grimshaw*	*Connor Joe*	*Hill/Alford*
								Ref: I Hendrick	Town are outdone yet again by non-league opposition at the Shay. The only real surprise is that they manage to take Witton to extra-time. The linesman rules Thomas' header goes over the line. Andy Grimshaw is left unmarked for his goal. Richardson's raking shot is too little, too late.											

League fixture with defunct Aldershot, expunged from League records																				
	A	ALDERSHOT		14	W	3-1	1-1	Bradley 26, Norris 55p, 63	Gould	Barr	Kamara	Graham*	Richards	Bradley	Paterson	Norris	Juryeff	Richardson	Cooper	Abbott
20/9			2,695	*13*				*Hopkins 1*	*Granville !*	*Brown*	*Cooper*	*Hopkins*	*Ogley*	*Berry*	*Rees*	*Puckett*	*Cole^*	*Henry !*	*Heath**	*Stewart/Burvill*
								Ref: R Bigger	Town recover to win despite conceding a goal after only 45 seconds. Shots keeper John Granville is sent off for handling outside the box and Mark Rees goes in goal for the remaining 65 minutes. Charlie Henry up-ends Norris for his penalty and is also ordered off, somewhat harshly.											

		Home					Away					
	P	W	D	L	F	A	W	D	L	F	A	Pts
1 Burnley	42	14	4	3	42	16	11	4	6	37	27	83
2 Rotherham	42	12	6	3	38	16	10	5	6	32	21	77
3 Mansfield	42	13	4	4	43	26	10	4	7	32	27	77
4 Blackpool*	42	17	3	1	48	13	5	7	9	23	32	76
5 Scunthorpe	42	14	5	2	39	18	7	4	10	25	41	72
6 Crewe	42	12	6	3	33	20	8	4	9	33	31	70
7 Barnet	42	16	1	4	48	23	5	5	11	33	38	69
8 Rochdale	42	12	6	3	34	22	6	7	8	23	31	67
9 Cardiff	42	13	3	5	42	26	4	12	5	24	27	66
10 Lincoln	42	9	5	7	21	24	8	6	7	29	20	62
11 Gillingham	42	12	5	4	41	19	3	7	11	22	34	57
12 Scarborough	42	12	5	4	39	28	3	7	11	25	40	57
13 Chesterfield	42	6	7	8	26	28	8	4	9	23	33	53
14 Wrexham	42	11	4	6	31	26	3	5	13	21	47	51
15 Walsall	42	5	10	6	28	26	7	3	11	20	32	49
16 Northampton	42	5	9	7	25	23	6	4	11	21	34	46
17 Hereford	42	9	4	8	31	24	3	4	14	13	33	44
18 Maidstone	42	6	9	6	24	22	2	9	10	21	34	42
19 York	42	6	9	6	26	23	2	7	12	16	35	40
20 HALIFAX	42	7	5	9	23	35	3	3	15	11	40	38
21 Doncaster	42	6	2	13	21	35	3	6	12	19	30	35
22 Carlisle	42	5	9	7	24	27	2	4	15	17	40	34
	924	222	121	119	727	520	119	121	222	520	727	1265

* promoted after play-offs

Odds & ends

Double wins: (0).

Double losses: (7) Blackpool, Burnley, Gillingham, Mansfield, Northampton, Rotherham, Scunthorpe.

Won from behind: (4) Wrexham (h), Carlisle (h), Crewe (h), Aldershot (a).

Lost from in front: (4) Lincoln (h), Crewe (a), Tranmere (LC) (h & a).

High spots: scoring four goals against Wrexham.

Taking 1st Division Tranmere to extra-time in the Rumbelows Cup.

Low spots: Losing more than half their league games.

Being beaten by non-league Witton in the FA Cup.

Only 881 turning up for the visit of Wrexham.

Town failed to win two consecutive matches.

Players' league appearances do not include the match against Aldershot, who resigned from the Football League on 25 March.

Player of the Year: Lee Bracey.

Ever-presents: (0).

Hat-tricks: (0).

Leading scorer: Nick Richardson (10).

	Appearances						Goals			
	Lge	*Sub*	LC	*Sub*	FAC	*Sub*	**Lge**	LC	FAC	**Tot**
Abbott, Greg	**24**	*5*	2		2		**1**			**1**
Barr, Billy	**35**	*1*	2		2		**3**	2		**5**
Bracey, Lee	**32**									
Bradley, Russell	**26**	*1*			2		**3**			**3**
Brown, Nick	**1**									
Cooper, Graham	**20**	*3*	2				**3**	1		**4**
Donovan, Kevin	**6**									
Ellis, Mark	**6**	*1*			2					
Evans, David	**26**	*5*	1		2					
German, David	**2**	*1*								
Gould, Jonathan	**10**		2		2					
Graham, Tommy	**13**	*2*	2							
Gregory, Tony	**5**									
Griffiths, Neil		*2*								
Hardy, Jason		*4*								
Hildersley, Ronnie	**14**	*4*				*2*			1	**1**
Hutchinson, Ian	**4**	*1*					**1**			**1**
Juryeff, Ian	**38**		2		2		**4**	1		**5**
Kamara, Alan	**35**	*1*	2							
Lewis, Dudley	**11**				1					
Longley, Scott	**1**									
Lucketti, Chris	**31**	*5*			1					
Matthews, Neil	**3**									
Megson, Kevin	**8**	*2*	1	*1*						
Norris, Steve	**18**		2		2		**7**	1		**8**
Paterson, Jamie	**14**	*2*		*1*			**2**			**2**
Richards, Steve	**25**	*1*	2		2					
Richardson, Nick	**42**		2		2		**8**	1	1	**10**
Wilson, Paul	**23**						**5**			**5**
29 players used	**473**	***41***	**22**	***2***	**22**	***2***	**37**	**6**	**2**	**45**

BARCLAYS DIVISION 3 (New Style) | Manager: McGrath ⇨ Mick Rathbone | SEASON 1992-93

No	Date		Att	Pos	Pt	F-A	H-T	Scorers, Times, and Referees	1	2	3	4	5	6	7	8	9	10	11	subs used
1	A	ROCHDALE			W	3-2	1-0	Hildersley 45, 55, Wilson 66p	Bracey	Megson	Wilson	Lucketti	**Thompst'ne**	Bradley	Matthews	**Case**	Thomas	Juryeff*	Hildersley	**Gayle**
	15/8		*2,497*		3			*Flounders 59, Milner 61*	*Rose*	*Thackeray*	*Graham*	*Reid*	*Brown*	*Bowden*	*Ryan*	*Payne*	*Flounders*	*Whitehall**	*Milner*	*Reeves*
								Ref: K Lupton	A season that will end in tears starts in such fine style. Hildersley scores two cracking volleys but the Shaymen then go to sleep and allow Dale back into the game. Shaun Reid spoils the home side's comeback by taking Thomas' legs and Wilson makes no mistake with the penalty.											
2	H	SCUNTHORPE		5	D	0-0	0-0		Bracey	Megson	Wilson	Lucketti	Thompstone	Bradley	Matthews	Case^	Thomas	Gayle*	Hildersley	Greenwood/German
	22/8		1,793	*14*	4				*Samways*	*Stevenson*	*Longden*	*Hill*	*Elliott*	*Humphries*	*Martin*	*Alexander*	*Daws*	*Buckley**	*Helliwell*	*White*
								Ref: T Lunt	The Iron missed out on promotion last season in the play-offs. They've had it easy at the Shay over recent seasons, but not this time. Halifax have the best of what few chances there were. Thomas lifts the ball over Mark Samways but sees it come back off the underside of the bar.											
3	A	CARDIFF		7	L	1-2	0-1	Thompstone 54	Bracey	Megson	Wilson	Lucketti	Thompstone	Bradley	Matthews	Case	Thomas	Gayle*	**Peake^**	Lewis/German
	29/8		*7,692*	*3*	4			*James 31, Dale 58*	*Grew*	*James*	*Searle*	*Millar*	*Perry*	*Brazil*	*Ramsey !*	*Richardson*	*Pike**	*Dale*	*Blake*	*Griffith*
								Ref: M James	Town create enough chances to win this but fail to cash in. Welsh international Robbie James scores a 25-yarder for Cardiff. Damon Searle opens up Town's defence for Carl Dale to score after Town had hauled themselves level. Paul Ramsey walks for a foul on debutant Peake.											
4	A	CREWE		18	L	1-2	0-2	Wilson 73 (og)	Bracey	Megson	Wilson	Lucketti	Lewis	Bradley	Matthews	Case	Thomas	Greenwood^	Peake*	**Hardy**/Gayle
	1/9		*3,228*	*3*	4			*Naylor 11, 25*	*Greygoose*	*McKearney*	*Annan^*	*Wilson*	*Hughes*	*Macauley*	*Hignett*	*Naylor*	*Clarkson**	*Harvey*	*Walters*	*Garvey/Smith*
								Ref: P Harrison	More chances are missed as Town slip to a second successive defeat. Tony Naylor curls the ball against the post in the fifth minute, then gets a double strike. Gus Wilson gives Town a chance, deflecting Thomas's header over the line. In injury-time Gayle has an effort scrambled clear.											
5	A	LINCOLN		22	L	1-2	0-1	Lucketti 56	Bracey	Megson	Wilson	Lucketti	Thompstone	Bradley	Matthews^	Case*	Thomas	Greenwood	Peake	Lewis/Gayle
	12/9		*2,689*	*7*	4			*Carmichael 45, Lee 54*	*Bowling*	*Smith*	*Clarke*	*Carmichael*	*Dunphy*	*Brown*	*Schofield*	*Bressington*	*Lee**	*Kabia*	*Puttnam^*	*Alexander/Barraclo'*
								Ref: A Flood	The fixtures have been cruel to Town. This is their third consecutive away game. Lincoln are 9-1 favourites to win the division but need a gift to win. Bracey spills the ball to Jason Lee and it goes in off his shin. Influential Case is injured on 43 minutes, then Matt Carmichael scores.											
6	H	DARLINGTON		17	W	1-0	1-0	Greenwood 34	Bracey	Megson	Wilson	Lucketti	Thompstone	Bradley	Matthews	Case	Thomas*	Greenwood	Peake	Hildersley
	15/9		1,287	*18*	7				*Prudhoe*	*Hinchley*	*Pickering*	*Gaughan*	*Parkin*	*O'Shaughn'*	*Mardenboro'*	*Toman*	*Juryeff*	*Dobson**	*Dowson*	*Shaw*
								Ref: J Worrall	The Shaymen become the last team in the League to register its first home win, but this is only their second at the Shay. A moment of magic from Greenwood settles it, volleying past Prudhoe from 18 yards. On 63 minutes Bracey claws Nick Pickering's vicious shot round the post.											
7	H	SCARBOROUGH		18	L	3-4	1-3	Greenwood 5, Wilson 60p, Hirst 65 (og)	Bracey	Megson	Wilson	Lucketti	Thompstone	Bradley	Matthews	Case^	Thomas*	Greenwood	Peake	Kamara/German
	19/9		1,230	*8*	7			*Lee 2, Jules 15, Foreman 29, 54*	*Evans !*	*Thompson*	*Mudd*	*Lee*	*Hirst*	*Curran*	*Ashdjian*	*Murphy^*	*Mooney*	*Foreman**	*Jules*	*Himsworth/Mockler*
								Ref: K Lynch	Ref Lynch is conspicuous, making a series of mystifying decisions. Town are 1-4 down when he sends off Boro keeper Mark Evans for fouling Thomas. The ball goes in the net but he awards the penalty. Tommy Mooney goes in goal. He is static when Lee Hirst heads into his own net.											
8	A	NORTHAMPTON		11	W	**5-2**	2-0	Thompstone 32, 43, 71, Lucketti 47,	Bracey	Megson	Wilson	Lucketti	Thompstone	Bradley	Matthews*	Case	Lewis	Greenwood^	Peake	Hildersley/German
	26/9		*2,021*	*20*	10			*Wilkin 50, Brown 62* [Greenwood 69]	*Richardson*	*Parsons*	*Chard^*	*Beavon*	*Angus*	*Terry*	*Burnham*	*Benton*	*Scott**	*Brown*	*Wilkin*	*Bell/Lanb*
								Ref: R Pawley	Sweeper Thompstone switches to the attack and pays instant dividends. He scores a terrific solo goal, a cracking 30-yarder and a simple tap-in for Town's first hat-trick away since Davison ten years ago. The last time Town scored five on their travels was at Accrington in April 1960.											
9	A	CARLISLE		13	D	1-1	0-1	Bradley 50	Bracey	Barr	Wilson	Lucketti	Thompst'ne^	Bradley	Matthews	Case*	Lewis	Greenwood	Peake	German/Hildersley
	3/10		*3,824*	*19*	11			*Watson 14*	*Craig*	*Williams**	*Thorpe*	*Holmes*	*Holliday*	*Edmondson*	*Gabbiadini^*	*Davey*	*Oghani*	*Watson*	*Potts*	*Walsh/Sendall*
								Ref: J Rushton	It should have been another goal feast for the Shaymen but for the heroics of Carlisle stand-in keeper, 18-year-old Anthony Caig. When former Shayman Andy Watson scores early on it looks like being enough for them. Fortunately for Town, Bradley's rocket drive finds a way through.											
10	H	COLCHESTER		17	L	2-4	0-2	Matthews 75, German 80 *[Bennett 77]*	Bracey	Barr	Wilson	Lucketti	Thompstone	Griffiths	Matthews	Case*	Lewis	Greenwood	Peake	German
	10/10		2,445	*15*	11			*Kinsella 13, Oxbrow 35, McDon'gh 47,*	*Newell*	*Grainger*	*Roberts*	*Kinsella*	*Cawley*	*Oxbrow*	*Ball**	*Bennett*	*McDon'gh^*	*McGavin*	*Smith*	*Donald/Devereux*
								Ref: A Wilkie	At times Town outplay Colchester, but they have a habit of gifting goals. The visitors are fortunate to have a two-goal half-time lead. They do, however, have the best player on view in Mark Kinsella. Sub David German gets his first ever senior goal following Thompstone's low cross.											

No	Venue	Opponent	Att	Pos	Pt	F-A	H-T	Scorers, Times, and Referees	1	2	3	4	5	6	7	8	9	10	11	subs used
11	A	WALSALL		13	W	2-1	1-0	Smith 18 (og), Peake 87	Bracey	Barr	Wilson	Lucketti	Thompstone	Bradley	Matthews	German^	Hildersley	Greenwood*	Peake	Lewis/Case
	17/10		*3,867*	*6*	14			*Clarke 48p*	*Gayle*	*Williams*	*Statham*	*O'Hara^*	*Cecere*	*Smith*	*West*	*Clarke*	*Marsh*	*Edwards*	*McDonald**	*Ntamark/Oller'nsh'w*
								Ref: K Burge	Injuries before and during the game handicap the Shaymen. Walsall keeper Mark Gayle smashes the ball against defender Dean Smith for an own-goal. Cecere then stumbles over Lucketti for Walsall's equaliser. Peake's late winner for Town is just reward for a battling performance.											
12	H	GILLINGHAM		10	W	2-0	1-0	Matthews 3, Thompstone 75	Bracey	Barr	Wilson	Lucketti	Thompstone	Bradley	Matthews	German*	Lewis	**Wright**	Peake	Case
	24/10		**1,216**	*22*	17				*Lim*	*Green*	*Henry*	*Butler*	*Breen*	*Smith*	*Clark*	*Eeles**	*Crown*	*Lovell*	*O'Connor*	*Forster*
								Ref: K Leach	Town's league position looks quite healthy after this. Not so Gillingham's. They now lie three points adrift of Northampton. Harvey Lim is a victim of the new backpass rule when he clears the ball straight to Matthews. He then plays a blinder but can't prevent Thompstone's header.											
13	A	HEREFORD		13	L	0-3	0-3		Bracey	Barr	Wilson	Lucketti	Thompstone	Bradley	Matthews	German*	Hildersley^	Lewis	Peake	Case/Paterson
	31/10		*1,936*	*17*	17			*Browning 4, 42, Davies 34*	*Judge*	*Fry*	*Downs*	*Davies**	*Smith*	*Devine*	*Hall*	*Jones*	*Browning*	*Pickard*	*Rowbotham*	*Theodosiou*
								Ref: S Dunn	Struggling Hereford make this win look easy. Subdued Town don't trouble Alan Judge in the first half. Former Shayman Derek Hall has a hand in all three goals and admits afterwards, 'It was nice to beat them.' On-loan Marcus Browning gives Bradley a real chasing and gets two.											
14	A	SHREWSBURY		15	L	0-1	0-1		Bracey	Lewis	Wilson	Lucketti	Thompstone	Bradley	Matthews	Case	Greenwood	Thomas*	Peake	Paterson
	3/11		*2,704*	*3*	17			*O'Toole 11*	*Edwards*	*Haylock*	*Lynch*	*Taylor*	*Spink*	*Blake*	*Brough**	*Clark*	*Lyne*	*Griffiths*	*O'Toole*	*Williams M*
								Ref: D Allison	The Shrews, under former Norwich and Man City boss John Bond, are attempting to get out of Division 3 at the first attempt. Carl Griffiths spins off his marker to set up Pat O'Toole's winner. Town shade the second half but only Bradley's last-minute header troubles Paul Edwards.											
15	H	TORQUAY		15	L	0-2	0-2		Bracey	Lewis	Wilson	Lucketti	Thompstone	Bradley	Matthews	Case	Thomas	Greenwood*	Peake	Hildersley
	7/11		1,651	*19*	17			*Foster 29, Fashanu 37*	*Sommer*	*Gardiner*	*Herrera**	*Salman*	*Curran*	*Johnson*	*Hall*	*Trollope*	*Fashanu*	*Myers^*	*Foster*	*Colcombe/Joyce*
								Ref: I Cruikshanks	The tragic Justin Fashanu, who once cost Forest £1m, has an eventful afternoon. He takes stick off the Shay crowd because of his off-the-field lifestyle, sets up Adrian Foster for his goal, then scores one himself. Later, he appears to stamp on Lewis, and is the centre of ensuing scuffles.											
16	A	WREXHAM		16	D	1-1	0-1	Hardy 87	Bracey	Megson	Wilson	Lucketti	Lewis	Barr	German^	Case	Paterson	**Lancashire**	Hildersley*	**Edmonds**/Hardy
	21/11		*1,873*	*13*	18			*Connolly 31*	*Morris*	*Jones*	*Hardy*	*Phillips*	*Humes*	*Pejic*	*Bennett*	*Owen*	*Connolly*	*Watkin*	*Cross*	
								Ref: T Fitzharris	After the humiliating FA Cup defeat at Marine, injury-ravaged Town need to restore some much-needed confidence. They do so courtesy of Jason Hardy, who curls in a late free-kick. This cancels out Karl Connolly's goal, scored when he stole in to meet Jonathan Cross's free-kick.											
17	H	CHESTERFIELD		17	D	1-1	0-0	Hardy 59	Bracey	Thompstone	Wilson	Lucketti	Lewis	Bradley	Matthews	Case*	Paterson	Lancashire	Hardy	Megson
	28/11		1,432	*9*	19			*Lancaster 61*	*Leonard*	*Lemon*	*Carr*	*Fee*	*Brien*	*Rogers*	*Hebberd*	*Williams*	*Lancaster*	*Turnbull**	*Kennedy*	*Morris*
								Ref: A Dawson	The Shaymen should be winning games like these. It's a poor one, but Hardy does manage to score his second goal in consecutive matches, crashing home the loose ball. However, Dave Lancaster powers in the equaliser after former Southampton star Steve Williams makes inroads.											
18	H	BARNET		18	L	1-2	1-1	Greenwood 32	Bracey	Megson	Wilson	Lucketti	Thompstone	Bradley	Matthews^	Barr	Hildersley	Greenwood	Peake*	German/Edmonds
	5/12		1,253	*2*	19			*Stein 38, 51*	*Phillips*	*Huxford*	*Cooper*	*Bodley*	*Howell*	*Horton*	*Payne*	*Stein^*	*Bull*	*Lowe**	*Hunt*	*Showler/Carter*
								Ref: G Singh	Stan Flashman sacked Barnet boss Barry Fry during the week. Fry, however, travels to the game and stands with the Bees supporters on the terracing. His 'old' side takes control to win after going behind. Town manager McGrath has had enough and tenures his notice two days later.											
19	H	BURY		19	L	0-1	0-0		Bracey	Megson	Wilson	German	Lucketti	Barr	**Williams***	Peake	Thompstone	**Brown**	Hildersley	Paterson
	19/12		1,760	*16*	19			*Hulme 55*	*Kelly*	*Hughes*	*Kearney*	*Daws*	*Valentine*	*Knill*	*Lyons*	*Sonner**	*Hulme*	*Reid*	*Ward*	*Branch*
								Ref: A Smith	Kevin Hulme will become a folk hero at the Shay in a few years time. Right now, though, he is not so popular. In a drab contest, he wins Bury the throw-in, when the ball clearly came off him, which leads to his goal. It's a disappointing start for Mick Rathbone, the new Town boss.											
20	H	DONCASTER		18	D	2-2	1-0	Megson 10, Thompstone 72	Bracey	Megson	Wilson	German	Lucketti	Barr	Williams	Peake	Thompstone	Brown	Hardy	
	26/12		1,854	*15*	20			*Richards 89, 90*	*Crichton*	*Rowe*	*Prindiville*	*Reddish^*	*Richards*	*Crosby**	*Hewitt*	*Hodson*	*Heritage*	*Morrow*	*Gormley*	*Felena/Reddish*
								Ref: J Key	The icy pitch does no one any real favours. Still, the Shaymen aren't complaining when they are sitting on a two-goal lead with only three minutes to play. But it is former Town defender Steve Richards who has the last laugh, popping up with two headers, the second in injury-time.											
21	A	YORK		18	D	1-1	0-1	Williams 58	Bracey	Megson	Wilson	German	Lucketti	Barr	Williams	Peake	Thompstone	Brown	Hardy	
	29/12		*4,068*	*2*	21			*Barnes 2*	*Kiely*	*McMillan*	*Hall*	*Pepper*	*Stancliffe*	*Atkin*	*McCarthy*	*Borthwick**	*Barnes*	*Swann*	*Blackstone*	*Tilley*
								Ref: W Burns	The Minstermen blow the chance to go top as a gritty display from Town belies their lowly position. On-loan Williams is caught napping and this leads to Paul Barnes' goal, but he makes amends with the deserved equaliser. He skips into the box and beats Dean Kiely with a low shot.											

No	Date		Att	Pos	Pt	F-A	H-T	Scorers, Times, and Referees	1	2	3	4	5	6	7	8	9	10	11	subs used
22	A	DARLINGTON		17	W	3-0	1-0	Ridings 4, 61, Thompstone 81	Bracey	Megson	Wilson	German	Lucketti	Barr	Williams	**Ridings**	Thompstone	Paterson	**Christie**	
	9/1		*1,984*	*15*	24				*Prudhoe*	*Fickling*	*Pickering**	*Gregan*	*Parkin*	*O'Shaughn'*	*Mardenboro'*	*Toman*	*Juryeff^*	*Dobie*	*Dowson*	*Gaughan/Dobson*
								Ref: K Breen	Mick Rathbone includes trialists Ridings and Christie in the side. The former makes a dream start by scoring twice, the first a header off Megson's cross when he is practically on his knees. Barr sets up Thompstone for his goal as Town complete their first double of the season.											
23	H	NORTHAMPTON		17	D	2-2	0-0	Ridings 67, 68	Bracey	Megson	Hardy	German	Lucketti	Barr	Williams	Ridings	Thompst'ne*	Paterson	Christie	Hildersley !
	16/1		1,323	*21*	25			*Harmon 50, McParland 59*	*Richardson*	*Parsons*	*Curtis*	*Harmon*	*Angus*	*Terry*	*Burnham*	*Wilkin**	*Bell*	*Brown*	*McParland !*	*Scott*
								Ref: D Shadwell	Dave Ridings is again the toast of the Town. In only his second game he gets another brace. This time he smashes home two in a minute to rescue a point. Over-zealous ref Dave Shadwell sends off sub Hildersley and Cobblers' Ian McParland for handbags stuff in the last minute.											
24	A	SCARBOROUGH		18	L	0-2	0-1		Bracey	Megson*	Hardy	German	Lucketti	Barr	Williams	Ridings	Thompst'ne^	Paterson	Christie	Peake/Hildersley
	23/1		***1,552***	*8*	25			*Mooney 34, 71*	*Ford*	*Barrow*	*Mudd*	*Lee*	*Ormsby*	*Hirst*	*Jules**	*Mockler*	*Mooney*	*Foreman*	*Lightbourne*	*Ashdjian*
								Ref: I Hemley	At times the Shaymen look the better side, but it is Boro's Tom Mooney who scores twice this time. His first is a rising shot that gives Bracey no chance. Town throw caution to the wind in the second half. Mooney's second comes after the Shaymen have won a corner at the other end!											
25	H	CARDIFF		18	L	0-1	0-0		Bracey	German	Hardy	Peake	Lucketti	Barr	Williams	Ridings	Thompstone	Paterson	Christie	
	26/1		1,339	*4*	25			*Stant 88*	*Ward*	*James*	*Searle*	*Matthews*	*Perry*	*Ratcliffe*	*Millar*	*Richardson*	*Stant*	*Blake*	*Griffith*	
								Ref: R Hart	Town can't be faulted for effort but Eddie May's promotion-seeking side are clearly a class above. Their late winner is highly controversial, though. Scorer Phil Stant looks clearly offside and Bracey claims that he stopped the ball before it crossed the line after it came back off a post.											
26	A	SCUNTHORPE		18	L	1-4	0-3	Paterson 90 [Buckley 73]	Bracey	German	Hardy	Peake	Lucketti	Barr !	Williams	Ridings	Thompstone	Paterson	Christie*	Case
	30/1		*2,460*	*7*	25			*Helliwell 3, 30, Martin 20,*	*Samways*	*Joyce*	*Stevenson*	*Martin*	*Elliott*	*Humphries*	*Buckley*	*Daws*	*Helliwell*	*Alexander**	*Farrell^*	*Greaves/White*
								Ref: P Danson	On this display Town are heading in only one direction – downwards. Scunthorpe canter to victory and there's a goal for former Town player Dean Martin. Out of frustration Barr stamps on Tony Daws and is sent off. Paterson's consolation comes when he charges Samways' kick out.											
27	H	ROCHDALE		18	L	2-3	2-2	Jones 13 (og), Barr 42p	Bracey	German	Hardy	Case*	Lucketti	Barr	Williams	Ridings	Thompstone	Greenwood	**Peel**	Bradley
	6/2		1,906	*9*	25			*Butler 1, Reid 38p, Mulrain 47*	*Rose*	*Butler*	*Graham*	*Reid*	*Reeves*	*Jones*	*Ryan*	*Doyle*	*Bowden*	*Whitehall*	*Mulrain*	
								Ref: P Vanes	Town are twice behind but have no answer a third time once Steve Mulrain's early second-half header goes in. Alex Jones clumsily knocks in Thompstone's cross for the first equaliser. Hardy up-ends Alan Reeves for Shaun Reid's penalty, then Reeves pushes Thompstone for Barr's.											
28	H	LINCOLN		17	W	2-1	2-1	Case 2, Greenwood 29	Bracey	German	Hardy	Case	Lucketti	Bradley	Peake	Ridings	Thompstone	Greenwood	Peel	
	16/2		1,260	*8*	28			*West 21*	*Pollitt*	*Smith*	*Barraclough*	*Finney*	*Carmichael*	*Brown*	*Schofield*	*West*	*Lee*	*Costello**	*Matthews*	*Parkinson*
								Ref: C Trussell	The performance isn't pretty but Rathbone isn't complaining. It's Town's first win at home since October. Case scores his first for the club from 40 yards. Lincoln dispute it but the linesman reckons keeper Mike Pollitt carried the ball over the line. Greenwood drives in the winner.											
29	H	CREWE		17	L	1-2	1-1	Case 42	Bracey	German	Hardy	Case	Lucketti	Bradley	Peake^	Ridings	Thompstone	Greenwood*	Peel	Paterson/Christie
	20/2		1,604	*11*	28			*Edwards 40, Carr 68*	*Greygoose*	*Lennon*	*Smith*	*Evans*	*Carr*	*Macauley*	*Ward*	*Naylor*	*Clarkson*	*Walters*	*Edwards*	
								Ref: T Lunt	The trumpeter among the Crewe supporters gets round to playing 'The Last Post'. It may be apt. The Shaymen lack any sort of inventiveness. Ashley Ward centres for both Crewe goals. Case's equaliser is a deflected free-kick. The ref prolongs the agony with ten minutes injury time.											
30	A	COLCHESTER		18	L	1-2	1-1	Thompstone 8	Bracey !	German	Hardy	Matthews	Lucketti	Bradley	Megson	Ridings	Thompstone	Greenwood	**Everingh'm**	
	26/2		*3,007*	*12*	28			*McGavin 30, Grainger 56*	*Emberson*	*Grainger*	*Roberts*	*Kinsella*	*Cawley*	*English*	*Betts*	*Hopkins*	*McDon'gh**	*McGavin*	*Smith*	*Abrahams*
								Ref: P Alcock	The Shaymen take the lead then nothing goes right. Steve McGavin equalises when Bradley fails to control Matthews' backpass. Bracey is sent off for pulling down McGavin when put clear. Greenwood goes in goal but is beaten only three minutes later by Martin Grainger's 35-yarder.											
31	H	CARLISLE		18	L	0-2	0-1		Bracey	German	Everingham	Matthews	Lucketti	Bradley	Barr	Ridings	Thompstone	Greenwood*	Hardy^	Paterson/Christie
	6/3		1,309	*15*	28			*Oghani 6, Arnold 60p*	*O'Hanlon*	*Burgess*	*Thorpe*	*Walling*	*McCreery**	*Holden*	*Oghani*	*Dawes*	*Arnold*	*Proudlock*	*White*	*Gabbiadini*
								Ref: T Fitzharris	Carlisle is striker George Oghani's sixth club. How Town must wish they had him in their team. He causes problems all afternoon, scoring the first then being upended by Bradley for Ian Arnold's penalty. Bracey keeps the score down. Paterson blazes over from six yards on 85 minutes.											

No	Date	H/A	Opponent	Att	Pos	Pts	Res	F-A	H-T	Scorers, Times, and Referees	1	2	3	4	5	6	7	8	9	10	11	subs used
32		A	TORQUAY		20		L	0-2	0-0		Brown	German	Hardy^	Matthews	Lucketti	Bradley	Barr	Ridings	Thompst'ne*	Paterson	Peake	Greenwood/Megson
	13/3			*3,345*	*18*	28				*Kelly 51p, Trollope 77*	*Blackwell*	*Barrow*	*Colcombe*	*O'Riordan*	*Moore*	*Kelly*	*Trollope*	*Curran*	*Sale*	*Muir**	*Foster*	*Chapman*
										Ref: M Pierce	The 'Evening Courier' has launched the 'Staying Alive' Town lifeline. The Shaymen need all the help they can get, but get none from referee Michael Pierce. He turns down their appeals for a clear penalty, then gives one at the other end when Lucketti halts Gulls sub Gary Chapman.											
33		H	SHREWSBURY		20		D	1-1	1-0	Barr 20	Bracey	German	Barr	Matthews	Lucketti	Bradley	Peake	Ridings	Greenwood	Paterson	Christie	
	20/3			3,872	*6*	29				*Blake 65*	*Edwards*	*Clark*	*Lynch*	*Taylor*	*Williams*	*Blake*	*Brown*	*Summerf'ld^*	*Piggott**	*Griffiths*	*Smith*	*Mackenzie/O'Toole*
										Ref: J Rushton	Town put on a carnival for the fans. There's a brass band, balloons, and a pre-match firework display. Barr dispatches a rocket of his own from 40 yards to score Town's Goal of the Season. Mark Blake spoils the party, reacting first to the loose ball when his header rebounds off the bar.											
34		A	CHESTERFIELD		22		L	1-2	1-1	Thompstone 3	Bracey	German	Barr	Matthews	Lucketti	Bradley	Peake	Ridings	Greenwood	Paterson	Thompstone	
	23/3			*2,382*	*11*	29				*Morris 34, Turnbull 77*	*Marples*	*Rogers*	*Carr*	*Clarke*	*Brien*	*Williams*	*Morris*	*Dyche*	*Lancaster*	*Turnbull*	*Hebberd*	
										Ref: A Smith	Mick Rathbone's men create a hatful of early chances but fail to build on Thompstone's solo goal. John Duncan's Chesterfield take control and there is only going to be one winner once Andy Morris heads in the equaliser. Lee Turnbull scores the inevitable winner and Town go bottom.											
35		H	WREXHAM		22		L	0-1	0-0		Bracey	German	Barr	Matthews^	Lucketti	Bradley	Peake	Ridings	Greenwood*	Paterson	**Craven**	Thomas/**Circuit**
	26/3			3,970	*2*	29				*Watkin 55*	*Morris*	*Jones B*	*Hardy*	*Owen*	*Humes*	*Pejic*	*Bennett*	*Lake*	*Connolly*	*Watkin*	*Cross*	
										Ref: E Wolstenholme	The gulf between the sides is obvious as Brian Flynn's promotion seekers dominate. There's no denying Wrexham victory but their winner is controversial. They sweep upfield for Steve Watkin to score easily while Town appeal for a penalty for a push on Paterson at the other end.											
36		A	BARNET		22		D	0-0	0-0		Bracey	German	Barr	Hardy	Lucketti	Megson	Peake	Ridings	Greenwood*	Paterson	Craven	Thomas
	3/4			*3,042*	*2*	30					*Phillips*	*Huxford*	*Naylor*	*Bodley*	*Howell*	*Sorrell*	*Payne*	*Stein*	*Bull*	*Evans**	*Hunt^*	*Lowe/Carter*
										Ref: M Bailey	Two days earlier Barry Fry left Barnet for the last time to take up at Southend. Mark Stein has taken over but his team are lucky not to lose. Normally a draw here would be a great result, but Town need victories now. They nearly get one when Hardy's lob over Phillips hits the bar.											
37		A	DONCASTER		21		W	1-0	1-0	Barr 3	Bracey	German	Barr	Hardy	Lucketti	Megson	Peake	Ridings	Thomas*	Paterson	Craven	**Obebo**
	10/4			*2,160*	*18*	33					*Crichton*	*Masefield*	*Prindiville*	*Reddish**	*Crosby*	*Hicks*	*Hine*	*Moss*	*Heritage*	*Jeffrey*	*Gormley*	*Douglas*
										Ref: J Kirby	Billy Barr pops up in the box to score an early goal which, for the time being, has the Shaymen moving in the right direction. They dig deep to protect their goal and leap over Torquay. Sub Godfrey Obebo, a Nigerian international, comes up with a few tricks, but misses a simple header.											
38		H	YORK		21		L	0-1	0-0		Bracey	Megson	Hardy	Barr	Lucketti	Bradley	Peake	Ridings	Greenwood*	Paterson	German	Obebo
	12/4			3,983	*2*	33				*Barnes 87*	*Kiely*	*McMillan*	*Hall*	*Pepper*	*Stancliffe*	*Atkin*	*McCarthy*	*Canham*	*Barnes*	*Swann*	*Blackstone*	
										Ref: J Brandwood	York's Paul Barnes scores his 20th goal of the season, when Jon McCarthy's shot hits his torso and deflects in. It follows a corner that Town feel should not have been given. It's cruel luck and there's little time to respond. But Town hardly look like winning. Only Paterson goes close.											
39		A	BURY		21		W	2-1	1-0	Paterson 42, German 86	Bracey	German	Barr	Hardy	Lucketti	Bradley	Peake	Ridings	Megson	Paterson	Craven	
	17/4			*3,069*	*6*	36				*Adekola 54*	*Kelly*	*Ward*	*Stanislaus*	*Daws^*	*Reid*	*Knill*	*Adekola**	*Rigby*	*Kearney*	*Stevens*	*Fitzpatrick*	*Mike/Hughes*
										Ref: G Singh	The Shaymen are still alive, thanks to David German's cool piece of finishing. This time Bury have little time to reply. Megson intercepts the ball to set up Paterson. Bury come storming back and David Adekola barges in the equaliser. Bad news, though, is that Torquay have also won.											
40		H	WALSALL		22		L	**0-4**	0-1		Bracey	German*	Barr	Hardy^	Lucketti	Bradley	Peake	Ridings	Megson	Paterson	Craven	Obebo/Christie
	24/4			2,929	*6*	36				*Cecere 11, 85, 88, McDonald 78*	*Gayle*	*Knight*	*Methven*	*Smith*	*Ntamark*	*Ryder*	*MacDonald**	*Clarke*	*Cecere*	*O'Connor*	*McDonald^*	*Kelly/Marsh*
										Ref: B Hill	The Saddlers expose everything that's bad about the Shaymen. In the second half, with Town already behind because of Mike Cecere's early strike, Rathbone takes off both full-backs. The result – Walsall score three in the last twelve minutes and Cecere completes an easy hat-trick.											
41		A	GILLINGHAM		22		L	0-2	0-0		Bracey	German*	Barr	Hardy	Lucketti	Bradley	Peake	Ridings	Megson	Paterson	Craven	Greenwood
	1/5			***7,151***	*19*	36				*Eeles 49, Baker 52*	*Barrett*	*Dunne*	*Martin*	*Green*	*Carpenter*	*Smith*	*Clark*	*Crown**	*Baker*	*Eeles*	*Forster*	*Crane*
										Ref: P Jones	The Gills ensure their own safety at the same time as breaking Town's hearts. The Shaymen actually look the better side but Gillingham score with two spectacular efforts by Tony Eeles and Paul Barker. Town are denied a certain penalty, and Lucketti deflects the ball onto the post.											
42		H	HEREFORD		22		L	0-1	0-0		Bracey	German*	Barr	Hardy	Lucketti	Bradley	Peake	Ridings	Megson	Paterson	Craven	Greenwood
	8/5			**7,451**	*17*	36				*Hall 61*	*Judge*	*Downs*	*Anderson*	*Davies*	*Abrahams*	*Morris*	*Hall*	*Pickard*	*Rowbotham*	*Jones*	*Nicholson*	
			Home	Away						Ref: J Winter	All roads lead to the Shay as the biggest crowd in years witness Town's last stand. Ridings goes desperately close early on and Town create a number of other chances. Craven's cross even hits the bar. But when former Shayman Derek Hall sidefoots home, the writing's on the wall.											
Average			2,232	3,169																		

Coca-Cola Cup			F-A	H-T	Scorers, Times, and Referees	1	2	3	4	5	6	7	8	9	10	11	subs used
1:1 H HARTLEPOOL		L	1-2	0-1	Megson 71	Bracey	Megson	Wilson	Lucketti	Thompstone	Bradley	Matthews	Case	Thomas	Juryeff*	Hildersley	**Greenwood**
18/8	1,370 *2:*				*MacPhail 23, Johnrose 80*	*Hodge*	*Cross R*	*Cross P*	*Tait*	*MacPhail*	*Emmerson*	*Johnrose*	*Olsson*	*Saville*	*Honour !*	*Gallagher**	*Southall*
					Ref: I Hendrick	Hartlepool are deserving winners. They must be clear favourites to go through. Bracey lets a cross from Paul Cross slip from his grasp to allow John MacPhail to score. Len Johnrose scores off Brian Honour's corner, but in the next minute Honour is sent off for chopping down Bradley.											
1:2 A HARTLEPOOL	5	L	2-3	2-2	Thomas 7, Lucketti 9	Bracey	Megson	Wilson	Lucketti	Lewis	Bradley	Matthews	German	Thomas	Greenwood	Hildersley*	Thompstone
25/8	*2,191 2:17*				*Johnrose 30, 85, Southall 45*	*Hodge*	*Cross R*	*Cross P*	*Tait*	*MacPhail*	*Olsson*	*Johnrose*	*Emmerson*	*Saville*	*Honour*	*Southall*	
					Ref: K Redfern (Halifax lost 3-5 on aggregate)	Town almost pull this one out of the fire. Lucketti launces a clearance that Thomas instantly loops over Martin Hodge, then he himself gets on to the end of Wilson's cross. Nicky Southall crucially races through to wipe out Town's advantage. Johnrose scores off Honour's quality cross.											

FA Cup																	
1 A MARINE	15	L	1-4	0-3	German 88 *[Camden 54]*	Bracey	Lewis	Wilson	Lucketti	Thompstone	Bradley*	Matthews	Case	Thomas	Paterson	Peake^	Megson/German
14/11	1,892 *HFS:6*				*Ward 31, Gautrey 37, Rowlands 42,*	*O'Brien*	*Ward*	*Johnson*	*Roche*	*Draper*	*Gautrey**	*Murray*	*Rowlands*	*Ross*	*Camden^*	*Dawson*	*McDonough/Grant*
					Ref: J Rushton	The Shaymen are in deep financial trouble and desparately need a good money-spinning cup-run. Unfortunately they plumb new depths with this gutless display. Marine are managed by window-cleaner Roly Howard, and his team harry and hastle Town into complete humiliation.											

		Home					Away					
	P	W	D	L	F	A	W	D	L	F	A	Pts
1 Cardiff	42	13	7	1	42	20	12	1	8	35	27	83
2 Wrexham	42	14	3	4	48	26	9	8	4	27	26	80
3 Barnet	42	16	4	1	45	19	7	6	8	21	29	79
4 York*	42	13	6	2	41	15	8	6	7	31	30	75
5 Walsall	42	11	6	4	42	31	11	1	9	34	30	73
6 Crewe	42	13	3	5	47	23	8	4	9	28	33	70
7 Bury	42	10	7	4	36	19	8	2	11	27	36	63
8 Lincoln	42	10	6	5	31	20	8	3	10	26	33	63
9 Shrewsbury	42	11	3	7	36	30	6	8	7	21	22	62
10 Colchester	42	13	3	5	38	26	5	2	14	29	50	59
11 Rochdale	42	10	3	8	38	29	6	7	8	32	41	58
12 Chesterfield	42	11	3	7	32	28	4	8	9	27	35	56
13 Scarborough	42	7	7	7	32	30	8	2	11	34	41	54
14 Scunthorpe	42	8	7	6	38	25	6	5	10	19	29	54
15 Darlington	42	5	6	10	23	31	7	8	6	25	22	50
16 Doncaster	42	6	5	10	22	28	5	9	7	20	29	47
17 Hereford	42	7	9	5	31	27	3	6	12	16	33	45
18 Carlisle	42	7	5	9	29	27	4	6	11	22	38	44
19 Torquay	42	6	4	11	18	26	6	3	12	27	41	43
20 Northampton	42	6	5	10	19	28	5	3	13	29	46	41
21 Gillingham	42	9	4	8	32	28	0	9	12	16	36	40
22 HALIFAX	42	3	5	13	20	35	6	4	11	25	33	36
	924	209	111	142	740	571	142	111	209	571	740	1275

* promoted after play-offs

Odds & ends

Double wins: (1) Northampton.
Double losses: (5) Cardiff, Crewe, Hereford, Scarborough, Torquay.

Won from behind: (0) .
Lost from in front: (3) Barnet (h), Chesterfield (a), Colchester (a), Hartlepool (CCC) (a).

High spots: Winning two consecutive matches during October.
Scoring five goals away from home, at Northampton, for the first time since April 1960.

Low spots: Two runs of four consecutive defeats.
Losing 13 league games at home.
Losing at non-league Marine in the FA Cup.

Halifax finished bottom of the league for the first time since 1947 and were demoted.
Town only managed three home wins – the fewest in the club's history.
The attendance of 7,451 for the visit of Hereford on the last day was the highest in the League at the Shay since 8,077 watched the game against Sheffield United in April 1982.

Player of the Year: Billy Barr.
Ever-presents: (1) Chris Lucketti.
Hat-tricks: (1) Ian Thompstone.
Leading scorer: Ian Thompstone (9).

	Appearances						Goals			
	Lge	*Sub*	LC	*Sub*	FAC	*Sub*	Lge	LC	FAC	Tot
Barr, Billy	28						3			3
Bracey, Lee	41		2		1					
Bradley, Russell	29	*1*	2		1		1			1
Brown, Linton	3									
Brown, Nick	1									
Case, Jimmy	17	*4*	1		1		2			2
Christie, David	6	*3*								
Circuit, Steve		*1*								
Craven, Peter	7									
Edmonds, Darren		*2*								
Everingham, Nick	2									
Gayle, Howard	2	*3*								
German, David	28	*7*	1			*1*	2		1	3
Greenwood, Nigel	21	*4*	1	*1*			5			5
Griffiths, Neil	1									
Hardy, Jason	20	*2*					2			2
Hildersley, Ronnie	7	*6*	2				2			2
Juryeff, Ian	1		1							
Kamara, Alan		*1*								
Lancashire, Graham	2									
Lewis, Dudley	10	*3*	1		1					
Lucketti, Chris	42		2		1		2	1		3
Matthews, Mick	23		2		1		2			2
Megson, Kevin	24	*2*	2			*1*	1	1		2
Obebo, Godfrey		*3*								
Paterson, Jamie	18	*5*			1		2			2
Peake, Jason	32	*1*			1		1			1
Peel, Nathan	3									
Ridings, Dave	21						4			4
Thomas, John	10	*2*	2		1			1		1
Thompstone, Ian	31		1	*1*	1		9			9
Williams, Michael	9						1			1
Wilson, Paul	22		2		1		2			2
Wright, Paul	1									
(own-goals)							4			4
34 players used	**462**	***50***	**22**	***2***	**11**	***2***	**45**	**3**	**1**	**49**

No	Date		Att	Pos	Pt	F-A	H-T	Scorers, Times, and Referees	1	2	3	4	5	6	7	8	9	10	11	subs used
1	H	KETTERING			D	0-0	0-0		Bracey	Barr	Craven	**Edwards**	**Filson**	Lucketti	Peake	Ridings	**Cameron**	Paterson	Gregory	
	21/8		**1,810**		1				*Hoult*	*Reed*	*Ashby*	*Price*	*Oxbrow*	*Taylor*	*Wright*	*Brown*	*Loughlan**	*Donald*	*Roderick*	*Clarke*
								Ref: C Gordon	The curious are out in force for Town's first Conference game. Many won't return for a while. Graham Carr is now manager of Kettering, and are well drilled in non-league football. Their keeper, however, is slightly the busier of the two. Halifax get familiar with time-wasting tactics.											
2	A	SOUTHPORT		12	D	2-2	0-1	Lucketti 60, Harvey 73 (og)	Brown	Barr	Craven	Edwards	Filson	Lucketti	Peake	Ridings*	Cameron^	Paterson	Gregory	**Constable**/German
	24/8		***2,423***		2			*Comstive 21, Haw 52*	*Moore*	*Dove*	*Fuller*	*Mooney*	*Goulding*	*Harvey*	*Lyons*	*Walmsley*	*Haw^*	*Comstive**	*Withers*	*McDonald/Mullen*
								Ref: M Pike	Bracey has got his wish and moved back into league football. Nick Brown takes his place, and is at fault for Southport's second goal, when he lets Haw's header slip through his hands. Town fight back, but it's home defender Jim Harvey, ex-Hereford, who deflects in their equaliser.											
3	A	SLOUGH		17	L	0-2	0-1		**Heyes**	Barr !	Craven	Edwards	Filson !	Lucketti	Peake	Greenwood	Ridings*	Paterson	Gregory	Constable
	28/8		*1,170*	*1*	2			*Hazel 21p, Scott S 82*	*Bunting*	*Quamina*	*Dowson*	*Hazel*	*Briley*	*Lee*	*Scott S*	*Stanley*	*Sayer**	*Scott M*	*Fiore*	*MacPherson*
								Ref: G Monks	John Docherty's side make it three wins out of three, but not without a little help from the referee. He rules that Filson has handled for Hazel's penalty, then sends off Filson and Barr in the 54th and 62nd minute respectively. Town then push forward, but leave Scott free to make it 0-2.											
4	H	STAFFORD		17	D	1-1	1-1	Paterson 20	Brown	German	Hardy	Barr	Lucketti	Gregory	Peake	Greenwood	Constable	Paterson	Craven*	Cameron
	30/8		1,228		3			*Burr 45*	*Price*	*Wood*	*Bradshaw*	*Simpson*	*Hope*	*Hemming*	*Williams*	*Hanlon*	*Burr*	*Massey^*	*Mettioui**	*Clayton/Boughey*
								Ref: G Grandidge	Wragg calls for his players to end the frustration. Paterson does his best with a perfect lob over Price to score Town's first goal home goal in 540 minutes. Burr gets above Lucketti to head the equaliser just before the break. Stafford look a dangerous outfit and could easily have won.											
5	H	YEOVIL		16	D	1-1	0-1	Filson 87	Heyes	German	Hardy	Barr	Lucketti	Constable	Peake	Greenwood^	Gregory*	Paterson	Craven	Filson/Megson
	4/9		1,152	*7*	4			*Sanderson 42*	*Coles*	*Dobbins**	*Ferns*	*Sherwood*	*Bye*	*Leonard*	*Sanderson*	*Wallace*	*Connor*	*Spencer*	*Harrower*	*Coates*
								Ref: P Elwick	Former Shayman Paul Sanderson returns to put Yeovil ahead following Heyes' weak punch. But although Steve Rutter's side remain unbeaten, for the most part they are under the cosh. Town batter away without success until Filson forces the ball over. The fans then dance on the pitch.											
6	A	RUNCORN		20	L	**0-5**	0-2	*[Connor 87, Parker 89]*	Heyes	Craven	Hardy^	Edwards	Lucketti	Ridings*	Peake	**Saunders**	**Hanson**	Paterson	Constable	Gregory/German
	11/9		*732*	*6*	4			*Hardy 15 (og), Brady 44, McInerney 73,*	*Williams*	*Bates*	*Robertson*	*Brady*	*Hill*	*Brown*	*Thomas*	*Connor*	*McInerney*	*McKenna**	*Brabin*	*Parker*
								Ref: F Taylor	Having beaten Bradford City in a memorable final of the Yorkshire Cup in midweek, Town get the shock of their lives at Canal Street. Hardy has a nightmare. As well as being overrun by Connor, he lobs the ball over Heyes for Runcorn's opener. There is no respite for hapless Town.											
7	H	WITTON		21	D	0-0	0-0		Heyes	German*	Barr	Lucketti	Edwards	Megson	Peake	Saunders	Constable	Paterson	Craven	Filson
	17/9		1,099	*8*	5				*Mason*	*Senior*	*Timmons*	*Edey*	*Thorpe*	*Hall*	*Rose*	*Cunningham*	*Maynard*	*Burke**	*Toal*	*Blackwood*
								Ref: M Douglas	Town at least restore some pride, but they are still looking for their first win in the Conference. Former Town assistant Oshor Williams is now second in charge to Witton boss Mike McKenzie. Honours are pretty even, but Megson goes closest in injury-time with a shot against the bar.											
8	A	WOKING		14	W	6-2	2-0	P'son 3, 50, Saund'rs 26, 60, H'son 74,	Heyes	Filson^	Barr	Lucketti	Edwards	Megson	Peake	Saunders	Constable	Paterson*	Craven	Hanson/German
	25/9		*1,848*	*19*	8			*Puckett 56, Walker 81* [Peake 80]	*Batty*	*Clement*	*Brown K*	*Berry*	*Fielder*	*Steele**	*Brown D*	*Biggins*	*Walker*	*Swift^*	*Heritage*	*Rattray/Puckett*
								Ref: P March	The Shaymen do it in style! This is their first six-goal haul away from home since December 1911. Without getting on the scoresheet, Shaun Constable is outstanding. Paterson rifles home to start the ball rolling. Saunders walks in his second goal with Woking's defence at a standstill.											
9	H	TELFORD		13	W	**6-0**	4-0	Peake 13, Paterson 21, 25, 80p,	Heyes	Filson	Barr	Edwards	**Lambert***	Megson	Peake	Saunders	Constable	Paterson	Craven^	Hardy/German
	2/10		1,118		11			[Saunders 30, 88]	*Acton*	*Pritchard*	*Statham**	*Ferguson*	*Gaunt*	*Parrish*	*Bignot*	*Mitchell^*	*Whitehouse*	*Myers*	*Muir*	*Gernon/Taylor*
								Ref: T Helbron	This time it's crisis-torn Telford, who sacked manager Gerry Daly yesterday, who are hit for six. The home supporters get well-accustomed to the sight of Paterson's celebratory cartwheel. Victory for Town is their first at home since February, but Wragg still reckons, 'We were awful.'											
10	A	STALYBRIDGE		12	D	1-1	1-1	Megson 31	Heyes	Filson	German	Edwards	Lambert	Megson	Peake	Saunders	Constable	Paterson	Craven	
	5/10		*1,233*		12			*Jackson 18*	*Hughes*	*Bennet*	*Coathup*	*Dixon*	*Aspinall**	*Boyle*	*Anderson*	*Jackson*	*Bunn*	*Kirkham*	*Locke*	*Brown*
								Ref: A Leake	Sky Sports film the game for a special feature on the Conference newcomers. The game is delayed for ten minutes, but Town then struggle to get to grips with tough-tackling Celtic. Megson's error lets in Jackson to score from 25 yards, but redeems himself with a 20-yard blockbuster.											

No	Venue / Date	Opponent	Att	Pos	Res / Pts	F-A	H-T	Scorers, Times, and Referees	1	2	3	4	5	6	7	8	9	10	11	Subs used
11	A	MERTHYR		12	L	1-2	1-0	Lambert 31	Heyes	Filson*	German	Edwards	Megson	Lambert	Peake	Saunders	Paterson	Constable^	Craven	**France/Crosby**
	9/10		*911*		12			*Rogers 55, Williams C 66*	*Wager*	*Williams M*	*Davies*	*Lewis*	*Trick*	*Holtan*	*James Rob**	*Coates*	*Tucker*	*Williams C*	*Rogers*	*James Ryan*
								Ref: K Pike	A game of two halves sees a Robbie James-inspired Merthyr come from behind to record their first Conference win. After Trick miscontrols the ball, Peake crosses for Lambert to head Town into a deserved lead. But the home side respond after the break and could have won by more.											
12	A	DAGENHAM		16	L	0-3	0-2		Heyes	**Rathbone***	Craven	Edwards	Lambert	Megson	Barr	Saunders^	Constable	Paterson	Filson	Ridings/France
	16/10		*1,303*	*14*	12			*De Souza 9, Broom 21, 84*	*McKenna*	*Stebbing*	*Watts*	*Butterworth*	*Conner*	*Reed*	*Broom*	*Owers*	*Crown*	*De Souza*	*Richardson*	
								Ref: G Barber	Dagenham were pre-season title favourites, but the scoreline here flatters them. De Souza looks well offside when he runs through to score the first. Injury and illness affects Town's line-up. Basil Rathbone plays his first game for three seasons as the supporters call for Wragg's sacking.											
13	H	WOKING		17	L	2-3	2-0	Lambert 6, Paterson 8	Brown	German	Craven	Barr	Filson^	Lambert	Peake	**Costello**	Constable*	Paterson	Megson	Edwards/Hardy
	23/10		1,201		12			*Clement 67, Tucker 73, Puckett 87*	*Batty*	*Clement*	*Agboola*	*Tucker*	*Berry*	*Brown K*	*Brown D*	*Puckett*	*Gray*	*Rattray*	*Walker*	
								Ref: S Mathieson	Heyes is left out of the side after being shaken up attending to a car accident victim. Town are in dreamland after only eight minutes. Woking's fightback stuns the home fans. Puckett, ex-Aldershot, robs German before firing in the winner. Wragg admits that he 'really has no answers.'											
14	A	BATH		18	D	2-2	2-2	Paterson 26, Peake 34	Heyes	Barr	Craven	Edwards	Filson	Megson !	Peake	Costello !	Lambert^	Paterson	Saunders*	Constable/German
	23/10		*712*	*10*	13			*Hobless 16p, Boyle 40*	*Mogg*	*Hedges*	*Dicks !*	*Weston**	*Crowley*	*Cousins*	*Banks*	*Gill*	*Adcock*	*Boyle^*	*Hobless*	*Smart/Vernon*
								Ref: M Warren	Peake's transfer to Scunthorpe is put on hold. He takes his place in the Town side, concedes a penalty, then makes and scores to put Town in front. Boyle makes it 2-2 before the ref dismisses Costello (44 minutes), and Megson and Grantley Dicks (60), brother of Liverpool's Julian.											
15	H	BROMSGROVE		16	W	3-0	1-0	Saunders 30, 53, Megson 90	Heyes	German	Craven*	Edwards	**Boardman**	Barr	Peake	Saunders	Ridings	Paterson^	Megson	Hardy/Constable
	6/11		1,003	*19*	16				*Cooksey*	*Stott*	*Brighton*	*Richardson*	*Wardle*	*Skelding*	*Carty*	*Shilvock*	*Hanks*	*Crisp*	*Radburn*	
								Ref: D Laws	Bromsgrove are looking to extend their run of twelve undefeated Conference and cup matches. They cause Town a few problems, but Saunders settles a few home nerves with two well-taken goals. He's on for a hat-trick but when his header comes back off the bar, Megson reacts first.											
16	H	WELLING		17	D	1-1	0-0	Lambert 57	Heyes	German^	Craven	Edwards	Boardman	Barr	Peake	Ridings	Lambert	Paterson	Saunders*	Constable/Filson
	20/11		1,035	*5*	17			*Abbott 47*	*Williams*	*Steffe*	*Robinson*	*Ransom*	*Burgess*	*Clemence*	*White*	*Hales*	*Abbott**	*Robbins*	*Reynolds*	*Slater*
								Ref: R Pearson	After the heroics of the West Brom game, Town find this a frustrating contest. Despite dominating, they are rocked when Abbott scores from eight yards following a free-kick, but respond through Lambert's header off Craven's free-kick. Williams in the Welling goal plays a blinder.											
17	A	WITTON		18	D	2-2	1-2	Lambert 40, 58	Heyes	Barr	Craven	Edwards	Boardman	Constable	Peake	Ridings	Lambert	Paterson	Saunders	
	26/11		*846*	*17*	18			*Burke 28, 41*	*Mason*	*Senior*	*Thomas*	*Edey*	*Henry*	*Garton*	*Tobin*	*Rose^*	*Maynard*	*Burke*	*Dixon**	*Pritchard/Gallagher*
								Ref: A Ogden	It's a mystery as to how Town fail to win this one. Peake hits the bar before Burke scores against the run of play. Burke nets his second within a minute of Lambert equalising. The second half is a one-sided affair. Lambert heads in his second, but the Shaymen can't finish off the job.											
18	A	DOVER		15	W	2-1	1-0	Paterson 10, Peake 75	Heyes	Barr	Craven	Edwards	Boardman	Megson	Peake	**Burr**	Ridings	Paterson*	Saunders	German
	18/12		*1,348*	*4*	21			*Leworthy 60p*	*Munden**	*Donn*	*Bartlett*	*Dixon A*	*O'Connell*	*Walker*	*Jackson*	*Walsh*	*Lewis*	*Leworthy*	*Milton*	*Dixon T*
								Ref: W Norbury	The fortunes of former leaders Dover are fading fast. Here, the 20th-minute withdrawal of injured keeper Munden doesn't help their cause, but Town are always on top. Lewis goes in goal but fails to stop Peake's 25-yard winner. Heyes upends Leworthy, who nets the resultant penalty.											
19	A	KIDDERMINSTER		19	L	1-2	0-0	Peake 81	**Wilmot**	Barr	Craven	Edwards	Boardman	Ridings*	Peake	Burr^	Lambert	Paterson	Saunders	Megson/Constable
	4/1		*2,016*	*1*	21			*Humphries 62, Cartwright 68*	*Rose*	*Hodson*	*Bancroft*	*Weir*	*Brindley*	*Forsyth*	*Deakin*	*Grainger*	*Humphries*	*Davies**	*Purdie*	*Cartwright*
								Ref: J McGrath	Graham Allner's Kidderminster set the standard that Town must aim for. Defeat all but spells the end of Halifax challenging for the title. The contest is settled in a six-minute spell. Cartwright sets up Humphries, then is on hand to net the second. Peake's 30-yarder just about creeps in.											
20	A	KETTERING		14	W	1-0	0-0	Ridings 49	Wilmot	Barr	Craven	Edwards	Boardman	Ridings	Peake	Burr	Lambert	Paterson	Saunders*	Megson
	8/1		*2,409*	*3*	24				*Benstead*	*Price*	*Ashby*	*Holden*	*Oxbrow*	*Taylor**	*Wright*	*Brown*	*Martin*	*Donald*	*Graham^*	*Ashdjian/Reed*
								Ref: N Barry	It's five years and a day since Town drew here in the FA Cup, before losing the replay. This time they respond to a 45-minute no holds barred dressing room showdown before kick-off to go one better. Dave Ridings scores the only goal from 20 yards, with the aid of a slight deflection.											
21	H	STALYBRIDGE		14	W	2-1	1-0	Ridings 38, 85	Wilmot	Barr	Craven	Edwards	Boardman	Ridings	Peake	Burr	Lambert	Paterson	Megson	
	11/1		1,012	*22*	27			*Aspinall 75*	*Hughes*	*Harold*	*Richards*	*Dixon*	*Aspinall*	*Ogley*	*Anderson*	*Leicester*	*Lutkevitch**	*Jackson*	*Blain*	*Bunn*
								Ref: B Polkie	Ridings is again the hero, as Town under-perform but get away with it. He opens the scoring with another long-range deflected effort. Celtic, equally as bad, hit back with Aspinall's bullet header. A draw looks likely when Ridings' header deceives Hughes and nestles in the corner.											

No		Date	Att	Pos	Pt	F-A	H-T	Scorers, Times, and Referees	1	2	3	4	5	6	7	8	9	10	11	subs used
22	H	RUNCORN		12	D	1-1	1-1	Lambert 22	Wilmot	Barr	Craven	Edwards	Boardman	Ridings	Peake	**Collins**	Lambert	Paterson	Burr*	Constable
		15/1	1,196	*8*	28			*Brady 31*	*Williams*	*Bates*	*Hill*	*Brady*	*Lee*	*Anderson*	*Thomas*	*Connor*	*McInerney*	*McKenna*	*Brabin*	
								Ref: D Morrall	Not for the first – or last – time the Town fans are chanting 'Wragg out' after his side fails to dispose of a poor Runcorn side. Paterson sets up Lambert, who gives Town the lead. Wraggs feels Town then become arrogant but they have no answers once Ian Brady slides in the equaliser.											
23	A	WELLING		10	W	2-0	1-0	Megson 14, Ridings 66	Wilmot	Barr	Craven	Edwards	Boardman	Megson	Peake	Ridings	Lambert	Paterson*	Burr	Collins
		29/1	*1,121*	*8*	31				*Williams*	*Hone*	*Robinson*	*Ransom*	*Copley**	*Clemence*	*White*	*Rutherford*	*Abbott^*	*Robbins*	*Reynolds*	*Finnan/Smith*
								Ref: P March	The Shaymen are full of ideas and catch Terry Robbins' side on the hop. Lambert sends Megson away to round Williams before scoring their first. Ridings forces in Burr's angled header. Welling's Steve Robinson is booked for a foul on Barr, who is then also booked for over-reacting.											
24	H	SOUTHPORT		10	D	2-2	1-0	Lambert 11, Barr 90	Wilmot	Barr	Craven	Edwards	Boardman	Megson	Peake	Ridings	Lambert	Paterson	Burr	
		2/2	1,310	*2*	32			*Quinlan 78, 90*	*Moore*	*McDonald*	*Fuller*	*Dove*	*Goulding*	*Lodge*	*Mitchell**	*Comstive*	*Haw*	*Gamble*	*Withers^*	*Quinlan/Williams*
								Ref: S Race	Brian Kettle's side move into second place, but he's fuming that his side didn't win the game. Trailing to Lambert's early strike, Quinlan pulls Southport level, then in injury-time he sweeps them in front. As the home fans head for the exits, Barr equalises with 93 minutes on the clock.											
25	A	STAFFORD		12	D	1-1	1-0	Hemming 1 (og)	Wilmot	Barr	Craven	Edwards	Boardman	Megson	Peake	Ridings	Lambert	Paterson*	Burr	Collins
		5/2	*1,082*	*10*	33			*Mettioui 76*	*Price*	*Berry*	*Bradshaw*	*Simpson*	*Essex*	*Hemming*	*Williams**	*Bodkin*	*Boughey*	*Mettioui*	*Foy*	*Mee*
								Ref: D Mansfield	Town's Steve Burr signed from Stafford and knows them well. 'They can be a funny lot,' he says. How true. Hemming jabs out a foot to turn in Paterson's cross for a 50-second own-goal. Town miss a hatful of chances, and pay for it when Moroccan Mettioui turns in Boughey's cross.											
26	A	TELFORD		14	L	2-3	0-1	Edwards 55, Lormor 56	Wilmot	Barr	**Prindiville**	Edwards	Boardman	Megson	Peake	**Lormor**	Lambert	Paterson	Craven	
		19/2	*1,072*	*10*	33			*Bignot 42, Sleeuwenhoek 83, 85*	*Hughes*	*Pritchard*	*Parrish*	*Niblett*	*Ford*	*Ferguson*	*Bignot*	*Whiteh'se**	*Taylor*	*Myers*	*Statham^*	*Sleeuwenh'k/Foster*
								Ref: E Walsh	After the sacking of Peter Wragg, Town have turned to John Bird to help keep the momentum going. He brings in Prindiville and Lormor, and the latter walks the ball in to put Town ahead. But the near-unpronounceable Kris Sleeuwenhoek comes off the bench to turn the game around.											
27	H	DOVER		18	L	0-1	0-0		Wilmot	Barr	Prindiville	Edwards	Boardman	Constable*	Peake	Lormor	Lambert	Paterson	Hanson	Higgins
		12/3	760		33			*Donn 78*	*Munden*	*Scott*	*Bartlett*	*Dixon*	*O'Connell*	*Walker*	*Jackson*	*Browne !*	*Blewden*	*Donn*	*Milton*	
								Ref: K Lynch	Halifax plum new depths with this awful performance. Matters are made worse by the fact that Dover play for an hour with only ten men, after Browne is sent off for dissent. Town force 18 corners but rarely look dangerous. Boardman's poor clearance provides Donn with his chance.											
28	A	MACCLESFIELD		15	W	1-0	0-0	Peake 54	Wilmot	Barr	Prindiville	Edwards	Boardman	German	Peake	Lormor	Lambert	Paterson	Hanson	
		19/3	*1,115*	*10*	36				*Farrelly*	*Shepherd*	*Bbimson*	*Kendall*	*Howarth*	*Sorvel*	*Askey**	*McDonald*	*Lillis*	*Power^*	*Sharratt*	*Adams/Lyons*
								Ref: P Devine	Bird is a relieved man as he picks up his first win. The unthinkable scenario of relegation had become a possibility. Both sides create chances, but there's only Peake who's able to snap one up. It's his parting gift – the following week he moves to Rochdale in exchange for Alex Jones.											
29	H	BATH		15	D	0-0	0-0		Wilmot	Barr	Prindiville	**Jones**	Boardman	Megson	German	Lormor	Lambert	Paterson	Hanson	
		26/3	1,008	*6*	37				*Mogg*	*Gill*	*Dicks*	*Crowley*	*Smart^*	*Cousins*	*Banks*	*Chenoweth*	*Adcock*	*Thaws**	*Vernon*	*Lucas/Ricketts*
								Ref: G Bradbury	Last week's win has helped push up the attendance, but at home the Shaymen disappoint. Like Bath, this is their 13th draw so far. German has a chip pushed onto the post by Mogg and Lormor misses from close range. For Bath, Banks sees his header cleared off the line by Prindiville.											
30	H	MERTHYR		13	W	2-1	1-0	Hanson 43, 73	Wilmot	Barr	Prindiville	Jones	Boardman	Megson	**Smith**	Hanson	Lambert*	Paterson	Constable	German
		29/3	771	*15*	40			*Dyer 90*	*Williams*	*Williams M*	*Jones N*	*Lewis D^*	*Davies*	*Lewis A*	*Tucker*	*Holtam**	*Benbow*	*Dyer*	*James R*	*Jones M/Drewitt*
								Ref: P Joslin	'Prove your worth,' Bird tells his players. They respond in positive fashion, and are deserving winners. Debutant Nigel Smith impresses on the wing. Town have 22 attempts on goal, two of which are headers from Hanson that go in. Dyer scores at the death with Merthyr's second shot.											
31	A	NORTHWICH		11	W	2-0	1-0	Hanson 20, Barr 85	Wilmot	German	Prindiville	Jones	Boardman	Megson	Smith	Hanson	Barr	Paterson	Constable	
		2/4	*927*		43				*Bullock*	*Tinson*	*Parker*	*Hancock*	*Boyd*	*Jones M*	*Hardy**	*Butler*	*Bunter*	*Adebola*	*Westray^*	*Norman/Jones T*
								Ref: B Rudkin	With a strong wind making life difficult, Town bring an end to Northwich's eleven-match unbeaten run. Hanson squeezes the ball home from a corner for the first. Just after half-time, Westray is unlucky to see his shot fly off the inside of the post. Barr's crossface header settles the issue.											

No		Date / Opponent	Att	Pos	Res / Pts	F-A	H-T	Scorers, Times, and Referees	1	2	3	4	5	6	7	8	9	10	11	subs used
32	A	GATESHEAD		11	L	1-2	0-1	Paterson 82	Wilmot	German	Prindiville	Jones	Boardman	Megson	Lormor^	Hanson*	Barr	Paterson	Constable	**Horsfield/Gray**
		4/4	**659**	*13*	43			*Dobson 21, 84*	Smith	Watson	Wrightons	Hine	Corner	Harvey^	Farrey*	Dobson	Proudlock	Rowe	Parkinson	Nobbs/Whitmarsh
								Ref: S Mathieson	Paul Dobson, once on loan at the Shay, takes his tally for the season to 25. He lobs Wilmot from 30 yards for his first. Hanson misses from six yards, but Paterson looks to have saved the game with a late equaliser. Two minutes later, Boardman's stray pass lets Dobson in for the winner.											
33	H	ALTRINCHAM		11	D	0-0	0-0		Wilmot	German	Prindiville	Jones	Boardman	Megson	Horsfield	**O'Toole***	Barr	Paterson	Constable	Higgins
		7/4	1,019	*18*	44				Collings	Cross	Heesom	France	Reid	Dempsey	Green A	Terry*	Green R	Carmody	Sharratt	Cockram
								Ref: G Cain	John King's Altrincham side play a frustrating offside game, and are clearly here for a point. They have only six attempts at goal. When Jamie Paterson gets clear only to mis-hit his shot, it's a sign that this game is heading for a goalless draw. Geoff Horsfield also fluffs a one-on-one.											
34	A	YEOVIL		14	D	0-0	0-0		Wilmot	German	Prindiville	Jones	Boardman	Megson	Lormor	Hanson*	Barr	Paterson	Horsfield	Constable
		16/4	*1,823*	*21*	45				Mason	White	Ferns	Sherwood	McClelland	Cordice	Coates N*	Wallace	Coates M	Wilson	Dobbins	West
								Ref: K Pike	37-year-old former Northern Ireland international John McClelland comes down from his Leeds home to aid struggling Yeovil. Jones is lucky to stay on the field after felling Marc Coates. The ref gives a corner. Yeovil boss Brian Hall says, 'You have to live with decisions like that.'											
35	H	NORTHWICH		14	L	1-2	1-1	Smith 11	Wilmot	German	Prindiville	Jones	Boardman	Megson	Lormor	Higgins*	Barr	Paterson^	Smith	Horsfield/O'Toole
		19/4	803		45			*Adebola 18, Hardy 69*	Bullock	Tinson	Simms	Hancock	Boyd	Parker	Westray	Norman	Bunter	Adebola	Hardy	
								Ref: U Rennie	Bird is trying a host of trialists, but results are suffering. Smith fires the Shaymen in front, but a howler from Wilmot lets in Adebola for Vics' equaliser. Attendances are falling, too. After Neil Hardy fires in the winner for Northwich, even fewer are expected for the visit of Gateshead.											
36	H	GATESHEAD		14	W	3-1	0-1	Paterson 51, 88, Barr 56	Wilmot	Barr	Prindiville	Jones*	Boardman	Megson	Constable	Hanson	O'Toole	Paterson	Smith	German
		23/4	760	*7*	48			*Dobson 4*	Smith	Higgins	Sweeney*	Hine^	Wrightson	Nobbs	Proudlock	Dobson	Sharpe	Rowe	Parkinson	Harvey/Lamb
								Ref: A Ogden	Wilmot blunders when he fails to control a backpass for Dobson's early goal. Town then lose Jones with a broken nose in the 32nd minute, but they turn the game around after half-time. Paterson charges down Simon Smith's kick-out for the equaliser, then the Shaymen don't look back.											
37	H	MACCLESFIELD		15	L	1-2	1-0	Smith 30	Wilmot	Barr	Prindiville	Jones	Boardman	Megson	Constable	Hanson	O'Toole	Paterson	Smith	
		26/4	732	*8*	48			*Power 49, 75*	Farrelly	Shepherd	Bimson	Lillis	Howarth	Sorvel	Lyons	McDonald	Alford*	Power	Adams	Powell
								Ref: A Leake	Cable TV are filming this one, and they capture Macclesfield skipper Bimson and keeper Farrelly almost coming to blows following a mix-up in the defence. They are already trailing to Smith's goal, but regroup after the break. Phil Power arrives to head the winner off Lyons' corner.											
38	H	DAGENHAM		15	L	0-1	0-0		Heyes	German	Prindiville	Barr	Boardman	Megson	Constable	Hanson*	O'Toole	Paterson	Smith	Horsfield
		29/4	**643**	*6*	48			*Payne 77*	McKenna	Stebbing	Watts	Butterworth	Blackford	Livett	Richardson	Sorrell	Cavell	Crown	Payne	
								Ref: E Lomas	David Crown, a thorn in Town's side over the years for Gillingham and Southend, is still doing the business. His pull-back allows Payne to score the only goal. After that, John Still's Dagenham dig in and hold onto their lead. Barr goes close when he hits the bar with a thunderbolt.											
39	A	ALTRINCHAM		16	D	0-0	0-0		Heyes	German	Prindiville	Barr	Boardman	Megson	Rathbone*	Horsfield	O'Toole	Paterson	Constable^	Smith/**Hook**
		30/4	*799*		49				Collings	Cross	Heesom	France	Reid	Dempsey*	Green A	Harris	Terry	Carmody	Sharratt	Green R
								Ref: D Morrall	For the first time since the 1980-81 season, the Shaymen play two games in two days. Rathbone plays his second game but ends up in hospital suffering from concussion. Altrincham come closest to breaking the deadlock on 65 minutes when Sharratt's inswinging corner hits the bar.											
40	H	KIDDERMINSTER		13	W	1-0	1-0	Barr 14	Heyes	German	Prindiville	Jones	Boardman	Megson	Horsfield	Barr	Hanson	Paterson	Hardy	
		2/5	1,141	*1*	52				Rose	Hodson	Bancroft	Weir*	Brindley	Forsyth	Cartwright^	Grainger	Humphries	Davies	Palmer	Woodhall/Deakin
								Ref: J Winter	Excerpts from this game will feature in an episode of 'A Touch of Frost', starring David Jason. Graham Allner's Kidderminster were hoping to clinch the title here, but Town throw a spanner in the works. Horsfield lays the ball off for Barr to crack home the only goal for a shock win.											
41	A	BROMSGROVE		13	L	0-1	0-1		Heyes	German	Prindiville	Jones	Boardman	Megson	Smith^	Barr	Horsfield	Paterson	Hardy*	O'Toole/Higgins
		5/5	*1,050*	*18*	52			*Stott 20*	Green	Skelding	Young	Richardson	Clarke	Gaunt	Burgher	Stott	Taylor	Shilcock	Carter	
								Ref: J Hubbard	Town go into this game knowing they are safe, whilst Bromsgrove are still scrapping for their lives. Bobby Hope's men are clearly up for this game the more, and continue to push Town back even after Stott's volleyed goal. Taylor hits the post, whilst Heyes has to be at his very best.											
42	H	SLOUGH		13	W	1-0	0-0	Paterson 79	Wilmot	German	Prindiville	Jones	Boardman	Megson	Horsfield	Barr	Hook	Paterson	Higgins*	Constable
		7/5	935	*21*	55				Bunting	Whitby	Dowson	Hancock	Lee	Hazel	Manning	Stanley	Scott M	Sayer	Smith*	Scott S
		Home	Away					Ref: B Coddington	Les Briley's Slough side need to win if they are to avoid relegation to the Diadora League on the final day. They give it their all, but this time Wilmot stands between them and survival. Town introduce Constable after 70 minutes, and when he sets up Paterson, Slough's fate is sealed.											
Average		949	1,267																	

FA Cup						F-A	H-T	Scorers, Times, and Referees	1	2	3	4	5	6	7	8	9	10	11	subs used
1	H	WEST BROM		14	W	2-1	2-0	Peake 6, Saunders 36	Heyes	German	Craven	Edwards	Boardman	Barr	Peake	Ridings	Lambert	Paterson*	Saunders	Constable
		14/11	4,250	*1:19*				*Hunt 81*	*Lange*	*Coldicott*	*Ampadu^*	*McNally*	*O'Regan*	*Burgess*	*Hunt*	*Hamilton*	*Taylor*	*Ashcroft*	*Donovan**	*Mellon/Reid*
								Ref: A Flood	Sky TV show this game live on a Sunday afternoon. Baggies boss Keith Burkinshaw won the Cup twice for Spurs, but his side are up against it once Peake walks through the defence for the first goal. Saunders scoots away for 2-0. Hunt heads in for the Baggies to set up a tense finish.											
2	A	STOCKPORT		18	L	1-5	0-1	Barr 84p *[Wallace 86]*	Heyes	German^	Craven	Edwards	Boardman*	Megson	Peake	Barr	Ridings	Paterson	Saunders	Constable/Cameron
		4/12	*5,496*	*2:2*				*Frain 38, Francis 53, 73, Beaumont 81,*	*Edwards*	*Todd*	*Wallace*	*Frain*	*Flynn*	*Gannon*	*Miller*	*Emerson*	*Francis**	*Beaumont*	*Preece*	*Ryan*
								Ref: M Peck	The 6'7" giant frame of Kevin Francis poses the biggest threat to Town. He is almost on his knees when he heads in his first to put County 2-0 up. The game slips way from Town, but they enjoy stroking the ball around. Paterson wins the penalty before Wallace curls in County's fifth.											

FA Trophy																				
1	H	EMLEY		12	W	2-1	1-1	Paterson 13, Baker 48 (og)	Wilmot	Barr	Craven	Edwards	Boardman	Ridings	Peake	Collins	Lambert	Paterson	Burr*	Megson
		22/1	1,579	*NP:P*				*Clarke 45p*	*Winstanley*	*Johnson*	*Jerome*	*Lockwood*	*Baker*	*Bondswell*	*Bradshaw*	*Clarke*	*Tunnacliffe*	*Burrows*	*Alcide**	*Reynolds*
								Ref: J McGrath	Town's first ever venture into the competition sees them installed as third favourites to win it. In this first meeting between near neighbours, they need Baker's unlucky own-goal to go through. Clarke's penalty, after Lambert fells Andy Bondswell, shakes up Town for the second half.											
2	A	SPENNYMOOR		12	W	2-1	0-0	Paterson 62, Peake 68	Wilmot	Megson	Craven	Barr	Boardman	Ridings	Peake	Burr*	Lambert	Paterson	Collins	Hanson
		12/2	*1,426*	*NP:1*				*Gorman 86*	*McNarry*	*Watson*	*Petijean*	*Goodrick*	*Saunders*	*Healy*	*Ainsley*	*Cook*	*Shaw*	*Gorman*	*Veart*	
								Ref: N Barry	On a sloping pitch, Town ride their luck as Spennymoor hit the post twice and the bar once, but they just about scrape through. The Shaymen are now unbeaten in eight matches, but rumours are spreading over Wragg's future. They are confirmed the following day when he is sacked.											
3	A	RUNCORN		15	D	1-1	0-0	Brabin 90 (og)	Wilmot	Barr	Prindiville	Edwards	Boardman	Craven*	Peake	Lormor^	Lambert	Paterson	Hanson	German/**Higgins**
		5/3	*1,302*	*6*				*Thomas 50*	*Williams*	*Bates*	*Hill*	*Brady*	*Lee*	*Anderson*	*Thomas*	*Connor*	*McInerney*	*McKenna*	*Brabin*	
								Ref: B Priest	Hanson is trying to claim Town's last-gasp equaliser. With their last throw of the dice, he dives to meet Barr's cross, but the ball is deflected into goal by Gary Brabin. Otherwise, Karl Thomas's close-range goal looked good enough for the home side. Bird admits, 'We got out of jail.'											
3R	H	RUNCORN		15	L	0-2	0-1		Wilmot	Barr	Prindiviller	Edwards	Boardman	Craven*	Peake	Lormor	Lambert	Paterson	Hanson^	German/Higgins
		8/3	1,406	*6*				*Anderson 5, Thomas 81*	*Williams*	*Bates*	*Hill*	*Brady*	*Lee*	*Anderson*	*Thomas*	*Connor*	*McInerney*	*McKenna**	*Brabin*	*Shaw*
								Ref: B Priest	Gateshead await the winners. Town get all fired up for the game – Bird's first at the Shay – but within five minutes they are a goal down. Gary Anderson is left free to put Runcorn ahead. Town's woe is complete when Thomas, the Conference's leading scorer, heads in Connor's cross.											

	P	Home W	D	L	F	A	Away W	D	L	F	A	Pts
1 Kidderminster	42	13	5	3	31	12	9	4	8	32	23	75
2 Kettering	42	9	7	5	23	14	10	8	3	23	10	72
3 Woking	42	12	5	4	35	25	6	8	7	23	33	67
4 Southport	42	10	7	4	26	21	8	5	8	31	30	66
5 Runcorn	42	12	6	3	41	26	2	13	6	22	31	61
6 Dagenham	42	12	5	4	41	23	3	9	9	21	31	59
7 Macclesfield	42	7	8	6	24	18	9	3	9	24	31	59
8 Dover	42	9	3	9	28	24	8	4	9	20	25	58
9 Stafford	42	10	7	4	39	22	4	8	9	17	30	57
10 Altrincham	42	8	5	8	23	22	8	4	9	18	20	57
11 Gateshead	42	10	6	5	23	18	5	6	10	22	35	57
12 Bath	42	6	8	7	28	21	7	9	5	19	17	56
13 HALIFAX	42	7	9	5	28	18	6	7	8	27	31	55
14 Stalybridge	42	6	6	9	27	30	8	6	7	27	25	54
15 Northwich	42	7	9	5	26	19	4	10	7	18	26	52
16 Welling	42	7	7	7	25	23	6	5	10	22	26	51
17 Telford	42	8	7	6	24	22	5	5	11	17	27	51
18 Bromsgrove	42	5	8	8	26	32	7	7	7	28	34	51
19 Yeovil	42	7	4	10	23	26	7	5	9	26	36	51
20 Merthyr*	42	8	7	6	34	26	4	8	9	26	35	49
21 Slough	42	8	8	5	30	24	3	6	12	14	34	47
22 Witton	42	4	8	9	18	30	3	5	13	19	33	34
	924	185	145	132	623	496	132	145	185	496	623	1239

* 2 points deducted

Odds & ends

Double wins: (0).

Double losses: (1) Dagenham.

Won from behind: (1) Gateshead (h).

Lost from in front: (5) Macclesfield (h), Northwich (h), Woking (h), Merthyr (a), Telford (a).

High spots: Beating 1st Division West Brom in the FA Cup.

Scoring six goals away, in a 6-2 win at Woking, for the first time since December 1911.

Scoring six goals for the second successive match in a 6-0 win over Telford.

Six games unbeaten up to 2 February.

Beating Bradford City 4-2 at Valley Parade to win the Yorkshire Cup.

Low spots: Failing to win the first seven Conference matches.

Three consecutive defeats in October.

Losing 0-5 at Runcorn.

Losing the replay at home to Runcorn in the FA Trophy.

Striker Steve Saunders having to retire due to ill-health.

Player of the Year: Craig Boardman.

Ever-presents: (1) Jamie Paterson.

Hat-tricks: Jamie Paterson (1).

Leading scorer: Jamie Paterson (15).

	Appearances Lge	*Sub*	FAC	*Sub*	FT	*Sub*	Goals Lge	FAC	FT	Tot
Barr, Billy	**39**		2		4		**4**	1		**5**
Boardman, Craig	**28**		2		4					
Bracey, Lee	**1**									
Brown, Nick	**3**									
Burr, Steve	**8**				2					
Cameron, Jim	**2**	*1*		*1*						
Collins, Simon	**1**	*2*			2					
Constable, Shaun	**20**	*9*		*2*						
Costello, Peter	**2**									
Craven, Peter	**26**		2		4					
Crosby, Andy		*1*								
Edwards, Elfyn	**25**	*1*	2		3		**1**			**1**
Filson, Martin	**10**	*3*					**1**			**1**
France, Darren		*2*								
German, David	**20**	*8*	2			*2*				
Gray, Ryan		*1*								
Greenwood, Nigel	**3**									
Gregory, Tony	**5**	*1*								
Hanson, Dave	**12**	*1*			2	*1*	**4**			**4**
Hardy, Jason	**5**	*3*								
Heyes, Darren	**18**		2							
Higgins, David	**2**	*3*				*2*				
Hook, Steve	**1**	*1*								
Horsfield, Geoff	**6**	*3*								
Jones, Alex	**12**									
Lambert, Colin	**20**		1		4		**7**			**7**
Lormor, Tony	**7**				2		**1**			**1**
Lucketti, Chris	**8**						**1**			**1**
Megson, Kevin	**29**	*3*	1		1	*1*	**3**			**3**
O'Toole, Pat	**5**	*2*								
Paterson, Jamie	**42**		2		4		**13**		2	**15**
Peake, Jason	**27**		2		4		**6**	1	1	**8**
Prindiville, Steve	**17**				2					
Rathbone, Mick	**2**									
Ridings, Dave	**15**	*1*	2		2		**4**			**4**
Saunders, Steve	**14**		2				**6**	1		**7**
Smith, Nigel	**7**	*1*					**2**			**2**
Wilmot, Richard	**20**				4					
(own-goals)							**2**			**2**
38 players used	**462**	***47***	**22**	***3***	**44**	***6***	**55**	**3**	**3**	**61**

No	Date		Att	Pos	Pt	F-A	H-T	Scorers, Times, and Referees	1	2	3	4	5	6	7	8	9	10	11	subs used
1	A	WOKING			W	3-1	2-1	Prindiville 19, German 32, Jones 47	Heyes	German !	Prindiville	Jones	Boardman	**Langley**	Paterson	Lambert	Hanson	**Flounders**	**Kiwomya**	
	20/8		*1,760*		3			*Steele 45*	*Batty*	*Tucker*	*Wye*	*Berry^*	*Brown K*	*Tierling**	*Brown D*	*Fielder*	*Steele*	*Hay*	*Walker*	*Dennis/Rattray*
								Ref: A D'Urso	Town get off to a great start, beating one of the fancied teams against the odds. There is drama in first half injury-time. Steele chips Heyes to halve the deficit, then German is sent off for stamping on a Woking player. Earlier, he had scored the goal of the game, a volley from 30 yards.											
2	H	NORTHWICH		6	D	0-0	0-0		Heyes	German	Prindiville	Jones !	Boardman	Langley	Paterson	Lambert	Hanson	Flounders*	Kiwomya	**Sunley**
	24/8		994	*7*	4				*Greygoose*	*Tinson*	*Jones*	*Abel*	*Parker*	*Gallagher*	*Boyd*	*Butler*	*Oghani*	*O'Connor**	*Snowdon*	*Cooke*
								Ref: G Spooner	Whistle-happy referee Spooner spoils an otherwise entertaining game, awarding 39 free-kicks. Town skipper Jones is sent off after 66 minutes for a second bookable offence. Heyes is lucky not to join him after hauling down Joe O'Connor. He stays on to save his resultant penalty kick.											
3	H	BROMSGROVE		2	W	4-2	1-2	Prindiville 9, Jones 64, Worthington 77,	Heyes	German	Prindiville	Jones	Boardman	Langley	Paterson	Lambert	Hanson	Flounders*	Kiwomya	**Worthington**
	27/8		1,047		7			*Carter 24, 32* [Power 89 (og)]	*Judge*	*Clarke*	*Power*	*Richardson*	*Skelding*	*Gaunt*	*Shilvlock*	*Stott*	*Taylor !*	*Carter*	*Gray**	*Young*
								Ref: G Frankland	Prindiville runs forward to hammer home from 20 yards, but at half-time, the Shaymen are behind. Steve Taylor's 48th-minute sending off for stamping does his side no favours. Town then turn on the style. Paterson's low cross is turned in by the hapless Power to complete the scoring.											
4	A	STALYBRIDGE		5	D	1-1	1-1	Flounders 38	Heyes	German	Prindiville	Jones	Boardman	Langley	Paterson	Lambert	Hanson	Flounders	Kiwomya*	**Fowler**
	29/8		*1,337*	*12*	8			*Langley 12 (og)*	*Hughes*	*Edmonds*	*Coathup*	*Ogley*	*Dixon*	*Megson*	*Bennett**	*Clayton*	*Shaughn'sy^*	*Wheeler*	*Ryan*	*Anderson/Bauress*
								Ref: G Bradbury	Peter Wragg, now manager of Celtic, is taunted by the travelling Town supporters. Halifax have the chance to go top, but they fail to get into gear. Flounders pounces to net the equaliser after Langley heads a brilliant own-goal. John Bird says it's the best goal he's ever seen him score.											
5	A	DOVER		7	D	1-1	1-1	Kiwomya 15	Heyes	Sunley	Prindiville.	Jones	Boardman	Langley	Paterson	Lambert	Hanson	Flounders	Kiwomya	
	3/9		*1,654*	*3*	9			*Eeles 12*	*Munden*	*Budden*	*Bartlett*	*Dixon*	*Scott*	*Walker*	*Eeles**	*Lewis*	*Milton*	*Blewden*	*Leworthy*	*Browne*
								Ref: E Green	Both sides start, and end, the day unbeaten, but the Lilywhites lose top spot. Eeles' looping header over a stranded Heyes gives them a dream start, but their joy is short-lived when Kiwomya scores from 25 yards. The game proceeds to be a thrilling contest, but it lacks any more goals.											
6	H	SOUTHPORT		6	W	2-0	0-0	Paterson 74, 80	Heyes	Sunley	Prindiville	Jones	Boardman	Langley	Paterson	Hanson*	Lambert	Flounders	Kiwomya	**Lancaster**
	6/9		1,308	*11*	12				*McKenna*	*Ward*	*Simms*	*Dove*	*Goulding*	*Lodge*	*Clark**	*Comstive*	*McDonald*	*Cuningh'm^*	*Thomas*	*Haw/Gamble*
								Ref: N Riley	Town set a new club record of six unbeaten games since the start of the season. Brian Kettle's side put up a stern resistance, but the Shaymen are patient and get their just reward. Flounders is easily the star of the show, and he sets up both Paterson's goals, the first of which is a header.											
7	H	FARNBOROUGH		7	L	0-1	0-0		Heyes	Sunley	Prindiville	Fowler	Boardman	Langley^	Paterson	Hanson*	Lambert	Flounders	Kiwomya	Lancaster/Worth'ton
	10/9		1,143	*3*	12			*Terry 86*	*Taylor*	*Semp*	*Pratt*	*Coney*	*Day*	*Turkington*	*Boothe*	*Jones*	*Baker*	*Read^*	*Horton**	*Terry/Thompson*
								Ref: T Heilbron	Bird hauls his players in for a Sunday morning lecture after this dreadful display. Farnborough, promoted to the Conference last season, look a dangerous side and 54th-minute sub Pete Terry's goal, following Boothe's breakaway, was always on the cards. Heyes keeps Town in the game.											
8	A	KIDDERMINSTER		10	L	0-3	0-3		Heyes	German	Prindiville	Jones	Fowler	Langley	Paterson	Lambert	Lancaster^	Flounders	Kiwomya*	Worthington/Hanson
	17/9		***2,062***	*9*	12			*Forsyth 11, 34p, Davies 41*	*Rose*	*Hodson*	*Webb*	*Weir*	*Brindley*	*Forsyth*	*Yates*	*Grainger !*	*Humphries**	*Davies*	*Hughes*	*Palmer*
								Ref: T Stephens	Kiddy won the title last season, but were denied entry to the Football League because their ground wasn't ready in time. They will struggle this time around, but not in this game. Town, however, feel the real turning point is the penalty, awarded when Humphries goes down under Heyes.											
9	A	MACCLESFIELD		10	D	1-1	0-1	Lancaster 83	Heyes*	German	Prindiville	Jones	Fowler	Langley"	Paterson	Flounders	Lambert	Worthington	Kiwomya^	Wilmot/Hanson/Lanc'
	24/9		*1,010*		13			*Tobin 27*	*Farrelly*	*Shepherd^*	*Bimson*	*Payne*	*Howarth*	*Sovell*	*Tobin*	*McDonald*	*Wood**	*Power*	*Lyons*	*Crisp/Kendall*
								Ref: D Adcock	Trailing at the interval, Bird changes tack, with the introduction of firstly Hanson, and then Lancaster. They play route-one stuff, and it pays off when the latter heads in Town's equaliser. For the first time, Town use three subs, including keeper Wilmot at half-time for a hobbling Heyes.											
10	A	DAGENHAM		9	W	4-1	2-0	P'son 29, Worth'ton 39, Kiwomya 65,	Heyes	Sunley	Prindiville	Jones	Fowler	Langley	Paterson	Lambert	Lancaster	Worthington	Kiwomya	
	1/10		*952*	*16*	16			*Richardson 74* [Lancaster 90]	*Boulder*	*Stebbing*	*Watts*	*Livett*	*Moore*	*Sorrell*	*Fowler*	*Richardson*	*Cavell*	*Greene*	*Broom*	
								Ref: T Howes	The Town players don't reach the Victoria Ground until 3.05 because of heavy traffic, but their performance on the field is well worth waiting for. Daggers' Bob Bolder is making his home debut, but he's badly at fault for the second goal. Kiwomya's goal is a stunning individual effort.											

No	Venue	Opponent / Date	Att	Pos	Res / Pts	F-A	H-T	Scorers, Times, Referees	1	2	3	4	5	6	7	8	9	10	11	subs used
11	H	ALTRINCHAM		10	D	1-1	1-1	Worthington 26	Heyes	Sunley	Fowler	Jones	**Hall**	Langley	Paterson	Lambert	Lancaster	Worthington	Kiwomya	
		8/10	1,175	*7*	17			*Terry 45*	*Collings*	*Cross*	*Heesom*	*France*	*Reid*	*O'Neill^*	*Terry*	*Harris*	*Green*	*Carmody**	*Sharratt*	*Butler/Ramoon*
								Ref: G Gordon	Leaders Altrincham arrive at the Shay with a 100% away record, having scored 18 goals from five matches. They prove a useful yardstick for Town, who actually go in front. Terry dispossesses Fowler to equalise right on half-time, and the Robins go on to dominate the second period.											
12	A	SOUTHPORT		11	L	0-4	0-1		Heyes	Sunley	Hall	Jones	Fowler	Circuit^	Leitch*	Lambert	Lancaster	Worthington	Kiwomya	Paterson/Langley
		11/10	*1,236*		17			*Cunningham 30, 60, Gamble 68, [Goulding 70]*	*McKenna*	*Ward*	*Fuller*	*Dove*	*Goulding*	*Lodge*	*Clark**	*Comstive*	*Haw^*	*Gamble*	*Cunningham*	*McDonald/Blackh'rst*
								Ref: J McGrath	This is another game covered by cable station Wire TV. They capture a wonder goal from ex-Town player Harvey Cunningham from all of 30 yards. After that, there's only one team in it. Southport's last two goals come from free-kicks, the first of which Gamble curls in from 20 yards.											
13	H	BATH		8	W	4-2	1-0	Kiwomya 29, 78, Lancaster 72, [Worthington 79]	Wilmot	Leitch	Hall	Jones*	Fowler	Sunley	Langley	Martin	Lancaster	Worthington	Kiwomya	Paterson
		15/10	775	*10*	20			*Mings 50, 68*	*Mogg*	*Gill*	*Taylor*	*Cousins*	*Brooks*	*Dicks*	*McLoughlin**	*Mings*	*Adcock*	*Birkby*	*Smart*	*Chenoweth*
								Ref: J Douglas	There are cries of 'Bird out' from the terracing as Town surrender their half-time lead and go behind. But then the players respond, and Bath are cleaned out. Lancaster equalises, then sets up Kiwomya for his second. Within seconds, Worthington lobs an amazing fourth from way out.											
14	A	FARNBOROUGH		10	L	0-2	0-1		Wilmot	Leitch	Prindiville	Jones*	Boardman	Hall	Martin	Langley	Lancaster	Worthington	Kiwomya	Fowler
		29/10	*815*	*8*	20			*Langley 28 (og), Baker 73*	*Taylor*	*Stemp*	*Pratt*	*Terry*	*Walters*	*Turkington*	*Boothe*	*Jones Mark*	*Baker*	*Jones Mur*	*Horton*	
								Ref: J Ross	Farnborough make amends for a 1-5 Cup defeat by Tiverton in midweek. They get lucky, though, when Kiwomya somehow hits the post from just five yards, and when Langley slices the ball over Wilmot. Baker gets the second from 25 yards after Boothe's shot comes back off the bar.											
15	H	STAFFORD		9	W	**6-0**	3-0	Lanc' 9, P'diville 28, Kiwomya 35, 67, [Lambert 46, Worthington 76]	Heyes	Fleming	Prindiville	Jones	Boardman	Martin	Fowler	Lambert	Lancaster	Worthington	Kiwomya	
		5/11	750	*22*	23				*Walker*	*Boughey*	*Bradshaw*	*Simpson*	*Penney*	*Smith*	*Williams*	*Crisp*	*May*	*Drewitt*	*Hassall**	*Griffiths*
								Ref: A Leake	In this 1.00 kick-off, Lancaster gives Town the lead after only nine minutes when Walker drops the ball. Halifax score at regular intervals, but Stafford's Leroy May could have scored three himself. Best goal of the day is Kiwomya's second, a magnificent solo effort beating three men.											
16	A	YEOVIL		11	L	1-3	0-0	Paterson 59	Heyes	Fleming	Prindiville	Jones	Boardman	Martin	Paterson	Fowler	Lancaster	Worth'gton^	Kiwomya*	Lambert/Flounders
		19/11	*1,801*	*21*	23			*White 80, Coates 82, 90*	*Mason*	*White*	*Ferns*	*Conning*	*McClelland*	*Cordice*	*Evans*	*Wallace*	*Wilson*	*Spencer**	*Flory^*	*Dobbins, Coates*
								Ref: P Briggs	Yeovil teenager Marc Coates played for the juniors in the morning. He comes off the bench in the 73rd minute to win the game and keep boss Brian Hall in a job. Town look to be heading for victory until White scores from 25 yards. Coates then scores twice, his second a lovely chip.											
17	H	KETTERING		9	W	2-1	2-1	Lambert 18, Paterson 41	Heyes	German	Prindiville	Jones	Boardman	Fowler	Paterson*	Lambert	Lancaster	Worthington	Kiwomya	Martin
		26/11	1,021	*7*	26			*Alford 4p*	*Benstead*	*Smith*	*Ashby*	*Saddington*	*Clarke*	*Taylor*	*Wright*	*Stringfell'w**	*Alford*	*Thomas*	*Brown*	*Barnes*
								Ref: R Pearson	With only four minutes gone, Heyes brings down Phil Brown, and Alford nets the penalty. Paterson sends over the corner for Lambert's quick response, then curls in another which is deflected straight in. His goal turns out to be the winner, despite the cut and thrust nature of the game.											
18	A	WELLING		11	D	1-1	1-0	Kiwomya 16	Heyes	German	Prindiville	Jones	Boardman	Fowler	Martin	Lambert	Lancaster	Worth'gton*	Kiwomya	Flounders
		10/12	*712*		27			*Copley 80*	*Hopping*	*Copley*	*Barrett**	*Ransom*	*Brown*	*Robinson*	*Hales*	*Barnes*	*Quamian*	*Robbins*	*Farley*	*Collins*
								Ref: P March	Town miss Paterson, who is finalising a £40,000 move to Scottish Premier League Falkirk. Still, without him, this game is there for the taking. Kiwomya makes the most of Worthington's deflected pass to put them ahead. Heyes should have cut out Robbins' cross for Welling's leveller.											
19	H	RUNCORN		10	W	4-0	1-0	Lancaster 36, Leitch 51, Worth'ton 71, [Kiwomya 78]	Heyes	Fleming	Prindiville	Jones !	Boardman	German*	Leitch	Lambert	Lancaster^	Worthington	Kiwomya	Hall/Hanson
		20/12	**733**	*15*	30				*Morris*	*Bates*	*Robertson*	*Ruffer*	*Hill*	*Byrne*	*Thomas*	*Connor*	*Hughes^*	*Brady*	*Smith**	*McInerney/Doherty*
								Ref: C Bassingdale	The only blot on this convincing win is Jones' 73rd-minute sending off for throwing the ball away, deemed by the referee as a second bookable offence. Leitch makes the most of a rare first-team start by scoring with a soft header. Kiwomya latches onto Hill's stray pass to net the fourth.											
20	A	GATESHEAD		8	W	2-1	2-1	Kiwomya 43, Worthington 44p	Heyes	Fleming	Prindiville	Jones	Boardman	Rathbone	Leitch*	Lambert	Lancaster	Worthington	Kiwomya	German
		26/12	*932*	*2*	33			*Boardman 10 (og)*	*Taylor*	*Watson**	*Farrey*	*Hine*	*Lacey^*	*Wrightson*	*Rowe*	*Dobson*	*Cavell*	*Cramman*	*Parkinson*	*Nobbs/Proudlcok*
								Ref: T Heilbron	The game is spoilt by gale-force winds, pouring rain, and a whistle-happy ref, who awards 45 free-kicks. Gateshead are having a good run this time, but after Boardman's headed own-goal, Halifax get two in a minute to win the game. Watson fells Kiwomya for Worthington's penalty.											
21	A	ALTRINCHAM		8	L	1-3	1-0	Hanson 22	Heyes	Fleming	Prindiville	Jones	Boardman	Rathbone	Hanson	Lambert	Lancaster	Worthington	Kiwomya*	German
		31/12	*1,059*		33			*Terry 68, Green 82, 88*	*Collings*	*Cross*	*Heesom*	*France*	*Shaw*	*Morton*	*Terry*	*Butler*	*Green*	*Martindale**	*Sharratt*	*Constable*
								Ref: S Baines	Bird is furious at the way his side collapses. Town hold a deserved first-half lead, but fortunes change after the break. Both sides have chances, but it's the Robins who take theirs. Terry picks up a loose ball to score the equaliser from long range. Green volleys Altrincham's killer third.											

No	Date		Att	Pos	Pt	F-A	H-T	Scorers, Times, and Referees	1	2	3	4	5	6	7	8	9	10	11	Subs used
22	H	GATESHEAD		8	W	3-2	1-2	Kiwomya 11, Worthington 73p,	Heyes	Fleming	Prindiville	Jones	Boardman	**Trotter**	Hanson	Lambert	Lancaster	Worthington	Kiwomya*	Gray
	2/1		1,099	*3*	36			*Lacey 25, Dobson 37* [Hanson 78]	*Taylor*	*Watson**	*Farrey*	*Hine !*	*Lacey*	*Wrightson*	*Rowe*	*Dobson*	*Cavell^*	*Cramman*	*Parkinson*	*Nobbs/Proudlock*
								Ref: F Taylor	The home fans are crying for the game to be postponed when Town trail at the interval. The pitch is frozen and acts like a skating rink. But it's a different tale when Worthington equalises with a penalty. Hine is sent off for handling on the line. Hanson then curls in a sensational winner.											
23	H	DOVER		7	W	4-0	1-0	Hanson 40, Rathbone 54, Lancaster 59,	Heyes	Fleming	Prindiville	Trotter	Boardman	Rathbone	Hanson	Lambert	Lancaster	Worthington	Kiwomya*	Gray
	7/1		1,017	*17*	39			[Prindiville 90]	*Williams*	*Budden*	*Carter*	*O'Connell*	*Scott*	*Walker*	*Donn*	*Browne**	*Blewden*	*Leworthy*	*Milton*	*O'Brien*
								Ref: D Laws	When 'Basil' Rathbone, one of the most popular characters ever at the Shay, despatches the ball into the net from just outside the box, he runs 60 yards with teammates in hot pursuit. It's the 36-year-old's first goal for over four years, and together with his performance, inspires the rest.											
24	H	WOKING		7	W	4-0	1-0	Hanson 32, 63, Lancaster 67,	**Pettinger**	Fleming	Prindiville	Jones	Boardman	Rathbone	Hanson	Lambert	Lancaster*	Worthington	Leitch	Trotter
	4/2		1,038		42			[Worthington 81]	*Batty*	*Tucker*	*Wye L*	*Fielder*	*Brown*	*Tierling**	*Wye S*	*Ellis^*	*Steele*	*Payne*	*Walker*	*Rattray/Alexander*
								Ref: G Bradbury	Chairman Jim Brown descibes this game as 'make or break'. Geoff Chapple's Woking, also hoping to catch leaders Macclesfield, are a tough side, and the scoreline doesn't do them justice. Two goals in a four-minute spell effectively end the contest. Worthington squeezes in the fourth.											
25	A	STAFFORD		5	W	1-0	0-0	Hanson 49	Pettinger	Fleming	Prindiville	Jones	Boardman*	Trotter	Hanson	Lambert	Lancaster	Worthington	Kiwomya^	German/Fowler
	7/2		*844*	*22*	45				*Walker*	*Brown*	*Hassall*	*Simpson*	*Squires*	*Bradshaw*	*Griffiths*	*O'Toole*	*Boughey*	*Drewitt*	*Williams*	
								Ref: N Hancox	In front of the Wire TV cameras, Hanson scores for the fifth consecutive Conference match. He shrugs off Bradshaw's challenge before firing home. Yet the league's bottom side give Town a fright. Both Drewitt and Simpson see efforts hit the post, and Williams misses an open goal.											
26	H	DAGENHAM		4	D	1-1	0-0	Kiwomya 85	Pettinger	German	Prindiville	Jones	Boardman	Trotter	Hanson	Lambert	Lancaster*	Worthington	Kiwomya	Rathbone
	14/2		927	*20*	46			*Haag 76*	*Bolder*	*Stebbing*	*Watts*	*Greene*	*Conner*	*Groves**	*Cook*	*Richardson*	*Haag*	*McDonough*	*Devereux^*	*Gammons/O'Sullivan*
								Ref: M Mountain	Third place is up for grabs if Town can win. In the end, though, they have to rely on Kiwomya's fluke 40-yard free-kick, carried by the wind, to gain only a point. It's better than nothing. Haag's goal, after Pettinger fails to gather the ball, threatens to win it for the struggling Daggers.											
27	H	MERTHYR		5	D	2-2	2-1	Hanson 7, Kiwomya 27p	Pettinger	Fleming	Prindiville	Jones	Boardman	Rathbone*	Hanson	Lambert	Lancaster	Leitch	Kiwomya	German
	25/2		910	*19*	47			*Webley 25, 89*	*Wager*	*York*	*Hopkins^*	*Beattie*	*Abrahams*	*Jones*	*Rogers*	*Williams**	*Mitchell*	*Webley*	*Dyer*	*French/Jenkins*
								Ref: F Taylor	Jim Brown has threatened to quit if the councillors don't approve a plan to develop a new stadium at Thrum Hall. At the Shay, Merthyr leave it late to gain a draw. The linesman awards a penalty, scored by Kiwomya, when Hopkins handles, but Webley's weak shot denies Town victory.											
28	A	NORTHWICH		5	L	0-3	0-2		Pettinger	German	Prindiville	Jones	Boardman	Trotter	Hanson	Lambert	Lancaster^	Leitch*	Fowler	Kiwomya/**Beddard**
	28/2		*831*	*10*	47			*Cooke 32, 38, Williams 64*	*Greygoose*	*Tinson*	*Jones*	*Abel*	*Parker*	*Walters**	*Duffy*	*Butler*	*Cooke*	*Williams*	*Baah*	*Oghani*
								Ref: G Shaw	Brown has indeed gone, after councillors voted against selling the Shay, therefore scuppering plans for a ground-share scheme with the rugby club. Football League status seems light years away after this defeat. Northwich's fourth successive victory is aided by two goalkeeping errors.											
29	H	MACCLESFIELD		5	L	0-1	0-1		Pettinger	German	Prindiville	Jones	Boardman	Trotter	Hanson	Lambert	Lancaster	Hutchinson	**Adekola**	
	7/3		1,002	*1*	47			*Lyons 42*	*Farrelly*	*Norman**	*Bradshaw*	*Payne*	*Howarth*	*Sorvel*	*Askey*	*Lyons*	*Wood*	*Power*	*Monk^*	*Tobin/Murray*
								Ref: G Frankland	John Stockwell is the new chairman, but he, like John Bird, knows that any faint title hopes Halifax may have had have disappeared after this defeat. Town show too much respect for Sammy McIlroy's table-toppers. Darren Lyons gets the all-important goal, heading in at the far post.											
30	A	KETTERING		7	L	**1-5**	0-1	Beddard 85 *[Brown 88]*	Pettinger	Fleming	Prindiville	Jones	Boardman	Hutchinson	Hanson	Lambert	German*	Adekola	Kiwomya^	Trotter/Beddard
	11/3		*1,330*	*6*	47			*Arnold 12, 54, 67, Thomas 63,*	*Gleasure*	*Reed*	*Ashby*	*Holden*	*Saddington*	*Donald*	*Brown*	*Thomas*	*Alford*	*Stringfellow*	*Arnold*	
								Ref: K Taylor	Dave Lancaster is not included in the squad, and he will be offloaded to Bury as Town look to make cuts. Without him, the Shaymen start well, but Adekola rues his 41st-minute penalty miss. Arnold goes on to complete a simple hat-trick, but best goal of the day is Beddard's 25-yarder.											
31	H	WELLING		7	W	4-0	3-0	Hutchinson 19, Kiwom' 21, Flem'g 44,	**Ford**	Fleming	Prindiville	Jones	Boardman^	Trotter	Hanson*	Lambert	Leitch	Hutchinson	Kiwomya	Beddard/German
	18/3		783	*18*	50			[German 64]	*Williams*	*Horton*	*Barrett**	*Hales^*	*Brown !*	*Robinson*	*Quamina*	*Farley*	*Copley*	*Robbins*	*Barnes*	*Smith/Burgess*
								Ref: G Laws	Town have been hit with a £140,000 tax bill and Rathbone has left the club. But a week of trauma is ended with this easy victory. Hutchinson strokes home the first, and Welling are three down when they lose Brown for a second bookable offence. Town could easily have scored more.											

No	Date	H/A	Opponent	Att	Pos	Pts	Res	F-A	H-T	Scorers, Times, and Referees	Line-up and match report
32	20/3	A	STEVENAGE	*1,293*	7 *8*	50	L	0-1	0-0	*Venables 71* Ref: E Green	Ford, Fleming, Prindiville, Jones, Trotter, Hutchinson, German, Lambert, Beddard, Worthington, Kiwomya *Gallagher, Webster, Sodje, Smith, Rattle, Simpson, Beevor, Hayles, Crawshaw, Venables, Lynch* Victory for the Shaymen could have lifted them into second place. But they are left to look back at Worthington's costly 49th-minute penalty miss as the game's turning point. He crashes his kick against the bar, then at the other end Venables scores when Town fail to clear a corner.
33	25/3	H	YEOVIL	816	5 *21*	53	W	2-1	1-1	German 44, Lambert 70 *Whale 13* Ref: D Bryan	Ford, Fleming, Prindiville, Jones, Trotter, German, Leitch*, Lambert, Beddard, Worthington, Hutchinson, Hanson *Mason, Llewellyn, Hornby, Cordice, Benbow, Dillon, Brock, Whale*, Black, Le Bihan, Coates^, Evans/Powell* The accountants tell the club to go into voluntary liquidation. With the game being billed as Town's last ever, they come from behind to win. Ford hands Whale a tap-in, then German pounces after Worthington's volley comes back off the bar. Lambert's header from a corner wins it.
34	27/3	A	BATH	*475*	3 *14*	54	D	0-0	0-0	Ref: P Armstrong	Ford, Fleming, Prindiville, Jones, **Dunphy**, Trotter, German, Lambert, Beddard, Worthington, Hutchinson *Mogg, Gill, Dicks, Cousins, Crowley, Birks, Hedges, Smart, Birkby, Adcock*, Chenoweth, Spencer* Typically, Tony Ricketts' Romans side hold Town to a draw – it's their twelfth of the season. Bird has had to release Kiwomya now, so under the circumstances he's happy with the point. Beddard has the best chance, but after rounding keeper Mogg, Hedges clears his shot off the line.
35	1/4	H	STEVENAGE	753	7 *8*	54	L	0-2	0-2	*Venables 40, Fortune-West 45* Ref: J Devine	Ford, Fleming, Prindiville, Jones, Dunphy*, Trotter, German, Lambert, Hanson, Worthington, Hutchinson^, Boardman/Beddard *Gallagher, Sodje*, Rattle, Webster, Fortune-West, Simpson, Hayles, Beevor, Venables, Lynch, Smith, Hedman* This is a lacklustre performance from the Shaymen. Stevenage clearly want to win the game more and do so courtesy of Venables' goal, made by Lynch following hesitancy in the Town defence, and through Fortune-West in first-half injury-time. John Bird feels sympathy for the fans.
36	8/4	H	STALYBRIDGE	802	8 *15*	55	D	1-1	1-1	Beddard 31 *Megson 32* Ref: D Oliver	Heyes, Fleming, Prindiville, Jones, Boardman, Trotter, Leitch, German, Hanson, Worthington, Beddard *Cooksey, Ogley, Coathup, Frain, Shaughn'sy, Hall, Burke, Megson, Anderson*, Clayton, Ryan, Wheeler* The only good thing about this game is the sunny weather. Peter Wragg makes his first return to the Shay, but the game is a poor one. Beddard puts Town in front, but within a minute the scores are level again. Megson enjoys scoring against his old club, a 20-yard shot high into the net.
37	11/4	A	MERTHYR	***403***	8 *20*	55	L	0-2	0-0	*Rogers 80, Webley 85* Ref: N Hancox	Heyes, Fleming, Prindiville, Jones, Boardman, Trotter, German*, Lambert, Hanson, Worthington, **Johnson**, Beddard *Wager, Holtam, York, Davies, O'Brien, Rogers, Loss, Jones N, Dyer, Webley, Jenkins*, Scott* Wire TV are filming Town for the third time this season, but this is their second defeat in front of the cameras. Victory for Merthyr helps them steer clear of the relegation zone. They rely on two late goals. Rogers scores off a corner, before Webley makes the most of slack defending.
38	15/4	H	TELFORD	609	8	56	D	1-1	0-0	Prindiville 67 *Griffiths 72* Ref: S Griffiths	Heyes, Fleming, Prindiville, Trotter, Boardman, Hutchinson, German, Lambert, Hanson, Worthington, Johnson *Goodwin, Fowler, Foster, Kearney, Niblett, Wilcox, Myers, Crisp, Wilson, Griffiths, Holden*, Crookes* In the 60th minute, Johnson has the ball in the net. The ref gives a goal, but changes his mind when he sees Goodwin lying in a heap, and gives a free-kick. The keeper is at fault for Prindiville's legal goal, a cross-cum-shot he fails to deal with. Griffiths sees to it that the lead doesn't last.
39	17/4	A	TELFORD	*829*	8	57	D	1-1	1-0	Johnson 6 *Myers 58* Ref: M Fletcher	Heyes, Fleming*, Prindiville, Jones, Boardman^, Trotter, Hutchinson, Lambert, Hanson, Worthington, Johnson, German/Beddard *Hughes, Fowler, Foster, Kearney, Niblett, Wilcox, Myers, Crisp, Wilson, Griffiths, Holden*, Crookes* The two sides meet again in a quick return. This time Johnson scores a goal that does count when he pounces with the game in its infancy. He could have had a hat-trick. But while Town are readjusting following injury to Boardman, Myers scores off a free-kick for a repeat scoreline.
40	22/4	A	BROMSGROVE	*897*	7 *11*	60	W	1-0	0-0	Hanson 73 Ref: K Woolmer	Heyes, Fleming, Prindiville, Jones, Boardman, Trotter, German, Lambert, Hanson, Worthington, Johnson*, Beddard *Judge, Clarke, Brighton, Richardson, Skelding, Gaunt, Smith*, Stott, Taylor, Warner, Marlowe, Whitehead* For all the world, it looks as if Halifax Town will fold at the end of the season. For the players, however, it has to be business as usual as they make the trip to the Victoria Ground. Dave Hanson's goal ends a run of six games without a win, although Bromsgrove claim he used his hand.
41	29/4	H	KIDDERMINSTER	**1,754**	8	60	L	1-2	1-0	Bancroft 45 (og) *Dearlove 72, Yates 85* Ref: C Webster	Heyes, Fleming, Prindiville, Jones, Boardman*, Trotter, German, Lambert, Hanson, Worthington, Beddard, Hutchinson *Steadman, Hodson, Bancroft, Webb, Brindley, Forsyth, Deakin*, Cartwright^, Yates, Dearlove, Hughes, Eades/Palmer* The club will package a video of this game, with the words 'We will fight until the end' emblazoned across the front. In the match, ironically, they don't. They take the lead on half-time when Bancroft turns in Prindiville's cross, but surrender when Kiddy score with two simple goals.
42	6/5	A	RUNCORN	*985*	8 *9*	63	W	3-0	0-0	Hanson 49, 60, 71 Ref: C Gordon	Heyes, Fleming, Prindiville, Jones, Boardman, Trotter, **Horner***, Lambert, Hanson, Worthington, Beddard, Hutchinson *Morris, Bates, Robertson, Byrne, Finley, Doherty, Thomas, Connor, Hughes*, McInerney^, Ellis, Smith/Taylor* With the fans' help, an initial target of £30,000 has been met. In glorious sunshine here, Halifax finish in style, with Hanson scoring a rocket from 20 yards to complete a memorable hat-trick. At the end, the travelling army invades the pitch, singing, 'There'll always be the Shaymen.'

	Home	Away
Average	974	1,106

FA Cup

Rd		Opponent	Pos	Res	F-A	H-T	Scorers, Times, and Referees	1	2	3	4	5	6	7	8	9	10	11	subs used
4Q	H	LANCASTER	8	W	3-1	1-0	Worthington 10, 90, Lancaster 75	Wilmot	Leitch	Hall	Jones	Boardman	Langley	Fowler*	Lambert	Lancaster	Worthington	Kiwomya	Paterson
22/10		779 *NPL*					*Diggle 90*	*Newall*	*Wooleson^*	*Stimpson*	*Eatough*	*Byrom**	*Hartley*	*Kennedy*	*Sharples*	*Diggle*	*Borrowdale*	*Flannery*	*Curwen/Baker*
							Ref: W Burns												

Town are playing in the qualifying rounds for the first time since 1923-24. They never look like losing, but leave it late to seal victory. Halifax sit on a one-goal lead until the aptly-named Lancaster scores a close-range second. Worthington's chipped effort in injury-time is the best goal.

Rd		Opponent	Pos	Res	F-A	H-T	Scorers, Times, and Referees	1	2	3	4	5	6	7	8	9	10	11	subs used
1	H	RUNCORN	9	D	1-1	0-0	Kiwomya 60	Heyes	German	Prindiville	Jones	Boardman	Fowler	Paterson	Lambert	Lancaster	Worth'gton*	Kiwomya	Flounders
12/11		1,286 *13*					*Thomas 57p*	*Morris*	*Bates*	*Robertson*	*Lee**	*Hill*	*Anderson*	*Thomas*	*Connor*	*Hughes*	*Ruffer*	*McInerney*	*Smith*
							Ref: P Rejer												

Halifax are concerned at dwindling crowds, but are heartened by this attendance. Despite not winning, they will welcome the revenue another game will bring. Runcorn's Morris is outstanding, but he can't stop Kiwomya scoring just after Thomas's penalty for hands against Boardman.

Rd		Opponent	Pos	Res	F-A	H-T	Scorers, Times, and Referees	1	2	3	4	5	6	7	8	9	10	11	subs used
1R	A	RUNCORN	11	W	3-1	0-0	Lancaster 77, 97, Lambert 95	Heyes	German	Prindiville	Jones	Boardman	Fowler	Paterson	Lambert	Lancaster	Worthington	Flounders	
21/11		*1,288* *18*			*aet*		*Pugh 87*	*Morris*	*Bates*	*Robertson*	*Ruffer*	*Hill*	*Anderson*	*Thomas*	*Connor^*	*Hughes**	*McInerney*	*Smith*	*Pugh/Godfrey*
							Ref: P Rejer												

After a fire at their Canal Street ground, Runcorn are temporarily playing their home games at Witton's Wincham Park. In this cracking replay, Pugh's curling shot sends the game into extra-time. But headed goals by Lambert, the game's best player, and Lancaster, send Town through.

Rd		Opponent	Pos	Res	F-A	H-T	Scorers, Times, and Referees	1	2	3	4	5	6	7	8	9	10	11	subs used
2	H	MANSFIELD	9	D	0-0	0-0		Heyes	German	Prindiville	Jones	Boardman	Fowler	Paterson	Lambert	Lancaster	Worth'gton*	Kiwomya	Flounders
3/12		2,396 *3:13*						*Ward*	*Boothroyd*	*Barraclough*	*Holland*	*Howarth*	*Aspinall*	*Ireland*	*Doolan*	*Wilkinson*	*Hadley*	*Campbell*	
							Ref: P Harrison												

Town are favourites to win, and have the better of things in this all-ticket match. But Kiwomya fluffs the game's best chance after 21 minutes. He rounds Ward, only to see Aspinall clear off the line. Andy King's Stags are disappointing, and are happy to take Town back to Field Mill.

Rd		Opponent	Pos	Res	F-A	H-T	Scorers, Times, and Referees	1	2	3	4	5	6	7	8	9	10	11	subs used
2R	A	MANSFIELD	11	L	1-2	1-0	Lancaster 26	Heyes	German	Prindiville	Jones	Boardman	Fowler*	Martin	Lambert	Lancaster	Flounders	Kiwomya	Hall
13/12		*2,648* *3:14*					*Aspinall 71, Holland 90*	*Ward*	*Boothroyd*	*Barraclough*	*Holland*	*Aspinall*	*Peters*	*Ireland*	*Campbell*	*Wilkinson*	*Pearson*	*Noteman*	
							Ref: P Harrison												

A home tie with Graham Taylor's Wolves looks to be Town's reward when Lancaster puts them ahead. Aspinall is fortunate when his soft shot loops over Heyes. Town more than match their 3rd Division opponents, but with extra-time looming Paul Holland heads in a dramatic winner.

FA Trophy

Rd		Opponent	Pos	Res	F-A	H-T	Scorers, Times, and Referees	1	2	3	4	5	6	7	8	9	10	11	subs used
1	A	BAMBER BRIDGE	7	L	0-1	0-1		Wilmot	Fleming	Prindiville	Trotter	Fowler	Rathbone^	Hanson*	Lambert	Lancaster	Worthington	Kiwomya	Leitch/German
24/1		*1,058* *UL:1*					*Mayers 23*	*Berryman*	*Brown*	*McHugh*	*Milligan*	*Baldwin*	*Senior*	*Black*	*Mayers*	*Greenwood**	*Thomas*	*Leaver*	*Crabbe*
							Ref: J McGrath												

Bamber Bridge, recently only playing parks football, include in their side ex-Shaymen Nigel Greenwood and John Thomas. The original game was postponed because of a waterlogged pitch. Town underperform, whilst Kenny Mayers' goal from 20 yards gives Bamber their finest hour.

		Home						Away					
		P	W	D	L	F	A	W	D	L	F	A	Pts
1	Macclesfield	42	14	3	4	39	18	10	5	6	31	22	80
2	Woking	42	11	8	2	46	23	10	4	7	30	31	75
3	Southport	42	13	4	4	46	21	8	5	8	22	29	72
4	Altrincham	42	10	3	8	34	27	10	5	6	43	33	68
5	Stevenage	42	10	4	7	40	27	10	3	8	28	22	67
6	Kettering	42	12	5	4	40	25	7	5	9	33	31	67
7	Gateshead	42	12	4	5	28	13	7	6	8	33	40	67
8	HALIFAX	42	11	6	4	46	20	6	6	9	22	34	63
9	Runcorn	42	11	7	3	39	28	5	3	13	20	43	58
10	Northwich	42	7	8	6	39	30	7	7	7	38	36	57
11	Kidderminster	42	6	5	10	28	29	10	4	7	35	32	57
12	Bath	42	10	6	5	35	26	5	6	10	20	30	57
13	Bromsgrove	42	9	7	5	42	35	5	6	10	24	34	55
14	Farnborough	42	8	5	8	23	31	7	5	9	22	33	55
15	Dagenham	42	8	5	8	28	32	5	8	8	28	37	52
16	Dover	42	6	10	5	28	25	5	6	10	20	30	49
17	Welling	42	9	3	9	31	33	4	7	10	26	41	49
18	Stalybridge	42	9	6	6	29	27	2	8	11	23	45	47
19	Telford	42	9	9	3	30	20	1	7	13	23	42	46
20	Merthyr	42	10	4	7	37	27	1	7	13	16	36	44
21	Stafford	42	5	5	11	29	34	4	6	11	24	45	38
22	Yeovil*	42	5	8	8	29	31	3	6	12	21	40	37
		924	205	125	132	766	582	132	125	205	582	766	1260

* 1 pt deducted

Odds & ends

Double wins: (1) Woking.
Double losses: (0).

Won from behind: (6) Gateshead (h & a), Bath (h), Bromsgrove (h), Kettering (h), Yeovil (h).
Lost from in front: (4) Kidderminster (h), Altrincham (a), Yeovil (a), Mansfield (FAC) (a).

High spots: Unbeaten in the opening six games – a then club record.
Six games unbeaten, including four consecutive victories, up to 25 February.
Beating Stafford 6-0 on 5 November.
Winning 3-0 at Runcorn on the final day.
The supporters dipping into their own pockets to help save the club.
Mick Rathbone's stunning goal against Dover at the Shay.

Low spots: Three consecutive defeats up to 11 March.
Six games without a win up to 22 April.
Losing 1-5 at Kettering.
Losing at Bamber Bridge in the FA Trophy.
The announcement in March that the club is heavily in debt and being on the verge of extinction.

Player of the Year: Steve Prindiville.
Ever-presents: (0).
Hat-tricks: Dave Hanson (1).
Leading scorer: Andy Kiwomya (15).

	Appearances						Goals			
	Lge	Sub	FAC	Sub	FAT	Sub	Lge	FAC	FAT	Tot
Adekola, David	2									
Beddard, Elliott	6	7					2			2
Boardman, Craig	32	1	5							
Circuit, Steve	1									
Dunphy, Sean	2									
Fleming, Paul	23				1		1			1
Flounders, Andy	9	2	2	2			1			1
Ford, Stuart	5									
Fowler, Lee	12	3	5		1					
German, David	22	6	4			1	3			3
Gray, Ryan		2								
Hall, David	4	1	1	1						
Hanson, Dave	26	4			1		11			11
Heyes, Darren	28		4							
Horner, Noel	1									
Hutchinson, Ian	9	2					1			1
Johnson, Simon	4						1			1
Jones, Alex	39		5				2			2
Kiwomya, Andy	29	1	4		1		14	1		15
Lambert, Colin	38	1	5		1		3	1		4
Lancaster, Dave	21	3	5		1		7	4		11
Langley, Kevin	13	1	1							
Leitch, Grant	11		1			1	1			1
Martin, Dean	5	1	1							
Paterson, Jamie	13	2	3	1			5			5
Pettinger, Paul	7									
Prindiville, Steve	39		4		1		4			4
Rathbone, Mick	5	1			1		1			1
Sunley, Mark	7	1								
Trotter, Mick	18	2			1					
Wilmot, Richard	2	1	1		1					
Worthington, Gary	29	3	4		1		9	2		11
(own-goals)							2			2
32 players used	**462**	**45**	**55**	**4**	**11**	**2**	**68**	**8**		**76**

No	Date	Att	Pos	Pt	F-A	H-T	Scorers, Times, and Referees	1	2	3	4	5	6	7	8	9	10	11	subs used
1	A HEDNESFORD			L	0-3	0-0		Heyes	**Thompson**	Prindiville	**O'Regan**	**Stoneman**	**Timons**	Horner	Johnson*	Beddard^	Worthington	**Brown**	**Ludlow/Midwood**
	19/8	*1,594*		0			*Essex 56, Lambert 69, Wright 83*	*Cooksey*	*Yates*	*Collins*	*Simpson*	*Essex*	*Fitzpatrick*	*Street*	*Lambert*	*Hanson*	*Devine**	*O'Connor*	*Wright*
							Ref: S French	Hednesford are new to Conference football, and they have a new ground, too. New-look Halifax are the first visitors to Keys Park. The Pitmen have signed two Town players in Lambert and Hanson, and the former stabs home their second goal, as Hednesford stroll to a comfortable win.											
2	H MACCLESFIELD			W	1-0	0-0	Stoneman 85	**Woods**	Thompson	Brown	Horner	Stoneman	Timons	O'Regan	Johnson	Midwood	Worthington	Beddard	
	22/8	**1,169**		3				*Williams*	*Locke*	*Bradshaw*	*Payne*	*Howarth !*	*Sorvel*	*Lyons**	*McDonald*	*Coates^*	*Power*	*Margison*	*Cavell/Clark*
							Ref: B Lowe	Woods plays because Heyes, with Prindiville, is stuck in traffic. Margison puts a first-half penalty wide for Macclesfield, then on 57 minutes, Howarth is sent off for a second bookable offence. A draw looks likely until Stoneman goes on a run, then fires in off the post from 25 yards.											
3	H SLOUGH		18	L	1-2	1-0	Johnson 33	Heyes	Thompson	Prindiville	Trotter	Stoneman	Timons	O'Regan	Johnson	Midwood*	Worthington	Brown	**Wilson**
	26/8	917		3			*Baron 56, 90*	*Preddie*	*Clement*	*Fiore*	*Harvey*	*Baron*	*Connor**	*Lee^*	*Pye*	*West*	*Bushay*	*Blackman*	*Blunden/Bateman*
							Ref: D Morrall	When Johnson scores after Midwood's header comes back off the bar, Town look good for a convincing win. But Slough skipper Trevor Baron pops up with two identical headers from corners, his second in injury-time, to win it. Minutes earlier, Worthington sky-highed a penalty kick.											
4	A STALYBRIDGE		20	L	0-1	0-0		Heyes	Thompson	Prindiville	Trotter	Stoneman	Timons	O'Regan	Wilson*	Johnson	Worthington	Horner	Beddard
	29/8	*905*		3			*Wheeler 90*	*Sherwood*	*Jones S*	*Coathup*	*Frain*	*Jones A*	*Hall*	*Shaw*	*Bauress*	*Higinb'th'm**	*Birk*	*Ryan*	*Wheeler*
							Ref: A Butler	The Shaymen are sunk by another injury-time goal. This time it's sub Paul Wheeler who does the damage with a looping shot into the corner. John Bird is happy with his side's performance. Stoneman goes closest, but his header is cleared off the line by former team-mate Alex Jones.											
5	H WELLING		14	W	2-1	2-1	O'Regan 17, Johnson 21	Heyes	Timons	Prindiville	Brown*	Stoneman	Trotter	Thompson	O'Regan	Johnson^	Worthi'gton"	Midwood	Horner/W'son/Bed'rd
	2/9	766		6			*Copley 42*	*Harris**	*Brown*	*Horton*	*Watts*	*Copley*	*Berry*	*Wordsworth*	*Rutherford*	*Sykes^*	*Farley*	*Barnes*	*Wastell/Smith*
							Ref: D Oliver	Injuries hinder Town's chances, and Brown, Johnson and Worthington all have to leave the field. But to their credit, Town hang on for a hard-earned victory. They go two goals up, but Copley's header sets up an interesting second half. Town survive, but are clearly relieved at the end.											
6	H GATESHEAD		11	W	2-0	1-0	Beddard 25, Midwood 83	Heyes	Timons	Prindiville	Brown	Stoneman	Trotter	Thompson	O'Regan	Midwood	Wilson*	Beddard	Ludlow
	5/9	743	*19*	9				*Musgrove*	*Watson*	*Dowson*	*Hine*	*Wrightson*	*Rowe*	*Ord^*	*Thompson*	*Proudlock*	*Cramman**	*Kitchen*	*Farrey/Dobson*
							Ref: G Atkins	Heyes is Town's hero, as he makes four excellent point-blank saves to keep out a useful Gateshead side that Bird knows quite a bit about. Four of their side used to play under him at Hartlepool. Beddard heads Halifax in front, but it needs Midwood's late strike to make the game safe.											
7	A WOKING		13	L	0-2	0-1		Heyes	Timons*	Prindiville	Brown	Stoneman	Trotter	Thompson	O'Regan	Midwood	Worthington	Beddard^	Wilson/Horner
	9/9	***2,065***		9			*Walker 29p, Steele 68*	*Batty*	*Tucker*	*Wye*	*Fielder*	*Brown*	*Crumplin*	*Reid*	*Ellis*	*Peters*	*Hay*	*Walker**	*Steele*
							Ref: G Wilard	Woking make it four wins out of four at home, whilst for Town, it's a third successive away defeat. After dominating the early stages, Town concede a penalty when O'Regan hauls down Walker, who scores from the spot. It's their first shot on target. Steele scores with their other.											
8	H NORTHWICH		8	W	2-0	1-0	Stoneman 31, Simpson 66 (og)	Heyes	Timons	Prindiville	Brown	Stoneman	Trotter	Thompson	O'Regan	Midwood	Beddard !	Constable	
	12/9	829		12				*Newall*	*Burgess^*	*Jones !*	*Tinson*	*Simpson*	*Walters*	*Duffy*	*Butler*	*Humphries*	*Clayton**	*Vicary"*	*Ogh'ni/McA'y/Hugh's*
							Ref: P Joslin	There is a double sending off in the 58th minute, when Beddard lashes out after Mark Jones' rash challenge. Beddard was a lot happier when his header set up Stoneman for a simple opener. Constable, back for a second spell, curls in a free-kick which Simpson turns into his own net.											
9	H KIDDERMINSTER		11	L	0-2	0-0		Heyes	Timons	Prindiville	Brown	Stoneman	Trotter	Thompson	O'Regan	Midwood	Beddard*	Constable	Worthington
	16/9	1,008	*2*	12			*Casey 64, May 90*	*Steadman*	*Hodson*	*Bancroft*	*Webb*	*Brindley*	*Yates*	*Hughes*	*Casey*	*May*	*Davies*	*Cartwright*	
							Ref: C Foy	High-flying Kiddy are grateful for Stoneman's weak header that lets in Casey to give them the lead and put them joint top of the table. Town feel fortunes are against them. May's injury-time goal is blatantly offside, an incensed O'Regan has to be retrained by colleagues at the end.											
10	A GATESHEAD			L	2-3	0-3	Worthington 62, Midwood 73	Heyes	Timons*	Prindiville	Brown	Stoneman	Trotter	Thompson	O'Regan	Midwood	Worthington	Constable	Beddard
	20/9	*559*		12			*Th'pson 23, Marquis 29, Cramman 45*	*Musgrave*	*Watson*	*Dowson*	*Marquis*	*Wrightson*	*Rowe*	*Cramman*	*Thompson^*	*Trott**	*Proudlock*	*Kitchen*	*Dobson/Hine*
							Ref: G Laws	Town's miserable away form continues, despite a sterling second-half fightback. Cramman sprints clear to score Gateshead's third goal in first half injury-time to give Town a mountain to climb. They attempt it, Midwood's low shot takes them close, but Town just fail to save the game.											

No	H/A	Opponent	Att	Pos	Res	F-A	H-T	Scorers, Times, and Referees	1	2	3	4	5	6	7	8	9	10	11	subs used
11	A	ALTRINCHAM		13	L	2-3	0-2	Trotter 46, Worthington 68	Heyes	Timons	Prindiville	Brown	Stoneman	Trotter	Thompson	O'Regan	Midwood	Worthington	Constable*	Hendrick
	23/9		1,085		12			Sharratt 17, Green 33, Hardy 53	Collings	Cross	Heesom	France	Butler	Hardy	Terry*	Whalley	Green	Carmody	Sharratt	Allan
								Ref: S Brand	The Shaymen play their part in a thriller, but still come off second best. Green's 35-yard lob over a stranded Heyes is worth going miles to see, and puts the home side 2-0 up. Town make a fight of it after the break. In the last minute, Midwood's shot is pushed onto the post by Collings.											
12	H	MORECAMBE			D	1-1	1-1	Midwood 41	Heyes	Thompson	Prindiville	Brown	Stoneman	Trotter	Hendrick	O'Regan	Midwood	Worthington	Graham	
	26/9		910		13			Norman 33	Banks	Burns	Rushton	Grimshaw	Hughes	Maddock	Knowles*	Comstive	McCluskie !	Ceroalo^	Norman	Harvey/Coleman
								Ref: J Robinson	A shortage of stewards means the supporters can't change ends at half-time. Halifax don't play well, but at least they bring an end to a run of three successive defeats. John Norman puts the visitors ahead, but Midwood equalises following a scramble which sees Worthington hit a post.											
13	H	DOVER		9	W	1-0	0-0	Hendrick 48	Heyes	Thompson	Prindiville	Timons	Stoneman	Trotter	Brown	Brook	Midwood	Worth'gton*	Hendrick	Hart^/Horner
	30/9		905		16				Ebbli	Donn	Dalli	Foot	Budden	Strouts^	Darlington*	Furney"	Restarick	Leworthy	Hayes	Theo'/Rogers/Walker
								Ref: M Pike	Former England winger Peter Taylor has taken over at Dover following John Ryan's sacking. Their keeper Ebbli looks like one of the Beatles. Bird includes a 'proven goalscorer' in Gary Brook in the Town side, but it's Hendrick who grabs the only goal – and he does play in a band.											
14	A	RUNCORN		7	W	1-0	1-0	Midwood 44	Heyes	Thompson	Prindiville	Timons	Stoneman	Trotter	Brown	Johnson	Midwood	Brook	Hendrick	
	7/10		637		19				Thomson	Bates"	Robertson	Ellis	Brady	Byrne	Warder*	Doherty N	Doherty M	Bignall^	McInerney	Smith/Taylor/Ruffer
								Ref: T Jones	Runcorn have won their last three games at Canal Street, but Town are happy to end that sequence, and also one of their own. Victory means they collect their first away points. It's a scrappy game won by one fleeting moment of quality, Midwood's header in from Prindiville's cross.											
15	H	STEVENAGE		9	L	2-3	2-3	Brown 27, Johnson 31	Heyes	Thompson	Prindiville	Timons*	Stoneman	Trotter	O'Regan	Johnson	Midwood	Worth'gton^	Brown	Hendrick/Beddard
	14/10		858	11	19			Lynch 16, Smith 23, Sodje 41	Wilmot	Webster	Mutchell	Sodje	Smith	Barrowcliff	Simpson	Browne	Crawshaw	Lynch	Hayles	
								Ref: G Laws	The game starts with heavy mist hanging over the ground. By the time it has lifted, Town are 0-2 down. Lynch scores the first from 25 yards. Halifax do well to pull it back, but Sodje, who is refused permission to wear his bandana, heads what proves to be the winner before the break.											
16	A	FARNBOROUGH		11	D	0-0	0-0		Woods	Smith	Prindiville	O'Regan	Trotter	Brown !	Hendrick	Cochrane	Midwood	Worthg'ton*	Horner	Beddard
	28/10		908		20				Mackenzie	Baker S	Stemp	Coney	Day	Robson	Boothe	Harlow	Senior	Denny	Baker K	
								Ref: D Crick	Farnborough fail to make it a twelfth win in a 13-match unbeaten run, but Woods has to work overtime. Halifax play for 26 minutes without Brown, sent off for the second successive game, this time for a professional foul. Non-playing sub for Farnborough is ex-Shayman Ian Juryeff.											
17	H	BATH		9	W	3-1	3-0	Midwood 13, 45, Cochrane 20	Woods	Smith	Prindiville	O'Regan	Trotter	Hendrick	Horner	Cochrane	Midwood	Worthington	Annan*	Thompson
	4/11		811	18	23			Chiverton 52	Mogg	Hedges	Dicks	Cousins	Graham	Gill	James	Chenoweth*	Chiverton	Birkby	Adcock	Smart
								Ref: M Messias	An inexperienced Town side rises to the task. Midwood takes the plaudits. He pokes home Worthington's cross for the first, then heads in the third right on half-time. In between, local lad Cochrane scores with a classic diving header. Halifax take the foot off the gas after the interval.											
18	H	KETTERING		7	W	2-0	2-0	Worthington 14, 32	Woods	Smith	Prindiville	O'Regan	Stoneman	Trotter	Hendrick	Cochrane	Midwood	Worthington	Thompson	
	11/11		929	8	26				Judge	Hunter	Norman"	Holden	Ibrahim*	Harmon	Mustafa	Stringfellow	Alford	Scott^	Pope	Trigg/McP'nd/March
								Ref: G Shaw	Heavy rain makes the pitch slippery, but Worthington doesn't mind. He scores twice to win the game for Town. His first is a beauty – a shot on the run, with the ball going in off the post. Victory is soured by racist taunts from a section in the crowd aimed at Kettering's Junior Hunter.											
19	A	DAGENHAM		7	D	1-1	1-1	Midwood 34	Woods	Smith	Annan	O'Regan	Stoneman	Trotter	Hendrick	Cochrane	Midwood	Worthington	Thompson	
	18/11		701	22	27			Bennett 1	Williams	Stebbing	Conner	Culverhouse	Crookes	Taylor	Graham	Dyer	Bennett	Reed*	Broom	Hughes
								Ref: P Armstrong	Steve Prindiville has left the Shay for Dagenham, but an agreement between the clubs means he can't play in this game. Town are a goal down after only 15 seconds. Midwood heads the equaliser, but the Shaymen miss a catalogue of second-half chances, and it's two points dropped.											
20	A	WELLING		10	D	0-0	0-0		Woods	Smith	Annan	O'Regan	Stoneman	Trotter	Hendrick	Cochrane	Midwood	Worthington	Thompson	
	25/11		666		28				Harris	Ash	Horton	Tierling	Copeley	Berry	Wordsworth	Rutherford	Morah	Henry	Brown*	Farley
								Ref: W Norbury	Town dominate this game, and though they fail to win, Bird is delighted with his side's performance. They survive a Welling penalty appeal in the second minute, then miss several chances and are thwarted by keeper Harris. In the last minute, Cochrane's cross-cum-shot grazes the bar.											
21	H	BROMSGROVE		10	D	1-1	1-0	Worthington 13	Woods	Smith	Annan	O'Regan	Stoneman	Trotter	Hendrick	Cochrane*	Midwood	Worth'gton^	Thompson	Johnson/Brook
	2/12		843		29			Skelding 56p	Taylor	Skelding	Power*	Richardson	Clarke	Randall	Smith A	Crisp	Hunt	Carter	Grocutt	Dowling
								Ref: J Jones	Thick fog helps disguise just how poor a game this is. Even so, Worthington's curler into the top corner looks like setting Halifax up for a third successive home win. It doesn't materialise, however, after Stoneman up-ends John Hunt in the box. Skelding makes no mistake from the spot.											

No	Date	Att	Pos	Pt	F-A	H-T	Scorers, Times, and Referees	1	2	3	4	5	6	7	8	9	10	11	subs used
22	A SLOUGH		7	W	3-2	0-1	Beddard 71, 74, Midwood 75	Woods	Smith	Annan	O'Regan	Stoneman	Trotter	Hendrick	Beddard	Midwood	Johnson	Brown	
	9/12	*862*		32			*Hercules 45, Catlin 55*	*Bunting*	*Clement^*	*Lee*	*Paris*	*Baron*	*Catlin*	*Rake**	*Pye*	*West*	*Hercules*	*Fiore*	*Bushay/Blackman*
							Ref: K Hill	With 20 minutes to go, Slough are coasting, with Woods looking suspect. He's already handed Hercules the opener. Then suddenly the game turns on its head, as Town score three in five minutes. Midwood beats the offside for the winner. The home fans vent their anger at their team.											
23	H RUNCORN		10	L	1-3	1-1	Johnson 45	Woods	Smith	Annan	O'Regan	Stoneman	Trotter !	Hendrick	Beddard*	Midwood	Johnson	Brown	Cochrane
	16/12	834	*19*	32			*Bignall 43p, 70, Eyre 63*	*Cartwright*	*Bates*	*Eyre*	*Ellis*	*Byrne*	*Finlay*	*Clowes**	*Docherty*	*Bignall*	*Taylor !*	*Ruffer*	*Brady*
							Ref: B Lowe	Stoneman crashes a 35th minute free-kick against the bar, but then Town lose their way. Bignall's penalty gets Runcorn going. Though Town draw level, they are decidedly second best. Runcorn, now under former England winger Peter Barnes, have Taylor sent off in the 89th minute.											
24	A SOUTHPORT		12	D	0-0	0-0		Woods	Smith	Annan	O'Regan	Stoneman	Brown	Hendrick	**Scaife**	Midwood	Johnson	Cochrane	
	1/1	*1,318*	*7*	33				*McKenna*	*Fuller**	*Farley*	*Cochran*	*Goulding*	*Lodge*	*Horner*	*McDonald*	*Davenport*	*Blackstone*	*Griffiths^*	*Thomas/Whittaker*
							Ref: C Foy	Billy Ayre is now in charge at Haig Avenue, but he despairs when Woods saves Griffiths' 27th-minute penalty. For most of the time, his side plays second fiddle to a Town side that just fails to find that cutting edge. Nick Scaife (York) is on loan, as was his father Bobby 21 years ago.											
25	H DAGENHAM		9	W	**3-0**	2-0	Cochrane 6, Johnson 29, O'Regan 68	Woods	Smith	Annan	O'Regan	Stoneman	Brown	Hendrick	Scaife	Midwood	Johnson	Cochrane	
	6/1	729		36				*Williams*	*Reed**	*Prindiville*	*Conner*	*Crookes*	*Wilson^*	*Stebbing*	*Worth'gton"*	*Stringfellow*	*Taylor*	*Broom*	*Dyer/Hewes/Gothard*
							Ref: G Shaw	Dagenham come to the Shay with three former Town players in their side, Prindiville, Wilson and Worthington. But they are taken apart by a relatively young Town side, with Midwood making all three Town goals. When Worthington goes off, reserve keeper Gothard takes his place.											
26	A STEVENAGE		11	L	0-2	0-2		Woods	Smith	Annan	O'Regan	Stoneman	Trotter^	Hendrick	Brown	Midwood*	Johnson	Cochrane	Beddard/Horner
	13/1	*1,841*	*2*	36			*Venables 36, 39*	*Wilmot*	*Webster*	*Sodje*	*Smith*	*Mutchell*	*Venables**	*Berry*	*Barrowcliff*	*Beeke*	*Browne*	*Hayles*	*Vier*
							Ref: R Coxhead	England non-league international Dave Venables hits Halifax with a double blast against the run of play to decide the outcome. Barry Hayles makes both, his cross being parried by Woods for the first. Wilmot is in great form, and denies his old side with two point-blank saves late on.											
27	H HEDNESFORD		11	L	1-3	0-1	Brook 75	Woods	Smith	Annan	O'Regan	Brown*	Trotter	Hendrick	**Benn^**	Midwood"	Johnson	Cochrane	Brook/Horner/Bed'rd
	3/2	859	*3*	36			*Devine 18, O'Connor 54, 88*	*Cooksey*	*Yates*	*Collins*	*Simpson*	*Essex*	*Carty*	*McNally*	*Fitzpatrick*	*Lambert*	*Devine*	*O'Connor*	
							Ref: B Bello	Town call for volunteers to help clear the pitch of snow so the game can go ahead. Their side is then blitzed by the high-flying Pitmen, who go on to record their ninth away win. Brook's exquisite chip gives Town some hope, but O'Connor's late goal reflects a more honest scoreline.											
28	A NORTHWICH		13	D	1-1	1-0	Brook 22	Woods	Smith	Brown	O'Regan	Stoneman	Trotter	**Lee**	Hendrick	**Sansam**	Brook	Annan*	Horner
	17/2	*879*		37			*Jones 65*	*Greygoose*	*Duffy*	*Jones*	*Burgess*	*Abel*	*Simpson*	*Ward*	*Butler*	*Cooke*	*Humphreys*	*Vicary*	
							Ref: C Webster	At the end of the game, Greygoose is hit by a brick thrown by a Town yob and the police are called in. Town were knocked out of the County Cup by Farsley in midweek, but their response is positive. Mark Jones denies them victory while the bar is still shaking from Cooke's header.											
29	A BATH		13	L	1-2	1-1	Sansam 1	Woods	Smith	Annan	O'Regan	Stoneman	Trotter	Lee	Hendrick	Sansam*	Brook	Midwood	Cochrane
	24/2	***547***		37			*Withey 19, Mings 56*	*Mogg*	*Gill*	*Dicks*	*Cousins*	*Sherwood*	*Sugar**	*Vernon*	*Chiverton*	*Withey"*	*Mings^*	*Wigley*	*S'ders/Smart/Adc'ck*
							Ref: J Griffiths	This game is in doubt until an hour before kick-off, with huge pools of water lying on the pitch. Sansam is happy it goes ahead when he tucks away Lee's corner with only 60 seconds gone. It's a different story at the end, though, as Town make two mistakes and are clinically punished.											
30	A DOVER		13	L	2-3	0-1	Lee 48, Midwood 90	Woods	Smith	Annan	O'Regan	Stoneman	Trotter	Lee	Hendrick*	Sansam^	Brook	Horner	Midwood/Cochrane
	2/3	*895*		37			*Harris 17, 50, Leworthy 67*	*Ebbli*	*Budden**	*Pilkington*	*Campbell*	*Daniels*	*Lewis*	*Darlington*	*Lindsey*	*Harris"*	*Leworthy^*	*Strouts*	*Donn/Jones/O'Brien*
							Ref: L Cable	Struggling Dover have signed 19-year-old Jason Harris from Crystal Palace, and he makes a dream debut with two goals that help sink a lively Town side. He uses his pace to score both, then chips Woods for Leworthy's tap-in that effectively puts the game out of the Shaymen's reach.											
31	H STALYBRIDGE		13	L	2-3	0-3	Trotter 76, O'Regan 78	Woods	Smith	Annan*	O'Regan	Stoneman	Trotter	Lee"	Horner	Sansam	Midwood	Thornber^	Br'wn/H'ick/Cochr'n'
	5/3	**509**		37			*Goodacre 16, 29, Jones 31*	*Willietts*	*Edmonds*	*Coathup*	*Frain*	*Hall*	*O'Shaughn'*	*Burke*	*Goodacre*	*Jones*	*Arnold*	*Ellis*	
							Ref: A Hogg	Town's first-half display leaves Bird 'shocked and embarrassed'. Stalybridge's three goals all come from the left flank as Annan has a personal nightmare. Town pull two back, the second a pile-driver from O'Regan, but it isn't enough. Prodigal son Steve Thornber plays in the first half.											

No	Venue / Date	Opponent / Att	Pos	Res / Pts	F-A	H-T	Scorers, Times, and Referees	1	2	3	4	5	6	7	8	9	10	11	subs used
32	A	MACCLESFIELD	15	L	**0-7**	0-3	*[Lyons 74p, Hemmings 78]*	Woods	Smith	Annan	O'Regan	Stoneman	Trotter	Brown	Horner*	Sansam	Midwood	Cochrane	Lee
	9/3	*1,348*	*1*	37			*Hulme 17, 29, Payne 24, Power 61, 75,*	*Price*	*Tinson*	*Bradshaw*	*Payne"*	*Howarth*	*Sorvel^*	*Wood*	*Hulme**	*Coates*	*Power*	*Hemmings*	*Gardiner/Lyons/Edey*
							Ref: M Mountman	The lowest point of Bird's management career. He says, ' I won't be sleeping tonight. There were too many players hiding today and it's not acceptable.' Town look so demoralised, the margin of victory could actually have been more. Relegation, once so remote, now looks possible.											
33	A	MORECAMBE	14	W	1-0	0-0	Cochrane 66	Heyes	Smith	Annan	O'Regan	Stoneman	Trotter	Brown	Horner	Brook	Midwood	Cochrane	
	12/3	*645*		40				*McIlhargey*	*Burns*	*Armstrong*	*Dullaghan*	*Lavelle*	*Sang*	*Monk^*	*Knowles*	*Ceroalo**	*Norman*	*Cain*	*Jackson/Comstive*
							Ref: M Pike	Bird picks up his troops, and they respond in the right manner. The Town players, though, have their hearts in their mouths when the recalled Heyes brings down Norman. The referee doesn't see foul play, and, from his clearance, Cochrane holds off a defender and coolly slots home.											
34	H	ALTRINCHAM	14	D	1-1	0-0	Stoneman 68	Heyes	Smith	**Mudd**	O'Regan	Stoneman	Trotter	Brown	Horner*	Brook	**Daws**	Cochrane	Annan
	16/3	755		41			*Terry 77*	*John*	*Cross*	*Heesom*	*France*	*Reid*	*Butler*	*Terry*	*Harris*	*Pritchard*	*Carmody**	*Kelly*	*Hughes*
							Ref: D Oliver	Town feel there is no justice in the game. They dominate the second period and go in front when Stoneman heads in at the second attempt off a corner. But the Robins find an equaliser through Terry, but he's lucky still to be on the field after assaulting debutant Mudd in the 54th minute.											
35	A	KIDDERMINSTER	14	L	1-6	1-4	Johnson 38 *[May 31, Davies 73]*	Heyes	Smith	Annan	O'Regan^	Stoneman	Trotter	Brown	Mudd	Brook*	Midwood	Cochrane	Johnson/Horner
	18/3	*1,168*		41			*Brindley 13, Hughes 16, Casey 21, 54,*	*Steadman*	*Hodson*	*Willetts*	*Dearlove*	*Brindley*	*Yates*	*Cartwright*	*Casey*	*May**	*Davies ^*	*Hughes*	*Shepherd/Purdie*
							Ref: K Hawkes	The Conference have announced that only two clubs will be relegated, which at this stage is good news for Halifax. But it makes this second heavy defeat no less palatable. Injuries compound Town's woes, and not even Johnson's fizzing strike can prevent Bird handing in his notice.											
36	H	SOUTHPORT	14	D	2-2	1-1	Horner 26, O'Regan 78	Woods	Smith	Mudd	O'Regan	Stoneman	Brown	Horner	Hendrick	Trotter	Daws	Midwood	
	26/3	694		42			*Davenport 29, Whittaker 76*	*Croasdale*	*Clark*	*Fuller*	*Dove*	*Goulding^*	*Lodge*	*McDonald*	*Whittaker*	*Davenport*	*Gamble**	*Haw*	*Griffiths/Cochran*
							Ref: C Foy	Assistant manager George Mulhall, in charge here in the Seventies, has taken over the reigns temporarily. His first move is to stick Trotter up front. O'Regan fancies the Town job, and leads by example. He fires in a stunning equaliser that overshadows Noel Horner's sweeping opener.											
37	H	FARNBOROUGH	15	D	0-0	0-0		Woods	Smith	Mudd	O'Regan	Stoneman	Brown	Horner*	Hendrick	Trotter	Daws	Midwood	Brook
	30/3	697		43				*Rowe*	*Stemp*	*Underwood*	*McAvoy*	*Day*	*Robson*	*Boothe*	*Harlow*	*Gavin*	*Baker*	*Wingfield*	
							Ref: A Breckell	Rough Quest wins the Grand National, and it also sums up Town's attempt to win this game. The most pleasing aspect of it is that Conference top scorer Chris Boothe is kept in check. Woods makes a stunning fingertip save from Gavin, whilst Midwood fluffs a great chance at the death.											
38	H	TELFORD	16	D	0-0	0-0		Woods	Smith	Mudd	O'Regan	Stoneman	Brown	Horner*	Hendrick	Trotter	Daws	Midwood !	Cochrane
	6/4	771		44				*Hughes*	*Eccleston*	*Fowler*	*Wilcox^*	*Foster*	*Kearney*	*Myers*	*Langford**	*Gray*	*Turner*	*Adams*	*Purdie/Bignot*
							Ref: C Webster	O'Regan and Trotter both hit the bar, and three minutes from the end Midwood is shown a red card for a second bookable offence. But these incidents stand out in a game that never promised much, and served up even less. Telford's Myers is booked for arguing a non-penalty award.											
39	A	KETTERING	12	W	2-1	1-0	Daws 14, Hendrick 64	Woods	Smith	Mudd	O'Regan	Stoneman	Brown	Horner	Hendrick	Trotter	Daws	Midwood	
	8/4	*1,317*		47			*Benjamin 89*	*Judge*	*Harmon*	*March*	*Norman*	*King*	*Nyamah*	*Mustafa*	*Pope*	*Scott*	*Fowler**	*Thomas^*	*Benjamin/Miles*
							Ref: A Bates	Tony Daws is set to return to Lincoln, so his goal, off Horner's cross, is a parting gift. It also sets up Town for their only win under Mulhall's present spell in charge. Hendrick doubles the lead, before Poppies' sub Ian Benjamin scores the late goal that leads to a nerve-wracking finish.											
40	A	TELFORD	13	D	1-1	1-0	Trotter 26	Woods	Smith	Annan	O'Regan	Stoneman	Brown	Horner*	Hendrick^	Trotter	Brook	Midwood	Cochrane/Johnson
	13/4	*708*		48			*Eccleston 50*	*Hughes*	*Bignot^*	*Kearney*	*Eccleston*	*Foster*	*Niblett*	*Myers*	*Langford**	*Gray*	*Turner*	*Adams*	*Purdie/Clarke*
							Ref: B Polkey	John Carroll and assistant Billy Rodaway are introduced to the players just before kick-off. But Mulhall is in charge today, and his five-game stint as caretaker ends unbeaten. Trotter gives Town a shock lead, then they defend desperately. Eccleston heads Telford's deserved equaliser.											
41	H	WOKING	13	D	2-2	1-0	Brook 18, 66	Woods	Smith	Annan	O'Regan	Stoneman	Brown	Horner^	Hendrick	Johnson !	Brook	Cochrane*	Beddard/Constable
	20/4	1,064	*2*	49			*Walker 81, Baron 86*	*Batty*	*Tucker*	*Wye**	*Fielder*	*Brown*	*Crumplin"*	*Thompson*	*Ellis*	*Steele*	*Adams^*	*Walker*	*Hay/Timothy/Baron*
							Ref: T Jones	Keen to impress their new boss, the Shaymen give it their all against promotion-seeking Woking. But their efforts are hampered when Johnson is sent off after only 16 minutes. Brook gives Town an incredible 2-0 lead, before evergreen Walker starts the fightback with a clinical finish.											
42	A	BROMSGROVE	15	W	1-0	0-0	Midwood 60	Woods	Smith	Annan	O'Regan	Stoneman*	Brown	Horner	Hendrick	Midwood	Brook	Cochrane	Beddard
	4/5	*887*		52				*Taylor*	*Skelding*	*Brighton*	*Richardson*	*Clarke*	*Smith*	*Young*	*Amos^*	*Hunt**	*Carter*	*Crisp*	*Marlowe/Gardner*
	Home	Away					Ref: P Roberts	Town end the season by extending their unbeaten run to seven games. Rovers have a Spalding Cup Final to look forward to, so find it hard to get motivated here. Midwood doesn't care, and takes advantage of an error by Adie Smith – Rovers' player of the year – to score the only goal.											
Average	838	1,025																	

FA Cup			F-A	H-T	Scorers, Times, and Referees	1	2	3	4	5	6	7	8	9	10	11	subs used
4Q A RUNCORN	9	L	1-2	0-1	Worthington 67	Woods	Smith	Prindiville	O'Regan	Trotter	Brown !	Thompson	Johnson	Midwood	Worth'gton*	Horner	Beddard !
21/10	*901 18*				*Taylor 10, Bignall 79*	*Morris*	*Bates*	*Robertson*	*Ellis*	*Byrne*	*Brady*	*Ruffer*	*Doherty N*	*Taylor*	*Bignall**	*Smith M*	*Clowes*
					Ref: A Leake	Town bow out at the first hurdle in dramatic fashion. Chasing the game after Bignall had restored Runcorn's lead and with time running out, Jon Brown is sent off for retaliation. A minute from time, Beddard joins him, for arguing that his effort had crossed the line. He had a case.											

FA Trophy																	
1 H SOUTHPORT	11	W	2-1	2-1	Johnson 3, Cochrane 9	**Buxton**	Smith	Annan	O'Regan	Stoneman	Trotter	Hendrick	Brown*	Midwood^	Johnson	Cochrane	Horner/Beddard
20/1	966 *5*				*Whittaker 28*	*McKenna*	*Clark*	*Farley*	*Dove*	*Goulding*	*Lodge*	*McDonald*	*Whittaker*	*Davenport*	*Gamble^*	*Blackstone**	*Griffiths/Haw*
					Ref: K Breen	Town feel that this could be their year. They shock the Sandgrounders with two goals in the first nine minutes, then after Whittaker pulls one back, hang on for dear life. Nick Buxton (Eastwood Town), called up for injured Heyes, is relieved to see Griffiths' shot come back off the bar.											
2 H BROMSGROVE	11	L	0-1	0-1		Woods	Smith	Annan	O'Regan	Brown	Trotter	Hendrick	Beddard	Midwood	Brook	Cochrane*	Benn
10/2	887 *9*				*Smith 25*	*Taylor*	*Skelding*	*Brighton*	*Richardson*	*Clarke*	*Gaunt*	*Smith*	*Amos*	*Hunt*	*Crisp*	*Grocutt*	
					Ref: C Webster	It isn't Town's year. Their Wembley dream is ended - ironically - by a removal man, Adrian Smith. Town pile on the pressure, but know their luck is out when, in the space of a minute, Brook hits the bar, then O'Regan has a penalty saved. In injury-time, Brook claims another penalty.											

		Home					Away					
	P	W	D	L	F	A	W	D	L	F	A	Pts
1 Stevenage	42	13	6	2	51	20	14	4	3	50	24	91
2 Woking	42	16	5	0	47	13	9	3	9	36	41	83
3 Hednesford	42	13	3	5	38	21	10	4	7	33	25	76
4 Macclesfield	42	12	5	4	32	16	10	4	7	34	33	75
5 Gateshead	42	9	7	5	32	24	9	6	6	26	22	67
6 Southport	42	10	7	4	42	25	8	5	8	35	39	66
7 Kidderminster	42	13	4	4	49	26	5	6	10	29	40	64
8 Northwich	42	9	3	9	38	35	7	9	5	34	29	60
9 Morecambe	42	12	2	7	51	33	5	6	10	27	39	59
10 Farnborough	42	8	6	7	29	23	7	8	6	34	35	59
11 Bromsgrove	42	11	6	4	33	20	4	8	9	26	37	59
12 Altrincham	42	9	6	6	33	29	6	7	8	26	35	58
13 Telford	42	8	7	6	27	23	7	3	11	24	33	55
14 Stalybridge	42	9	3	9	29	37	7	4	10	30	31	55
15 HALIFAX	42	8	7	6	30	25	5	6	10	19	38	52
16 Kettering	42	9	5	7	38	32	4	4	13	30	52	48
17 Slough	42	4	6	11	35	44	9	2	10	28	32	47
18 Bath	42	9	4	8	29	31	4	3	14	16	35	46
19 Welling	42	6	8	7	21	23	4	7	10	21	30	45
20 Dover	42	8	1	12	29	38	3	6	12	22	36	40
21 Runcorn	42	4	5	12	25	43	5	3	13	23	44	35
22 Dagenham	42	5	7	9	31	34	2	5	14	12	39	33
	924	205	113	144	769	615	144	113	205	615	769	1273

Odds & ends

Double wins: (1) Kettering.
Double losses: (4) Kidderminster, Stevenage, Hednesford, Stalybridge.

Won from behind: (1) Slough (a).
Lost from in front: (2) Slough (h), Bath (a).

High spots: Unbeaten in seven games up to 9 December.
Unbeaten in the last seven games of the season.
Beating last season's champions Macclesfield in the first home match.

Low spots: Losing the first five away games, the first three without scoring a goal.
Four consecutive defeats in a run of seven games without a win.
Losing 0-7 at Macclesfield, Halifax's heaviest Conference defeat.
Losing to Farsley Celtic in the County Cup.

The attendance of 509 for the visit of Stalybridge was the lowest at the Shay during Town's five years in the Conference.

Player of the Year: Kieran O'Regan.
Ever-presents: (0).
Hat-tricks: (0).
Leading scorer: Michael Midwood (10).

	Appearances						Goals			
	Lge	*Sub*	FAC	*Sub*	FAT	*Sub*	**Lge**	FAC	FAT	**Tot**
Annan, Richard	**20**	*1*			2					
Beddard, Elliot	**8**	*9*		*1*	1	*1*	**3**			**3**
Benn, Wayne	**1**					*1*				
Brook, Gary	**11**	*3*			1		**4**			**4**
Brown, Jon	**33**	*1*	1		2		**1**			**1**
Buxton, Nick					1					
Cochrane, Karl	**16**	*6*			2		**3**		1	**4**
Constable, Shaun	**4**	*1*								
Daws, Tony	**5**						**1**			**1**
Graham, Deniol	**1**									
Hart, Ian		*1*								
Hendrick, John	**25**	*3*			2		**2**			**2**
Heyes, Darren	**17**									
Horner, Noel	**17**	*7*	1			*1*	**1**			**1**
Johnson, Simon	**14**	*3*	1		1		**6**		1	**7**
Lee, Glen	**4**	*1*					**1**			**1**
Ludlow, Lee		*2*								
Midwood, Michael	**36**	*2*	1		2		**10**			**10**
Mudd, Paul	**6**									
O'Regan, Kieran	**40**		1		2		**4**			**4**
Prindiville, Steve	**17**		1							
Sansam, Christian	**5**						**1**			**1**
Scaife, Nick	**2**									
Smith, Paul	**27**		1		2					
Stoneman, Paul	**39**				1		**3**			**3**
Thompson, Simon	**19**	*1*	1							
Thornber, Steve	**1**									
Timons, Chris	**14**									
Trotter, Mick	**36**		1		2		**3**			**3**
Wilson, Lee	**2**	*3*								
Woods, Andy	**25**		1		1					
Worthington, Gary	**17**	*1*	1				**5**	1		**6**
(own-goals)							**1**			**1**
32 players used	**462**	***45***	**11**	***1***	**22**	***3***	**49**	**1**	**2**	**52**

No	Date		Att	Pos	Pt	F-A	H-T	Scorers, Times, and Referees	1	2	3	4	5	6	7	8	9	10	11	subs used
1	A	STEVENAGE			L	**0-6**	0-2	*[Sodje 67, Browne 71, 82]*	Woods	Brown	Mudd	O'Regan	Trotter	**Lee**	Cochrane*	Stoneman !	Worthington	Brook	Midwood^	Horner/Hendrick
	17/8		*2,117*		0			*Bignall 10, 18, Barrowcliff 46,*	*Gallagher*	*Webster*	*Paris*	*Sodje*	*Smith*	*Barrowcliff*	*Beevor^*	*Browne*	*Venables*	*Catlin*	*Bignall**	*Trebble/Ugbah*
								Ref: D Bryan	Former Runcorn striker Mark Bignall chose Stevenage in preference to Halifax during the summer. He plays his part in this demolition job as Town suffer their heaviest-ever opening-day defeat. A nightmare start is worsened by Stoneman's 47th-minute sending off for using an elbow.											
2	H	ALTRINCHAM		18	D	1-1	1-1	Brook 44	Woods	Brown	Mudd	O'Regan	Trotter	Lee*	Hendrick	Stoneman	Worthington	Brook	Davison	Horner
	20/8		842		1			*Terry 10*	*Dickens*	*Maddox*	*Heesom*	*France**	*Butler*	*Doherty*	*Terry*	*Harris*	*Cain"*	*Horrigan*	*Sharratt^*	*Pybus/Reid/Carroll*
								Ref: G Shaw	Some sanity is restored, though Town are far from convincing. Terry reacts first to the loose ball following a corner to stun the Shaymen, but Brook pops up with an unexpected equaliser. A torrential downpour spoils the second half, as does the referee, who disallows two Town goals.											
3	H	SLOUGH		11	W	**4-1**	0-0	W'ton 46, Horner 54, Brown	Woods	Horner	Mudd	O'Regan	Trotter^	Brown	Hendrick*	Stoneman	Worth'gton"	Brook	Davison	**Brown J'm**/C'rane/Midw'd
	24/8		793		4			*Hercules 78* [James 84, Midwood 85]	*Wilkerson*	*Smart**	*McGinnis*	*Micklewhite*	*Hercules*	*Bateman*	*Blackford*	*Stapleton*	*West*	*Abbott*	*Bolt*	*Walton*
								Ref: G Shaw	Slough arrive at the Shay having scored nine goals in their opening two matches. Town give them a taste of their own medicine, but only after a dismal first half. Worthington strikes 45 seconds into the second half. Unknown Jimmy Brown plays the last 28 minutes and is outstanding.											
4	A	SOUTHPORT		17	L	1-2	0-1	Horner 89	Woods	Horner	Mudd	O'Regan	Stoneman	Brown	Hendrick^	Cochrane*	Worth'gton"	Brook	Davison	M'w'd/Brown J'm/**Cam'n** !
	26/8		*1,543*		4			*Gamble 44p, 72p*	*Stewart*	*Clark !*	*Jones*	*Horner*	*Farley*	*Gamble*	*Carroll*	*Butler*	*McDonald*	*Davenport*	*Griffiths^*	*Vickers/Whittaker*
								Ref: S Brand	The referee is kept busy. He awards Southport two penalties, the first for Stoneman's trip on McDonald, the second when Woods brings down Carroll. Then, with two minutes to go, he sends off Clark for throwing the ball at Cameron, and Cameron for reacting. Horner's goal follows.											
5	A	KETTERING		21	L	1-4	1-1	Norbury 29 *[Lynch 88]*	Woods	Horner !	Brown	O'Regan	**Harold**	Lee	Midwood^	Brown Jam	**Norbury**	Brook*	Worthington	Hendrick/Cochrane
	31/8		*1,541*		4			*Mustafa 24, Nugent 70, Pope 80,*	*Judge*	*Marshall^*	*Gaunt*	*Norman*	*Nugent*	*Mustafa*	*Berry*	*Nyamah*	*Lynch"*	*Pope*	*Carter**	*Harding/March/Stoch*
								Ref: P Barnes	Town at last get to play £10,0000-buy Norbury, after he's served a four-match ban held over from last season. He scores into an unguarded net, but Horner's 42nd-minute sending off hinders Town's chances. Nugent's headed goal is a killer, but two further strikes really flatter Kettering.											
6	H	GATESHEAD		17	W	2-0	0-0	Norbury 62, Brook 66	Woods	Horner	Mudd	O'Regan	Harold	Lee	Hendrick^	Brown	Norbury*	Brook	Brown Jam	Davison/Worthington
	3/9		679		7				*Sherwood*	*Watson*	*Ord*	*Robson G*	*Hague !*	*Kitchen*	*Proudlock*	*Foreman**	*Thompson*	*Lowe*	*Pearson^*	*Harkus/Robson J*
								Ref: A Hogg	Exactly 75 years ago, Halifax beat Darlington 5-1 in their first ever game at the Shay. The team of '96 ensures a happy anniversary. Gateshead are a ruthless lot, and have Hague sent off for a vicious tackle. From the free-kick he conceded, Norbury scores after Brook's shot hit the bar.											
7	H	RUSHDEN		18	L	1-3	1-1	Norbury 21	Woods	Horner	Mudd"	O'Regan	Harold	Lee	Hendrick*	Brown	Norbury	Brook^	Brown Jam	Worth'gton/Davison/Trotter
	7/9		948	*13*	7			*Rodwell 29, Collins 58, Cramman 74*	*Davies*	*Wooding*	*Ashby*	*Stott*	*Rodwell*	*Wilson*	*Wilkin*	*Butterworth*	*Alford**	*Collins*	*Cramman*	*Furnell*
								Ref: J Devine	Newcomers Rushden, out of the Beazer Homes League, record a history-making first-ever win in the Conference. The game often gets out of hand, but they take advantage of Town's inept second-half display. Town actually took the lead, looking good for a ninth unbeaten home game.											
8	A	ALTRINCHAM		21	L	1-2	1-1	Brook 22	Woods	Horner	Trotter*	O'Regan	Harold	Lee	Stoneman	Brown	Norbury	Brook	Brown J'm^	Davison/Hendrick
	10/9		*673*	*7*	7			*Hardy 11, Terry 59*	*Dickins*	*Maddox*	*Heesom*	*France**	*Butler*	*Doherty*	*Terry*	*Williams*	*Hardy !*	*Carmody*	*Horrigan*	*Cain*
								Ref: P Eastwood	Town huff and puff, but don't show any quality against a Robins side that not only wins the game, but does so with only ten men for half the match. Hardy is sent off for violent conduct on half-time, but Terry still finds his side a winner. Carroll blasts his team – 'Improve or clear off'.											
9	H	STALYBRIDGE		16	W	**4-1**	2-1	Ellison 8, Norbury 39, 60, Trotter 69	Woods	Horner	Brown	O'Regan	Trotter	Stoneman	Hendrick	**Ellison^**	Norbury	Brook"	Brown J'm*	McInerney/W"ton/Davison
	17/9		664	*22*	10			*Charles 14*	*Willetts*	*Bates*	*Coathup*	*Hine*	*Boardman*	*Hall*	*Burke*	*Todd**	*Trott !*	*Arnold*	*Charles*	*Vine*
								Ref: P Canadine	Stalybridge have Trott sent off in the 38th minute for dissent, but Town do better this time against ten men. Lee Ellison scores an early opener, then is never heard of again. Trotter heads in Town's fourth, then celebrates another goal Ravanelli-style while the linesman flags for offside.											
10	A	HAYES		16	D	0-0	0-0		Woods	Horner	Brown	O'Regan	Lee	Stoneman	Hendrick	Worth'gton	Norbury	Brook	Brown Jam	McInerney
	21/9		*521*		11				*Meara*	*Goodliffe*	*Cox*	*Wilkinson*	*Kelly*	*Adams*	*Brady*	*Sugrue*	*Williams*	*Haynes*	*Ulasi*	
								Ref: J Ross	It's not pretty, but Town's defensive ploy at least is effective. It brings their run of four away defeats to an end. Dover have been hit by injuries but they swamp the Town goal, without success. Andy Cox has a header cleared off the line, and Woods makes a string of outstanding saves.											

No	Venue	Opponent	Pos	Res	F-A	H-T	Scorers, Times, Referees	1	2	3	4	5	6	7	8	9	10	11	subs used
11	H	TELFORD	17	L	0-3	0-2		Woods	Horner	Brown	O'Regan	Lee	Stoneman	Hendrick	Worth'gton	Norbury	Brook	Brown J'm^	Cameron/Ellison
	24/9	663	*9*	11			*Russell 1, 44, Niblett 52*	*Jones*	*Eccleston*	*Kearney*	*Robinson*	*Foster*	*Niblett*	*Ashley*	*Russell**	*Gray*	*Turner*	*Page*	*Fowler*
							Ref: C Bassindale	Damon Russell heads the visitors in front after only 45 seconds, and it's downhill all the way for the Shaymen. His second goal is an absolute gift. The fans want O'Regan as manager, and there are incessant chants of 'Carroll out'. Mark Cameron responds with a two-fingered gesture.											
12	A	MACCLESFIELD	18	L	0-1	0-0		Woods	Brown	Mudd	O'Regan	Trotter	Stoneman	Horner	**Beckford**	Davison	Brook	McInerney	
	1/10	*951*		11			*Circuit 76*	*Price*	*Edey*	*Bradshaw*	*Payne*	*Howarth*	*Sorvel**	*Askey*	*Circuit*	*Mottram*	*Power*	*Mitchell^*	*Wood/Hemmings*
							Ref: B Bello	Despite home defeat by Bishop Auckland in the Cup, the board give their backing to Carroll. But the manager has to do without Norbury here, who claims he is working. Town battle until the end, but are sunk by Circuit, who never made it at the Shay, when he bundles the ball in.											
13	H	KIDDERMINSTER	19	L	2-3	0-2	Norbury 49, Horner 59	Heyes	Brown	Mudd	O'Regan	Trotter	Stoneman	Horner	Beckford	Davison*	Brook	McInerney^	Norbury/Midwood
	5/10	786		11			*Willetts 30, Yates 33, Hughes 60*	*Steadman*	*Bignot*	*Prindiville*	*Weir*	*Brindley**	*Yates*	*Cartwright*	*Willetts*	*Hughes*	*Olney*	*Doherty*	*Webb*
							Ref: G Atkins	The players leave the field to a standing ovation, after playing their part in a rousing contest. Halifax dominate, but concede two headed goals. Horner makes, then scores, a goal to get Town level, but his joy is short-lived. Davison is disgusted at being subbed a minute before the break.											
14	H	WOKING	21	L	0-4	0-0		**Gibson**	Horner	Mudd	O'Regan	Stoneman !	Beckford	Francis !	**Hulme**	Norbury	Davison*	McInerney	Horsfield
	19/10	807		11			*Grazioli 61, 76, 83, Walker 68p*	*Batty*	*Howard*	*Taylor*	*Foster*	*Brown*	*Jones*	*Thompson**	*Wye*	*Grazioli*	*Payne*	*Walker^*	*Ellis/Steele*
							Ref: M Ryan	Referee Michael Ryan ruins this game. He sends off Francis, on his return to the club he left in 1985, and Stoneman for innocuous challenges. The game ceases to be a contest, particularly after he awards the Cards a soft penalty. After the game, Ryan is attacked by a fan on crutches.											
15	A	DOVER	21	D	2-2	1-1	McInerney 39, Hulme 58	Gibson	**Cox**	Mudd	O'Regan	**Goulding**	Trotter	Horsfield	Hulme	Norbury*	Brook	McInerney	Worthington
	2/11	*1,038*	*13*	12			*Dobbs 4, Strouts 90*	*Horne*	*Munday*	*Barber*	*Budden^*	*Daniels**	*O'Connell !*	*Stebbing*	*Dobbs*	*Strouts*	*Leworthy*	*Lindsey*	*Theodosiou/Jones*
							Ref: D Crick	As John Hendrick tells the club he's had enough, Town's ever-changing team comes close to snatching their first Conference away win of the season. Hulme volleys Town in front, but Strouts rescues his side, down to ten men after O'Connell's 67th-minute dismissal, in injury-time.											
16	A	BATH	21	D	0-0	0-0		Gibson	Cox	Mudd	O'Regan	Goulding	Stoneman	Horsfield	Hulme	Norbury	Brook	McInerney	
	9/11	*567*	*22*	13				*Hervin*	*Cross*	*Dicks*	*Davey*	*Crowley*	*Brooks*	*Honor*	*James*	*Adcock*	*Penny^*	*Wyatt**	*Harrington/David*
							Ref: M Warren	Town travel down to Bath on the preceding day so that they can prepare in readiness for this basement battle. For the most part, the Romans are on top, but find Town hard to break down. Paul Gibson, on loan from Man Utd, pulls off four terrific saves to keep Town off the bottom.											
17	H	WELLING	19	D	1-1	1-0	Brook 5	Woods	Cox	Mudd	O'Regan	Goulding	Stoneman	Horner^	Hulme	Horsfield	Brook	McInerney*	Worthington/Brown
	23/11	**608**		14			*Smith 90*	*Knight*	*Watts L*	*Farley*	*Trott*	*Copley^*	*Horton*	*Brown**	*Rutherford*	*Morah*	*Dennis*	*Lakin*	*Watts S/Smith*
							Ref: M Pike	With injuries mounting, 37-year-old boss Carroll has registered himself as a player. He's not needed here, where Town look to have the game won courtesy of Brook's early 25-yarder. The ref adds on over 90 seconds of injury-time, enough time for Danny Smith to head the equaliser.											
18	H	KETTERING	20	W	2-1	0-1	Horsfield 61, Davison 74	Woods	Cox	Mudd	O'Regan	Goulding*	Stoneman	Horner	Hulme	Horsfield	Brook^	McInerney	Brown/Davison
	30/11	790		17			*Norman 37p*	*Shoemake*	*Marshall*	*March*	*Gaunt*	*Norman*	*Berry*	*Harmon*	*Stock*	*May*	*Lynch*	*Pope^*	*Judge/Mustafa*
							Ref: R Pashley	Kettering's Shoemake is hurt after only ten minutes, so sub keeper Alan Judge comes on. They lead thanks to a debatable penalty, but Halifax turn the game around with two significant strikes. Horsfield's is his first for the club, whilst Davison's winner is his first for Town since 1982.											
19	A	STALYBRIDGE	18	W	3-2	2-0	Stoneman 13p, 35, Horsfield 79	Woods	Brown	Mudd	O'Regan	Cox	Stoneman	Horner	Hulme^	Horsfield	Davison*	McInerney	Brook/**Kelly**
	7/12	*814*	*16*	20			*Burke 66, 69*	*Williams*	*Powell M*	*Coathup*	*Hine*	*Boardman*	*Hall*	*Burke*	*Jones*	*Trott*	*Arnold*	*Charles*	
							Ref: M Warren	Celtic's eight-match winning streak comes to an end. After Stoneman gives Town a two-goal lead, they look to have blown their chances when Burke scores a quickfire double. Then Horsfield dispossesses Williams for the winner. Wound-up Hulme is substituted to avoid being sent off.											
20	H	MORECAMBE	17	D	1-1	0-1	Brook 90	Woods	Brown	Mudd	O'Regan	Cox	Stoneman	Horner*	Hulme	Norbury	Davison^	McInerney"	Worth'gton/Brook/Midwood
	14/12	883		21			*Jackson 1*	*Banks*	*Knowles*	*Annan*	*Miller*	*Hughes*	*Burns*	*Monk*	*McKearney*	*Jackson**	*Norman*	*Shirley^*	*Ceroalo/Grimshaw*
							Ref: D Messias	Jim Harvey's high-flying Morecambe are close to pulling off a real smash-and-grab victory. Justin Jackson's headed goal only 37 seconds into the game looks like being enough for them, with reserve keeper Andy Banks looking unbeatable. However, in injury-time, Brook heads home.											
21	A	WOKING	17	D	2-2	0-2	Horsfield 58, Lyons 80p	Woods	Cox	Mudd	O'Regan	Goulding^	Stoneman	**Lyons**	Worthington	Norbury !	Horsfield*	McInerney	Brook/Davison
	21/12	*2,331*		22			*Steele 3, 26*	*Batty*	*Howard*	*Wye*	*Foster*	*Brown*	*Jones*	*Thompson*	*Wye*	*Steele^*	*Hay**	*Walker*	*Hunter/Ellis*
							Ref: M North	Carroll claims the Woking players got Norbury sent off when he plays on after the ref has blown. It's his second bookable offence. Town feel justice is done, though, when the ref awards them a penalty when Foster brings down O'Regan. Newly-signed Lyons confidently tucks it away.											

No	Date		Att	Pos	Pt	F-A	H-T	Scorers, Times, and Referees	1	2	3	4	5	6	7	8	9	10	11	subs used
22	H	NORTHWICH		20	L	0-3	0-1		Woods	Cox"	Mudd	Horner*	Goulding	Stoneman	Lyons	Hulme	Norbury	Horsfield^	Worthington	Brook/Davison/**Place**
	26/12		1,078		22			*Simpson 18, Steele 87, 89*	*Greygoose*	*Ward*	*Duffy*	*Crookes*	*Simpson*	*Bishop**	*Reddish*	*Walters*	*Steele*	*Tait*	*Vicary*	*Stannard*
								Ref: J Devine	At half-time, fitness trainer Tommy Gildert breaks the World Superstars record by doing 144 press-ups in 60 seconds. It's all the home fans can cheer, as Town hardly compete. Northwich lead through Simpson's header, and compound the misery with two more in the closing stages.											
23	A	GATESHEAD		18	W	1-0	0-0	Norbury 89	Woods	Horner	Mudd	Martin	Goulding	Stoneman	Lyons*	Brook	Norbury	Horsfield^	Worthington	Davison/Place
	28/12		***466***	*15*	25				*Harper*	*Watson*	*Ord*	*Pearson*	*Wrightson*	*Kitchen*	*Dixon**	*Dia*	*Thompson*	*Lowe*	*Rowe*	*Proudlock*
								Ref: A Butler	Gateshead have now failed to score in their last six matches. They have their chances here, as do the Shaymen, but a goalless draw looks to be the likely outcome. That is until Mick Norbury chests down Stoneman's free-kick, then smashes the ball home to score a sensational winner.											
24	H	BROMSGROVE		16	W	1-0	0-0	Norbury 89p	Woods	Brown	Mudd	McInerney"	Cox	Stoneman	Lyons*	Hulme	Norbury	Brook	Worth'gton^	Horsfield/Davison/Horner
	28/1		**608**	*20*	28				*Taylor C*	*White*	*Gardner*	*Crisp*	*Wardle*	*Skelding*	*Peters*	*Smith*	*Amos**	*Mainwar'g^*	*Hunt*	*Trowman/Nesbitt*
								Ref: C Webster	Bromsgrove boss Brian Kenning can't believe it as his side totally outplay the Shaymen, but leave with nothing. He's cursing the referee when he awards Town a last-gasp penalty after Horsfield goes crashing down. Biggest obstacle barring Bromsgrove's way is the outstanding Woods.											
25	A	BROMSGROVE		19	L	0-3	0-2		Woods	Brown	Mudd	O'Regan	Cox	Stoneman !	Horsfield	Hulme	Norbury"	Brook*	Worth'gton^	Davison/Horner/Lyons
	1/2		*686*	*20*	28			*Mainwaring 11, 45, Crisp 59*	*Taylor C*	*Smith A*	*Gardner*	*Hunt**	*Wardle*	*Skelding*	*Taylor"*	*Smith C*	*Mainwari'g*	*Crisp*	*Peters^*	*White/Brighton/Trowman*
								Ref: A Hall	Revenge is sweet for Bromsgrove. Town's cause isn't helped by Stoneman's 43rd-minute sending off, but the home side are already dictating things. They lead by Mainwaring's goal when the ball comes back off the post. Victory could have been more but for three goalline clearances.											
26	H	BATH		20	L	4-5	2-3	Horsfield 15, 81, Lyons 32, Martin 71	Woods	Brown	Mudd	O'Regan	Goulding	Cox	Francis	Martin	Horsfield	Brook*	Lyons	Davison
	15/2		655	*21*	28			*H'ton 31, Davis 41, 82, Colb'ne 43, 86*	*Hervin*	*Davey*	*Hedges*	*Brooks N*	*Towler*	*Harrington*	*James*	*Hirons**	*Colbourne*	*Davis*	*Wyatt*	*Harvey^/Brooks M*
								Ref: B Bello	It's all over for Carroll now. Bottom club Bath gain their first away win in an extraordinary game where Town actually led three times. With nine minutes to go, Halifax go 4-3 up, but awful defending sees Bath take a decisive lead. After the game, Carroll leaves 'by mutual consent.'											
27	H	FARNBOROUGH		19	W	3-0	1-0	Brook 13, Horsfield 61, Day 72 (og)	Woods	Brown	Mudd	O'Regan	Cox*	Horner	Horsfield	Davison	Norbury	Brook	Martin	Goulding
	22/2		694		31				*MacKenzie*	*Stemp*	*Hedges*	*Coney**	*Harford*	*Robson*	*Boothe*	*Harlow*	*Gavin*	*Baker^*	*Wingfield*	*Day/Mintram*
								Ref: P Pawson	George Mulhall – again – and Kieran O'Regan have been handed the job of steadying the ship. They do away with the direct style and go for a more passing game which pays dividends. Brook turns on a sixpence for the opener. Keith Day's bullet header into his own net stuns everyone.											
28	A	WELLING		16	W	1-0	0-0	Brook 90	Woods	Brown	Mudd	O'Regan	Cox	Horner	Hulme	Horsfield*	Norbury	Brook	Martin	Davison
	1/3		*688*		34				*Knight*	*Watts L*	*Cooper^*	*Trott*	*Copley**	*Horton*	*Brown D*	*Farley*	*Morah*	*Smith*	*Dakin*	*Dimmock/Watts S*
								Ref: A Harvey	The board tell Mulhall and O'Regan, 'Keep us in the Conference and the job's yours.' Town record a second successive victory, whilst at the same time ending Welling's run of five straight home wins. Nobody is quite sure how, though. Brook's late strike is Town's first shot on goal.											
29	H	HEDNESFORD		14	W	1-0	0-0	Brook 64	Woods	Brown	Mudd	O'Regan	Cox	Horner	Hulme	Davison	Norbury	Brook	Martin	
	4/3		623	*5*	37				*Cooksey*	*Carty"*	*Mason**	*Comyn*	*Essex^*	*Collins*	*Devine*	*Lambert*	*Russell*	*Fitzpatrick*	*O'Connor*	*Harnett/Street/Hemmings*
								Ref: E Tarry	The players are given a standing ovation after this rousing contest. Scott Cooksey keeps the visitors in the game in the first half, but he can't prevent Brook's effort from twelve yards after the break. Thick fog makes visibility difficult. The tannoy announcer credits the goal to Martin.											
30	A	KIDDERMINSTER		16	L	0-3	0-1		Woods	Brown*	Mudd	O'Regan	Cox	Horner	Hulme	Davison	Norbury	Brook	Martin	Lyons
	8/3		*2,523*	*2*	37			*Doherty 7, Hughes 70, 81*	*Barber*	*Bignot*	*Willetts*	*Weir*	*Brindley*	*Yates*	*Webb*	*Deakin*	*Hughes*	*Davies*	*Doherty*	
								Ref: K Ingram	Kidderminster keep up the pressure on leaders Macclesfield with this comfortable win. Disappointingly, Town are never in the game after they fall behind to Doherty's early goal from an acute angle. Hughes scores two headers for an emphatic win. 'It was men against boys,' – Mulhall.											
31	H	DOVER		17	L	1-3	1-2	Stoneman 15	Woods	Horner	Mudd	O'Regan	Norbury	Cox !	Hulme	Stoneman	Horsfield	Brook	Worthington	
	15/3		703		37			*Adams 37, 47, Strouts 41*	*Fearon*	*Lindsey*	*Palmer*	*Daniels*	*Budden*	*Barber*	*Dobbs*	*Strouts*	*Reina*	*Adams*	*Milton**	*O'Connell*
								Ref: A Hogg	Joe O'Sullivan's Dover, one of the form teams in the Conference, make it five wins from their last seven outings. Town never get a hold on the game, even after Stoneman's goal. Dover take contol with a three-goal blast before the break. Cox is unlucky to receive a second yellow card.											

32	A	NORTHWICH	16	D	2-2	1-2	Norbury 34p, Horsfield 66	Woods	Horner	Mudd	O'Regan	Norbury	Martin	Hulme	Stoneman*	Horsfield	Brook	Worthington	Cox
	17/3	*911*		38			*Walters 3, Tait 6*	*Greygoose*	*Stannard"*	*Fairclough*	*Crookes^*	*Simpson*	*Bishop*	*Reddish*	*Walters*	*Humphreys*	*Tait*	*Vicary**	*Steele/Cooke/Ward*
							Ref: B Bello	Mulhall describes this fixture with fourth placed Vics as 'crucial'. But within six minutes, Town are 0-2 down. Worthington's woeful backpass lets in Walters for Northwich's first. Brook is felled for Town's penalty. Mulhall's half-time roasting sees Town respond in the right manner.											
33	H	SOUTHPORT	16	W	2-0	2-0	Murphy 36, Martin 38	Woods	Brown	Mudd	O'Regan	**Murphy**	Cox	Lyons	Martin	Horsfield	Horner	Worthington	
	28/3	792		41				*Stewart*	*Farley*	*Rogers*	*Horner P^*	*Horner R**	*Moran"*	*Clark*	*Whittaker*	*Duerden*	*Gamble*	*Sharratt*	*Dove/Blakeman/Haw*
							Ref: E Tarry	Town launch their 'Shaybuilder Premier Bond Club', as they attempt to raise money for Phase One of their redevelopment programme. In the game, two headed goals by newly-signed Jamie Murphy (Doncaster) and on loan Dean Martin prove enough to ease Town's relegation fears.											
34	A	FARNBOROUGH	18	L	0-3	0-3		Woods	Horner	Mudd	O'Regan	Murphy	Brown	Lyons	Martin	Horsfield	Brook	Worthington	
	31/3	*675*		41			*Boothe 15, Harlow 25, Wingfield 31*	*MacKenzie*	*Stemp*	*Mintram**	*Baker*	*Day*	*Robson*	*Boothe*	*Harlow*	*Gavin*	*Underwood*	*Wingfield*	*Haywood*
							Ref: M North	Halifax badly miss either suspended or injured Norbury, Cox, Hulme and Stoneman, and Mulhall admits that without them the side isn't good enough. Woods is backpeddling when Boothe lobs the opener. The game is won by half-time when Farnborough get two more from set pieces.											
35	A	SLOUGH	18	L	0-1	0-1		Woods	Brown"	Murphy	O'Regan	Norbury	Cox	Martin	Hulme	Horsfield	Brook*	Worth'gton^	Mudd/Lyons/Davison
	5/4	*760*		41			*Hercules 15*	*Miles*	*Smart*	*Hardyman*	*Bateman*	*Hercules*	*McMinn*	*Fiore*	*Owusu**	*Brazil*	*Abbott*	*McGinnis*	*Blackford*
							Ref: K Hill	Cliff Hercules heads the decisive goal off McMinn's free-kick to put the pressure back on the Shaymen. Though Halifax enjoy long spells of possession, and have a howling wind behind them after the break, they can't save the game. Hulme tries, but his penalty appeal is turned down.											
36	A	HEDNESFORD	18	D	1-1	0-0	Lyons 67	Woods	Brown	Mudd	O'Regan	Cox	Murphy	Lyons	Hulme*	Norbury	Horsfield	Martin	Horner
	7/4	*1,017*	*7*	42			*Fitzpatrick 63*	*Brant*	*Cotterill*	*Collins*	*Simpson*	*Comyn*	*McNally**	*Carty*	*Fitzpatrick*	*McKenzie*	*Hemmings*	*Francis*	*Rowland*
							Ref: P Carradine	This precious draw means Town are now six points clear of the relegation zone. They actually look disappointed not to have won. Fitzpatrick pokes the ball home for Hednesford, but Lyons, who might have scored a hat-trick, latches on to Mudd's through ball for a quick equaliser.											
37	A	TELFORD	18	D	1-1	1-1	Norbury 39	Woods	Brown	Mudd	O'Regan	Cox	Murphy	Lyons	Hulme*	Norbury	Horsfield	Martin	Horner
	12/4	*759*		43			*Wilding 6*	*Dudley**	*Naylor*	*Fowler*	*Joseph*	*Wilding*	*Niblett*	*Challinor*	*Ashley*	*Gray^*	*Williams*	*Purdie*	*Jones/Langford*
							Ref: J Hubbard	Telford are there for the taking, but Town don't seem to realise it. They fail to test sub keeper Jones, who replaces injured Dudley after half-time. Pete Wilding is granted a free header early on. Norbury heads the equaliser, but it's Woods who earns Town a point with two vital saves.											
38	A	MORECAMBE	18	L	0-1	0-0		Woods	Brown	Mudd	O'Regan	Cox !	Murphy	Lyons*	Worthington	Norbury	Brook^	Martin	Stoneman/Horner
	16/4	*711*		43			*Monk 90*	*McIlhargey*	*Knowles*	*Burns*	*McKearney*	*Hodgson*	*Grimshae*	*Monk*	*Healy*	*Bignall^*	*Norman*	*Williams**	*Cain/McCluskie*
							Ref: B Bello	Town complete a difficult period – this game at Christie Park is actually their fifth consecutive away match. It ends in frustating fashion when Ian Monk fires in the only goal in injury-time. Cox receives his second red card in the 58th minute for hauling down Bignall when he is clear.											
39	H	HAYES	18	D	2-2	1-0	Norbury 41, Lyons 75	Woods	Brown	Mudd	O'Regan^	Cox !	Murphy	Lyons	Worthington	Norbury"	Brook*	Martin	Stoneman/Horner/Horsfield
	19/4	684		44			*Goodliffe 55p, Cox 83*	*Meara*	*Brady*	*Duncan**	*Goodliffe*	*Cox*	*Williams*	*Roddis*	*Francis*	*Randall*	*Roberts*	*Hyatt^*	*Wotton/Bunce*
							Ref: P Eastwood	This game is sponsored by a Mr Geoff Hayes, with his five sons. With Town leading, Cox is sent off again and Mulhall will make an example of him. O'Regan is hurt when he concedes the penalty. Lyons makes it 2-1 with a scuffle going on at the other end. Andy Cox scores for 2-2.											
40	A	RUSHDEN	19	L	0-1	0-0		Woods	O'Regan	Mudd	Martin	Stoneman	Murphy	Lyons	Hulme	Norbury^	Brook*	Horner	Worthington/Davison
	26/4	***2,629***	*15*	44			*Hackett 79*	*Cherry*	*Hodge*	*Peaks*	*Cramman*	*Rodwell*	*Scott*	*Collins*	*Butterworth*	*Alford*	*Leworthy*	*Hackett*	
							Ref: M Tingey	Rushden are not out of danger themselves, and need four points from their last three games to be safe. They get three of them here. Town are unlucky to go down, but defeat leaves them staring relegation in the face. Brendan Hackett scores the all-important goal, in off the woodwork.											
41	H	MACCLESFIELD	19	D	3-3	1-2	Murphy 45, Horsfield 81, Hulme 85	Woods	Brown	Mudd^	Martin*	Stoneman	Murphy	Lyons	Hulme	Norbury	Brook	O'Regan	Horner/Horsfield
	30/4	**2,191**		45			*Byrne 3, Sorvel 21, Davenport 79*	*Price*	*Tinson*	*Edey*	*Payne*	*Howarth*	*Sorvel*	*Askey*	*Wood*	*Davenport*	*Power*	*Byrne*	
							Ref: A Hogg	Macclesfield need to win to clinch the title and promotion. When Murphy is caught in possession, Davenport puts them 3-1 up and they think it's in the bag. But Town aren't finished. Horsfield's shot goes in off a post, then a delighted Hulme sweeps the ball home to deny his old club.											
42	H	STEVENAGE	19	W	4-2	2-2	Norbury 27, 41, 56, Horsfield 90	Woods	Brown	Mudd	Martin	Stoneman	Murphy	Lyons	Hulme*	Norbury	Brook^	O'Regan	Horner/Horsfield
	3/5	1,191	*3*	48			*Stoneman 20 (og), Hayles 39*	*Wilmot*	*Kirby**	*Mutchell*	*Sodje*	*Smith*	*Barrowcliff*	*Hooper*	*Mison*	*Crawshaw*	*Trebble^*	*Hayles*	*Cretton/Browne*
	Home	Away					Ref: M Jones	Only victory will ensure Town's safety. Stoneman's own-goal doesn't help. Norbury saves them with a priceless hat-trick. He completes it off an indirect free-kick inside the box. With Bath now winning, Town want a fourth to be certain. Horsfield's goal is greeted by wild celebrations.											
Average	842	1,139																	

FA Cup					F-A	H-T	Scorers, Times, and Referees	1	2	3	4	5	6	7	8	9	10	11	subs used
1Q	A	OLDHAM TOWN	20	W	3-2	1-0	Hendrick 11, Brook 48, 50	Heyes	Lee	Brown	O'Regan	Trotter	Stoneman	Hendrick^	Davison"	Norbury*	Brook	Brown Jam	W'ton/**McInerney**/Midw'od
14/9		*445 NWC*					*Hession 51, 72*	*Shepherd*	*Everett*	*Hughes*	*Greaves*	*Hoolickin*	*Thompson*	*Hession*	*Bowler*	*Butterworth*	*Carty*	*Livesey*	
							Ref: J Hardy	Wembley looks a million miles away as Town start the competition at the first stage. Hendrick's lobbed goal puts Town ahead, but though they go 3-0 up, those who reckoned, like vice-chairman David Greenwood, that defeat was unthinkable are relieved at the end, as Halifax hang on.											
2Q	H	BISHOP AUCKL'D	17	L	1-4	1-3	Norbury 32 *[Mulroy 67]*	Woods	Horner	Mudd	O'Regan	Lee	Stoneman	Hendrick*	Brown	Norbury	Brook	Brown J'm^	Davison/McInerney
28/9		628 *UL*					*Bolam 3, Scaife 15, Dixon 45,*	*Bishop*	*West*	*Lynch**	*Waller*	*Lobb*	*McKinley*	*Dixon*	*Scaife*	*Mulroy^*	*Bolam"*	*Banks*	*Driscoll/Adams/Carter*
							Ref: W Markham	The lowest point of Town's FA Cup history? They were looking for a good run in the competition, but that's virtually over by the 15th minute. Town look disorganised and in disarray. Defeat prompts an invasion by the fans, a delegation of which get to speak with Carroll and directors.											

FA Trophy																			
1	A	STALYBRIDGE	19	W	1-0	1-0	Brook 14	Woods	Brown	Mudd	McInerney*	Goulding	Stoneman	Horner	Hulme	Horsfield^	Brook	Worthington	Davison/Cox
18/1		*973 11*						*Williams*	*Powell*	*Coathup**	*Hine*	*Boardman*	*Hall*	*Burke*	*Jones*	*Trott*	*Arnold^*	*Thomas G*	*Thomas K/Vine*
							Ref: F Stretton	Gary Brook plays because Norbury is suspended, but it's his header from Horsfield's corner that sends Town through. In a gripping and tense encounter, he also misses a 30th-minute penalty. The Town fans are baying for the final whistle after Stalybridge had twice rattled the crossbar											
2	A	GLOUCESTER	19	L	0-3	0-0		Woods	Cox	Mudd	O'Regan	Goulding	Stoneman	Horner	Hulme	Norbury*	Horsfield	McInerney^	Brook/Davison
8/2		*1,118DM:3*					*Thorne 63, Watkins 66, 79*	*Coles*	*Thorne*	*Johnson*	*Ferguson*	*Kemp*	*Burns^*	*Kirkup*	*Cooper*	*Holmes**	*Watkins*	*McGrath*	*Webb/Tucker*
							Ref: G Ashby	John Carroll's position looks precarious after this shocking defeat. Leroy Rosenior's Dr Marten's League side take the lead in bizarre fashion, when Thorne's long punt upfield deceives Woods and bounces in. But it's no more than they deserve. Watkins outpaces Goulding for the third.											

		Home					Away					
	P	W	D	L	F	A	W	D	L	F	A	Pts
1 Macclesfield	42	15	4	2	41	11	12	5	4	39	19	90
2 Kidderminster	42	14	4	3	48	18	12	3	6	36	24	85
3 Stevenage	42	15	4	2	53	23	9	6	6	34	30	82
4 Morecambe	42	10	5	6	34	23	9	4	8	35	33	66
5 Woking	42	10	5	6	41	29	8	5	8	30	34	64
6 Northwich	42	11	5	5	31	20	6	7	8	30	34	63
7 Farnborough	42	9	6	6	35	29	7	7	7	23	24	61
8 Hednesford	42	10	7	4	28	17	6	5	10	24	33	60
9 Telford	42	6	7	8	21	30	10	3	8	25	26	58
10 Gateshead	42	8	6	7	32	27	7	5	9	27	36	56
11 Southport	42	8	5	8	27	28	7	5	9	24	33	55
12 Rushden	42	8	8	5	30	25	6	3	12	31	38	53
13 Stalybridge	42	9	5	7	35	29	5	5	11	18	29	52
14 Kettering	42	9	4	8	30	28	5	5	11	23	34	51
15 Hayes	42	7	7	7	27	21	5	7	9	27	34	50
16 Slough	42	7	7	7	42	32	5	7	9	20	33	50
17 Dover	42	7	9	5	32	30	5	5	11	25	38	50
18 Welling	42	9	2	10	24	26	4	7	10	26	34	48
19 HALIFAX	42	9	5	7	39	37	3	7	11	16	37	48
20 Bath	42	9	5	7	27	28	3	6	12	26	52	47
21 Bromsgrove	42	8	4	9	29	30	4	1	16	12	37	41
22 Altrincham	42	6	3	12	25	34	3	9	9	24	39	39
	924	204	117	141	731	575	141	117	204	575	731	1269

Odds & ends

Double wins: (2) Gateshead, Stalybridge.
Double losses: (2) Kidderminster, Rushden.

Won from behind: (2) Kettering (h), Stevenage (h).
Lost from in front: (3) Bath (h), Dover (h), Rushden (h).

High spots: Defeating Stevenage on the last day to avoid relegation to the Unibond League.
Three consecutive wins after Mulhall and O'Regan take over.
Winning the West Riding Senior Cup.

Low spots: Losing four consecutive matches in a run of eight games without a win.
Failing to win any of the first eight away matches.
Losing 0-6 at Stevenage on the opening day.
Presenting Bath with their first away win of the season.
Losing 1-4 at home to Bishop Auckland in the FA Cup.
Losing at Gloucester, of the Dr Martens League, in the FA Trophy.

Only relegated Bromsgrove scored fewer goals away from home than Town's 16.

Player of the Year: Andy Woods.
Ever-presents: (0).
Hat-tricks: Mick Norbury (1).
Leading scorer: Mick Norbury (14).

	Appearances						Goals			
	Lge	*Sub*	FAC	*Sub*	FAT	*Sub*	**Lge**	FAC	FAT	**Tot**
Beckford, Jason	**3**									
Brook, Gary	**34**	*4*	2		1	*1*	**8**	3	1	**12**
Brown, Jimmy	**7**	*2*	2				**1**			**1**
Brown, Jon	**31**	*2*	2		1					
Cameron, Mark		*2*								
Cochrane, Karl	**2**	*2*								
Cox, Paul	**22**	*1*			1	*1*				
Davison, Bobby	**11**	*14*	1	*1*		*2*	**1**			**1**
Ellison, Lee	**1**	*1*					**1**			**1**
Francis, John	**2**									
Gibson, Paul	**3**									
Goulding, Derek	**8**	*1*			2					
Harold, Ian	**4**									
Hendrick, John	**8**	*3*	2					1		**1**
Heyes, Darren	**1**		1							
Horner, Noel	**27**	*10*	1		2		**3**			**3**
Horsfield, Geoff	**19**	*5*			2		**9**			**9**
Hulme, Kevin	**21**				2		**2**			**2**
Kelly, Tony		*1*								
Lee, Andy	**8**		2							
Lyons, Darren	**14**	*3*					**4**			**4**
Martin, Dean	**17**						**2**			**2**
McInerney, Ian	**11**	*2*		*2*	2		**1**			**1**
Midwood, Michael	**2**	*4*		*1*			**1**			**1**
Mudd, Paul	**36**	*1*	1		2					
Murphy, Jamie	**10**						**2**			**2**
Norbury, Mick	**30**	*1*	2		1		**14**			**14**
O'Regan, Kieran	**39**		2		1					
Place, Damian		*2*								
Stoneman, Paul	**26**	*2*	2		2		**3**			**3**
Trotter, Mick	**8**	*1*	1				**1**			**1**
Woods, Andy	**38**		1		2					
Worthington, Gary	**19**	*7*		*1*	1		**1**			**1**
(own-goals)							**1**			**1**
33 players used	**462**	***71***	**22**	***5***	**22**	***4***	**55**	**4**	**1**	**60**

No	Date		Att	Pos	Pt	F-A	H-T	Scorers, Times, and Referees	1	2	3	4	5	6	7	8	9	10	11	subs used
1	A	HAYES			W	2-1	1-0	Horsfield 29, Lyons 67	**Martin**	**Thackeray**	**Bradsh'w***	O'Regan	**Jackson**	Stoneman	Paterson	Hulme	Brook	Horsfield	Brown	**Griffiths^**/Lyons
	16/8		*907*		3			*Flynn 75*	*Meara*	*Brady*	*Flynn*	*Sparkes^*	*Cox"*	*Goodliffe*	*Francis*	*Pye**	*Randall*	*Roberts*	*Wilkinson*	*Haynes/Bunce/Duncan*
								Ref: D Bryan	Horsfield arrives hot from the building site but gets the nod to play, then nods Town in front. Griffiths, a 25th-minute sub, takes a knock in the face and doesn't appear after the break. His replacement Lyons curls in a free-kick. Town survive a late scare after Flynn's opportunist strike.											
2	A	SLOUGH		8	D	1-1	0-1	Paterson 72p	Martin	Thackeray	Bradshaw	O'Regan	Jackson	Stoneman	Paterson	Hulme	Brook*	Horsfield	Brown	Lyons
	23/8		***740***		4			*Browne 41*	*Miles*	*Smart*	*Hardyman*	*Randall*	*Hercules*	*Angus*	*Bailey*	*Browne*	*Brazil*	*Abbott*	*Bolt*	
								Ref: B Baker	The Rebels have played two games and seen twelve goals, but it's difficult to see how. The Shaymen, despite going behind, are the better side. Paterson is brought down, then nets the penalty that gets Town level. Five minutes from time, Hardyman handles Jackson's effort on the line.											
3	A	SOUTHPORT		11	D	0-0	0-0		Martin	Thackeray	Bradshaw	O'Regan	Jackson	Stoneman	Paterson	Hulme	Lyons	Horsfield*	Brown	Brook
	25/8		*1,889*	*3*	5				*Stewart*	*Farley*	*Ryan*	*Deary**	*Dove*	*Futcher*	*Butler*	*Kielty*	*Ross*	*Thompson*	*Formby*	*Mitten*
								Ref: P Eastwood	Ex-Shayman Paul Futcher is now in charge at Southport, but his side are more relieved to hear the final whistle. Despite the scoreline, there's plenty of excitement, not least that provided by Paterson who might have had a hat-trick. But three unbeaten away games set Halifax up nicely.											
4	H	WELLING		7	W	1-0	1-0	Paterson 31	Martin	Thackeray	Bradshaw	O'Regan	Jackson	Stoneman	Lyons !	Paterson	Brook	Horsfield	Brown	
	30/8		**1,011**		8				*Knight*	*Watts*	*Dolby**	*Martin*	*Copley^*	*Horton*	*Chapman !*	*Rutherford*	*Watson*	*Cooper*	*Lakin*	*Farley/Dimmock*
								Ref: R Pashley	Ref Ray Pashley's performance is diabolical, and two fans try to tell him so at half-time. Lyons is sent off for retaliation, whilst his assailant Dolby is withdrawn at half-time. Chapman is sent off on 49 minutes for a second bookable offence. Paterson rounds Knight for the only goal.											
5	A	TELFORD		2	W	3-0	2-0	Brook 13, Horsfield 35, 47	Martin	Thackeray	Bradshaw	O'Regan	Jackson	Stoneman	Lyons	Paterson	Brook	Horsfield	Brown	
	2/9		*805*	*11*	11				*Jones*	*Ashley*	*Colcombe"*	*Wilcox*	*Bentley*	*Eccleston*	*Turner*	*Bennett**	*Gray^*	*Langford*	*Fowler*	*Palmer/Colley/Daley*
								Ref: S French	Steve Daley's Telford are simply not in the same class as Town. Mulhall says of his side's display, 'We were superb. The passing frightened me in the first half it was so good.' Brook's bullet header starts things off. Horsfield volleys his first, then taps home a rebound for his second.											
6	H	YEOVIL		1	W	3-1	1-1	Horsfield 42, 55, 75	Martin	Thackeray	Bradshaw	O'Regan	Jackson	Stoneman	Lyons	Paterson	Brook	Horsfield	Brown	
	5/9		1,515	*5*	14			*Patmore 25*	*Pennock*	*White*	*Harvey*	*Roberts**	*Hannigan*	*Cousins*	*Fielder*	*Kemp*	*Patmore*	*Pickard*	*Winter*	*Pounder*
								Ref: P Dowd	This game is brought forward a day because of the funeral of Princess Diana tomorrow, but Town take advantage to go top. Patmore's volley rocks them, but when Lyons's shot comes back off the bar, Horsfield puts Town in front. He completes his hat-trick from an impossible angle.											
7	H	TELFORD		1	W	**6-1**	2-1	Horsfield 2, 9, 60, O'Regan 46,	Martin	Thackeray	Bradshaw	O'Regan	Boardman	Stoneman	Paterson*	Hulme	Brook"	Horsfield^	Brown	Griffiths/Horner/Place
	16/9		1,119	*17*	17			*Daley 24* [Stoneman 48, Hulme 70]	*Dudley*	*Ashley*	*Colcombe^*	*Palmer*	*Bentley*	*Turner*	*Cartwright**	*Wright*	*Bennett*	*Daley*	*Colley*	*Collins/Charlton*
								Ref: C Webster	Telford decide their best tactic to stop the Shaymen is to kick them to bits. At half-time, they are still in with a chance. O'Regan's delightful free-kick gives Town breathing space. Horsfield completes his second hat-trick by coolly rounding the keeper. Hulme heads in Town's sixth.											
8	A	FARNBOROUGH		1	W	2-1	1-1	Horsfield 45, Brook 60	Martin	Thackeray	Bradshaw	O'Regan	Boardman	Stoneman	Paterson	Hulme	Brook	Horsfield	Brown	
	20/9		*919*	*11*	20			*Boothe 35*	*Rowe*	*Stemp*	*Rowlands*	*Robson*	*Miller*	*Harford*	*Baker*	*Harlow**	*Boothe*	*Mehew*	*Underwood*	*Laidlaw*
								Ref: M North	Games like this will decide the destiny of the title. Town hardly play well, yet grind out the win. They go behind to Boothe's soft goal from a corner. Horsfield weaves his way into the box for the equaliser. Brook's winner is fortunate, as Rowe lets his header slip through his hands.											
9	H	LEEK		1	W	2-1	1-1	Paterson 27, Bradshaw 67	Martin	Thackeray	Bradshaw	O'Regan	Jackson	Stoneman	Paterson	Hulme	Brook	Horsfield	Brown	
	30/9		1,329	*21*	23			*Biggins 12*	*Newlands*	*Brunskill*	*Hawtin*	*Walker*	*Filson*	*Cun'ingh'm^*	*Ellis*	*Tobin*	*Diskin*	*Biggins**	*Trott*	*Leicester/Beeby*
								Ref: A McGee	Peter Ward's Leek side look like ending a run of three consecutive defeats when Biggins lashes home a corner. They are a tough nut to crack, but Town come through. Paterson's equaliser takes a deflection. Bradshaw wins it, keeping his cool when the ball comes back off Newlands.											
10	H	KETTERING		1	W	3-0	2-0	Hulme 26, Bradshaw 43, Thackeray 63	Martin	Thackeray	Bradshaw	O'Regan	Jackson	Stoneman	Paterson	Hulme	Brook	Horsfield*	Brown	Lyons
	4/10		1,836	*22*	26				*Quy*	*Berry*	*Mutchall*	*Devito*	*Tucker*	*Vowden*	*Ridgeway*	*Norman*	*Wilkes*	*Costello*	*Adams**	*Miles*
								Ref: A Hogg	Kettering, still looking for their first win, put their entire first team squad up for sale last week. This is Town's seventh consecutive league win, equalling the class of 1963-64. Wing-backs Bradshaw and Thackeray pop up with headers. In the 59th minute, Quy saves a Paterson penalty.											

No	Date	Venue	Opponent	Att	Pos	Pts	Res	F-A	H-T	Scorers, Times, and Referees	1	2	3	4	5	6	7	8	9	10	11	subs used
11		H	STEVENAGE		1		W	4-0	1-0	Horsfield 29, 65, Hulme 46,	Martin	Thackeray	Bradshaw	O'Regan	**Kilcline**	Stoneman	Horner	Hulme	Brook*	Horsfield	Brown	Lyons
	18/10			2,139	*10*	29				[Bradshaw 52p]	*Gallagher*	*Kirby*	*Love*	*Smith*	*Trott*	*Barrowcliff*	*Stevens**	*Perkins^*	*Crawshaw"*	*Trebble*	*Beevor*	*Holden/March/Gallen*
										Ref: M Hall	Former Coventry skipper and FA Cup winner Brian Kilcline joins Town after a local plumber tells George Mulhall he's doing nothing. He has an easy debut. Horsfield opens the scoring when Gallagher spills O'Regan's cross. He's later brought down by Love for Bradshaw's penalty.											
12		A	MORECAMBE		1		D	1-1	1-0	Horsfield 18	Martin	Thackeray	Bradshaw	O'Regan	Kilcline	Stoneman	Horner	**Hurst**	Brook*	Horsfield	Brown	Lyons
	28/10			***3,940***	*3*	30				*O'Regan 60 (og)*	*Banks*	*Burns*	*Hughes*	*Miller**	*McKearney*	*Grimshaw*	*Monk*	*Healy*	*Ceroalo*	*Norman*	*Shirley*	*Mayers*
										Ref: G Shaw	This top-of-the-table clash captures the imagination of the fans, around 1,000 of whom make the trip from Halifax. Kick-off is delayed by ten minutes, then the spectators watch a thriller. Horsfield sticks his head out to put Town ahead. O'Regan slices Shirley's cross over Martin.											
13		A	CHELTENHAM		2		L	0-4	0-0		Martin	Thackeray	Bradshaw	O'Regan	Kilcline	Stoneman	Paterson	Hurst*	Brook	Horsfield	Brown	Lyons
	1/11			*2,508*	*4*	30				*Eaton 61, 63, 73, Bloomer 67*	*Book*	*Duff*	*Victory*	*Banks*	*Freeman*	*Smith"*	*Howells*	*Knight*	*Eaton**	*Watkins^*	*Bloomer*	*Wright/Crisp/Benton*
										Ref: G Beale	Newly promoted Cheltenham, under young manager Steve Cotterill, show that they will be threat to Town this season. The game is won in a twelve-minute spell. The killer is the second goal when Town's Killer slips. Eaton grabs a hat-trick, but Bob Bloomer's volley is the best goal.											
14		H	KIDDERMINSTER		2		W	2-1	0-0	Paterson 52, Kilcline 77	Martin	Thackeray	Bradshaw	O'Regan !	Kilcline	Stoneman	Paterson	Hulme	Brook	Lyons	Brown*	Horner
	8/11			1,799		33				*Willetts 48*	*Steadman*	*Clarke*	*Prindiville*	*Smith*	*Brindley*	*Yates*	*Deakin^*	*Willetts*	*Olney**	*Arnold*	*Doherty*	*Robinson/Casey*
										Ref: A Butler	Horsfield is suspended, but Town manage to win without him and keep up their 100% home record – just. After trailing, Kilcline's header off Paterson's free-kick puts Town ahead. But at the death, O'Regan is sent off for cynically scything down Ian Arnold, who is heading for goal.											
15		A	STALYBRIDGE		1		W	1-0	1-0	Stoneman 43	Martin	Thackeray	Bradshaw	O'Regan	Kilcline	Stoneman	Paterson	Hulme*	Brook^	Lyons	Horner	Murphy/Hurst
	15/11			*1,421*	*20*	36					*Statham*	*Bates*	*Coathup*	*Lonegan*	*Daley*	*Gouldbourne*	*Burke*	*Jones*	*Sullivan*	*Storey*	*Thomas**	*Trees*
										Ref: C Webster	The Bower Fold pitch doesn't make for pretty football, but Town's battling performance sends them back to the top of the table. Kick-off here is delayed by ten minutes. Stoneman moves into midfield following Hulme's 34th-minute injury, and nets the only goal from twelve 12 yards.											
16		H	HEREFORD		1		W	3-0	0-0	Horsfield 64, 78, 88	Martin	Thackeray	Bradshaw	Murphy	Kilcline	Stoneman	Paterson	Horner	Lyons	Horsfield	Brown	
	22/11			2,214	*9*	39					*Quy*	*Warner^*	*Fishlock*	*Pitman*	*Brough*	*Walker*	*Hargreaves*	*McGorry*	*Grayson*	*McCue**	*Mahon*	*Foster/Cook*
										Ref: P Eastwood	Graham Turner's Hereford, relegated from the League last season, make their first return to the Shay since that fateful day when Halifax lost their League status. In a game played in fog, Horsfield returns to the side to grab a second-half hat-trick. He cuts inside to score his solo third.											
17		A	WOKING		1		D	2-2	0-2	Horsfield 62, Paterson 72p	Martin	Thackeray	Bradshaw	Murphy	Kilcline	Stoneman	Paterson	Horner*	Lyons	Horsfield	Brown	O'Regan
	29/11			*3,319*	*5*	40				*Betsy 3, Taylor 41*	*Batty*	*Betsy*	*Taylor*	*Saunders*	*Brown*	*Danzy*	*Thompson*	*Ellis*	*West*	*Payne*	*Steele*	
										Ref: S Tomlin	Woking are roared on by their biggest crowd so far, and look to be heading for victory when Robin Taylor volleys in spectacularly for a 2-0 lead. But Horsfield's sweeping goal, and Paterson's penalty, after Batty hauled down Thackeray, ties the game up. Lyons nearly wins it late on.											
18		H	STALYBRIDGE		1		W	3-1	2-0	Lyons 34, Horsfield 45, 57	Martin	Thackeray*	Bradshaw	Murphy	Kilcline^	Stoneman	Paterson	O'Regan	Lyons	Horsfield	Brown	Horner/Boardman
	5/12			2,453	*19*	43				*Jones 58*	*Ingham*	*Bates**	*Coathup*	*Hine*	*Daly*	*Hall*	*Burke*	*Powell*	*Jones*	*Thomas*	*Sullivan^*	*Trees/Storey*
										Ref: S Brand	Stalybridge have just dismissed manager Brian Kettle, so defender Mark Hine picks his first team. He packs the defence and hopes for a draw. But when Lyons' shot is deflected in, the outcome is a formality. Horsfield's second, flicking in Lyons' cross, takes his tally so far to 23.											
19		H	NORTHWICH		1		W	4-2	0-1	Lyons 59, B'shaw 70, Pat'son 81, 87	Martin	Thackeray	Bradshaw	Murphy	Boardman	Stoneman	Paterson	O'Regan	Lyons	Horsfield	Brown	
	9/12			2,165	*15*	46				*Walters 20, Cooke 82*	*Greygoose*	*Ward*	*Fairclough*	*Crooks*	*Simpson !*	*Duffy*	*Collins^*	*Walters*	*Tait**	*Cooke*	*Williams*	*Billing/Stannard*
										Ref: M Ryan	Town go seven points clear after sweeping Northwich aside in the second half. The visitors have Simpson sent off in the 63rd minute, but by then, Lyons had crashed in the equaliser. Bradshaw glides the ball in for 2-1. Paterson's second somehow slips under the body of Greygoose.											
20		A	LEEK		1		L	0-2	0-2		Martin	Thackeray	Bradshaw	Murphy	Boardman*	Stoneman	Paterson	O'Regan	Lyons	Horsfield	Brown	Horner !
	13/12			*1,282*	*14*	46				*Soley 6, Ellis 21*	*Cutler*	*Beeby*	*Hawtin*	*Tobin*	*Diskin*	*Soley*	*Ellis"*	*Brunskill*	*McAuley^*	*Biggins*	*Leicester**	*Trott/Cunningham/Callan*
										Ref: M Warren	Paterson is a marked man, and is kicked in the air within five seconds of the start. Leek continue to be ruthless, even after they go 2-0 up. Both are scored when Town fail to clear their lines. Horner replaces Boardman after 71 minutes, but lasts only five minutes, sent off for a bad tackle.											
21		H	HEDNESFORD		1		D	1-1	0-0	Horsfield 56	Martin	Thackeray	Bradshaw	Murphy	Kilcline*	Stoneman	Paterson	O'Regan	Lyons	Horsfield	Brown	Horner
	20/12			3,338	*3*	47				*O'Connor 80*	*Cooksey*	*Carty*	*Hemmings*	*Blades*	*Comyn*	*Niblett*	*Ware*	*Simpson*	*Fitzpatrick*	*Dennison**	*O'Connor*	*Norbury*
										Ref: G Shaw	This is a massive game, with John Baldwin's Hednesford lying in second place. Honours end even, and Town drop their first home points of the season. Horsfield latches on to Horner's pass to put Town ahead, but O'Connor punishes their defence when they fail to clear a free-kick.											

No	Date	Att	Pos	Pt	F-A	H-T	Scorers, Times, and Referees	1	2	3	4	5	6	7	8	9	10	11	subs used
22	A GATESHEAD		1	D	2-2	2-2	Paterson 5, Horsfield 7	Martin	Thackeray	Bradshaw	Murphy	O'Regan	Stoneman	Paterson	Horner	**Philliskirk**	Horsfield	Brown	
	26/12	*1,239*	*22*	48			*Harkus 22, 35*	*Williams*	*Scott"*	*Wells*	*Robson**	*Marquis*	*Kitchen*	*Bowey*	*Harkus^*	*Carter*	*Lowe*	*Rowe*	*Proudlock/Innes/Ord*
							Ref: B Bello	It's top versus bottom, but with ex-Halifax boss John Carroll now in charge at Gateshead, extra spice is added to the game. On a difficult pitch, Paterson and Horsfield give Town a quick-fire lead. Two headers from Harkus level the scores. Town bombard the home goal without success.											
23	A KETTERING		1	D	1-1	0-1	Philliskirk 49	Martin	Thackeray	Bradshaw	O'Regan	Murphy	Stoneman	Midwood	Hulme	Philliskirk	Horsfield	Brown	
	29/12	*2,276*	*20*	49			*Van Dulleman 43*	*Taylor*	*Ridgway*	*Mutchell*	*Moore*	*Cox*	*Vowden*	*Sandeman*	*Adams*	*Pearson*	*V Dulleman*	*Berry**	*Norman*
							Ref: R Beeby	Town slip up against lowly Kettering. It's their fourth game without a win, but Mulhall maintains, 'I feel more confident now than I did two months ago.' On-loan Philliskirk fires in a sweet equaliser as Town dominate the second half. Stoneman has a 60th-minute header ruled out.											
24	H GATESHEAD		1	W	2-0	0-0	Horsfield 64, 77	Martin	Thackeray	Bradshaw	Murphy	O'Regan	Stoneman	Midwood	Hulme*	Philliskirk^	Horsfield	Brown	Kilcline/Brook
	1/1	3,149	*22*	52				*Williams*	*Scott*	*Wells*	*Robson*	*Marquis*	*Kitchen*	*Bowey*	*Harkus**	*Carter*	*Lowe*	*Rowe*	*Innes*
							Ref: G Atkins	Closest rivals Cheltenham lost at Yeovil earlier today, so Town know a win will increase their lead at the top. Gateshead are the poorest side at the Shay this season, and come looking for a point. When Williams spills the ball, Horsfield pounces for 1-0, and the result is never in doubt.											
25	A STEVENAGE		1	W	2-1	0-1	Hulme 58, Philliskirk 89	Martin	Thackeray	Bradshaw	Murphy	O'Regan	Stoneman	Paterson	Hulme	Philliskirk	Horsfield	Brown	
	17/1	*2,946*	*15*	55			*Trott 27*	*Gallagher*	*Dillnut*	*Love*	*Smith*	*Trott*	*Soloman*	*Perkins*	*Trebble**	*Crawshaw*	*Wordsw'th^*	*Fenton*	*Dixon/Inman*
							Ref: J Ross	Philliskirk is set to return to Cardiff, but signs off with a priceless winner. He stoops to head the ball over Gallagher off a short-corner routine. It completes a second-half revival after Town were outplayed up to the break. Philliskirk claims the equaliser, but Hulme gets the last touch.											
26	H SLOUGH		1	W	1-0	1-0	Horsfield 24	Martin	Thackeray	Bradshaw	Murphy	O'Regan	Stoneman	Paterson	Hulme	Hanson	Horsfield	Brown	
	24/1	2,098	*10*	58				*Miles*	*Smart*	*Fiore**	*McGinnis*	*Hercules !*	*Angus*	*Bailey*	*West^*	*Brazil*	*Browne*	*Bolt*	*Abbott/Simpson*
							Ref: C Webster	Work has begun on the Hunger Hill terracing. Halifax need it completed by 31 March to meet the Football League deadline – should they win the Conference. The legendary Nat Lofthouse, a guest of Mulhall, watches the game, and sees Horsfield get free to score at the second attempt.											
27	A RUSHDEN		1	L	0-4	0-2	*[Underwood 65]*	Woods	Thackeray	Bradshaw	Murphy	Kilcline	Stoneman !	Paterson*	Hulme	Midwood	Horsfield	O'Regan	Lyons
	7/2	*3,675*	*3*	58			*Collins 1, 53, Butterworth 31,*	*Smith M*	*Wooding*	*Bradshaw*	*Mison^*	*Cramman*	*Whyte*	*Hamsher*	*Butterworth*	*West**	*Collins"*	*Underwood*	*Smith C/Cooper/Capone*
							Ref: J Hubbard	Woods, who earlier walked out on the club, gets called up. He won't play again after this heavy defeat against Brian Talbot's side. They go in front after only 28 seconds. Town claim the ball earlier went out of play. Stoneman's 86th-minute sending off rounds off a bad day for Halifax.											
28	A DOVER		1	W	1-0	1-0	Paterson 2	Martin	Thackeray	Bradshaw	Murphy	Kilcline	Stoneman	Paterson	Hulme	Brook*	Horsfield	O'Regan	Hanson
	14/2	*1,316*	*13*	61				*Davies*	*Munday*	*Palmer*	*Budden*	*Shearer*	*Stebbing**	*Clarke*	*Stouts*	*Alford*	*Le Bihan*	*Adams^*	*Le Beri/Dobbs*
							Ref: G Hedgley	Town survive a few scares, but with other results going for them, Paterson's strike is enough to send Town nine points clear at the top. He gets it after only one minute and 53 seconds, a soft shot that bounces over Davies' outstretched arm and trickles in. Paterson says, 'It was a classic.'											
29	A YEOVIL		1	W	1-0	1-0	Paterson 45p	Martin	Thackeray	Bradshaw	Murphy	Kilcline	Horner	Paterson	Hulme	Brook*	Horsfield^	Brown	Hanson/Lyons
	21/2	*2,584*	*11*	64				*Pennock*	*Thompson*	*Pounder*	*Howard*	*Hannigan*	*Cousins*	*Fielder*	*Stott**	*Patmore*	*Pickard"*	*Calderwood*	*Spencer^/Denys/Birkby*
							Ref: B Beale	Town return from their third successive away trip, having travelled a total of 1,200 miles, with all three points. Paterson again scores the only goal, this time with a penalty after Pennock up-ends Horsfield. Martin protects the lead with a close-range stop from Cousins in the last minute.											
30	H FARNBOROUGH		1	W	1-0	1-0	Horsfield 35	Martin	Thackeray	Bradshaw	Murphy	Kilcline	Horner	Midwood	Hulme	Hanson	Horsfield*	Brown	Kiwomya
	28/2	2,352	*15*	67				*MacKenzie*	*Stemp*	*Baker*	*Miller*	*Und'rwood**	*Harford*	*Baker*	*Harlow*	*Robson*	*Mehew*	*Rowlands K*	*Rowlands M*
							Ref: A McGee	This is a 5.00 kick-off to accommodate L!VE TV, who are piloting a series of Conference matches. Mulhall and O'Regan celebrate their first anniversary in charge with a win, though Town don't play well. They rely on Horsfield's header, off Midwood's free-kick, to claim the points.											
31	H DOVER		1	D	1-1	1-1	Hulme 45	Martin	Thackeray	Bradshaw	Murphy	Kilcline	O'Regan	Midwood*	Hulme	Brook^	Horsfield	Brown	Kiwomya/Hanson
	7/3	1,949		68			*Strouts 12*	*Mitten*	*Le Beri*	*Palmer*	*Budden*	*Shearer*	*Stebbing*	*Dobbs**	*Strouts*	*Alford*	*Adams*	*Henry*	*Jones*
							Ref: G Shaw	Town give a big hand to Bradshaw, who became the club's first-ever international when playing – and scoring – for the England semi-pro side against Holland in midweek. There's nothing much to cheer in the game, except Hulme's equaliser, after unmarked Strouts' put Dover ahead.											

No	Venue / Date	Opponent / Att		Res / Pos	Pts	F-A	H-T	Scorers, Times, and Referees	1	2	3	4	5	6	7	8	9	10	11	Subs used
32	A	HEDNESFORD	1	D		0-0	0-0		Martin	Thackeray	Bradshaw	Murphy	Kilcline	Stoneman	Paterson	Hulme	O'Regan	Horsfield	Brown	
	14/3	*1,856*		*7*	69				*Cooksey*	*Sedgemore*	*Lake*	*Blades*	*Brindley*	*Collins*	*Ware*	*Beeston*	*Eccleston*	*Fitzpatrick*	*Francis**	*O'Connor*
								Ref: M Cooper	Former Town striker Mick Norbury, now at Telford after moving from Hednesford, backs Town to win this clash. Yet the Pitmen's home form is impressive, so the Shaymen do well to hold out for a point on a terrible sand-covered pitch. Lee Martin suffers a 13th-minute neck injury.											
33	H	MORECAMBE	1	W		5-1	2-1	B'shaw 34, Thackeray 38, Pat'rson 46,	Martin	Thackeray	Bradshaw	Murphy	Kilcline	Stoneman	Paterson	Hulme^	O'Regan*	Horsfield"	Brown	Horner/Lyons/Kiwomya
	17/3	2,507		*5*	72			*Norman 13* [Kilcline 57, Horsfield 58]	*Banks*	*Lowe*	*Kennedy**	*Rushton*	*Mayers*	*Drummond*	*Knowles^*	*Healy*	*Milner"*	*Norman*	*Shirley*	*Ceroalo/Hodgson/Hunt*
								Ref: B Bello	Town look nervous in the opening 25 minutes, and fall behind to Norman's free-kick. Bradshaw and Thackeray put Halifax ahead, and when Paterson breaks free for the third, it's siesta time. Horsfield scores the fifth after Andy Banks fails to hold Brown's 40-yard lob under the bar.											
34	H	RUSHDEN	1	W		2-0	0-0	Wooding 72 (og), Paterson 85	**Morgan**	Thackeray	Bradshaw	Murphy	Kilcline	Stoneman	Paterson	Hulme	O'Regan	Horsfield	Brown	
	21/3	3,951		*2*	75				*Smith M*	*Wooding*	*Bradshaw*	*Mison^*	*Cramman*	*Whyte*	*Hamsher*	*Butterworth*	*West**	*Foster*	*Underwood*	*Mehew"/Capone/Rawle*
								Ref: M Hall	The Shaymen feature on BBC's Football Focus, as they wise up to their achievements. On loan Phil Morgan (Stoke) plays his only game. This is an all-ticket game dominated by Town throughout. Wooding turns the ball into his own net, then Paterson rounds the keeper for the second.											
35	H	HAYES	1	D		1-1	1-1	Horsfield 13	**Rhodes**	Thackeray	Bradshaw	Murphy	Kilcline	Stoneman	Paterson	Hulme*	O'Regan	Horsfield	Brown	Lyons
	28/3	2,506		*9*	76			*Domingos 27*	*Meara*	*Watts*	*Beer*	*Bunce*	*Cox*	*Sparks*	*Metcalf*	*Hall**	*Domingos^*	*Randall"*	*Taylor*	*Brady/Hammett/Boothe*
								Ref: M Warren	Morgan has been recalled, so Andy Rhodes (Airdrie) signs until the end of the season. In his first match, he has little to do, but is beaten once by Domingos, who stabs in Watts' cross. This cancels out Horsfield's 31st goal of the season. Halifax fail to match their efforts of last week.											
36	H	WOKING	1	W		1-0	1-0	Hulme 22	Rhodes	Thackeray	Bradshaw	Murphy	Kilcline	Stoneman	Paterson	Hulme*	O'Regan	Horsfield	Hanson	Horner
	4/4	2,826		*3*	79				*Batty*	*Smith*	*Taylor*	*Saunders !*	*Sutton*	*Danzey**	*McAree*	*Ellis*	*Payne^*	*West*	*Hayward"*	*Betsy/Hay/Steele*
								Ref: B Bello	The new North Terrace has been passed fit by Football League officials, and is used for the first time here. Town extend their lead to 13 points when Horsfield plays Hulme in. Woking hit both posts, but concede the game when Saunders receives his marching orders in the 86th minute.											
37	A	HEREFORD	1	D		0-0	0-0		Rhodes	Thackeray	Bradshaw	Murphy	Horner	Stoneman	Paterson	Hulme	O'Regan	Horsfield	Hanson*	Kiwomya
	11/4	*3,304*			80				*Quy*	*Rodgerson*	*Fishlock*	*Pitman**	*Brough*	*Matth'wm'n*	*Hargreaves*	*McGorry*	*Agana*	*Williams*	*Mahon*	*Warner*
								Ref: S Castle	The south-west of England has suffered heavy flooding, but an 8.30 pitch inspection sees this game given the go-ahead. Town never look like scoring until the 85th minute, when Horner puts wide. The Bulls pile on the pressure, but the Town defence holds firm. Murphy is outstanding.											
38	H	SOUTHPORT	1	W		4-3	1-0	Paterson 43, Hulme 50, Hanson 82, 84	Rhodes	Thackeray	Bradshaw	Murphy	Kilcline	Stoneman*	Paterson	Hulme	O'Regan !	Horsfield	Brown	Hanson
	13/4	4,701		*13*	83			*Ross 49, O'Reilly 67, 69*	*Stewart*	*Farley*	*Ryan*	*Horner*	*Bolland*	*Futcher^*	*Thompson**	*Butler*	*Ross"*	*Morris*	*Formby*	*O'Reilly/Jones/Gamble*
								Ref: P Eastwood	A real cliff-hanger. Town lead for a second time when O'Regan is sent off on the hour for retaliation. O'Reilly then takes advantage of slack defending to put Southport 3-2 up. Hanson then comes off the bench for his moment of glory. He heads the equaliser, then slips in the winner.											
39	A	KIDDERMINSTER	1	W		2-0	1-0	Horsfield 42, Paterson 80	Rhodes	Thackeray	Bradshaw	Murphy	Kilcline	Stoneman	Paterson	Hulme	O'Regan	Horsfield	Brown	
	18/4	*3,151*		*17*	86				*Steadman*	*Willetts*	*Prindiville*	*Weir*	*Pope*	*Yates*	*Webb*	*Davies*	*Bignall*	*Arnold*	*Deakin*	
								Ref: P Walton	Kiddy secretary Roger Barlow reckons Town won't clinch the title here, but he's wrong. Rhodes saves Arnold's 21st-minute penalty. Horsfield latches on to Steadman's dreadful error to fire in the first. Paterson scores a screamer from 25 yards with his right foot, then bursts into tears.											
40	A	NORTHWICH	1	L		0-2	0-1		Rhodes	Thackeray	Bradshaw	Murphy	Horner"	Stoneman	Paterson	Hulme^	Hanson	Horsfield*	Brown	Kiwomya/Brook/Lyons
	20/4	*2,106*			86			*Illman 22, 90p*	*Greygoose*	*Ward*	*Gardiner*	*Crookes*	*Simpson*	*Milligan*	*Duffy*	*Walters^*	*Cooke**	*Tait*	*Illman*	*Vicary/Bishop*
								Ref: M Ryan	The Northwich players form a guard of honour as Town take the field, and Queen's 'We Are The Champions' plays over the tannoy. But the Shaymen can't motivate themselves. Rhodes lets Illman's shot trickle through his fingers, then brings down the same player for his penalty.											
41	H	CHELTENHAM	1	D		1-1	1-1	Horsfield 41	Rhodes	Lyons	Bradshaw	Murphy	Kilcline	O'Regan	Paterson	Hulme	Hanson*	Horsfield	Brown	Brook
	25/4	**6,357**			87			*Watkins 25*	*Book*	*Knight*	*Duff*	*Eaton*	*Jackson*	*Walker*	*Grayson*	*Banks*	*Wright*	*Watkins*	*Victory*	
								Ref: S Brand	There is a party atmosphere, and hundreds of balloons are released just before kick-off. Town fail to win, but do preserve their unbeaten home record. Watkins punishes Murphy's stray pass, but Horsfield equalises off Kilcline's header. The Conference trophy is presented afterwards.											
42	A	WELLING	1	L		**2-6**	1-3	Horsfield 21, Brook 78 *[Cooper 62]*	Rhodes	Thackeray	Bradshaw	Murphy*	Kilcline	Stoneman	Paterson	Hulme	Brook	Horsfield	Brown	Horner
	2/5	*1,344*			87			*Hynes 4, 22, 43, Farley 51, Vercesi 54,*	*Knight*	*Watts*	*Dolby*	*Farley*	*Skiverton*	*Vercesi^*	*Hanlon**	*Rutherford*	*Hynes*	*Cooper*	*Chapman*	*Abbott/Side*
	Home	Away						Ref: M Yearby	A disappointing end to a great season. Only Horsfield gets something out of it. His headed goal ensures he's the Conference's leading scorer with 30, one ahead of Rushden's Darren Collins, and he scoops £1,000 in prize money. But in the 77th minute he sees Knight save his penalty.											
Average	2,539	2,073																		

FA Cup					F-A	H-T	Scorers, Times, and Referees	1	2	3	4	5	6	7	8	9	10	11	Subs used
1Q	H	DROYLSDEN	1	W	4-1	1-1	Brook 37, 51, Paterson 54 Horsfield 90	Martin	Thackeray	Bradshaw	O'Regan	Jackson*	Stoneman	Paterson	Hulme	Brook	Horsfield	Brown	Boardman
13/9		799 *UL:1*					*Kinney 39*	*Williams*	*Lattie*	*Diggle^*	*Hughes*	*Tunnicliffe*	*Harley*	*Fahy"*	*Morley*	*Green**	*Kinney*	*Hall*	*Ashton/Hall/Blain*
							Ref: L Mason	Relegated from the Unibond's Premier division, Droylsden have won all their matches so far. They prove to be no pushovers, as Kinney's goal after Hall's shot comes back off the post, indicates. Brook comes into his own with two goals, but the final scoreline certainly flatters Town.											
2Q	H	LEIGH RMI	1	W	4-0	1-0	Paterson 32p, 64, Brook 51, [Horsfield 90]	Martin	Thackeray	Bradshaw*	O'Regan	Jackson"	Stoneman	Paterson	Hulme	Brook^	Horsfield	Brown	Lyons/Horner/Boardman
27/9		1,103 *UL:P*						*Felgate*	*Anderson*	*Schofield*	*Hill*	*Smythe*	*Booth^*	*Williams*	*Ridings*	*Shaw*	*Cruer*	*Jones**	*James/Evans*
							Ref: S Eaton	Dave Ridings returns to the Shay for the first time since 1994, but he's guilty of giving away the penalty, which Paterson scores, when the ball hits his hand. Leigh are no match for the Shaymen. Brook rounds David Felgate, ex-Bolton, for 2-0. Horsfield isn't left out – he scores a tap-in.											
3Q	H	OSSETT TOWN	1	W	5-0	4-0	H'rsf'd 15, Hulme 20, 45, Brook 39, 52	Martin	Thackeray	Bradshaw	O'Regan	Brown	Stoneman	Paterson	Hulme*	Brook^	Horsfield	Lyons"	Horner/Place/Griffiths
11/10		1,060 *NC:P*						*Leneghan*	*Dodd G*	*Oliver"*	*Adams*	*Danby*	*Edmundson*	*Warburton*	*Portray**	*Sayar^*	*Dodd D*	*Shaw*	*Wright/Crowther/Fellowes*
							Ref: G Salisbury	There is disappointment at the Shay as Peter Jackson leaves to take over as manager of Huddersfield. Town have also lost their first game in the Spalding Cup. No chance of losing this one, for Ossett are as poor as the scoreline suggests, and Town ease off after Brook heads the fifth.											
4Q	A	GAINSBOROUGH	1	L	1-2	1-1	Horsfield 34	Martin	Thackeray	Bradshaw	O'Regan	Kilcline	Stoneman	Horner	Hulme*	Brook^	Horsfield	Brown	Lyons/Griffiths
25/10		*1,730 UL:P*					*Morrow 45, Bradshaw 75 (og)*	*Sherwood*	*Hanby*	*Limber*	*Ogley*	*Timons*	*Ellender*	*Brown*	*Price*	*Morrow*	*Riley*	*Dennis*	
							Ref: K Lynch	Gary Brook was once in charge at Gainsborough, and actually recommended present manager Ernie Moss to the post. Moss continues a good record against Town. Steve Sherwood, a Cup finalist in '84, denies Horsfield, before Bradshaw bundles Morrow's mis-hit shot over the line.											

FA Trophy																			
1	H	BLYTH	1	W	2-1	1-0	Brook 11, Lyons 90	Martin	Thackeray	Bradshaw	Murphy	O'Regan	Stonemam	Paterson	Hulme	Brook !	Horsfield*	Brown	Lyons
10/1		1,712 *UL:P*					*Moat 71*	*Jones*	*Farrey*	*Pike*	*Tinkler*	*McGarrigle*	*Cole*	*Ainsley*	*Atkinson**	*Renforth*	*Fletcher^*	*Hislop*	*Moat/Walker*
							Ref: A Bates	Soccer eccentric John Burridge is player-manager at Blyth, but the keeper with more than 600 league appearances to his name sits this one out, literally – on top of the dug out. Town struggle, and Brook's 83rd-minute sending off doesn't help. Lyons' last-gasp curler sees them through.											
2	H	SLOUGH	1	D	1-1	0-0	Paterson 51	Martin	Thackeray	Bradshaw	Murphy	O'Regan	Stoneman	Paterson	Hulme*	Hanson^	Horsfield	Brown	Kilcline/Lyons
31/1		1,633 *10*					*West 84*	*Wikerson*	*Smart*	*Hardyman*	*McGinnis**	*Hercules*	*Angus*	*Bailey*	*Abbot^*	*Brazil*	*Browne*	*Bolt*	*Stowell/West*
							Ref: S Brand	Slough were beaten here last week in the Conference and offered little in attack. It's a different story this time, and Paterson's shot on the turn that gives Town the lead actually comes against the run of play. Their luck runs out when Mark West heads home a free-kick to force a replay.											
2R	A	SLOUGH	1	L	0-2	0-1		Martin	Thackeray	Bradshaw	Murphy	Kilcline	Stoneman	O'Regan	Hulme	Hanson*	Horsfield^	Brown	Lyons/Midwood
3/2		*876 10*					*Brazil 17, Abbott 64*	*Wilkerson*	*Smart*	*Hardyman*	*McGinnis*	*Hercules*	*Angus*	*Bailey*	*Browne*	*Brazil*	*Abbott*	*Bolt*	
							Ref: D Gallagher	Town's priority is the Conference, and this is a replay they don't need. Interest in the Trophy ends here, but it might not be a bad thing. Rivals Cheltenham will pay the price for winning it. At Wexham Park, Town arrive late, play well, but fall to Brazil's tidy shot and Abbott's header.											

	P	Home W	D	L	F	A	Away W	D	L	F	A	Pts
1 HALIFAX	42	17	4	0	51	15	8	8	5	23	28	87
2 Cheltenham	42	15	4	2	39	15	8	5	8	24	28	78
3 Woking	42	14	3	4	47	22	8	5	8	25	24	74
4 Rushden	42	12	4	5	44	26	11	1	9	35	31	74
5 Morecambe	42	11	4	6	35	30	10	6	5	42	34	73
6 Hereford	42	11	7	3	30	19	7	6	8	26	30	67
7 Hednesford	42	14	4	3	28	12	4	8	9	31	38	66
8 Slough	42	10	6	5	34	21	8	4	9	24	28	64
9 Northwich	42	8	9	4	34	24	7	6	8	29	35	60
10 Welling	42	11	5	5	39	27	6	4	11	25	35	60
11 Yeovil	42	14	3	4	45	24	3	5	13	28	39	59
12 Hayes	42	10	4	7	36	25	6	6	9	26	27	58
13 Dover	42	10	4	7	34	29	5	6	10	26	41	55
14 Kettering	42	8	6	7	29	29	5	7	9	24	31	52
15 Stevenage	42	8	8	5	35	27	5	4	12	24	36	51
16 Southport	42	9	5	7	32	26	4	6	11	24	32	50
17 Kidderminster	42	6	8	7	32	31	5	6	10	24	32	47
18 Farnborough	42	10	3	8	37	27	2	5	14	19	43	44
19 Leek	42	8	8	5	34	26	2	6	13	18	41	44
20 Telford	42	6	7	8	25	31	4	5	12	28	45	42
21 Gateshead	42	7	6	8	32	35	1	5	15	19	52	35
22 Stalybridge	42	6	5	10	33	38	1	3	17	15	55	29
	924	225	117	120	785	559	120	117	225	559	785	1269

Odds & ends

Double wins: (6) Farnborough, Kidderminster, Stalybridge, Stevenage, Telford, Yeovil.
Double losses: (0).

Won from behind: (8) Kidderminster (h), Leek (h), Morecambe (h), Northwich (h), Southport (h), Yeovil (h), Farnborough (a), Stevenage (a).
Lost from in front: (1) Gainsborough (FAC) (a).

High spots: Twelve matches unbeaten from the start of the season.
Another run of twelve unbeaten matches up to 18 April.
Clinching the title at Kidderminster.
Eight consecutive league wins up to 18 October – a club record.
New terracing at the Shay being ready for Football League inspection, and being approved.

Low spots: Two 0-4 defeats, at Cheltenham and Rushden.
Failing to win the last three matches.
Losing 2-6 at Welling on the final day.

Halifax lost only five games in the league – a club record.
Geoff Horsfield was the Conference leading scorer with 30 goals, one ahead of Rushden's Darren Collins.

Player of the Year: Jamie Paterson.
Ever-presents: (1) Mark Bradshaw.
Hat-tricks: Geoff Horsfield (3).
Leading scorer: Geoff Horsfield (34).

	Appearances Lge	*Sub*	FAC	*Sub*	FAT	*Sub*	Goals Lge	FAC	FAT	Tot
Boardman, Craig	**4**	*1*		*2*						
Bradshaw, Mark	**42**		4		3		**5**			**5**
Brook, Gary	**18**	*4*	4		1		**3**	5	1	**9**
Brown, Jon	**37**		4		3					
Griffiths, Willie		*2*		*2*						
Hanson, Dave	**6**	*4*			2		**2**			**2**
Horner, Noel	**10**	*8*	1	*2*						
Horsfield, Geoff	**40**		4		3		**30**	4		**34**
Hulme, Kevin	**30**		4		3		**7**	2		**9**
Hurst, Chris	**2**	*1*								
Jackson, Peter	**8**		2							
Kilcline, Brian	**23**	*1*	1		1	*1*	**2**			**2**
Kiwomya, Andy		*5*								
Lyons, Darren	**13**	*11*	1	*2*		*3*	**3**		1	**4**
Martin, Lee	**32**		4		3					
Midwood, Michael	**5**					*1*				
Morgan, Phil	**1**									
Murphy, Jamie	**27**	*1*			3					
O'Regan, Kieran	**36**	*1*	4		3		**1**			**1**
Paterson, Jamie	**36**		3		2		**14**	3	1	**18**
Philliskirk, Tony	**4**						**2**			**2**
Place, Damian		*1*		*1*						
Rhodes, Andy	**8**									
Stoneman, Paul	**38**		4		3		**2**			**2**
Thackeray, Andy	**41**		4		3		**2**			**2**
Woods, Andy	**1**									
(own-goals)							**1**			**1**
26 players used	**462**	***40***	**44**	***9***	**33**	***5***	**74**	**14**	**3**	**91**

No	Date		Att	Pos	Pt	F-A	H-T	Scorers, Times, and Referees	1	2	3	4	5	6	7	8	9	10	11	subs used
1	A	PETERBOROUGH		4	W	2-0	0-0	Hanson 48, Horsfield 75	Martin	Thackeray	Bradshaw	**Lucas**	Stoneman	**Murphy S**	**Duerden**	Hulme	Hanson	Horsfield	Brown	
	8/8		*5,746*		3				*Tyler*	*Scott*	*McMenamin*	*Castle*	*Bodley*	*Edwards*	*Farrell**	*Payne^*	*Carruthers"*	*Quinn*	*Houghton*	*Gill/Hooper/Grazioli*
								Ref: E Lomas	Kieran O'Regan took over only two days ago but his makeshift side comes up trumps before 1,000 travelling supporters. Posh's Jimmy Quinn squanders an early chance. Mark Bodley falls over to let in Hanson for the first. Horsfield dances through the defence to seal a memorable win.											
2	H	BRENTFORD		3	W	1-0	1-0	Horsfield 31	Martin	Thackeray	Bradshaw	Sertori	Murphy S	Stoneman	Lucas	Hulme	Hanson	Horsfield*	Brown	Duerden
	15/8		3,876	*7*	6				*Dearden*	*Boxall*	*Watson*	*Cullip**	*Powell*	*Bates*	*Rowlands*	*Aspinall^*	*Quinn*	*Rapley*	*Scott*	*Owusu/Freeman*
								Ref: C Foy	League football returns to the Shay. Brentford, under the wing of chairman Ron Noades, who also picks the team, are fancied to win promotion at the first attempt. They look useful, but leave empty handed. Hanson has hit the bar before Horsfield nets the only goal off Murphy's corner.											
3	A	DARLINGTON		2	D	2-2	0-1	Horsfield 73, 78	Martin	Thackeray	Bradshaw	Sertori	Lucas	Stoneman	Butler	Hulme	Hanson	Horsfield	Brown*	O'Regan
	22/8		*4,200*	*14*	7			*Naylor 1, Gabbiadini 58*	*Preece*	*Pepper*	*Hope*	*Liddle*	*Tutill**	*Devos*	*Gaughan"*	*Naylor*	*Dorner^*	*Gabbiadini*	*Atkinson*	*Tutill/Shutt/Roberts*
								Ref: P Richards	Naylor lobs over Martin with the game only 37 seconds old. Town are second best for most of the time, and when Gabbiadini (ex Sunderland and Derby) fires in, they look out for the count. Then Horsfield strikes twice, running at the defence to score the equaliser from a narrow angle.											
4	H	SHREWSBURY		1	W	2-0	1-0	Hulme 41, Horsfield 62	Martin	Thackeray	Bradshaw	Lucas	Sertori	Stoneman	Butler	Hulme	Hanson	Horsfield	Brown	
	28/8		3,424	*16*	10				*Edwards*	*Seabury*	*Hanmer*	*Wilding*	*Preece**	*Gayle*	*Berkley*	*Jagielka*	*White*	*Evans*	*Jobling*	*Brown*
								Ref: J Robinson	This Friday night switch gives Town the chance to go top overnight, which they take. It's easy to see how Jake King's side lost 0-3 at home to Cardiff last weekend. They have no ideas once Hulme crashes in a shot that Edwards never sees. Brian Gayle blunders for Horsfield's strike.											
5	A	PLYMOUTH		4	L	0-1	0-1		Martin	Thackeray	Bradshaw	Sertori	Lucas	Stoneman	Butler	Hulme	Hanson	Horsfield	Brown	
	31/8		*6,544*	*3*	10			*Gibbs 42*	*Sheffield*	*Flash*	*Gibbs*	*Mauge**	*Heathcote*	*Wotton*	*Barlow*	*McCarthy*	*Jean^*	*Collins*	*Hargreaves*	*Power/McCall*
								Ref: R Styles	Martin makes a series of fine saves, but is beaten by a fluke cross. Argyle's full-back floats the ball over from near the touchline, only to see it deceive everyone and end up in the net. Town's unbeaten start comes to an end, but may have been still intact had Horsfield not headed over.											
6	H	HARTLEPOOL		2	W	2-1	2-0	Hulme 21, Horsfield 22	Martin	Thackeray	Bradshaw	Sertori	Lucas	Stoneman	O'Regan	Hulme*	Hanson	Horsfield	Brown	Murphy J
	4/9		3,820	*5*	13			*Beech 49*	*Hollund*	*Knowles*	*Ingram*	*Barron*	*Lee*	*Beech*	*Miller*	*Midgley"*	*McDonald**	*Howard*	*Clark^*	*Evans/Irvine/Pemberton*
								Ref: M Pike	Sky TV screen this one live. Town under-perform and are grateful for two goals in the space of a minute. Both are from close range, Horsfield scoring a brave far-post header. The second half is delayed by irate visiting fans who have a poor view. Beech runs unchallenged for his goal.											
7	A	SOUTHEND		5	D	0-0	0-0		Martin	Thackeray	Bradshaw	Sertori	Lucas !	Stoneman	Butler	Hulme	Hanson*	Horsfield	Brown	**Williams^**/O'Regan
	8/9		*3,620*	*8*	14				*Margetson*	*Halls*	*Stimson**	*Morley*	*Newman*	*Dublin*	*Maher*	*Gooding*	*Conlon*	*Whyte*	*Burns*	*Jones*
								Ref: P Walton	Former West Ham and England defender Alvin Martin is manager at Roots Hall. He includes in his side £90,000 Barry Conlon from Man City. Halifax battle gamely for a point. Peter Butler, a former Southend player, leaves a free-kick to Lucas, who then gets sent off for time wasting!											
8	H	CARDIFF		5	L	1-2	0-0	O'Regan 60	Martin	Thackeray	Bradshaw	Sertori	Lucas	Stoneman	Butler*	Hulme	Hanson	Horsfield	Brown	O'Regan
	11/9		2,814	*10*	14			*Fowler 80, Thomas 84*	*Hallworth*	*Delaney*	*Eckhardt*	*Mitchell*	*Jarman*	*Carpenter*	*Bonner*	*Brazier*	*Thomas*	*Nugent^*	*O'Sullivan**	*Fowler/Williams*
								Ref: P Dowd	Town blow their chance to go back to the top. The side's performance is baffling. Horsfield hits the bar in the first half, but it takes O'Regan's deflected free-kick to put Town ahead. Cardiff look dangerous and turn the game around. Dai Thomas runs from halfway to score the winner.											
9	A	HULL		5	W	2-1	0-0	Horsfield 63, Hanson 79	Martin	Thackeray	Bradshaw	Sertori	Lucas*	Stoneman	O'Regan	Hulme	Hanson	Horsfield	Brown	Paterson
	19/9		*4,719*	*23*	17			*McGinty 81*	*Wilson*	*French**	*Mann*	*Hocking*	*Whitworth*	*Hawes*	*Peacock*	*D'Auria*	*Brown^*	*Saville*	*McGinty*	*Rioch/Morley*
								Ref: R Furnandiz	Hull are in all sorts of trouble at the foot of the table, with the Tigers' fans urging owner David Lloyd to leave the club. But they welcome back old favourite Andy Saville. Manager Tony Hateley despairs at his side's amateurish defending that allows Town to put the game out of reach.											
10	H	TORQUAY		6	D	1-1	0-0	Paterson 76	Martin	Thackeray*	Bradshaw	Sertori	Butler	Stoneman	Paterson	Hulme	Hanson^	Horsfield	O'Regan	Williams/Lucas
	26/9		2,753		18			*McFarlane 83*	*Gregg*	*Gurney*	*Herrera*	*Robinson*	*Thomas*	*Monk*	*Clayton^*	*Leadbitter*	*Donaldson**	*Partridge*	*Waddle*	*McFarlane/McGorry*
								Ref: M Cowburn	Former England forward Chris Waddle is the star attraction. He's helping out old colleague Wes Saunders, boss at Torquay, and is barracked by the Shay crowd. But he has the last laugh by sending over the free-kick for McFarlane's equaliser. Horsfield played in Paterson for his goal.											
11	A	SCUNTHORPE		3	W	4-0	0-0	Paterson 49, 76, Williams 58, 81	Martin^	O'Regan*	Bradshaw	Sertori	Murphy J	Stoneman	Paterson	Hulme	Williams	Butler	Lucas	Brown/**Carter**
	3/10		*4,989*	*1*	21				*Clarke*	*Fickling"*	*McAuley*	*Logan*	*Wilcox*	*Hope*	*Walker*	*Forrester**	*Eyre*	*Gayle^*	*Calvo-Garcia*	*Stamp/Bull/Marshall*
								Ref: P Danson	Brian Laws has taken Scunthorpe to the top of the table and has just been named Manager of the Month for September. The Shaymen then take his side apart. Horsfield is ruled out with a virus, but Marc Williams shows he isn't missed. He scores twice, and makes the others for Paterson.											

No	Venue	Opponent	Att			F-A	H-T	Scorers, Times, and Referees	1	2	3	4	5	6	7	8	9	10	11	subs used
12	A	ROCHDALE		5	L	0-1	0-1		Martin	Thackeray	Bradshaw	Sertori	Murphy J	Stoneman	Paterson	Hulme*	Williams	Butler	Lucas	Brown
11/10			*3,628*	*18*	21			*Williams 44*	*Edwards*	*Williams*	*Barlow*	*Hill*	*Jones*	*Johnson*	*Diaz*	*Painter*	*Lancashire**	*Bryson*	*Peake*	*Leonard*
								Ref: P Rejer	All talk is about Horsfield's impending move to Kevin Keegan's Fulham. At Spotland, an uninspired Town fall behind to Mark Williams' free-kick. Brown almost equalises with a shot that comes down off the bar and somehow bounces over. Sertori and Hill come to blows at the end.											
13	H	BARNET		4	D	1-1	1-0	Guinan 30	Martin	Thackeray	Bradshaw	Sertori	Murphy J	Stoneman	Paterson	**Guinan**	Williams*	Butler	Lucas	Brown
16/10			2,223	*19*				*Charlery 90*	*Harrison*	*Stockley*	*Sawyers**	*Alsford*	*Basham*	*Arber*	*Searle*	*Doolan*	*Charlery*	*McGleish*	*Simpson*	*Devine*
								Ref: R Pearson	Horsfield has moved to Fulham in a record deal, so O'Regan takes Steve Guinan on loan from Forest. He makes a pleasing debut, and dances into the box to put Town ahead. In injury-time, Martin spills the ball, Stoneman miskicks, and Charlery stabs home Barnet's deserved leveller.											
14	H	CAMBRIDGE		8	D	3-3	2-2	Stoneman 20, Thackeray 25, Paterson 60	Martin	Thackeray	Bradshaw	Sertori	Murphy J	Stoneman	Paterson	Guinan	Williams	Butler	O'Regan	
20/10			**1,906**		23			*Butler 5, Russell 40, Ashbee 65*	*Marshall*	*Chenery*	*Mustoe*	*Duncan*	*Joseph*	*Campbell*	*Wanless*	*Taylor**	*Butler*	*Young*	*Russell*	*Ashbee*
								Ref: D Laws	A passionate encounter where the action swings from one end to the other. Williams hits the post for Town, then Butler puts Cambridge ahead. They are temporarily down to nine men when Stoneman equalises. Paterson makes it 3-2, then Cambridge level it from a debatable free-kick.											
15	A	LEYTON ORIENT		8	L	0-1	0-1		Martin	Thackeray	Bradshaw	Sertori	Murphy J	Stoneman	Paterson	Guinan	Williams	Butler	O'Regan	
24/10			*3,655*	*10*	23			*Inglethorpe 7*	*MacKenzie*	*Walschaerts*	*Lockwood*	*Smith*	*Hicks*	*Clark*	*Ling*	*Joseph*	*Richards^*	*Simba"*	*Inglethorpe**	*Ampadu/Griffiths/Watts*
								Ref: A D'Urso	Games around London are being called off left, right and centre, but referee Tony D'Urso elects to play this one. It is played in near-gale force winds, and the pitch is covered in water. After Alex Inglethorpe's early goal, both sides struggle, although Andy Thackeray twice hits the post.											
16	H	SWANSEA		6	W	2-0	1-0	Hulme 35, Paterson 88	Martin	Thackeray	Bradshaw	Sertori !	Murphy J	Stoneman	Paterson	Hulme*	Williams	Guinan	O'Regan	Brown
31/10			2,383		26				*Freestone*	*Jones*	*Howard*	*Jenkins*	*O'Leary**	*Bound*	*Price^*	*Thomas*	*Alsop*	*Watkin*	*Appleby*	*Bird/Roberts*
								Ref: M Messias	Hulme comes into the side because of injury to Butler, but pops up to convert Bradshaw's cross. Swansea manager John Hollins, ex-Chelsea star, describes his side's display as the worst of the season. Town have Sertori sent off in the 88th minute, then Paterson blasts in a right-footer.											
17	A	CARLISLE		4	W	1-0	0-0	Stoneman 89	Carter*	Thackeray	Bradshaw	Sertori	Murphy J	Stoneman	Paterson	Hulme	Williams	Guinan	Brown	Lucas
7/11			*3,636*	*19*	29				*Caig*	*Bowman*	*Searle*	*Whitehead*	*Brightwell*	*Pokas*	*Hopper*	*Clark**	*Stevens*	*Thorpe*	*Finney*	*Dobie*
								Ref: M Dean	Tim Carter comes in for unwell Lee Martin, but he only lasts 45 minutes. He takes a nasty knock from Jeff Thorpe, and doesn't reappear after the break. Hulme takes over in goal and makes a string of fine saves. Stoneman rounds off an eventful day by heading in Paterson's free-kick.											
18	H	CHESTER		1	W	3-2	1-0	Paterson 21, Thackeray 70, 74	Martin	Thackeray	Bradshaw	Sertori	Murphy J	Stoneman	Paterson	Hulme !	Williams*	Guinan	Brown	Lucas
10/11			2,427	*19*	32			*Beckett 53, Murphy 68*	*Cutler*	*Davidson"*	*Cross*	*Richardson*	*Crosby*	*Woods*	*Flitcroft**	*Priest !*	*Murphy*	*Beckett^*	*Smith*	*Reid/Wright/Shelton*
								Ref: A Leake	Halifax go top in dramatic fashion. The scores are level, when a mass 22-man brawl breaks out in the 55th minute. Hulme and Priest are both sent off, but Hulme wants to continue things in the tunnel. Chester then go in front, but Thackeray pops up twice, sticking out a leg to win it.											
19	A	BRIGHTON		1	W	1-0	1-0	Paterson 7	Martin	Thackeray	Bradshaw	Lucas	Murphy J	Stoneman	Paterson	Butler	Williams*	Guinan	Brown	Murphy S
21/11			*3,305*	*13*	35				*Ormerod*	*Browne*	*Sturgess**	*Minton*	*Bennett*	*Johnson*	*Thomas*	*Arnott*	*Hart*	*Barker"*	*Culverhouse^*	*Mayo/Storer/Moralee*
								Ref: R Oliver	Brighton are playing all their home games at Gillingham's Priestfield Stadium. Defeats like this won't help manager Brian Horton's chances of staying in the job. One piece of Paterson magic sees his 15-yarder go in, then it's a backs-to-the-wall job as Brighton pile it on without success.											
20	H	MANSFIELD		1	D	2-2	0-2	Thackeray 63, Paterson 90p	Martin	Thackeray	Bradshaw	Lucas	Murphy J	Murphy S*	Paterson	Butler	Williams	Guinan	Brown	**Newton**
27/11			3,227	*5*	36			*Ford 4, Peacock 19p*	*Bowling*	*Ford*	*Harper*	*Peters !*	*Clarke*	*Hackett*	*Schofield^*	*Walker"*	*Lormor**	*Peacock*	*Tallon*	*Christie/Kerr/Williams*
								Ref: K Hill	The ageless Tony Ford gives Mansfield the lead early on, but lose Peters minutes later, sent off for a two-footed tackle. They go 2-0 up with a dubious penalty for hands, but Town claw their way back. Paterson's cool penalty, deep into injury-time, enables Town to go three points clear.											
21	A	SCARBOROUGH		5	L	0-1	0-1		Martin	Thackeray	Bradshaw	Lucas	Murphy J	Stoneman	Paterson	Butler	Williams	Guinan^	Brown*	**Power**/Newton
12/12			*2,251*	*23*	36			*Brodie 31*	*Weaver*	*Jackson*	*Atkinson*	*Robinson^*	*Lydiate*	*Marinkov"*	*Bullimore*	*Hoyland*	*Brodie*	*Greenacre*	*Dablesteen**	*Campbell/Russell/McNaughton*
								Ref: A Butler	Mick Wadsworth's struggling side may have only scored five goals in their last eleven matches, but they only need one to win this game. It's scored by Steve Brodie, following a breakaway move. Scarborough look as poor as Town, but O'Regan says, 'You have to beat sides like that.'											
22	H	EXETER		4	D	1-1	0-1	Williams 86	Martin	Thackeray	Bradshaw^	Sertori	Lucas	Stoneman	Paterson	Butler	Williams	Guinan*	Brown	Hanson/Newton
19/12			2,342	*18*	37			*Lucas 33 (og)*	*Bayes*	*Fry*	*Power*	*Baddeley*	*Cale*	*Gittens*	*Rowbotham*	*Holloway*	*Flack*	*Curran*	*Gardner*	
								Ref: G Cain	Exeter, under Peter Fox, have not won away for 26 matches, but look like ending that depressing run with just five minutes remaining. They lead thanks to an own-goal that is eventually credited to Richard Lucas. Williams saves the day for Town by converting Hanson's knockdown											
23	H	DARLINGTON		5	D	0-0	0-0		Martin	Thackeray	Bradshaw*	Sertori	Murphy J	Stoneman	Newton	Lucas	Williams	Hanson	Brown	Power
26/12			3,557	*11*	38				*Preece*	*Brumwell*	*Barnard*	*Liddle*	*Tutill*	*Bennett*	*Leah*	*Oliver*	*Naylor**	*Gabbiadini*	*Atkinson*	*Roberts*
								Ref: M Warren	Darlington, like Halifax, topped the table earlier this season, but they've fallen away quite a bit. They contribute as little as the Shaymen do in this Boxing Day fixture, played in strong winds and driving rain. O'Regan is so annoyed with his players, he locks them away for 30 minutes.											

No	Date		Att	Pos	Pt	F-A	H-T	Scorers, Times, and Referees	1	2	3	4	5	6	7	8	9	10	11	subs used
24	A	ROTHERHAM		6	L	1-3	1-2	Guinan 2	Carter	Thackeray	Bradshaw	Sertori	Murphy J	Stoneman	Power	Butler*	Hanson^	Guinan	Brown	Lucas/Williams
	28/12		4,728	8	38			Roscoe 22, Knill 31, Raven 84	Pollitt	Ingledow	Hurst	Garner	Knill	Raven	Warner	Thompson	White	Glover	Roscoe	
								Ref: S Mathieson	Guinan gives Town a dream start when presented with an open goal 30 yards out. But a howler from Carter, allowing Roscoe's weak shot to slip through his hands, gets the Millers level. Former Shayman Alan Knill nets their second as some Town fans turn on chairman Jim Brown.											
25	A	SHREWSBURY		6	D	2-2	1-1	Power 41, O'Regan 88	Carter	Thackeray	Bradshaw	Sertori	Murphy J*	Stoneman	O'Regan	Power	Hanson	Guinan	Brown	Williams
	2/1		2,806	20	39			Preece 23, Kerrigan 48	Edwards	Seabury	Hanmer	Wilding	Whelan	Gayle	Berkley	Kerrigan	Jagielka	Evans	Preece	
								Ref: P Richards	Player-manager O'Regan makes his first start since the end of October and fires in a 30-yarder to earn his side a deserved point. He also sets up Power for his first Town goal that cancels out a 30-yarder by Shrews' player-coach Preece. Kerrigan restores their lead by heading in a corner.											
26	H	PETERBOROUGH		6	D	2-2	0-1	Stoneman 51p, Williams 73	Carter	Thackeray	Lucas	Sertori	Butler	Stoneman	O'Regan	Hulme	Williams	Hanson*	Power	Newton
	9/1		2,784	8	40			Castle 13, Butler 46p	Tyler	Scott^	Drury	Hooper	Rennie	Edwards	Davies	Castle	Broughton*	Carruthers"	Farrell	Butler/Haan/Grazioli
								Ref: R Furnandiz	Barry Fry sees his Posh side go two goals ahead when Carter needlessly gives away a penalty. Town fight back, and then have O'Regan's goal mysteriously ruled out. Never lost for words, Fry claims Town's first goal was 'never a penalty', and Williams' equaliser was 'miles offside'.											
27	H	PLYMOUTH		6	W	2-0	0-0	Williams 62, 74	Carter	Thackeray	Bradshaw	Sertori	Stansfield	Stoneman	O'Regan*	Hulme	Williams	Power	Butler	Brown
	23/1		2,762	10	43				Sheffield	Ashton	Beswetherick	Wotton*	Branston	Collins	Barlow	Hargreaves	Marshall"	McCall^	Forinton	Bastow/Sweeney/Jean
								Ref: M Jones	There has been much recent off-field criticism aimed at O'Regan and Jim Brown, but the players, at least, put this to the back of their minds to end a run of seven league games without a win. Power, a Plymouth player at the start of the season, sends Williams away for his second goal.											
28	H	ROTHERHAM		8	L	2-4	1-1	Stoneman 28, Power 69	Carter	Thackeray	Bradshaw	Sertori	Murphy J*	Stoneman	Brown	Hulme	Williams	Power	Butler	Hanson
	30/1		4,251	5	43			Thompson 8p, Warne 55, 63, Jackson 90	Pollitt	Warner	Hurst	Garner	Knill	Strodder	Berry	Thompson	Jackson	Warne	Dillon	
								Ref: M Brandwood	Tim Carter made a bad error at Millmoor, and he makes another one here. He fails to hold Garner's 30-yarder and Warne nips in to restore the visitor's lead. Thackeray concedes the early penalty against Knill, who is almost apologetic. Lee Power's goal for 2-3 is a brave overhead kick.											
29	A	HARTLEPOOL		9	L	0-2	0-2		Carter	Thackeray	Bradshaw	Sertori	Stansfield	Stoneman	**Etherington**	Murphy S*	Williams	Power	Butler	Hanson
	6/2		2,374	20	43			Howard 3, 15	Hollund	Knowles	Ingram	Barron	McGuckin	Elliott	Stephenson	Beardsley	Howard	Midgley*	Brightwell	Irvine
								Ref: C Foy	With Lee Martin already ruled out with a back injury, Carter ends up playing despite having pulled a hamstring. He fails to reach a corner and Howard scores his first. He heads in his second to put Pool in control. Former England star Peter Beardsley works diligently in their midfield.											
30	H	SOUTHEND		7	W	3-1	0-0	Hulme 49, Power 50, 90	Martin	Thackeray	Lucas	Sertori*	Stansfield	Stoneman	Etheringt'n^	Hulme	Williams	**Jackson**	Power	Brown/Grant
	13/2		2,302	19	46			Rapley 55	Margetson	Beard	Booty	Gooding^	Hunter	Coleman	McGavin	Unger	Campbell*	Rapley	Houghton	Conlon/Burns
								Ref: T Jones	Southend can consider themselves unlucky to let this one slip. They enjoy a large share of the possession, but two close-range goals just after half-time put Town in control. Kevin Rapley nips in to give Halifax a nervy last 35, but in injury-time Power scores again – from close range.											
31	A	CARDIFF		6	D	1-1	0-1	Bradshaw 66	Martin	Thackeray	Lucas	Sertori	Stansfield	Stoneman	Etherington	Hulme*	Power^	Jackson"	Bradshaw	Brown/Hanson/Williams
	19/2		8,570	1	47			Eckhardt 45	Hallworth	Young	Legg"	Mitchell	Eckhardt	Carpenter	Fowler	Delaney	Williams*	Nugent	Middleton^	Bowen/Hill/O'Sullivan
								Ref: M Halsey	The Shaymen halt table-topping Cardiff's run of eight consecutive home wins. They keep things tight, but when Jeff Eckhardt heads in on the stroke of half-time the Bluebirds look like extending their run. However. Bradshaw's deflected 25-yarder earns battling Town a deserved point.											
32	H	HULL		10	L	0-1	0-0		Martin	Thackeray	Lucas	Sertori	Stansfield	Brown	Etherington	Hulme	Jackson^	Hanson	Bradshaw*	Grant/Williams
	27/2		4,455	23	47			Brown 54	Wilson	Swales	Greaves	Edwards	Whittle	Brabin	Joyce	D'Auria	Brown	Alcide	Williams	
								Ref: M Pike	Earlier this season Hull looked out for the count. Now, under player-boss Warren Joyce, they are enjoying something of a revival. It's his free-kick that leads to David Brown heading the only goal. But in truth, there is only one team in it and the Shaymen are lucky not to lose by more.											
33	A	TORQUAY		10	L	0-4	0-1	[Bedeau 67]	Martin	Thackeray	Lucas	Sertori	Stansfield	Stoneman !	O'Regan^	Hulme*	Jackson	Hanson	Butler	Brown/Grant
	6/3		1,715	19	47			Robinson 43, Donaldson 48, Hill 54	Southall	Tully*	Nichols	Robinson	Thomas	Leadbitter	Aggrey	Hapgood	Bedeau	Donaldson	Hill^	Jermyn/Worthington
								Ref: A Hall	O'Regan states there is no margin for error as his side hopes now for a play-off spot, but though Torquay hadn't scored for three games, four different players get on the scoresheet. Former Wales keeper Neville Southall has little to do. Stoneman is sent off unluckily in the last minute.											
34	H	CARLISLE		10	W	1-0	0-0	Bradshaw 81	Martin	Murphy J	Bradshaw	Brown	Stansfield	Stoneman	O'Regan	Murphy S^	Jackson	Power	Newton*	Hanson/Lucas
	13/3		2,432	21	50				Caig	Bowman	Searle	Whitehead	Brightwell	Clark	Dobie*	Boertien	Stevens^	Bridge-Wilk'n	Anthony	Tracey/Finney
								Ref: R Oliver	Billy Barr returns to the Shay with Carlisle, but is ruled out through injury. O'Regan overrules assistant-boss Andy May to keep himself on the pitch and perhaps justifies his decision. It's a lifeless affair, and Bradshaw's exquisite 22-yarder is out of character with the rest of the match.											

No	Venue	Opponent	Att	Pos	Res	F-A	H-T	Scorers, Times, and Referees	1	2	3	4	5	6	7	8	9	10	11	Subs used
35	A	BRENTFORD		9	D	1-1	1-1	Stansfield 45	Martin	Murphy J	Bradshaw	Sertori	Stansfield	Stoneman	O'Regan	Brown	Jackson	Power	Butler	
	16/3		*3,713*	*3*	51			*Partridge 29*	*Woodman*	*Boxall*	*Anderson^*	*Hreidarsson"*	*Powell*	*Mahon*	*Folan*	*Partridge*	*Owusu*	*Rowlands**	*Evans*	*Quinn/Scott/Oatway*
								Ref: C Wilkes	The rough pitch doesn't make for pretty football, but Town roll their sleeves up and come away with a point. The Bees break for their goal, but Stansfield's header right on half-time bounces up and in. Woodman may have used his hand to deny Jackson late on. Nine players are booked.											
36	A	SWANSEA		8	W	2-1	0-1	Murphy J 76, Paterson 90	Martin	Murphy J	Bradshaw	Sertori	Stansfield*	Brown	O'Regan^	Hulme	Hanson	Power	Butler	Paterson/Lucas
	20/3		*4,974*	*9*	54			*Cusack 17*	*Freestone*	*O'Leary*	*Howard*	*Cusack*	*Smith*	*Bound*	*Roberts*	*Casey**	*Alspo*	*Watkin*	*Coates*	*Lacey*
								Ref: A D'Urso	A play-off place is still in sight after this important win. Town leave it late after falling behind to Cusack's first goal of the season. Paterson, a 60th-minute sub, delivers the corner that transfer-listed Jamie Murphy heads home, then in injury-time his 25-yarder creeps in at the far post.											
37	H	LEYTON ORIENT		9	L	1-2	0-2	Butler 68	Martin	Brown	Bradshaw	Sertori	Murphy J	O'Regan*	Paterson	Hulme	Jackson	Power	Butler	Hanson
	26/3		2,978	*6*	54			*Omnymni 3, Clark 25*	*Barrett*	*Walschaerts*	*Lockwood*	*Ampadu*	*Hicks*	*Clark*	*Beal*	*Joseph M^*	*Watts**	*Richards*	*Omnymni"*	*Morrison/Joseph R/Maskell*
								Ref: T Heilbron	Ref Tony Heilbron was in charge of last week's Worthington Cup Final, won by Spurs. This is by far a better game. Headers from Omnymni and Clark put the O's in the driving seat. Town have plenty of possession, but only have Butler's deflected 25-yader to show for their efforts.											
38	A	BARNET		11	D	2-2	1-1	Paterson22, Bradshaw 82	Carter	Brown	Bradshaw	Sertori	Murphy J	Stansfield	Paterson	Lucas^	Jackson	Power*	Butler	Hanson/Murphy S
	3/4		*2,055*	*15*	55			*Charlery 35, Onwere 54*	*Harrison*	*Onwere*	*Sawyers*	*Basham*	*Heald*	*Arber*	*Currie*	*Doolan*	*Charlery*	*McGleish*	*Wilson**	*Hackett*
								Ref: K Hill	Town travel to Underhill without five regular first-teamers. Paterson fires them in front, then in the 60th minute, scores direct from a free-kick that was awarded indirect. The ref rules it out. Town fall behind, but equalise through Bradshaw's 35-yarder that may just have been a cross.											
39	H	ROCHDALE		11	D	0-0	0-0		Carter*	Brown^	Bradshaw	Sertori	Murphy J	Stansfield	Paterson	Hulme	Jackson	Power	Butler	O'Regan/Newton
	5/4		2,759	*17*	56				*Edwards*	*Carden*	*Barlow**	*Bayliss*	*Monington*	*Farrell*	*Stoker*	*Painter*	*Morris*	*Peake*	*Lydiate*	*Bryson*
								Ref: P Dowd	The inability of the Shaymen to beat a poor side like Rochdale is one reason why O'Regan is about to lose his job. Tim Carter fails to reappear after the break, so the sight of Kevin Hulme between the sticks for the second time this season makes the game only slightly more interesting.											
40	A	CAMBRIDGE		11	L	0-4	0-0	*[Taylor 87]*	Martin	Brown*	Bradshaw	Lucas	Stansfield	Stoneman	Newton	Murphy S	Jackson	Hanson	Butler	Paterson
	10/4		*4,838*	*1*	56			*Walker 51, Wanless 66, Butler 82,*	*Marshall*	*Ashbee*	*Mustoe^*	*Duncan*	*Eustace*	*Campbell*	*Wanless*	*MacKenzie"*	*Butler*	*Benjamin*	*Walker**	*Taylor/Bruce/Joseph*
								Ref: J Kirkby	Dave Worthington has taken over as caretaker manager. He couldn't have wished for a harder start. Lee Martin makes a fine double save from Butler's controversial penalty for hands in the 37th minute, but the league-leaders take control. Taylor's goal is his 75th for the club - a record.											
41	A	MANSFIELD		9	W	1-0	1-0	Thackeray 31	Martin	Thackeray	Bradshaw	Lucas	Brown	Stoneman	Newton	Hulme^	Jackson"	Murphy S*	Butler	Sertori/Power/Hanson
	13/4		*2,471*	*8*	59				*Bowling*	*Williams*	*Harper*	*Willis*	*Allardyce*	*Linighan*	*Kerr"*	*Ford^*	*Lormor**	*Peacock*	*Clarke*	*Christie/Walker/Schofield*
								Ref: B Knight	Town make up the points on the Stags, who were lying seventh, four points above them. Thackeray's side-footed goal, off Jackson's pull-back, proves enough. Margin of victory could have been more. The ref originally awards Town a penalty, then decides to book Newton for diving.											
42	H	BRIGHTON		7	W	1-0	1-0	Jackson 28	Martin	Thackeray	Bradshaw	Sertori	Brown	Stoneman	Newton"	Hulme*	Jackson^	Lucas	Butler	Paterson/Murphy J/Hanson
	17/4		2,773	*15*	62				*Ormerod*	*Bennett^*	*Mayo*	*Minton*	*Hobson*	*McPherson*	*Storer**	*Arnott*	*Hart*	*Moralee*	*Sturgess"*	*Barker/Smith/Ansah*
								Ref: G Laws	Like Town, Brighton have dispensed with their manager. Mickey Adams has taken over from Jeff Woods, and this is his first game. It is also Worthington's first at home. Justin Jackson, who badly needs a goal, scores a beauty. He cuts in and lets fly with a shot that goes in off the bar.											
43	A	CHESTER		8	D	2-2	1-1	Newton 44, Bradshaw 86	Martin	Thackeray	Bradshaw	Sertori	Brown	Stoneman	Newton	Hulme	Jackson*	Lucas	Butler^	Paterson/Hanson
	24/4		*2,461*	*15*	63			*Priest 20, Beckett 65*	*Cutler*	*Davidson**	*Cross*	*Richardson*	*Crosby*	*Woods*	*Flitcroft*	*Priest*	*Murphy*	*Beckett*	*Fisher^*	*Reid/Shelton*
								Ref: L Cable	Chester earlier survived a financial crisis, and so are happy still to be here. They have nothing to play for, but make life hard for the Shaymen, who find themselves twice behind. Newton's first senior goal from outside the box is bettered by Bradshaw's late 30-yarder into the top corner.											
44	H	SCUNTHORPE		7	W	1-0	0-0	Stoneman 68	Martin	Thackeray	Lucas	Sertori	Murphy S	Stoneman	Paterson	Hulme*	Jackson	Newton	Butler	Hanson
	27/4		3,486	*4*	66				*Evans*	*Witter*	*Dawson*	*Logan*	*Harsley*	*Hope*	*Walker*	*Forrester*	*Eyre*	*Gayle**	*Calvo-G'rcia^*	*Wilcox/Sheldon*
								Ref: M Fletcher	Scunthorpe still have an outside chance of automatic promotion. They try to muscle the Shaymen out of the game with their physical approach. Chances are few, but Stoneman gets his head to Paterson's hanging cross, and the ball, Evans, and the onrushing Hulme all end up in the net.											
45	H	SCARBOROUGH		7	L	1-1	1-2	Jackson 24	Martin	Brown*	Bradshaw	Sertori	Murphy S	Stoneman	Paterson^	Newton"	Jackson	Hanson	Butler	Thackeray/Power/Lucas
	1/5		3,308	*24*	66			*Atkinson 7, Brodie 9*	*Parks*	*Russell*	*Atkinson*	*Worrall*	*Renison*	*McNaughton*	*Hoyland*	*Jones*	*Tate*	*Brodie**	*Roberts^*	*Carr/Robinson*
								Ref: K Lynch	A minute's silence is observed for Alf Ramsey, who died in midweek. Scarborough, fighting for their lives, have lost their last five matches but are two up within nine minutes. Town, wearing their new striped kit, pull one back but struggle thereafter, although Hanson hits the post.											
46	A	EXETER		10	L	1-2	1-1	Jackson 43	Martin	Thackeray	Lucas	Sertori	Murphy S	Stoneman	Paterson	Hulme*	Jackson	Brown^	Butler	Hanson/Newton
	8/5		3,180	*12*	66			*Thackeray 44 (og), Curran 90*	*Potter*	*Curran*	*Power*	*Holloway"*	*Richardson*	*Gittens*	*Rowboth'm^*	*Rees*	*Flack*	*Fry*	*Wikinson**	*Breslan/Smith/Waugh*
		Home	Away					Ref: D Crick	It's a painful last game in charge for Worthington. He watches on crutches after ripping a knee running for the team bus, then sees the play-off disappear. But Swansea's win makes it all academic. Thackeray's headed own-goal cancels out Jackson's strike which put Town in dreamland.											
Average		3,002	3,921																	

Worthington Cup						F-A	H-T	Scorers, Times, and Referees	1	2	3	4	5	6	7	8	9	10	11	subs used
1:1	A	WREXHAM		4	W	2-0	1-0	Horsfield 11, Hanson 81	Martin	Thackeray	Bradshaw	**Sertori**	Stoneman	Murphy S !	Lucas	Hulme	Hansonˆ	Horsfield*	Brown	**Overson**/Duerden
	11/8		2,655	*2:*					*Cartwright*	*McGregor*	*Brace*	*Owen*	*Humes*	*Carey*	*Chalkˆ*	*Russell**	*Connolly*	*Rush*	*Ward*	*Brammer/Skinner*
								Ref: S Mathieson	Ex-Liverpool striker Ian Rush, now player-coach at Wrexham, jointly holds the record with Geoff Hurst of most goals in this competition, but he is upstaged by Town's strike-force. Town have to manage for 62 minutes without Stephen Murphy, sent off for a crude challenge on Owen.											
1:2	H	WREXHAM		3	L	0-2	0-1		Martin	Thackeray	Lucas	**Butler** !	Sertori	Stoneman	Murphy S	Hulme	Hanson	Horsfield*	Brown	O'Regan
	18/8		2,692	*2:*				*Roberts 26, Connolly 76p*	*Cartwright*	*McGregor*	*Hardy**	*Brammer*	*Ridler*	*Carey*	*Roberts*	*Owen*	*Connolly*	*Rushˆ*	*Ward"*	*Skinner/Spink/Russell*
								Ref: T Heilbron (Halifax won 4-2 on penalties)	Neil Roberts halves the deficit after 26 minutes, but Town suffer the loss of debutant Peter Butler, sent off just before the interval. Connolly's penalty brings the tie level. Town dig deep in extra-time, but the game goes to penalties. Town go through when Martin saves from Brammer.											
2:1	H	BRADFORD C		5	L	1-2	0-1	Hanson 57	Martin	Thackeray	Bradshaw	Sertori	Lucas	Stoneman	O'Regan*	Hulme	Hanson	Horsfield	Brown	Paterson
	15/9		5,716	*1:*				*Moore 33, Beagrie 68*	*Walsh*	*Wright*	*Jacobs*	*McCall*	*Moore*	*Dreyer*	*Pepper*	*Blake**	*Mills*	*Whalley*	*Beagrie*	*Watson*
								Ref: J Kirkby	Paul Jewell has been appointed the Bantams' boss but his side have made a slow start in Division One. They leave the Shay with an advantage, though. Moore heads in their opener. Hanson replies with a diving header, but Town are out-done when Peter Beagrie cuts inside and lets fly.											
2:2	A	BRADFORD C		5	L	1-3	0-0	Paterson 53	Martin	Thackeray	Bradshaw	Sertori	Butler	Stoneman	Paterson	Hulme	Hanson	Horsfield	O'Regan*	Williams
	22/9		6,237	*1:21*				*Blake 56, Beagrie 77p, Pepper 81*	*Walsh*	*Wright*	*Jacobs*	*McCallˆ*	*Moore*	*O'Brien*	*Pepper"*	*Blake*	*Watson**	*Whalley*	*Beagrie*	*Edhino/Ramage/Dryer*
								Ref: B Coddington (Halifax lost 2-5 on aggregate)	The ref is the only person to see Hulme's tug on Blake. He awards City a crucial penalty, and the tie slips away from Town. Earlier, Paterson sees Walsh save his spot kick, but he nets the rebound. Town's interest ends when Stoneman falls on the ball to allow Pepper to get the third.											

FA Cup																				
1	A	MANCHESTER C		1	L	0-3	0-2		Martin	Thackeray	Bradshaw	Sertori	Murphy J	Stoneman	Paterson	Lucas*	Williams	Butler	Brown	Murphy S
	13/11		11,106	*2:7*				*Russell 6, 34, Goater 64*	*Weaver*	*Crooks*	*Vaughan*	*Morrison*	*Wiekens*	*Horlock**	*Bishopˆ*	*Mason*	*Goater*	*Dickov*	*Russell*	*Brown/Pollock*
								Ref: R Pearson	This game evokes memories of the 1980 meeting, won by Town, and is played on a Friday night for the Sky TV cameras. Halifax do without Hulme, suspended by the club for his part in the Chester brawl, but never get into gear. Transfer-listed Craig Russell proves to be City's hero.											

		Home						Away					
	P	W	D	L	F	A	W	D	L	F	A	Pts
1 Brentford	46	16	5	2	45	18	10	2	11	34	38	85
2 Cambridge	46	13	6	4	41	21	10	6	7	37	27	81
3 Cardiff	46	13	7	3	35	17	9	7	7	25	22	80
4 Scunthorpe*	46	14	3	6	42	28	8	5	10	27	30	74
5 Rotherham	46	11	8	4	41	26	9	5	9	38	35	73
6 Leyton Orient	46	12	6	5	40	30	7	9	7	28	29	72
7 Swansea	46	11	9	3	33	19	8	5	10	23	29	71
8 Mansfield	46	15	2	6	38	18	4	8	11	22	40	67
9 Peterborough	46	11	4	8	41	29	7	8	8	31	27	66
10 HALIFAX	46	10	8	5	33	25	7	7	9	25	31	66
11 Darlington	46	10	6	7	41	24	8	5	10	28	34	65
12 Exeter	46	13	5	5	32	18	4	7	12	15	32	63
13 Plymouth	46	11	6	6	32	19	6	4	13	26	35	61
14 Chester	46	6	12	5	28	30	7	6	10	29	36	57
15 Shrewsbury	46	11	6	6	36	29	3	8	12	16	34	56
16 Barnet	46	10	5	8	30	31	4	8	11	24	40	55
17 Brighton	46	8	3	12	25	35	8	4	11	24	31	55
18 Southend	46	8	6	9	24	21	6	6	11	28	37	54
19 Rochdale	46	9	8	6	22	21	4	7	12	20	34	54
20 Torquay	46	9	9	5	29	20	3	8	12	18	38	53
21 Hull	46	8	5	10	25	28	6	6	11	19	34	53
22 Hartlepool	46	8	7	8	33	27	5	5	13	19	38	51
23 Carlisle	46	8	8	7	25	21	3	8	12	18	32	49
24 Scarborough	46	8	3	12	30	39	6	3	14	20	38	48
	1104	253	147	152	801	594	152	147	253	594	801	1509

* promoted after play-offs

Odds & ends

Double wins: (4) Brighton, Carlisle, Scunthorpe, Swansea.
Double losses: (3) Leyton Orient, Rotherham, Scarborough.

Won from behind: (2) Chester (h), Swansea (a).
Lost from in front: (3) Cardiff (h), Exeter (a), Rotherham (a).

High spots: Being unbeaten in the first four matches to go top.
Four consecutive wins up to 21 November.
Beating Chester in a stormy game on 10 November go top again.
Beating 2nd Division Wrexham on penalties in the Worthington Cup.

Low spots: Seven games without a win up to 9 January.
Losing home and away to Scarborough, who were demoted.
Selling top scorer Geoff Horsfield to Fulham in October.
Failing to make the play-offs.

The Worthington Cup-tie with Bradford City realised new record receipts of £36,267 at the Shay.

Player of the Year: Paul Stoneman.
Ever-presents: (0).
Hat-tricks: (0).
Leading scorer: Jamie Paterson (11).

	Appearances						Goals			
	Lge	*Sub*	LC	*Sub*	FAC	*Sub*	Lge	LC	FAC	Tot
Bradshaw, Mark	**41**		3		1		**4**			**4**
Brown, Jon	**32**	*8*	3		1					
Butler, Peter	**33**		2		1		**1**			**1**
Carter, Tim	**9**	*1*								
Duerden, Ian	**1**	*1*		*1*						
Etherington, Craig	**4**									
Grant, Gareth		*3*								
Guinan, Steve	**12**						**2**			**2**
Hanson, Dave	**19**	*12*	4				**2**	2		**4**
Horsfield, Geoff	**10**		4				**7**	1		**8**
Hulme, Kevin	**28**		4				**4**			**4**
Jackson, Justin	**16**						**3**			**3**
Lucas, Richard	**29**	*7*	3		1					
Martin, Lee	**37**		4		1					
Murphy, Jamie	**21**	*2*			1		**1**			**1**
Murphy, Steve	**12**	*2*	2			*1*				
Newton, Chris	**8**	*6*					**1**			**1**
O'Regan, Kieran	**15**	*4*	2				**2**			**2**
Overson, Vince				*1*						
Paterson, Jamie	**19**	*5*	1	*1*	1		**10**	1		**11**
Power, Lee	**14**	*4*					**4**			**4**
Sertori, Mark	**39**	*1*	4		1					
Stansfield, James	**12**						**1**			**1**
Stoneman, Paul	**40**		4		1		**4**			**4**
Thackeray, Andy	**37**	*1*	4		1		**5**			**5**
Williams, Marc	**18**	*6*			1		**6**			**6**
26 players used	**506**	***63***	**44**	***3***	**11**	***1***	**57**	**4**		**61**

Southend United back-peddle during Town's 3-1 home win (February 1999)

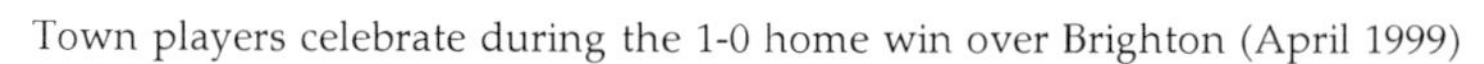

Town players celebrate during the 1-0 home win over Brighton (April 1999)

SUBSCRIBER	FAVOURITE PLAYER
Charlie Adamson	Jamie Paterson
Nick Annetts	Bobby Davison
Mr David Ashton	Geoff Horsfield
Philip Ashworth	Mike Norbury
Allan Baker	Tony Rhodes
Keith N Barraclough	Rick Holden
Mr Robert Bateson	Rick Holden
David Beecham	Jamie Paterson
Roger Bottomley	Freddie Hill
Paul Brown	Geoff Horsfield
S J Brown	Peter Butler
Stephen Bush	Freddie Hill
Gavin Butler	Jamie Paterson
Mr Ian Byng	Bill Atkins
Steve Charlesworth	Phil McCarthy
Mr Peter Chilcott	Jamie Paterson
Mr R Chymycz	
Andy Connell	Bill Atkins
Jon Crowther	Jamie Paterson
Joe Dennison	Geoff Horsfield
Simon Denton	Paddy Roche
Bob Eastwood	Les Massie
Jack Ellis	Jamie Paterson
Peter Frankland	Freddie Hill
Martin Furness	Phil McCarthy
J H Gaimster	Les Massie
Graham Gent	Jamie Paterson
Mr Alan Gill	Jamie Paterson
William Harper	Jamie Paterson
Richard S Harrison	Paul Stoneman
Paul Helliwell	Bobby Davison
Mr C D Kendrick	
Michael Kingston	Jamie Paterson
Micheal Lasota	Steve Norris
Stephen Lumb	David Shawcross
Ian Mackintosh	Bill Atkins

SUBSCRIBER	FAVOURITE PLAYER
Christopher Marsh	Jamie Paterson
Mick McCaul	Paul Hendrie
David Millington	Dave Gwyther
Trevor Morrell	Geoff Horsfield
John Motson	Billy Barr
Ray N	Dave Evans
Dave Neatby	Les Massie
David Normanton	Rick Holden
Andrew Nunwick	Mick Kennedy
Mrs Brenda Nuttall	Bobby Davison
David Oates	Jamie Paterson
John Rawnsley	
Mark Reynolds	Rick Holden
Paul Robinson	Chris Nicholl
Charles Sargeant	
David Shaw	Les Massie
Mr G B Simpson	David Longhurst
Henry Skrzypecki	Jamie Paterson
Brian Smith	Bill Atkins
Mr G Sutcliffe	Bill Atkins
Mike & Jan Torevell	Jamie Paterson
Antony Tune	Geoff Horsfield
Claire W	Paddy Roche
David Walker	Dave Chadwick
Richard Walker	Geoff Horsfield
Howard Wilcock	Bill Atkins
Stephen Wilson	David Longhurst

MOST POPULAR HALIFAX TOWN PLAYER 1968-1999

23 different players received votes

1 Jamie Paterson
2. Bill Atkins
3. Geoff Horsfield
4. Les Massie
5. Rick Holden